I0199370

Smorgonie, District Vilna; Memorial Book and Testimony (Smarhon, Belarus)

Translation of
Smorgon mehoz Vilno; sefer edut ve-zikaron

Editors: Abba Gordin and Honoch Levin

Association of Emigrants of Smorgon in Israel and USA
Published in Tel Aviv, 1965

Published by JewishGen

An Affiliate of the Museum of Jewish Heritage—A Living Memorial to the Holocaust
New York

Smorgonie, District Vilna; Memorial Book and Testimony (Smarhon, Belarus)
Translation of *Smorgon mehoz Vilno; sefer edut ve-zikaron*

First Printing: January 2020, Tevet 5780

Translation Project Coordinator: Marc D. Hodies
Layout: Donni Magid
Cover Design: Nina Schwartz artstop@impulsegraphics.com

Published by JewishGen, Inc.
An Affiliate of the Museum of Jewish Heritage
A Living Memorial to the Holocaust
36 Battery Place, New York, NY 10280

Printed in the United States of America by Lightning Source, Inc.

Library of Congress Control Number (LCCN): 2019954862
ISBN: 978-1-939561-85-5 (hard cover: 780 pages, alk. paper)

Cover Credits:
Front cover: New *besmedresh* (house of study and prayer) under construction, circa 1930. Courtesy of the YIVO Institute for Jewish Research, Digital Archive on Jewish Life in Poland, http://polishjews.yivoarchives.org/archive/index.php?p=digitallibrary/digitalcontent&id=4342#.
Map: Courtesy of Topographic Maps of Eastern Europe, easteuropetopo.org.
Back cover: Wilenskiej Street on market day, 1930; photo by A. Wysocki. Plaque in memory of the prisoners of the Smorgon Ghetto. Source: Wikimedia Commons.

JewishGen and the Yizkor Books in Print Project

This book has been published by the **Yizkor Books in Print Project**, as part of the **Yizkor Book Project** of JewishGen, Inc.

JewishGen, Inc. is a non-profit organization founded in 1987 as a resource for Jewish genealogy. Its website [www.jewishgen.org] serves as an international clearinghouse and resource center to assist individuals who are researching the history of their Jewish families and the places where they lived. JewishGen provides databases, facilitates discussion groups, and coordinates projects relating to Jewish genealogy and the history of the Jewish people. In 2003, JewishGen became an affiliate of the **Museum of Jewish Heritage—A Living Memorial to the Holocaust** in New York.

The **JewishGen Yizkor Book Project** was organized to make more widely known the existence of Yizkor (Memorial) Books written by survivors and former residents of various Jewish communities throughout the world. Later, volunteers connected to the different destroyed communities began cooperating to have these books translated from the original language—usually Hebrew or Yiddish—into English, thus enabling a wider audience to have access to the valuable information contained within them. As each chapter of these books was translated, it was posted on the JewishGen website and made available to the general public.

The **Yizkor Books in Print Project** began in 2011 as an initiative to print and publish Yizkor Books that had been fully translated, so that hard copies would be available for purchase by the descendants of these communities and also by scholars, universities, synagogues, libraries, and museums.

These Yizkor books have been produced almost entirely through the volunteer effort of researchers from around the world, assisted by donations from private individuals. The books are printed and sold at near cost, so as to make them as affordable as possible. Our goal is to make this important genre of Jewish literature and history available in English in book form, so that people can have the personal histories of their ancestral towns on their bookshelves for themselves and for their children and grandchildren.

A list of all published translated Yizkor Books in the project with prices and ordering information can be found at:
http://www.jewishgen.org/Yizkor/ybip.html

Lance Ackerfeld, Yizkor Book Project Manager
Joel Alpert, Yizkor-Book-in-Print Project Coordinator

This book is presented by the
Yizkor Books in Print Project
Project Coordinator: Joel Alpert

Part of the
Yizkor Books Project of JewishGen, Inc.
Project Manager: Lance Ackerfeld

These books have been produced solely through volunteer effort of individuals from around the world. The books are printed and sold at near cost, so as to make them as affordable as possible.

Our goal is to make this history and important genre of Jewish literature available in English in book form so that people can have the near-personal histories of their ancestral towns on their bookshelves for themselves and for their children and grandchildren.

Any donations to the Yizkor Books Project are appreciated.

Please send donations to:
Yizkor Book Project
JewishGen
36 Battery Place
New York, NY 10280

JewishGen, Inc. is an affiliate of the
Museum of Jewish Heritage
A Living Memorial to the Holocaust

Acknowledgements

Special thanks to the National Yiddish Book Center in Amherst, Massachusetts and the New York Public Library for supplying the high resolution images used in this book.

Frieda Lewin with parents

Dedication

IN LOVING MEMORY OF MY FATHER CHAIM LEVIN

AND BROTHER SHLOMO,

MY GRANDMOTHER CHAJA LAPIDUS LAPYDA),
NEE KATZKOVITCH

MY UNCLE AND AUNT, LEIZER AND FANIA AND FAMILY

MY UNCLE AND AUNT BEREL AND MINCHA AND FAMILY,

PARENTS OF HANOCH LEVIN, THE WRITER
AND ALL MY FRIENDS AND RELATIVES IN SMORGON
AND THE SURROUNDING REGION

FRIEDA LEVIN DYM AND FAMILY

Levine and Lewin are the same

Introduction to the Translation

In 1970, I was a 7-year-old boy visiting my Smorgon-born grandmother, Freda Hodies (nee Horowitz), in a Brooklyn Jewish home for the aged. I saw many elderly people in wheelchairs, who seemed to stare at me in an unsettlingly way; sometimes smiling, but most often expressionless. Years later, I know what they were thinking: they were seeing a young boy, free from persecution, hate, and violence, with his entire life in front of him. As a kid, I had no idea that they were immigrants, who courageously started a new life in America with their only possessions toted in a suitcase. If I could turn back the clock, I would ask them about their life in Europe, their experiences in steerage for three weeks, and how they felt when they first glimpsed the Statue of Liberty. I was too young to be able to reflect on the significance of the moment. How I wish I could go up to them now and ask them about their lives.

Halfway between Minsk and Vilna, Smorgon was at the crossroads of history during World War I and II with battles fought within the city limits. The translated Yizkor book reveals the rich history of the town including a renowned Bear Academy, where bears were trained to perform for crowds, a rich cultural theatre scene where actors traveled from other cities to perform, and a thriving Jewish population with seven synagogues, active Zionist groups, and rich rabbinical heritage. The original Yizkor book was published in 1965 in Tel Aviv by the Association of Former Residents of Smorgonie (in Israel and USA) and contains much history (beginning in the 1300s), a detailed discussion and mention of the Rabbis of Smorgon, both wars, memoirs and personal anecdotes, stories of community and political life, and the Holocaust. There are also various photographs and maps appearing in the book.

I am forever grateful to Anita Gabbay who not only personally invested her time, skills, and resources in getting the book translated, but also in securing funding from other generous benefactors. If not for Anita, we would have only the Introduction to the Smorgon Yizkor book to read. Most of the translations were authored by Jerrold Landau, whose careful attention to accuracy and explanations resulted in a Yizkor book that will endure for future generations. The Smorgon Yizkor book has a significant number of footnotes to assist the next generation of Smorgon descendants in understanding the colloquial reference, thought, or idea. I am very proud of that feature.

When there was a need for a project coordinator for the Smorgon Yizkor book, I jumped at the chance. It truly was an honor, and I increasingly felt a connection to my Smorgon heritage as the project progressed. To open up these treasures of stories, poems, and memories, which reveal the daily life of town folk, religious and political figures, and heartbreaking stories of the Holocaust survivors was an opportunity to pay tribute to the Smorgon community which came before me.

My grandmother, Freda, did not share many early life details with my dad, despite his pleading. Her memories were too hard and painful, and consequently my dad only got bits and pieces. She had over ten brothers and sisters but we only know of three who survived. Her parents were apparently killed in a horrible manner, most likely when the town was torched in 1915, and Smorgon Jews incurred unprintable atrocities. Freda spoke five languages and with the assistance of friends, survived through World War I by working in a bakery in an adjacent town. Her two older brothers, Ike and Avraham (whom my brother and I are named after respectively), came to America prior to 1911 and ultimately saved for their baby sister's ticket of passage, bringing her over in 1924, almost 14 years later.

To Ike, Abe, Freda of Blessed Memory, and to the many Smorgoners past and present, born or descendant, I hope we honor you with this translated Yizkor Book of Smorgon.

Marc D. Hodies

Young Freda

Notes to the Reader:

We apologize ahead of time for the poor quality of images in the book. Often these images had been scanned from the original Yizkor books which were of poor quality to begin with, being copies of old photographs. Each transfer results in loss of quality. We have done the best we could, given the original material and the resources and technology at hand. Even though images often appear of higher quality on computer screens, that does not transfer to high quality images in print. A reader can view the original scans on the web sites listed below.

Within the text the reader will note "{34}" standing ahead of a paragraph. This indicates that the material translated below was on page 34 of the original book. However, when a paragraph was split between two pages in the original book, the marker is placed in this book after the end of the paragraph for ease of reading.

Also please note that all references within the text of the book to page numbers, refer to the page numbers of the original Yizkor Book.

The original book can be seen online at the New York Public Library site:
https://digitalcollections.nypl.org/items/f3fe2ac0-3a16-0133-1c1f-00505686a51c
or at the Yiddish Book Center web site:
https://www.yiddishbookcenter.org/collections/yizkor-books/yzk-nybc314002

In order to obtain a list of all Shoah victims from Smarhon, the reader should access the Yad Vashem web site listed below; one can also search for specific family names using family name option. These lists are continually updated by Yad Vashem, so it is worthwhile to periodically search these lists.

There is much valuable information available on this web site, including the Pages of Testimony, etc.
http://yvng.yadvashem.org

A list of this book and all books available in the Yizkor-Book-In-Print Project along with prices is available at:
http://www.jewishgen.org/Yizkor/ybip.html

Geopolitical Information:

Smarhon, Belarus is located at: 54°29' N, 26°24' E

In NW Belarus, 45 miles ESE of Vilnius (Vilna), 21 miles W of Vilyeyka, 19 miles ENE of Oshmyany.

Alternate names for the town are: Alternate names: Smarhon' [Bel], Smorgon [Rus, Yid], Smorgonie [Pol], Smurgainys [Lith], Smorgone, Smarhoń, Smurgainiai

Belarusian: Смаргонь. Russian: Сморгонь. Yiddish: סמורגון

Period	Town	District	Province	Country
Before WWI (c. 1900):	Smorgon	Oshmyany	Vilna	Russian Empire
Between the wars (c. 1930):	Smorgonie	Oszmiana	Wilno	Poland
After WWII (c. 1950):	Smorgon'			Soviet Union
Today (c. 2000):	Smarhon'			Belarus

Jewish Population in 1900: 6,743

Nearby Jewish Communities:
- Soly 9 miles WNW
- Zaskevichi 10 miles ESE
- Krevo 12 miles SSW
- Zhuprany 13 miles W
- Liebiedzieva 17 miles SE
- Ashmyany 19 miles WSW
- Astravyets 20 miles WNW

Smorgon located in Belarus

Hebrew Title Page of Yizkor Book

סמורגון

מחוז וילנא

ספר
עדות
וזכרון

הוצאת ארגון יוצאי סמורגון בישראל
תשכ"ו ישראל 1965

Translation of the Title Page of Original Yizkor Book

Smorgon

Vilna District

Book of Testimony And Memories

Published by the Association of Emigrants of Smorgon in Israel

Israel 1965 5725

Table of Contents

The Town and its Residents
A. Till the First World War

The Town and its Residents
B. Between the Wars

Few out of Many
Images from the town

The Holocaust and the Destruction
Chapters of Testimony

[Page 2]

Map of the City of Smorgon

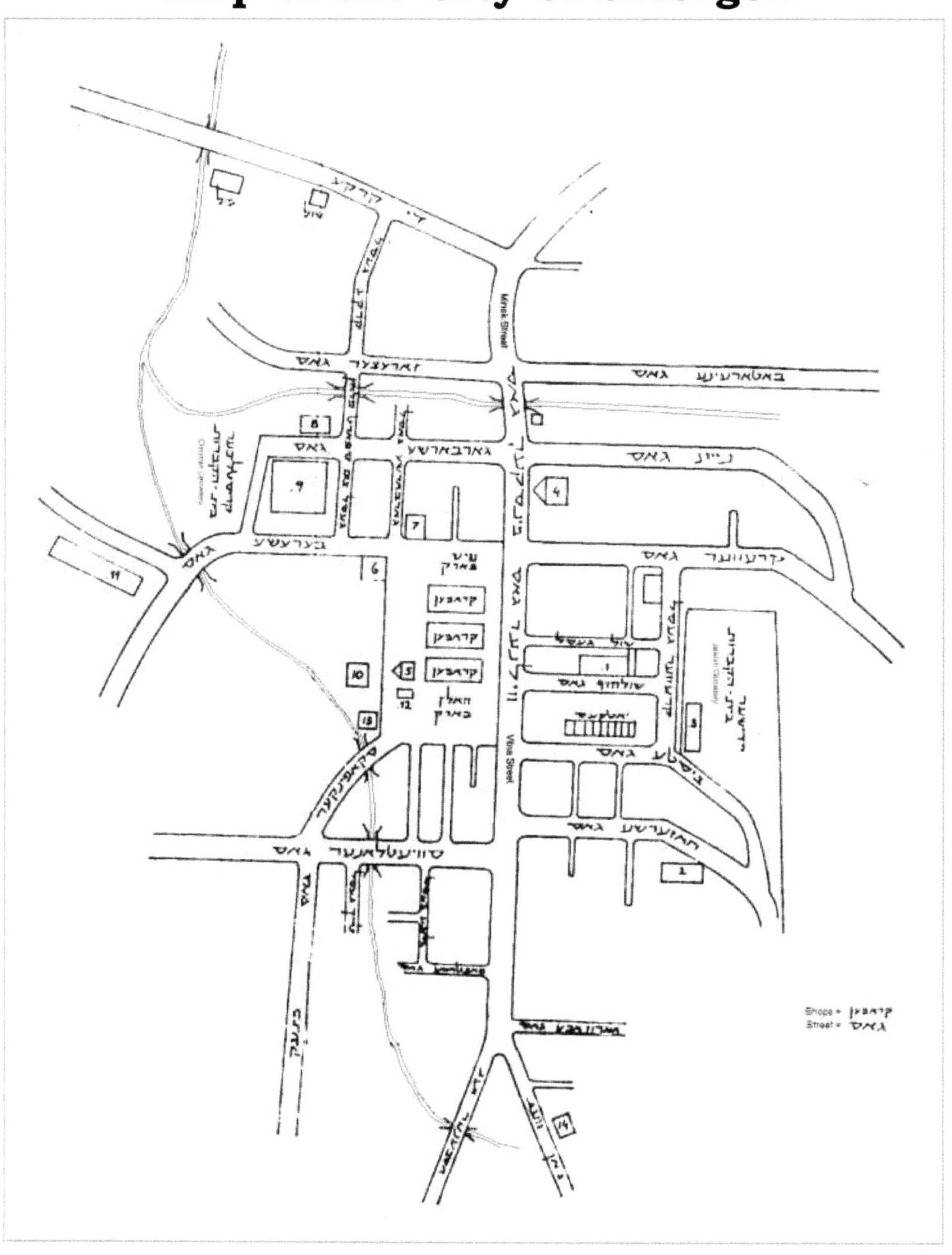

דער פּלאַן פֿון סמאָרגאָן	**The Plan of Smorgon**
1 די גרויסע שול	The Big Shul (Synagogue)
2 דער אינטערנאַט (תרבות שולע)	The Internat (Tarbut School)
3 תלמוד תורה	Talmud Torah
4 די קריסטליכע קירכע	The Christian Church
5 די פּראַוואָסלאַווע קירכע	The Pravoslavic Church
6 דער מאַגיסטראַט	The Magistrate
7 די פּאָסט	The Post Office
8 די פּאָליציי	The Police
9 דער ספּאָרט פּלאַץ	The Sport Square
10 די פּוילישע פֿאָלקס־שולע	The Polish Elementary School
11 די האַנדלס שולע	The Business School
12 די פֿייער לעשער קאָמאַנדע	The Fire Station
13 די באָד	The Bath
14 די באַן סטאַנציע	The Train Station

Prepared by Elyezer Karpel, Mordechai Tabouriski & Israel Levinson

[Page 3]

Preface to the Book

Translated by Jerrold Landau

When the pillar of fire rose up from the beacons of the Jewish communities of the Diaspora, and other disturbances arose from one end to the other, pillars of smoke from the terrible inferno ignited by the cruel, bloodthirsty nation, who jumped out from their dark hiding places like beasts of the field – we, the orphans of the nation, ran out, one from a city and two from a country, among the waves of filth of the great inferno, to salvage the last relics and give of them to the People of Israel as a final light.[1]

As the voice of the cries of the members of our nation bursts forth, the voice of defeat of those taken to their deaths in the vale of murder, citizens of the other planet who were burned at the stake in all the camps of "enlightened" Europe, and the voice of bravery of the few fighters of the ghettoes and forests who gave their souls for the honor of Israel and the honor of humanity – we captured the voices from their to imbue them in our blood, to incorporate them in all our senses, so that they will not be silenced — —

Then our town of Smorgon, killed, slaughtered, and burnt, was also seen by us. You too drank from the cup of poison along with the Jewish communities of the Diaspora.

You, the merciful one, the city in which Torah and worldly life, where grace and kindness, scholarliness and secular wisdom, were gathered together.

You the mourning one, who gave a structure of truth with your toiling hand to go forth to all strata of the nation and humanity, to build "a world that is built on justice"...

You, the one that was wiped away, who gave a weight and measure to grace the soil of our Land here, as you sent forth your pioneers before the camp; as well as to heal the ruins of life in the Diaspora when you attached yourself to any spark of existence.

Oh, how have you been destroyed, our town Smorgon...

Oh, how were the pits of destruction opened to swallow you alive, with your masses of people.

Oh, how you once were and are no more.

See, how our hearts are full of tears, and our eyes are wellsprings of agony.

Now that the book is placed before us, we feel with greater strength the anguish of the lost life, for which there is no atonement. We feel with all strands of our soul the living spirit coming forth from the chapters of this book – this is the spirit of our town Smorgon that was wiped out.

We did not have the intention to place all this material, rescued from forgetting and oblivion, gathered up in these folios of agony – as something hidden away for the generations, without forming it and embalming it within the realm of history.

We attempted to forge it into a living path for the hearts of the natives of Smorgon, to level out a pathway into our own structures, to arouse the feelings of a changed reality, and to store away in our souls the good, sublime memories of the life that was cut off.

With all this, to move one stone, a sorrowful one, to the perpetual pantheon, as a monument to the splendor of life of the Diaspora of Israel in every place.

The community of Smorgon will also shed tears into the cup of agony of our nation.

This memorial book is the fruit of good intentions and toil of the masses. The signature of the community of Smorgon natives is upon it.

Its beginning – with the idea hatched by our native, Isser Ish-Ahuvi of blessed memory, with the initiative of Bertha Shein of blessed memory, and the wise advice of Mr. Gershon Weinstein and his son Raphael, may they live – these were the first of its producers.

Set up the portals of this book – all those who were included in the writing.

The editors of the Book of Smorgon

Translator's Footnote

The reference "one from the city and two from a country" is most likely inspired from Jeremiah 3.14, https://www.mechon-mamre.org/p/pt/pt1103.htm. The phrase means that very few survived.

[Page 4]

Abba Gordin - editor (1887–1964)

Words in Memory of Abba Gordin

by Chanoch Lewin

Translated by Jerrold Landau

This man came from the roots of precious stones.

The rock that forged him consisted of prominent rabbis, but his environment of the downtrodden, toiling masses shaped him.

His roots were very strong with all the changes of the times. It is self-evident that these roots were grounded in the foundations of national and human existence.

The changes in the world during the latter three generations, which imprinted themselves to no small degree on the spiritual life of humanity, and broke down the preconceived notions of individuals and the masses - were unable to shake his great faith in rectifying the world with the rule of justice, peace, and brotherhood of man.

He was faithful to the house of Israel until his final day. He unearthed the good and sublime from within the hiding places of that nation, and emmeshed them, as they were, among the pages of his many books.

He had a role and contributed to all streams of Jewish and human thought. He was at home with all the schools of the spirit in the development of human thought.

He spent time in the depths of the ways of the generation and was alert to all human pathways.

At times, he was strange to his brethren, the members of his nation. The multitude of his ideas, just like the complicated, intertwined paths that signified his generation, were a wonder in their eyes. In the character of the ways of the world between the wars and great revolutions of the 20th century, he stood at the pathway with the giants of the world. He expressed his opinions in the ears of captains and leaders. He did neither cowered before them, nor trembled in fear. He followed his unique path with strength of heart and dedication of the soul.

Toward the end of his days, he found his path in the ways of his fathers, leaving behind an army of students with a doctrine and a path, so that they would continue to cleave to their "rabbi" from afar. His old age did not betray the charm of his youth. He was like an overflowing wellspring in his conversations, his achievements, and when he picked up the writers' pen, even in his old age – until his final day.

Many storms of his heart were calmed. Many twists of his soul were straightened. The sting was removed from his thorns and briars. He made peace with himself and with the god of his spirits. There are tens of pages of this book that he started but did not live to see its conclusion. Yet within these pages are the sparks of his spirit and the etched events of his life—all woven and bound into the story of the life of the spirit of his town and our town – Smorgon.

Let this book serve as a miniature sanctuary to mark the memory of Abba Gordin.

[Page 5]

Words in Memory of Abba Gordin

by Eliezer Steinman

Translated by Jerrold Landau

Abba Gordin, the man of the world, has left the world. He was a man who was a complete world [himself], who worked all his days to repair the world. He went out in secret, as is the way of a good person who does good, without bothering people during his life or after his death.

Even now that he has reached the Heavenly court, the writers of articles from among us have not reached the stage of levelheadedness to be able to tell even a portion of his praise and honor in any sort of publication. This [inability] is no surprise.

Abba Gordin was at home in many streams of thought: in logic and in poetry, in his sense of understanding, as well as his command of social sciences. He was a linguist, pedagogue, raconteur and researcher, a master of memories, a seer for the House of Israel and the gentiles, a communal leader, and also a wise and attentive man. His delving into the fields of Judaism was particularly deep. He authored tens of books and hundreds of articles. He was able to write quickly in four languages: Hebrew, Yiddish, Russian, and English. There was nobody as daring and sharp as he in both written and oral debates. He stood on podiums with literal self–dedication and without fear. Abba Gordin's field of endeavor was very broad, and he imbued his soul into all his literary efforts. One would have to dedicate a great deal of time, energy, goodwill, and love of the truth in order to encompass all his arenas. He was not a man of the hour of a passing vision. His field of influence was broad as well as long. He was modest, with great patience. He had the time and patience to wait until the [community] came to appreciate him (as was appropriate).

I hereby give, for the sake of a memorial, only a few kernels from the chief of the stalks. Not a bundle, but rather a harvested sheaf.

Words in Memory of Abba Gordin

by Chaim Dan

Translated by Jerrold Landau

In [the town of] Ramat Gan, he would sit separate and isolated in his dwelling with his weapons: a pen in his hand, deliberating over manuscripts, immersed in battle and creativity. And he was over 70.

He was a remnant of the active generation that established Russian and Polish Jewry at the beginning of the 20th century – a generation when the nation ruled over the individual. He was a personality of rich spirit, a scholar and the son of a scholar, expert and sharp. He bound together the ideas of the early ones and later ones in his articles and books. He swam in the sea of Talmud and Zohar, and his hands were in Marx and Kropotkin; he frequently brought ideas from one side to the other, without a division between them. His interests lay in many fields: science and philosophy, prose and poetry, proportions and numbers, articles and feuilletons. He possessed an insatiable intellectual curiosity that knew no bounds.

The man went through many incarnations. From Poland to Russia, from Russia to America, and, at an old age, from America to Israel. From Orthodoxy to apostasy, and from orthodoxy in apostacy to anarchism[1].

In Russia, during the revolution, he was one of the chief spokesmen of the anarchists who were competing with the Bolsheviks to take hold of the government. He came into contact with the giants of the revolution: Lenin, Kamenev, Dzerzhinsky, and others. He was an opponent to their ploys in the name of the consistency of the revolution. How did he, the son of a rabbi, a supporter of tradition and splendor, careful about the honor of every person, become involved in such an environment? [Ah], the irony of fate.

His beliefs stood for him. The fire of his youth was not quenched even with the changing times and climate in the surroundings and environment. In his latter days, he immersed his spirit in the worlds that were close to him from his early youth. In his final years, he was involved in writing a novel from the era of King Solomon, and a book on the Maharal[2].

Translator's Footnotes

1. Orthodoxy in apostasy is intentional and infers that Gordin moved from a traditional version of apostacy to anarchism.
2. See https://en.wikipedia.org/wiki/Judah_Loew_ben_Bezalel

[Page 6]

Members of the Editorial Board

Translated by Jerrold Landau

Baruch Sutskover

Chanoch Levin – vice editor

Leah Bondor–Bubis

Avigdor Jacobson

[Page 7]

Mordechai Taborisky

Shoshana Danishevsky – Flavski

Yisrael Levinson

Liza Kat–Levinson

[Page 8]

Yisgadal VeYiskadash[1]

by Chanoch Levin

Translated by Jerrold Landau

How can I sing to you with songs, and praise your name in the gate?
You are sealed in the hearts of your survivors in a chant of tears and light:
From your rebellion – for then they quarried the wheel of the storm,
Your tanners, harbingers of peace and freedom.

In you was Menashe of Ilya, the holy rabbi, alone like a juniper,
Aspiring to do good to his nation and rectifying the damage of the exile.
In you was Kabak, envisioning his rule, treading through the narrow path
And Kulbak wandered, escaped, from you to the lost path.

Oh Kulbak, even the smoke of his pyre flowed like a path
Dragged and attached to your memory that flailed in the fire;
Even though he did not gather most of your essence – deeds,
But "Montag" — The Messiah the son of Joseph, passed over your face.[2]

As I recall the day, it caused my heart to pulsate,
Before we went out, without returning, to naught
In my pitiful town, to the mezuzah of my parental home
His soul fluttered about then – and perhaps still now.

As he went, he said as follows, as if slowly to himself:
"Who knows if he did not set up a lodging
The redeeming Messiah, who will redeem his nation
On Mount Zion with the pioneers of Smorgon..."

Regarding your pioneers, the poet D. Shimoni speaks a poem
"In the Forests of Hadera" they drilled and danced with "The Wagoners' Jubilee."
With youthful enthusiasm, they broke through the iron fetters and poverty
They were the first to draw the vehicles of the fighters and the builders.

I will sign today with my heart, I rember of all your martyrs
Whomever still pulsates with you and still senses you within their blood,
We, the few survivors of your flock,
Stand enveloped in grief, with *Yisgadal VeYiskadash.*

Tel Aviv 5725 / 1965

Translator's Footnotes

1. Magnified and sanctified – the opening words of the Kaddish prayer.
2. The Messiah the son of Joseph is a Jewish Messianic figure who died in battle prior to the final victory of the Messiah the son of David.

[Page 9]

Historical Introduction

by Abba Gordin

Translated by Ron Arons

Edited by Jerrold Landau

Smorgon, like the district of Vilna, was considered to belong to Lithuania, without precise consideration of the geographical location.

1. Beginning

Already in the year 1388, we find a considerable Jewish community in Brisk (or Brest Litovsk) that received a bill of rights similar to the bill of rights that had already been granted to the Jews of Lwow. The bill of rights of Lwow was given by the Grand Duke Witold (Vytautas).

One of the rights the Jews received exempts them from the duty to harbor Christians in their houses.

In 1389, we find a Jewish community in Grodno as well. The community has a cemetery and a synagogue. On June 18, 1389, the Jews of Grodno received the same rights that the Jews of Brisk enjoyed. They are as follows: freedom to engage in business and trades, to work the land, to make and sell alcoholic drinks, to perform *shechita* (ritual slaughter) on cattle, and to sell meat wholesale.

The Jews of Grodno used the rights that were given to them. They dealt in agriculture and engaged in all kinds of craftwork and artisanry as detailed in the bill of rights.

In 1399, Witold brought prisoners of war, amongst them Jews, from southern Russia and the Crimean Peninsula. Karaites taken as prisoners of war were separated from the other Jews and settled them in Trakai, which, after a while, became the spiritual center of Karaism.

In 1441, the Jews of Trakai were granted a bill of rights. They received full autonomy in accordance with the Magdeburg charter.[1]

In April 1495, the Jews of Lithuania were expelled, and their property was confiscated. However, after eight years transpired, in 1503, the Jews returned to their places in Lithuania. The Jews of Brisk, Grodno and Trakai returned and re–established their communities according to their previously received bill of rights.

In 1506, three years after the cancellation of the expulsion edict, a community was formed in Pinsk. Jews received the same rights that the community of Brisk enjoyed.

The Jews of Grodno established two more communities in 1522 - one in Tykocin and one in Nowydwor.

In 1525, the Grand Duke granted the wealthy Jew, Michael Josepowicz of Brisk. the status of a nobleman, for him, and his children after him. Since he attained greatness, he was appointed as head of all the Jews of Lithuania. However, this appointment was a disappointment to the Jews of Lithuania. They did not.

[Page 10]

They wanted to recognize a leader that was foisted on them by the government of the land.[2] They yearned for independence in terms of community affairs.

In 1529, there were communities in Pinsk, Grodno, Brisk, Trakai, Tykocin, Nowydwor, Kobrin, Kletzk, and Ludmir.

Brisk, the first and oldest of the communities, became the center of Torah from which G–d's word went forth to all of the cities of Lithuania. A Jewish printing house was established, and the *Chumash* was published in 1546. Around 1550, approximately four years after the *Chumash* was released, a kind of *Yeshiva* was formed in the town.

In that year, 1550, the number of Jews in Lithuania grew to about 10,000.

In 1551, we find communities in Slonim, Mstibovo, and Kremenetz. That same year, permission was granted to two wealthy Jews from Krakow to rent stores and houses in Vilna and to conduct business there as guest businessmen, but not to reside there. The right to live in Vilna and build a community was not granted to the Jews because of Vilna's importance as a capital city. The same difficulties and obstacles were met by Jews in Kovno.

After a while, Jews were permitted to come and settle in the city on condition that they would live in houses that were purchased by members of the Duke's Council, because the citizens and guild members did not want to give the Jews the opportunity to freely set foot wherever they wanted in their rich city.

The Jews of Pinsk founded the community of Kletzk.

The Jewish communities of Lithuania paid about a quarter of the total taxes collected from all of the cities of Lithuania.

In 1555, we find Jews in Zaselye. In 1556, Jews were permitted to reside only on one street that was reserved for them in the city of Kowel. This street belonged completely to the Jews and the Christian citizens were not allowed to build houses there.

In 1560, there were three streets in Grodno that were designated for the settling of Jews: Street of the Jews, Street of the Synagogue, and Narrow Street of the Jews. The Jews were concentrated onto a specific street in Nowogrodek as well.

In 1563, the communities of Usterkhi, Dvoretz, Lachowitz, and Turets were founded.

In 1563 a special tax was levied on the Lithuanian Jews – 4,000 groszy. The taxes were divided among the Jews of Lithuania as follows: Usterkhi – 600; Stroja – 600; Luck – 550; Ludmir – 500; Trakai – 376; Brisk – 264; Grodno – 200; Kremenets – 140; Tykocin – 100; Dvorets – 60; Nowogrodek – 30; Lachowitz – 30; Kletzk – 15.

In 1564 an epidemic erupted in Vilna. Everybody ran away, including the ruler.

[Page 11]

Before he ran away for his life, the Duke's representative elected two de facto rulers. One was a Jew by the name of Shmuel Ben–Israel of Lachowitz.

In 1566, we count in Brisk 85 homeowners, in Grodno – 60, Luck – 56, Kremenits –48, Tykocin – 37, Ludmir – 30; Pinsk – 24, Kobrin – 22, Novydwor – 12, and in Kletzk – 4.

In the census conducted in 1566 in Brisk, a printer named Yaakov is mentioned; and the son–in–law of Reb Shmuel Wohl, was listed as Dovid Druker.

In the same year, taxes were levied on the Jews of Lithuania in the amount of 6,000 shok groszy. Of the sum, the communities were ordered to pay 3,670 shok, divided as follows: Brisk – 1,300; Luck – 500; Usterkhi – 500; Ludmir – 300, Trakai – 300; Grodno – 200; Tykocin – 170; Kremenets – 150; the Jews of Nowogrodek, Slonim, Lachowitz, Kletzk, Turets, Chochora and the Vilna and Kovno tax lessees– altogether – 250.

Exports of the Lithuanian Jews

Merchandise was shipped by boat down three rivers – the Bug, the Wisla, and the Neman. Through Kovno, primarily grains were sent to Konigsberg, which was called Krolewiec at the time, and salt was imported from there. The well–known merchants from Lithuania at that time were Michael Josepowicz and Yitzchak Borodawka from Brisk, and Ephraim son of Yerachmiel from Mohilev.

Lithuanian Jews maintained business connections with Germany and Poland. Lithuanian merchants would go to Leipzig, Wroclaw (currently Breslau) in Silesia, Poznan, Krakow, etc. They conducted business with Turkey, Moldavia, and Wallachia. They would import bulls, spices, and various other merchandise from those places. They also tried to penetrate the Duchy of Moscow, but all of their efforts were for naught, because Ivan the Terrible was afraid of the "bad" influence of the Jewish Lithuanian businessman on his subjects, lest they lead his subjects away from their Greek Orthodox faith. He even denied with much anger Zygmunt August's request.[3] The fear of "Judaizers" (Jews that try and convert others to Judaism) fell on Ivan because rumors were spreading that several members of that "sect" ran away to Lithuania and were circumcised and turned into Jews.

In 1573, a synagogue was established in Vilna. The building was purchased from a nobleman and was outside the jurisdiction of the municipality.

Stefan Batory was chosen as king (1575–1586). He ascended the throne with the help of the Jewish merchant, Shlomo Ashkenazi.

Stefan Batory was well disposed to the Jews. He defended the Lithuanian Jews against the blood libels that their enemies and haters would spread about them. In 1576, he allowed the Jews to conduct business, and to buy and sell with no obstacles, even on Christian holidays. He ruled that anyone who killed a Jew would be punished with the death penalty, just like the murderer of a Christian. He placed complete responsibility on the municipal leadership any damage by mass incitement to synagogues, cemeteries, and Jewish deceased. Whomever perpetrates incidents against Jews or steals their belongings would pay a penalty of 10,000 Polish Marks, and an equal penalty would be paid by the Polish authorities for neglecting their job and failing to defend the Jews living under their jurisdiction. A fear of his authority prevented anti–Jewish incitement.

[Page 12]

During the rule of this benevolent king, the Jews founded a community in Minsk and received a bill of rights. However, when the city dwellers of Mohilev, which sits on the river Dnieper, requested from the king to disallow Jews from living in their city, he fulfilled their request in 1585.

One of the important administrators of the community in Minsk was Rabbi Shaul Ben–Yehuda (Wahl Katzenelboign). Rabbi Ben–Yehuda was a learned and extremely wealthy Jew, a tax lessee and received the title of King's Servant in 1589.

Legend has it that Shaul (Ben–Yehuda) Wahl was chosen as the king of Poland after the death of Stefan Batory, and fulfilled the role for one night.

In 1590 Rabbi Mordechai Yaffa (1530–1612), Rabbi of Lublin, signed, along with 30 other Rabbis of Poland and Lithuania, an agreement that prohibited a rabbi from receiving any money or gifts or loans for the role of rabbi, either directly or to themselves or to other people.

In 1592, the Jews were permitted a legal *Yeshiva* in the city of Vilna. In the bill of additional rights, they were explicitly permitted to establish public amenities, such as cemeteries, slaughterhouses, stores, bathhouses, etc.

In Grodno, however, the anti–Semites had the upper hand and the Jews were forbidden from conducting business in grains, salt, and salted fish.

The large Jewish communities spread their influence and authority on the smaller Jewish settlements in their neighborhood. This pattern is how the regions were established: Brisk and its region, Grodno and its region, Vilna and its region, etc. Occasionally a dispute would break out as to which larger Jewish community a smaller settlement belonged to.

The major communities, i.e. Brisk, Pinsk, Grodno, and Pinsk, established the Council of the State of Lithuania. Belonging to it were – "the heads of the state", and the rabbis of these three communities. The council dealt with all of the common matters of the communities and Jews of Lithuania, and their relationships to each other on matters of economy, culture, and custom: communal elections, institutions, economy, leasing, education, religion and morals, charity, settling of the Land Israel, and many other things.

The Council of Four Lands

During the reign of Sigismund III (1532–1587), the Jews of Poland established an institution that had no historical precedent in the Diaspora, which bestowed on certain designated communities autonomy and power, as well as importance both internally and externally. Up to this point this function was carried out informally. During the period when rabbis and *Yeshiva* heads would gather together with their students at large fairs in Poland, they would deal with various important issues, adjudicate disputes, deliberate over conflicts, and agree on general decisions. These original gatherings brought a great deal of benefit in the private and communal lives of the Jews. It was under their influence that the idea was hatched to convene formal periodic gatherings of the leaders of the major communities, with the aim of reaching decisions and issuing directives to all the communities in the country, which they would be obligated to follow. Apparently, the communal administrators were in an atmosphere of peace at that time, and they agreed to meet, cooperate, organize, and create some sort of cohesive unit from the independent communities. At the outset, the communities of countries of Lesser Poland, Greater Poland, and Reisen (White Russia) merged to form a permanent council that would meet regularly.

[Page 13]

The government decided on the total amount of taxes that would be imposed upon the Jews, and they used the council as a tool to apportion and collect the taxes. Most of the meetings were held in small towns in order to get away from the sphere of influence of the leading communities. The council worked on remaining issues in a free environment, where they could make decisions and judgments about private people and communities without surrendering to pressure and interest groups. That way, the council was able to judge clearly and truthfully, without playing favorites, when disputes between large communities and their dependent communities were brought before them.

The primary communities sent wise men as representatives. The representatives elected a chairman to preside over the deliberations of the issues at hand. He would record in a book the minutes along with the decisions that were reached during the meetings. Conflicts between communities were resolved. Anything that made life for Jews difficult were deliberated, such as issues of imposition and collection of taxes, religious and moral enactments, procedures and means of keeping danger away from the communities. Financial aid was allocated for people suffering from want. The leadership of the council also conducted an audit. It issued permits to print and distribute important books. They also censored other books that were considered to be detrimental and bad influences upon the Jews by not allowing such books to be printed or distributed.

Later, when Lithuania was annexed to these countries, the council was called the Council of Four Lands.

The council concerned itself with enactments regarding daily life and morals. It prohibited borrowing money from Christian clergy, military personnel, and even from students without the knowledge and approval of the community. This was because many problems arose with such loans.

"And he who enslaves his wife and children to non-Jewish is cast away from two worlds."[4]

From this clear ruling ,we learn that there were incidents where heads of families would put their family members on the line as collateral for the loans. From the ban in the enactments, we learn what sort of activities would take place. Nobody prohibits an act that does not cross an individual's mind.

[Page 14]

In 1623, the Lithuanian council separated from the general council and its first rulings date from the month of Elul 1623.

The first ruling of the Council of Four Lands is from November. 22, 1580.

The Council of Lithuanian Jews carried on until 1764 and then was annulled.

Prior to the Tribulations of Ta'ch[5], the Council would convene a convention of the major communities approximately once every two years. Between the years 1662 and 1700, they would convene once every three years.

Rabbi Mordechai Yaffa (1530–1612), who occupied the rabbinical seat of Lublin, was apparently the founder of the Council of Four Lands. Following him, the chairman was Rabbi Yehoshua Falik Hacohen, the author of the book "*Pnei Yehoshua*" and the head of the *Yeshiva* in Lwow (1592–1616).

In 1619 the Jews in Grodno received permission to build a synagogue, with the restrictions that it could neither be taller than any of the other buildings nor similar in outside appearance to the beautiful churches.

The community of Vitebsk was founded and received a bill of rights.

In Vilna and in other cities, there were forms of ghettos under the pretext of providing safety for the Jews against the murderousness and burglary of fanatics who were in the cities populated by believers in Jesus.

Between the years of 1633 and 1648, there was a very strong conflict between the Jewish artisans and the organized guilds of the Christians.

In Vilna, Jewish tailors were only allowed to make clothes for Jews so as to keep them out of competition.

The sons of Rabbi Nathan Shapira, head of the rabbinical court of Krakow and author of *Migalei Amukot*, published their father's books three years after his death in 1636. His son, Rabbi Moshe Shapira, was the son–in–law of Rabbi

Eliezer Katzin, one of the heads of the community. He lent money to publish the Talmud in Lublin. Along with his brother, he made efforts and received permits from the issuers of rights to the Jews of Lithuania and Vilna.

In 1637, a fire broke out in Brisk. Hooligans pillaged and robbed Jewish shops and homes during the fire and the great chaos that ensued. The Jews defended themselves and their property. In order to maintain good order from that point on, a guard was formed that was made up of equal numbers of Christians and Jews.

The Vilna community, which was the youngest of all of the major communities, grew very quickly in large steps. It became both a center of Torah and a pillar of wisdom that everyone went to. It surpassed all of the other communities.

In 1622, Shabtai Cohen was born in Vilna (the author of the *Sha'ch* commentary on *Yoreh Deah*). He was one of the students of Yehuda Falik Hacohen, known as "Hecharif" (born in Vilna in 1580, and died in 1616), head of the *Yeshiva* of Lwow. The *Sha'ch* published his book in Krakow in the year 5406 (1646) at the age of 24.

[Page 15]

Rabbi Moshe, the son of Yitzchak Yehuda Lima, served as rabbi in Vilna. He was also one of the students of Rabbi Yehuda Charif ("the sharp one"). He wrote the book *Chelkat Mechokek*, a commentary on the *Even HaEzer* section of the Code of Jewish Law. The members of the rabbinical court of Vilna in his days were the *Sha'ch*; Rabbi Ephraim, the son of Aharon and the author of the book *Shaar Ephraim*; Rabbi Aharon Shmuel Kaidanover; the Maharsha'k (the father of the author of *Kav Hayashar*, Zvi Hirsch); and Rabbi Hillel, author of *Beit Hillel* on the Code of Jewish Law.

In 1652 the Vilna community received representation on the Council, however the city did not have equal rights as the more, well–established, older communities.

In Grodno in 1653, the Jewish artisans came to an agreement with the Christian tailors. According to the agreement, they were to pay 6 guilders (gold coins) and 2 liters of gunpowder every year to the guild of Christian tailors. Reciprocally they were allowed to deal freely in tailoring and the fur trade. They were even permitted to employ Christian workers and apprentices.

The palace of Prince Radziwill was located in the suburbs of Vilna . There, Ysh'r (Yosef Shlomo Rofeh) of Candia Delmedigo (1591–1656)[6], served as the doctor in the palace. He was one of the most enlightened and scientific Jews of that time. He studied at a scientific institute in Padua and learned doctrine[7] from the great Galileo (1564–1642), through whom he became familiar with the theories of Copernicus (1473–1543). He became famous in Poland as a great doctor. A large number of young men and people interested in knowledge would gather around him, especially Karaites.

During the Shoah[8] (1654–1655), many great rabbis fled. Among the few that returned was Rabbi Moshe Rivkash, the author of the *Be'er Hagolah*, the son–in–law of the Vilna Gaon.

In the years 1669–1673, King Jan Sobieski authorized the bill of rights of the Jews and defended them against the citizens who opposed Jewish settlement in the cities. In 1676 he authorized the bill of rights of the Jews of Brisk after the city was rehabilitated. (In 1660, the city had been burned down and completely vandalized by the Russians.) They were granted the rights to pursue trades without belonging to any of the Christian guilds, and they were allowed to conduct business in shops and on the streets.

In 1673 the tinsmiths and needle makers guild in Vilna agreed that there could be four Jewish tinsmiths that would be licensed to work, and those licenses would be inherited. In return, the Jewish artisans agreed to pay the guild 25 guilders annually.

The number of Jews in Lithuania in the years 1673–1677 was about 32,000, and in Poland about 150,000. The head tax that was levied on the Jews in Lithuania was 25,000 guilder and in 1677, the tax was 20,000 guilder, since the number of people dwindled because of the wars and the disturbances perpetrated by the evildoers.

Life in the large cities was difficult for the Jews because the municipal authorities persecuted them, and the Christian guilds opposed Jewish tradesmen. These difficulties were a catalyst to the founding of smaller settlements in remote places, i.e., the rest of Lithuania.

[Page 16]

In the year 1674, Rabbi Gershon Yissachar–Ber decided to build a Talmud Torah (school). This raised the level of the economic and cultural life.

Vilna was marching ahead and fighting for first place among the communities as a center for Torah and wisdom, which would be a blessing to them and to the country. The Jews developed business and artisanships, and they would teach destitute boys, whose parents could not afford to pay tuition to send them to private *cheders*. Rabbi Gershon committed 2,225 guilders to this holy endeavor. The Council of the state received this amount from the Vilna community and agreed to permanently allocate close to seven guilders every week for the needs of Talmud Torah.

Rabbi Yosef, the son of Mordechai, donated to the studiers of Torah or the Talmud Torah a sum of 675 guilders. From this fund they received 105 guilders every year.

Before his death, Rabbi Yehoshua Heshel Charif donated a large sum of money to found a *Beis Midrash*. His wealthy widow also added a large sum of money and built a tall, luxurious building.

The struggle between the Jewish communities and the municipalities continued unabated. The citizens of Pinsk complained that the Jews were taking over their city and pushing out their Christian neighbors. They complained that the Jews owned only 18 houses in the city in 1633 and yet in 1667, just 34 years later, they owned 600 houses. In 1717, the citizens of Pinsk brought forth a complaint against the Jewish residents, stating that almost all of the Christian houses and lots had passed to Jewish hands, including the houses of the guilds of the tailors, furriers, blacksmiths, butchers, and shoemakers. They complained that all of these were purchased by Jews that were taking advantage of Christians. These were routine exaggerations and complaints made by the haters of Israel that date all the way back to the days of Laban the Aramean: "Jacob took all that was our father's, and all this honor came from our father" (Genesis 31:1).

Jews settled in Kovno from the beginning of the 18th century, as well as in Slobodka, called Wiliampol in those days. In 1761, the Jews were expelled from Kovno, but they found a safe haven in Slobodka.

[Page 17]

2. Smorgon

Jews came to Smorgon during the 17th century. In 1634, Vilna was known as "The community of Vilna and its environs, excluding Smorgon." In 1637 the community of Smorgon joined Vilna.

In 1651 (5412), Smorgon existed as a separate unit that stood on its own and collected taxes for the Council of the State of Lithuania. The community of Minsk paid 16 shok (one shok equals 60 groszy), and Smorgon paid one shok. This meant that Smorgon was much smaller than its neighbor, Minsk. The head tax paid by Smorgon which, by this time, had already succeeded in establishing and broadening itself and having dependencies in the region, was 40 zloty – (a Polish zloty equaled 30 groszy). Minsk and its environs were paying 120 zloty.

In 1678 (5439), after 27 years, Smorgon was still paying only one zloty. After the war[9], all of the communities became smaller and they did not have the financial ability to pay more. However, after 42 years, the community of Smorgon and its environs was paying a head tax of 1,700. During this period, the community of Minsk and its environs was paying a tax of 5,500.

Rabbi Avraham Konki, who was an emissary from Hebron during the ten years between 1683 and 1694, and was one of the most important emissaries of the late 17th century, visited Smorgon in order to collect money for the community in the Land of Israel. He testified about the cities that he passed through, and among them he mentioned the community of Smorgon, noting and that they "generously gave of everything that they had, from silver to gold." (Lithuanian Jewry, Professor Y. Rivlin, p. 459.)

In 1765, the community of Smorgon numbered 649 people. But there were also many "evasive ones", those who were trying to avoid paying taxes.

In 1897 the population was 6,743 Jews and 2,165 Christians.

With the liberation of the vassals in 1861, the town began to develop. At that time, an academy for the training of bears to dance was built.

The area around Smorgon belonged to Prince Radziwill and Counts Potocki ,Tyszkiewicz and other feudal rulers. After the unsuccessful liberation of the areas, the liberated vassals were left bare and without any means, and especially without any land to farm. Worried about the outbreak of a revolt, Potocki came up with the idea that he would turn these unemployed people into bear hunters. The forests around Smorgon were full of bears.

The Radziwillites used to harness bears rather than horses to their wagons and their carriages, and drive down the streets of Smorgon, to the astonishment of the residents.

A small Jewish settlement was established near Smorgon during the days of Nikolai the First (1796–1853). During this time, the government was giving out lands for Jewish settlement (as tenant farmers.)

The settlement was divided into twenty parcels of land. Around the time of World War One, there were more than 40 families who farmed the lands, worked in agriculture, and earned their livelihood from the bounty of the land.

[Page 18]

Smorgon developed especially as an industrial city, i.e. a center for tanning. There were 54 tanneries and 30 other related workshops. The merchandise was marketed in Russian cities, the Caucasus, Siberia, Manchuria, and even Vladivostok. For a period of time they also sold their goods to Germany.

Aside from factories for leather work, Smorgon also had:

Two tobacco factories, Titon and Makhorka; one for soap; three for wool shearing; two (general) workshops, workshops for knitting socks and muskrat hides; warehouses for kerosene; two tea warehouses; two warehouses for sugar; and 175 shops. Cakes from Smorgon were famous throughout Russia and they were sold at all of the fairs. Since Smorgon was developing as an industrial city, a strong and revolutionary worker movement arose. Most of the Jewish workers were organized with the Bund[10].

In the beginning of the 1890s, a mass movement arose among the Jewish workers in Lithuania to improve the harsh working conditions. The workers, organizing in Vilna and Smorgon, demanded a shorter work day. There were strikes in 1893 and 1894 in Vilna and Smorgon. The government persecuted the strikers and many of them experienced hardships in Siberia. The government supported the employers against the workers.

Already in 1893, the tanners in Smorgon were celebrating May Day. In 1894 the strike fund had 200 members.

In 1895 the "Jargon Council"[11], through the initiative of the writer David Pinsky, founded workers' libraries in several cities, Smorgon among them.

At the end of 1895, 850 workers in Vilna went on strike. This strike led to the organization of 27 professional unions. At about the same time, an equal number of Jewish workers went on strike in Minsk. In the wake of Vilna and Minsk, workers from several other cities, among them Smorgon, joined the strikers.

"1892 through 1895 were the years in which we see the beginning of the workers' movement in in Smorgon." (A. Tratkower, History of the Jewish Workers' Movement, Volume 1, p. 36, Warsaw, 1929).

"The tanning industry centered in the Vilna District. The center of this manufacturing was in Smorgon, where there were 27 workshops. The methods for working leather in Smorgon were antiquated.

[Page 19]

They would place the leather in pits for soaking, and afterwards they would work them by hand. 461 workers were employed in the tanning workshops, among them 258 Jews." (Kagedan, History of the Bund, p. 38).

Social Democratic organizations were represented for the first time in the congress in London. The Russian delegation was made up of representatives of nine cities, including Smorgon. In 1896, the 4th International Socialist Congress convened in London. Of the four delegates, one was from Smorgon. This representative was Vera Zasulich.[12] (Kagedan, op. cit., pp .364–365)

The founding meeting of the Bund took place on October 7–9, 1897. The group from Smorgon could not participate in the meeting because of the harsh crackdown by the police, but they immediately announced their joining of the Bund. (Arkady Z. Zamelbuch, 163, Kagedan, Bs. Hmtz. 8, a, p. 366).

The regional organization of tanners started intensive work in 1897 (in both Krinik and Smorgon). Most of the workers were small storeowners whose situation had weakened or who had lost their social standing. The 'damp workers' were the ones that suffered the most from being taken advantage of. The working conditions were unbearable. During the winter days, their wet hands would freeze and stick to metal. (Despite the cold, employers refused to supply wood for heat in the tannery.) For the 'dry workers' in the drying rooms, the heat was unbearably high. The workers used to work in their underwear and would sweat nonstop from their faces and bodies.

There were 400 Jews among the 600 workers in the tanneries. The level of exploitation continually rose. They were afraid of both the employers and the government. (During visits of inspectors to the factories, the workers being so afraid of the employers, would give incorrect information regarding the length of the workday, etc. They used to hide the underage workers until the inspectors left and the danger passed.)

In 1896 there were ten cases of scurvy in Smorgon. Six of the (ten) ill people died.

These terrible conditions were the impetus for the workers to go to war. In 1896, strikes broke out frequently. During that year, there were 25 strikes in the factories and five in the workshops.

[Page 20]

The workers in Smorgon refused to accept their time cards at work. They were fighting for a 12–hour workday and an increase in salary of one ruble a week. The average salary during that time was four rubles a week.

Every strike brought arrests and crackdowns by the government. As the crackdowns increased, the conviction of the workers for battle grew too. In 1897, there were many arrests in Smorgon.

Because of the many prolonged strikes, the workday was indeed shortened to 12 hours.

The Jewish workers movement formed support groups of its own: strike funds and professional organizations on the one hand, and development and skills workshops on the other hand. The movement had grown beyond being limited to one region or sector. The movement united several cities, with Smorgon taking a respectable place among them. (Kagedan, the Book of Mtz. P. 109).

It was the year 1896. In the forefront of the revolutionary workers movements in Smorgon, we find Liba Ginzburg the daughter of Rabbi Menashe Ginzburg, Sara Mitlicikia, Shmuel Lewin, and Olga Burstein. They were under the influence of Rowanowa and Sinicki, both belonging to grassroots revolutionary movements.

Ivan Franciewicz Sinicki was a resident of Smorgon and a tax collector. Whenever he got ready to inspect the shops, he would warn the shopkeepers in advance to get rid of the "*chometz*" (illegal stuff) that was in their shop. Under his influence, we find Bila Ginzburg and the sister of Liba (sister–in–law of the poet Abraham Leissin), Dvora Szimszlewicz, Sonia Szpalter, Rivka Daniszewski, and Ida Hajlikman.

Sinicki was a grassroots revolutionary. He did not participate in the workers' movement. Shmuel Lewin, who leaned towards Marxism, invited Abraham Leissin (A. Walt) to a debate to argue against the harmful influence of Sinicki who treated with negativity the workers' movement that was based on the Social Democratic template.

The debate took place in Sinicki's home in the presence of six or seven of the movement's activists. Leissin opened by expounding the Marxist point of view.

Liba Ginzburg gave free private lessons to Smorgon workers. The students/workers who would gather in the house of Binyamin Szimszlewicz included Gershon Feldman, Yudel Krimer, Vilefka Minkus, and Bintsha Milkovski. Liba taught them Russian. After the lesson, she would conduct a propaganda session on Marxist Socialism, especially the ideas of class struggle. Shmuel Lewin, who was a private tutor in Smorgon, founded an aid fund and administered a study group for general education among the workers. This study group in natural sciences and sociology had 20–30 members.

The workers who had a class awareness would celebrate Mayday in the forests of Licznik (Litchnik) that was near Smorgon.

[Page 21]

As the movement grew and expanded, two provocateurs (informers in the secret intelligence service), Gorski and Sztrashinski, infiltrated it.

Lewin left Smorgon in the year 1896. That year, the first strike occurred. With the help of the informer Gorski, the police discovered the ledger of the Aid Association (Kupat Ezra) with all names of the membership payers. Yudel

Krimer and Eliakim Malkis, the treasurer of the fund, were arrested and exiled.

(A Jew named) Minka from the "Karke" (outlying area of Smorgon where the tenant farmers worked the land), Nechama Ginzburg the daughter of Yitzchak Tabacznik (tobacco salesman and industrialist), and Aharon Szimszlewicz organized the youth among the tanners in their workshops.

Approximately 400 workers participated in the demonstrations in the forest during the year 1897. In 1898, demonstrations were already taking place in the streets of Smorgon. In the years 1899–1900, workers organized funeral demonstrations in honor of the fighters who died in prison or shortly after their liberation; their deaths caused by long imprisonment that damaged their health. In Smorgon, a funeral demonstration of this nature also took place.

In the year 1901, political consciousness grew among Jewish workers. It was almost impossible for propagandists to provide for the workers' need for illegal literature (of socialist nature). Not only did the tanners organize an economic battle to improve their working conditions, but they also demonstrated for political reasons. (Kagedan ibid, p.170). That same year, workshop employees in Smorgon organized a general strike. Their workday was 15 hours, from 5:00 a.m. to 8:00 p.m. The strikers demanded a workday of 12 hours. The strike succeeded. The employers were willing to agree to the workers' demands. Nevertheless, in 1901 on Shmini Atzeret, on the last day of the Sukkot festival, a Cossack band of 100 individuals entered Smorgon. Thirty to forty of the striking workers were arrested. They were imprisoned in the Antokolsky Prison. The workers in Smorgon were not subdued. On the contrary, they overcame and organized a general strike of employees in all the factories and workshops in the city.

The factory inspector conceded that the workers' demand for a 12-hour workday was justified since, according to the laws of Catherina (1729–1796) who ruled from 1762–1796, it was prohibited to employ factory workers for more than ten hours a day. The mayor of Vilna had publicized this law in 1892. However, changing the workday was delayed because the workers were not content with merely economic demands, but also demanded political rights, the liberation of political prisoners, the right to free gathering, the right to a free press, and a constitutional assembly for all Russia. The strike continued from October 12th to 27th. The police subdued the strike. All 120 activists were arrested. Gershon Feldman was sentenced to two years in prison and deported to the Irkutsk district. He returned to Smorgon in the year 1903. Despite all the persecution and decrees, the workers achieved a shorter workday of 12 hours.

Pan Wahl, governor of the Vilna district, visited the prison where the Smorgon strikers were imprisoned.

[Page 22]

He attacked them with insult and curses and prohibited them from having interviews or visits from relatives.

At the same time, a group of Jewish workers was also brought into the prison in Vilna, which was packed with all types of political prisoners. They were tanners from nearby towns — Smorgon among them — and their crime was striking for higher salaries and improvement of their living conditions. Pan Wahl himself honored them with his visit to the prison cells. He came to speak with them. As he entered, he issued degrading commands not once but twice: *Zhidi Wofrijad*! But they didn't budge from their positions...

He ordered that the strikers be flogged on May 1, but Hirsh Likert shot him, and he (Hirsh) was hung by the Czar's hangmen (A. Sh. Stein. Comrade Arthur, p. 48, 5713 – 1953, Tel Aviv).

The police chief of Smorgon would arrest the workers for every conflict that occurred between the workers and their employers. He arrested the worker activists as if they were revolutionaries and sent them to prison in Vilna. The prisoners were forced to walk the whole way while the Cossacks beat them with deathblows. Even those who escorted them were beaten without mercy (Kagedan, ibid, p. 215).

Almost all the revolutionary political activists in Smorgon paid with their lives for their actions. They died untimely deaths. Liba Ginzburg died on August 18th, 1912. Sara Miatlickaja escaped to London and returned to Minsk. She was smuggled from Minsk to the United States by her friends. She became sick and committed suicide in the hospital. Nechama Ginzburg (daughter of Yitzchak the tobacco man), who organized a strike of the sewers, escaped to the United States, and returned to Kiev where she died suddenly. The famous student of Shmuel Lewin, Yitzchak Mayer Diwniszewski, was killed in 1919 by the Polish Legionnaires in Vilna. Lewin came to the United

States., graduated from medical school, and died suddenly from stomach ailment. This list was compiled by Bela Ginzburg in the year 1937. She too committed suicide a few years after her brother–in–law Abraham Leissin died.

In 1904, the Bund chapters conducted propaganda (agitation) against the draft. One of the active branches was in Smorgon. These activities led to conflicts with police, with subsequent arrests, and exile to Siberia (Lithuanian Jewry, p. 557).

3. Smorgon and Immigration to the Land of Israel

There were residents of Smorgon among the early pioneers who immigrated to the Land of Israel.

From among the students of Rabbi Chaim of Volozhin, who had a strong influence on generations to come, Rabbi Joseph Charif must be noted. He died in Jerusalem in 5600 (1861). He was the son of Rabbi Aharon Steinhardt of Smorgon. A regular visitor of Rabbi Chaim from Volozhin, who was supported at his table, Rabbi Charif was full of the virtues of his teacher and rabbi and (in turn) strongly influenced Rabbi Hirsh Michel Shapira, of blessed memory. one of the unique individuals of morality and Torah. He established a special school in Jerusalem, which was continued by Rabbi Yaakov Moshe Charlap. (Lithuanian Jewry, Prof. Y. Y. Rivlin, The Jews in Lithuania and the Land of Israel, p. 471).

[Page 23]

There also was a Smorgon resident among the Biluim: Shlomo Zalman Cukerman (Avinoam), was born in Smorgon, Vilna District, in 5627 (1867). He was educated in traditional and general schools. He joined the assembly of the "Dispersed of Israel" in Minsk and was transferred to the Land (Israel) by the association. He made *aliya* on the 3rd of Shevat, 5644 (1884), at the age of 17. He was accepted as a member of the Bilu (*Beit Yaakov Lechu Venelcha* – Sons of Jacob, Arise, and Let us Go), worked in Mikve Yisrael, and settled in Hadera at the time it was established. In 5665–6 (1905–1906), he participated in a delegation to America, together with Dov Leibovitch (Ariel) to distribute wines from the Land. He died in Gedera, on Iyar 19th 5687 (1927), at the age of 60. He left an extensive family. His sons Yoav and Asahel were among the redeemers of the lands of the Negev. (Arieh Tzantzifer, Footsteps of Redemption, p. 52, fig. 102, 177. Lithuanian Jewry, p. 498).

Here is a paragraph from the charter of Bilu. A. internal rules, the goal of the Bilu organization:

1. To settle and return the people of Israel to this ancestral land.
5. Those who join Bilu and become part of its society intend to give of all their energy and their time for the benefit of this organization and abstain from all their desires.
18. Only young men could join the organization: not older than 25 years, single, and free of burden of wives and children.
19. The member should not be the owner of any personal property. It is prohibited to make the effort to achieve this goal. Rather, all his resources, power and strength will be devoted to the benefit of the society.
20. It is prohibited for him to marry a woman during this period, until he becomes a landowner himself.
21. The entire society will have one treasury. Nobody may own any private property. Even his clothing and whatever he brings from his home or receives by shipment will be the property of the association.

The center of correspondence in Kishinev corresponded with 11 associations, Smorgon among them. (Lithuanian Jewry, p. 511).

Dr. Y. Czelnov could not continue to carry out the activity for the Keren Kayemet (Jewish National Fund) from Moscow, and he continued in Smorgon, Vilna district., (Lithuanian Jewry, p. 52). The delegate Meir Wernick from Smorgon took part in the Zionist conference of the Vilna district in the year 5660 (1900). (Tzantzifer ibid, p.142, figure 394).

Delegates from Smorgon also participated in the second conference of Russian Zionists in Minsk in 1902.

[Page 24]

Halperin approached Dr. Herzl during his visit in Vilna in 1903 and said: "The workers in Smorgon do not believe in Zionism."

Herzl responded: "Go and tell the workers of Smorgon that Zionism will be realized."

In 1905 in Smorgon, an S.S. Association (Socialist Zionists) was founded, their members were mostly tailors and commerce assistants.

In 1908, Wolfson returned from Petersburg, accompanied by Sokolow. He stayed in Vilna for one day. Many delegations came to his reception; one of them from Smorgon. In the delegation were Szimszelewicz and another delegate. They greeted Wolfson (Lithuanian Jewry, p. 521).

The district committee organized conferences ('weddings') in the districts. In that way, a conference of the associations in Vilna district took place in Smorgon, in Adar II 5679 – 1909. (ibid, p.525).

Dr. Ben Zion Mozesson visited Smorgon and lectured in 1909. A group of Zionists took pictures with the guest speaker. (Arie Tzantzifer, ibid, p.151, figure 438).

Smorgon continued to develop. It grew in population, industry, and trade. "Unemployed young people from the surrounding towns came to Smorgon and found work there." (B. Tz. Wolf, I Visited Smorgon Three times, p. 1272 in the book Lithuania edited by Dr. M. Sudarsky).

There were 25,000 Jews and 4,00 gentiles in Smorgon at the beginning of 1941. It had two splendid *Beis Midrashes* (Study Halls); seven *kloizes*, including the *shtibels* of Chabad Hassidim, Koidanov, and others; one Talmud Torah, three elementary *Yeshivas*; one old age home; one "*Beit Lechem*" (House of Bread) that supported the poor of the city, providing bread as well as firewood during the winter; one hospital; one charitable fund; one place for the housing of wayfarers; and a lodging house for poor from other cities who were passing through the city and stayed for a while; one "*Linat Tzedek*" organization whose members stayed overnight with sick people who had no family, supporting them on their sickbeds.

Among the honorable householders who built the aforementioned institutions, we must mention especially: Zalman and Gedalia Rothstein, Yaakov Piribozski; Yisrael Suczkower, Zalman Bickowski, Gedalia Solodochi, Yehuda Cukerman, and Yaakov Kowarski.

4. Smorgon in its Ruins and Partial Rehabilitation

In year 1915, World War I was in full force. Smorgon had achieved industrial and commercial climax when, unexpectedly, disaster and ruin came upon it.

In the Vilna district, 20 towns and cities suffered great damage, among them Smorgon, which became a heap of ruins.

Already by the beginning of 1915, the city had become part of the battle zone.

[Page 25]

Struggles between Christians and Jews concerned land, shortage of currency, and plots by speculators.

On August 7th, Cossacks entered the city. The gendarmes stirred them up against the Jews.

Several brigades of the German Cavalry broke through the front line and surrounded the Russian Corps near Smorgon from three sides.

On September 2nd, the Germans entered Smorgon. They conducted searches and confiscated leather, money, and items of value. The German commander captured Jewish hostages. The withdrawal of the Germans from Smorgon brought happiness among the whole population. However, joy did not last for long; the Cossacks reentered Smorgon in the wake of the retreating German soldiers. The Christian population informed on the Jews, saying they helped the Germans.

On the night of the 8th of that month, Jewish property was pillaged once again, and local Christians took part. Many Jews escaped through the forests on the way to Minsk. The tribulations continued and worsened. The soldiers broke into houses of Jews with the pretext of searching for Germans. They murdered and raped. A group of about 40 Jewish soldiers organized to protect the Jewish population. The group fought against the Cossacks in the front yard of the synagogue entrance, in the place where the Cossacks raped Jewish women who hid there. When the Jewish soldiers broke into the synagogue, a horrible sight appeared before them; the Cossacks were in the process of destroying ritual articles and tearing Torah scrolls. The corpses of women who had been raped and died of torture lay on the floor. Near one young girl's corpse lay her father's corpse. In the battle between the Jewish soldiers and the Cossacks, two of the defenders died and many were injured. The Cossacks were injured as well. A deportation command was added to the pogrom and, with the deportation, there was robbery, arrests and even killing. The burning of houses began. Whoever did not succeed in escaping or hiding, died in the fire. Fugitives were injured in the forests and on the roads by soldiers and peasants (Lithuanian Jewry, The History of the Jews in Lithuania, by Dr. Israel Kloizner, pp.120–121).

On September 11, the Jews of Smorgon were ordered to be exiled. The command was issued by junior officials on their own.

The Cossack captain entered the house of Avraham Sobol and ordered the family to hurry and leave the city. One of the sons, Leib Sobol, responded that he could not abandon his elderly father in his sickbed. The captain asked him to show him the sick man. When the son did so, the captain took out his gun and shot the sick father, killing him in front of his son's eyes, and told him – "Now you can leave the city, since you have no sick person to take care of." He deported the whole family and did not let them bury their father.

The Jews were deported, and their houses were burned. The Cossacks and their captains passed from house to house, setting the homes on fire. Some Jews hid in cellars, but the fire and smoke forced them to go out and run for their lives.

[Page 26]

(One Jew) Wilenczyk was captured as he left the bathhouse. He was sentenced to hanging for evading the deportation, but he saved himself by giving a ransom of 1,500 rubles to the captain.

Weinstein, who was paralyzed, asked to be pushed into the Lubavitcher Shtibel, where he was burned. Kalman Razowski was injured. Many Jews were burned alive. Among the pogromists, the Ukrainian Cossacks were noted for their cruelty and wildness.

Those who escaped were arrested on their way by the Russian soldiers and were injured, robbed and beaten with deathblows. The peasants also assaulted the refugees with batons. The Circassians told the peasants that the Jews are open for all (punishment with impunity), and they were allowed to cut off their heads without fear of punishment.

The soldiers prohibited the few good peasants from giving lodging to the refugees of Smorgon in their houses.

Many children died along the way; pregnant women miscarried.

The number of refugees that escaped to Minsk alone reached 8,000 (Chapter from: The Scroll of Destruction).

"During the course of several hours, the Jews of Smorgon were forced to leave the city in great haste. The scene was terrible. Men and women, with toddlers and babies in their arms and bunches of underwear and pillows on their shoulders, marched tens of verst[13]. More accurately, they ran in the cold and rain to arrive at the train station going to Minsk. Hungry and very tired, they ran away from the sword." (Mendel Sudarsky, Lithuania, Through the Towns, pp.1549–1550).

The exiled Smorgonians first dispersed all over Russia. Some arrived in Harbin and some even went to the United States. Afterward, they started to converge, and later had better days. When they had some relief, they congregated and established industrial centers for tanning.

They moved the factories to Bogorodsk, and invited tanners and tailors from Smorgon to come. The same was done in Kharkov and Rostov on the Don River.

During the war years, a severe shortage of processed leather was felt, and the Smorgonians organized and returned to their work. They continued to work in tanning and the connection between the Smorgon employee and his employer was not severed." (A. Rafels, Zamelbuch, Smorgon, 1937.)

In 1921, after their exile years, Smorgoners started to return to their hometown. The rehabilitation work started in full drive and strong momentum. The assistance committees (Yekofo) and their equivalents in the U.S. (Relief) came to the assistance of those who returned, by organizing the welfare relief.

The German forces flooded large areas in the Pale of Settlement.

"Under the whip of difficult decrees and cruel deportations perpetrated by enemies of Israel, Nikolai son of Nikolai (uncle of the King Nikolai II), the chief commander of the Russian troops and his chief of staff the General Yanushkevich, millions of Jews suffered. A wave of hundreds of thousands of homeless refugees spilled into Central Russia and Ukraine. As always in hard times and distress, the Jewish heart was pulsating and restless."

[Page 27]

"The Aid committee (The Jewish Committee for Assistance – Yekofo is the acronym) was founded with wondrous haste, with its new style." (Yosef Chernichow – Danieli, A Page of Memories, "Heint" Jubilee number 1908–1928, p. 186).

"During the war year of 1919, the Vilna Yekofo was established by the gathering of delegates of the communities and Aid Committees of the districts of Vilna and Nowogrodek. Included in its scope of activity were: juridical and legal aid, the rehabilitation of ruined towns, the economic situation of the refugees and returnees, the war orphans, immigration, cultural work and cooperation, and other branches of rehabilitation and welfare." (A.I. Grodzinsky, Vilna in the Past and Present, ibid, p.109.)

On February 2nd, 1921, a Smorgon representative participated in a Yekofo conference in Vilna.

The first returnees settled temporarily in cellars until their houses were completed. They barely made a living. A weekly market day took place, and peasants from the surroundings came and brought their produce and crops. The refugees bought from them vegetables, butter, cheese and eggs, and carried the goods to Vilna. Transportation of the merchandise by wagon and train was difficult because of the malicious behavior of the wagon drivers. With a payoff they often softened their rigidity.

The returnees showed their motivation, confidence, and independent initiative. First attempts were made to remove the logs from the foxholes on the front and reusing them as building material. In this way, the first houses in Smorgon were built.

In agriculture, the returnees managed more easily. They planted potatoes and vegetables, and ate their own produce. They ate of the fruits of their labor on their land.

5. Monetary Report – "Yekofo"

257,876 Polish Marks were allocated to Smorgon for building materials and reconstruction of the wreckage. 20 Polish Marks had the value of one dollar. On May 5th, 1921, 55 Jews returned, and 15 houses were built for them. On

October 22nd, there were already 600 returnees, and 30 houses were built. On December 5th, 37 houses had been built. October 31st, 1922, 91 houses were built. At the end of 1922, 60 more houses were built, and 105 houses were under construction.

On 3/31/1922, a report on the budget was received from "Smorgon Relief" in New York.

[Page 28]

David Brunda brought more than 8,000 dollars. From this pool of money, 15,000 Marks were given out as loans, 5,000 Marks were expended on the building of the elementary school. The fence around the cemetery cost 4,000 Marks. They established a refugee building with the dimensions of 10' x 21', which cost 3,000 Marks. The building of the "Karka"×£ *Beis Midrash* cost 15,000 Marks. The building of the bathhouse cost 1,000 Marks; the hospital was 1,000 Marks; the library was 1,000 Marks; salary for teachers in the elementary school was 1,000 Marks; refugees received 50 Marks. The interest free Benevolent Society received 500 Marks.

During 1922, 233 men, 247 women, and 268 children retuned to Smorgon. Altogether 738 people returned.

On March 12, 1922 a general meeting of the Jews in Smorgon took place, and a new executive committee of 14 members was elected. The chairman was Dr. Yaakov Provozski and the secretary, Gershon Weinstein. The following are the names of the members of the executive committee: Moshe Yehuda Kreines, Yosef Provozski, Yaakov Boaz Horowitz, David Miller, Baruch Daniszewski (from the Karka), Ephraim Gross (from the Karka), Yona Stricenski, Chaim Gorland, Moshe Szapira, Avraham Kac, Nota Kuborski, Zusman Jetes, and David Magids.

The supervision of the children who returned with their parents was handled diligently by a special physician. In August 1922, 211 children were examined. The buildings for the children were also to be finished that week. Negotiations were conducted with the Internat (an orphanage for children). They prepared furniture, beds, mattresses, sheets and blankets. A library for the children was to be established. The Internat would start to function in about two weeks.

In October 1922, teenagers between 14–18 who wanted to study arts in Smorgon, stood at 56 boys and 57 girls.

The returnees to Smorgon were delayed in Baranovichi and Stavich for about 2 to 3 months. They were forced to stay there until the authorities agreed to return them to their place of residence. When they arrived, they received first aid and especially constructional relief in the form of loans to rebuild their ruined houses.

In November 1922, 126 people were already residing in the public buildings. The winter led to cutbacks in building work, and the workers suffered from unemployment.

The Yekofo report stated that all the returnees were settled in dwellings. Nobody was homeless. Yekofo expended a total of 8,267,393 Marks, 4,070 of that on clothing shoes and food.

On March 31, 1922, 180 families received food, clothes, shoes, and, of course, medical care. In case of emergency, sick people were moved to a rest home for the ill in Vilna. A bakery was opened. Tailors and sewers purchased sewing machines. The carpenters, shoemakers and blacksmiths received support in order to enable them to buy tools for work. Health stations were established and supported a small pharmacy with a paramedic, with the help of EZA.

The returnees suffered from lack of ID cards, and they could not move out of the city.

[Page 29]

In 1920, Yekofo built the first house for the returnees. It was two rooms, 12' x 10'.

In the year 1921, sixty people lived in it. It served this purpose until 1922.

In the beginning of 1922, when the wave of returnees increased, the problem of dwelling became more serious. Therefore, they repaired the first story of the *Beis Midrash*, and prepared it to be used as an apartment house. They prepared and fixed the cellar of Ch. Greenhaus in a similar fashion and set it up to be used as an apartment house. Both houses served their purpose until September 1922. Sixty people lived in them.

In March of that year, a public building was erected near the cemetery. It measured 26' x 10', and was divided into two rooms. More than 70 people lived there. This house functioned as a dwelling for the returnees until the end of 1922. During the months of June and July of that year, two buildings of Magides were built. They were rented as dwellings for the returnees. In total, 500 people passed through those buildings until their private houses were built and ready to be settled.

On June 15, 1923, all those communal buildings were evacuated since it became too dangerous for the residents. People whose houses were not yet complete moved to private houses. For the new arrivals that kept on coming, they fixed an old abattoir.

Medical care was arranged by physicians that came from Vilna for visits.

Care for the Children

211 children of the ages 1 thru 16 were examined. All of them were anemic, 11 had ophthalmia, 3 had ear infections, 1 had a nasal and throat illness, 112 had internal illnesses, 31 were blind, 11 had orthopedic problems, 6 had mental and nervous illnesses.

Of all the children who were checked, 8 were orphans, 37 half orphans, 123 were children of the poor, and 18 were children of middle class parents.

The Internat opened. 36 children, orphans and non–orphans, from the children of families who resided in the communal houses, lived there. (With time, a new building was built for 100 children.) A kitchen was established for the children, with a capacity of preparing meals for 150 children. At this point, 130 meals were distributed once per day.

A two–story building was built by the Internat. The building was finished in the spring of 1923. Meanwhile, the Internat was resided in six wooden houses rented for that purpose. One house served a dormitory for 32 children. A dining room for 130 children was in a second house. Classrooms were in the third one. In the fourth, there reading and playrooms. The fifth and sixth were dormitories for personnel.

The former abattoir was renovated and functioned until spring as an entertainment place for sick children.

The public house near the cemetery was renovated and became the elementary school.

[Page 30]

Expenses for the renovations came equally from Yekofo and the local community.

The renovations started with one building for carpentry for child returnees.

In January 1923, there were 42 children at the Internat. They added one large room to the building as an additional playroom.

The children established a sports club, a court of justice for themselves, an executive committee, etc.

Lectures in geography and history were given.

143 meals were distributed by the kitchen once a day. The weak or sick ones received their meals twice a day, in accordance with the advice of the physicians.

All the children were under the supervision of the educators, who also supervised hygiene and clothing. The older children also participated in performances.

General Assistance

The committee supported 140 people who received medical aid, extra high nutritional food, and rent support.

In the elementary school, studies were already carried on in a normal fashion.

All the repairs in the carpentry shop were completed that month.

Out of 12 families who lived in damp cellars, five were moved to communal houses, three were moved to private houses, and four will find a place within a month.

General assistance was stopped in March 1923. It was given only for construction.

In April 1923, the carpentry shop was opened by Yekofo and ORT. Fifteen returnee children studied there. The workshop operated during the next 1 Â½ to 2 years. ORT will manage the institution and provide all its economic and educational needs. For this goal, the Yekofo provided ORT with the building for that duration, and was responsible for 75% of the budget. This annual amount of 2,000,000 Marks was paid in advance.

A two–story building was built with 14 rooms which housed the Internat.

On the first floor there was one bedroom with 30 beds; two bedrooms with 35 beds; for personnel: a two–room apartment and kitchen for the director; a room for clothes storage; a cellar; a room for food storage; a room for wood storage, a heated toilet; facilities, etc.

The building was built in the shape of the letter T. Sixty children of the poor of the city lived there. Some were orphans or half orphans. The Internat owned the carpentry building and the elementary school.

Out of 815 war orphans, 57 came to Smorgon.

It was not long before the Holocaust came upon Smorgon along with other towns and cities that drank from the cup of poison against their will. Jewish Smorgon was destroyed to its foundations during World War II.

Editor's Notes

1. https://en.wikipedia.org/wiki/Magdeburg_rights
2. The editor suspects the negative is missing in the original as there is a gap and thus the Jews did not want a leader that was *foisted* upon them.
3. Zygmunt August was a Polish King and presumably made a request to Ivan to allow Jews to trade.
4. A reference to punishment in this world (i.e. by the community), as well as in the World To Come (by G–d).
5. A reference to the tribulations related to the Chmielnicki uprising of 1648–1649.
6. See https://en.wikipedia.org/wiki/Joseph_Solomon_Delmedigo
7. Interestingly, the word used here is Torah, but it must refer to scientific doctrine.

8. Not referring to the Holocaust, although it is fascinating that the term Shoah is used. Likely referring to the outbreak of the Russo–Polish war (see https://en.wikipedia.org/wiki/Russo–Polish_War_(1654%E2%80%931667)

9. There is a footnote in the text as follows: "In my verses, I woke people up for *Selichot*" – thus writes Winchevsky himself about the character of his literary activity 35 years ago, when the writer of these lines first met himâ€¦ When his young guest was mentioning to him that they are waking up for *Selichot* in Vilna, Minsk and Smorgon as well due to his call, he was filled with world–changing enthusiasm." (A. Leisin, Memories and Experiences, p. 75, am Oved, 5703 (1943), Tel Aviv, Translated by A. Kariv). (Editor's note: *Selichot* are the penitential prayers recited early in the morning during the High Holy Day Season. Here it is seemingly alluding to a call to a new world order. For Winchevsky, see https://en.wikipedia.org/wiki/Morris_Winchevsky)

10. "After the war" may reference the Polish–Ottoman War (1672–76) or Lubomirski's Rebellion.

11. Jargon is at times used as a term for Yiddish.

12. There is a footnote in the text as follows; Vera Zasulich (1851–1919), the daughter of a noble family, was born in the village of Mikhaylovka, Smolensk Governorate. In 1868, G. Nechayev convened (a gathering) in Smolensk. She was imprisoned in 1869, and spent two years in jail. She joined the group of modernists in Kiev. She came to Peterburg in 1877. She went to Switzerland in 1878. She returned to Russia in 1879, and stood at the head of the "Black Division" together with Plekhanov. She was also among the founders of the "Freedom of work" Marxist organization. She translated Engel's book "The Development of Socialism, From Utopia to Science," and Marx's book "The Poverty of Philosophy" into Russian. She was a member of the editorial board of "*Hanitzutz*" (Iskra) and of *Hashchar* (Zaria). Vera took the side of Plekhanov during the schism between Lenin and Plekhanov. The Bolsheviks denigrated her as a traitor due to her opposition to the October revolution (Editor's note: see https://en.wikipedia.org/wiki/Vera_Zasulich)

13. An old Russian unit of length, about .66 mile.

[Page 31]

A Conversation from Ancient Times

by Chanoch Lewin

Translated by Jerrold Landau

In memory of my parents: my father Reb Dov-Ber and my mother Minca, in holiness

A. Groyat and Okna

Smorgon is situated on the route between Minsk and Vilna, between the surrounding walls of forests. Its northern bounds almost touch the banks of the calm Viliya, flowing somnolently and thoughtfully through its channel of greenery. From the city's other sides, the boundaries of Smorgon touch two rivers, tributaries of the main river Viliya – the Groyat and the Okna. The first is a proud, strong river, flowing with strength, always hurrying as if it had to get somewhere quickly. The second one, the Okna, is calm, gentle, and weak, as if saying: "See, I am slow and sandy..." The "Beradim," wandering poets and instrumentalists of Lithuania, would issue from the depths of their soul, through the strings of the bandura, the musical instrument of that area – a song of legend and story. The puffy [literally "full of skin"] eyes of the Beradim wandered through the space of the cottage of the farmer, into which old and young, women and children, gathered to hear stories from olden times – the extinguished eyes of the poets wandered through the space of the farmer's hut, imagining that they are seeing the young, brave Lithuanian prince Groyat, and his beautiful bride Okna.

The elderly "Wydolta," the first of the poets and instrumentalists, who played the antique instrument and told in verse the story of the young prince who descended from the heights of the town of his father, the great ruler Gydmin [Gediminas]. The young knight descended from his white horse, and found the maiden Okna in the field. -- -- --

Okna stood before him, clear as the sun, decorated with dew-laden, perfumed, and decorated graceful flowers.

Then the knight Groyat took her, seated her on his white horse, and galloped away with the maiden, the queen of his dreams, to the palace of his father, the ruler, in order to request his blessing.

The father hardened his heart and said: "This one is not fitting for you, my son the knight. She is the daughter of a village, and you are a prince."

Gydmin, the great ruler of a large city, sent the maiden Okna away. The sorrowful, morose maiden went down to the banks of the Viliya, flowing and descending eastward. The young prince Groyat followed in her wake, absorbing her shadow and concerned about the breath of her spirit. Thus did both of them go for two days and one night until they reached a rocky pillar on the banks of the Viliya River. They met at the top of the rock. The lovers embraced each other, and their golden joy lit up the waves of the river. Then Groyat said:

"My bride, perhaps the Viliya, the mother of rivers, will gather us up. In its depths we will build an abode of love forever." Okna said:

[Page 32]

"Take me with you, Groyat my beloved, take me into the calm Viliya, where our life will flow forever."

They spoke, and did not continue. Then they jumped into the river.

The mother Viliya took the lovers into its bosom. As they jumped, the rock upon which they stood split, and two rivers broke forth from the sides, forging for themselves paths through the forests and the fields in a joyous and splendorous stream – are these not the rivers Groyat and Okna?

People say, as time went on, a human settlement arose between these rivers, ruling over their dual essence.

This is the mighty Groyat bursting forth, and the dreamy gentleness of the Okna.

B. Smorgon, the Interpretation of the Name

It is said: Smorgon had a difficult name to identify. More difficult is the pronunciation of this name in the mouths of the gentile: Smorgonia. The interpretation of the name was not known for many years. Many worked on it. They asked the historians and turned to the secrets of legend – but came up with nothing.

It is said: The interpretation of the name is shrouded in mystery, and its meaning is obscured in the clouds of the past. Nevertheless, the tradition of the elders is the desire to solve the hidden secrets of the past, to reveal all, or at least some part of the footnotes of long-gone days. [Who really knows?] In any case, the following is told to us:

On the face of the wide world, situated between the Lycznik [Litchnik] and Przyboz forests, with the Viliya closing in on it from the north and the south, and from Zlasia (meaning: opposite the forest)[1], on the way to the "Dark Forest" on the route to Soli from the east and west – farmers of White-Rus[2], connected to the "*Panim Lachim*" (Polish nobility) who worked the land, and who ignored the law.

All the storehouses of the landlords were full of grain – while they and their households hungered for bread.

The houses of the nobility were constructed with planks, from the best forests of the area – while they lived in dirt shacks on the banks of the rivers.

The noblemen had relations with their brides first, and while they sent their children to forced labor.

When their souls became entangled [enwrapped] from agony and hunger, the farmers of White Rus composed a revolutionary song. From the depths of their being, the degraded souls of the vassals shouted out:

"You, oh Viliya, have you not seen how downtrodden [we are] from the contact with the lashes of the whip – the end shall come, the yoke will be removed!" (From a Byelorussian national song). Then it happened that the farmers could no longer keep the words of the son in their hearts. They took their axes and scythes, went up to the rocky hill, shouted with a bitter cry and said:

"We will no longer work for the landowners until we get land to grow bread for our children and wives." When the voice of the farmers was heard through the decorated wall of the young nobleman of the Tyszkiewicz ruling family, the brave man rounded up his men and galloped over to the camp of the protesting farmers. They came to the edge of the camp, stood across from them, and the young "*Pan*"[3] called out in a loud voice:

[Page 33]

"Farmers, abandon your weapons and return to your houses!"

The farmers answered him in unison: "Only death will cause us to abandon our weapons. We will not move until our property will be secure in our hands."

"So it will be," said the young *Pan*, "Your property will be established."

"And how will this be established?" asked the farmers of White Rus of the Polish nobleman.

"Did you not know, did you not hear that the land is measured by *morag*[4], a large unit of measure, and, v unit, its younger sister, called *hajunja* – for every *morag* of my estate, you will receive one *hajunja* for your inheritance. And now, tell me if I have spoken in justice?" They all answered: "Our master has spoken justly, thus let it be." All the farmers rose up and stood on one side, and the young *Pan* of the Tyszkiewicz dynasty stood on the other side. They took an oath of faith, and wrote the words of the agreement in a book. They wrote it and sealed it, some with a seal of a man, and others with a sign of blood from their thumb – to keep and establish the words of this oath until the end of days.

When the people, the farmers of White Rus, returned to their homes, the women and children went out to greet them and asked:

"From where are you coming?"

The husbands and father answered in one word: "From Smorg-hajunja"

It is not known whether they succeeded in explaining the meaning of the name to their wives and children. It is known that the farmers were cheated by the ruling *Pans*, as [only] a small measure was given to them – a small amount of land, and the land was measured with a stingy eye.

After a long time passed, a human settlement sprung up there. In memory of the breakdown of brotherhood between the landlords and their serfs, the place was called:

Smorgon.

A second version of the ancient legend follows:

In the decorated castle of Prince Tyskiewicz lived a Jewish steward of Khazar extraction, named Reb Avraham Kuzari. The prince brought the Jew from the large city of Kiev to be the steward of his house. The prince placed everything he had into the hands of Reb Avraham, for the man was wise and resourceful. His advice was always logical.

There was none like him in the country who conducted himself with such wisdom wherever he went. *Pans* from afar would frequent his door to get advice from him, and also to settle their disputes, both internal and external.

The young prince of the Tyskiewicz family took none other than he, Reb Avraham the Kuzari, on the day of the great dispute between himself and his servants, the farmers of White Rus. He,

[Page 34]

Reb Avraham and none other gave the wise advice regarding the distribution of land in measures of *morag* and *hajunja* – to assuage the anger of the serfs who were rebelling against their masters.

According to a different version of the legend, his wife and children came out to greet him upon his return to his city, and asked him:

"Is all well with you, my husband and our father?"

"*Shalom*," answered Reb Avraham.

"And from where are you coming?" they further asked him.

"From Smorgon," responded Reb Avraham.

It is unknown if he succeeded in explaining the meaning of the name to his wife and children. It is known that due to his good advice, the prince of the Tyskiewicz family gave him a large inheritance upon which to build his house, in the place where the deal was struck.

Reb Avraham the Kuzari called the place Smorgon. As time when on, Reb Avraham brought in Jews from his native land, settled them there, and distributed to them land from his inheritance. He brought in a large population. They built many houses. There was a street which the gentiles called the Street of the Khazars. Future generations changed the name of the street to the Street of the Pigs [*chazirim*][5].

Let the name be a reason to nod the head, and [be] a joke and source of derision.

C. Bear Hunters

1.

From time immemorial, the nickname “Bear Chasers” was attached to the Jews of Smorgon. It is possible for the distributor of nicknames to all living beings[6] to attach this nickname to the Jews of the city, and did not find any other suitable name for them other than this. They were not pursuers of profit, not even pursuers of pleasure, not pursuers of spirit, and not even pursuers of peace... but, specifically, pursuers of bears.

The writer[7] is speaking of the Jews of Smorgon to exclude the local gentiles, for we have never heard the gentiles being called such a name by their friends, even though, according to all opinions, they were closer to the boundary of the forests than the children of Abraham, Isaac, and Jacob.

The bears of Smorgon achieved renown, and their fame went afar. We are not talking about regular bears, as such are found in all forests; not of the sweet-toothed glutton that puts its paw in its mouth during a long slumber in its den for the entire winter as it watches a pleasant dream of the honey of the world, and not of its sting – but rather of that trained bear, with a beautiful back and a beautiful soul, whose paws are made up and whose breath is sweet, walking upright and standing on its hind paws, understanding hints and distancing itself from the fist. All its steps are human steps, bearing grace and charm to its owners and to everyone, knowing how to dance according to the musical instruments and the tunes. After each dance, “our master the bear” would place itself before its audience, spread its arms, as if to say:

[Page 35]

“I did my part, and now you do your part...” During its performance, it did not intend anything other than the good taste of this sweetness, the honey liquid that is called mead.

From which house of study did this “child” learn its teaching? – not from the *Beis Midrash* of Shem and Japheth, but rather from that of Ham. Ham in the literal sense – in the academy of bears that was founded by Count Potocki himself.

Where was this school of bears founded?

In Smorgon, at the end of the long road, as you come to the wide market along the way to the Przyboz Forest. There, Potocki founded it and set up its doors. From time immemorial, this street has been called "The Street of the Bears" (Berishe Gasse)[8].

2.

There was a Jewish man
In Smorgon the capital.
Bedecked and decorated.
But not graced with property.
Lit up with good deeds.

The man's name was Moshe Ber (Moshe the bear). Not that his education was such, but rather because of something that happened with him.

This is what transpired: Reb Moshe was a straightforward man, happy with his lot. He was also poor, may it not befall you. He lived in a small hut, with his wife and many children. And his work? – he put his hand [in] at all jobs.

He was a water drawer, he lit the oven in the bathhouse, but his main livelihood was from the trees of the forest. Immediately after the High Holy Days, Reb Moshe would go out to the nearby forest, cut down trees, and load them on his wagon. Together with his children, he dragged them back to town to sell the wood to the residents. Reb Moshe conducted great publicity for his merchandise. He stood in the market, and declared to the public:

"In the Forest of Przyboz I was.
Lofty trees I saw
I cut down the tree – I will gird my loins
I will bring it to your houses, and pay, my sirs!"

The children saw and responded:

"We will bring the wood, we will light the fire
The heat will spread, and the cold will disappear."

Once, in the middle of the winter, the householders of Smorgon saw Reb Moshe return from his work in the forest. He was pulling his wagon laden with wood, and the *kozowka* (the furs, a short winter coat made of hides with the hair inside) was not on him. They went to greet him, and found that he was only wearing his kaftan, and was shivering from cold and hunger. They asked him to explain the situation, but he did not answer them. He only gestured to his wagon laden with wood. The people standing around turned their eyes, and saw his outer coat, the *kozowka,* folded on top of an [obscure] bundle atop the wood in the wagon. One of them approached and opened the bundle. What do you think they saw there? A wounded bear cub.

[Page 36]

After some time, Reb Moshe told his story in short form:

"In this forest, there are chopped trees.
Among the trees, there was an abandoned bear cut.
He removed his coat and wrapped up the animal
He brought it hope, and raised it with the children."

One cannot describe the great joy when Reb Moshe brought the little "child of the forest" to his home. The joy of the children was boundless. He fed it of their bread, gave it to drink from their cup, and set up a bed for it atop the hot stove.

When the stove was especially hot, the "berish", the little bear, stood up on his hind legs. The children stood below, turned their thin necks upward toward the oven, shouted out loud, clapped their hands, and the "berish", this little bear, danced to the tempo of their song.

As time went on, the cub grew up and became an [adult] bear. His "beary" soul was bound to the members of the household. He was their guard and their shadow.

"They gave it food at the right time
And it kept them from its kicks
It rejoiced and danced on the oven.
And drank a pitcher full of mead."

From that time, Moshe Ber Dov was given the nickname Moshe "the bear."

3.

News spread through Smorgon: the only daughter of Count Potocki, the apple of his eye and breath of his spirit, was dying.

Already this news had stopped being a secret, for the young princess had fallen into a "black melancholy," may G-d protect us, some time before, and she was "flickering like a candle." All the physicians that her father brought from the large land of Poland as well as from overseas left as perplexed as they came. Even the various soothsayers and strange women in white could not find any cure – nothing helped. The delicate girl sat dully, in a room inside a room. Food did not enter her mouth, and a smile did not appear on her pale lips. She only stared ahead with hollow eyes. People said, "She is flickering like a candle."

A Jew, Reb Shmelke of Danyshev lived on the estate of Count Potocki. He was the steward of his house, and a wonderful advisor to his master. Count Potocki did not do anything simple or complex without asking the advice of "his" Jew. With time, Reb Shmelke married off his daughters to the sons of householders of Smorgon. He regarded himself as a resident in all aspects in his new city of residence.

[Page 37]

One day, Reb Shmelke was sitting with the elderly count, conducting business with his merchandise and discussing many business matters. The door of the parlor [opened] in which the count and the Jews were sitting, and the elderly nanny burst in, wailing:

"My master, your graciousness, a terrible thing has happened. Your daughter the princess has fallen down, and who can raise her up?

The elderly count was perplexed, and called out loudly.

"Please save, oh Jew, pray to your G-d, Shmelke Sardacza!"

The steward responded:

"I will do as you say, only be strong and brave."

After he spoke, he hastened out to the street, running the entire way.

The Jews of Smorgon were standing in the market, perplexed and astonished – where is Reb Shmelke from Danyshev running? The women looked out the windows of their houses and said to each other:

"What happened to Reb Shmelke?"

The children of the *cheders* [9] heard the tumult from the street. They peered through the cracks and said:

"Our master, Reb Shmelke, is running..."

And he, the Danyshever, Reb Shmleke, arrived at the house of Moshe "the bear," roused up the residents of the house, and called out, saying:

"Reb Moshe, take the bear and follow me!"

"To where?" asked the owner of the bear to Reb Shmelke, "What is the hurry?" Even though he [intuitively] knew that if Reb Shmelke was saying something, he knew he what he was talking about.

Reb Moshe took the bear down from the oven in his house. He whispered in its ear, placed a sugar cube in its mouth and a chain around its neck, and pulled the bear after him. The bear uttered a growl of understanding, as if to say: "I am invited to a celebration." It lifted its legs, shook its head this way and that, blinked its eyes as the dandies do, wiped its nose with its paw, spat out its spittle – and went onward! As if to say, "Take me after you, let us hurry!"[10]

Reb Shmelke of Danyshev ran
Reb Moshe "the bear" ran after him
Dragged behind them like a householder sitting
Our good "berish".
The town was in ferment
The householders shouted in anger:
"To where, is this convoy going,
If not to Potocki the count?
The convoy already passed the market
Along the way to the Przyboz Forest.

[Page 38]

The lambs [i.e., young children] had already left the *cheders*
In which their souls were marching mightily
And the good animal was then pacing
Up the steps of the palace

To save the dying daughter of the count
To prevent a tragedy for Potocki.

You have probably figured out for yourselves that the Danyshever went to the count in this manner, and Reb Moshe "the bear" and the good berish following after them.

They were brought into the room of the dying princess. The delicate one was lying on a shiny silk mattress. A dull light shone whiteness on her golden hair, as the white rose of death sprouted upon her lips.

Then Reb Moshe approached the good "berish" and whispered in its ear... The bear checked and lifted one paw, and then checked its other paw. It stood upright, grasped the cymbals in its front paws, and clanged them!

"Clang the cymbal
And sing with all strength
A Divine song, the hymn of life
From the angels with white wings."
And the "berish" is dancing and dancing, clanging the cymbals,
Say to the eyelids of the delicate girl
Open her eyes, the pitiful one.
Let the agony disappear, let the grief pass
From the bitterness of death that is with her – let her rise.
-- -- -- -- -- -- --
-- -- -- -- -- -- --

When Count Potocki saw the charm of life that was in the dancing bear, he commanded his servants to go out to the forests and hunt bears, starting from the forests of Smorgon and reaching to the forests of Bilo Bzh' – throughout the entire lands of Count Potocki.

Then, through the advice of Reb Moshe, the count built a brick, two-story house, with a large opening between each floor. The bears were placed in the second floor. A large oven was built for the house, whose fire did not extinguish day or night. Tongues of flames rose up from the oven, flowing through the heat ducts leading to the open space under the floor of the second floor. The floor got hot, and who would not be burnt through the heat?

The bears stood on top, checked their paws, which were indeed burnt by the fire. They began to jump and grunt in anger. They could not stand on their paws, for the fire was burning hot. They ran and danced, the poor things.

[Page 39]

Boiling tears flowed from their eyes, and their noses sniffed with flames. Reb Moshe "the bear" and his sons stood below, on the first floor, throwing blocks of sugar to the bears.

This did this task for many days. They heated and cooled the floor in succession, and the bears danced.

After a time, Reb Shmelke of Danyshev brought an instrumental troupe of Jews, who played below while the bears danced above.

When the bears concluded their "course of study", their bellies were filled with Torah and wisdom: How, does one dance before the bride?[11] And how does one pace upright? And how do you execute a bow with a friendly face, and other such manners and customs? They would sell each bear separately for a great deal of money, in royal currency, to gypsies who traverse many countries, to distribute them throughout the wide world, where they would stand in the markets as the bears danced to the enjoyment of the audience. Then the gypsies would fill their pockets with "jingles"[12], so that they could sustain their bones with all good food as for Olnmishke the bear. Thus they called it (perhaps on the name of the first benefactor Reb Moshe "the bear"), so that it would not forget its master:

"The block of sugar will be put in its mouth
And its cheeks will be full of sweet mead
For who is as nice as he
Understanding music and dancing in a circle"

This bear school existed for many years in Smorgon. It was the famous Bear Academy. It existed all the days of Reb Moshe the Bear, and his sons who followed after him, "the bear pursuers."

And I was still a youth, in my young days

I did not stand among the adults, I did not demonstrate in the gates.

My ears only heard legends and isolated stories

Told by my blind grandfather, to the honorable gathering

The story of Reb Moshe and the good "berish"

Who danced in the markets and growled on the street

Who tasted sweetmeats and sampled nectar

I will conclude my story with wishes of "all the best".

D. The Story of the Cakes

"The cakes of Smorgon" were famous throughout the world. There is a story of a certain Jewish native of Smorgon who wandered afar during the time of the great world war, and ended up in Harbin. From there, he wandered southward through the Asian Continent and reached the isles of the sea. In the isles of the sea, the local children dressed up, as is known, in necklaces of colorful flowers on every holiday and birthday. They tied the wreaths on their necks, and went out in dances as the drum beat in front of them.

What did that Jew do? Since he ended up among them, he did as they did. However, instead of a floral wreath, he produced and affixed a wreath of small cakes, made by a baker, who colored them in all the colors of the flowers known in the isles of the south. The local residents came and asked him:

[Page 40]

"What does this necklace around your neck do?"

He stood up and responded them in brief:

"Come to me tomorrow."

This Jew from Smorgon returned to his home, called his wife, and said to her, "Quickly, knead dough."

The two of them, the husband and his wife, stood the entire day and night making dough. They rolled it into long strips, and tied the strips around the finger, in the measure of a ring. They would pull and grab the edges. Later, they would place the dough-rings on the burning oven until they changed to a sparkly color like gold. In honor of the location, and in accordance with the custom of the people there, the small, brown cakes would be dyed in the color of live flowers. They would be place in strings to create a necklace of cakes.

The residents of the island came the next day and saw the necklaces that were tied on beams of reeds on the wooden hut. They tasted the small cakes, and praised their taste and aroma. The people purchased the cake necklaces for themselves and their relatives, paying in the national currency. They left, returned, and added more purchases to what they had already purchased. That Jew of our town earned the merit of the ancestors and the merit of the cakes – and earned his livelihood in a bountiful manner. After time, he affixed a sign onto the front of his house, advertising his trade:

"Smorgon Bagels"

Written in the vernacular, in the language of the natives, and the Yiddish language.

That is the end of the story of the Jew of Smorgon who found himself in the islands of the south. While he was still there, the making of cakes did not stop in Smorgon. Many residents of the town, especially the gentiles, did so in public in every place. They would export to the markets of the towns in the country of Poland, and advertise their merchandise. There were gentiles who purchased their cakes and tied them to their belts and the necks of their children, making necklaces of cakes, large, medium sized, and small. Their tastes were different: some sweet, other salty, and others lukewarm. Some of the dough was kneaded with eggs – they were crisp and tasty – an enjoyment to the palate. They spread their own fame, and were called Kazimir in the city of Vilna, the Jerusalem of Lithuania. There, they were publicized with words of song:

Here it is in our language:

Cakes from Smorgon,
Gather together in crowds.
Purchase from morning until night
And in your houses – there will be food.

So what was the beginning of the cakes of Smorgon?

About this, I heard in the cellar of Reb Nota Kowarski. In his attic, Reb Nota worked in communal affairs and brought medicine to the sick of his nation, with healing for all their ailments. For Reb Nota Kowarski was a first class feldscher[13]. The large cellar of his stone house was dedicated to his wife and children to work in the baking of cakes. They were assisted by proper gentile women from the nearby villages and hamlets.

[Page 41]

During winter evenings, gentiles would gather from all the nearby homes to the cellar of Kowarski. Children, students returning from *cheder* as well as their sisters all sprouted to life at the light of the wide oven, which contained long iron grates with various cakes atop. At times, several elderly women would come to the basement to warm their old bones at the oven and feast "their souls" with gossip and chit-chat.

The main point of the matter was that Welinka, an orphaned daughter of farmers, a Pole with a prying face, was present. She was raised in the house of old man Mytropan. By your life, if you have ever seen a gentile such as him – large, bony, and instilling fear.

But with the "instrument" in his hands – you have also not seen the dream. Mytropan knew how to play, and he made his musical instrument with his own hands. In form, it was unclear whether it was a double bass, or a drum with various extra strings stretched across it, some thick as rope, and some thin and thread.

Mytropan would bang this instrument with his right thumb, and strum the strings with all the fingers of his left hand. Simultaneously, he would open his empty mouth and expose his solitary tooth that remained, instilling fear on all the children sitting before him. "Welinka Dosza," the old man would turn to his granddaughter, "Now, tell them stories from Grandmother, the refined soul. And I will make sounds with the strings of the instrument."

"Welinka, begin your story
And I will make ringing sounds with my instrument
The story is sad, but not scary."

And in the space of the cellar, the cellar of Reb Nota Kowarski, Welinka the orphan relates the gloomy story of the past.

"Mitka from the Chotor[14] loved the very beautiful Marilka, the daughter of the merchants. Her father refused to give her to him, for the lad was poor, not of a good family. Mitka had nothing other than the cloak on his body and his shepherd's flute. What would the lad do with his great love, where would he bear his pain? Perhaps the Okna, the ancient stream, would sweep away the flames of his pain with its current. Or perhaps he should give his oppression, and place his supplication before Jabducha, who weaves quaint strands of silver in the foliage of the trees on moonlit nights?

The Okna will carry Mitke's agony with its waves to the great sea – where it would be lost in the depths.

[Page 42]

Mitka went from Chotor to Marilka, the daughter of the merchants. He went directly to her house. For unfortunate Mitka?

And the witch Jabducha – to her must be brought a gift in the currency of sorcery, and where would he obtain such? Nobody was at the home of the merchant. They had all gone to a festive meal of the gentiles. Only the youngest daughter, the most beautiful Marilka, remained. The girl was standing, kneading dough to make cakes for their holiday that was to take place the next day. Her voice was raised in pleasant song.

Mitka opened the door quietly, stood before him at his full height, pale and sad.

"What is with you, Mitinka, that you came? And why do you look sad?"

"You asked two things, my beautiful one. To the first, to ask if you will come with me today. To the second, because I have no life without you..."

Then Marilka responded to Mitka from the Chotor.

"How can I follow after you, if you do not betroth me with a gold ring, as is the custom of men. Mitinka, purchase a ring. Buy a gold ring. Then I will stretch out my finger to you, and you can betroth me as a wife in accordance with the law and custom."

Then the forlorn lover stood up, and responded to the beautiful one with the emotion of his heart.

"From where can I get a gold ring, my Marilka, being that I am a poor orphan, and have nothing in the world other than the love in my heart." He did not reply anything [additional] for his heart was seething inside him, and his dark eyes were ignited with a strange fire. Then he turned to and fro, and saw Marilka busy with working the dough, and the oven was burning.

Mitinka quickly approached the dough. Before the eyes of his beloved, he took off a piece of the kneaded dough, made it into a ring around his finger, and then approached the burning oven and placed his hand in the flame. Thus did he hold his hand in the flame for a long time. Mitinka's face became pale, and his burning eyes dwindled, and were extinguished.

Then Marilka screamed. She hurried to her beloved and removed Mitka's hand from the fire. The finger was completely roasted, and, closed around it, was a wonderful ring, the work of an artist, in a form of beaten gold.

"Mitinka, my love," whispered the lovely maiden, as she melted down in tears, "take me with you, my darling. Wherever you go, I shall go, for your love is as strong as fire, your heart is like a long hearth that will never extinguish."

Then the two of them went to the Chotor, Mitka the shepherd, and the beautiful Marilka, the daughter of merchants.

Her father stood in his refusal, and did not bless the match. He also cut his daughter off from her property, so how would they sustain themselves?

Marilka kneaded the dough into wraps. Mitka would wrap them around his finger, as he had done at the time of the great ordeal. They would bake rings of dough in the oven. They would make cakes, and tie them onto strings so they would become a single unit. They would go out to the markets and proclaim:

[Page 43]

"Buy cakes for a penny
Then we can live, and not die.
Buy, matrons, and you too, oh master,
The best of the small cakes of Smorgon."

Mytropan's strings became silent. A tear fell from Wilenka's eyes, and those seated in the cellar were all agitated and afraid.

The storyteller relates:

It is ended, but not complete
In writings such as this, you find but do not dream.

The wise person believes and the fool ceases
For at the end – my heart mourns.

Translator's Footnotes

1. 'las' is forest in Polish.
2. White Rus may not be geographically equivalent to White Russia. See https://en.wikipedia.org/wiki/White_Ruthenia and https://en.wikipedia.org/wiki/Ruthenia
3. Sir or Mister in Polish. See https://culture.pl/en/article/pan-poland-word-by-word
4. A morgen is an obsolete unit of measure in Poland and other places.
5. A play on words: *Kuzarim* and *chazirim*.
6. A play on words of "The distributor of life to all living beings" – a description of G-d.
7. The author is referring to himself.
8. The following article provides some context: https://vetliva.com/tourism/what-to-see/pamyatnik-medvezhey-akademii-v-smorgoni/
9. Cheders are traditional Jewish elementary schools
10. Song of Songs 1:4.
11. A well-known Jewish wedding melody, based on a Talmudic statement. See http://www.zemirotdatabase.org/view_song.php?id=150
12. Jingling coins – i.e. pocket change.
13. A medic. See https://en.wikipedia.org/wiki/Feldsher
14. Seemingly a location.

[Page 44]

Smorgon– The Story of Its Town and Destruction

by A.Y. Goldschmidt*

Translated by Anita Frishman Gabbay and Frieda Levin Dym

A Short Story of Smorgon

Smorgon is situated in the Vilna district, between the small rivers Neris and Vilnia (or Vilnele). When the town was founded–historians do not know exactly when—a small Jewish community began growing according to different legends. But in the famous Pinchas, "Kingdom of Lita", which is found in the famous Strashun Library in Vilna, Smorgon is already mentioned as an outstanding Jewish settlement. From 1628 onwards, Smorgon was able to pay taxes to both the local community and the Lithuanian Kingdom.

Three years later, the residents were delighted to have their city of Smorgon enlarged and given the status of a city.

With time, the renown and importance of Smorgon grew among all the other towns, and the city evolved into an industrial and cultural center during the 17th and 18th centuries. In 1765, there were 649 Jews in Smorgon. In 1847, the Jewish numbers increased to 16,212 along with the non Jewish population slightly larger[1]. But Smorgon was still considered a small town of the Oshmiany region, similar to the times when it was considered part of Poland. When the Libava–Romener Railroad was built, Smorgon began to be recognized as a city of great status, and from this point on, its ties to the great and vast Russia were strengthened.

[Page 45]

After the peasants were freed (from the revolution), a rebirth of rebuilding and industrialization began, and Smorgon slowly gained a new and improved status as an industrial and commercial center. In parallel, a very strong populist movement grew within the city. In 1897 there were 6743 Jews in Smorgon; in 1900, there were over 10,200 Jews. And by 1914, there were over

31,000 people, of which 25,000 were Jews[2]. From this time on, Smorgon had the status of a large city.

At one time [beginning in the 17th century], Smorgon was known mainly for its "Berentreiber" industry (trained bears that performed for crowds). The largest part of the land was owned by the princely Radziwill family, the Potovskis, the Titchkevitchs and other noble families. Peasants remained loyal to their landowners. They all depended on one another.

The ruins of Smorgon after the First World War

The nobility were afraid to loose the loyalty of their peasants. This was the reason that they opened a school in Smorgon to train bears and to give the "Berentreiber" [bear trainers] a livelihood. In this way, they enabled a large part of the poor peasant population to start an industry in order to survive. These bears were plentiful in the nearby forests of Smorgon. The trainers with their students, known collectively as " Smorgon Academia" and also known as "Honey– eaters", (a Yiddish expression, meaning licking the benefits from the people), would travel all through the towns through Russia and Europe. The bears were transported in chains through the towns and they would dance for the audience who were drinking brandy and eating sweets: La–La–La[3]. This pleasant form of entertainment led to the development of breeding bears and consequently, the bear show would go from street to street through towns like Smorgon and Neazvich with the townsfolk deriving much pleasure.

[Page 46]

The people would gladly pay a few pennies for this form of entertainment. The Radziwill family earned quite a bit from this enterprise.

Eventually Smorgon, renowned as a city of "Berentreiber,"also became noted for its leather industry. There were 54 leather factories and 30 workshops, and their manufactured products were sent all over Russia: Carpathians, Siberia, Manchuria and Vladivostok, and throughout Germany. In Smorgon, there were also two tobacco factories, one soap factory, three seltzer warehouses, and two beer breweries. The town was also known for its bagels, "Smorgon Barankis"; the bagels were renowned all through Russia. In addition, there were 175 stores and shops, two sugar and two tea warehouses, a kerosene warehouse, an industry for wool shearing and knitting, and production facilities for knitting socks.

Most of the industry, the warehouses and the production [facilities], was in the hands of the Jewish population and not owned by the Christian population. This demographic was unusual; the Jewish workers were not discriminated against and worked alongside other workers, Lithuanians, Polish and Russians. No where in the world was an economy run by so many Jews.

Smorgon was also noted for its "farming colony" run by Jewish farmers in an area [a suburb of Smorgon] which was known as the "Karke". The plots of land were given to those early settlers in the time of Nicolai the First which was during the Russian regime that was greatly influenced by Yitzhak Ber Levinson. Jews were given such parcels of land in the Ukraine, Reisen and Lita. The colony [Karke] was divided into 20 parcels and farmed by over 40 Jewish families until the outbreak of the First World War. The farmers worked the land and lived like Jewish peasants. They had their own Rabbi, a separate lifestyle and their own religious institutions.

Smorgon, as a new century unfolded, was no longer used to the old way of life. Yet, rich and educated Jews still did stick to the old traditions of helping the needy and doing good deeds.

[Page 47]

Jewish Smorgon, was endowed with fine religious institutions: two beautiful synagogues, seven "kloizim" (smaller synagogues), a Talmud Torah and three Yeshivas. Also, there was an Old Peoples Home, a Hospital, a "Gemilut Hesed" (loans for the needy), a Soup Kitchen which looked after the basic needs of the poor with bread and wood in the wintertime, a shelter for poor folks passing through, a special place for the beggars hanging around the Cemetery, and a place where poor widows and widowers would come to sleep and sort out clothing.

It should be noted that the founders of these institutions were: Zalman Rothstein, Gedalia Rothstein, Mendel Fineberg, Israel Sutzkever, Perevoztski, Zalmen Bitzkovski, Gedalia Solodocha, Avraham Yehuda Zvi Kerman, and Yacov Kavarski.

This patriarchal philanthropy which existed in Smorgon was very usual for those times. The livelihood of the entire community was directly related to the religious and pious duty of all.

The basis were the Kloizim, the Rabbis, the Heders and the Yeshivot.

The pride of Smorgon was the Rabbi Menashe of Ilya–most renowned throughout the Vilna community. Why was he the Rabbi of Smorgon but called himself "from Ilya"? The answer is that he got married in Ilya and lived there for many years. His father was then [living] in Smorgon, when Rabbi Menashe was born in 1767.

Rabbi Menashe from "Ilya" was one of the famous personalities that Jewish Russia produced. No one could measure up to his greatness. His greatness was like that of a "GAON" and a great idealist. He understood German and Polish and was educated in philosophy, mathematics and physics, chemistry and engineering. Even 150 years ago, he presented [ideas] in a speech that Jews should share their ways of earning a living from farming and adopt new ideas to build a better future in industry and commerce. His whole life was devoted to improve the lives of the poor Jewish masses. He even handed out newsletters in Yiddish to reach the most people. In those times, it was quite unusual for a "Gaon" to speak about those new, forward–looking ideas and teachings in those times, and with such vigor, determination and antagonism.

He did not [initially] want to be a Rabbi. In his later years, the people of Smorgon had to plead with him to become their Rabbi. He only retained the position for a year and a half. He stepped out of line with a fiery speech against the "Grabbers" (greedy people) which were spreading rumors.

[Page 48]

They demanded an apology and he got frightened. The townsfolk asked him to refrain from such speeches and distance himself from such controversial matters. So immediately insulted, he resigned from the Rabbinate. He could not remain silent when such issues needed to be addressed.

The Smorgon Rabbinate was also blessed with historical figures from the Shapira family, which goes back to the 12th century. More recently, in the first half of the 19th century in Smorgon, the most important of the rabbis was the Gaon, Rabbi Leibele Shapira, who was well known amongst his peers. He was also part of the Enlightenment and intellectual world as was Rabbai Menashe of Ilya and Rabbi Yossel Mazel. Rabbi Leibele Shapira was also a student of theory and mathematics. He was even well known in Israel by the name Rabbi Leibele of Kovno (Kovner) when he was the Rabbi in Kovno in his later years.

After [the tenure] of Rabbi Leibele in Smorgon, his son became Rabbi: Rabbi Chaim Avraham Shapira. Famous and smart, he sacrificed a lot in order to instill the Torah in Smorgon and to make the city a Center for Torah Study by founding an important Yeshiva. Three Yeshivas were opened in the city of Smorgon, and they became known to all the Torah scholars of Lithuania, Russia and Poland.

After the death of Rabbi Avraham Shapiro, his son in law, Rabbi Menashe Ginsberg became the Rabbi in Smorgon. Rabbi Menashe, extremely religious and of wise character, would spend his days and evenings studying the Torah and dictating sound advise. For this reason, the population held him in the highest esteem. One of Rabbi Menashe's sons, Rabbi Eischer, was the Rabbi in Paris; currently he is the Rabbi in Bronx, New York. Here in New York, Rabbi Menashe's two daughters, Baila and Perel, also lived.

Another Rabbi that lived in Smorgon was Rabbi Yehuda Leib Gordin (from Rechitza). He was important because of his New Age thinking, and his presence was held in great esteem throughout [the area]. Anti–Semitic rants and pamphlets started to appear in Russian and German against the Talmud, the Shulhan Aruch (Jewish code of law), and other [sacred writings within the] Jewish community, so Rabbi Yehuda Leib Gordin undertook to write "Explanations of the Talmud", in which he explained and revealed the writing of Brachman, Luntostofski, Steker and other known writers. Rabbi Gordin explained the "High" (or Holy) morale and ethical teachings of the Talmud, built on the ethics of the spiritual teachers of that time. He sent his explanation to the Russian authorities, and he received their approval and many thanks.

[Page 49]

Rabbi Gordin also had a son, Abba Gordin, who rose to great fame as a writer in Yiddish–Hebrew–English circles.

Later, Smorgon, the once production oriented and cultured city, became broken and destroyed. Smorgon was at one point a city of industrial strength with thousands of workers and a wealthy middle class. However, exploitation grew and over time, and got out of hand. As a result, the Worker's Movement was established and its direction was towards Socialism. The pioneers of this movement were naturally the oppressed from Smorgon's society.

In the front row of this movement was the daughter of Rabbi Menashe's daughter–Liba Ginsberg, Sara Metlitzkaia, Schmuel Levin and Olga Bornstein. Their lives were entwined with martyrdom. From the very beginning, they were under the influence of the Narodnikas (a labour movement), Rubanova and Sinitski. (Exact information on their lives and their revolutionary activities can be read in the pages of the "Revolutionary Works of Smorgon–red[4].

Smorgon endured through all of the stages of Soviet political storms and grew alongside the new socialism of mother Russia. In the period starting June 1905, Smorgon was in the front row of the beginning of a colossal framework of a new world order. When the revolutionary cavalry fled, the situation was ripe for a cultural revolution. And so the building of a Romantic period of culture began (from 1907–1914). That began when Dovid Einhorn wrote "We will be left behind in our Synagogues according to our historical nature"[5]. Again, Smorgon survived this period. Here in Smorgon, a movement was started to "Russify" the school system (Russian–Hebrew/Jewish Cultural Institute). The Institute was formed to monitor the education system by modeling it on the system already established in Russia [which was funded] with private Russian "pensions" for Jewish children—essentially a state school that would teach Yiddish and Hebrew. Dr.Tzemach Schabad, the chairman of the Vilna committee of the brothers of "Friends of Higher Learning", came to establish such a school.

[Page 50]

In 1912, they invited a teacher named Israel Gurevitch from Nevernatzia Outchelitche. He was familiar in this form of Jewish/Russian education and met with important personalities of Smorgon to propose and discuss ideas to establish this type of Jewish School. The meeting took place in the house of Dr. Epstein, and the workload was divided among other modern–thinking individuals such as Arkady Gurevitch. After many discussions, large opposition arose, and the School was never established. However, they began to re–organize so children would be tutored in the evenings in Yiddish and Hebrew.

A large contribution to Yiddish education in Smorgon was made by the sons of Rabbi Gordin "The Gordin Brothers", who were deeply immersed and broadly educated in new pedagogical and open minded ways of thinking (ideas). They wanted to institute a new and original way of learning that would produce a new generation of Jews. They started a school with new methods of teaching and upbringing. The children were proud of their teachers, and the name "The Brothers Gordin" became very well known throughout all of Lita (Lithuania). All their earnings were reinvested in their Cheder (school), and they devoted all their time and love for the Yiddish and Hebrew culture and language, a new pedagogical approach which they founded. In this new approach, new ideas were taught, sometimes revolutionary and controversial. Someone in the community started to spread rumors that the Heder should be closed. The "Cheder Metukan" was home to the famous poet Moyshe Kulback. Another Yiddish poet that comes from Smorgon is Abraham Sutzkever.

Smorgon used to publish all Yiddish and Hebrew newspapers, and bought Hebrew and Yiddish Literature books for their library. The "Yiddishe Welt" (The Jewish World) published by "Kletzkind", was distributed to hundreds in Smorgon as well as the Hebrew publications "HaShiloach", "Achiasaf", "Tushiya". Smorgon became a cultural center of great importance and [produced] youth with great and new ideals.

*

The First World War engulfed the world, and pogroms against the Jews began. Immediate assistance was needed, and food and lodging was provided all through the Kovna Gubernia (province). The expelled Jews from Kovno were forced to flee during [the holiday of] Smorgon Erev Shavuot. The entire population came to their assistance.

[Page 51]

Immediately, an organization sprung up to provide the necessary help, food and a warm place to stay, and also, medical help.

At nighttime, the first part of those fleeing from Kovno arrived. The entire town prepared [and] welcomed the folk during the evening and the entire next day of Shavouot. New arrivals came, over 600 people, mostly women and children, without their husbands. There were some rich folk, but the larger portion were without means. The greeting by Smorgon was heartwarming and honest, and the energetic youth were ready and able to help in this time of need. We gave them the food and special holiday treats that we prepared, and found them lodging and took care of all their basic needs.

Due to this outpouring of warmth and brotherly love for a people fleeing persecution and fearing for their lives, especially during the holiday of Shavuot, the expelled Jews did not feel alone, and for the second day of Shavuot, we all celebrated as brothers. This coming together in such a time of need with the outpouring of generosity and togetherness amongst all kinds of folk, regardless of their class, became very dear to us.

In several months, however, it was the Smorgoners turn to flee. The front was closing in, and the destruction of Smorgon began. The Jewish population was forced out with such haste and brutality that the Jewish folk, full of fear and chaos, scattered in all directions and throughout all of "mother Russia".

There was no one there to welcome them with open arms and brotherly love as the Smorgoners did for their fellow brothers from Kovno. The bestiality of the Czarist army is characterized according to some folk by the following:

An officer saw a student, [named] Sobol, and yelled at him, "Did anyone remain in Smorgon? Remove yourselves immediately from here!"

[Sobol] replied, "My grandfather is in his sickbed, how can I leave him here?"

"Where is your grandfather?" demanded the officer.

[Page 52]

So the grandson took him home and showed him. Immediately the officer shot the sick man. Now, you can go, he [the officer] yelled like a beast!

Smorgon became a war zone. Death and destruction was everywhere, and until today, there is no place to return. From a 25,000 person city, fewer than 600 Jewish families returned. After 1917–1918, the city no longer grew and neither did the Jewish community. The wealthy Jews were no longer. Two World Wars took its toll.

There were no more factories and no more workers. No more Shapiros, no more Ginzbergs, no more Levins and no more Mitlitskis—only the bestial Russian "Endecas". After this time, our lives were filled with the Nazis to torment us day and night. Our youth feels lost. No where to run! Doors are closed wherever they run! And they ask: G–d help us! Where will our help come from? Please help us!

(Smorgoner Memorial Book 1934— New York)

* Murdered in the Vilna Ghetto

Translator's Footnotes

1. There is a wide discrepancy in reporting the number of Jews in Smorgon in the late 19th and early 20th centuries. The number of Jews in Smorgon was likely lower than referenced in this chapter. https://www.encyclopedia.com/religion/encyclopedias–almanacs–transcripts–and–maps/smorgon
2. See Footnote 1.
3. A likely reference that everyone was being happy and maybe even singing.
4. The color red being a reference to communism.
5. http://www.jewishencyclopedia.com/articles/5483–einhorn–david

[Page 54]

Rabbi Menashe from Ilya
(1767- 1831)
by Abba Gordin
Donated by Eilat Gordin Levitan

Rabbi Menashe

Rabbi Menashe was born in the city of Smorgon in 1767, where his father, Rabbi Joseph, served as a spiritual teacher and judge. From an early age, Menashe was known as a prodigy and a genius of sorts. His elders foresaw a great future for him and believed he would become both a leader and a symbol to his People.

In Vilna, the spiritual capitol of Lita (Lithuania), the story was told of a 4-year-old boy, the son of the rabbi of Smorgon, that had memorized the whole sidur (prayer book) by heart from beginning to end, as well as backwards, from the last chapter to the first. His critical nature, which was already evident at a very young age, never failed to provoke and anger in all who knew him, or of him. As a consequence, his life was plagued by much pain and suffering. At the tender age of 5, Menashe had already memorized the five books of the Torah, as well as Rashi's commentary. Once, he read this next verse out loud to his teacher “And when the woman saw that the tree was good for food, and that it was a delight to the eyes, and a tree to be desired to make one wise, she took of its fruit, and did eat, and gave also to her husband with her.” (Genesis 3:6). He went on to quote Rashi's commentary from memory, and turned to his teacher and asked how Rashi could have known Eve's intention when handing Adam the forbidden fruit. How could Rashi know she did so out of fear that Adam would live on after her and would then wed another woman? How did he know she didn't do so because she wanted to share with him this most wondrous fruit, simply out of her true love and adoration for him?

His teacher responded by telling him that Rashi had based his commentary on our sages' commentary on this verse. But this response did not satisfy the young boy, who went on and asked how our sages knew Eve's intention.

Vexed by his pupil's audacity, he irately replied that there was nothing our Great Sages did not know, and that it is not for a young boy, such as himself, to question their teachings.

After a short pause, young Menashe defiantly retorted that it seems that they made their “speculations” based on their personal interpretation of the biblical text. He then articulated that he believed the sages induced this from the words “with her” in the biblical verse, which were superfluous!

By stating that she “...gave also to her husband with her”, the text suggests that she avoided eating the forbidden fruit before he did, because she feared she would perish and he would live on and wed another woman.

The young Menashe knew the entrails of Shulchan Aruch, the Jewish book of laws and regulations, written by Joseoh Kalo, and it was told that when he was only 8 years old he would often be asked to partake in the trials of Smorgon to help the judges come to a verdict when they were perplexed by the case at hand. The city of Smorgon was well known for its wealth and its many wise residents, and the reputation of its spiritual teachers' reputation proceeded them. Yet, when Menashe, son of the famed Rabbi Joseph, was 10 years old there was no one to be found that was able to further educate him in the teachings of the Torah. In his book on the life of Hagr”a (1914) Rabbi Y. L.

Hacohen wrote that upon his father's decree, Menashe went to study at the Great School of Torah Studies, which was home to some of the finest minds, who dedicated their every waking hours to the study of the Torah. There, Menash devoted all his time to his diligent studies of the Gemara, of Rashi, of addendums, of early interpretations, of commentaries and of other religious teachings.

The older pupils at the school of Smorgon, who were themselves known throughout Lithuania for their great wisdom and knowledge, would look upon young Menashe with envy, for he surpassed them with his brilliance, his memory, and his tenacity. The famous verse "...and thou shalt meditate therein (the Torah) day and night." (Joshua 1:7), was literally taken and brought to life by Menashe until the age of 15 when his father wrote to him on behalf of one of Smorgon's wealthiest and well respected families, and ordered him to marry this man's daughter. As was customary at the time, he did not ask the boy if this was how he felt about this life changing decree, or if the girl was to his liking. Sadly, when the children did not appreciate their father's intension, such pre-arrange marriages often ended in much distress and pain. After the terms of the transaction were drawn, the two were wed, and the match left Menashe miserable and distressed. Rabbi Hacohen wrote in his book that the sire's spoilt daughter would consistently harassed and belittle her young groom, who was kind and noble by nature .

She demanded of him to show his appreciation for marrying into a family of such high stature and to behave accordingly. But Menashe did not wish to change. By nature, he was drawn to the poor and less fortunate people of the lower social classes. He chose not to flaunt his wealth or to interact only with those of a high social standing. His wife was relentless in her efforts to change him and her father also actively tried to influence his young son in law to abide to her demands, but to no avail.

One day, his father in law went so far as to quote the book of Genesis, imploring with him that God himself told Abraham that he must heed everything his wife Sarah bid him (21:12). He went on to say that Abraham did all that his wife requested of him, even if it did not coincide with his own wishes and inclinations and asked why he was intent on defying his spouse.

Menshe broke his silence and asked his father in law's forgiveness, as he pointed out that one shouldn't ignore Rashi's commentary on that very verse.

Rashi, he elaborated, noted that in encouraging men to listen to their wives and to heed their directives, he referred only to those women who expressed the spirit of God and his way. God did not intend for any man to follow a woman who did not possess such insight. There for, it would be wrong to take God's words to Abraham literally and apply any case in which a man's spouse lacked an inherent knowledge of our Lord's intensions. Rashi, was also perplexed by this biblical verse, and drew upon our sages conflicting commentary which suggests that he who heeds his wife's every word may unwittingly lose himself on hell highway. His point being that God's words to Abraham were in no way meant to be taken literally, and if taken so, they would surely distance one from God's true intension. Man should, in essence, heed the words spoken by women imbued with, and expressing the spirit of God, but in no way should one follow a woman devoid of spirit and of any comprehension of God.

Some months later Menashe shared his distress with his father, telling him he could neither love nor respect his wife. His father, who loved him dearly, was saddened by this and regretted having made such a rash decision, which brought his beloved son such distress and sorrow. And so, he made up his mind to correct his error and spoke to his in-law, asking him why should his son pay for his mistakes? Then he went on to ask If he had wronged him, was it not his responsibility to undo the unfortunate consequences of his actions?

Menashe's father in law understood this and agreed with rabbi Joseph [Menashe's father], although it broke his heart, and agreed to grant his daughter a divorce from this fine young man.

Rabbi Menashe returned to his religious studies, until one day, a man visited Smorgon. This man, rabbi Abraham, was a great scholar and a tradesman from the town of Ilya. He stayed in Smorgon for a few days to complete his business there. While there, he heard much praise of the young Menashe, that was said to be a great pupil and of a sharp mind.

He contacted the boys father and told him he had a fine and virtuous daughter, as well as a large dowery and much possessions to give him for years to come. Menashe's father agreed, on one condition, that Rabbi Abraham took his son back to his home for a few days, to see if Menashe liked the girl and approved of this marriage. So, as agreed, Menashe returned to Ilya with Rabbi Abraham, who then introduced him to his daughter. The two immediately took a liking to each other and sent for Menashe's father, and a marriage agreement was drawn. Soon, the young couple was wed in a majestic ceremony. In Sarah he found a loyal spouse, who appreciated him, and did all she could to forward and satisfy all of his needs.

In the city of Ilya, Rabbi Menashe's reputation preceded him, as one of the greatest scholars of his time. He dedicated all of his time and energy to his studies of the Torah.

It is told, that when focusing on a given issue his concentration was so complete and intense that he was oblivious to everything around him.

Once, as Rabbi Menashe sat in his room, immersed in his studies, a young men entered the room and began blowing the Shofar very loudly. Upon hearing the is great racket, a well-respected neighbor rushed over and reprimanded them for disturbing the rabbi, immersed in his studies, reminding them that this was a terrible sin. Puzzled, Rabbi Menashe did not know who or what he was talking about. So great was his concentration when immersed in his studies. Even though he dedicated all of his time to his studies, he found the time to observe the people around him, and contemplate the ways of the world he lived in. His perceptive and curious nature aroused many questions in his mind. He responded to the happenings he witnessed, by gentle intervention. He had great faith in the power of the human mind and believed that if shown the way, any person would instinctively follow it. He truly believed all social problems could be solved by the use of common sense, which was given to all people by God. He believed everyone was born with inherent intelligence and that our minds are our portal to wisdom and to the discernment of truth.

Of his profusions writings, in which he put down his thoughts in the form of questions and answers, only two pages remained. These were from his book “sema dechayai”, written in both Hebrew and Yiddish, counterpoised page by page, and named in Yiddish “Labness meytell”.

When Rabbi Menashe's in-laws passed away a short time after their wedding, she (his wife) never complained, even when they lost much of their wealth. She never requested his help with her daily chores, so as not to take any of his time or energy from his arduous studies. She knew he was destined for greatness and provided for them and their children by her own labor.

Although they were no longer wealthy, she managed to put food on their table and clean clothes on their backs.

They had two daughters, [one daughter - Rokha (Rokhel) Blitznstein 1794 - 1850+] and a son named Joseph [1798-1847]. It was her work and devotion that made it possible for Rabbi Menashe to publish his life's works. Although he was often asked to lead and teach different congregations, he declined. He was skeptical of anyone accepting and following his radical teachings and life altering beliefs, recognizing their innovative nature. Rabbi Menashe knew that nothing was harder for people than rejecting old habits and embracing the new.

"I, the writer of these lines, have seen the distress and sorrow of the beings in this world. Their sorrow and destitution make my heart ache. Although they are many and I cannot name them all, I will shortly articulate my observations. Everywhere, oppression is evident. The large devours the small, the strong is empowered, as the weak perishes. Yet, the greatest of all evils is poverty. People fight to make a living every day, while few succeed. Famine is all too common. The masses walk the streets, plagued by hunger and thirst, homeless, seeking shelter from the elements. All this is compounded by sickness and plagues, God help them. This is the reality I witness day after day, and which fills my heart with sorrow. Wherever I turn, this reality haunts me and as much as I try to find a solution, I am forever helpless and distressed. Every day I pray that God will show me the way to bring welfare to all." (taken from Rabbi Menashe's preface to his book Tikun-Klali).

In his treatise, Rabbi Menashe prays to God to find a solution for societies ailments, a way to set right its inherent corruption. Questioning his own intelligence, he ponders the morbid condition of humanity. In "Sama DeChayai" he is convinced he has found the solution, the way to correct the injustice of the human condition, by the application of the rules of justice and logic.

Prone to question every new phenomenon he encounters, Rabbi Menashe was avid about sacrificing his old ways of thought and action for innovative ones, which never failed to amaze and startle his peers. Aware of the transitive nature of life, he was burdened by the plight of man and by the thought of what would come to be after he was gone. So much so, that he no longer enjoyed the simple things in life. He was dismayed by people's complacence and lack of forethought, thinking only of the present moment, not giving a second thought to what the future holds for them. The rich, content in their riches, the wise, content in their intellectual endeavors, and the warriors in their victories.

Although of different walks of life, they had one thing in common. They all focused on the present. all satisfied with their lives, like animals fattened before they are fed on, unaware of the slaughter that awaits them. These up thoughts would forever occupy Rabbi Menashe's mind, until he came up with what he believed, was a solution which was in accordance both with the Torah and with common sense (Sama DeChayai, page 15).

Rabbi Menashe was a man of great conscience and of fine perception. One could justly say of him that he had more awareness and sorrow for the human condition in his smallest finger, than others had in their whole body. His comprehension of the Jewish moral code was so complete, that it not only touched upon the righteous interaction of men, but also covered our interaction with the animals, which he loved and befriended. To his mind, we were all children of God, forever bound in the same universe expected to heed God's law. Rabbi Menashe did not condone cruelty to animals, and believed their suffering and ours were not to be differentiated. He compared man not only to a tree whose roots reach deep into the ground that sustains it, as written in the book of Psalms, but also to the worms and the maggots, as expressed by king Solomon there in chapter 22, verse 7: "But I am a worm and no man". Rabbi Menashe believed that an unseen bond, impervious to the naked eye and to conventional scrutiny, exists between both man, nature, and all living beings, maggots and all.

His religious ethics surpassed the boundaries of humanity and permeated all realms of existence. Rabbi Menashe extended the Jewish directive for good-will and universal comradely beyond human relations, to include the universe in its entirety. He understood this next verses from the book of Proverbs in this light: "The lord is good to all, and his tender mercies are over all his works" (there:145:9). "...O Lord thou preserves man and beast." (there:36:7)

Rabbi Menashe recognized the diversified nature of people.

"Some are stoic, unless their own well being and goals are at risk. Others are concerned with the well being of there family and friends, as well. This is true of the majority of people. But the enlightened, those who appreciate the hardship of sorrow and suffering, God bless them, are passionate about the well being and happiness of all who can experience pain, and there heart goes out to all animals as well as all men." (Alphey-Menashe, pg. 58. Vilna, 1904)

Rabbi Menashe believed it was every man's responsibility to make every effort to polish his own personality, and to ford his courage to such a degree that he realizes the interconnectedness of all beings, and see them all as essential parts of one great vessel, (there, page 16).

"...and as I have noted, it is our inherent responsibility to aspire to, and reinforce all that is good, and to distance the harmful...we should distinguish between the transitive good, the longer lasting good, and both these from the eternal, or ultimate, good... and to sacrifice the first two, for the achievement of the latter. The enlightened person, one who can picture both the joy and the pain experienced in life, cannot help but wish for the well being of all those who can experience them, and nothing less. Anything else would be almost inconceivable. Such a person that sees the essence of all beings and of life itself, will no doubt sense all the sorrow and the suffering of all the beings, as if they were their own. No shade of distress or agony would be foreign to him, whether he had experienced them himself, or whether he had imagined them."

Rabbi Menashe Ben Porat was such a man. He truly felt that as long as there was one distressed worm in the world, stuck in crevice too narrow for it to advance, to withdraw, or to turn – the world was not right nor truly merciful, and he, Rabbi Menashe could not be at peace, nor complacent, nor serene.

Rabbi Menashe's ultimate goal was to correct all that is wrong in the world, and to bring Tikun to all, by spreading good and dispersing harm. He would rarely delve into his personal needs or comfort and always focused on the general good. "What am I, and what is my value in comparison to the countless other natural beings living in this world? And if God had blessed me and my family and my friends with health and wealth and success for all times, yet someone in the world was still miserable, I would renounce it all.

How could I enjoy my life when somewhere there is some living being that is unable to realize himself completely, as God intended? Unable to seek and realize the good, as he perceives it, in accordance with his true nature. I am certain that this is not what God meant by directing us to pursue the correction of the world(Tikun Klali)." (from the preface of Ha'amek she'ela/Seeking the Truth). Rabbi Menashe could never differentiate his well being from the common good. The transitive nature of life made this bond even stronger for him, perceiving his own life as meaningless in comparison to his mission to rid the world of misery and suffering. He spoke of a story his mother once told him of she had nursed her sick baby girl on Yom Kipur's eve. Agonized by her suffering, she left the girl with a servant, and crept off to the synagogue to pray.

It was then that his father was preparing to go pray at the synagogue, dressed in white, covered by his Talit, that he heard the little girl cry, and realized his wife had left the girl with the servant and left the house. He then removed his Talit and outer garment, and sat down by the infant's cradle, to gently rock it and give her medicine. He sent the servant to tell his wife that he would remain at home, and would not leave the baby's side, until she returned. His point being that nursing the sick is of greater importance than the practice of religion.

Rabbi Menashe often cried out to God, imploring him to help him understand the miserable reality of human existence. He couldn't understand why God would create a world in which man was so powerless against plagues, hunger, and poverty. A world in which parents can't afford to feed their young. And if one generation sins, why must the next pay for their sins? And why some should live in lavish wealth, while others fight day in and day out, to just barely survive? (from Sama DeChayai)

Tormented by these social queries, he knew no peace, until he found what he believed was the answer. Given his radical approach to these issues, it was no wonder that he was targeted by many fanatics. One day, Rabbi Menashe visited a town nearby the city of Smorgon, where he was born. Although Rabbi Menashe did not appreciate the resident rabbi, nor did he agree with his teachings, he decided to visit him, as not to appear disrespectful. He was startled to find him sitting alone in his court house. "Why", asked Rabbi Menashe, "would your honor agree to sit alone in judgment? Have you forgotten the written rules forbidding this?" (Avot:84, chapter 8). "But can you not see", replied the rabbi, "that I am not alone? I have before me the great book Shulchan Aruch, the cornerstone of all laws. So, you see, we sit here together in judgment." Rabbi Menashe then replied, with the slightest smile on his lips, "I am surprised that your honor would share his court with one who is oblivious of his existence...?"

When the great controversy broke out between the Hasidim and the traditionalists who bitterly opposed them, Rabbi Menashe took no part in their fanatical persecution of this innovative school of thought. Unwilling to judge them simply because his peers found them abominable, he decided to go and see for himself what the Hasidic school of thought was about, and if there was any basis for the claims made against them, and visited the city of Liyadi, home of rabbi Sneyor Zalman.

In doing so, he acted in accordance to our sages directive, not to judge another unless you are in his position, and able to see things from where he stands. When he returned, he said he found fault both in the traditionalists and in the Hasidim, and that both would eventually bare the consequences of their actions. The traditionalists were wrong for thinking that because we have the Torah and our traditional writings, we don't need a rabbi, and the hasidim, for arguing that because they have a rabbi, they no longer need the books. Another source, quotes him as saying, “the one group is wrong in believing they have no need for a rabbi, and the other is wrong in believing they have found one. The truth being that we all need a rabbi, but where is he to be found?”.

Rabbi Menashe admired and venerated the Gaon of Vilna, Rabbi Eliyahu, for turning his back on the interpretive reading of the Torah, and returning to the literal understanding of the holy texts. He believed that too many rabbis were so busy with their elaborate interpretations of the Torah, that they lost sight of its literal meaning. Rabbi Menashe also said that if rabbi Eliyahu had not made this bold return to the primary meaning of its texts, the Torah would have been lost from our People forever. And he didn't do so because he lacked ingenuity or because he was not familiar with the countless interpretations of his peers. The opposite was true. In spite of his brilliance and his sharp perception, he valued simplicity, and made a point of not looking beyond the immediate sense of the texts he studied, and relishing in their literal meaning.

Rabbi Menashe was very interested in mechanics, and mechanical inventions, that saved the time and effort of manual jobs, and believed they were omens of man's forthcoming salvation from too much hard labor, which drained him both physically and emotionally. When he heard that a gentile in his town had bought a machine that breaks the seeds and distributes them across the field, he was fascinated, and studied it for hours, until he understood completely how it was built and how it operated. Seeing this, he wondered, if there existed such a machine, that could replace long days of arduous manual labor, why not build a machine to till the fields, to replace the people slaving to do the same job? He then ingeniously invented a mechanical plow. One machine that plowed more in one day, than it would have taken twenty men, with twenty bulls to till in the same time.

Rabbi Menashe showed his mechanical plow to the gentile, and to others, but they were not interested in the invention of a Jewish rabbi, who knew nothing about agriculture. He also went to rich Jewish land owners with his plowing machine, but they laughed to his face, saying they had no need for such gadgets, and suggesting he showed his invention to the farmers, and not to them.

One day, a rabbi approached him with a book full of elaborate disputes of some textual interpretations. Rabbi Menashe invited him to his house on Saturday eve. During dinner, the guest went on and on about different interpretations of a given text, but Rabbi Menashe rejected them all and offered simple literal explanations for these same verses.

When the soup was served, the guest was startled to find a before him a fork, and no spoon. He asked Rabbi Menashe if this too was one of his inventions, eating soup with a fork? The Rabbi replied mockingly that he thought he would prefer it, hinting at his useless interpretations. “If fish are eaten with a spoon, and not a fork, i thought you would prefer to eat your soup with a fork....”.

Like the Maharal and the Gaon of Vilna, Rabbi Menashe opposed the talmudic, interpretive readings, which would ignore the obvious, and would come to ridiculous conclusions, based on dubious conjectures. He even wrote a book named “Understanding a Text's Literal meaning”.

Rabbi Menashe often rejected Rashi's interpretations, and provoked many of his peers, including Hagra, who criticized him for this and stood by Rashi's traditional interpretations.

But nothing in Rabbi Menashe's writings warranted the attacks against him, by those fanatics, who would not stand for any explanation that slanted even slightly from the traditional school of thought, and were known to have killed people for lesser “transgressions”. In this context, Rabbi Menashe, spoke of Abraham, our forefather, who rejected his elders paganism ways.

"Condemning them, he chose not to explain their beliefs and their actions as being of an occult nature, which lay beyond the grasp of simple comprehension, as some people do now" (hinting to the Cabbalist and Hassidic schools of thought).

"A wise man will not opt to believe everything he hears. Even if it is told by a reputable person. Especially if what he says is of an outrageous nature. A wise man will believe only what he can judge for himself, and will not take as a fact anything he cannot see for himself, say if they are said to exist in a distant land. A gullible person, on the other hand, will believe anything. Even something he could easily judge for himself, if he only opened his eyes. This is even more evident when it comes to the issue of beliefs. The stranger a proposition is, the more prone a foolish man is to believe it. For, how could such wise men be wrong? He lacks the power of judgment and the common sense to think that they based their beliefs on the words of their friend, who was led astray by taking the word of another person, to begin with. And so, in this manner, one person takes the word of another, who, with no ill intent, takes as a fact the mistaken beliefs of his predecessors" (there, page 17).

"And so, the stranger the doctrine, the more people will profess that it is a deep, unfathomable/clandestine truth, beyond the grasp of the human intellect. By doing so, the queries of the thinking man are disregarded, and the more inept a man is, and the stronger his belief is in these non-truths, the more he will tend to consider himself a holy person. While the enlightened, thinker that wants to study the issue with his mind, is cast out as a non-believer, and not of the Jewish People, for they have always been distinguished by their undying devotion to their beliefs" (there, page 51).

In his books, written between 1822-1823, Rabbi Menashe insisted it was essential to change the school's curriculums. He advocated the addition of secular classes, to the traditional religious studies, as well as the teaching of trading skills and of practical crafts. He didn't want the younger generations to grow up to be intellectuals, with no understanding of economy. He also hoped to weaken the existing economical structures, and encouraged the involvement of the students in agriculture, believing that as an institution, schools must rely on a sound and stable economical system. In his book Shekel Hakodesh, Rabbi Menashe expressed his strong objection to pre-arranged marriages of children, and also harshly criticized many other traditions that were practiced in his days, and were founded on superstitions, that plagued the thought of orthodox jewelry. He perceived the Jewish faith as a guide for living life in a way that could be grasped by human rationality, and was mapped out by men who told us what is good and righteous (referring to the prophets).

"His books were burned by the extremists, whose fanaticism outweighed their sensibility, and neither had anything to do with the love of God, but rather with the fear of common sense and of science" (rabbi Yizchak Spalter of Smorgon, in Alphey Menashe, page 70). [Menashe's great grandson]

Rabbi Menashe often visited the nearby city of Vyajin, to see his relative, Rabbi Joseph Mazel, who was a well-respected man of means. He always sent his horse drawn carriage to take him to and from his house. When there, Rabbi Menashe would lose himself in the lord's lavish library, feverishly reading the religious book's of the Spanish authors, as well as books in philosophy, in scientific research and in kabala. Aware of his insatiable thirst for learning, Rabbi Joseph bought more and more books for him to study, so much so, that his library became the largest in the state.

By the request of his friend, Rabbi Shmaryahu Luria, Rabbi Menashe went to lecture a few times in the large temple in the town of Mohilov, situated on the shores of the Denayphir river.

His lectures were always very vivid and eloquent. Everyone would come to hear him and listen to his potent lessons. But one day a fanatic orthodox student was present, and when Rabbi Menashe mentioned the writings of the Greek philosophers Plato and Aristotle, he began screaming out loud that it was a mortal sin to speak of foreign places and beliefs before the tabernacle, where the scrolls of the Torah were kept. The minister of the temple, of course, chastised and reprimanded him, and Rabbi Menashe waited until the everyone was silent, before he continued his lecture, unaffected.

And not only did the heckler not apologize to Rabbi Menashe, he had the audacity to approach and tell him to never repeat such a sermon, which went against the spirit of the Jewish faith. Rabbi Menashe ignored him, and did not respond, as though he had not heard his insolent remark.

Rabbi Shmaryahu Luriya was thrown by his reaction, and on their way back to his home, respectfully asked him how could he ignore such audacity. Rabbi Menashe did not respond.

But as they were making their way home something happened to Rabbi Shmaryahu. A calf thwarted him, and he fell to the ground. Once he stood again, Rabbi Menashe asked him in jest, why did he not reprimand the calf for his audacity. Rabbi Shmaryahu replied, saying that the calf lacked intelligence, and that its actions were hardly premeditated. Rabbi Menashe smiled at him and said "the same is true of the young student that had hackled him earlier. He too, lacked intelligence, and was not unlike the calf".

At one of the town assemblies, in Ilya, rabbi Joshua Tseitlis of Shkalov, a local writer, malevolently told all present that Rabbi Menashe had said that some of Rashi's interpretations, as well as parts of the addendums, were superfluous. And that he had also stated that portions of the Mishna were not interpreted correctly, or literally, by the Talmudic sages.

The town's people were enraged and wanted to banish Rabbi Menashe, who said in his defense that everything rabbi Joshua said was true, but that his sole intention was to uncover the truth. Afterwards, Rabbi Menashe visited rabbi Joshua to prove to him that it was appropriate for him to criticize his predecessors, just as they had criticized theirs. His excommunication was retracted once the crowd realized that Rabbi Menashe was truly one of the greatest thinkers of his time. But the persecutions did not cease. Even though he continued the tradition of the Gaon of Vilna, which valued the literal meaning of the sacred texts, and discarded the complexities and the implications of the homiletic interpretations. Yet, what was alright for the Gaon, was not permissible where Rabbi Menashe was concerned, and he was forever hounded like a sheep by a pack of menacing wolves. Because of these endless persecutions, Rabbi Menashe left his home in Ilya, and traveled from town to town seeking a teaching position. One day he arrived at the city of Brisk, where rabbi Shaul Katzanelboygen served as head rabbi. He welcomed Rabbi Menashe graciously and appointed him to teach his children. But with one stipulation, that he would never mention any of his personal interpretations.

But although he valued his employment, Rabbi Menashe could not help but defy the rabbi's request. One day, when reading a verse from the Gmara (Shabbat 14:1) about rabbi Yochanan and the rites of handling the Torah book, after he had quoted the traditional reading, saying that he who held an uncovered Torah book (unclothed), would be berried bare, meaning, without his last rites, Rabbi Menashe swerved. He elaborated on his own interpretation, by which the person referred to in the Mishna was bare, and not the Torah book, which he held, and as punishment he would be berried unrobed, without his Tachrichim (wrapping). For this diversion from the Amoraic interpretation, Rabbi Menashe lost his job. Rabbi Menashe moved on to the town of Brodi, and visited the home of rabbi Yaacobke, the Gaon. He told him of his innovative teachings and of his objections to Rashi's interpretations. His host was not pleased by what he heard and refused to listen. He could not understand how a relatively unknown person, such as Rabbi Menashe, had the gall to dispute the works of better and greater men.

Rabbi Menashe explained that his opposition did not rely on who he was, or where he lived, it relied solely on the explicit meaning of the written texts. But the rabbi would not be moved. Given the rabbi's rejection of Rabbi Menashe and of his beliefs, no one else wished to listen to him. Despondent, he returned to Ilya. One time, Rabbi Menashe wanted to travel to Berlin, to meet with the members of Baaley Hamehashef and ask their advice about his situation, and on how he should deal with his ceaseless persecution. After much hardship, he arrived at Koenigsberg, where he met a group of Jewish men from Lithuania. They tried to convince him not to visit Berlin, because many of the Jews were corrupted, saying that they wore short pants, instead of suits, and shaved their beards and sideburns. Rabbi Menashe disregarded their warnings. But they were adamant, and influenced the officials to deny him passage, leaving him no option but to return home. But Rabbi Menashe did not return empty handed. He had in his possession many books that he had received from the scholars of Brodi. Unknown to anyone, he began learning foreign languages. But he was spied on, and when word of this got to the town's people, he was again chastised and persecuted.

Not long after that, Napoleon came to power, and Russia became interested in the fate of the Jewish communities. In 1801 Alexander the czar was enthroned, and made a revolution with his new decree regarding the Jews. He ordered that their restrictions be lessened and their freedom enhanced. In 1804 Jewish children were allowed to attend public schools, and Jews were granted the right to own lands. And Jewish tradesmen were permitted for the first time to live anywhere in Russia.

In 1807, Alexander established the Sanhedrin (the supreme Jewish judicial body during and shortly after the period of the Second Temple), and Jews from other countries were invited to participate in its meetings.

At that point, the Pravo-Slavian church declared war on Napoleon, claiming that he had made an alliance with Jews , and the Russian minister of interior affairs said that the Sanhedrin meeting that was to be held in Paris was a mortal threat to all European countries.

Rabbi Menashe made a point of closely following world events. In the library of rabbi Joseph Maazel he found a lot of information about the French revolution. And in March of 1789 a Hebrew journal was published, that covered all major world events.

In 1797 the Jews in Holland were granted equal political rights. This was documented in a report written by Hirsh Ilfeld about the Jewish controversy. Rabbi Menashe was then inspired to write a book in which he argued that the Jewish communities deserved equal rights. He explained that they were well educated and did not require schooling, as many other communities did, in order to qualify as civilized people. Thus, he wrote, they were a community worthy of comprehensive citizenship.

Rabbi Menashe wanted to send his book to the government in Petersburg, but first consulted his friend, rabbi Joseph Maazel. Rabbi Joseph then called together the town's people to listen to a reading of the book. The entire community gathered and listened as the manuscript was read out to them in its entirety. After having heard it, they were startled and overcome with anxiety. They believed the publication of the book was a dangerous threat to them all, and that if the rulers would learn of its contents, they would persecute the Jews even more passionately than they did at the time. Then, by the decree of the community's leaders, the book was burned and no copy of it survived.

In 1807 Rabbi Menashe published his essay "Pesher Davar" (the meaning of it all), where he encouraged the Jewish community to actively seek employment in their local communities. In it, he articulated the books' objective, and explained how he wished to consolidate the great leaders of the Jewish congregations, alluding to the Gaon of Vilna, rabbi Eliyahu and rabbi Shneyor Zalman, writer of the Tanyah and the leader and founder of the Chabad movement. Once again, the book was eradicated, and only a single copy survived (in the British Museum). But unlike Rabbi Menashe's other writings, it was not burned in public, nor was its author ostracized. This was due to the distinguished position he had acquired in the community. Yet, none the less, his book was perceived as an outrageous insult to the Gaon of Vilna and was destroyed.

When Rabbi Menashe wrote his book "Alphey Menashe", he could not find anyone in Lithuania who was willing to set and publish it, for fear of the assured repercussions. He managed to find a publisher in Vohlin, who began printing it, but then a fanatic from Lithuania arrived and defamed Rabbi Menashe and his work. After hearing this, the publisher retracted his obligation to Rabbi Menashe, and to avoid his incrimination for aiding the culprit author, burned the few pages he had already printed. He also burned the original manuscript.

In his steadfast dedication to his ideas, Rabbi Menashe rewrote the text and published it in Vilna, in 1822. He was then called to appear before rabbi Shaul Katzanelboygen, who served as arbitrator at the time. Rabbi Shaul demanded that he emit the passage in his book where he stated that in their day and age rabbis were called upon and permitted to change the laws of the Jewish constitution. He threatened Rabbi Menashe that if he failed to do so, he would burn his book in the entrance to his center of Torah studies. In order to save the complete text, Rabbi Menashe erased the passage.

As he explained, all Rabbi Menashe wanted was that "...the opposing leaders of the Jewish communities would join together and agree on all the amendments that had to be made, and only then we (the Jewish congregation) would follow them, without hesitation" (Alphey Menashe).

But the resistance to his ideas was relentless. Fanatics found his notes to "Sehma Dechayai", brought them to Vilna, and burned them in public. The text enraged them because in it Rabbi Menashe criticized the corruption existing in the world of commerce, and the immoral nature of the tradesmen who benefited from it. In their defense, the vandalisms claimed that in his book, Rabbi Menashe was empowering their sworn enemies, and may as well have armed them with live ammunition.

Given the lack of support he found in the larger cities, Rabbi Menashe returned to the city of Smorgon, where he was born. Surprisingly, he was honored and revered by the town's people, who took no notice of all the allegations made against him. It is said that a prophet, however great, is never appreciated where he was born and raised, it was there, in the city of

Smorgon, that he was recognized as the brilliant and conscionable man he truly was.

Every Friday, he would gather the uneducated people of Smorgon, and teach them basic Hebrew grammar so that they too could properly read Hebrew texts. And on Saturday evenings, he gathered them and taught them ethics and the importance of helping and caring for one another. The city's dignitaries and students implored with him to fill the position of the official rabbi of Smorgon. Rabbi Menashe had always despised the closed mindedness of the rabbinate. But, given his weariness and his disheartened disposition, after decades of relentless persecution, he accepted. And there, for the first time in his life, he was comforted by the reverence the local community showed him, and by their recognition and appreciation of his truly unprecedented stature and integrity.

Throughout his residency in Smorgon, Rabbi Menashe gave his devoted congregation daily lessons in the Talmud and the Bible. Both accomplished scholars and admiring young pupils would come from Smorgon and from all the neighboring towns to listen to his enlightening teachings.

The elders of Smorgon spoke of how every day before his sermon, Rabbi Menashe would read verses from the book of Psalms, tearfully beseeching the Lord to guide him, so that he would not misinterpret any of the verses he read, and would remain true to the meaning of the sacred texts. And when he read before his congregation, he did so with awe, love, and humility. Rabbi Menashe always encouraged his congregation to be kindhearted and charitable in their daily lives, and to love all living creatures. He also emphasized the importance of avoiding at all cost the practice of gossip and hate. Rabbi Menashe mediated in personal disputes, and everyone honored his opinion, both if his judgment relied on the holy books and civil law, and if it expressed his very personal logic, insight and intuition. Each day he presided as rabbi and arbitrator of Smorgon, his brilliance and virtuous nature were unwavering and evident to all.

But, sadly, he held his position in Smorgon for only eighteen months. At the time Jewish children were being abducted from their families throughout Russia and forced to serve in the Russian army. Rabbi Menashe saw that the elders and leaders of the Jewish communities were assisting the dark forces for profit. They would mostly kidnap the children of poverty-stricken families, as well as poor orphans, and hand them over to the Russian monarchy.

The notorious czar Nicholas the I (1796-1855), took the throne in 1825, had expedited the process when in 1827 he issued a law regarding the recruitment of Jews to the Russian army. In it he declared that 18-year olds would serve in his army for no less 25 years. He also decreed that Jewish children who were recruited at the age of 12, would be designated as junior soldiers until they reached the age of 18, and that the years they served during those years would not apply to the 25 years of service they were required to serve. Every year, the Jewish community was ordered to "supply" a certain quota of children between the ages of 12 to 18, and seldom would they hear from or see them ever again. Rabbis and of registered tradesmen, as well as pupils and graduates of public schools, craftsmen, factory workers and farmers were exempt from service and were not drafted. The word of the decree spread and shocked the Jewish community of Lithuania. They mourned the news and were horrified by its implications.

The decree was first announced on the Jewish new year of 1828. Everyone was anguished and demoralized by it. Children as young as 8 years were taken from their families, and were transported to far away destinations. Many of them died of starvation or froze in the process.

To meet the quota, the leaders of the Jewish communities opted to draft the children of underprivileged families and of anyone they did not favor. Many left their homes and hid, to avoid having their children abducted, and many cities and towns remained empty. Yet, even in these trying times of the cantonic horror, the saints and geniuses of the Jewish communities continued their feverish Torah studies and religious practices. The light of the Hasidic school of the rabbi of Lubavitz never dimmed, and the fiery Torah studies in Volozhin never ceased. As thousands of Jewish children were being tortured in nameless barracks throughout the Siberian wastelands, the religious rites and the Torah studies of Jews and Hasidim throughout Russia continued. Until, the despair and horror so overwhelmed the Jewish People, there were no more intellectuals left to go out to the Siberian wilderness to try to comfort and cheer up the destitute children of Israel.

Rabbi Menashe, who had witnessed the demoralization of his People, publicly condemned all the Jews who participated in the abductions, as well as anyone who abetted them. The leaders of the Jewish communities came to Rabbi Menashe and warned him that his actions could be construed as treason by the wretched Russian authorities. And that as a consequence, they may penalize the entire Jewish community. Rabbi Menashe told them that if he as head rabbi and arbitrator could not publicly express how he felt, and could not shout out against the oppression of his People, that he would have the moral obligation to resign from his lofty position. Although he had no other source of income, it was on that same day that Rabbi Menashe resigned from the rabbinate of Smorgon. Rabbi Menashe went back to grinding tobacco leaves with the machine he had once invented and made barely enough money to sustain himself and his family on bread and water. In 1831, at the age of 64, Rabbi Menashe fell ill with cholera and on the fourth day of Menachem Av [July 14, 1831], he returned his soul to his maker. Rabbi Menashe devoted the last three years of his life to writing. He did not leave his house and worked feverishly day and night. He put all his manuscripts in a chest for safekeeping. Tragically, the chest perished along with all of Rabbi Menashe's writings in the fire that consumed Smorgon in 1884. Nothing survived*, but the memory of this great man of undying faith, boundless love, and a beautiful vision that preceded its time.

*In 1807 Rabbi Menashe published his essay "Pesher Davar" (the meaning of it all), where he encouraged the Jewish community to actively seek employment in their local communities. In it, he articulated the books' objective, and explained how he wished to consolidate the great leaders of the Jewish congregations, alluding to the Gaon of Vilna, rabbi Eliyahu and rabbi Shneyor Zalman, writer of the Tanyah and the leader and founder of the Habad movement. Once again, the book was eradicated, and only a single copy survived (in the British Museum).

Towering above all the disciples of the Gaon, the most outspoken in behalf of enlightenment is Manasseh of Ilye (1767-1831). At a very early age he attracted the attention of Talmudists by his originality and boldness. In his unflinching determination to get at the truth, he did not shrink from criticising Rashi and the Shulhan 'Aruk, and dared to interpret some parts of the Mishnah differently from the explanation given in the Gemara. With all his admiration for the Gaon, but for whom, he claimed, the Torah would have been forgotten, he also had points of sympathy with the Hasidim, for whose leader, Shneor Zalman of Ladi, he had the highest respect. Like many of his contemporaries, he determined to go to Berlin. He started on his way, but was stopped at Königsberg by some orthodox coreligionists, and compelled to return to Russia. This did not prevent his perfecting himself in German, Polish, natural philosophy, mechanics, and even strategics. On the last subject he wrote a book, which was burnt by his friends, "lest the Government suspect that Jews are making preparations for war!" But it is not so much his Talmudic or secular scholarship that makes him interesting to us to-day. His true greatness is revealed by his attempts, the first made in his generation perhaps, to reconcile the Hasidim with the Mitnaggedim, and these in turn with the Maskilim. He spoke a good word for manual labor, and proved from the Talmud that burdensome laws should be abolished. His Pesher Dabar (Vilna, 1807) and Alfe Menasheh (ibid., 1827, 1860) are monuments to the advanced views of the author. In the Hebrew literature of his time, they are equalled only by the 'Ammude Bet Yehudah and the Hekal 'Oneg of Doctor Hurwitz.

[Page 71]

Our Master Rabbi Avraham Yitzhak HaCohen Kook

In the company of Rabbi Chaim Avraham in Smorgon

by Ephraim Tzoref

Translated by Sara Mages

R' Avraham Yitzchak's great thirst for knowledge grew from day to day. He traveled to centers of study from which perpetual light glowed to a distance. And here, when he was trave;omg to his destination, an incident happened to him on the way and the wagon broke. Therefore, they were forced to stop for a long time in Smorgon, the district of Vilna. In the meantime, he went to visit the city's rabbi who known as one of the greatest of the generation, and indeed:

[Page 72]

He is Rabbi Chaim Avraham Shapira. In his conversation with the young guest the rabbi was amazed at his knowledge. He immediately persuaded him not to continue to his destination and influenced him to stay in Smorgon, which was also a city of many scholars

Avraham Yitzchak accepted the advice of the city's rabbi and remained to study in Smorgon. The beauty of the place and its inhabitants - the great Torah scholars and the piety in it - had a great influence on his personality. Throughout his life he remembered them in his thoughts for the better. In one of the letters he sent to his brother, R' Shaul Hanna, in the days that he also studied in Smorgon, he wrote to say:

The name and memory (of Smorgon) is engraved in my heart for love from the dawn of my childhood. The city, in which I found affection for the sacred in my early days, is full of sages and authors, sharp and learned, who fear God and think of his name. Their company expanded my heart and also helped me to train my childhood talent

HaRav HaGaon, A. Y. HaCohen Kook zt"l realized the magnitude of his knowledge

The elders of Smorgon told of his stay in their city and noted that his diligence, in studies and work, was an incomparable vision. His diligence stemmed from the purity of his soul, out of piety, love of the Torah and the purposes for which the Torah was given. During the time he spent in Smorgon he studied ethic books, especially the Gemara and Poskim. He was knowledgeable in "Mesillat Yesharim" ["Path of the Upright"], a book of ethics by Moshe Chaim Luzzatto, and knew it by heart. Later, it was discovered that he had virtues that are only awarded to wise students and unique individuals

He greatly admired all moralists, even those whose methods were different from his methods, like R' Yisrael Salanter. HaRav Kook did not study morality with excitement and enthusiasm, but calmly and moderately

The people of Smorgon saw it as their right that the young prodigy lived among them and provided all his needs with great devotion. When he returned to his hometown, Griva, at the end of his year in Smorgon, scholars wrote him from there and pleaded before him to return to them, but, for various reasons, he had to stay in Griva

During his stay in Smorgon his name reached ADeReT (Rabbi Elijah David Rabinowitz-Teomim), the Rabbi of Panevėþys. This rabbi decided to appoint R' Avraham Yitzchak's as a groom to his daughter and performed the engagement ceremony

(Efraim Tzoref, The life of HaRav Kook)

[Page 73]

Two Lions

by Abba Gordin

Translated by Sara Mages

It is difficult for a son to write, to testify, about his father objectively. Twice as hard - for a rebellious son, who was in dispute and conducted a "culture struggle," on a small scale, with his father. Therefore, we will begin with the conventions that are not dependent on reason or evaluation.

My father z"l, was a rabbi who fulfilled the expression of *Chazal* ["Our Sages may their memory be blessed] - "and hate mastery" [*Avot* 1:10]. He used to repeat the popular saying, "a rabbi is not Jewish," and gave it a reason and definition of his own. A Jew is the one who pays a high price for his Jewishness, whereas a rabbi is the one who receives a payment, a salary, sometimes high, for his Jewishness

When he was a rabbi in Augustów, and he was thirty years old then, he signed the letter he had sent to the famous Rabbi of Brisk, R' Yehoshua Ber Soloveitchik, "Rav - or in Russian Raab', meaning - slave.

He used to say: a rabbi is like a gypsy. A gypsy is a nomad, and sò is a rabbi, he moves from city to city. Indeed, my father started his service in the small town of Mikailiðkës [Michaliszk] - from there he moved to Augustów, from Augustów to Ostrov, later he came to Smorgon, from Smorgon to £om¿a - and finished in Chicago

And he also said: "my sons aren't wicked sons of a righteous father, maybe they're good sons of a good father, but their wine is wine offered to idols which is forbidden to enjoy."

I remember, once we walked down a street in the city of Smorgon, a poor man approached us and held out his hand. My father dropped ten kopecks into the open hand. I did not give him anything.

When the poor man parted from us with a blessing and went away, my father turned to me with a question: Abb'ke, why didn't you give him a handout?"

"My father" - I answered - "we have a method, and when we fulfill it the poor will cease out of the land and also the rich will cease to exist"...

How long will it take you to introduce this new regime? - my father asked

"I think, about sixty years"... - I answered, it was in 1908, and I was twenty-one then

"Could this poor man wait so long? Surely, in the meantime he would die of starvation. When there will be no poor people, it is clear that we'll not deal with charity then, but, as long as they are with us, we must to give them alms... and next time, when a poor man meets you, give him what he deserves and don't reject him with a flimsy excuse of a "method"...

[Page 74]

My father wasn't in complete agreement with the "*Mussarnikim*" [members of the "Musar Movement"] from the school of R' Yisrael of Salant [Lithuania]. He thought that their preoccupation with morality, and constant struggle between good and evil inclination, was completely unnecessary He used to say: "when a person studies twenty-four hours a day, he has no time to sin, and this nasty man, even the evil inclination wouldn't dare to approach him!"...

HaRav R' Yehudah-Leib z"l, author of "*Teshuvot Yehudah*"

My father was very diligent and studied incessantly, in the literal sense of the saying, as if, organically, he could not tolerate idleness. He counted his hours and minutes like *drachmonim* [gold coins] and hid them from those who were afraid to lose their money but wasted their time recklessly He sat and studied day and night and during the break he wrote "*Chiddushei Torah.*" The books, in his private library, were granted with notes on their pages. Once, during an angry argument, I told my father:

[Page 75]

"What are you, the rabbis who fear God's word, who take pride in the Jewish world that is not yours. If, at least, you brought the Messiah, I would admit that your strength is better than our strength, the free secular people. But, you have not brought the Messiah, and without bringing it, we can be like you"...

On that he answered me: But. do you know how to wait every day for his arrival like us? That is the question"...

I heard my father explain, in his own way, the saying - "In every generation one must look upon himself as if he personally had gone out of Egypt." We are leaving Egypt also in our generation, because is happening right now if we look at it over one of the distant stars to which this sight of exit had now come. He gave this interpretation a number of years before the relativity theory was widespread, and the explanation of the phenomenon of "simultaneity."

My father wrote two books of questions and answers on the four sections of "*Shulchan Aruch*," and also wrote a booklet in Russian called " What is Hassidut?" which was published in 1903 in Warsaw, and a book in Russian called "What is the Talmud?" which was published in 1909.

The booklet in Russian about the Hassidut came in response to a question from the Governor of Poland to my father. The Hasidim were slandered that they were "involve in different matters," and the authority asked my father to give his opinion on this sect among the Jews

A very positive review of this booklet came at the time in "Ha-Tsfira." The reviewer was Pesach Kaplan, the author and teacher from Bialystok who perished in the Holocaust.

The book, "What is the Talmud,?" came as an answer to the booklet of the anti-Semite, B. O, Grosicki, called "Mystery in the Talmud," which was published in Warsaw in 1903 and distributed in tens of thousands of copies. In his introduction, the oppressor turned to Jewish communities with a challenge to try to deny his words, and if they prove his injustice, he was willing to pay a fine in the amount of 1000 ruble.

A number of prominent members of the communities of Warsaw and Lodz turned to my father with a request to answer something to Grosicki who was insulting the Oral Torah, and to fulfill - "Give a foolish man a foolish answer, or he will seem wise to himself " (Proverbs 26:5) - especially in the eyes of others.

The book "What is the Talmud?" contains two sections. Section 1 - "There is no mystery in the Talmud." Section 2 - " The essence of the Talmud." In his introduction the author writes: When we read the booklet mentioned above we notice... that the author, B. O. Grosicki, though severely criticizes the Talmud, had never seen it and, in any case, he wouldn't understand a single article written in it." And the author adds - it is clear to him that, his words and his denials, wouldn't influence people of this type, to whom Mr. Grosicki belongs to. His way is to harm with lies, forgery and plots that have no foundation. Nevertheless, we wrote this volume, "There is no mystery in the Talmud," because we set ourselves a double goal: A) To erase in refutation the dirty footprints that the false booklet "Mystery in the Talmud" left behind in literature. B) To offer the truth to those who seek it.

[Page 76]

The book, "What is the Talmud?" was published in Warsaw in 1909. My father sent a copy to Ahad Ha'am, who lived at that time in London, and a second copy to Leo Tolstoy in Yasnaya Polyana, Tula Oblast.

And how different were the reactions. Ahad Ha'am replied in a letter filled with spite: "I love the honor of the Torah and I am sorry to see those, who bear its banner, humiliating themselves to stand before the gentiles as accused, to justify and bring many proofs that our Torah does not oppose moral laws."

And another passage from the letter: Books, of this kind, do not appeal to me because they have no purpose. Do you believe that the gentiles hate us because they believe, in good faith, the words of charlatans like Grosicki, and if a rabbi will come and show them that Grosicki does not know the Talmud, would they repent? The truth is the opposite. Since the gentiles hate us, they believe, whole heartedly, in all words of hatred against us even though their forgery is evident in them. And just as all the apology books, which were written before, did not help, neither will the book of Your Honor will remove, even as a drop from the sea, all the lies that they fabricated, and fabricate, on us.

We will bring another small passage from the same letter of Ahad Ha'am, written in the bitterness of a cranky editor and a meticulous teacher: “And maybe, Your Honor will forgive me if I tell him that it is necessary to correct his style in the Russian language.”

What is the difference between my son and son-in-law: L. N. Tolstoy received the same book, read it and highly praised it. Praised it for its content and style, and was so affected by it that he came up with a proposal. He asked the rabbi-author to write for, “Posrednik Publishing House” in Moscow, a book on the “Ethics of the Talmud." The last words in Tolstoy's letter were deeply etched in my memory even though I had read them fifty years ago: “My millions of readers will be grateful to him.” Yes, Tolstoy had millions of readers and he promised them to my father if he would accept his offer and write the requested book.

Gorbunov Posadov established “Posrednik” (the mediator) in 1887 and was its director. Gorbunov was one of Tolstoy's oldest students, both in faith and morality, and in free education

My father sat to write the proposed book at the beginning of 1910 - but, suddenly an urgent letter was received from Tolstoy's wife in which she pleaded to cease this task and correspondence. Her excuse: her husband, Tolstoy, is weak, sick and should not be bothered. A slight harassment, like the exchange of letters, will cost him his life.

Apparently, Tolstoy's wife was afraid that the correspondence of her husband the author with an orthodox rabbi would hurt his name, and his sworn enemies from the “Holy Synod” [ruling body of the Georgian Orthodox Church] would spread a rumor that he intended to accept the Jewish faith...

[Page 77]

Under these complicated circumstances, my father was afraid to put his head between the lion and the lioness. So, as not to increase the controversy in Tolstoy's home - he ruled: “not to act in doubtful cases is better.”

A few months after his wife's interfering Tolstoy fled his home and died on the way, in a monastery, on 19 November 1910, at the age of 82.

My father passed away at the age of 72, on the intermediate days of Passover 5685. An "*Ohel*" was erected on his grave and a perpetual light is lit inside it.

I sold the letters of Tolstoy and Gorbunov Posadov, which were in my possession, to the Yiddish author, Herman Gold, and he sold them to Brentano, and the letters were purchased from Brentano by Yale University in New-Haven, United States.

ספר
תשובות יהודה
כולל
שאלות ותשובות
בארבעה חלקי הש"ע

ווילנא

תרס"ח

[Page 78]

Rabbis of the Community of Smorgon

by Moshe Tzinovitz

Donated by Jerrold Landau

A. Rabbi Chaim HaCohen, the First Rabbi

The Jewish settlement of Smorgon first appears [documented] as an independent community in the "State of Lithuania" in the year 5412 (1652). From 5439 (1679) and onward, we see this Jewish settlement and its environs called by the name "Smorgon and the region". Despite this [recognition], the name of the rabbis who served in the (Smorgon) community as heads of the rabbinical court or rabbis (*Moreh Tzedek*) have not been preserved for us.

One possible explanation [for the lack of rabbinical preservation] is because "Smorgon and the region" in those days belonged to the military district of Vilna during the kingdom of Poland. Since the Jewish community in Vilna began to be a chief community in the "Council of the State of Lithuania" beginning in the year 5412 (1652), similar to the older nearby communities of Brisk, Grodno, and Pinsk, the community of Smorgon may not have had its own rabbi and head of the rabbinical court, for it and its region were affiliated with the official rabbinical court of Vilna.

If Smorgon indeed had second tier rabbis with the title of *Moreh Tzedek*, *Yeshiva* Head, or Preacher of Righteousness, they were not considered important enough for their names to be registered and preserved for the generations. Our words are stated on the following authority: in the writ of appointment of the *Gaon* and rabbi, Rabbi Shmuel the son of Rabbi Avigdor as the final head of the rabbinical court of Vilna on 28 Adar II 5510 (1750) it is stated that he also has the authority as "the Head of the Rabbinical Court of the Region of Smorgon" (according to the book "*Kiriya Neemana*" by Rabbi Sh. Y. Fein).

Apparently, this form of precedence that was useful long ago, but was forgotten completely with the passage of time, and this last attempt of resurrecting it took place during the appointment of the aforementioned Rabbi Shmuel on account of the merits of his father-in-law, the author of the "Yesod" (Rabbi Yehuda the Scribe and Rabbinical Judge), an administrator (*parnas*) and intercessor in the community of Vilna at that time.

Around that time, we know that Rabbi Chaim HaCohen served as the "Head of the Rabbinical Court of the District of Smorgon." Rabbi Chaim HaCohen was also known as the famous rabbi and *Gaon* Rabbi Chaim Cohen, "the son of the great rabbi Rabbi Aryeh Leib (who was) the son of the *Gaon* Rabbi Kalonymos HaCohen, head of the rabbinical court of Nemirov." We have information about this rabbi of Smorgon, who was no longer alive in the year 5529 (1769), from his son-in-law, the husband of his daughter, Rabbi Shlomo Zalman (who was) the son of Rabbi Yehuda Leib (who was) head of the rabbinical court of Mir, in his booklet "*Darush Hesped*," which was published later when this rabbi was already serving as a rabbi in Konigsberg, the capital of East Prussia.

[Page 79]

This booklet includes the eulogy delivered by the author (Moshe Tzinovitz), the rabbi of Mir, on three rabbis and *Gaonim* who died at that time in Germany: Rabbi Netanel Weil Ashkenazy, head of the rabbinical court of Karlsruhe (author of "*Korban Netanel*" on the Ro'sh); Rabbi Mordechai the head of the rabbinical court of Duesseldorf (author of "*Maamar Mordechai*" Responsa); and Rabbi Avraham Abosh, the head of the rabbinical court of Frankfurt am Main. In the booklet, the author eulogizes his brother-in-law (brother of his wife) "the bright, great, famous Rabbi David, the son of my father-in-law, Rabbi Chaim HaCohen who served as the head of the rabbinical court of Smorgon, may his memory be a blessing." From here we learn that Rabbi Chaim HaCohen was no longer alive in the year 5529 (1769), and certainly died several years before that since by 5529 his son Rabbi David had died, and Rabbi Chaim's son-in-law, Rabbi Shlomo Zalman, was already an elderly man. Zalman, according to the sources ("*Or Vilna*" by the Maggid Steinschneider) died just a few years later, in 5535 (1775).

We can state that Rabbi Chaim HaCohen died prior to the year 5510 (1750) since in that year, Rabbi Shmuel, the son of Avigdor, received his certificate of appointment, in which he was called "the head of the rabbinical court of the District of Smorgon."

The reason that the rabbinate of Smorgon and its district neither passed to Rabbi David, the son of Rabbi Chaim, who was alive at the time, and nor to his son–in–law the rabbi and *Gaon* Rabbi Shlomo Zalman who was at the time the head of the rabbinical court of Mir and was appropriate for that post since he was great in Torah and also a splendid orator, is from the power and strength of Rabbi Yehuda the author of "Yesod." This issue caused a communal and social crisis in Vilna, and even led to the abolishment of the post of head of rabbinical court there until the final period prior to the Holocaust.

Regarding the state of the rabbinate in Smorgon during the era of Rabbi Shmuel of Vilna, with the worsening of relations between him and the new administrators chosen by that community, and also with the abrogating of government certification of the communal districts and the official power of the primary community (with the disbanding of the Council of the Four Lands of Poland and the Council of the State of Lithuania in the year 5524 – 1764), Smorgon probably became completely independent from Vilna, something that previously only occurred on paper.

From that time forward with respect to Smorgon, we find rabbis with the title "Head of the Rabbinical Court" whom we know by name. We also find second level rabbis, and at time rabbis who served on the rabbinical courts of these heads of rabbinical courts. These rabbis (*Morei Tzedek*, *Magidei Meisharim*) were at time "replacements" for the head of the rabbinical court between "kings" when the official position of head of rabbinical court was vacant. Thus, we know that in the year 5527 (1767) Rabbi Yosef Ben–Porat served as a rabbi (*Moreh Tzedek*) in Smorgon, and that year, his son, Rabbi Menashe Ish Ilya, who later became famous as a *Gaon*, researcher, critic and sage, was born in that city.

[Page 80]

B. The second rabbi, Rabbi Eliahu

From sources, we know the name of this rabbi as "Rabbi Eliahu from Volozhin," who served as the head of the rabbinical court of the community of Smorgon and the other communities. With respect to the "other communities" – one was Zaskovich. (In the latter years, it was half village, and half small town, but in those days, it was considered an important community and a town full of sages and scribes.)

We do not have details regarding the history of this Rabbi Eliahu, but something remains in our hands thanks to the history of *Gaonim* Rabbi Menashe Mailia and Rabb Shmuel Strashon, who were both relatives of this rabbi of Smorgon.

Rabbi Eliahu is described in "*Kiriya Neemana*" of Rabbi Sh. Y. Fein as a "*Gaon* and *Tzadik*, famous for his piety and character traits." Alongside him, Rabbi Yosef served as a rabbi (*Moreh Tzedek*) in Smorgon in the year 5527 (1767). From this reference, we can determine that Rabbi Eliahu was already appointed as rabbi in Smorgon before this date. We know that the young rabbi Menashe studied Torah from this uncle (brother of his mother) during his childhood in his native town of Smorgon.

The son-in-law of Rabbi Eliahu, Rabbi of Smorgon, was Rabbi Yosef (who was) the son of Rabbi Shmuel (who was) the head of the rabbinical court of Zaskovich. When rabbi Shmuel died in the year 5552 (1792), his in-law, Rabbi Eliahu of Smorgon, filled his place in the rabbinate of that town, and died there eight years later, on the first day of *Rosh Chodesh Tevet* 5560 (1800).

We do not know the reason that Rabbi Eliahu preferred Zaskovich to Smorgon, even though the community of Smorgon was already larger than Zaskovich. Perhaps this preference was caused by conflicts with strongmen in Smorgon. However, it is possible that Rabbi Eliahu was attracted to Zaskovich because it was the hometown of his family. The family had been involved in commercial and economic life in this town, and maintained contact with the large-scale landowners who owned estates next to this town. The town had many small Jewish settlements around it, so perhaps it was worthwhile for Rabbi Eliahu to move from Smorgon to Zaskovich. As support for our theory, after the death of Rabbi Eliahu, his grandson and great-grandson: the father and son Rabbi Menashe the eldest son of his son-in-law Rabbi Yosef, and Rabbi Elazar (who was) the son of Rabbi Menashe followed him in this rabbinate.

Rabbi Yosef the son of Rabbi Shmuel lived for a period of time with his father-in-law Rabbi Eliahu in Smorgon, and moved with his father-in-law from there to Zaskovich. From there he moved to Vilna, to be with his son the *Gaon* Rabbi Shmuel. He died there in his prime in the year 5589 (1829). This Rabbi Yosef was also an honorable man, and he played a significant role among the important people of the Jerusalem of Lithuania[1]. The following is written on his gravestone: "The precious, prominent rabbi, a G–d fearing man, with an upright path. His name was greatly known among the graspers of Torah."

[Page 81]

C. In Smorgon between Kings[2]

Rabbi Yehoshua Heshel the *Moreh Tzedek* and *Mara Mesivta*

He came from central Poland. During his youth, he excelled as a "great sharp person" and would generate many new ideas through didactics. He took on the goal of answering all the questions of the *Tosafos*[3] in cases where they were left with questions on the *Gemara*, and especially when the authors of the *Tosafos* had difficulty with *Rashi* in determining the straightforward explanation. However, his writings on many tractates in Talmud have been lost.

With the passage of time, we see that Rabbi Heshel settled in Lithuania and White Russia and established himself as a rabbi and author. During the years 5527–5542 (1767–1782), we see Rabbi Yehoshua Heshel as a *Moreh Tzedek* and *Yeshiva* Head in Old Bichov (District of Mohilev), and later filling this role in Minsk and Smorgon. (We know about his tenure in Smorgon from the book "Toldot Chachmei Yerushalayim" by Frumkin, Section 3). When Heshel was already in Lithuania and White Russia, this sharp man was influenced strongly by the school of learning of the *Gaon* of Vilna. In the book "Aliyot Eliahu" (by the *Gaon* Rabbi Yehoshua Heshel Levin), it is stated about Rabbi Heshel that "he merited to see the face of the Divine Presence, the holy of holies, our Rabbi the *Gaon* of Vilna."

Through his closeness to the G'ra [*Gaon* of Vilna] and his group in Vilna, Rabbi Yehoshua Heshel departed from the path of extreme didactics and concentrated in an exacting fashion on the words of the early sages through studying their works in depth. This observation can be recognized from the two books that he wrote during that time. His first book was "Matzmiach Yeshua" (Nowy Dwór, 5542 – 1782), which is a commentary on Sefer Mordechai on the two Mishnaic orders of Zeraim and Moed, as well as on the laws of Alfasi. In his second book "Yeshua Berosh," this author explains the words of the R'osh on the three tractates of Bava Kama, Bava Metzia, and Bava Batra, and delves into commentaries on the difficult issues of the R'if and Maimonides (Rambam). These two books are adorned with approbations from the Torah giants of Lithuania and famous rabbis from other places, including Rabbi Avraham Katzenelboigen, the head of the rabbinical court of Brisk of Lita [Brest Litovsk] and Rabbi Yisrael Mirkin, the head of the rabbinical court of Minsk (grandson of the *Gaon* Rabbi Chaim HaCohen, the rabbi of the district of Smorgon). The rabbi who provided the second approbation knew [the author] Rabbi Yehoshua Heshel personally. As the *Moreh Tzedek* in Minsk, Rabbi Mirkin wrote about this author (in his capacity as a sermonizer) regarding his great prowess, that "his lips drip myrrh and honey from a rock, and oil from a flintstone, as his mouth speaks great things." The rabbi who wrote an approbation, the *Gaon* Rabbi David Tebeli, head of the rabbinical court of Lissa (in Greater Poland), writes about this author that "they left him a place in Heaven to close himself off with his novel ideas." We should also note that Rabbi Yehoshua Heshel was the scion of a great lineage from his both his father's and mother's sides. He was named for after his ancestor Rabbi Heshel, the head of the rabbinical court of Lublin and Kraków. When Rabbi Yehoshua Heshel was a rabbi in Smorgon, he was involved with the group of the *Gaon* Rabbi Yisrael Parosh (the author of "Peat Hashulchan") who made aliya to the Land of Israel in the year 5570 (1810) and settled in the city of Safed (where those who came with the first waves of immigration of the *Perushim*[4], the students of the G'ra from Lithuania, settled). After several years, this rabbi from Smorgon went to his final resting place there.

[Page 82]

D. Rabbi Michel the son of Rabbi Feibish

We only know about this rabbi, who served as a *Moreh Tzedek* in Smorgon, from Rabbi Sh. Y. Fein in his book "*Kiriya Neemana.*" No other sources are left for us about him.

Rabbi Sh. Y. Fein tells us only that Rabbi Michel (the son of Rabbi Feibish) moved from Smorgon to Vilna, where he took an honorable place among the notables of that faithful city. His is buried among the notables in the old cemetery of Vilna. From the lists of other deceased people in the book "*Kiriya Neemana,*" we learn that this rabbi of Smorgon died in the year 5573 (1813).

Apparently, Rabbi Michel served as a rabbi in Smorgon after Rabbi Yehoshua Heshel, the author of "Matzmiach Yeshua" made aliya to the Land of Israel.

E. Rabbi Eliahu (who is) the son of Hillel HaLevi (Altz-Gut), the rabbinical judge in Smorgon until the year 5586 (1826).

The book "Ir Vilna" [City of Vilna] by Hillel Noach Magid Shteinshneider (Vilna 5660 – 1900) serves as a source for our words on this topic.

Rabbi Eliahu was born in the year 5546 (1786) in Vilna to his father Rabbi Hillel, who served as a communal rabbinical judge there. He got married in Smorgon to the daughter of "the wealthy man, upright in his ideas" Reb David Dnoszber, and served there as the communal rabbinical judge. Rabbi Eliahu returned to Vilna at the age of 40 and was referred to as "the Smorgonie Judge" by everybody, due to his former place of residence. Rabbi Eliahu filled the role of rabbinical judge in Vilna in a blessed manner for approximately 39 years and died close to the age of 80.

[Page 83]

In the year 5623 (1863) he wrote the book "Yad Eliahu" (didactics and novella) that has remained in print. The author of "Ir Vilna," who knew Rabbi Hillel at the time of his old age in Vilna, writes about Rabbi Eliahu that he was "great in Torah, with immense knowledge, great content, and a splendid author [who wrote] in clear, pure language. He was the fourth generation of rabbinical judges, and his family name was Altz Gut."

The following fact testifies to the Talmudic greatness of Rabbi Eliahu. One of his students was appointed at a young age – this student was the *Gaon* and wealthy man Rabbi Eliezer Landau of Vilna and Horodno, who later became famous for his outstanding composition "Damesek Eliezer," on the commentary of the Gr'a of Vilna on the *Orach Chaim* section of the code of Jewish Law. Apparently, Rabbi Eliahu Altz Gut filled the place of the rabbi and head of rabbinical court of Smorgon around the year 5567 (1826), for one year later, in the year 5587 (1827), Rabbi Menasha of Ilya was appointed to this role. Only after intensive persuasion did the *Gaon* Rabbi Menashe agree to occupy the rabbinical seat in his hometown.

F. The *Gaon* Rabbi Menashe the son of Yosef Mailia

Rabbi of Smorgon 5587–5588 (1827–1828)

The talented writer and analyst Mr. Abba Gordin, the editor of this book, has written an interesting and important research work on the learned *Gaon*, researcher and critic Rabbi Menashe of Ilya, shedding light onto the spiritual image of this wonderful man and earning a special blessing in its own right.

I will therefore suffice myself within the confines of this article on the rabbis of Smorgon to matters that have direct relevance to the relations between Rabbi Menashe of Ilya and the Jews of his hometown, whom he knew from up close for more than 60 years. In Smorgon, as one of the householders of that city, he taught students, both during his short tenure in the rabbinate, as well as when he lived there at the end of his days as a private individual.

The most prominent thing regarding this relationship was that Rabbi Menashe was beloved and accepted by all the Jews of Smorgon who looked upon him as a sublime man, even from the perspective of a rabbi and religious leader. As a proof, they selected him to be their rabbi and head of their rabbinical court, which Rabbi Menashe agreed only after lengthy persuasion, since his desire was not for this position, as he distanced himself from benefiting from the crown of the rabbinate. This stance was despite the fact that Rabbi Menashe was estranged and even distant from the circles of the great rabbis of Lithuania of those days due to his fundamental ideas and unique approach to the study of Torah, as especially seen in his words published with regards to "amendments to the understanding of the society and community, and preaching about deliberate, practical erudition and imparting a profession to the next generation" – matters that were a daring innovation at that time. The brazenness of his sermons caused him great suffering throughout his life. Furthermore, these statements were made publicly by a Torah author and major scholar. Nevertheless, the Jews of Smorgon, who knew Rabbi Menashe closely, regarded him as a leader in the paths of belief as one of the most patriarchal Orthodox rabbis, taking interest in the lives of the workers and laborers, doing things for their benefit and concern about the education of their children. He would gather the fine students of the *Beis Midrash* and pay attention to their Torah accomplishments. All these fine traits of their fellow native, Rabbi Menashe, served as a faithful guarantor for the scholarly Jews of Smorgon, and the broad masses that this man, the son of the rabbinical judge, was appropriate to be the religious leader of their community.

[Page 84]

Regarding the activities of Rabbi Menashe in Smorgon, we know from the writers of his story, that he would gather the masses of the city folk together on Sabbaths and teach them the principles of Hebrew grammar, so that they would be able to read Hebrew properly and would not be mocked by the scholars. On Saturday nights, he would invite all the townsfolk to teach them principles of morality, as he had formerly done when he lived in Ilya. He similarly later led the morality teachings in Smorgon when he served as rabbi and head of the rabbinical court, as well as when he lived there as a private householder (5587–5591 - 1827–1831).

Rabbi Menashe would also supervise the studies of the children and lads in the *cheders*, by taking interest in the level of their studies as well as the special abilities of the students with regard to their spiritual and professional futures. He got to know his students and consequently influenced and worked for the benefit of talented Torah youth with scholarly traits. He became particularly close with several of them and encouraged and guided them in everything related to their progress in Torah and spirituality. He mentored those who were fitting to be rabbis or *Yeshiva* heads in matters of leading a community, congregational relations, pedagogy, Talmudic methodology, as well as subjects related to deliberation and deciding Jewish law in interpersonal judgments and in communal and organizational edicts. This circle of instruction that was created by Rabbi Menashe in Smorgon (and previously in Ilya) can be regarded as a sort of Torah academy for independent study that was composed of young Torah scholars, with unique souls, who absorbed spiritual paths into their souls from the spiritual legacy of their prominent teacher and rabbi – each according to their individual talents. This Torah academy had an indirect effect (from the perspective of "the wind goes around and around"[5]) on the latter generations of rabbinics and scholarship in Lithuania, the land of classic Torah. All of this influence is thanks to the power, and power of power (through the students) of this pedagogue from Ilya–Smorgon.

The following rabbis and *Gaonim* were among the students of Rabbi Menashe during the period of his activities in Smorgon: Rabbi Aryeh Leib

Shapira, Rabbi Aryeh Leib Ihuminer, and the youngest of the group, Rabbi Reuven HaLevi Levin, a native of Smorgon. In this article, we will include specific words of appreciation of these individuals.

[Page 85]

As is known, Rabbi Menashe spent the end of his days in his native city of Smorgon during the period of 5587–5591 (1827–1831), and only spent about a year and a half in the role of head of the rabbinical court of that city. Most of his family lived in Ilya, for he had made his home there for decades. Several manuscripts written by Rabbi Menashe existed privately for more than 50 years with his family in Smorgon before finally being published. However, these manuscripts were burnt during the large fire that afflicted Smorgon in the year 5644 (1884). The few that survived remained in the hands of the author's great-grandson, Rabbi Yitzchak Spalter, as a legacy from his ancestors.

Rabbi Yitzchak Spalter, who served as a second rabbinical judge and *Yeshiva* head in Smorgon, published these remnants in the year 5665 (1905) under the name "*Alfei Menashe*" (first volume), which includes "Life-providing knowledge that is beneficial to the behavior of its possessors, and an opening to solve difficult matters in *Agada*, and explanations in *Halacha*." The second volume, which was published about 74 years after the death of its author, includes approbations from the great rabbis of Lithuania – not only from Rabbi Y. Y. Reines[6] of Lida, but also from Rabbi Yitzchak Blazer, the pillar of "*mussar*" (moral teachings), and Rabbi Refael Shapira (the son of the *Gaon* Rabbi Aryeh Leib Shapiro), as well as the two primary rabbis of Vilna: Rabbi Shlomo HaCohen, and Rabbi Chaim Ozer Grodzinski.

These rabbis who provided approbations already saw the light of outlooks that were different from those of the generation of Rabbi Menashe, and they knew how to positively appreciate the praiseworthy activities of Rabbi Menashe of Ilya regarding the books that he wrote in his time.

In his approbation to the book "*Alfei Menashe*," Rabbi Y. Y. Reines writes the following: "The author was among the excellent *Gaonim* and rabbis. Many of his generation did not appreciate his great heart at that time, but anyone who thinks carefully about the words in his few books that were published during his lifetime will see that his words are very precious, and there is no limit to their benefit."

Rabbi Shlomo HaCohen regards Rabbi Menashe as "A wonderful *Gaon* and *Tzadik*, learned, and teaching knowledge to the nation, to lead them to understand wisdom, morality, and fear of G–d."

Even more typical are the words of the approbators Rabbi Chaim Ozer and Rabbi Yitzchak Blazer, who were considered representatives of the extreme right wing of the rabbis of Lithuania during the latter two eras. Rabbi Chaim Ozer expressed his positive opinion of Rabbi Menashe with these words, "In truth, it is not necessary to provide an approbation for this man, for the name of the *Gaon* Rabbi Menashe is known throughout the entire Diaspora as a mighty *Gaon* and researcher in every area. I cast light on this rabbi, (for aside from the preciousness and importance of his writings in of themselves), as his ideas and thoughts are also worthy of publication for the members of the current generation, and will provide proof that it was for naught that they hung empty people on the tree (he was referring to Rabbi Mordechai Flungian, who in his book on the annals of Rabbi Menashe Ilya, '*Porat Yosef*,' portrays him as a progressive rabbi who diverges from the image of a Talmudic rabbi dedicated to the Code of Jewish Law and ancestral tradition). When they see these writings, they will understand that they tried to darken his great light for naught, and their attributed opinions to him that were not in accordance with his spirit."

[Page 86]

The *Gaon* Rabbi Blazer, the student and spiritual heir of Rabbi Yisrael Salanter, regards Rabbi Menashe as a "Great *Gaon*, and all that he has published is 70–fold refined silver. His holy words are fit to be published so that the masses can benefit from his light."

It must be noted that the *Gaon* Rabbi Avraham Abli Paswalier, the head of the rabbinical court of Vilna, served as a protector and shield for Rabbi Menashe against certain rabbis who cast venom at him. He was his relative and friend, and was content when the words of wisdom and thought of Rabbi Menashe were published. He also gave an approbation to the first book of Chaim Zelik Slonimski.

That these words of appreciation from the approbating rabbis regarding Rabbi Menashe were true and trustworthy can be seen from the fact that all his descendants remained within the realm of Torah heritage. Some of them were even famous rabbis and expert Torah giants. This is a situation that not all rabbis and Orthodox families succeed in.

According to the words of the aforementioned Rabbi Yitzchak Spalter at the beginning of the book "*Alfei Menashe*" (volume II), we know the following details about the descendants of Rabbi Menashe:

Rabbi Menashe had one son who was a great scholar and an honorable merchant. He drowned in the Neman River near Tilsit, East Prussia, where he is buried. This was the grandfather of Rabbi Yitzchak Spalter of Smorgon.

Rabbi Menashe had two daughters. The eldest married Rabbi Baruch Blidstein in Ilya, who was the father-in-law of the aforementioned *Gaon* Rabbi Aryeh Leib Ihuminer. Rabbi Baruch's son, Rabbi Avraham, was the one by whom a large chest of letters of Rabbi Menashe was burnt. (Rabbi Menashe was his maternal grandfather. Rabbi Avraham Blidstein married his two daughters to two great scholars: to Rabbi Yitzchak Pines, one of the first to serve the role as *Moreh Tzedek* in Minsk, and to Rabbi Yoel Shlomo Sherman, the head of the rabbinical court of the large community of Rovno in Volhynia.

The aforementioned Rabbi Yoel Shlomo is described by Rabbi Yehuda Leib HaCohen Fishman (Maimon), who knew him personally from when he was once his guest in Rovno: as "one of the great ones of the generation, with a sharp mind and deep knowledge in Torah, the splendor of his community (Rovno) for all the time he lived there. He left behind a good name and a memory for generations." This rabbi, who was already elderly at the time, told him (Rabbi Maimon) about his wife's grandfather Rabbi Menashe of Ilya, and about his Torah and greatness.

Further details about this rabbi of Rovno can be found in the article "Rabbis and rabbinical judges of Rovno" in the Yizkor Book of that community published in 5717, edited by Aryeh Avitachi, and published by Yalkut Volhyn. It should be noted that the descendants of Rabbi Menashe also included three famous rabbis: Rabbi Yitzchak Eliahu Ginzburg, the official city rabbi of Bialystok (died in 5683 - 1923), whose wife was the daughter of the *Gaon* Rabbi Aryeh Leib Adler (the son of the *Gaon* Rabbi Yisrael of Salant), and granddaughter of the *Gaon* Rabbi Yom Tov Lipman Heilprin (author of "*Oneg Yomtov*") head of the rabbinical court of Bialystok; Rabbi Glidstein, the son-in-law of the *Gaon* Rabbi Zalman Sender Kahana Shapira, rabbi of Choroszcz near Bialystok, and previously the *Mashgiach* (spiritual supervisor) of the *Yeshiva* of his father–in–law the *Gaon* of Malcz; and Rabbi Simcha Zelig Reier, the chief *Moreh Tzedek* in the rabbinical court of Rabbi Chaim HaLevi Soloveitchik in Brisk (Brest Litovsk). Rabbi Reier was Rabbi Soloveitchik's right hand and assistant in all matters of rabbinical decisions and teaching, as well as one of the primary *Yeshiva* heads in the *Yeshiva* of *Toras Chesed* of Brisk.

[Page 87]

G. The Rabbi and *Gaon* Rabbi Aryeh Leib Shapira

Rabbi Aryeh Leib Shapira is known in the rabbinical world as Rabbi Leibelie of Kovno, since Kovno was the location of his final rabbinical post (during the years 5609–5614 (1849–1854)). He was considered as one of the *Gaonim* of Lithuania and Reisin of his generation. His methodology of study and learning was unique: straight, clear depth without any abstruse didactics, combined with a significant spirit of research in his approach and outlook related to the understanding of the early sages as well as the greats of the latter sages. His second characteristic in learning came from a blend of the spiritual force of his teacher and rabbi, Rabbi Menashe of Ilya with his own individual personal characteristics. He forged his personal scholarly and spiritual approach through these attributes.

Rabbi Leibele expressed his Talmudic novella in brief prose that clarified and purified the Talmudic discussion under consideration, in a straightforward manner, as something that can be self–understood – a form of a second edition of the commentary of *Rashi*. At first glance, an intermediate scholar would not understand the essence of the new ideas of Rabbi Leibele, as expressed with complete simplicity as if it was swallowed up in the storm of his studies. However, the advanced scholars from among his students would listen to the utterances of his mouth with suspense and deep concentration, regarding the terse words of their teacher and rabbi as feeding off the direct essence of the difficult words of the *Gemara* in a manner that made sense. He answered all questions through his brief explanations, and there was no room for didactics among the various commentaries on the essence of this matter.

In addition to his greatness in Talmud, this rabbi was held in esteem by the elders of the generation and considered great in both wisdom and sciences, including technology, engineering, religious research, as well as mysticism. It is said that the rabbi once expressed: "From the time the *Gaon* of

Vilna died there is nobody who understands Kabbala, and if someone says that there are such people, then I am among them." He would say, "If only I had attentive students, I would give them lessons in technology and engineering." His great knowledge in these areas would be exposed publicly when he would study sections of *Gemara* relevant to those fields.

[Page 88]

Apparently, Rabbi Leibelie was born in Ivenets, where his father Rabbi Yitzchak Zundel served as the town rabbi. He lost his father at the age of six, and he was raised by his maternal grandfather, Rabbi Eliezer the head of the rabbinical court of Lyubcha, near Novhorodok. Rabbi Eliezer's father, the *Gaon* Rabbi Aryeh Leib Shapira, the scribe and rabbinical judge in Vilna, is known throughout the rabbinical world through his book "*Nachalat Ariel*" on Tractate *Sofrim*. Rabbi Leibel also took on the family name Shapira from his mother's side. The name stems from the great ones and martyrs of Shapira–Speyer[7]. His first rabbinical post came through the special recommendation of his teacher, Rabbi Menashe of Ilya. The appointment was unanimous because everyone knew that whomever Rabbi Menashe of Ilya nominates, is chosen. Rabbi Leibele served in this rabbinical post in Smorgon for eleven years, from 5588–5599 (1828–1839). From there he moved to Kalwaria until 5609 (1849), and then to Kovno, where he eventually died. Rabbi Leibele was the first rabbi of Kovno with the title "Head of the Rabbinical Court" since the earlier rabbis were only given the title of *Moreh Tzedek* due to their dependence on the rabbinate of nearby Slobodka. Their rabbinical authority was restricted, and only the head of the rabbinical court of the community of Slobodka could give direction on unique matters requiring special attention.

The *Gaon* Rabbi Leibele Shapira did not concern himself with publishing his Torah novella, and only bits of it are included in the works of other authors of his time. In the *Mishna Berura* commentary on the Code of Jewish Law by the Chafetz Chaim, it is brought down in his name that he annulled the custom of standing during the reading of the Ten Commandments in the Torah portions of *Yitro* and *Vaetchanan*, as well as on Shavuot. His reasoning was that it would seem that this is the main point, and the rest [of the Torah] is subordinate to it, as if it was not uttered by G–d like the Ten Commandments.

During the time of the rabbinical tenure of Rabbi Leibele in Kovno, the *Gaon* Rabbi Yisrael Salanter set up his *Beit Hamusar* [House of Moral Teachings], but the *Gaon* Rabbi Leibele, the head of the rabbinical court of the city, was among the opponents of this new idea. That rabbi of Kovno expressed his opposition by saying: "In *Hallel*, it says 'the House of Israel shall bless G–d, the house of Aaron, etc., fearers of G–d, etc.' but it does not say 'the house of those that fear G–d.'" There is a proof from here that there is room for individual fearers of G–d, but not for a special group of that nature...

Despite Rabbi Leibele's distance from special routines between man and G–d and between man and his fellow, he was accepted as a prominent rabbi among all the rabbinical circles, both as a Tamudic *Gaon* and also as a person who conducted himself with holy purity, very immersed in holy service. When he died in the year 5614 (1854), he was eulogized even in far off cities. The *Gaon* Rabbi Yosef Chaver, head of the rabbinical court of Dubno (near Łomża), in his special eulogy that he delivered in memory of his father, the *Gaon* and Kabbalist Rabbi Yitzchak Izak, head of the rabbinical court of Tyktin and Suwalki, who died around that time, mentions in his memorial, "And from afar, we heard about the honor and splendor of the great and famous *Gaon*, Rabbi Aryeh of blessed memory, the head of the rabbinical court of Kovno, and my eyes fill with tears. For the flock of G–d was taken captive, the horn of Israel has declined drastically due to the (death) of these two prominent figures."

[Page 89]

The *Gaon* Rabbi Leibele Shapira merited to be the ancestor of a famous rabbinic dynasty that wrote a bright page in the annals of the rabbinate of Lithuania in the patriarchal Orthodox fashion. One of them, the *Gaon* Rabbi Rafael, even joined the famous family of "*Beit Harav*" in Volozhin. This dynasty was established by six famous sons that Reb Leibele left after him: Rabbi Yitzchak Menachem Zundel, Rabbi Shlomo, Rabbi Chaim Avraham, Rabbi Levi, Rabbi Rafael, and Rabbi Moshe Shmuel, as well as one daughter who married Rabbi Moshe Shlomo Ginzburg. All of them had a direct connection with Smorgon – having been born or raised and educated there. They were nurtured by their illustrious father, grew their wings in Smorgon, and were raised to the pinnacles of the rabbinate, earning a special recognition in this article. In this section about their father, we will note something about only one of them, Rabbi Shlomo, about whom only one fact is known to us: that he was a rabbi in the district city of Perm in central Russia, and died in the year 5646 (1886). His son Rabbi Zundel changed his family name from Shapira to Rabinovitch. We do not know any other details of Rabbi Shlomo or his descendants.

H. Rabbi Yitzchak Menachem Zundel

The eldest of Rabbi Leibele Shapira's sons, filled the place of his father in the rabbinate of Ilya after his father moved from there to Smorgon. He died in his prime, in the year 5601 (1841) during the lifetime of his father. His son, Rabbi Chaim Yaakov, lost his father at the age of nine, and was raised in the home of his grandfather in Kovno. He was nurtured by his uncle Rabbi Chaim Avraham in Smorgon, and was ordained as a rabbi at a young age by the *Gaonim* Rabbi Yosef Feimer of Slutsk and Rabbi David Tebali of Minsk. He served for some time as a rabbi in Ivenets as the replacement for the *Gaon* Rabbi Reuven HaLevi. From there he moved to Kovno where he served as a *Moreh Tzedek* for more than 20 years in the rabbinical court of the *Gaon* Rabbi Yitzchak Elchanan Spector. Then he moved to Jerusalem where he was appointed as a *Moreh Tzedek* in the Ashkenazic–*Perushim* rabbinical court, headed by the *Gaon* Rabbi Shmuel Salant. He did not become involved in the issues of the city, but rather remained fully immersed in his studies and his service as a rabbinical judge and teacher – roles he filled with dedication and faithfulness for a period of 18 years. When he died in the year 5688 (1919), an article about him appeared in Chavatzelet in Jerusalem. The husband of his granddaughter, Rabbi Tzvi Pesach Frank, a native of Kovno (husband of the daughter of his son Rabbi David of Kovno) took his place as a judge in the rabbinical court. Rabbi Tzvi Pesach Frank eventually became the head of the Ashkenazic rabbinical court of Jerusalem.

[Page 90]

I. Rabbi Levi Shapira was famous as a *Gaon*

He was raised and educated by his father in Smorgon and Kovno. He married the daughter of Rabbi Avraham Rabinovitch of Neustadt–Sugintai in Zamot, where he lived with his father–in–law for several years. In the year 5624 (1864), he became the rabbi of Tryškiai, and later in Novoaleksandrovsk (a regional town in the Kovno district), where he died in his prime at the age of 42 in the year 5640 (1880). There is a memorial to that late rabbi in *Hamelitz* of that year. He is described there as a man who blended Torah and wisdom. In the book "*Nachalat Avot*" by Rabbi Levi Ovchinsky, it is written about him that he was "a great and wise rabbi, expert, with splendid praises." Many years later (in the year 5673 – 1913), Rabbi Chaim Tzvi Shapira (the nephew of the aforementioned Rabbi Levi), the rabbi of Lapichi, wrote a book of responsa and Torah novella of his uncle, the rabbi of Novoaleksandrovsk, called "*Beit Levi.*" Rabbi Moshe Shmuel, the brother of this author (the father of rabbi Cham'ol) wrote about the late rabbi and author: "the brother of the great, true *Gaon*, who was set to become the most prominent rabbi of the entire Diaspora had he not been cut off from the world while still in his prime, at the age of forty." His other brother, the *Gaon* Rabbi Shapira of Volozhin, described him as "the Great *Gaon*, the famous Sinai and uprooter of mountains in his Torah and fear of Heaven"[8]. In his book "*Beit Levi*" (which contains only a small portion of his many Torah writings) Rabbi Levi Shapira discussed halachic responsa and novel Torah ideas with famous rabbis, including his two famous brothers, as well has his third brother, "The sharp Rabbi and *Gaon*, expert as a Sinai and uprooter of mountains – Rabbi Chaim Avraham, the head of the rabbinical court of Smorgon."

[Page 91]

J. Rabbi Chaim Avraham Shapira

Rabbi Chaim Avraham served in the rabbinate of Smorgon for 33 years (5614–5646 – 1854–1886) following his father the *Gaon* Rabbi Aryeh Leib. He was born around the year 5581 (1821) in Ilya. He was raised by his father the *Gaon* of Smorgon, from whom he gained most of his Torah knowledge. He is described by those who knew him personally as a "*Gaon* and a wise man with general intelligence." The wisdom of Rabbi Chaim Avraham, when he was 13 years old, is included in the book "History of the Jews of Kovno." The story is as follows: One time, his father, Rabbi Leibele of Smorgon, traveled to a town and left the *Moreh Tzedek* Rabbi Meir as his fill–in to respond to questions. Rabbi Meir was an irritable person by nature and stringent in his directives. As he was sitting in the *Beis Midrash*, a young girl entered and asked a question regarding [the kashruth of] a chicken. Rabbi Meir briefly glanced at her, and immediately decided: It is *treif*! [not kosher]

The lad Chaim Avraham was present at that time. When he heard the decision of the *Moreh Tzedek*, he ran after the girl, caught up to her, and told her, "And I tell you that this chicken is kosher, and if you do not believe me, I am prepared to buy it from you with cash." Rabbi Meir nurtured a hatred against this brazen youth. When the *Gaon* Rabbi Aryeh Leibele returned home from his journey, Rabbi Meir went to greet the rabbi, and told him about the incident with Chaim Avraham. Rabbi Leibele summoned his son and asked him to explain his behavior, and about the basis that he gave a permissive answer to the question. The son answered, "Based on such and such a place in the Code of Jewish Law, *Yoreh Deah*." Since that was the case, his father Rabbi Leibele answered him, "Indeed you are correct, but you are still deserve a lashing." Rabbi Chaim Avraham, the rabbi of Smorgon, was not dependent on the community for his salary. He was a wealthy man, and his salary from the community of Smorgon was designated for charity. He also supported his sons–in–law at his table, along with their families, for many years, until they were appointed as rabbis in Jewish communities. In the book "*Responsa Beit Levi*" by his brother the *Gaon* Rabbi Levi Shapira, a responsa of this author is included regarding the designation of the precise day of yahrzeit of their father the *Gaon* Rabbi Aryeh Leib, due to a dispute among his children as to whether the death took place on the 17th or 18th of *Shvat* (5614 – 1854), since the death took place at dusk[9]. His brother, the rabbi, informed him in a decisive fashion that "our father died immediately after the time of the Maariv service on the night of the 18th of *Shvat*."

Rabbi Chaim Avraham is described in the book "*Nachalat Avot*" as "A great, wise, and renowned rabbi" and who symbolized the "splendor of the rabbinate" in the most sublime fashion. When he died in the year 5646 (1886), the news was published in the Hebrew newspapers as well as the "*HaAsif*" of Nachum Sokolov, volume II (5647 – 1887) in the memorial section, where it is written: "aside from his great expertise in Talmud and rabbinic decisions, the late rabbi was also a very wise in worldly matters. The soul of his community cleaved to him greatly, and that his rabbinical brothers came from various towns to eulogize and weep for him."

Regarding his activities as Rabbi of Smorgon, it is mentioned in *HaLevanon* in the year 5641 (1881) (number 19) that in that year, that the activists of that city decided along with the *Gaon*, the head of the rabbinical court, to impose a "small tax" on all types of grain for the purposes of charity in the city. They money was also designated to grant travel expenses to lads going to the army. The small tax along with the meat tax added up to a sum of 2,000 rubles.

K. The *Gaon* Rabbi Chaim Yehuda Litwin

Rabbi Chaim Yehuda Litwin was considered as a Talmudic *Gaon* with a great memory and depth of sharpness. The great rabbis were in awe when they met him, and none other than the *Gaon* Rabbi Yosef Shaul

[Page 92]

Nathanson, the head of the rabbinical court of Lwów in Galicia, mentions him several times in his well–known book "*Shoel–Umeishiv*" regarding his clarity in matters of rabbinical decisions requiring special adjudication and clarifications.

Rabbi Chaim Yehuda went through a tense period in his personal life. According to the history of those times, when he arrived in Smorgon in the year 5646 (1886) he was known as the "Rabbi of Brody" of eastern Galicia. He was born in Bobriusk (White Russia) in the year 5600 (1840) and was known already in his youth as a genius [*iluy*]. He got married in Sośnica (district of Czernihów). From the name of this town, he gained his nickname "The *iluy* of Sośnica," which stuck with him throughout his life. He was employed there in commerce and business through his wealthy father–in–law. When his father–in–law's situation weakened, he too lost his fortune. When he later resided in Minsk, the greats of that city, especially the wealthy scholar Rabbi Zusia HaCohen Rappaport, drew him near to assist. However, all of this comfort did not satisfy him. He became sick from all the anguish and traveled abroad to consult with physicians. He spent time in Germany, Hungary, and Galicia. In Lwów, he was approached by the rabbi of the city, the aforementioned *Gaon* Rabbi Yosef Shaul Nathanson. He received spiritual and material support from Rabbi Nathanson.

At that time, in the year 5629 (1869), the *Gaon* Rabbi Shlomo Kluger, the head of the rabbinical court and rabbi of the splendid community of Brody, died. The "Sosnicani" who was a "Russian" guest, was appointed to take the place of the late illustrious leader of Brody, thanks to the special recommendation of the *Gaon*, the head of the rabbinical court of Lwów. He filled this role successfully for close to 18 years (until the year 5645 – 1885), and became the expert in responding on matters of halachic decisions for famous rabbis from near and far, as he expressed his opinion in serious elements of Jewish law.

Two family disasters overcame Rabbi Chaim in the year 5645 (1885). The wife of his youth, and his son, the young *Gaon* Rabbi Shimshon, the son-in-law of the *Gaon* and head of the rabbinical court of Stryj, both died. He left Brody because of these events, and returned to Russia. He married for a second time to the daughter of the *Gaon* Rabbi Eliezer Moshe Horowitz, the head of the rabbinical court of Pinsk. He waited to obtain an important rabbinical position, appropriate to his honor. He agreed to come to occupy the rabbinical seat of Smorgon and served there as the head of the rabbinical court for 17 years (5646–5663 – 1886–1903).

This *Gaon* and head of the rabbinical court of Smorgon died after a lengthy illness that left him bedridden for two years. Words of appreciation were published in the three Hebrew newspapers of that time: *Hamelitz*, *Hatzefira*, and *Hatzofeh* (of Warsaw). In the first newspaper it was written that during the funeral of this *Gaon*, as he was being brought to his final resting place, "all the shops in Smorgon were closed and locked. All the workers in the factories and the tradesmen ceased their work," and that "all of them took care to give final honors to their rabbi." It was also written there that six eulogizers delivered bitter (sorrowful) eulogies over the deceased and described the value of his greatness in Torah.

The name of this *Gaon* of Smorgon was perpetuated in his responsa book "*Shaarei Deah*" that was already printed in the year 5644 (1884) when he was the rabbi of Brody. This book includes many responsa from this author with significant content and scope on various issues in the sections of the Code of Jewish Law, and especially in matters of marital law and the releasing of *agunot*[10] which require expert scholarship. This great author took a place for himself in these difficult, thorny matters with his scholarly deliberations and decisive opinions.

[Page 93]

His solutions in matters of matrimonial law were very appropriate and realistic in the community of Brody, a border city near the division between Austrian Galicia and Russia, at the beginning of the 1880s. During that time, thousands of Jewish refugees gathered in Brody. These refugees included men and women of various types who had no knowledge of their family pedigree with respect to marriage and divorce. This made it difficult to work out such matters in the court of the rabbi of Brody. Several matters required exacting and detailed deliberation based on the facts together with the Halachic clarification.

Rabbi Chaim Yehuda writes the following in one of his responsa: "In the year 5642 (1882), our city of Brody was a gathering point for immigrant refugees from Russia who had been persecuted there. Many passed through here to America, the place of freedom and liberty in the human kingdom as well as the Kingdom of Heaven. In our great sins, many of the travelers cast off the yoke of Torah and proper behavior. Therefore, we deal with many *gittin* [bills of divorce] in our court on a daily basis, for the husband wants to travel afar whereas the woman does not – or vice versa."

The painful points in these types of situations are the dangers of Jewish women becoming an *agunah* [10] because such husbands are trying to evade their wives as they travel afar, far from their acquaintances, townsfolk, and environment; as well as the concern of the large number of such women who know or do not know their status. Such questions kept Rabbi Chaim Yehuda very busy. He did the best he could with his deep expertise and sharpness. With his clear and wise deliberation, he knew how to decide such matters and determine a clear, incisive decision in such cases.

Regarding the unique realities that were created at that time in Brody and the region due to the waves of refugees that swept into the cities, we find a discussion in a second responsa in the book "*Shaarei Deah*" beginning with the following words: "In the wake of the tribulations, disturbance, and persecutions of the masses of Jewish residents of greater Russia..." These two sources are not known to Jewish researchers who concerned themselves and wrote about that era.

I will note one more interesting detail: during those times (after Passover of 5642 – 1882), the *Gaon* Rabbi Shmuel Mohilever[11] came from Brody to Lwów with a unique focus to personally determine the status of these refugees in the two cities and to judge and clarify regarding the preparations and references for these refugees to immigrate to America or the Land of Israel. When he was in Brody, the *Gaon* Rabbi Shmuel Mohilever got to know the *Gaon* Rabbi Chaim Yehuda, head of the rabbinical court of the city. When they sat down together to deliberate over this actual problem in the city, Rabbi Chaim

Yehuda supported the idea of the *Gaon* Rabbi Shmuel Mohilever to turn and direct his personal activity in this matter for the good of the Land of Israel. However, their desire did not succeed fundamentally. The vast majority of the massive waves of immigration streamed to America for several reasons. From that time on, the activities and communal work of Rabbi Shmuel Mohilever [were no longer directed to resolving the refugee immigration problem] but now dedicated solely to the Chibbat Zion Movement and the principle of renewing settlement in the Land of Israel. We can relate this [change of direction] to that meeting in Brody with Rabbi Chaim Yehuda, the head of the rabbinical court o the community, who strengthened the opinion of Rabbi Shmuel Mohilever for the benefit of this matter. This was the final stroke of the hammer relating to this. (From A. Sh. Hirshberg of Bialystok).

[Page 94]

Rabbi Chaim Yehuda himself found it difficult to become active in Chibbat Zion for personal reasons relating to his family situation and his weak health. His activities as rabbi of Brody and later of Smorgon were tied to the place itself, as well as to the fact that his personal nature was to "sit in the tent"[12]. Nevertheless, he followed the development of the movement with great interest. He held the blessed activities of Rabbi Shlomo Mohilever in great esteem, and he considered him to be a "praiseworthy *Gaon*" in the field of Torah as well as in all matters relating to the development of the Chibbat Zion movement and the advancement of aliya and settlement in the Land of the Patriarchs. He would publicly declare his faithfulness to this movement and to the local expansion activities by the activists of Chovevei Zion in Smorgon. Through these efforts, they began to become a recognizable force in communal and social affairs in the city. The correspondence from Smorgon that appeared in *Hatzefirah* in the year 5659 (1899) (number 266) confirms what was stated above. It tells us about the large-scale activities of the Chovevei Zion chapter in that city: "About 60 regular members participated in the Odessa Committee (meaning that they paid monthly dues). Aside from this, many others pay periodically to that committee." The main point: "the head of the rabbinical court of the city, the well-known *Gaon*, may he live long, expresses his goodwill and great desire to increase the honor and might of the chapter."

The person who wrote that article, under the name of "Yehudi" (Dov Ber Shimshelevitch) also informs us about the general meeting of the Chovevei Zion members on *Rosh Chodesh Tevet* in 5659 (1898), where the executive committee of the chapter in Smorgon was elected. The meeting included members as follows: Rabbi of the community (government appointed rabbi) Tzvi Fridensohn, *Magid Meisharim* (Preacher of Righteousness) of the city Rabbi Shlomo Yitzchak Schwartz, Shabtai Frankfurt, Chaim Bodnes, Moshe Levinson, Chalvina Kowarski, Idel Broda, Shmuel Mordechai Marsha'k, Avraham Yehuda Zuckerman, Baruch Leib Vinch, Rafael Parishtat, and Dov Ber Shimshelevitz (aforementioned).

[Page 95]

The rabbi of Smorgon, Rabbi Chaim Yehuda Litwin, was already a follower of political Zionism during its first years. His opinion on this subject was published by one of the Zionists of Smorgon, David Kopiliovitch, on the pages of *Hamelitz*, year 5660 (1900) (no. 72). In this article, Rabbi Chaim Yehuda reacts sharply to all those rabbis who oppose Zionism. He regards this as "folly and a great evil." "His heart is so bitter over this brazenness that he uses the term evil" regarding those people who endanger the soul of the "Israelite." He states that "Zionism and Zionists are occupied in a great commandment and a major principle of religion, and that someone occupying himself in this movement fulfils the greatest commandment upon which our faith is founded, and establishes the abode of our life."

L. Torah *Kibbutz* in Smorgon during the years 5656–5669 (1896–1900)

Under the supervision of the *Gaon* and head of the rabbinical court, Rabbi Chaim Yehuda Litwin

During the period of the rabbinate of the *Gaon* Rabbi Chaim Yehuda Litwin in Smorgon, a Talmudic *Kibbutz* (Talmudic Gathering) was set up in the city for several years for talented lads and young married men, under the supervision of the rabbi and *Gaon*.

This Talmudic *Kibbutz*, which was not technically a *Yeshiva*, and did not follow the customary protocols of *Yeshiva* life as defined by *Yeshiva* heads under the supervision of the *Yeshiva* overseers – set up its headquarters in one of the *Beis Midrashes* of the city. The Torah study was primarily based on imparting proper Talmudic knowledge in the rabbinic decisors and especially in the study of the *Yoreh Deah* section of the Code of Jewish Law at the level of a *Moreh Tzedek* – so that ordination of "*Yoreh Yoreh*" and "*Yadin Yadin*"[13] could be granted by the *Gaon*, the head of the rabbinical court.

In order to obtain a certificate of ordination from the *Gaon*, the head of the rabbinic court, students had to become close with him, and assist in the giving of rabbinic decisions for a certain period. Only those whose souls were fit for this assignment, and who amassed practical rabbinical knowledge in *Halacha* were able to obtain such ordination. Among the students of this Torah *Kibbutz* were a number of graduates of large *Yeshivas*, whose aim was to become expert in issuing rabbinical decisions. They accomplished their objective in Smorgon and over time became famous rabbis in important communities.

However, among this *Kibbutz* of Smorgon were students of other *Yeshivas* who were also attracted as the status of oversight was less stringent that in other, older *Yeshivas*. In Smorgon, they found a place that was comfortable for everyone interested in personal growth of knowledge as an extern (similar to a non–resident student). Some succeeded in this objective after many searches and challenges throughout their journey. However, there were also students who did not succeed due to a lack of diligence or appropriate opportunity, and they remained bereft on all counts. Some of the *maskilim* of both types of students of the *Kibbutz* became attracted to Zionism, Socialism, or ideas of Tolstoyism that were disseminated by a Russian intelligentsia named Sinichki.

[Page 96]

The following excellent students were among the "*Perushim*" (A term used in the cities of Lithuania for young men in the *Yeshiva Kollels* who were destined for the rabbinate – and this term also became used for *Yeshiva* lads):

a. the Iluy of Uzde, Rabbi Uri Moshe Gordin (later the son–in–law of the pious wealthy man, Reb Sender Ziskin of Łódź, and thereby the brother–in–law of the renown *Gaon* and researcher Dr. Chaim Heller).

b. Rabbi Meir Karelitz, the son of Rabbi Shmarya Yosef of Kosowo (the brother of the Chazon Ish[14]). He later became the son–in–law of the *Gaon* Rabbi Shlomo Cohen, the first *Moreh Tzedek* of Vilna. He served as a *Moreh Tzedek* in Vilna, as a rabbi in Lachowice, and later as the spiritual leader of the Poalei Agudas Yisrael movement.

c. Rabbi Shaul Elchanan Kook of Griva (near Dvinsk – Daugavpils) – the brother of the *Gaon* Rabbi Avraham Yitzchak HaCohen Kook, the chief rabbi of Jerusalem and leader of the rabbis of the Land of Israel. He later became one of the first residents of Tel Aviv and a founder of the Mizrachi movement in the Land of Israel. Notably during his time at the Talmudic *Kibbutz* in Smorgon, Rabbi Shaul Elchanan Kook became known as the first Torah researcher who appeared in the *Hapisgah* rabbinical anthology of Rabbi David HaCohen Treivish, the rabbi of Vilkija.

d. Mr. Mordechai Rosenson (Raziel), the son of Rabbi Ovadia Nissan of Vandžiogala (near Kovno), who was formerly educated in the *Yeshivas* of Eishishok (Eišiškės) and Volozhin. He graduated from the "Grodno Courses" for Hebrew teachers. He married the daughter of the *Gaon* Rabbi Yehuda Leib Gordin, the head of the rabbinical court of Smorgon, and lived with his father-in-law, the rabbi of that city, for a period. Later, Rabbi Mordechai Raziel became one of the first teachers of the Tachkemoni School in Tel Aviv. He was considered one of the first national–religious Torah scholars and educators in this Hebrew city and many of the finest builders of the renewed settlement were among his students. His daughter Esther Raziel–Naor, also a teacher, was a member of Knesset. The lad Avraham Meir Devnishki was also among those who studied in the *Kibbutz* of Smorgon. He was nicknamed "the Benikani" after his native town of Benikan (Bieniakonie), a stop between Vilna and Lida. This "*Parush*" later became more renown as one of its students, A. Vayter, became an expert Yiddish writer and one of the leaders of the Bund in Russia during the period of 1904–1906.

Due to the prolonged illness of Rabbi Chaim Yehuda, he was not able to supervise the spiritual matters of this Talmudic *Kibbutz*. In the meantime, the police began to cast an evil glance at several youths of this *Kibbutz* who belonged to the Socialist underground. Householders who were formerly committed to the physical upkeep of these "*Perushim*" became weary of continuing with this burden of oversight. A large portion of the *Perushim* left Smorgon which became known as a center of Socialism. New Torah forces did not come to this town to refresh those leaving. Therefore, this Talmudic *Kibbutz* disappeared on its own, without fanfare and undue scrutiny.

[Page 97]

It should be noted that the most dedicated students of this *Kibbutz*, who made the Torah their vocation, entered the new Talmudic *Kibbutz* that was formed in Vilna, under the supervision of the *Gaon* Rabbi Chaim Ozer Grodzinski. Rabbi Uri Gordin, Rabbi Mendel Danishevski (a native of Smorgon), and Rabbi Eliezer Silver[15], the son of Rabbi Bunim Tzemach of Dosiat (Dusetos) were among the Smorgon *Perushim* who transferred there. Rabbi Eliezer Silver, a friend of Rabbi Shaul Chuna Kook of Smorgon, later became one of the scholarly rabbis of the United States of America. He served at various times as the president of the Union of Orthodox Rabbis of the United States and Canada. He was a founder of the Orthodox Rescue Committee of Holocaust Victims, and a leader of Agudas Yisrael in North America. Notably among the famous rabbis of America who served in giving rabbinical decisions in Smorgon under Rabbi Chaim Yehuda Litwin (as they were in the process of receiving their rabbinical ordination from him) were: Rabbi Nachman Tzvi Ebin, a rabbi in Brooklyn; and Rabbi Shmuel Tzvi Glick, a rabbi in the Bronx, a founder of the Rabbinical Committee of Greater New York and its chief secretary for many years. Rabbi Sh. Tz. Glick translated the *Ein Yaakov* book on the *Agadaic* sections of the Talmud into clear English, thereby earning recognition and appreciation among all the English-speaking religious Jewish circles in America, Great Britain, and beyond.

M. The Rabbi and *Gaon* Yehuda Leib Gordin

Born in Rezitza (Vitebsk district), 5613 - 1853
Died in Chicago, United States, 5685 -1925

He was the son of Rabbi Meir Avraham Abba, one of the notables of the city of Rezitza. He received excellent Torah education and was considered a genius (*iluy*) during his youth. He already knew the Talmudic tractates of two orders, *Nashim* and *Nezikin*, at the time of his Bar Mitzvah. Along with this knowledge, he knew how to speak and write in Russian, which later helped him greatly as a rabbi and communal leader in congregations in Israel and Russia. As a young man, he maintained correspondence in Torah matters with the *Gaonim* Rabbi Yosef Zecharia Stern of Šiauliai, and the Cohen brothers, Rabbi Betzalel and Rabbi Shlomo, leading Moraei Tzedek in Vilna, the Jerusalem of Lithuania. (Clarify)

Later, when he was once in the town of Svir, he got to know the rabbi of Svir, the *Gaon* Rabbi Moshe Danishevski (later the head of the rabbinical court of Slobodka, the author of "Beer Moshe" on the Code of Jewish Law), and remained to study under his supervision. Rabbi Danishevksi guided his learning methodology and also served with him as a decisor of practical *Halacha*. In Svir, the young Rabbi Yehuda Leib studied with deep diligence the Talmud and halachic decisions. He also completed his studies in Russian literature and general knowledge.

[Page 98]

His rabbi and teacher matched him with the daughter of a wealthy Torah Jew, Reb Sender Miller, who owned an estate near the town of Svir. He spent several years immersed in the tents of Torah while supported by his father-in-law. At that time, he was already regarded as an expert scholar, and a man of fine mannerisms and politeness - destined to be a great rabbi in a large Jewish community Indeed, all of these predictions came true.

In the year 5643 (1883), he was appointed on the recommendation of his teacher and rabbi, Rabbi Moshe, to be the rabbi in the nearby town of Michalishki. That town was small, but it was known as a town of Torah and erudition. It was a tradition in that town from past years that honorable rabbis were active there. Of note are the father-in-law and son-in-law Rabbi Baruch and Rabbi Leib Karelitz, whose son Rabbi Shaul Binyamin was known as the "Rabbi Shikovitzai" and who forged and broadened the primary education of the Old *Yishuv* in the Holy City of Jerusalem. The well-known poet and Hebrew linguist Adam HaCohen Levinson also lived in that town. His name was also known as Reb "Ber Michalishker" on account of this town - and this is the explanation of the "mem" in his literary name Ada'm – i.e. Avraham Dov Michalishker[16].

The famous rabbi and preacher Rabbi Eliahu Sharazon was also a native of that town. He was an expert in the research of religious literature, as can be seen in his book "*Ugat Eliahu*" on *Pirkei Avot*. The previous rabbi of that town, Rabbi Aharon HaLevi, served as eyes for him in that matter.

Michalishki only served as Rabbi Gordin's first stop in his holy service. Later, during the years 5646–5647 (1886–1887), he served as the rabbi in Augustów, a regional town in the district of Suwałki. This community was partially Lithuanian–Polish and *misnagdic* (opposing Hassidism) from its foundation. Later, during the years 5657–5665 (1897–1905) he served as the rabbi of Ostrów, a regional town in the district of Łomża, whose vast majority of the community were Hassidic, following various *Admorim*, primarily Ger.

Rabbi Y. L. Gordin was also accepted by the Hassidim of this city. He received approval for his appointment from the most veteran Hassid of the town, Reb Ben–Zion, one of the remaining students of Reb Mendel of Kock, and one of the first Hassidim of the *Admor* of Ger.

Despite all this support, when two of his sons began to stray from the path of belief, he was no longer content to remain in Augustów, and Rabbi Y. L. Gordin willingly responded to the invitation of the community of Smorgon to accept the city's rabbinical post which had become vacant in 5663 (1903) after the death of their previous rabbi, the *Gaon* Rabbi Chaim Yehuda Leib Litwin. In the beginning of the year 5770 (1909), Rabbi Gordin was appointed as the head of the rabbinical court as well as the official religious rabbi (as was the custom in Poland) in the district city of Łomza[25]. He served that honorable community for about eight years, for the benefit of the members of that community and the tens of communities that belonged to that district, to the point where he was considered to be the general rabbi of all the Jews of that district.

Those days (5674–5682 1914–1922) were a time of emergency for the Jews of that area, for their city, a border city, was close to East Prussia, and was in a state of lawlessness for the Russian units and the inimical (hostile) Polish population. Rabbi Gordin then dedicated his entire effort and power as a rabbi to save those Jews. He conducted those efforts to the best of his ability, and saved the Jews of Łomża and the area from the decrees and libels of individuals and the public.

[Page 99]

When the Russian–German front approached the fortified regional city of Łomża, there was the danger of expulsion as happened in the nearby cities of Jedwabne, Nowygrod, Wyzna, and Ostroleka. At that time, Rabbi Gordin traveled to Vilna and appeared before the military commander. Thanks to his strong intercession, the Jews were able to remain in their place. Later, when the Jews of Łomża were accused of spying for the Germans, and the anti–Semitic commander of the regional army demanded hostages, Rabbi Gordin risked his life by going straight to the enemy and requesting that the commander annul the decree. He was received coarsely by the commander, but the Łomża rabbi responded with pride, and without submitting to him. He presented his words to the enemy and offered himself as a hostage. His bravery influenced the commander, and the decree was annulled.

The *Gaon* Rabbi Yehuda Leib Gordin was also very active in the area of the local rabbinate and Torah education. As a Torah scholar, he was considered the expert rabbinic decisor, even in comparison to elderly rabbis of nearby towns, including such scholarly rabbis as Rabbi M. A. Miel in Grajewo, Rabbi B. A. Ramigolski of Stawiski, Rabbi Yosef HaCohen of Szczuczyn, Rabbi Yitzchak Bursztejn of Ostrołęka, Rabbi Avigdor Bialistocki and Jedwabne, and others.

Rabbi Gordin's primary concern was for the local Talmud Torah in Łomża, which served as a large house of learning for 600 students and for the upper level *Yeshiva* in Łomża which was famous throughout Poland and Russia. As the local rabbi, Rabbi Gordin invested a great deal of energy to renew this *Yeshiva* during the time of the first German occupation, and especially to free its principal and primary *Rosh Yeshiva*, Rabbi Yechiel Mordechai Gordon, from the financial straits and economic burden which were especially heavy during those years. Rabbi Y. L. Gordin also concerned himself with the spiritual encouragement of the senior students in the *Yeshiva*. The students found an open house with the rabbi to discuss their situation. He would generously give permits for issuing rabbinic decisions to the most talented of them. He regarded this as a fine prize for the benefit of their physical and spiritual futures, and something that served as a guarantee that they would become firmly dedicated and complete their studies. In the year 5681 (1921), when the material (financial) situation of the *Yeshiva* worsened, he responded to a request from the principal, the *Gaon* Rabbi Y. M. Gordon, (today the main Rosh *Yeshiva* and principal of the *Yeshiva* of Petach Tikva, founded as a continuation of the *Yeshiva* of Łomża) to travel to the United States of America to conduct a collection campaign for the benefit of the *Yeshiva*.

The *Gaon* Rabbi Y. L. Gordin agreed to this and travelled to the United States. The collection was successful. Thanks to this effort, the *Yeshiva* of Łomża reestablished itself and maintained a strong physical and spiritual stand until the destruction of the community and the *Yeshiva* during the Holocaust period.

Thanks to the special intercession of the *Gaon* Rabbi Y. L. Gordin, the Łomża Talmud Torah was renewed. A large, three-story building was built, and this educational institution served as the central educational institution for Torah and religion for the city of Łomża and the towns of the area- until these communities existed no longer due to the great destruction.

[Page 100]

Rabbi Yehuda Leib Gordin did not return to Poland. In the year 5682 (1922), he was accepted as the head rabbi of Chicago, a position that he occupied until the day of his death on 16 Nisan 5685 (1925). He succeeded in endearing himself and gaining acceptance in all the synagogues of greater Chicago, the largest city after New York. All the rabbis in this metropolis and the area consulted him and listened to his words in matters of religion, Jewish law, and topics of what is forbidden and what is permitted. He was also a principal force in the founding of the Bais Medrash L'Torah educational institution of Chicago, patterned after the Rabbi Yitzchak Elchanan *Yeshiva* of New York[17]. This Torah institution educated rabbis and religious leaders for the Chicago area. It is today headed by Rabbi Y. L. Gordin's son-in-law, the rabbi and *Gaon* Rabbi Dr. Chaim Dov Regensberg, who serves as a *Rosh Yeshiva* and a member of the leadership committee. He was educated in Slobodka and Telz. He is the son of the rabbi and *Gaon* Rabbi Menachem David, may G-d avenge his blood, the head of the rabbinical court of Zambrów near Łomża.

Rabbi Gordin was also an active member of the leadership of the Union of Orthodox Congregations of the United States and Canada. Every difficult matter for this union in halachic, religious, social, or communal issues would be brought to him and his logical and well-reasoned opinions were considered (in high esteem) in such matters.

In accordance with his spiritual outlook, Rabbi Y. L. Gordin tended toward the Zionist movement. However, due to the unique conditions that affected the rabbis of Poland, he could not publicly support that movement, so he followed its progress and development from afar. The situation changed after the Balfour Declaration in 1917. He was already the head of the rabbinical court of Łomża, a fundamentally *Misnagdic* city[18] and tended toward Zionism. Then he already found it possible to affix his signature on the collections for the Keren HaGeula and Keren Hayesod funds, and even to preach publicly for their benefit, and for the benefit of religious Zionism that was organized in Poland at that time under the flag of the Mizrachi organization.

In the year 5679 (1919), Rabbi Y. L. Gordin signed, together with the Łomża *Moreh Tzedek*, the rabbi and *Gaon* Rabbi Yosef Avraham Cinowicz, a proclamation from a group of rabbis in Poland to "our brethren, the Children of Israel" "to organize under the flag of the Mizrachi movement. This movement aspired to the revival of the Torah of Israel, the Land of Israel and the People of Israel in truth and honesty. The movement raised the flag of Torah and commandments within the nationalist Zionist movement, and participated in all the activities of that the movement that have taken place to this point, with the help of G–d." (*Hamizrachi* weekly, 5779 – 1991, issue 18).

The *Gaon* Rabbi Y. L. Gordin left behind three important Talmudic works: 1) "*Divrei Yehuda*" (Warsaw, 5665 1905) including responsa on the Code of Jewish Law, *Orach Chaim* and *Yoreh Deah*, 2) "*Teshuvot Yehuda*" (Vilna 5668 – 1908) on all the sections of the Code of Jewish Law, and 3) "*Diglei Yehuda*" (Warsaw 5664 –1904). In "*Teshuvot Yehuda*", he outlines a Torah and halachic debate with the famous *Gaon* Rabbi Avraham Bornstein, the *Admor* of Sochaczew. He describes his view on the debate with that *Gaon* with the self–confidence and convention that emanates from the correctness of his opinion. Because of the opposition of the Hassidim of that *Admor*, Rabbi Gordin was denied the opportunity to accept the position of the head of the rabbinical court of Łódź after the death of the *Gaon* Rabbi Eliahu Chaim Meisel, even though he had every possibility to be appointed to that important office.

[Page 101]

It is very interesting that the third book of the *Gaon* Rabbi Y. L. Gordin, "*Diglei Yehuda*", includes two large sermons from the period when he served as the rabbi and head of the rabbinical court of Ostrava. Those sermons are "*Degel HaGadol*" for *Shabbat HaGadoll*, and "*Degel Hamishna*" on the occasion of the completion of the six orders of Mishna. In this composition, the *Gaon* Rabbi Y. L. Gordin displays his expertise in philosophy and comprehensive, encyclopedic general knowledge in all branches of practical and social sciences. He even demonstrates his knowledge of what took place in the issues of societies and movements among the young generation of Russian Jews at that time. A hint to his stance and outlook on that matter, which was not stated directly due to the conditions of censorship, can be seen in his first sermon, which reacts to some degree to the relationship between the Jewish community with regard to the awakening of new somnolent powers that began to change the color of progressive social life in a Jewish city.

However, the *Gaon* Rabbi Y. L. Gordin shows himself not only as an adjudicator of opinions and a great expert in general sciences, but also as an expert preacher, with a mouth that exudes pearls, both in form and in content. Every sermon of his was a communal event in the towns in which he served as rabbi. He attracted an audience from all circles. In Łomża, even people from the extreme intelligentsia circles of that district city attended his sermons.

He also excelled as a fine orator in the Russian language, with his public speeches and sermons on official festive occasions, with the participation of the Russian officials. He made a deep impression on these officials, sanctifying the Divine Name in public.

His great prowess in the Russian language and literature was utilized in the publication of three special booklets in that language, to shut the mouths of the accusers and anti–Semites who stood up against the Jews of Russia during that period. In one of his Russian booklets, "*Nyet Tayn*" (No Mysteries), published in 1911 when he was the rabbi of Smorgon, he provides a response to one Russian enemy who published a booklet in Russian "*Tayni Talmuda*" (Mysteries of the Talmud) promising a reward of 1,000 rubles to anyone who would find fault in his accusations against the Talmud. Rabbi Gordin responded to him from Smorgon in his booklet, exposed his lies and forgeries, and demanded from him the 1,000 rubles which he would dedicate to the poor without differentiating by religion. However, the aforementioned anti–Semitic author made himself disappear and evaded fulfilling his words. (See the *HaYehudi* weekly, London, 5771 – 1911, issue 33).

In his second booklet "What is the Talmud" published earlier, Rabbi Gordin disproves the libels of the anti–Semites against the Talmud, starting from apostate Pfefferkorn[19], Eisenmenger[20], Rohling[21], all the way to the enemies of the Jews in the latter times. In his third booklet, "What is Hassidism," Rabbi Gordin explains the theory of Hassidism in the proper light, and proves that it is not a hidden sect, separate from the general Jewish community, as the anti–Semites believed and acted upon (for this reason) during the well–known Kiev blood libel of 1913 during the Beilis trial[22]. The defenders of

Beilis, who were the defenders of Judaism in general, used the aforementioned books of Rabbi Gordin to demonstrate and prove the justice of the Nation of Israel from the aforementioned libel, and the prohibition of Jews using blood for based on the sources in the Talmud and Hassidic literature.

[Page 102]

While Rabbi Gordin was the head of the rabbinical court of Smorgon, he also maintained a correspondence with L. Tolstoy, one of the giants of Russian literature, regarding the editing of a special anthology in Russian that would include a choice selection of moral statements of the Talmudic sages. That great Russian writer Tolstoy wrote the following to the Rabbi of Smorgon, "I would be greatly indebted to you if you would publish for me a selection of Talmudic adages. Not only I but also millions of readers would thank you for this favor for it would give them the opportunity to appreciate the great wisdom of the teachers of the Jewish religion."

This idea did not come to fruition due to the death of the aforementioned great writer.

Thanks to his genius in Torah, his ability to sermonize with his mouth dropping pearls of wisdom in general knowledge, and his excellent fluency in the vernacular both in speaking and writing, Rabbi Gordin attained great fame during the period as Rabbi of Smorgon. In the year 5770 (1910), things reached the point where Rabbi Gordon, the rabbi of Smorgon, was the second candidate from among the rabbis of the Vilna district to [serve as a delegate to] the general rabbinic conference that took place in the Russian capital of Peterburg (currently Leningrad). The first candidate was Rabbi Chaim Ozer Grodzinski. RabbI Gordin was only short a few votes in obtaining a majority in this election. In his place, [another candidate] Rabbi Chanoch Henech Ages, the *Moreh Tzedek* of Vilna, was chosen. Incidentally, he was a friend and admirer of the rabbi of Smorgon.

It should be noted in his book *Teshuvot Yehuda*, the rabbi / author expresses his gratitude and blessing to "those who excel in distribution of charity in the city of Smorgon and who support me in honor, and have taken care of all my needs for the past five years." Additionally about this famous rabbi, exemplifying his spiritual makeup with complete fullness, that a few weeks before his death, Rabbi Gordon sent a telegram of blessing from

Chicago on the occasion of the opening of the Hebrew University in Jerusalem, as follows:

> "Mazel Tov! I hereby declare on the occasion of the opening of the university on Mount Scopus in our holy city. I pray that the studies there will be appropriate with the scriptures of Judaism and traditions, and will not become involved in Biblical criticism and other such things. Then, the grace of G–d will be upon all the teachers and students. The university will flourish and rise to great heights in the spirit of Jewish tradition, and will become a source of glory for all humanity in general, and for our nation in particular.
>
> Yehuda Leib Gordin, chairman of the rabbinical office in the community of Chicago."

We should also mention that a large crowd of thousands of people participated in his funeral in Chicago, and many eulogizers described the extent of the great loss with the passing of this *Gaon*.

[Page 103]

N. Rabbi Menashe Yosef Ginzberg

Rabbi Menashe Yosef was born in the year 5611 (1851) in Kovno during the time that his father, the *Gaon* Rabbi Moshe Shlomo, was supported by his father–in–law, the *Gaon* Rabbi Aryeh Leib, the head of the rabbinical court of the city. Rabbi Yosef served his father–in–law by issuing rabbinic directives and answering halachic questions. Rabbi Menashe Yosef later served with his father in Ilya, the town where his father was the rabbi. He spent some time in the *Yeshiva* of Volozhin, where his uncle, the *Gaon* Rabbi Rafael Shapira, served as a head of the *Yeshiva*. He married the daughter of another uncle, the *Gaon* Rabbi Noach Chaim Avraham Shapira. After marriage, he became a constant resident of Smorgon through the rest of his life.

After the death of his father–in–law, the *Gaon* and head of the rabbinical court of Smorgon, in the year 5646 (1886), Rabbi Menashe Yosef submitted his candidacy for the office of rabbi of the city. The wealthy people of the city agreed to this on the pretext of "*chazaka*"[23], and the general rights of the former "household of the rabbi" from a financial perspective. These wealthy individuals regarded this candidate as an upright rabbi, immersed in the world of Torah and diligent in its study. From this perspective, it would be appropriate for him to fulfil the role of their rabbi. On the other hand, another group of Smorgon residents felt that they required a famous rabbi and *Gaon*, with great rabbinical experience in the world of the rabbinate, as well as a history of being active in the religious community in a manner appropriate to their city. The Smorgon scholar Rabbi Eliahu Leib Brodna joined the second group, who brought in the *Gaon* Rabbi Chaim Yehuda Litwin, who was known as the "genius of Sośnica" to occupy the rabbinic seat. That side was victorious.

At the outset, the first side separated from most of the city. Even after that time, they regarded Rabbi Menashe Yosef as their rabbi, and gathered around him in their own *kloiz*. They became known as the "Poles" due to their rebellion, as Poles were considered rebellious. However, this opposition eventually abated and then stopped completely. The *Iluy* [genius] of Sośnica was considered the rabbi of the entire city, and Rabbi Menashe Yosef served only as a *Moreh Tzedek*. Rabbi Yosef continued in that role throughout the tenure of the *Gaon* Rabbi Yehuda Leib Gordin, who followed the Sośnica rabbi as the head of the rabbinical court of that community (5665–5673, 1905–1913). When Rabbi Gordin moved to become the head of the rabbinical court of the regional city of Łomża in Poland, the *Moreh Tzedek* Rabbi Menashe Yosef served as the chief *Moreh Tzedek* of Smorgon between "reigns." In the interim, the First World War broke out. Smorgon, which was close to the front, was destroyed, and its Jews were exiled to various points inside of Russia. Rabbi Menashe Yosef was among them. When a portion of the Jews of Smorgon returned after the war, and the Jewish community was reconstituted in a smaller fashion to its previous incarnation, Rabbi Menashe Yosef returned as well and served as the de factor rabbi, in the position of "fill in" for Jewish community of Smorgon – in accordance with Polish regulations. The veteran rabbi, *Moreh Tzedek* of Smorgon, served in this role until his death in the year 5685 (1925). We should note his two–volume work "Givat Olam" (Vilna 5658 – 1898). The first volume includes novel ideas and didactics on various sections of the Talmud, and the second volume includes explanations and ideas on *Agada* (the lore portion of the Talmud).

[Page 104]

News of the death of Rabbi Menashe Yosef was included in the rabbinical anthology "*Shaarei Zion*" (5685 – 1925), published in Jerusalem. In that document, he is described as the rabbi and *Gaon*, head of the rabbinical court of Smorgon.

O. Rabbi Shmuel Aharon HaCohen Plotkin

Rabbi Shmuel HaCohen Plotkin's father, Rabbi Yitzchak Elchanan, was the head of the rabbinical court of Krievi, where he died in the year 5684 (1914)[24]. Rabbi Plotkin served as rabbi in Derechin in the district of Slonim for 20 years. He saved tens of people from death during the time of the emergency of 1920. He later spent some time in America and then returned to Poland where he became the rabbi of a suburb of Grodno ("Behind the River"), and then in Smorgon. He was only active there for a few years (following the death of Rabbi Menashe Ginzberg in 5685 – 1925), and he died in the year 5691 – 1931. After his death, a dispute broke out among the people of Smorgon regarding the appointment of a new rabbi. The "bundle separated" and two rabbis served: Rabbi Yitzchak Markus and Rabbi Zelig Slodzinsi. Rabbi Yitzchak Markus was a native of Zettel in the district of Slonim and was one of the excellent students of the *Yeshiva* of Radin. He obtained the rabbinate of Smorgon as a fill–in for his father–in–law, the aforementioned Rabbi Plotkin. Rabbi Zelig Slodzinski was a native of Kobrin and equally one of the excellent students of the Mir *Yeshiva*, who served Rabbi Yerucham Leibowitz, the spiritual leader of the famous Mir *Yeshiva*, and one of the pillars of the *mussar* movement of the previous generation. Rabbi Markus was the son–in–law of Rabbi Yitzchak Halevi Shuster, the rabbi of Sokółka, whose wife was the daughter of Rabbi Shlomo HaCohen, the first *Moreh Tzedek* of Vilna. Those two rabbis perished in the Holocaust in the year 5703 (1943), may G–d avenge their blood.

Translator's Footnotes

1. A well–known nickname for Vilna.
2. i.e. between chief rabbis.
3. *Tosafos* is a collection of commentaries on the Talmud.
4. See https://en.wikipedia.org/wiki/*Perushim*
5. *Kohelet* (Ecclesiastes) 1:6
6. Rabbi Reines was a founder of the Mizrachi movement, and Rabbi Blazer was a disciple of Rabbi Yisrael Salanter, the founder of the Musar movement.

7. See https://en.wikipedia.org/wiki/History_of_the_Jews_in_Speyer

8. In rabbinic terminology, a "Sinai" is a person who is a repository of Torah knowledge, whereas an "uprooter of mountains" is a person who is able to make derivations and deductions from his knowledge. There is an ongoing debate as to which trait is preferable."

9. Between sunset and the time the stars come out, when there is a dispute as to when the halachic day changes over.

10. See https://en.wikipedia.org/wiki/*agunah*

11. See https://en.wikipedia.org/wiki/Samuel_Mohilever

12. "Sitting in the tent" is the rabbinical term for a person who prefers the study hall over worldly affairs or communal activism.

13. A high level of rabbinic ordination, allowing the rabbi to judge court cases. See https://judaism.stackexchange.com/questions/38703/yoreh-yoreh-vs-yadin-yadin?utm_medium=organic&utm_source=google_rich_qa&utm_campaign=google_rich_qa

14. See https://en.wikipedia.org/wiki/Avrohom_Yeshaya_Karelitz

15. See https://en.wikipedia.org/wiki/Eliezer_Silver

16. Ber is the Yiddish form of the Hebrew name Dov.

17. The rabbinical seminary of *Yeshiva* University.

18. Religious opposition to the Zionist movement was strongest among the Hassidic stream, rather than the *Misnagdic* stream.

19. See https://en.wikipedia.org/wiki/Johannes_Pfefferkorn

20. See https://en.wikipedia.org/wiki/Johann_Andreas_Eisenmenger

21. See https://en.wikipedia.org/wiki/August_Rohling

22. See https://en.wikipedia.org/wiki/Menahem_Mendel_Beilis

23. *Chazaka* is a term for the right of possession of a privilege or an office.

24. Unlike other Hebrew / Secular dates in this section, where I translated the Hebrew year into English (and I could be off by a year in some cases, as the Hebrew year starts at a different time than the secular year), both dates were included here in the text. There is an obvious error, as 5684 corresponds to 1924 rather than 1914. I maintained the error in the text, and am noting it here.

25. A document contradicts the 1909 date: https://www.jewishgen.org/Yizkor/ostrow1/ost029.html

[Page 105]

Natives of Smorgon Serving as Rabbis in Other Communities

Translated by Jerrold Landau

Rabbi Shlomo the son of Rabbi Shimon

In the year 5542 (1782), we find the Smorgon native Rabbi Shimon, the son of the eminent rabbi and Hassid Rabbi Shimon, may the memory of the righteous be a blessing, roaming through various Jewish communities of Germany to collect funds for his journey to the Holy Land. In the interim, he spent some time in Altona and Hamburg. He published the book "Rules of Oaths and Laws of Business" of Rabbi Hai Gaon, which had been published more than 200 years previously, and "cannot be found presently."

There is an approbation at the beginning of the book from the *Gaon* Rabbi Rafael HaCohen, the head of the rabbinical court of the two united communities. Many years earlier, Rabbi Rafael had served as the rabbi in the Lithuanian cities of Minsk, Pinsk, and Vilkomir[1]. In his approbation, he describes the author as "the wonderful scholar, the son of the Rabbi and Hassid from the community of Smorgon, Lithuania."

We do not now whether he succeeded in making *aliya* to the Land of Israel or remained in Hamburg as one of the "Polish" scholars.

Rabbi Pesach the son of Rabbi Moshe HaCohen

Rabbi Pesach HaCohen was a principal student of the *Gaon* Rabbi Aryeh Leib Shapira, who appointed him as a *Moreh Tzedek* in his rabbinical court. Later, he served in that position during the period of the rabbinate of the Gaon Chaim Avraham of Smorgon.

He died in the year 5635 (1875) at the age of 84.

In his book of memoirs, Rabbi Tzvi Shimshi recalls being told in his youth that Rabbi Pesach HaCohen received five silver coins from his father, Reb Reuven Yisrael, as his redemption[2].

Rabbi Avraham Moshe Halperin

Rabbi Avraham Moshe was born in the year 5578 (1818) in Vosiliškis. He was a descendent of the rabbi, kabbalist *Tzadik*, and *Hassid*, Rabbi Moshe Ashkenazi from his father's side. He was a descendent of the *Gaon* Rabbi Yechiel Luria of Minsk, the author of the book "*Sefer HaDorot.*"

[Page 106]

He spent more than 20 years in Smorgon immersed in Torah and Divine service. He married the daughter of Reb Moshe Nachum, an honorable man of the city. Rabbi Avraham Moshe served as a *Moreh Tzedek* without expectation of a salary, while his diligent wife managed a textile shop in the center of town. One of his daughters, Esther, married Reb Reuven Yisrael Shimshelevitch, the grandfather of Yitzchak Ben Zvi of blessed memory, the second president of Israel.

The Rabbi and *Gaon* Rabbi Moshe Danishevski

He was born in 5590 (1830) in Minsk. He died in 5670 (1910) in Slobodka, Kovno.

He served in the rabbinate of the city of Svir for 25 years, and for seven years in Altomorantz. He then became the honorable rabbi of Slobodka. In the year 5657 (1897), when the *Yeshiva* Knesset Beit Yitzchak was founded, Rabbi Moshe was appointed to its main leadership group.

In his book "*Beer Moshe*," he offers words of blessing to his father-in-law: Zeev Wolf Vishniavski of Smorgon, "Where I stayed in his house, spending nights as days in the study of Torah for about ten years after my marriage." He writes about his father-in-law, "A rabbi known for his Torah, righteousness, and great action for the sake of Torah."

The Rabbi and Gaon Meir Feimer (5594 – 5541 1834-1881)

Rabbi Meir Feimer was the son-in-law of the *Gaon* Rabbi Chaim Avraham Shapira. He was supported at the table of his father-in-law, the rabbi of Smorgon, for 12 years, as he studied Torah diligently. He left Smorgon in the year 5624 (1864) and was accepted as the rabbi of Slutsk to replace his father, who in his time was one of the primary students of the *Gaon* Rabbi Chaim when he founded the *Yeshiva*.

The *Gaon* Rabbi Rafael Shapira

He was born in Smorgon in the year 5597 (1837) to his father the Rabbi and *Gaon* Aryeh Leib Shapira, the rabbi of the city.

He studied with his father until the age of 15, and excelled in his sublime talents and wonderful diligence. He married the daughter of the Netzi'v (Rabbi Naftali Tzvi Yehuda Berlin), the head of the rabbinical court and *Rosh Yeshiva* of Volozhin. He assisted his father-in-law in editing his book "*HaEmek Sheelah.*"

[Page 107]

He began to deliver a class three times a week in that famous *Yeshiva* in the year 5625 (1865). He served in that position until the year 5641 (1881), when he was appointed as the rabbi of Novoaleksandrovsk. He gave his position in the *Yeshiva* to his son-in-law, the *Gaon* Rabbi Chaim Soloveitchik, the son of the Gaon Rabbi Yosef Dov, the rabbi of Brisk.

In the year 5646 (1886), Rabbi Rafael accepted the rabbinical pot in Bobruisk (in the *Misnagdic* community). In the year 5659 (1899), he was called to the honorable position of head of the rabbinical court and *Rosh Yeshiva* and principal of the *Yeshiva* of Volozhin, when it was reopened after having been closed by the government. He served in this holy position until the outbreak of the First World War. He escaped to Minsk, and died on the 23rd of *Adar* II, 5685 (1925).

He excelled in his trait of quietness. His book "*Torat Rafael*" was published by his sons, the rabbis: Rabbi Aryeh Leib Shapira, head of the rabbinical court of Bialystok; and Rabbi Yisrael Isser Shapira, a resident of Tel Aviv.

Rabbi Shabtai Mordechai Feinberg

Rabbi Shabtai was born in the year 5610 (1850). He was the son-in-law of Avraham Brodna of Smorgon.

Rabbi Shabtai worked in hide production in Smorgon. In truth, however, his wife Ethel ran the factory, while he dedicated his time in Smorgon to Torah. He learned in order to teach. After the *Shacharit* service, he would deliver a lesson in *Gemara*. In the afternoon he taught the Code of Jewish Law, section *Yoreh Deah*, in the *Kibbutz* of the *Perushim*. He gave a class in *Orach Chaim* between *Mincha* and *Maariv*.

He was appreciated and beloved by all the people of Smorgon.

Later, when he lost his fortune, he was accepted as the rabbi of Mikailiškia. He served in this position for 23 years.

He died in Berlin in 5669 (1909), and was burned in the Adas Yisrael Cemetery of the Orthodox community in the capital of Germany.

Rabbi Yehuda Leib Gordin eulogized him in Smorgon.

His books "*Afikei Maginim*" and "*Meshivat Nefesh*" were published posthumously by his son.

The famous poet Abraham Sutzkever[3] was his grandson, the son of his daughter.

The Rabbi and *Gaon* Rabbi Shlomo Mordechai Brodna

Rabbi Shlomo Mordechai was born in Smorgon in 5592 (1832). His father was Reb Eliahu Leib Brodna (5576-5653 1816-1893), an honorable merchant. His mother was the daughter of the renowned Rabbi Aryeh Leib HaLevi Friedberg.

[Page 108]

At the age of 12, he studied in the *Yeshiva* of Volozhin, which was headed by the *Gaon* Rabbi Yitzchak, the son of the *Gaon* Rabbi Chaim, the founder of the *Yeshiva*.

Rabbi Shlomo Mordechai lived in Smorgon. His wife worked in business and he sat in the tents of Torah. The scholars of the city were among those who attended his sharp classes.

He served as rabbi of the community of Radoshkovichi for about ten years. In the year 5648 (1888) he became the rabbi of Stowbtsy, and continued in that post for 14 years. He returned to his hometown of Smorgon in the year 5662 (1902). He did not receive any position there. He dedicated himself to the study of Torah. He died on the 20th of Tammuz 5669 (1909).

His book "*Ohel Shem*" was published posthumously.

The third president of Israel, Zalman Shazar, describes him in his memoirs. His grandson is Broli.

The rabbi and *Gaon* Rabbi Mordechai the son of Yoel Kopelovich

Rabbi Mordechai Kopelovich was the son-in-law of Rabbi Eliahu Brodna. He dwelled in the tents of Torah for many years in Smorgon. He studied especially with his brother-in-law, the brother of his wife, the Gaon Rabbi Shlomo Mordechai, as well as with Rabbi Shlomo Slosch, who was at that time supported at the table of his father-in-law Rabbi Avraham Moshe Halperin.

He was appointed as the rabbi of Krasni, Vilna District, in 5638 (1878). He served there for approximately 50 years. He died on 3rd *Shvat,* 5685 (1925).

He was very diligent, and excelled with the sharpness of his mind. He was described by the greats of Lithuania as a rabbi, a *Gaon,* righteous, and upright.

Rabbi Moshe Aharon Rabinovitch, one of the founders of Hadera

Rabbi Moshe Aharon was born in Smorgon in the year 5598 (1838) to his father, the rabbi and *Tzadik* Rabbi Yaakov the son of Rabbi Moshe, the head of the rabbinical court of Krivi. He was from the family of the great Rabbi Yeshaya the Blind of the Gramir family, one of the great wise men of Torah and teaching in Vilna.

He was ordained by the *Gaon* Rabbi Avraham Shmuel the author of the book "*Amudei Eish*" in Eišiškės. He also received ordination from the *Gaon* Rabbi Eizel Charif, the head of the rabbinical court of Slonim. He was appointed as rabbi of the town of Varakļāni, Vitebsk District. He stopped working in the rabbinate and came to Vilna, where he engaged in commerce and was successful. However, most of his interest was in Torah. He exchanged correspondence with questions and responsa in *halachic* matters with the greats of the generation.

Rabbi Moshe Aharon was an enthusiastic lover of Zion. When there was discussion about the founding of the Moshava of Hadera in Samaria, he registered as a member with full rights. He purchased a plot of land there, and invested his entire means in it. His vision was to settle in the Land of Israel as a farmer. However, his vision did not materialize, for he died suddenly in Vilna in the year 5657 (1897). He was eulogized by the Torah giants and heads of Chovevei Zion.

[Page 109]

The Chofetz Chaim[4]

The *Gaon* and *Tzadik* Rabbi Yisrael Meir HaCohen [known popularly as the Chofetz Chaim] was in Smorgon in the year 5632 (1892).

One of the Chofetz Chaim's acquaintances, Rabbi Mordechai Bik of Eišiškės, lived in Smorgon.

The Chofetz Chaim was then busy preparing his book "*Chofetz Chaim*" for print. The book is based on the verse (Psalms 34: 14-15) "Who is the person who desires life, loves days to see good? Withhold your tongue from evil and your lips from speaking deceit." The book discusses at length "guarding the tongue" and emphasizes the seriousness of the sin of speaking bad about people, and spreading tales and slander.

The Chofetz Chaim, who lived in Radin, found the impetus to write a book on speech, with life and death under its control, from a dispute that broke out in that town against Rabbi Eliahu Margolis, who was a student of Rabbi Menashe of Ilya. In the heat of the anger, the disputants, of course, were not careful with their language, and the issued baseless accusations. The Chofetz Chaim kept back from the words of dispute and denigration that flew about without any sense of responsibility, and decided to write a book to warn against this severe sin.

The Chofetz Chaim came to Smorgon to complete his book and to give to the young man Mordechai Bik to copy over in clear script to make it easier for the typesetter.

The Chofetz Chaim came to Smorgon with his young son, Reb Aryeh Leib, and they were hosted in the home of Rabbi Chaim Ora's, the father-in-law of Reb Mordechai Bik, who was pious an upright in his deeds, and supervised the *Gemilut Chesed* [charitable fund] of the city.

The young man, Reb Mordechai, who was great in Torah and fear of heaven, was familiar with sickness. He died after a few years. The *Gaon* and *Tzadik*, the Chofetz Chaim, always remembered him with great grief.

Rabbi Shimon Mordechai the son of Yeshaya Dubinsky

From his mother's side, Rabbi Mordechai was a member of the family of the *Gaon* Rabbi Chaim, the founder of the *Yeshiva* of Volozhin. Born in that famous town Volozhin, he married a wife from Smorgon and lived there [in Smorgon] for many years. He would go to the two rabbis of the city: Rabbi Chaim Leib the Socenicani and Rabbi Yehuda Leib Gordin. In Rabbi Gordin's book *"Teshuvot Yehuda",* Torah novella of Rabbi Shimon Mordechai are included. Rabbi Shimon Mordechai was famous in the Torah world for his book *Mashmoni* (Vilna 5663 – 1903) in which he collects all the opinions of the early and latter sages on Tractate *Eruvin,* in the form of"An anthology of opinions on this difficult tractate, with their explanations and novella on every page, and including his own notes and novella."

[Page 110]

The *Gaonim* of the generation testify to the importance of that work with their approbations:

First, we should note the words of praise of the head of the rabbinical court of Smorgon, Rabbi Chaim Leib the Socenicani, who notes that this book is a precious one of its genre. He also notes the sharpness of the author in Talmud and the early and latter rabbinical decisors. Along with this praise, the Rabbi of Smorgon also notes that this author had already been ordained by sages, *Gaonim* of the generation of past years, and "the *halacha* is taught as he states."

Rabbi Rafael, the head of the rabbinical court and *Rosh Yeshiva* of Volozhin, who knew Rabbi Shimon already from the time when he was studying in that *Yeshiva,* writes about the author that "He enlightens the eyes of the studiers by gathering precious scattered lights in the commentators and responsa of the early and later rabbis. The notes and novella that the rabbi and *Gaon* added on his own demonstrate his sharpness and expertise in Talmud and rabbinic decisors, and are very pleasing in my eyes."

Rabbi Yitzchak Blazer (formerly rabbi of Petersburg) writes in his approbation to this book that even though he refrains from giving approbations to new books, this one is different, since the author did a great thing in his work to define a path through this tractate, of which very few writers have written anything about. Now the reader will see the words of the early sages and latter sages anthologized together.

In his approbation to this book, Rabbi Chaim Ozer Grodzinski also stresses the special importance "For there are very few commentaries on the tractates of *Eruvin*, *Nidda*, and *Yevamot*, and the words of the sages that are meager in this place are rich in other places – so he has done well by gathering them like bundles of grain to the barn. Anyone studying and interested will find connections to purity in this composition.

The famous rabbis -- Rabbi Chaim Meir Noach Levin, *Magid Meisharim* and *Moreh Tzedek* of Vilna; Rabbi Zalman Sender Kahana Shapira, head of the rabbinical court and *Rosh Yeshiva* of Maltz (and later Krinki) refers to the author as "my friend and relative," as does the *Gaon* Rabbi Eliezer Rabinovitch, rabbi of Minsk. Rabbi Eliezer also notes that, in addition to the novel ideas of his own that the author elaborates, Rabbi Mordechai includes an anthology from the books of our early and latter rabbis. He brings into the composition anything relating to the decision of law. This is a great benefit for the students, who will find everything prepared for them, in fine, enlightening words.

In this composition, the author discusses *halachic* matters related to the repair of *eruvs*. He includes correspondence with the famous rabbis: Rabbi Eliezer Simcha Rabinovitch, head of the rabbinical court of Kalwaria; Rabbi Yaakov Rabinovitch of Ponovezh; Rabbi Avraham Yitzchak Maskil Le'eitan of Chasloviche; and Rabbi Mordechai Kopelovitch of Krasni.

In writing this composition, which is like a "*Shita Mekubetzet*" [An anthology of opinions] on Tractate *Eruvin*, the author from Smorgon required a rich Torah library. He found this in the famous Strashon Library of Vilna, which he visited often, as well as in the praiseworthy Torah library of the Gaon Rabbi Chaim Ozer Grodzinski.

[Page 111]

Rabbi Shimon the son of Michel Suchkover

He was born in Lebedovo (district of Vilna), and was educated in the *Yeshiva* of Volozhin. He also studied in the *Yeshiva* of the *Perushim* in Smorgon, and got married there. He was one of the excellent students of the *Kibbutz* in Vilna, under the supervision of protection of the Gaon Rabbi

Chaim Ozer, in which there were many young men with great talents. At that time, he rounded out his education with languages and general sciences. He became an expert in Hebrew translation, and gained fame as a well-known grammarian. He wrote the booklet "*Hanetiyot VeHashemot*" under the name of Sh. Shimoni, and also published monthly articles on issues of Hebrew grammar in the "*Hasafah*" Hebrew.

He did not earn his livelihood from Torah. Rather, he earned his living in Smorgon as an accountant in enterprises and factories. He was a refugee in Ukraine during the First World War. He later returned to a Poland that was broken and shaken. He no longer found his place in Smorgon, which was destroyed at that time, so he settled in Vilna. Since he was a modest, discreet man by nature, Rabbi Shimon Suchkover earned a meager livelihood by giving Hebrew lessons or functioning as an accountant in various businesses. The *Gaon* Rabbi Chaim Ozer Grodzinski recalled the younger days, and was almost the only one who concerned himself with his economic existence. He died at the age of 51 in the year 5686 (1926) in Vilna. A brief article of appreciation for this great man in Torah and wisdom was published in the "*Dos Vort*" Orthodox weekly in Vilna.

The *Gaon* Rabbi Avraham Yitzchak HaCohen Kook

During the period that Rabbi Gershon Tanchum lived in Smorgon – in the year 5643 (1883), a lad from Griva (near Dvinsk – Daugavpils), Rabbi Avraham Yitzchak HaCohen the son of Rabbi Shlomo Zalman Kook, established his place of study in that city. He became known as one who frequented the *Beis Midrash* of that town, and was known by the name of his hometown ["Lad from Griva"]. This wonderful youth aspired to spent time in the Torah centers of Lithuania – as a place to perfect his studies. Later, he studied in the *Yeshiva* of Volozhin. He favored Smorgon as a place to actualize his study, since that town had a Torah atmosphere for anyone who aspired to such, and many local youths set aside times to study Torah in their town. There were groups of isolated *Perushim*, and especially expert Torah scholars from other places who were supported by their fathers-in-law in Smorgon.

The "Lad from Griva" succeeded in raising his standing in Smorgon, where he spent an entire year immersed in Torah and Divine service. This period of study was through his friendly relations with the young scholar Rabbi Gershon Tanchum, the son-in-law of the *Gaon*, head of the local rabbinical court, Rabbi Chaim Avraham Shapira. The spirit of innovative Torah ideas began to pulsate in Rabbi Avraham Yitzchak Kook in Smorgon, and he succeeded in writing an entire composition of his novella, "*Kinyan Daled Amotav.*"

[Page 112]

About 15 years after the lad from Griva had already become famous publicly as the rabbi of Bauska, Latvia, we know that his younger brother Shaul Chuna Kook set his place of study in the new *Yeshiva* of the *Perushim* in Smorgon, because he wrote his brother a letter of encouragement for choosing that place to ascend in his *Yeshiva* studies. In his letter, he reminisces about the time when he spent studying Torah in that city, in the following words: "The city in which I found my first path, a city filled with sharp and expert sages and scribes, G-d fearing who are concerned with G-d's Name, whose friendship broadened me and caused me to perfect my talents with greater strength. Its name and memory are etched on the tablet of my heart in love from the early period of my youth" (From the book "*Azkara*" in his interesting article about Rabbi Y. L. Fishman Maimon. "The annals of the *Gaon* Rabbi Avraham Yitzchak HaCohen Kook.) We can also add that when the lad Avraham Yitzchak returned to his parents' home in Griva from Smorgon, and then moved to nearby Dvinsk to get to know the *Gaon*, head of the rabbinical court of that town, Rabbi Reuven HaLevi Levin, who himself was a native of Smorgon - they had the opportunity to discuss the town of Smorgon, its general makeup, its scholars and students. Along with this, he extended to him a greeting from the head of the rabbinical court of Smorgon, Rabbi Chaim Avraham, the childhood friend of that great *Gaon*.

Translator's Footnotes

1. Lithuania here refers to the broader sense of the area, rather than the boundaries of the present-day country.
2. Referring to the redemption of the first born (*Pidyon HaBen*), in which five silver coins must be given to a Cohen (a member of the priestly group) as a redemption for a first-born son.
3. See https://en.wikipedia.org/wiki/Abraham_Sutzkever
4. See https://en.wikipedia.org/wiki/Israel_Meir_Kagan

[Page 113]

Abridged autobiography

by Tzvi Shimshi (Shimshelevich) (1862-1953) (5623 – 5714)
Father of the president
Yitzchak Ben-Zvi of blessed memory

From the book "*Zichronot*" (Memoirs) by Tzvi Shimshi,
Jerusalem 5698 (1939),
and "*Megilat Yuchsin*" (Family Tree), Jerusalem

Translated by Jerrold Landau

I was born in the city of Smorgon, Vilna District, on 15 Kislev, 5623 (end of 1862 according to the secular year). My parents were young, about 18-19 years old, when I, their eldest child, was born. Our family grew in honor with sons-in-law who were great in Torah and wise of heart, such as Rabbi Eliahu Chaim Meisel, the rabbi of the community of Łódź; Rabbi Elyakim Shlomo Shapira, the rabbi of the community of Grodno; and others. My mother's family was proud of its own pedigree, for my maternal grandfather, Avraham Moshe Heilprin, was a descendent of the author of "*Seder Hadorot*"[1] and the Kabbalist Rabbi Moshe of Ibya, a friend of the G'ra [Gaon of Vilna], and a descendent of Rashi – whose genealogy can be traced to King David in accordance with the determinations in "*Seder Hadorot.*"

My father occupied the respectable office of postmaster in the town of Voronovo, on the main road from Grodno to Lida. My mother and father, carrying along with my young brother who was still nursing, moved to their new place of residence. I, three years old, was left with my paternal grandparents in Smorgon.

I did not know my parents until I was seven years old. I only heard about them incidentally without great content.

I recall from my childhood that I called her [seemingly the grandmother] Mother Rachel. Her husband, Avraham, the teacher of young children, taught me the *aleph beit*, and the teacher Zecharia taught me Bible.

My father came and took me to him when I was six years old.

When I arrived at my father's house, there was already a teacher ready for me to teach me Bible, as well as *Chumash* with Rashi's commentary.

My first impetus toward reading Hebrew secular books came from the war between France and Germany in 1870-1871. At the end of the war, I could easily read the news from the battlefields in the *HaMagid* weekly and could provide highlights to the "*Perushim*" – i.e. the lads from the nearby area studying in the *Beis Midrash.*

[Page 114]

After the war, I did not suffice myself with reading "*HaMagid*", and I began to inspect my father's bookcases. I searched through the bottom dwellers on the lowest shelves, and found *Sefer HaYashar*[2] and Josephus. I read them, and my eyes lit up. Additionally in the lower shelf of the bookcase, I incidentally encountered "*Ahavat Zion*" and "*Ashmat Shomron*" by A. Mapu. The first lines of *Ahavat Zion* captivated my heart, and in my eyes [view], the words were like an addition to the Bible stories that I loved.

When I was still a nine-year-old child, I founded a group called "*Tiferet Bachurim*" to purchase specific holy books that were collected by the members[3]. The members gathered together every Friday. They brought to the *Beis Midrash* a Torah scroll, books of the prophets, *Megillot,* the Talmud, *Tur,* and Code of Jewish Law, and bound all the torn books that were on the bookshelves of the *Beis Midrash.* In that way, I became known as a communal activist who functioned in good faith, so nobody accused me later when I founded a library for books of *Haskalah.*

When I was 12 years old, I began to study Russian reading and writing from a language teacher, but I did not take interest in this language until 1876, when the Russian-Turkish War broke out in the spring, and the appetite for news from the front gave me the impetus to read with care the government newspaper "*Hamevaser HaVilnai.*"

From the age of 15 to 18, I wavered between Torah and *Haskalah.* During those days, I merited to see the first fruits of my pen, my unripe writing, published in the newspapers "*Ruski Yevrei*" (the Russian Jew), and "*Halevanon*".

When I turned 18, my father concerned himself with the future in saving me from army duty when my turn would come two years later. My brother was only two years younger than me, whereas the law only freed the older son from army duty in the event that his brother was four years younger. My father sent a notice to the army courts stating that a mistake was made with my age, and that in reality, I was already 20 years old.

I left my both parents home and the town at the age of 19, full of dreams and hopes for a bright future. My first stop was the city of Minsk. I found a good teacher and became a student of the eighth grade of the gymnasium. I dedicated myself diligently to my gymnasium studies. There was a large number of Jewish externs [students] in Minsk. The directors of the gymnasium and the examining teachers related to the students in a way that they would have no chance in passing the examinations. Therefore, they turned toward the cities of the south where the examinations were easier. That idea also inspired me to leave Minsk after a year of living there. I moved to Poltava, where I continued to study and prepare for the examinations.

The group of youths in Poltava responded to the call of Bilu: "House of Jacob arise and let us go!" Of them, only four took the leap of Nachshon and made *aliya*: Shalit, Cohen, Swerdlow, and his sister.

The rest of the members of the circle were obligated to help locally their brethren who were making *aliya* until they got set up in the Land, and then they too would make *aliya*. These were the first active members of Chovevei Zion. Their first activity was to send a delegate to the Katowice convention, where they banded together. All of the Chovevei Zion members got together and formed a single center.

[Page 115]

At first, the *aliya* of the Bnei Zion group of Poltava took on the form of a charitable organization, with trustees who took upon themselves the task of collecting donations from like-minded people for the purposes of settling into the Land of Israel. I was accepted as a member of the Bnei Zion group by paying six silver rubles a year.

{Photo page 115: Tzvi Shimshi, the father of President Yitzchak Ben Zvi of blessed memory.}

Already that winter, in the year 5644 (1884), I entered the confidence of the committee and became an assistant to the secretary. After some time, when he left the town, I took his place as secretary of the Bnei Zion organization of Poltava for many years.

We issued raffle tickets. The price of each ticket was three and a quarter rubles. We were unsure of how to distribute them, for sending them by mail was dangerous. The members approached me and asked me to travel with the tickets to distribute them among the organizations in the cities throughout the country.

I went to Odessa. This was the time of the formation of the Bnei Moshe organization. We discussed the raffle. I went to Smorgon, where there were individual members of Chovevei Zion. While I was there, I gathered together approximately 30 people. They formed an organization, and they took half a series of tickets.

[Page 116]

In the summer of 5649 (1889), I traveled to Vilna on a mission from the committee to bless Reb Sh. Y. Fein on his 70th birthday, and Reb K. Shulman on reaching his literary jubilee.

Around that time, Reb Yehoshua Barzilai-Eisenstat came to our town to attract members to the Bnei Moshe organization. After that, we both traveled to Kharkov, where we set up a chapter of Bnei Moshe there as well. Also set up in our town were a Hebrew library, a modern *cheder*, and a girls' school for handicrafts and for the study of Hebrew. The committee set up a plan whereby four wealthy people from our town who knew each other would band together to purchase a plot of land and found a Moshava within five or six years. When everything was set up, the settlers would come to their plots. The committee and the members in charge of the purchase selected me and one of the shareholders, Mr. Dribin, to travel to the Land of Israel and purchase the land. We were given 4,000 silver rubles for the down payment on the purchase. The rest would be sent as we requested it.

I left Poltava on the day of Lag B'Omer, May 15 5651 (1891). I arrived in Nikolayev the next day at 8:00. I waited for about an hour on the deck of the Argonbat ship, travelling to Odessa. I turned over the money that was in my hands for the purchase of the lands to Dr. Pinsker in the presence of M. L. Lilenbaum, in exchange for a check to the active committee in Jaffa.

With great difficulty, after I almost had given up, I received a passport for travel abroad. I then arranged my Turkish visa easily and boarded the Austrian ship Midviza on 9 Sivan, travelling to Kushta (Constantinople). I and my travel mate from Poltava were lodged in third class. There were approximately 100 travelers there, all Jews heading toward the Land of Israel. In Kushta, we transferred to the Austrian ship Sturna, that set sail eastward. Our ship passed through the Dardanelles on 12 Sivan, and reached Izmir on 14 Sivan. The ship arrived in Beirut on 19 Sivan, and reached Haifa at 2:00 a.m. The boat set sail from Haifa at 4:00 a.m. The city of Jaffa could be seen in the horizon at 10:00 a.m.

I finally succeeded in making *aliya* and coming to the Land of Israel. I toured the land. When I returned to Jaffa from my tour, I found a letter from the committee of the organization in Poltava, stating that the article of Ahad Ha'am "Truth from the Land of Israel" melted the hearts of those who wanted to settle there, and they retracted their desire to purchase land. Therefore, I was to extricate ourselves from the purchase and return home[4].

I succeeded in visiting the Land of Israel again in the year 5665 (1905), 14 years after my first visit. I was in Haifa on the 10th of July. It had advanced significantly since the time I left it in the year 5651 (1891). I returned to Jaffa on July 14. I returned to my home in Poltava at the end of the month of August.

The world movement spread out primarily among the middle-class circles . There was no activity among the working ranks. That task was filled by Poalei Zion, headed by the young Zionists, members of the committee Borochov and Y. Ben-Zvi.

Poalei Zion walked hand in hand [agreed] with the committee on issues of Zionism as well as on many other questions. The joint work was especially noticeable during the times of the disturbances following the "honeymoon" of October 1905. News that the police were inciting the masses against the Jews, and helping the hooligans beat and pillage the Jews, arrived from places near and far. Then the members of the committee spoke with Poalei Zion about organizing a properly armed Jewish self-defense in our town, so we would be able to protect ourselves and not be like lambs to the slaughter. It is in fact thanks to the organized self-defense, our city avoided pogroms with their terrible disgraceful consequences.

[Page 117]

The transgressions of the self-defense were elusive to the police, and they were unable to forgive their failure. They began to search for the defenders. The shadow of suspicion fell upon me. On June 28 (July 11)[5] 1906, a squad of police surrounded my house. The search lasted for approximately eight hours. The results were that they found guns, bullets, and other types of weapons in my son's room. In the coat of my eldest son, which he left behind when leaving the house, they found documents proving that he stood at the head of the Poalei Zion organization. They immediately informed my wife and I that we were under arrest. They hauled us to jail at midnight, and gave us over to the chief jailer. After they searched my clothing and checked my pockets in his office, they took me to an isolated cell and locked me in.

The writ of accusation was finally received in the fall of 1907. The four of us – I, my wife, my son, and my daughter – stood trial in January 1908 before a group of judges in the Kharkov district.

The trial lasted for two days. The verdict was issued to exonerate my wife and daughter and free them immediately, but to permanently deport me and my son to Siberia and have all rights stripped. From the court, we were immediately sent back to jail.

My only comfort was that my wife decided to travel with me, to help and to arrange things as a free woman in all matters that were forbidden to me as someone who was stripped of his rights.

In the morning of June 23 (July 10), they brought me to the clothing warehouse and ordered me to strip to put on prison clothes. I was given over to a squad of soldiers to take care of me. They handcuffed me, led me to the train, and seated me in a car full of prisoners, most of whom were bound at their hands and legs, as was the law for those sentenced to hard labor. They also brought my son to the car.

The journey of torment began. Tula, Samara, Krasnoyarsk, Irkutsk.

My wife arrived with a permit from the minister of the Poltava District to join the caravan of prisoners and to accompany me in my place of exile. According to an edict from the minister of justice, the Jewish exiles were allotted a place in the Preobrazensk District. In accordance with the edict, my name had already been listed in the list of deportees, and it was impossible to change. What was the situation in the place? It was 1,500 kilometers north of Irkutsk. Rumor had it that one eats little and sleeps a great deal there, but one does not rely on rumors. The Jews of Irkutsk who knew the place said that the region is a place of business and livelihood related to the plentiful animal hunting. The valuable furs were exported to the world market for a high price.

[Page 118]

The journey continued: My son and I traveled from Irkutsk to Aleksandrovsk by wagon. We left Aleksandrovsk on August 7. My wife joined me after an absence of two years[6]. We arrived in Zhigalovo on the Lena River. In Zhigalovo, we set out on large barges. We spent five days on our boat until a steamship met us and took us on board quickly. Those with families were permitted to transfer their seats from the barges to the halls of the ship.

We arrived in Kirensk – the chief city in a region with the same name. Preobrazensk, my destination, was in that region. The area of this region was similar to Germany and France combined, although there were very few populated areas scattered on the banks of rivers: a few here and a few there.

After a journey of eight days by wagon and twelve days by ship from Kirensk, we arrived in Chechyusk, from where started the sole road to the Preobrazensk Region, designated as the residence of the Jews. 135 Jews and five gentiles were given over to the commander of the region and transferred to our place of exile. The elder of the region in Chechyusk informed us that we were free to sail on the river and house ourselves wherever we liked until they would find sufficient horses to transport us to the edge of the Preobrazensk Region. From there, they would take us further on, until we reach the office of the command of that region.

My wife remained in Chechyusk until I returned. My son and I joined the final caravan, departing from the command office to go to Zbolok, the first village in the Tunguska River valley that surrounds the Preobrazensk Region. My son remained to live temporarily in Nepa. From Nepa, I and two others traveled by vehicle to Preobrazensk. When we arrived there at noon, we met with three of the exiles, who took us to the registration office so we can register our arrival in the book. The religious official, the elder of the region, the secretary, the police official, a public-school teacher, and the medic gathered in the office to greet us. All of them drank in our honor to the point of drunkenness, and we became good friends.

I decided to settle in the village of Moga and open a store there. A Jewish shopkeeper had lived there previously and succeeded in his business. He had died two years previously, and his widow liquidated the business and returned to her homeland of Poland.

The relationship between me and the farmers was very good. With some of them--the more progressive ones--I even became friends.

In 1913, at the conclusion of 300 years of Romanov rule, a Czarist edict was issued, proclaiming that the Czar had mercy upon all those who were sentenced to perpetual exile, and set the term of exile to ten years. The district officials had the right to change the status of those who had already completed five years of their term to the level of farmer, if they were fitting for this. Based on this, the registration office exonerated me without me knowing, and then officially informed me that they had registered me in the book of farmers. Thereby, I obtained rights to a parcel of the public land of the village.

[Page 119]

In the official document that I received, I was designated as a farmer in the Region of Preobrazensk, District of Irkutsk.

In the wake of the world war, all of Russia was in ferment [turmoil], and even the quiet, remote [town of] Tunguska was shaken up. I waited impatiently for the end of my exile in 1918. The day of my liberation came early due to the revolution of March 1917.

At the end of that year, I completed my accounts with my customers and liquidated my entire business. I left Tunguska at the beginning of 1918 with the hope of making *aliya* to the Land of the Patriarchs, to which my soul longed from the day that I began to have my own opinions. However, I encountered many obstacles and detours during my wanderings as I was returning from exile, for now the country was ruled by red, white, and green wild beasts[7] who desired blood and reward from oppression, and played with the lives of people.

The Lena River opened on the eve of *Rosh Chodesh Sivan* 5682 (1922). My wife, my daughter, and I set out to Kirensk on the first steamship. We celebrated the Festival of Shavuot in the village of Zhigalovo.

Very slowly, we made our journey on transport wagons in a caravan. After an eight-day journey, we arrived in Irkutsk on June 26. From there, we traveled by a train that wound through the interior of Russia. We crossed the Ural Mountains on July 16, and entered Europe, which I had left 14 years previously and did not believe that I would see again. We arrived in Moscow on July 23. We left Moscow on 13 *Tishrei* 5683 (1922), and passed through Latvia, Lithuania, Germany, Austria, Yugoslavia, and Italy. We finally arrived at our desired destination, the holy city of Jerusalem, on 17 *Cheshvan* 5683 (the end of 1922.

My son Aharon escaped from Siberia in 1909 and made *aliya* to the Land of Israel in the year 5670 (1910).

*[8]

He lived in the Land for 30 years. He merited to witness with his own eyes the establishment of the State of Israel, the burden of his soul for all his days.

The author died at an old age in Jerusalem on the eve of 26 *Cheshvan* 5714. He was about 91 years old when he died in 1953.

Translator's Footnotes

1. See https://en.wikipedia.org/wiki/Seder_HaDoroth
2. See https://en.wikipedia.org/wiki/Sefer_haYashar_(midrash)
3. The implication seems to be that used books were collected by members perhaps as a way of recycling them.
4. "Melted their hearts"—e.g. got scared. The phrase likely borrowed from the same term used in the Torah for what the report of the spies did to the Israelites.
5. Appears to be a Julian-Gregorian translation of dates.
6. The wife most likely got stranded in one of the towns during part of the journey and eventually rejoined two years later.

7. The colors likely represent a number of factions: the czarist flag was red and blue.

8. What follows is apparently the editor's note.

[Page 120]

Professor Nahum Slouschz

by David Tidhar

Translated by Sara Mages

Was born in Smorgon on 28 Kislev 5633 [28 December 1872] to his father, HaRav David Shlomo (one of the Valozhyn's best students. A rabbi and a preacher, a Hebrew writer and a member of the board of "*Hovevei Zion*"), and to his mother, Rivka Leah, daughter of HaRav Avraham Moshe Heilprin from Smorgon (according to family tradition he was one of Rasi's descendants). He grew up in Odessa and for a while in Kherson. When he was three, his father began to talk to him in *Leshon Hakodesh* [Hebrew], and at the age of six his father began teaching him the Bible. He studied Talmud and *Poskim* [Jewish law] with his mother's father, and general education and languages, Russian, German and French, with private tutors.From childhood he had read many research books, poetry in Hebrew and Hebrew newspapers. Later, he also read foreign literature, especially many travel books. He often visited the library of "*Bnei Zion*" in Odessa (his father was called to serve as a rabbi there) and read, under the guidance of the library's director, member of "*Hovevei Zion,*" Pinchas Friedman, who brought him closer to the matters of new settlement in Eretz-Yisrael and to the new literature that had been created there. When he was still a young boy, he started to send letters to Hebrew and Russian newspapers and wrote a detailed entry on the history of the city of Odessa in "*Eshcol,*" of Shaul Pinchas Rabinowitch. Because of his article, which was published in the monthly "*Beit Yisrael*" in Vienna, on "The Jews in Russia" (on which he established in 5648, at the age of 15, the hypothesis that the Jews of Russia were partly Khazars and, therefore, had the right to inherit citizenship in that country), the Russian censorship confiscated that monthly. Two years later, it also confiscated the newspaper, "*Ha-Chavacelet,*" which was published in Jerusalem, because of his article there on the persecution of Jews in Russia.

When he was in Odessa, the center of activity of "*Hovevei Zion*" and the seaport of immigrants to Eretz Yisrael, he devoted himself to Zionist activity and organized a group for settlement in the country. On the holiday of Shavuot, 5651 (at the age of 18), at the height of the days of glory of the "Tyomkin period," he arrived to the country on its mission to explore the conditions and prepare the ground. The decrees and failures stopped the immigration, but he remained in the country and tried to settle there as an agricultural laborer, but, for health reasons, he was forced to return to Russia in the winter of 5652. He worked for a living as an assistant in Russian papers, continued to write in Hebrew and make propaganda for the sake of Zion. At the same time he took part in the founding of the society, "*Yisrael HaTzair*" [Young Israel], the association of Hebrew speakers "*Sfateno Itano*" [our language with us], and a branch for the society, "*Safa Berurah*" [clear language]. In 1896, he visited Israel for the second time and the news about the publication of "*Medinat HaYehudim*" ["The Jewish State"], by Herzl, reached him there. He returned to Russia and devoted himself to organizing and propaganda for political Zionism. He participated as a delegate in the Zionist Congress in Warsaw and in the Second Congress of "*Bnei Zion*" association. After the congress he enrolled to study literature, science and oriental languages, at the University of Geneva. He graduated from the university and the seminary for new French, and continued to study at the Sorbonne in Paris and at the School for Oriental Languages (Arabic and Aramaic with professors Hartwig and Drenberg; Cushitic and Ancient Arabic - with Yosef HaLevi; Assyrian - with Jules Oppert and others).

[Page 121]

In 1903 he was granted a doctorate in literature on the basis of his book, "The revival of Hebrew literature," which was published in French. The book did a lot of publicity for the revival of the Jewish nation in the circles of scientists and literary figures in the world. It was also published in Hebrew, with the author's translation, by "*Tushita*" Publishing. In Paris, he participated in the foundation of a National Jewish University with a school for living Hebrew. He served as a teacher at the Teachers' Seminary for Oriental Countries, and lectured on Hebrew literature until the end of the First World War.

During those years he wrote extensively for the Hebrew and general press, and also for the scientific press.

[Page 122]

Participated in Zionist activity and Zionist congresses, wrote books on oriental studies and developed the theory regarding the ancient Hebrew people, that the Israelites and the Phoenicians were part of them, who created the culture and spread it in the Mediterranean Basin. He established his opinion on the study of Phoenician articles and other sources. Participated in research expeditions in North African countries and was especially interested in the study of ancient Jewish settlements in them. He was a member of the Committee for Semitic Sciences and editor of Phoenician articles of the Paris Academy. Was a teacher in the school for higher education in Rabat (Morocco) and received a medal of honor from the Sultan of Morocco. There, he helped to arrange the life of the Jewish communities. During the First World War he devoted himself to Zionist political work in Paris, demanding the establishment of a Jewish state in his meetings with French politicians. At the end of 1916, he traveled to America for the purpose of political action to establish inter-relations between France, America and Zionism. There, he lectured in Hebrew, at R' Yitzchak Elchanan's Yeshiva, on the history of the Jews in the Middle Ages, and was invited to lectures at Columbia University and Dropsie Collage. After the armistice, he returned to Paris on a mission to work alongside the Zionist delegation in the peace conference.

At the end of 1919, he immigrated to Israel and devoted himself to research and science. He participated in the activities of the Hebrew Society for the exploration of the Land of Israel and its antiquities and edited its files. He conducted excavations in Tiberias, discovered caves in "*Yad Avshalom*" [Tomb of Absalom], deciphered ancient inscriptions and, from time to time, spoke and wrote about current events. At different times he arranged classes in the Phoenician language at the British School of Antiquities in Jerusalem, and classes about the Jews of Africa in a seminar of the Youth Department of the Jewish Agency. In the last years he served as chairman of the "World Hebrew Alliance." He published many articles and pamphlets in Hebrew, and other languages, and these are the books he published:

"*Mah Ya'aseh ha-Adam we-lo Yeheteh*" [What will a man do not to get sick]. "*Ha-Osher me-Ayin Yimmatzeh*" [Where will happiness be found], both translated from French. "*Massa be-Lita*" [A journey in Lita] (5649), "Lamentation to R' Moshe Rimos" (with French translation), "*Keneset ha-Gedolah*" [The Great Assembly] (about the congress and Zionism, Warsaw, 5658), "Emile Zola, his life and books" (5650), "*Ha-Kongres ha-Ziyoni ha-Revi'i*" [The Fourth Zionist Congress] (Warsaw, 5660), "The stories of Guy de Maupassant" in seven volumes (translation from French), "On the Islands of the Sea" (about the Hebrew Mediterranean Sea, New-York, 5649), "Salammbô" (translation of Flaubert's book), "*Cohanim* in Djerba," "The *Anusim* in Portugal," "*Daya Ult Yenfaq*," "The Book of Travels" volumes A and B (about his travels in Libya), "The treasure of Phoenician articles," and "The Origin of the Israelites." Ready for publication: " Book of the Sea" in 3 volumes, "Book of Travels" (additional chapters), "Canaan and the Past." Some of his compositions appeared in foreign languages.

(David Tidhar), Tel-Aviv, Encyclopedia of the Founders and Builders of Israel, 1943

[Page 123]

Aharon Avraham Kabak

by T. Z. Weinberg

Translated by Sara Mages

In the days of my youth, as my hand tried to hold a writer's pen, I found myself, on my way to my destination, in his parents' hometown, Veisiejai, in the Suwalki Region, a colorful and spectacular landscape. In the house, where I was staying, was a scholarly girl who was proficient in our ancient literature and spoke Hebrew well. A vision didn't erupt in those days. I arrived there at twilight and had the feeling that I had reached a corner of wonders. In the morning, the girl led me to the rabbi's house, the father of the writer Kabak, and the eyelashes of her shy eyes, which were slightly scorched from the reading of the Torah, added grace to her modesty and her restrained smile when she talked to me about "*Levadah.*"[1] I thought - "she, she is the reader, the book was created for her." The street, with its ascents and slopes, the strange little houses with bushes around them, the solid church house that stretched out to the sky, and the synagogue, which was lower and narrower, stood out together at the top of the hill and appeared, by the side of the road, like tall towers where faithful guardians of God gathered, took me out of reality and put me in another world - into a realm of hallucination and dream. That day was a Christian holiday, a clear day. Crowds of gentiles streamed down the hill paths to their house of prayer. The sound of footsteps, the rustling of the leaves of the trees, the game of lights and shadows on the majesty of the day, and the seriousness on the face of the person ascending to the house of God, merged into one revered holiness, full of awe and majesty, and I was completely enchanted.

The old rabbi, with his majestic appearance, welcomed me and called the Rebbetzin, a noble old woman, quick and laborious, to rejoice together with the guest who knows their son, and not to let him go without refreshments. The drink, and the amazing sweets and jams made by the Rebbetzin and seasoned with cordial conversation about the writer son, and their affection and anxiety toward me, in which they surrounded me with simplicity and innocence, pleased me. The smell of the village, and its food, rose from their refreshments, touch, serene manners and speech and I felt the warm atmosphere in which the writer's first book, "*Levadah,*[1]" grew and developed.

A few years later, when the writer Kabak, a sturdy young man with wild black hair, full of vitality and freshness and wide cloak on his shoulders, visited me in my home, in Suwalki, on his way home from his parents' house. I smelt in him the smell of his parents' home, his kind eyes gleamed his father's sweet smile and the light of grace of the portrait of his mother's face.

Since then, I have not had any contact with him. We moved away from each other, the distance of place and time. He went abroad, to the vastness of the world, and I remained in Poland hoeing within my four walls. Every once in a while I followed him, read his books, checked his creation, its nature and essence, and did not find the man I had known for a long time. His books, which were full with plot, attracted me and aroused great participation in me, but the symbolism imbued in them, the external elegance, the sparkle of the tale and its complexity, which had a foreign flavor, blurred his source and muddied his lively spring. It seemed, as if the man had strayed from his way and moved away from himself. He became a multidimensional writer, a conductor on a large scale, but the main point, the central, was far from him.

[Page 124]

When I immigrated to Israel for the first time in 5681, I found him living in Jerusalem, and enjoying it, after his wanderings in foreign lands, and I recognized the great change that had taken place in him: he returned to his source and found himself. He was still confused in the country, the pondering was still in his eyes, the longing for what he had abandoned was still strong, but his movement was different, he recovered, his inner strength shook itself and grew stronger.

The foreign peels split off him and fell, the intranuclear, the fundamental, folded into its natural pouch, in its color and growth, a native of the land and the heritage of home, and the book. "Shelomo Molkho, " was created. I read this book in the Diaspora, when I was uprooted from Israel unwillingly, and the longings ate me. This man, who restored my soul, has risen in my eyes and his faithful words tied me to him again, and I said to myself, when I return to Israel I would thank him face to face. One of my visits, when I returned to Israel for the second time, was to Kabak in Beit HaKerem [Jerusalem], and how great was my anxiety when I saw him lying in a chaise longue, bound and motionless, after his severe illness. I was astonished at what I had seen, but his smile and warm greeting revived me. His lively conversation and vivid eyes, made me forget that before me was a man confined to his seat, weak and in pain, struggling for his life. At his wife's request, I, and his family, raised him and put him in his bed. The weight of his body and painful face, when we carried him, shocked me, but, as soon as he lay down his comfortable and pleasant expression returned. His silver hair, the smile on his lips and the light of his eyes projected before me the noble image of his father's face and his kind smile, a lost figure from many years ago that had now arisen before my eyes.

[Page 125]

I read his book, "*Ba Mishol ha-Zar,*"[2] which came to me after he had recovered and got to his feet, with unsaturated thirst. A supreme human interest, a combination of creation, torments and sufferings emerged from the pages of the book and fascinated me. The man, a weak and mortal creature, struggles with all his might with the difficulties of his life and snares of death, and overcomes them. A deep echo of thanksgiving of a man, who has risen from the realm of death, trembled in his verses and between his lines. It was clear that the man had written his book wholeheartedness and extracted, from the depths of the language, in a strength that wasn't his, the appropriate thought to express his feelings before God and man. Then, I saw him again, as I saw him a few years ago in his bed. A man without physical strength, heavy as a stone, that the light God did not leave him and his confidence in salvation beamed from his honest eyes in the faith of an artist. And like a vision, his birthplace, Veisiejai, from which the man was formed, passed before me with its houses, alleys and narrow paths extending to the houses of God, for a Jew and non-Jew alike. A distant vision was exposed to me from the mists of time, on the efforts of a fair man, a secular, son of a secular, who paves his way to the Supreme God. It is transparent in the plot of his book, in the drawings of the landscape of Israel, in the descriptions of the splendor of the Galilee and its greatness, the final transition from Veisiejai to Kfar-Nahum and wandering in countries and generations. In them, there is a great faith in a man who rises from poverty and believes that God will not abandon him. This time, the man had a hard experience in the struggle for life and the purity of his creation, and came out intact. From now on, he was ready for bold action and new attempts to uncover the layers of the last century, the glow of resurrection and the rebirth of man and nation, and started his book, "*Toledot Mishpahah Ahat.*"[3] I saw him quite often, alone and in a group, full of energy and strength, believing in his powers and purpose and the gift of his God, and didn't feel the burden he had imposed upon himself and the temptations spread out at his feet. In "Shlomo Molkho," and especially in, "*Ba Mishol ha-Zar,*" he managed to free himself from the foreign influence that had plagued him all his life, but it crept up again, a little bit here and there. The road was not smooth for a man who had great momentum and the obstacles in his path were not few. He sailed and strove to the depths and spread his arms to embrace a whole world. At the last meeting at his home, in the last summer, his wife complained bitterly before me that he was wasting his strength and neglecting his health, and he, in his good laugh, bitterly protested her rebuke and, with the stroke of his soft eyes, praised the anger of his loyal guard.

Translator's Footnotes

1. "*Levaddah*" - "By Herself"
2. "*Ba Mishol ha-Zar*" - "the Narrow Path"
3. "*Toledot Mishpahah Ahat*' - "History of One Family"

Lines to the image of Aharon Avraham Kabak (1880-1944)

by David Tidhar

Translated by Sara Mages

Was born on 29 Kislev 5641 (at the end of 1880) in Smorgon, in the Vilna province (White Russia), to his father R' Natan Kalonymus, a great Torah scholar, from the descendants of R' Menashe Me'Iliah. He later served as a rabbi in the community of Veisiejai, in the Suwalki region, composed and published a Jewish law book based on the composition, "*Torat HaChatat,*" by the "*Rema*" [Rabbi Moses Isserles].

He studied in *Hadarim* and *Yeshivot* until he was attracted in his youth to education. Studied the Russian language and literature privately and moved to Odessa for further studies in general education. After his twentieth year he began writing literary works in Hebrew. His first story, in the Zionist trend, was "*Ha-Ma'pil.*" It was published in "*Ha-Shilo'ah*" with a dedication in memory of Herzl who died shortly before, in 5664. A year later, in 5665, his novel, "*Levadah,*" was published by "*Ha-Shilo'ah.*" It was not only the first novel of his works, but also the first novel in the Hebrew language. It fascinated its readers in its plot, content and form, not like the novels that educated people, who knew the Bible, read for the *mitzvah* of reading Hebrew literature. Therefore, his Zionist trend had an enormous positive impact on the younger generation.

After the 1905 revolution in Russia he left for Istanbul, the capital of the Ottoman Empire, which, at that time, also contained the Land of Israel. He wanted to know a different world from the one he grew up in and also to get to know the focal point where the affairs of Eretz-Yisrael were decided. He spent a few years there as a reporter and sent articles to "*Ha-Zman*" ["The Time"] in Vilna, articles and stories to the Yiddish daily newspaper "*Der fraynd*" ["The Friend"] and the weekly Zionist "*Das Idishe fal?*" ["The Jewish people"]. He married Feiga, daughter of R' Alexander Ziskind Tchernovitz, and Leah, daughter of R' Shlomo Drozer (Feiga's brothers are the famous writers - HaRav Chaim Tchernovitz (pseudonym "Rav Za'ir") and Shmuel (pseudonym "*Sphog*" Tchernovitz).

He immigrated to Israel in 1911, engaged in teaching (for a while as a teacher of literature at "*Herzliya*" gymnasium in Tel-Aviv) and continues his literary work. He participated in the"Hebrew Writers Association in Israel," wrote the story "*Nano,*" several booklets published by *Keren HaKayemet* [JNF] with the signature of Eliezer ben Nathan, the play "The derailment of a Kingdom," translated Russian and French literature and edited the book "*Sefer* Klausner."

[Page 126]

His books: "*Levadh*" ("By Herself," Warsaw 1905), "*Ha-Ma'pil*" ("The Trailblazer," Odessa 1910), "*Me-al ha-Migdal*" ("Above the Tower," Warsaw 1910), "Stories" (Warsaw 1911), "Daniel Shfranov" (Warsaw 1911), "*Nizzahon*" (Victory), the stories "*Yezira*" ("Creation," Warsaw 1923), "*Ahava*" ("Love," Jerusalem 1923), "*Nano,*" "*Kol Ba-Afelah*" ("Sound in the Dark "), "*Ha-Navi*" ("The Prophet"), "Stories" (Tel-Aviv 1927), "Shlomo Molkho" (3 volumes, London 1927-29), "*Bein Yam u-vein Midbar*" ("Between the Sear and the Desert," 3 volumes, Tel-Aviv 1933), "*Ba Mishol ha-Zar*" ("In the Narrow Path," 2 volumes, Tel-Aviv 1937), "*Toledot Mishpahah Ahat'* ("History of One Family," volume 1). "*Be-Halal ha-Reik*" ("The Empty Space" book 2, Tel-Aviv 1943), "*Be-Zel Ez ha-Teliyah*" ("In the Shadow of the Gallows," Tel-Aviv 1944).

He also worked as an editor and translator. Published (together with A. Steinman) the "*Me'aasef*" of "The Hebrew Writers Association for Literature" (1940) and translated a line of novels from Yakov Wassermann, Pierre Loti, Dmitry Merszkowski, Stindal and others. Over the years he was a member of "The Hebrew Writers Association" and received the Bialik Prize of the Tel Aviv Municipality for significant accomplishments in Hebrew literature.

In his last years he was active in a circle of intellectuals who sought ways to revive the religion.

He died suddenly in Jerusalem on Saturday night, 12 Kislev 5705, 18 November 1944, and was buried in Jerusalem. His daughters: Bat-Ami and Edna.

(Tel-Aviv, Encyclopedia of the Founders and Builders of Israel)

[Page 129]

Drawings to the image of A. A. Kabak

by Lea A'mitan

Translated by Sara Mages

You have nothing as difficult as writing the memories of a person whose whole essence was love of life and love of man. It is certainly easier to sit down with Kabak, talk to him and take interest in his impulsive reactions - it is an almost childish naiveté and a daily re-admiration of the act of the Creator - who did not leave him even on the threshold of old age and during the difficult days of illness

I first met A. A. Kabak during the first week of my immigration to Israel (1925). My relatives told me that he would certainly agree to include me on a trip to Jericho and the Dead Sea which was organized by "*Ha-Gymnasia ha-Ivrit*" in Jerusalem where Kabak worked as a Hebrew and Bible teacher.

I headed towards the school building in the Bukharim Quarter and, when I entered one of the dark rooms and saw Kabak, it seemed to me as if the sun had suddenly rose and lit up the room. I kept this impression to the end of his days, not only because he was already a well-known author and received a shy young woman with warmth and friendly manner, but because there was something abundant and illuminating in him. Although he was not musical he was very fond of singing and in a loud bass voice he sounded, a little off-key, the "Elegy" of Massenet. Incidentally, this love for music, without knowing it, sometimes caused errors in his books. So, for example, in his novel, "*Ahava*" ["Love"], he described a concert in which a pianist played Tchaikovsky's "Barcaroolle" and her little boy turned the pages. When it was mentioned to Kabak that the "Barcaroolle" was so easy that even a novice student knows it by heart and there's no need for a page turner because it only contains 2-3 pages, Kabak received the comments in good spirits and said with a laugh that in the new publication of the book he would take the "child" off the stage...

On the above-mentioned trip with the gymnasia in Jerusalem, I marveled at the social relations between the teacher Kabak and his students. Many of his former students have not forgotten their teacher.

Kabak was among the first builders of the neighborhood Beit-Kerem in the western part of Jerusalem. Their home quickly became the center of the neighborhood and a meeting place for the intelligentsia in the full meaning of the word. Every writer, who came to Jerusalem, must have visited Kabak's home and enjoyed the simple and cordial atmosphere of him and his wife, Sara Feiga of the Tchernovitz family. But this house, built on rocks and later surrounded by a pine grove, caused quite a few troubles and concerns to its owners. Like all the settlers in Beit-Kerem, Kabak did not have the money needed for the construction - the loans, interest and the compound interest ate them, and it's possible to say that they shortened his life... and the life of his wife.

[Page 130]

During his difficult illness, I believe in 1931 or close to it, he underwent a great transformation, became religious and kept all the practical commandments that he abandoned when he was less than the age of Bar-Mitzvah - the age at which he left his father's house. The residents of Beit-Kerem joked a little, at the expense of the former atheist, and said that "Kabak converted to Judaism." Then he wrote his great and outstanding creation, "*Ba Mishol ha-Zar*" ["The Narrow Path"]. However, the Bialik Prize was not given to him for this work but for "Be-Halal Ha-Reik ["The Empty Space"].

It was interesting to look at Kabak when someone told him about a certain event or a movie. His wide face, his mouth wide with wonder, and his cries of admiration "really," "what do you say," reminded a little boy enjoying fairy tales. Indeed, there was something childish about this beautiful aging writer. His willingness to help, advice and encourage novice writers touched the heart. He was even willing to hear criticism from these writers and consider them. He was absent-minded and lacked sense of direction. He, for example, visited Shimoni's home in Tel Aviv many times, and every time he lost his way and had to ask how to get there.

A.A. Kabak preferred the company of women on that of men. In his books he often characterizes women. All his life he was free in his opinions. However, after he had a severe arterial disease (became slightly paralyzed and dragged a leg), he became pious and observant, kept the commandment and was careful with his blessings. He even blessed the tea and prayed three times a day.

It was easy to influence him since he was not familiar with political problems. However, when he was approached after Arlosoroff's murder and asked to sign a leaflet for Stavsky's defense, he signed. That's why he was considered to be revisionist

He had no coherent political views. He was a poet and succumbed to moods. He was an elegant man, pleasant in his ways and meticulously dressed. There was no speck on his clothes.

He lived in poverty, wasn't familiar with accounts, and started to build his house with forty pounds in cash and the rest in loans and mortgages.

In the last years, when he withdrew from teaching, he used to write in the morning and drank a lot of coffee at that time.

He deeply loved his two daughters and accused himself of neglecting their education. He used to say: Bat-Ami should have been a gifted actress. Edna, his youngest, should have been a sculptress.

He was not strict. He gave me his book, "*Bein Yam u-vein Midbar*" ["Between the Sea and the Desert"], and when he asked for my opinion I answered him: I only liked the name. He smiled and answered: my publisher, Tvresky, gave me the name.

[Page 131]

He was willing to admit his mistakes even in public. He made friends with Bialik, R' Binyamin, and especially with Yehezkel Kaufmann with whom he often walked in the evenings.

His wife, Sara Feiga, was smart and practical. She copied his writings until he purchased a typewriter and leaned to type on it with one figure of his right and left hand.

Sara Feiga used to say jokingly: I made my bathroom from "*Ahava*," meaning, she purchased it from the royalties that Kabak received for his book named "*Ahava*."

[Page 132]

Moyshe Kulback (1896-1937)

by Meir Alef

Translated by Anita Frishman Gabbay and Frieda Levin Dym

Moyhse Kulback was born in Smorgon. His father was worked in forestry. His mother came from the "Karke". Karke is a parcel of land on the outskirts of Smorgon where Jewish farmers tilled the land and harvested crops. Kulback got a religious Jewish education, but not an orthodox upbringing. He only went to the Yeshiva for one year, then, on his own time, he began reading Hebrew, Yiddish, and Russian literature.

During the First World War he was a Hebrew teacher in Kovno. He started writing poems. Moshe typically started to write the poem in Hebrew, but then reverted right back to Yiddish as that language was his preference. In 1916, he published his first poem "Little Stars". The poem became very popular. People liked the poem so much, he set it to music and folks start singing it. It became a very popular tune.

In 1920, in Vilna, he published his book of songs, called "Shirims" (or Poems). He was also a teacher in the Jewish folk school in Vilna. In the fall of the same year, he arrived in Berlin to study and expand his intellectual horizons. He became involved with the Berlin Yiddish Theatre. He read voraciously and had a lust for learning. In 1922, in Warsaw, he published the book "New Poems". Then in 1923, his drama, *Yacov Frank* was published in *Di-tsukunft* (a periodical based in New York). The drama was also released as a book six years later. In a short three years, Moshe Kulback became famous.

In 1923, he returned to Vilna. He obtained the position of a teacher in literature at the Jewish Gymnasium and in the Jewish teacher's seminary. He was involved his students in performing Yiddish plays and general repertoires. He was also a popular public speaker on literary themes and became one of the most popular figures in Yiddish cultural life.

[Page 133]

In 1924, his first prose work "Meshiekh ben Efraim" was published in Berlin.

In 1926, he published the poem "Vilna" and a small novella, "Montag" (Monday). In 1927, the long poem "Bunye and Bere" was published.

[Page 134]

In 1928, he left Vilna and moved to Minsk, in Soviet land.

In 1931, he published his work "Zelmanyaner", about the fate of a traditional Jewish family facing the new conditions of the Soviet Union after the October uprising. Life and ideologies were described as a "crooked mirror"—distorted and personally interpreted. It was written in an antagonistic style. The review of this work was divided between fans and critics. Under the circumstances of Soviet Union (censorship), it was difficult to continue writing, and he almost stopped writing lyrical poetry.

In 1933, he published his satire, a partly autobiographical poem, “Disner Tshayid-Harold, a harsh critique on Germany, in which a Russian Jew (perhaps himself) reflects on his intellectual growth after moving to Berlin from Jewish Lithuania. The satire was written in a mock-epic and self-reflective tone.

In 1935, he published his second volume of “Zelmanyaner”. It got the same mixed reviews as the first part. It concentrated on two generations of Jewish families who undergo profound lifestyle changes. It also contained a passage about the Smorgon leather industry.

In 1935, he writes a comedy “Boytre” in which the robber, steals from the rich and gives to the poor. In that communist era, his writing was published in the newspaper “Staren” (English equivalent is “Stars”) and located within pages 7, 9, 11.

When it was played again for the second time, he was arrested in the theatre and charged. The Bolsheviks probably realized that the satire was about the Russian revolution and the character Boytre was a mocking portrait of Lenin. On the orders of Lenin, the play was ended. Kulback was sent to a concentration lager in the Urals. He died when he was only 41 years old. No one knows of the precise day he died or the exact reason his life was cut short while in his prime. Only his colleagues knew. They are probably afraid to speak about the Stalin regime that is ruled with an iron fist.

[Page 135]

Characters from Karke

by Moyshe Kulback

Translated by Jerrold Landau

1.

Grandmother...
Grandmother was a modest Jewess
A master of children – a child every spring.
Easy, without pain, just as hens lay eggs
She gave birth to twins – a twin and another twin.
Three uncles did grandmother give birth to in the attic,
Two uncles did grandmother give birth to atop the oven.
Grandmother gave birth to my father in a barn
Then her womb was closed forever.
Grandmother sent diapers to the poor.
Grandmother, the dear one, did her thing,
She went around her home
Like a duck among ducklings

2.

Grandmother, of blessed memory, Went Outside

When Grandmother, in her old age, went outside
The birds sang
For with her charity, and with her good heart
The world resonated.

And when Grandmother passed away
Everyone was silent,
And without a sigh, the good old woman
Was laid into the earth.

[Page 136]

Grandfather went into his house
As a dead person,
For he, the old man, had told her
That he would die first.
And when they led the deceased through the town
The townsfolk said
"Niome Niome, the old Shlomoche is no longer here,"
And even Priest Vasily mourned.

And when the beadle took out the knife
To rend the garments[1],
Then, my uncles started to cry out
Like the murderers before a hanging.

3.

Grandfather Dies...
Grey, like a dove, did Grandfather come in from the field in the evening
He quietly made his bed and recited the confession,
In his heart, he made peace with the world
And then closed his eyes, devoid of energy, the weary one.

Then the uncles came to the head of Grandfather's bed,
Bowed down their grown-up heads and were silent.
Something closed up their hearts and did not let them speak.
Sealed hearts – they could not even let out a sigh.

Slowly Grandfather then opened his eyes.
A smile came over his face,
He sat on the bed, barely sitting up straight
And Grandfather then began to talk to his sons:

-- The first one, my firstborn, you are the foundation of the family!
The first in the field and the last to sit at the table.
The ground opens up warmly under your plow,
As the seeds in the earth should be fruitful and fresh.

[Page 137]

Rachmiel, who can compete with you in the meadow!
Your scythe in the grass is like a surge of fire,
You know the snakes in the swamps, the birds in their nests.
Blessing should rest with you in your stall, without bounds!

You Shmulia, the river man, there is nobody as smooth in the world!
Always with a lash over your shoulders, always wet.
The smell of the slime of the rivers sticks with you.
You should be blessed on the land, and you should be blessed – on the water!...

Night fell. The glistening tiles of the cottage
Cast a dark shine upon Grandfather.
My uncles were silent, my father was silent
Not wanting to miss a word of the blessings and speech.

Then Grandfather stopped talking. He brought in his limbs.
And the strong man quietly closed his eyes forever.
Those gathered looked at him, looked at the silent body,
They saw nothing, and not one tear was shed.

Somewhere in the forest, a bird chirped his lament during the night,
The last flickers of light in the hut were sparking
And the uncles stood with bowed heads toward Grandfather
The heavy, adult heads had sunk into the shoulders.

Translator's Footnote

1. Rendering of garments refers to the Jewish custom of the mourners tearing the garments of the deceased as an expression of grief prior to the funeral service.

[Page 138]

Avraham Sutzkever

From a conversation with Avraham Sutzkever

Translated by Anita Frishman Gabbay and Frieda Levin Dym

Avraham Sutzkever: A.S..

Y.P. Let us begin with the childhood years.

A.S. I was born in Smorgon, not far from Vilna, in 1913. I came from a well-known rabbinic family

Y.P. How did your family get from Smorgon to Siberia?

A.S. I'll start around the First World War. A rumour was going around and my family heard from a Jew "gutermacher" who said, "You will more likely be able to survive the war in Siberia"[1]

Y.P. Your father, Hershl, was a scholar and studied the Torah [with you] in Siberia. Hershl was also a fiddle player and brought his fiddle from Smorgon to play.[2]

A.S. The brightness of the Siberian fields was my inspiration. My first poem, called "Siberia" made me famous.

Y.P. I would like to hear more about your father, the scholar from Smorgon and the fiddler from Siberia.

A.S. At age 30, he had a heart attack while playing those Rabbi levi-itzhak's melodies.

Y.P. It was a difficult [time], but also a "bright" Siberia for the Sutzkever family. Your father was still young and was already supporting his family by peddling in the marketplace. After your father's death, your mother with her young family returned to Smorgon. At the time you were only 8 years old. Right before the First World War, your father had a leather factory in Smorgon. As your mother and children came back, they found everything burnt down. And, shortly after, your family left for Vilna.

A.S. My grandfather from my mother's side, was the Michalizker Rabbi, Rabbi, Shabtai Feinberg.[3]

[Page 139]

I remember from my Vilna years, [a} "yung vilna"— a club of young intellectuals and friends. Beside devouring books [of] Yiddish literature, I loved to wander through the Jewish quarter, the market, the Vilner shulhof—all with very sharp eyes and ears in order to absorb the rhythm of everything Yiddish around me. The group, "young vilna", which began in the 1930s, made their own impression in the literary circles, one did not envy the other.[4]

My mother Reinaz'l (Reina), with her holy prayer book in hand, was taken away to Ponar--that's the way it was. Actually, she did go [take] with her holy prayer book (siddur).

Y.P. Let us discuss the events from the Vilna ghetto, your memories and how you survived.

A.S. My entire Yiddish being was revealed to me in the Vilna ghetto. I can honestly say "life and death" were in the hands of the Yiddish language. Without which i could not have warded off death. My Yiddishkeit was my "magic wand", without which I could not have "warded" off death.

[Page 140]

I believed, that if I spoke with the purity of words, that death would not take over. It was divine justice.

Y.P. Afterwards came the partisan movement, each day and night [bringing] miracles. When the time came, when one did not have any more hope of survival, a Soviet airplane came to the rescue of the partisans. On this airplane you were saved. Thank G-d!

A.S. This is how it was: On the 12th of September, together with my wife and other partisans, we escaped through the barbed wire that surrounded the ghetto, to the Naroch woods, and to the Jewish partisan organization "Nekama".

When the Lithuanian partisan group in Moscow found out, that I was with the partisans, a telegram arrived to the commander of the Vorosilov-Brigade, Feodor Markov, stating that my wife and I should be brought to Moscow. So, in March of 1944, i am greeted by a group of partisans. I arrived in the Hushatsch province by plane, then airlifted again to Moscow. Here I was asked to be a witness in the Nuremburg trials. On the morning of February 27, 1946 my wife and I started our testimony. As I looked over to my right side, several feet from me, I saw those "murderers" sitting in two rows, may their memory be erased. The first one—Goering, like a wounded beast—here is Streicher, looking like a pregnant cow. I spoke for 38 minutes. I came to the land of Israel in September 1947.

Abraham Sutzkever[5] is the founder of the "Goldene Keyt', the golden chain, a literary quarterly, remaining its editor in Tel Aviv. To date, he has a collection of 47 works.

His poetic works include:

The Fortress, 1943
The Jewish Street, 1948
My Home Town, 1948
In the Fire Wagon, 1952
From Three Worlds, 1953

Ode to Death, 1955
In the Sinai Desert, 1957
Oasis, 1960
Holy Earth, 1961

[Page 141]

Siberia, with drawing by Marc Chagall, Jerusalem, 1953. In 1962, the poem [Siberia] was translated into English by Yacov Sontag; he was awarded a prize by UNESCO as well as from the International Pen Club[6]. The poem is included in the series of UNESCO works “of our time”.

Translator's Footnotes

1. Gutermacher meaning good man or a mensch.
2. Wikipedia has Abraham's father's name as Hertz, https://en.wikipedia.org/wiki/Abraham_Sutzkever/
3. Michalizker is referencing a person from the town of Mikaelishok.
4. Potentially a reference to the traditional or classic writers of Yiddish literature.
5. Abraham Sutzkever smuggled arms into the Vilna ghetto and concealed rare Jewish books and manuscripts of the YIVO collection, which he unearthed after the war. Writing poetry under aggravated conditions, he described several brushes with death: the murder of his mother and his new born son, the cultural underground resistance, and ghetto events and personalities. Admiration for his poems smuggled from the ghetto by a Lithuanian courier prompted the Jewish anti-fascist committee in the USSR to airlift Sutzkever to Moscow.
6. UNESCO, United Nations Educational, Scientific and Cultural Organization

[Page 142]

Abraham Sutzkever

by Aharon Rubin

Translated by Anita Frishman Gabbay and Frieda Levin Dym

The writer, Abraham Sutzkever, was born and bred in Smorgon, both on his father's side and his mother's side. Abraham Sutzkever's grandfather on his father's side was a "Hassidic" Jew through and through. In this [Hassidism] thinking, the study of the Torah was a great blessing. He was a wealthy leather manufacturer. The factory was situated on Vilner Gas (Street).Every week there were hundreds of clients. He had two sons, Shmuel and Naphtali Zvi–Hershl. When the grandfather died, the two sons inherited the factory. Shmuel, the older son, looked after the factory. Hershel was interested in studying, so he basically made an arrangement to receive an income from his brother from the factory.

This is the story of Zebulon and Issachar[1]:

Abraham Sutzkever's mother came from a Smorgon family deeply devoted to the study of Torah and were extremely religious. In Smorgon there was a Jew by the name of Itzele. He was the richest and most respected Jew in Smorgon, and he owned a row of shops in the market square along with a large home with a large property. And at the edge of Krever Gas, he had a watermill that was called the "Veiter Mill". (Veiter Mill likely translates into "further mill" so perhaps there was a closer one).

This [Rabbi Itzele] was Abraham Sutzkever's great grandfather. Rabbi Itzele had a son who was a devout Hassidic Jew, and therefore, he was nicknamed, the "Pashut", Avremele Itzele's. He married his daughter to a Rabbi Shabtai Feinberg. Rabbi Shabtai inherited his father–in–law's leather factory. However, he had very little interest in this enterprise. Rabbi Shabtai gave lessons in the large Synagogue.

[Page 143]

In those days, Smorgon was not only a center for the leather industry, but also a center for Torah study. Smorgon was famous for its Yeshiva. From near and far, students would come to the Synagogue to listen to Rabbi Shabtai's fiery sermons and discussions.

Commerce and Torah study did not go together, and Rabbi Shabtai was invited to preside over the Rabbinate in Mikaelishok. Rabbi Shabtai liquidated the factory and took the position in the Rabbinate. He is the author of "AKIKI – MAGINIM". His daughter Reina was Abraham Sutzkever's mother.

Translator's Note

1. Zebulon and Issachar represent two tribes referenced in the Torah where the former represented business and the latter representing study and learning. The two worked out an arrangement conducive to both.

[Page 144]

With Grandfather in Smorgon

by Avraham Sutzkewer

Translated by Jerrold Landau

Then, when my grandmother
Was busy with vinegar and honey
So noble,
She sent me for my birthday
A clock –
Then my time was
In the same manner.

It was a wall clock that originated from the moon.
The ink is insufficient to describe its style.
She saved it
(If my memory served me correctly)
At the time of her wedding, from a fire at grandfather's house in Smorgon,
That city, where in a wreath of laurels,
I was born.

It was handicapped
With crooked legs of lead;
With its bitter chains
That dangle from there.

A snowman, an androgynous
From red wood and steel.
With burning eyes
Like stars, twelve in number.

I have my guest, my dear one
Set at the head:
I will shine you and clean you
And there will be your throne.

[Page 145]

And even though it was cleaved
It then never cleave
My time.
It was all mine.
And if my grandmother had a desire
To knock with a blue umbrella
In the Garden of Eden –
The clock would not allow for us to be separated.
Grandmother had become a homey cuckoo.
Every hour she called out from her grave:
Cuckoo!
Yours is the time, and yours, yours:
Cuckoo!
Now, when that clock has been burnt
As well as my time like burnt-up rye,
Only, the blind cuckoo seeks a nest in my memory.

From Midbar Sinai, 1957

[Page 146]

The Sculptor Itkind

by Daniel Charni

Translated by Anita Frishman Gabbay and Frieda Levin Dym

The sculptor, Itkind, was not with us during the war. He started as a dyer in women's clothing in Smorgon. From time to time, Itkind would sculpt different forms and figures from “clay”. In Smorgon, it was evident, that there were not many buyers (market) for Itkind's “clay sculptures”. But, Latski-Bertoldi, who was known as a great connoisseur of art, would often come to Smorgon on business. He remembered Itkind and introduced him to a larger world audience.

Folks started to write about him in the newspapers and compared him to a second Antokolski. When the time of war arrived in Smorgon, when the Germans and their helpers descended upon us like a firestorm, Itkind, “naked” and “bare”, immediately went with me and several others to Moscow.

In Moscow, he found us a new home and a new life. One person, a Moscovite countess, began as Itkind's patron. She was involved with him for such a long time, that she eventually fell in love with him. Thanks to her connections and her means—the countess immediately found good clients for Itkinds' sculptures--the little boy from Smorgon became a very eligible bachelor and a “prince like figure” in Moscow.

He started wearing very fashionable and decadent clothing and outerwear and looked very aristocratic. So, Itkind, came visiting to me one day, by himself, and with a hearty welcome, brought me and my wife to his countess where we all were able to greet the New Year according to old Russian customs.

The family villa of this noble family was in a street with other nobles and wealthy folk, where they had their''atavkiakes”. The count's villa was completely “silvered” in the front, and looked like a frozen “ice palace”. Inside the salon, it looked gilded as well. The table was set with old family heirloom silver. Also, the very high candelabras were lit with star-bright candles, and the samovars (tea urns) were from massive silver.

Even the two steam ovens, from which the steaming samovar emitted its aroma, shone like silver. The four high wall mirrors, which were displayed in all four corners of the room, reflected the entire salon and the table in all its splendor. One imagined to be dreaming of a "thousand and one nights."

But the New Year of 1917-1918 it seems was the last night of the "thousand and two" nights! It was not only the last night for the nobility, but also for the people in general.

I never in my life saw or heard a new year celebrated in such a lavish style that a samovar was heated, not with water, but with...cognac!!!

I never in my life saw or heard that the new year be welcomed with flaming hats made of sugar and drenched with strong spirits. The blue flames of the flaming sugar hats danced and bounced off the 4 mirrors in all of the corners of the room. One could honestly say, that the new year of 1918 was being born to a sweet-blue new year that would bring only joy and prosperity to the whole world.

I had a sudden thought—that my small son will be born into such a sweet-blue atmosphere.

Our child, Rochel, will also be sweet-blue—I said this, under the steam of the heated samovar and burnt sugar, to my wife.

The sculptor Itkind, who sat next to us, suddenly interrupted us: "You know, Charni, my countess wants to have a child with me. But I suddenly realize, if it's a boy," she would no longer have use for me."

"I have already had enough", Itkind shortly stated, "My father comes to me nightly in my dreams and begs me to bury him in the land of Israel (or a Jewish burial).

It is known, that when Itkind's father "fled" to Minsk from the burning Smorgon, he was captured on the way. Together with other folks and Christians, he was murdered, and his remains lie in a field between Smorgon and Minsk.

So, because of how his Dad died, I feel badly for Itkind. That every night his dead father appears asking that he have a proper burial and every night the love-struck princess comes to him with a "bastard".

It suddenly becomes clear to me that his last exhibited sculpture was one of a lying female figure, distorted and crude, without feet!

This is "Russia", the old "Russia", (Russland it is now called), Itkind was now showing me new ideas for his new work. This is what the Bolsheviks were now preaching: the feet of old Russia will be chopped down—so that it will no longer continue (walk) in the same manner.

Also, his countess, the love-struck prize, suddenly, it seems, also felt that her noble upbringing would soon be over and her "Antokolski" Jew from Smorgon will be gone. She also made a resolution that very night (1917-1918 evening) to preserve her inheritance.

The flaming hats were now a long distant memory. And the samovars with the warm cognac were a memory of days gone by. Together with them, the days of the drunken Russia was no more.....extinguished! "Russia" was no longer, only the new "Soviet Russia".

[Page 150]

My Destroyed City
Holy Smorgon

by Eliahu Galob

Translated by Jerrold Landau

(Excerpts from the book "Destruction")

A.

Tell me, heavens, why do they lie
Dead and hollow in the city
Who sanctified their breath
Which is most desolate, G-d?

See the chimneys of the factories
Like a sparse forest
They stand up, above the living
Dark and cold.

And motionless machinery
Is silent, not active, desolate
Parts of rotting iron
Lying black in rubbish

And the streets stretched out
Like a long corpse;
Heads bent to the ground
Hanging on by a miracle.

Roofs half torn apart
Windows peering blindly.
Reveling freely in the palaces
Every evil wind.

[Page 151]

Balconies fell to the ground
Pillars were twisted,
Sculptures of gods, wildly damaged
Roll about dead.

And the orchards and the flowers
See, they cover the house –
See, the desolation devour still further
Not satisfied with its prey.

Reltzn[1] peer out from the grass
Broken, twisted;
And from afar, hangs wire
Twisted, mute.

Protruding, twisted pipes
Like withered hands,
Hang in pieces in the air
From the crooked walls.

And no drop of force flows
From energy-power;
Absorbed into the nerves
The entire life juices.

The city is covered with a white darkness
In the blind night.
The shadows are swallowed up in themselves,
Not protected by any beam.

Also over the dead does the desolation
Blow its sword,
Rotting bones lie around
On the damp earth.

Graves appears as the wounded
From a sick body,
Naked, dark – like worms
They slink around.

[Page 152]

Hunger begs from everywhere
Lamenting without a voice;
Dogs are gnawing on a human bone
Already for the tenth time.

Tell me, heavens, who harmed
The life source,
And the desolation calls out
Enjoying its celebration?

B.

Then the early morning is ill and pallid
And weary on the fields, the hollowness spreads out.
Somewhere, a lone bird with its melody
From the sparse grove, prepared for tomorrow.

From somewhere around, a weakened sky
Silently the clouds begged for rays
And just as they ruled palely from under the wings
Of the angel of death, they fled to save themselves.

And quietly in the heavens, and quietly in the fields
A quivering terror pervades –
Suddenly a flame bursts forth from somewhere
And is extinguished so quickly from somewhere.

And the air cuts as sharply as a knife
A shaking zuz-ziz[2]... and they were terrified,
An explosion went off, and immediately like a bomb
It had the power of thunder.

And it was calm again in the air –
But immediately the heart of the city felt its pain,
This was a greeting from there
Where life and death go arm in arm.

[Page 153]

And it became desolate. The streets died,
Winding long, without edges, and silently
Escaping in terror, and going somewhere into cellars,
And hiding in damp, crooked pits;

And then, there was a thunder, a second,
And from somewhere afar, a third answered;
These were hostile forces, with flames
Alternating around the city-head.

Lightning appeared high in the air
And cracking sounds shook the ground
Followed by thousands of small bangs
The kettle was boiling hot, as in hell.

The earth and the heavens moaned terribly
A lament of worlds stood in the air.
Tens of thousands of window panes shattered into pieces
And towers fell like shepherd's tents.

A mute fear wandered through the streets
The ill and tired glances gazed.
When will the world curse end
And the sun again send its rays from heaven?

The mother presses the child close to her heart
So that death will not beat him during the moments,
Every thunder rips the heart from the roots
And poisons the soul, and brings death to the blood.

The city is clothed as if in flaming chains
Corpses of horses and people already lie around
Bloody blossoms blanket the streets.

The houses nestled in silence
As the air became filled with death
And the flames frequently burst forth from above
A ball – and they are sent into burning graves.

[Page 154]

C.

Night
A night crept up
Black with silent winds,
Something thunders and crashes
Not sleeping and not calm.

Every knock in the city echoes
It beats against the hard walls
Lurking like a black god
Something is burning far in the heavens.

Red and colorless flames fall
Angry shadows cover
No light is burning on the street
Wandering at the edges of the sky
Quiet, no sound, desolate and silent
From a projector a sharp light,
A magical-red hand
Seeking something with the fingers.

One looks from the cellar of the house
A terror crawls deep into the heart,
Suddenly, tearing out of a pit
A cannon's angry caprice.

D.

A camp tore through
And entered the city
A thousand living heads move
Heavy with iron hanging through[3].

Breathing angrily with flames and fire
And they shudder for a thousand miles.
They step, hard, numbered, and certain
Going in quick, numbered, steps.

[Page 155]

Wagons with people move
Horses and men harnessed together
Both with a common intention,
Pushed far one from the other.

Suddenly, they move apart
On the courtyards, streets, and alleyways;
With angry, fierce eyes

And faces, wild and hot.

They pour out in blind fury
On the stone-gods, images,
They drag everything, to the abyss
Angry and wild words storm forth.

They tear into the cellars
Raping daughters with their mothers.
Beating, destroying everything without stop
Metal, stone, and people together.

The killed sick people in the beds
They tore the tongues out of the mouths
They robbed the dead of their belongings
They twisted the rings with the fingers.

Does it not seethe with wild anger?
That sullies the holiness, empty
It goes, drunken laughter
With the appearance of the faces of beasts.

It becomes wilder in its turbulence
Its evil fury is not satisfied
It attempted then to destroy the city
The creation of a thousand years.

[Page 156]

E.

Shadows wander through the street
Some of them crawling home,
Who will now interfere with the night
When no ray comes from above?

Something moves quietly and leisurely
Lying pale with a package
And a second near a flute
And a third accompanying him.

Flames leap out near a corner,
And hide in the yard
Going from place to place

Ascending into the air in rings.

Quiet, no word is heard,
Who obeys the warnings?
Which are still prepared
In the city that now lies dead?!

———

Suddenly an agonized shout bursts forth
Going forth from end to end –
It is burning!... It is burning!... the city, woe!
A red terror hovers in the air.

People wander outside
Women, children, naked, and bare,
One falls over the other
Who lost a child and a friend?

And from heaven, from the red
The city is decorated with flames
Flames burst forth from the roofs
Sending red tongues high up.

[Page 157]

And they twist about in clusters
Standing in black columns
Of smoke mixed with flames
Streets and alleyways are deserted.

Sighing from the high balconies,
And the walls tremble
Flames fall from cannons
In the red city that is burning!

Resounding with terror and angry pain
Street out and street in
Th city has become a sea of fire
The people run wildly from the flames.

They do not know where to run
Caught up in rings of fire,
And forgetting street and house
Seeking salvation in a pit.

Mothers grab strange kids
Mothers beat themselves with rage
They pull them out of the flames,
So they will not be lost in the smoke.

It becomes more terrible by the hour
Youth suddenly become grey
And darkening the judgment
They go to save a stone,
They throw themselves into a plume of fire
And are themselves burnt.

———

And from behind, charging
The entire people with a naked sword,
People free from the fiery kettle
Old, young, people, and horses,

[Page 158]

People run to the forests, the fields
There where the steps are cooking
Dark, but from afar fall
Flames are spreading far and wide.

Still echoing in the air, the knocking
Of collapsing walls
And, in contrast – shooting
Flying around endlessly.

One runs form one place to the next
Behind – terror, and in front – death
The clothes become heavy on the person
The last bread is cast away

They chase people and animals
And rob young and old;
They toss children off the wagons,
And drag women deep into the forest.

F.

The beast went through
And sowed destruction far and wide
A wagon stands in the middle of the path
With its wheels turned backward.

Blades of the windmill hang
Shot through, plucked apart,
And one solitary house protrudes
Without a roof, pushed to the ground.

Lying, tossed around, somewhere or another
Human limbs – covered with dust.
A cap lies without a person
With dark specks of brains.

And on the side, small graves
Without markers, quiet and silent –
Crows circle around in the air
Wolves smell the air around.

[Page 159]

A roar hovers in the air
Someone still moans in the forest,
Dug in the bushes
Orphan-guns stand cold[4].

And in the city, there remains
Not one person and not one house;
An insane person
Wanders around as if a grave.

The black night arrives, and shadows
Lie on the empty street –
The insane person goes around quietly
Digging and seeking in the black ash.

He drags himself around, half burnt,
His arm is bound with a string

He moves through the empty streets
And digs near a wall.

Dogs chase after the victim
A sorrowful hunger pervades on the street –
Death interrupts its desolate slumber
With a crazy scream.

Krakow, May 1918, "Kunst Ring", Literary and Artistic Almanac, Second Book, second edition, Publishing House, Yiddish.

Translator's Footnotes:

1. I am not sure of the translation of this word.
2. Zuz-zuz is a word sound like vroom, etc
3. Meaning is unclear.
4. Meaning of orphan-guns is unclear but perhaps guns whose owners died or abandoned them.

[Page 160]

Eliahu Golub
(Autobiography)

Translated by Anita Frishman Gabbay and Frieda Levin Dym

After the October Revolution, Eliahu Golub fought on the Ukrainian Front against the Germans. In 1918, he started to produce songs steeped in Yiddish Literature and embedded with Russian-Soviet undertones. His works include: "In the Storm", Poems, in 1934, Krakow 1918, "To a New World", Symbolic Drama in 4 parts, in 1948, in 1919, "Between two Worlds" (songs and poems), in 1971, Krakow 1921.

Note: the dates are transcribed exactly as in the original Yiddish

[Page 161]

Gershon Broide (1888-1947)

Translated by Anita Frishman Gabbay and Frieda Levin Dym

Gerhon Broide was born in Smorgon in 1888 into a wealthy family in the Leather Business.

He studied in Bern, Switzerland. During the years of the First World War and the October Revolution, he lived in Moscow. In 1921-1925, he remained in Berlin. In 1925, he immigrated to Israel. He died in 1947, at the age of 59.

[Page 162]

G–D and Samael (The Devil)[1]
by Gershon Broide

Translated by Anita Frishman Gabbay and Frieda Levin Dym

Samael, with might and fury, descended from the skies
Upon our land.
The first song, one in which the world had never known before
Was to G–D.

And we endured this Holy Melody for eternity
No one disturbed the choir!
He stood young and steadfast
He forgot about us in his Creation.

The world sang! And in every corner
Where there was silence–we felt the THUNDER!
Suddenly, the earth was destroyed
The song was forever silenced.

[Page 163]

Our voices, pitiful and tearful, from...
"Let go of me"
"The higher I raise my voice
Eventually you will succeed"

"If you want to leave me here in pain
A man who still believes in a G–D
A corpse from the earth–to remain on this earth
With hope to understand my request."

And G–D took a mountain of earth
And from it made a Holy corpse,
But before he could give him ....
He was lost in his thoughts.

In the meantime, Samael, flies down
From the skies, with speed, to attack
The corpse, and ....

With great stealth, he finished his work
G–D alone remarked!
And blew his spirit into the corpse
A spirit that is Holy and Pure!

Friday, July 13, 2018

Translator's Note

1. Samael "Venom of G–D" or "Poison of G–D" or "Blindness of G–D" is an important archangel in Talmudic and post Talmudic lore, a figure who is an accuser (satan), seducer, and destroyer, and has been regarded as both good and evil.

[Page 164]

Nissan Meckler

by David Yosifon

Translated by Sara Mages

Was born on, 11 Tevet 5662, in Smorgon, Russia, to his parents, Avraham Sheraga Feivel and Chana. At the age of five and a half he entered the "*Heder*" and a year later a disaster happened to him: one of his eyes was blinded in an accident. He continued to study at the "*Heder.*" A year and a half later he was hit on the head and lost sight in the other eye. His parents traveled with him to the best physicians in Russia and Germany, but to no avail. They were advised to put him in an institution for the blind in Europe, However, R' Avraham Sheraga Feivel, an honest Jew who read the Torah in his *Kloiz* (in return for his service he lived in a narrow and wet cellar without paying rent), absolutely refused to give his son to an institution where Christians were also educated. At that time the father was still working in his profession, shoemaking (and was very poor along with that), sent the boy, accompanied by his grandfather, to the Institute for the Blind in Jerusalem.

In 1913, a year before the outbreak of the First World War, Nissan was accepted as a student at the School for the Blind. It soon became apparent that the boy had excellent talents: was active, focused, a good friend, virtuous and level-headed.

Thirteen years later his younger brother, who left the Yeshiva, immigrated to Israel and became a laborer in the country. After that his parents and sister also immigrated.

When he got older, Nissan stood out in the institution as a young man of spirit, alert to public life, idealist, who was very interested in the life of his blind brothers' to faith. Over the years he became their spokesman in the institution and outside it.

To fulfill his aspiration to attain higher education he had to obtain a matriculation certificate, but, at that time, it wasn't yet customary to take external matriculation exams in our country. Meckler was examined at the Hebrew High-School in Jerusalem by the Board of Education, according to authorization and special arrangement, and passed the exams. He entered to study at the Hebrew University of Jerusalem and chose to study humanities: general philosophy, history and sociology. In 5695, he successfully completed his studies at the university and received, despite his blindness. a master's degree in humanities. He did not settle for the education he had acquired and aspired for further education. In the meantime, he also urged his friends at the institution to study in teachers' colleges and to continue their studies at the university. After graduating from the university, Dr. Sheraga Feivel Kalai, the principal of a high school in Baghdad, asked him to come to Baghdad and serve as a teacher at the Jewish school for the blind which opened there that year. Meckler, who already had an experience teaching at the institution where he had been educated, accepted the job and prepared to travel and teach reading and writing in Braille, crafts and musical instruments.

[Page 165]

But, in the meanwhile, Dr. Y. L. Megnes, who lived at that time in the United States, tried to get him a scholarship so he could study at Columbia College in New York in the Department of Blind Education. Meckler preferred to take this good opportunity and rejected the teaching work in an Arab country...

When he returned to Israel at the end of 1936, he entered to teach at the Institute for the Blind in Jerusalem, where he grew up and was educated, and immediately became the central figure in the teaching faculty. One of the teachers at the institution defined him well after she returned from the cemetery: “He was the conscience within us!” The conscience of the institution, that's how everyone knew him.

He acted according to justice and morality in matters between man and his friend. There's no one among the institution's employees, today and in the past, that Meckler did not make every effort to help him in time of need. He was the driving force behind the establishment of the employees' committee in the institution, and in 1946 he managed to reach an agreement between the institution's committee and the employees' committee that he headed from its inception to his last day. The agreement was signed at the initiative of "*Histadrut Hapkidim*" [The Office Workers' Union] in Jerusalem and at Meckler's initiative. Since then, all of Meckler's free time was given to the interest of the workers in general and the personal and professional matters of each of them in particular, without exception.

The night of the UN vote on Israel's independence, everyone is sitting by the radio tense and anxious, but Meckler, in his typical peace of mind, comments: "I'm sure that we will succeed." Jerusalem is shelled, especially in the vicinity of the institution. Everyone is sitting in the shelter, crowded and shaking. A fifty-kilogram shell explodes in the institution's yard destroying part of its building. Meckler sits and tells the students funny stories - childhood memories and mischievous acts, and fascinates the children with his stories. Everyone forgets the magnitude of the danger they face.

No one had ever heard Nissan Meckler slander anyone. He always spoke well about a person, could not see sin, understood everything and forgave. Loved peace and pursued peace. For that, everyone loved him - young and old students, employees and teachers, all of them did not take a step without him in the field of education and teaching at the institution. He was the fortress to which everyone turned to. He worked tirelessly at home, without getting paid, in different areas of the education system and in the area of printing Braille books by volunteers that he alone was in contact with them. He directed and guided, wrote and answered, in the field of improving the situation of the blind and rehabilitating them, even those who were outside the institution. For that reason the members of the blind association, "*Sheshet,*" canceled the party that was going to take place on the day of his burial and rushed to his funeral. Also all the members of the blind cooperative, "*HaTikvah,*" closed their workshop and came to Jerusalem to pay their last respect.

[Page 166]

He supported his family with all his savings. His niece wrote him that she had been sent home from high-school, where she was studying, because her father, who was out of work, could not pay the tuition, and the good uncle sent the required amount without hesitation, He did not build a family home for himself, but purchased an apartment in Beit-Hakerem and put in his old friend, Emanuel Schaffer and his wife, the printer at the school for the blind. Such was the man that few like him were in our generation.

He was the main speaker in all the teachers' meetings and, when Meckler spoke. everyone listened because his words were never empty, everything - to the point with no trace of selfishness, but, for the common good or for the individual to whom he came to help and fight his war of deprivation. Everyone knew that when Meckler opened his mouth, only justice and truth, to which he aspired, spoke from his throat.

May his memory be blessed!

[Page 167]

My Brother Avraham Forsite
(1896-1954)
by Benjamin Forsite

Translated by Anita Frishman Gabbay and Frieda Levin Dym

Avraham, while still in his younger years, brought into our home in Smorgon a new style and set of ideas and views of a broader world that lay beyond our shtetl.

Quite young, he left for the Ukraine and found work in a little town called Mena, in the district of Chernigov. Here he familiarized himself with the lives of the peasants (i.e. the peasant way of life).

When he returned home to us in Smorgon for the holidays, he brought with him the revolutionary (Russian) songs and taught them to us. He was being indoctrinated with Revolutionary ideals in Mena and was forced to flee. When he returned to Smorgon in 1915, he accompanied us on our wander-years through Smorgon- Moledechno, Minsk-Kharkov, and then Rostov on the Don.

He started working immediately as a bookkeeper and began to think of his future in the Commercial Institute. But the [political climate] state of affairs at that time, the Revolution and the civil struggle, beckoned him to abandon his studies.

He was tormented by his convictions. Not being able to pursue his dreams, he helped our father with his earnings.

These times were uneasy and turbulent. Pogroms organized by the White Russians were waiting for us in Rostov. Avraham immediately got involved, bringing home a revolver and teaching us how to defend ourselves in the event of a Pogrom. Times were always changing in the Ukraine. Jews were living in "Holy Fear"!

In 1921, our mother and father died, and the livelihood of the family was left to Avraham.

In 1922, we used up all our means, and our last option was immigrating to relatives in America. We arrived in New York in 1923.

[Page 168]

The process of starting life anew and adapting to a new profession became very difficult. Our relatives, to whom we arrived, were far from being rich folk, but Avraham developed an idea. He became a businessman. In 1925 he got married.

World War II began and our entire Jewish world suffered.

Avraham threw all his energy into relief work to help his fellow Smorgoners who persevered through these most difficult times and miraculously survived their destruction [lives].

He was weak and sick, but Avraham hid his sorrow and longing for our homeland Israel. He could not make himself too comfortable here and he was tormented by his yearning to be in the "Homeland".

Avraham arrived in Israel in 1954 with his wife Sima, his sister, and the Rebbetsin[1], Ester Warshavski, for a visit. On the second day of Pesach, he died suddenly.

He produced 3 works: one was "Bar Kochba" [published] in New York in 1941. It is a historical book. Below is an excerpt:

The Bar Kochba uprising, that started in 132 A.D. was a National Liberation War where the Zealots fought for over 60 years. The spirit of the Zealots, their idealism, courage and bravery and their willingness to fight until the end, surely found resonance in the ranks for the Bar Kochba"s heroes.

Bar Kochba's fighters are referred in this book as "Zealots" even though, in fact, the fighters actually were soaked in Blood and Fire in the destruction in the year 70 (the same year of the destruction of the Holy Temple). The Bar Kochba uprising serves as a symbol for the future Jewish struggle for National survival.[2]

The book was 256 pages. In 1947, his "In the Red Glow", is introduced (a work in 3 parts) and here is an excerpt from his book:

[Page 169]

The most important event in our time was the Russian Revolution, the events of which influenced the world and change the whole of mankind. I was in Russia in those fateful days, I lived and breathed the turmoil, and vowed to write my thoughts and remember those images of these times. During the moment, it was still so fresh and new. I would not have been able to put it in perspective and to comment objectively, so I held myself back from writing about these events for 20 years.

The rise of Fascism and more importantly, the years that the Nazis engulfed all of Europe, compelled the necessity to bring to the Jewish readers my modest works.

His third work was, "To a Bright Future", which was introduced in 1953, shortly before his untimely death.

[Page 170]

In this work, he goes back home to satisfy the great longing to return to his little shtetl of Smorgon among his old friends and personal belongings. He returns to his Jewish roots, to the Hassidic customs and to the Mitzvoth in all its Holiness. And he returned to his melodious songs that ring from the Torah, with the singing and blessings that remember "Israel" (In praise of Israel)

May his memory forever live on and be a blessing.

Translator's Notes

1. Rebbetsin or Rebbetzin is a wife of a Rabbi or alternatively a female teacher.
2. More information can be found here, https://en.wikipedia.org/wiki/Bar_Kokhba_revolt

[Page 171]

Yitzchak Bar'Eli (Izik Brudny)

(1888–1956)

Translated by Jerrold Landau

Yitzchak Bar'Eli, the director of Bank Hapoalim, died in Tel Aviv on Iyar 3, 5716 (1951). He was one of the heads of the workers' movement and forgers of the shape of the economic and financial institutions of the Israeli workers' movement. He was born 67 years previously, on Marcheshvan 1, 5649 (1890), under the name of Izik Brudny, in our town of Smorgon, to his father Meir Brudny and his mother Sheina (nee Sapir) Brudny.

He was the scion of a Smorgon family. Ten generations of his ancestors are buried in Smorgon, and he was able to discuss them all within the family circle. Apparently, the ancestors of the family arrived in Lithuania from the city of Brody (from where the name Brudny stems) during the time of the Chmielnicki disturbances. At the end of the 19th and beginning of the

20th centuries, this family was called by the Jews of Smorgon by the name of Eliahu–Leib (for example, Izak Brudny's father would be called Reb Meir Eliahu–Leib's)[1]. Therefore, the name was changed to Bar'Eli in Israel, named after that great–grandfather. In this rabbinical family, the grandfather of Izik Brudny, Shlomo Mordechai Brudny, stands out. He is a native of Smorgon who served for many years as the rabbi of Steibitz (Stolbtsy), and was the first teacher of Zalman Shazar (Rubashov), the third president of Israel. Shlomo Mordechai Brudny was the author of the “Ohel Shem” responsa book.

After *cheder* studies in Smorgon and *Yeshiva* in Slobodka, Y. Bar'Eli traveled to the Land. He toured it and then studied in the American University in Beirut, as a preparation for life in the Land of Israel. Only after he gave up on the educational level in Beirut did he transfer to Berne, Switzerland, where he completed his academic studies. During the First World War, when the retreating Russians burnt Smorgon [likely 1915], the family moved to Kharkov. This was a year after Bar'Eli married Dr. Chava Yahalom. He only succeeded in leaving the Soviet Union for Lithuania in 1921. He remained there for about five years. He built the largest banking institution of Lithuanian Jewry, the Central Bank, which he headed. His only son, Meir, was born there [in Lithuania].

He made *aliya* to the Land in 1926. He directed the Mashbir Hamerkazi [Central Distribution]. He took upon himself the leadership role during the period of the difficult depression, when the first Solel Boneh weakened, and the entire economy was in the pits. After he succeeded in extricating the central consumers' cooperative from its difficulties, he transferred to lead Bank Hapoalim. This became his life's work for close to 30 years.

[Page 172]

Even though he occupied himself in communal affairs to no small degree before his *aliya* to the Land, as one of the builders of Tzeirei Tzion and later, [another institution], Tz. S. (Socialist Zionists) (at first in Soviet Russia, and later in Lithuania); after he arrived in the Land, he dedicated his talents and energy solely to business. Even his communal work in Mapai (Israel Labor Party) was both directly and indirectly tied to economic affairs. He was a member of the directorship of almost all the important economic institutions of the Histadrut, and dedicated time, talent, and energy appropriate to what was needed in various eras. He was also a member of the leadership of several primary economic institutions in the Land, such as Bank Leumi LeYisrael.

Yitzchk Bar'Eli's work in Magbit Hitgaysut VeHatzala [Campaign for Enlistment and Rescue] was unique in his communal activities. He was a member of the leadership throughout all the years. In essence, this fund laid the groundwork for independent Hebrew taxation in the Land even before there was a sovereign Jewish state. He became ill during his final years yet he continued to work with great energy despite his

[Page 173]

physical weakness. He laid the foundations for a great expansion of Bank Hapoalim during the years of the state.

He was also a delegate to the Zionist congresses from the tenth congress until the end of his days (except for two or three congresses to which he was unable to travel). He was at the center of the financial activities of the congresses and headed a few of the financial committees. He was also the chairman of the budget committee of the Jewish Agency for many years.

His memory remains etched in the hearts of his friends and acquaintances, not only on account of his deeds and achievements, but also because of his personal integrity, his good heart, and his willingness to assist anyone in need of help. He assisted with a full heart and an abundance of charm, wisdom, human, and great knowledge of Jewish popular folklore.

Translator's Footnote:

1. Nicknaming after an ancestor with the possessive form was a common form of appellation among Eastern European Jews.

[Page 174]

David Raziel

Translated by Jerrold Landau

His remains were transferred from Iraq to Cyprus, and brought to burial in the Jewish Cemetery in Margo, near Nicosia, on December 20, 1955. They were transferred to a military grave on Mount Herzl in Jerusalem on March 17, 1961.

His Roots:

He was the descendent of rabbis, great in Torah and mighty in faith. David Raziel was born in the city of Smorgon, Vilna District, on 18th Kislev 5671 (1910) to his father Reb Avraham–Mordechai Rozenson and his mother Bluma.

In his parents' home, he was imbued with a nationalistic consciousness rooted in the early generations: the strong faith in the greatness of the chosen people and the pain from the degradation of the pride of our nation under the oppressive conditions of exile. From his ancestors who lamented the destruction of the temple during the nights, he inherited the burning desire for redemption and the feeling of the bitterness of Diaspora life that bent the Jewish image.

He was three years old when he made *aliya* with his parents to the Land of Israel in the summer of 5674 (1914). His father was invited from the Diaspora to serve as a teacher in the Tachkemoni School of Tel–Aviv Yafo[1]. After approximately a half a year, on account of the persecution and deportations by the Turkish Army during the First World War, the family was deported along with other Jewish families on account of their Russian citizenship. [The child] David wandered with his parents through Egypt to Ukraine, central Russia, Georgia, Moscow, and Kovno. They wandered from country to country, from exile to exile, for eight years. During this time, he received his education from his father and mother. He studied a great deal of Torah, and learned the Hebrew language from his early childhood. He already knew almost the entire Bible by heart by the age of eight. He knew the six order of Mishnah by heart by the age of 12.

During the years of wandering, David read a great deal of modern Hebrew literature. Through his reading and study of Bible, he became very impressed with the bravery and glory of our ancestors in the olden days. During his wandering, he saw the Jewish nation in the degradation of exile. The months of his childhood in which he lived in the Land of Israel with his parents remained etched in his memory. He aspired to return to the Land, and his will to follow the paths of our early heroes and to fight for the liberation of our homeland was great.

He returned to the Land with his parents at the age of 12, after his father was invited a second time to serve as a teacher in the Tachkemoni School. On Chanukah 5683 (1922), eight years after they were deported from the Land, David returned, rich in experiences from their time of wandering, and rich in the spirit that he absorbed from the study of Bible and Hebrew literature.

David Raziel completed his studies in Tachkemoni, and took the government matriculation exams. He studied in the Merkaz Harav *Yeshiva* of the Gaon Ra'yh (Rabbi Avraham Yitzchak Hakohen) Kook of blessed memory for two years. Then he began to study in the department of spiritual sciences at the Hebrew University. He also studied mathematics and philosophy, and excelled in those subjects.

[Page 175]

David Raziel's soul was a wonderful blend of the wisdom of Shem and Japheth[2]. His compositions from his childhood excelled in artistic sparks that foreshadowed the sprouting of great talent. He wrote a great deal about the heroes of the Bible. Two plays that he wrote have been preserved from that childhood era: The Spies, and Korach; as well as comprehensive monographs: Saul and David. These creations from his childhood days excelled in their artistic refinement and the enchanting spirit that testified to the strong yearning of the young author for ancient heroism, the judges and kings of

Israel, the greats of the nation and its martyrs. Later, the child became impressed with the bravery of the Hasmoneans, the heroes of the wars of the Second Temple period, Bar Kochba, and Rabbi Akiva. In his eyes, Rabbi Akiva was a symbol of the spirit with his studies and might, and he aspired to follow his path, to gather troops, to strengthen the hands of the fighters, and to teach the bow to the children of Israel[3].

His Activities

The bloody disturbances of 5689/1929 consolidated within him the consciousness that the redemption of Israel will not come without fighters for the redemption. The slaughter of the students of the Hebron *Yeshiva* without opposition created in him the strong desire to build up the strength of the Hebrew youth. His childhood dreams took on form [lit: skin and bones]. He joined a group of volunteers of the communal council of Jerusalem. His first task was to accompany the tens of *Yeshiva* students who were slaughtered in Hebron to their eternal rest.

[Page 176]

In the wake of the disturbances of 5689 / 1929, a portion of the important officers separated from the ranks of the Haganah and set up the Irgun Tzvai Leumi. David Raziel joined the separatists immediately upon the founding of the Irgun. From then, he dedicated his talents to studying military professions. On account of the dearth of Hebrew military literature, he went to foreign sources, and studied with great diligence until he became one of the top officers. He was given the responsibility for conducting courses for officers of the Irgun Tzvai Leumi, or, as the Irgun was nicknamed in those days "Haganah Bet". In order to instill, advance, and disseminate military training among the soldiers, he translated, edited, and authored professional manuals. David Raziel was a pioneer and guide in the writing of military books. His books served as the source of advanced study and knowledge during the early days of the rise of Hebrew military power.

The disturbances of 5696/1936 brought a fateful change to the life of David Raziel – a change that had a decisive influence on the history of our nation. Bloody disturbances broke out once again in the Land of Israel. Mass murder began. Much Jewish property was destroyed. The Arab enemy wished to stop the mighty stream of immigrants that stemmed from the countries of Nazified Europe, over whom the shadow of the Holocaust was already hovering. The official leaders of the Jewish community decreed "restraint," and preached restraint regarding the use of force amongst the Hebrew youth, proclaiming the command "Thou shalt not kill" even when the enemy rose up and murdered Jews, men, women, and children, on a daily basis.

At the beginning of the disturbances, the activity of Haganah Bet was still restricted to guarding activities, but its commanders quickly reached the conclusion that the policy of restraint was lacking in political propriety, and was certainly lacking in military correctness. It led to an increase of Jewish victims, and gave the British a pretext to accede to the demands of the Arab strongmen.

The official leaders opposed a change to the policy of restraint, and when Haganah Bet decided to begin retribution actions, some of its officers left and joined the Haganah. The fighters remained in the Irgun Tzvai Leumi.

David Raziel quickly became known as a revered commander. The chief of the organization, Zeev Jabotinsky of blessed memory, gave him the chief command. With his talents in work, his commitment to the goals, and his readiness to serve as a personal example of self–sacrifice, David Raziel earned the trust of the officers and the soldiers, some of whom were more veteran and older than he.

He organized the ranks around the battle flag and began to act. On 10 Kislev 5698 (November 14, 1937), known as "Black Friday" he conducted the first attack against Arab gangs in Jerusalem. The restraint was broken, to the dismay of the official leaders. The battle of the Irgun Tzvai Leumi began, and did not stop throughout the period of the disturbances that continued until the year 5699 (1939), and only stopped with the outbreak of the Second World War.

[Page 177]

David Raziel was the head of both the planners and the actualizers. He placed himself in danger before he endangered the life of others. He shocked the enemy and proved that Jewish blood was not wanton. He transferred the battle to the gates of the enemy who stood securely in the paths of murderers. However, he did not suffice himself with that. In his spirit, he saw the rise of a Hebrew army which will storm and liberate the homeland at an opportune time. He dedicated all his strength and talent to this goal, and spent days and nights studying books of tactics and strategy in order to prepare the generation of fighters for this goal.

During this period, Raziel wrote many booklets and books on military professions. Anything he learned from foreign sources he translated to Hebrew. His works that he authored during the underground war include: The Pistol, written together with Avraham Stern (Yair), may G–d avenge his blood; The Leadership Doctrine; Exercises in the Order of Consolidation and Dispersing, as well as Notes to Klausowitz; On Reality; Principles in the Giving of Orders and Fulfillment; and the Spirit of the Kibbutz.

* * *

His activities broadened and reached the centers of Hebrew youth in the Diaspora. Underground cells of the Irgun Tzvai Leumi arose in Poland, Lithuania, and other countries, and were prepared to serve as the reserve army of the army of liberated Israel.

The reserve army broke through and rose. The Haapala (Illegal Immigration) period began. The official leaders preached against the illegal immigration. They desired to preserve the selective *aliya* according to the certificates of the mandate government. However, the danger of annihilation was already hovering over Europe. Jabotinsky issued his call to liquidate the Diaspora, and the soldiers of the Irgun Tzvai Leumi from all locations began to break through to the shores of the Land. Masses of other Jews, including competitors, made *aliya* along with the soldiers of the Irgun Tzvai Leumi. This was the "Free aliya" and every Jew had the right to save himself and leave Europe through the Haapala and the Underground, under the command of David Raziel. Thousands upon thousands of Jews are alive and well today in the Land of Israel, having been saved from the vale of murder thanks to the activities of the Haapala.

Through the narrow path of the underground, David Raziel succeeded in going to the Diaspora, and meeting Zeev Jabotinsky face to face. During that historical meeting, the warlord of Etzel[4] expressed his reverence for the "Man of Steel" David Raziel. "Sir, I have waited for him for these past fifteen years," he said about him, and imbued him with his full reverence and trust. David Raziel bore the highest rank in Etzel, "Aluf ben Anat." He was the only person to bear the rank Aluf (Brigadier).

During this period, Etzel broadened its activities, and opened attacks against the British government, which had been subdued by Arab terror and proclaimed the decrees of the "White Paper" against the Hebrew settlement. From that time, Etzel took upon the goal of proving that giving in to the Arabs will not restore quiet to the Land, and that the Hebrew youth will fight with all their might against the strangling plots included in the "White Paper."

* * *

With the outbreak of the Second World War, Etzel decreed a truce in the battle against the British.

[Page 178]

A common enemy arose against humanity as a whole – the Hitlerist beast. The majority of the Etzel leadership reached the decision that the Irgun must decree a truce due to the immediate danger of physical destruction threatening the Jewish people by Hitler.

Through the intercession of Pinchas Rotenberg of blessed memory, Raziel was freed from prison a short time after the outbreak of the war[5]. The rest of the imprisoned Etzel members were freed after him, including Avraham Stern (Yair), may G–d avenge his blood. Then the schism in the ranks of the Irgun began, with a group of captains headed by Yair forming the Irgun Hatzvai Haleumi BeYisrael, later called "Lochmei Cherut Yisrael"[6]. David Raziel married Shoshana Spitzer, a commander in the Etzel, some time after being freed from prison.

The Final Mission

The German enemy threatened to conquer the Middle East. Rommel's army advanced through the deserts of Africa toward the Land of Israel. Anti–British ferment arose in the Arab lands, with the aim of helping the advancing enemy army. The "Revolt" of Rashid Ali broke out in Iraq, with the help of Germany and the support of the Mufti of Jerusalem, Hajj Amin El Husseini, who was responsible for the murderous acts perpetrated by the Arabs against the Jewish settlement in the Land.

The victory of Rashid Ali and his friend the Mufti was liable to bring the enemy armies and air force to the borders of the Land of Israel, whose fate would be sealed since the forces of the Jewish settlement were insufficient to defend it. The sword of destruction was waved with full threat over the Jewish settlement.

During those fateful days, David Raziel saw three primary goals for the Etzel:

To join the allies as a partner in the war against the Nazis.

To prevent the danger of Iraq turning into a German base.

To liquidate the "Jerusalem Mufti," whose existence is a danger to the Jewish nation.

When they [leaders of war effort] approached David Raziel with the proposal to directly help the allies by penetrating behind the lines of Rashid Ali, he did not hesitate, and accepted the role. In opposition to the opinion of his friends, he decided to go himself into the line of fire, at the head of a small group of daring youths who had no fear.

They went out and fulfilled one of the most important roles in subduing the rebels and conquering Baghdad. He himself planned the defense of the airport in Habbaniya. It is characteristic that his advice was taken as literal commands. Everyone felt that standing before them was a man who was proficient in military tactics.

The members of his group penetrated in disguise the besieged capital, which was surrounded by the allies. They stood firm and did not flinch from the fear of the Iraqi and German forces that were literally within the walls of the city. This hesitation was liable to decide the fate of the battle, for the rebels had the stronger force, and could only be subdued by a flash battle. To do so required information on what was transpiring within the besieged city. A group of Etzel men brought the information and salvaged the situation. They infiltrated the enemy lines at the risk of their lives.

[Page 179]

They carried out sabotage actions and determined that the Iraqi army was in a state of disorderly retreat, and there was no defense of Baghdad. This revelation surprised the British command, who decided to conquer Baghdad.

The efforts to assassinate the Jerusalem Mufti did not bear fruit. The Mufti escaped to Germany when the revolt failed, where [after] he collaborated with the Nazi enemy in the liquidation of European Jewry.

* * *

David Raziel went out on his rounds of the advancing lines on 23 Iyar, 5703 (1943). His group was attacked by the German air force, and he fell victim, far from the homeland. He was buried in the military cemetery in Iraq, with the name “Ben Moshe.”

The Funeral Cortege of David Raziel Sets Out for Mount Herzl

The funeral cortege of David Raziel, may G–d avenge his blood, the chief commander of Etzel who fell in Iraq more than 20 years ago, whose coffin was brought to Israel from Cyprus yesterday, set out this morning from Tel Aviv on route to Mount Herzl in Jerusalem. It was accompanied by a large procession of automobiles, in them thousands of Etzel people from the entire country. There was a delegation of Beitar veterans, communal personalities, and a large, variegated crowd.

Mr. Y. Ben–Zvi, the president of the state, delegated his military advisor, Major D. Hermon, to represent him today in the funeral of David Raziel.

The chairman of the Knesset, Mr. K. Luz, passed by the coffin of David Raziel of blessed memory at 8:45 this morning in the Metzudat Zeev meeting hall in Tel Aviv. The chairman of the Knesset tarried next to the coffin for several minutes.

Immediately following him were Knesset members Argov, the chairman of the foreign and security committee; and E. Govrin, the chairman of the Mapai faction in the Knesset and leader of the coalition.

David Raziel's close friends tarried next to his coffin during the night at Metzudat Zeev, taking turns in guarding. They brought forth memories of the era of the underground, and recited words of prayer.

The elder commanders of Etzel and members of his command conducted a mourning roll–call next to the coffin.

The coffin, draped in the national flag, was taken out to the square next to the fortress at 9:30.

Member of Knesset Y. Meridor, who was Raziel's deputy, spoke emotional words. Then, the coffin was placed in a command car, and the funeral procession set out, accompanied by brigades of Etzel and many delegations from the country and the Diaspora.

Six veterans of Etzel, bearing their arms, served as the honor guard in the command car.

[Page 180]

A group of nurses from the national Kupat Cholim in white uniforms were prominent among the cortege.

The coffin reached the Great Synagogue of Tel Aviv around 10:30. The Kel Maleh Rachamim prayer was recited there by the chief cantor. Eulogies were not delivered.

From the synagogue, the funeral procession set out to Rechov Haaliya, where cars were waiting to accompany the cortege to Jerusalem.

"You have returned to the homeland, our commander." The remains of David Raziel, may G–d avenge his blood, have come to their rest and inheritance after 20 years.

At a distance of several tens of steps from the grave of the visionary of the state, the grave of one of the choicest of the fighters for its independence was dug. Near to the burial place of many of the fallen of the Israel Defense Forces, the man who bore the vision of the Hebrew army is buried.

Soldiers of the Israel Defense Forces fired three volleys in his memory. David Raziel was buried for the third and final time.

All of those who knew him, who fought with him, and even who opposed him, came to accompany him on his final journey. There were members of his command from more than 20 years earlier. They marched in an upright position, in a united, honorable group. Many looked on. Others were unable to approach the event. Clods of earth were brought from atop the graves of those killed in defense of the State to be placed onto Raziel's grave.

There were younger people present, members of the generation who did not know David and his activities. These youths heard about Raziel from what was written, or from their parents.

Communal notables, the city fathers, rabbis, judges headed by the president of the supreme court, the delegate of the president, the secretary of the prime minister, and military personal followed after the coffin. *Yeshiva* students and workaday people who closed their businesses and locked their offices to pay their final respects to Aluf Ben–Anat marched en masse.

The elderly Rabbi Aryeh Levin, the rabbi of the underground prisoners, was present.

His faithful people stood there according to their flags: people of the command from all parts of the country came and wore black berets; members of Cherut and Beitar in blue uniforms, under their flags; nurses of the national Kupat Cholim in their white dresses; and behind them – thousands of people. Some were anonymous soldiers of the former underground. Others felt a personal need to accompany one of the first of these soldiers on his final journey.

Yafo Street, the main street of Jerusalem, changed its appearance yesterday afternoon. Instead of bustling traffic, thousands of residents of the city stood along its length, while many others filled the balconies above it. The long mourning cortege appeared before their eyes. In front was the coffin, covered with the flag of Israel. Behind it were the family members of the deceased. Marching behind them silently in one block was the group of former commanders, prisoners of Mizra, Latrun, Jerusalem, Sudan, and Eritrea – a group who believed in the path of David Raziel.

[Page 181]

David Raziel was an emissary of a mitzvah [holy task] – thus did [Chief] Rabbi Yitzchak Nissim state [utter] next to his grave. An emissary of a mitzvah – who gave his life for it. David Raziel raised the honor of his nation and was one of the renewers of the tradition of bravery of the Jewish nation.

Thousand surrounded the grave. The cold wind blew the clouds eastward. The final rays of sunlight caressed the peak of Mount Herzl.

“Fire!”, commanded the young army captain before the groups of his soldiers. The volley of gunshots resonated from one end of the mountain to the other: once, twice, and three times.

Wreaths of greenery were piled on the grave. The remains of David Raziel returned to the nation.

Translator's Footnotes:

1. The Diaspora refers to the corpus of the Jewish community in general outside the Land of Israel. So one can be invited by the Diaspora (i.e. from outside of Israel). The other references to Diaspora in this article are consistent with this meaning.
2. Referring to a blend of spiritual knowledge [Shem] and the arts [Japheth].
3. A reference to II Samuel 1:18, the dirge of David to Saul and Jonathan.
4. Alef Tzadi Lamed – acronym for Irgun Tzvai Leumi. Ie. Irgun and Etzel are synonymous.
5. Apparently he was captured by the British: https://www.jewishvirtuallibrary.org/david–raziel
6. Known as the Stern Gang.

[Page 185]

The Town and its Residents

A. Till the First World War

Segments of Memories

by Abba Gordin

Translated by Jerrold Landau

I was born in the town of Michaliszki. This was my first birth, as I was born a second time in Smorgon. That was my literary birth. I began to take up the writer's craft in Smorgon. That city, Smorgon, is dear to me because my cradle, the cradle of creativity, stood there.

A. We left Ostrów

The city was full of rumors. They complained about the children of the rabbi, who sinned and led the youth to sin, removing them from the faith in their Maker, bringing them in to a bad crowd called "Ivriya," introducing them to the malignant illness of Zionism, Heaven save us.

On the other hand, there was nothing with which to complain about the children of the rabbi. One could not place the mantle of wantonness upon them. They wore long *kapotes* [cloaks] – kosher even for the stringent, wore Jewish caps, and grew curly *peyos* [side curls] in accordance with the religion of Moses and Israel." They did not denigrate even the smallest custom. The clear sign of entering into a bad crowd was lightheadedness toward girls. The rabbi's sons were innocent of such sins. They set a covenant with their eyes, and why would they pay attention to a girl. Abba, the middle of the rabbi's children, was so dedicated, with all his soul and all his senses, to Hebrew and Zionism, to the point where he had no time or a scintilla of energy to dedicate to anything else. For Abba and Zeev [another son of the Rabbi], it was as if the better sex did not even exist.

In accordance with the understanding of the Hassidim of Ostrów, the casting off the yoke of Heaven was bound tightly with "licentiousness" and interest and connection with girls, one could not imagine such a sin with them and there were those Hassidim who even defended the rabbi's sons and the purity of their name, not allowing any denigration.

Reb Ben-Zion, the head of the Gerrer Hassidim, was among such defenders. He was a veteran student of the head of the Gerrer dynasty, Rabbi Yitzchak Meir Rotenberg-Alter, who was a student and son-in-law of Reb Mendele of Kock.

In the Gerrer *shtibel*, from which the accusation against the rabbi's sons emanated, Reb Ben-Zion stood up and declared in a loud and angry voice, "I will slap the face of anyone who is so brazen as to utter one derogatory word against the son of Rabbi ."

[Page 186]

In his eyes, the murmuring about them was false rumors.

Reb Ben-Zion's wife, Mrs. Chana Gittel, would come to visit the rabbi's wife. During a friendly conversation, she informed her that people were talking badly about Bluma the rabbi's eldest daughter. They were saying that she was teaching Hebrew to the daughters of important householders. She, Chana Gittel, did not believe that Bluma, a modest, proper, and G-d fearing Jewish daughter, would do such a deed, that ought not to be done.

Reb Ben-Zion came on a regular visit to the rabbi, discussed city issues with him, and strolled with him for long and short walks, [often] delving into a difficult Talmudic discussion on Tractate *Taharot*. And after all this, incidentally told the rabbi about what was going on in the *shtibel*[1]. Abba was present on that occasion, and was astonished at the great naivete of Reb Ben-Zion, who looked at the eyes and not at the heart, and placed his full faith in the sons of his friend, the rabbi, without investigation or inquiry.

Rabbi Yehuda-Leib listened to Ben-Zion's words, and was silent. However his face became cold. He knew very well that this was not slander. The words were completely true.

The rabbi began to seek think of ways to avert the evil, and to extricate himself from this crisis. It is clear that he could not leave the city before the storm broke regarding the venomous situation of his sons and household and the Hebrew spoken in the Sephardic pronunciation was heard within the walls of his house[2]].

He thought silently, did not say anything, but rather arose and did something. He traveled, so to speak, to visit his father-in-law Rabbi Sender of Niestaniszki, in order to obtain a rabbinic post in Lithuania. He placed his eyes upon Smorgon, Vilna District, which was close to Niestaniszki.

It was in this manner that he received the writ of rabbinical post from the holy community of Smorgon.

Rabbi Yehuda Leib returned from his journey with the news: to prepare to leave Ostrów and move to Smorgon.

The *Rebbetzin* was not particularly satisfied, knowing that "there is no honor for a prophet in his native land," and Smorgon was sort of the city of her birth. She suspected that they would not honor her appropriately, in accordance with what she was accustomed to. However, the situation could not be put off. There was no choice – they had to leave the city of Ostrów quickly. Even the rabbi was not satisfied. The existing conditions would mean that a change of place would lead to a change of fortune. It would be a form of salvation.

Abba, Zeev, and the sisters were in "seventh heaven" from great joy. They went from darkness to a great light. They would be liberated from the Hassidim who live in darkness, and would no longer have to be "Marranos." In Smorgon, they would have the opportunity of conducting Hebrew and Zionist publicity in the open without disturbance, and without complaints.

B. To Freedom and Disappointment

The rabbi, *Rebbetzin*, daughters, and youngest son went first. Abba and Zeev were last, and traveled alone.

[Page 187]

Abba took leave from his impoverished group, especially from his dear friend Shmuel Szwarc, whom he left behind to take his place and continue his holy work. Szwarc was full of agony and worry. In a tearful voice he said, "Now that you are leaving the city, zealousness will increase here. Your father , the rabbi of the city, had a restraining effect on the zealots. They could not do whatever they want in the community. They were afraid of the rabbi. Now, we remain as a flock of sheep among lurking wolves. They will tear us up, and nobody will be there to save us."

Abba and Zeev traveled via Białystok and reached the Smorgon station safely.

The winter was at its coldest point. They were both wearing new suits, new coats, and hats. It was possible to wish them "*titchadesh*"[31]] from head to toe. The sun was shining. The day was bright. The cold was freezing but refreshing. The snow crunched under their feet and shone in splendor, like countless pearls and diamonds sparkling over the fields on both sides of the steel tracks.

Both of them enjoyed walks. Walking a mile or two was their only physical outlet. They did not aspire simply to athletics. When they had to take advice from each other or to deliberate over some difficult matter, they would go out to stroll. They would solve the matter outside the city in accordance with the advice of the *Gemara* (*Berachot* 8). There, there was no wall with ears, and one can be sure that nobody is lurking behind the door or room.

They would stroll frequently even in Ostrów where strolling was considered as a "lighthearted pursuit" unfitting for a lad occupied in Torah. Sometimes, they would even go as far as the forest. There, they would go into seclusion and discuss amongst themselves in Russian to practice that foreign language without fear that their words would fall upon a pious ear.

In any case, their primary aim was a stroll for the sake of a stroll. The other reasons served as a pretext to justify their desire.

Since the snow was so sparkly that it blinded the eyes, and the skies were spiced with their blue, our "mighty ones" said not to go home to see the face of their parents, sisters, and brothers, but rather to set out through the sea of snow and splendor. They left the house of poor paths and went out afar to walk through the frozen snow covering the village streams. A group of policemen and gendarmes were standing next to the tracks, where the path crossed them. When Abba and Zeev approached them, they made way for them to cross with great politeness.

Of course, Abba and Zeev noticed the servants of the Czar, but they did not place any special importance on their gathering beside the railway tracks. Since they let them cross, and also because they treated them with honor, they did not try to figure out what the "satraps" were doing on such a cold day in the field.

They delved deeply into their conversation, which was no idle conversation, but rather a discussion as to how they should conduct their pure Zionist and Hebrew publicity in this new place, without any intermixture of religion. They valued Smorgon as an enlightened city, in which they would be free to continue their work without clashing with the unenlightened zealots. However, they would yet encounter numerous difficulties in their home. They would have to play the "Marrano" game for more time yet, and not in a restricted manner, for the "rabbi's home" forged their steps.

[Page 188]

An hour or two passed. The cold took its toll, penetrating through their coats, which were only a half or a third fit for the winter, reminding them that the time had come to return – that if they were to tarry, evening would fall and searching for the rabbi's house in the darkness of evening in an unfamiliar place would not be among the most pleasant of things.

When they approached the guards, the latter ones did not greet them as they had expected based on their early experience. Rather, they spread around them, surrounded them as if with an iron circle, and arrested them.

The questions rained forth quickly and urgently.

"From where did you come?"

"Where are you going?"

"Who are you?"

The questions were known to those asked. They were taken from *Pirkei Avot*, Chapter 3[4]], but the answers were different, not in accordance with the "writ."

They did not come from a putrid drop, but rather from a very large city, and they were not at all prepared to give an accounting.

The nostrils of the gendarmes were opened wide. They smelled the smell of explosives in the answer. Explosions.

Abba unintentionally removed his right glove. The gendarmes who had grabbed hold of his arm and were leading him as if to a wedding, suddenly let go, and jumped behind him with an acrobatic leap. At first, Abba did not know the meaning of their reaction. Why were the gendarmes so afraid? However, it immediately became clear to him: Since they were coming from Białystok, and Białystok was a den of terrorist anarchists, [they suspected] that he had a bomb in his pocket, and the gendarmes felt "fortunate is the man who is constantly afraid"[51]] and they were suspicious of the anarchists of Białystok.

In short, a comic-tragic situation of perverted girls and twisted explanations played itself out here.

"Why? Just for a stroll?"

"In such bloodcurdling cold? Who do you think you are fooling? We know you and we recognize you".

The truth was what does not make sense, what is not logical. Even if it is perfectly true, nobody would believe it.

What type of a crazy person would go out on a stroll on such a cold day. Furthermore, if they were coming from a far journey, they would go home immediately. Something like this deviates from the norm. The gendarmes had to know that there were two "characters" here, people who do not follow they normal path and do not act in accordance with generally accepted norms. Could they imagine that they caught two "prisoners" who had miraculously escaped from prison, and were celebrating their freedom at this time, both from a spiritual and a clothing perspective. They quickly freed themselves from the foolish Hassidim who regarded their manner of speaking as an unforgiveable capital crime. Now they could speak Hebrew and Russian to their heart's content – without complaint or outcry! They removed their dirty clothes, their *kapotes* and *gartels*, their hats and strange socks. Could the gendarmes have imagined that standing before them are two "Marranos" from the middle ages who were saved from the talons of the inquisition, and were now in Amsterdam in free Holland?

[Page 189]

The following is what took place. Nikolai II, Czar of all the states of Russia, wished to travel on that railway line this day or the next. The two brothers did not read the daily newspaper while they were on their journey, and did not know what was taking place in the country.

They were dedicated to Hebrew and Zionism with heart and soul. They often reviewed the story of Herzl and the lessons therein: A king should not seek the "status of a teacher of young children." Rather, they should obtain land, found a Jewish state, and not attain the "Greek" revolution through vinegar. Jews had to occupy themselves with one thing, and to place their entire interest there. They had to concentrate their willpower and all their thoughts – to liberation, complete redemption, leaving the destruction, freeing themselves from the enslavement to the exile – politically, spiritually, and culturally. To this end, every Jewish person must enlist all strands of their energy, every drop of blood flowing through their veins.

Both were imprisoned.

They swallowed their first morsel of food of "redemption."

This was the reception they received in free Smorgon.

C. Free

How should they inform their parents that they were imprisoned, all because of some misunderstanding? However, this communication was already done by others.

Smorgon was a major Jewish city. The Bund operated there. Other revolutionary activity took place there. Smorgon had a tradition of Sinitski, a known revolutionary who belonged to the Populist Party, which was now in exile in Siberia. There were tanning workshops and factories for the working of hides in Smorgon. The agents went to the edges of Russia with their merchandise. Nevertheless, Smorgon was a typical Jewish town in all its detail. It was a town in which everybody knew everybody else, and every detail of fresh news would immediately spread, go from mouth to mouth on the streets, alleyways, shops and stalls, in the *Beis Midrashes* and *kloizes*.

Nothing would be hidden. It was a given that everything hidden would be revealed, and every secret would be disclosed.

And, a frightening and startling event such as this took place here. In the afternoon, two lads were led through the city under the heavy guard of gendarmes.

The question was immediately asked: Who are they? What did they do? Why were they captured by the government? The Bundists knew all their members, as did the Social Democrats of the city. Therefore, these dandy lads were from the outside. They immediately surmised that they are probably the children of the rabbi who had recently arrived, for they were awaiting their arrival that day.

[Page 190]

When then rabbi found about the matter, he approached the city mediator, Yehuda Folkisz. He was known as a communal who stood in contact with the local and government officials. He used to blind their eyes with "secret gifts," whether from private individuals or the community – as an agent of the holy community.

In short, the conundrum was solved, and the strolling "criminals" were "freed" after spending the night in complicated Smorgon negotiations.

They returned home. The joy was great in their home, but not for long.

The friction lost its bitterness and sharpness. Zionism and Hebrew were not forbidden matters in Smorgon. However, extreme transgressions leading toward complete secularism or uncompromising atheism were not considered acceptable ideas, whether in the house of the rabbi or in the homes of the city notables. And the two sons of the rabbi had become heretics, opponents to the Diaspora way of life. They rejected the holy, well-rooted customs.

They maintained the externals of traditional Judaism. They washed their hands, seemingly recited their blessings, whispered the grace after meals, apparently prayed and put on their *tefillin*, as if forced by a demon.

How could they cast this burden off of their shoulders? This was a fundamental question that did not leave from them daily or given them rest.

D. The Announcers

The status of the "Marranos" was difficult. They wrenched their souls with the fulfilment of religious texts. They were tired of bearing such a heavy burden. However, they did not have the strength to cast off the practical commandments. They did not have the spiritual strength to break away from their father. However, to continue to bear the yoke for an unlimited period – they could not endure. It was impossible that times of wrath, and difficult and desperate battles would not come. They must gird their strength and be prepared to manage without gift and without prayer, but rather with battle[6]] – a battle over a problem more difficult than all civil wars.

What will be will be. From Egypt, from the dark Hassidic town, they extricated themselves from the fortress – even though they did not reach the open area. Nevertheless, they breathed freely. Now, the dual battle – they would connect with their father who would not receive support from the environment, from the Jew surrounding him.

They thought about their situation seriously. They did not give themselves false hopes. They realized that the patience of their father and mother would reach a certain point and stop. No rabbi, even the most enlightened, would make peace with militant, strong atheism. They must take good counsel, and hatch a well-thought-through strategic plan.

During their stroll, they discussed how they should act when they reached home. Therefore, they tarried in the field. They did not want to arrive unprepared and depend on improvisation. They regarded their imprisonment as an iniquitous event perpetrated by gendarmes ensconced in darkness. However, this imprisonment gave them a fateful hint, foreseeing and pointing to their pending luck.

[Page 191]

The first thing was to capture the *Beis Midrash* lads. They would come as if to a public prayer service. If they were already heretics, they would take advantage of their situation, use it to their benefit, and see if there were studying lads who could be "enlightened" and extricated from the pit.

How? They had to use discrete and well thought methods of publicity. They would use Bialik's poem "Hamatmid." It would act as a wedge. This poem would certainly attract the hearts of the *Beis Midrash* students.

They found two excellent students, one was the Genius of Godleib, and the other was younger than him. He was nimble and shrewd, and his name was Warszawski. They did not eat their meals on a rotation basis as did the "patrons," but rather received monthly support from the community such that they could solve their financial problems in a meager fashion and prepare themselves for the day that they would receive rabbinical ordination, and later, fine, gracious brides from wealthy families.

The Genius of Godleib would go backward, tending toward "black melancholy." He did not speak but rather strung his words like tarred strings. He went far with the rabbinical decisors and was on the threshold of receiving rabbinical ordination, and a bride that would come along with support from the table of the father-in-law. Further on, he had bright prospects: if G-d desires and the father-in-law would make the right contacts, he might receive a rabbinical post in a small town the length of a yawn.

Warszawski had bright hair, took joy in life, and had speaking talents of the sort of a "preacher". He was even developed in the art of homey conversation.

The brothers Abba and Zeev became friendly with the two lads. Bialik did a good service for them. He was the iron ram croaking at the spiritual fortress of the ghetto.

The two lads would frequent the house of the rabbi, and also got to know the rabbi's daughters. The Genius of Godleib even attempted to court the elder, Bluma, in a refined fashion, but was not successful. The lads began to study Hebrew diligently, and willingly practice Hebrew speaking.

Warszawski almost became the "assistant" of the brothers in their work of explanation and publicity, in winning over souls for Zionism and Hebrew from amongst the rest of the lads.

The third lad, upon whom they stormed to win him over and bring him under the Zionist-Hebrew canopy was Chaim Yisrael. He was the son of a Hassidic Rebbe. He was G-d fearing, with enthusiastic devotion. He was far from a scholar, but he occupied his bench in the *Beis Midrash* willingly. He was a "patron" in the full sense of the term. He ate his meals on a rotation basis, as was customary. His father "the good Jew" had passed away, and his only son was raised by relatives as an orphan. He was exacting in both the light and difficult commandments. The publicity toward secular Zionism and Hebrew was very difficult for the brothers. Chaim Yisrael was a hard nut that would not be easy to crack. Abba invited him to their house. After much urging, he came shyly, stayed a bit, and it seems that he felt himself in chains. He especially felt himself bound in iron chains in the presence of the older daughters of the rabbi. Through the united efforts of Abba, Zeev, Bluma, and Rachel, he was finally won over from this trap of zealous orthodoxy. He became a secular Hebraist and Zionist. When he received the "new religion" he transferred all his burning zeal and boundless dedication to it.

[Page 192]

The brothers found in him a particularly effective assistant.

There was only one point on which he did not give in. This was the question of Zion. All of their logical and revolutionary reasons about the benefits of Uganda were not effective with him. When he was pushed against the wall in the heat of the debate, he would admit that they were logically correct. However, when they met him the next day, they found that he was again a Zionist for Zion, not only partially, but fully, limb of his limbs and flesh of his flesh. He was connected by his belly to the Holy City of Jerusalem, to Mount Carmel, and to the other holy historical places. Late at night, when he left the rabbi's house after a lengthy discussion, he seemed to be a convinced Ugandist, but through the course of one night, all of his Ugandism flew away, and he returned to his previous beliefs, ready to dedicate his entire soul on the altar of the chosen Land.

Under the influence of the publicity of the brothers, he stopped observing the Sabbath, rejected the festivals, ceased praying, and even lost his belief in G-d – but he did not betray his love of Zion. It was impossible to uproot that love from his heart, literally to the end of his soul. It was as if he was connected to the soil of the Holy Land, and breathed its air. It was the place of his life in the full sense of the term.

E. Demonstrations

This was the second activity of the Gordin brothers in Smorgon.

They gathered the children of the *cheders* and Talmud Torah, and arranged a public gathering every Friday afternoon, where they taught them Hebrew. They organized them into small groups, and directed them to go out together on the Sabbath when the Jews of Smorgon would go out to stroll on the only wooden sidewalk on the main street. Their instructions were to mix in with the crowd and speak Hebrew out loud as a form of demonstration, to give the impression that Hebrew is a living language among the youth of Smorgon.

Chaim Yisrael Lezer was the head of the brothers in this activity. He was the chief commander of these demonstrations. It was as if he was created for that task.

Abba announced that he was prepared to teach Hebrew to all the private Jewish Russian teachers, an even to the *melamdim* [religious teachers of young children] Anyone who hungered [to know] should come and learn. They would receive free lessons.

Everything developed as planned. However, even here in free Smorgon, they began to murmur about the rabbi's sons, who removed the *Beis Midrash* lads from the knowledge of their Creator, and were destroying the remnant with their publicity toward secular Hebrew.

[Page 193]

Several important householders, headed by the banker Brodna, complained that the rabbi's sons were using the *kloiz* for organizing gatherings of *cheder* and Talmud Torah students. They claimed: the *kloiz* is a holy place, and these gatherings are regarding secularism leading to heresy. It is an idol in the sanctuary! Brodna got angry. These gatherings destroy the schoolchildren. Instead of Torah and the observance of the commandments, they are taught to mumble Hebrew in a gentile accent. Such should not be done in the *kloiz* in which he serves as first *gabbai* [trustee] He will stand in the breach. You must purge the evil from your midst[7].

At the urging of the brothers, Chaim Yisrael gathered a group of youths who chased Brodna out of the *kloiz*. He will learn a lesson, and will know that he is not the highest authority, and is not the ruler. The *kloiz* is not his private property.

This daring act was set up as a scandal. They blamed the sons of the rabbi. They claimed that their hand was moved by these brazen ones, for without their incitement, they would not have dared to embarrass this unfortunate "patron" at the head of the community, and chase him out of the *kloiz* in which he worshipped and sustained in all matters. However, they could not prove that Chaim Yisrael was an emissary of the sons of the rabbi for this act of deceit.

The brothers acted innocent and quiet as if they did not know anything about what took place.

Their father the rabbi did not react. It is possible that he was indeed satisfied at the impingement on the honor of this strongman who was haughty, who was sure of his wealth, and who conducted himself with excessive glory. He instilled fear more than he feared sin.

Further, a non-insignificant portion of the householders who were manufacturers and tanners regarded the rabbi's sons as a positive force, as a sort of counterbalance to the social forces leading to frequent strikes in the workshops. They determined that the rabbi's sons were fulfilling an effective role by turning some of the youth away from revolutionary activity. Let blessing fall upon them. They noted the daughters of Rabbi Moshe Gincburg, especially the eldest Liba, who disseminated the Socialist doctrine in Smorgon. She was one of the top students of a man named Sinicki, a Byelorussian, who had been exiled by the authorities to a far-off land for his destructive activities. It was good and fitting that the rabbi's sons disseminated Zionism and Hebrew.

Sinicki had a plot with a fruit orchard and vegetable garden behind the city. He built a spending house in the Swiss architectural form in the garden, which was surrounded by a fence. In an attic of the house, he taught the doctrine of populist Socialism to the progressive sons and daughters of Smorgon, as an addition to the art of conducting strikes.

In comparison to the curse that Liba, the daughter of the Hassidic rabbi, was disseminating in the city, the activity of the sons of the new rabbi was literally a blessing from G-d.

[Page 194]

F. The "Bachelor" Teacher

A rumor spread like good news that a German language teacher named Katriel Shoub was coming to settle in Smorgon. He lived in Switzerland, and concluded his course of studies in Berlin. He knew German and its literature fluently and did not demand a high price for a private lesson.

Abba and Zeev went to their mother to intercede. They knew German more or less, but now an important teacher was coming straight from Berlin. He would shorten the path toward fluency in this language and especially in its literature. They wanted to take two private lessons a week. The lessons would not cost a lot of money.

The mother gave her assent and finance this educational endeavor. The same day, they spoke to Katriel and came to an agreement, eagerly enjoying the first lesson on the spot. This was not a lesson in exact pedagogical-educational terms. He discussed with them the purity of the German language and read sections of the classics to them. Schiller's plays were especially dear to the teacher. He loved to read them. To him, the task of reading was almost at an artistic level. His voice was sweet, and his method of speaking was clear and sharp.

They became friendly with their teacher after several lessons. His father was a *shochet* and *bodek* [ritual slaughterer and checker of slaughtered meat] by profession, from which his name Shoub, the acronym for *shochet* and *bodek*, came. Katriel was a native of a small town. His soul loved philosophy, and he intended to become a philosopher of no less stature than Immanuel Kant. He went to Germany, suffered from want, ate bread with salt, slept on a bench, and toiled in philosophy for many years – and he did not even reach Kant's ankles. Katriel longed for Jews and was overtaken by a Jewish environment. The foreign country became revolting to him. He returned and stayed in Vilna. One of his friends gave him good advice: go to Smorgon, a bustling city filled with practical social and cultural life. There you will be able to give enough private lessons to provide for your livelihood.

He heeded the advice and came to Smorgon.

Katriel was not at all a pedagogue. However, the brothers did not require such. They had already absorbed the complex and pedantic German grammar, and were fluent in it. Their desire was to practice speaking and to enrich their vocabulary some. Katriel helped them with this to the best of his knowledge. They invited him to visit them, and he accepted their invitation willingly. Katriel visited and befriended the rabbi's daughters. They taught him Hebrew.

He had two male students, no more – the brothers Abba and Zeev. However, he had more female students – thirteen in number. On Friday nights, he would gather all his students and give them a reading, as a free bonus. Lovely girls would gather at the fine literary event. They were like a bundle of charming and aromatic flowers. They were lovely Jewish daughters, not sullied by poverty. His students came from the middle class, not the poor families. The brothers Abba and Zeev came to the readings, but did not take this opportunity to get to know the "lovely ones." "In my eyes, they are like white geese." (Tractate *Brachot,* 20).

[Page 195]

They stopped taking the lessons because their father made his usual complaint: I do not have to pay money to turn my sons into gentiles. The few rubles which are spent in vain can bring benefit elsewhere. Let us give them to charity.

Their father did not value teachers in general. According to his understanding, study is connected to desire, and someone who desires learning has no need of a teacher. Diligence and persistence are the best teachers. He did not hold by the adage, "make for yourself a rabbi"[8]]. He changed it to the following: "Make yourself into a rabbi." The best student is the best independent teacher.

He told his children, "You know enough German, and if you find you do not know some word, look it up in the dictionary." There were Russian and German dictionaries in their house. They continued to be invited to Katriel's readings even though they stopped being his students. The teacher's esteem increased as the size of the gathering increased. They were considered to be among his students. They continued their friendly relations, and he continued to be invited to their home often.

Everything went properly. The popularity of the teacher increased, and the number of female students increased. More than one maiden saw him as the fulfillment of her dreams. He was handsome, dark, had an upright posture, was manly, broad shouldered, and built like a butcher. His mannerisms were pleasant, he was exacting in politeness, he was foreign born, stimulating, and exotic.

It was as if Germany had a character in Smorgon. People learned the language for its own sake, for the sake of the teacher.

Then the disaster came suddenly, like lightning on a day with clear skies. He mentioned in his broken Russian.

"My married one is coming". "Married one" instead of saying wife.

The mockers in the city repeated the strange expression "married one is coming". There was no end to the mockery. A few girls groaned silently and bandaged their broken hearts. Woe to their dream that disappeared like smoke.

Bakunin[9]] would say: a revolutionary who gets married immediately loses 50% of his joy of battle. He destroyed half of his revolutionary tendencies.

Since the teacher was married, half of his charm of attraction disappeared. He lost his enchantment. Who needs German in Smorgon? To the extent that it is needed for the matriculation exams, German is available to any student. Is there any "Jew from the land of the Jews" who does not require that language? When Ovarov (Avar-Av in the flowery language of Y.L.G[10]), the Russian education minister, asked the *Rosh Yeshiva* of Volozhin whether he hears German, the *Rosh Yeshiva* responded, "*bevadai*"[11], thinking he was using a proper German word.

Who was Katriel Shoub's wife? She was dark, beautiful, and graceful, with dreamy black eyes. She never interjected a word into their conversations. She spoke Yiddish, and did not know other languages. She did not know how to read or write. Indeed, where did he find her? She was already pregnant.

[Page 196]

Where, how, when? The questions came out all at once.

According to his words, she was a maid at an inn in Vilna in which he was staying. He returned from Germany full of longing, and a charming Jewish girl stood before him. Should she pass her over and not pay attention. He married her. He did not go in the ways of Kant the bachelor, but rather in the ways of Heine who chose Mathilde.

The girls of Smorgon could not forgive Shoub for his crime of non-bachelorhood. However, the anger was even greater when they found out that his "helpmeet" [wife apparently] was lacking elementary education. They saw shame in his decision. He embarrassed all the enlightened girls of the city.

The lessons stopped. He was left without a staff of bread in the true sense of the term, without food for one meal. In the meantime, his wife gave birth to a son. He had no money with which to purchase diapers or a cradle.

He went around with faded clothing. His pants had holes in the backside. Yet, his enthusiastic smile did not leave his face for a moment. His strength of heart and sense of self-worth did not abandon him.

He was an activist in Poalei Zion during the tumultuous years of 1905-1906. He rose high in the party hierarchy, and became its chief spokesman. He reached the pinnacle of leadership.

He left his wife and young son to groan in Smorgon[12].

G. The *Tallit Katan*[13] and the Great Dispute

At this time, life was flowing quietly in the house of the rabbi of the free city of Smorgon. But this was the calm before the storm, that was liable to break sooner or later. Too many contradictions and contrasts existed, and one could not avoid the explosion.

The distance between the children and the parents continued to widen. The kulturkampf that began in the zealously Hassidic Ostrów continued secretly and without an audience, as if an underground warrior. It is true that Smorgon was a modern, Lithuanian city, but one must maintain tradition to an expected degree in the house of a rabbi. It was impossible to push it to the sides definitively, with the push passing in peace.

The *Rebbetzin*, Chaya Esther Sara, found the *tallit katan* of the youngest son, Moshe, by chance, lying under his bed, casted aside like a rejected object. What a disgrace this discovery was for this important piece of Jewish clothing! He was dragged after his older and wiser brothers. On his own, he would not be so brazen as to denigrate this commandment of *tzitzit* [wearing of fringed garments] about which is written “and you shall see, and you shall remember”[14]. She was not lazy, and she made a search that showed her that the *tallit katans* of the older sons were in the same disgraceful situation – that is, under their beds among the rags. A shudder overtook her, and after the shudder – astonishment. She had not imagined that her dear sons had cast off the yoke to that extent. Her soul suffered from much agony, anger, and pain.

[Page 197]

At that moment, the rabbi entered, returning from the *Shacharit* service in the *Beis Midrash*. She told him what she had discovered.

The rabbi immediately garbed himself in anger, called Moshke and began an investigation and inquisition. He gave him two ringing smacks on the cheek in front of all the children. Abba got angry, approached his father calmly, turned his cheek to him, and called out in anger:

"Smack! – and a curse word emanated from his mouth involuntarily.

He was astonished at the sound of the curse word emanating from his mouth. But can anyone return a word that came from one's mouth? This came from the great anger he had toward his father for not joining the Zionist camp. Abba regarded this as "careerism." Abba was convinced that a complete idealist would sacrifice his wife and children on the altar for the ideal of the nation, without any hesitation at all.

The father was shaken to the depths of his soul by the denigration. He was frightened by the spiritual and cultural gap that had opened between his sons and himself, to the point that one was so brazen as to curse him.

What had taken place in his home, in the nest of his family? How had this son fallen so drastically? He transgressed with such coarseness the commandment of honoring one's father , which is one of the Ten Commandments given to Moses on Sinai. How did he sin against his family such that one of them poured such denigrating invective upon him?!

He felt himself wounded, as if a poison arrow had struck his heart. He immersed himself in dark, bleak thoughts.

Rabbi Yehuda Leib was a democrat by nature and character. He did not enjoy being a sole judge, standing on his opinions. He would say, "Even The Holy One Blessed Be He took council with the ministering angels (Tractate *Sanhedrin* 38, *Bereishit Rabba* portion 8) and did not rely on His own knowledge and abilities. How much more so should flesh and blood do so. He had to ask for the advice of his friends and acquaintances. How flimsy is the knowledge of man, that he can err and commit a travesty especially when it affects himself. When one has a dispute with one's friend, one is not permitted to consider his opinion as the final verdict, to which there is no appeal."

Even as a judge, and serving as a judge is one of the tasks of a city rabbi, he would bring in arbitrators when disputants came before him.

Therefore, since he has an issue with his sons, and he knew that they were Hebrew Zionists, he would summon an honorable Zionist from the Mizrachi organization[15] of the city, who is acceptable to his friends. He would place his complaint before him, and he [the arbitrator] would adjudicate between he and his sons who had turned away from the straight path, and would issue his verdict.

The Zionist from Mizrachi in Smorgon was considered to be a proper person with a straight intellect.

The rabbi invited him to serve as a judge. Only Abba was invited to the judgement, as he was the one generally [accused] guilty. The rabbi began to complain about his son to the judge. He turned straight to Abba:

"Have you forgotten the commandment of honoring one's father that graces the Ten Commandments? This is a sublime Divine certificate. Is it possible for Abba to be wanton about this? Does he not talk about living in accordance with set principles, and is not simply a brazen person following an evil heart.

[Page 198]

Since his father laid his stake on the verse "Honor your father and your mother" (Exodus 20, 12; Deuteronomy 5:16), Abba answered him in brief with a strong sense of conviction.

"There are other positive commandments:"

"Honor your son and your daughter."

"Is that so? Is that so? From where do you get that? This is the first time in my life that I hear that commandment. On what basis do you tie that commandment? Who is the authority that issued such a command? And is it possible to arrange relations between parents and their children based on that? Who raises whom? Who sustains whom? Do not the parents sustain their children and educate them, and not the children to their parents"

"If that is so, we are obligated to express gratitude toward you, the parents. Who asked for you to give birth to children? Did you not bring us into being for your own benefit? We are your children forever. And now that we exist and have our own free will and opinions, you want to enslave us, to treat us like indentured servants![16] No and no! The young generation has rights and duties. Its rights are granted by virtue of the new consciousness, through knowledge that a young man is considered a man. A son or daughter is not property such as a part of the private property of the parents. They are not 'objects.' The parents have no ownership of them. They cannot do to them as they wish. They are not clay devoid of will and understanding, and the parents are not the potters to knead them as they wish, lengthening them at their will and shortening them at their will.[17]"

Abba began to discuss impromptu the theory of the battle of generations in the history of humankind. He cited a statement of the sages (Tractate *Kiddushin*, 31): When G-d said (Exodus 20), "I am... And there will be [no other]", the nations of the world said: He is expounding for His own honor. When He said, "Honor your father and your mother," they retracted and admitted to the first commandments." A covenant was struck between the Father in Heaven and the earthly father. They unite to oppress their children. The parents are obligated to respect their sons and daughter no less than the sons and daughters are obligated to respect their parents.

The father and judge allowed Abba to develop his ideas. They did not interrupt him with even one comment or auxiliary statement. When he finished, his father said in anger and with an anguished heart.

"Empty ideas, nonsensical words. They have no dawn. They will lead to the loss of the human race."

His father thought a great deal about the ideas printed and disseminated among the youth during the new time that fulfilled the adage, "The young will act arrogantly toward the elderly, and [similarly], the downtrodden to the honorable." However, he comforted himself with the though that just as they [the new ideas] came through the wind, a wind of breaches, they will pass and disappear when another wind comes by.

[Page 199]

H. The Rabbi and the Beggars

Rabbi Yehuda Leib had a good disposition. His world stood on two things, on Torah and on good deeds – meaning charity, donations to the poor, and gifts to the destitute.

Thus was his daily routine.

He went to worship in the *Beis Midrash*, not overly early. He was not among those who got up early, but rather among those who stayed up late. He often fulfilled the verse, “Arise, cry out at night, at the beginning of the watches” (Lamentations 2:19). He continued his studies until after midnight. He remembered well the words of the sages: “By day, the L-rd will command His lovingkindness, and in the night His song shall be with me, even a prayer to the G-d of my life.”[18] Everyone who occupies himself with Torah at night, G-d will place a strand of grace upon him during the day, as it says (Psalms 42): By day, the L-rd will command his lovingkindness. Why does G-d command His Lovingkindness? Because at night, His song is with him. (Tractate *Chagiga*, 12).

He was among the diligent ones. He studied day and night. He did not know how to sit idle. His pride was his “ledger.” He had all his times in his hands. He knew what he did at every hour in the day. He did not even waste one minute. He counted his minutes literally as a person counts his money, hiding it and guarding it from thieves. His mouth never desisted from learning. His thoughts were all directed to words of Torah or novel Torah ideas that he wrote down. All the books in his many-volume library were covered with notes in the margins. He could not bear an idle conversation. He repeated the [Talmudic] statement (Tractate *Yoma* 19): “Rabba says: someone who carries on an idle conversation violates a positive commandment, for it says (Deuteronomy 6): 'And you shall speak about them' and not about idle matters. Rav Acha the son of Yaakov said, He violates a negative commandment, as it says (Kohelet 1), 'All things toil to weariness; man cannot utter it.'[19]”

A person is obligated to speak in matters of Torah and Widsom, and even in matters of literature, which is in the category of *Agadata* [Talmudic lore], even about the affairs of the world, practical matters. A person must fulfil the verse “And you shall toil in it day and night” (Joshua 1:8). This is how explained that verse, not deviating from its simple meaning: A person is obligated to toil in the Torah of G-d day and night – in this Torah of which only a small portion is written with letters. The rest of the portions are written by the stars in their heavenly paths, and by the rivers, streams, lakes , springs, oceans, mountains, valleys, human beings, beasts of the field, winged birds, insects, crawling creatures and bugs. The entire Torah is identified with practicality, reality, and creation. “Fortunate is man who occupies himself with Torah day and night, for all these are phenomena and ways of “The words of the Living G-d" (Tractate *Eruvin* 13). G-d adds up in *gematria* to Nature[20], for the value of each of those words adds up to 86.

In general, he did not occupy himself with *gematria*. He did not value them, other than this *gematria* that he held in esteem.

He did not elongate his prayers.

[Page 200]

He returned from the *Beis Midrash*, and entered the "court of law." He placed his cane in the corner, and put down his *tallis* and *tefillin* bag.

At this point, the room was filled to the brim with beggars of all types. Some were equipped with "documents" from the rabbis of their cities, legitimate or forged. The rabbi called these documents "collection documents" with light mockery.

He came to the first one, who was sitting next to the door. He asked him, half seriously and half in jest:

"Do you have a document?"

The person showed him the "document" in which it was written that he was "burned" or was collecting for a poor bride – i.e. for his daughter who had come of age.

The rabbi pretended to read the document. In truth, he was glancing at the signature below. He asked, with tone half in jest:

"And how much, dear Jew, do I owe you?"

He received whatever he asked for. The small sums varied between ten and twenty coins. They were never greater than twenty, and never smaller than ten.

This is how he went from one to the next. When he finished his daily "circuit", he called out with satisfaction: "I paid everyone, I do not owe anything to anyone."

The courtroom emptied.

Only then did he enter the dining room to eat his morning meal.

I. Farewell

Abba was very vexed from the incident that impinged on the honor of his father, whom he appreciated and respected. He was also angry at him and condemned him for not affiliating with Mizrachi, as Rabbi Reines[21] had done, and for not dedicating his oratory and preaching skill to this ideal. He was a great orator, one of the few among the rabbis of his generation. Even though he appreciated and valued his talents, the tension grew due to the fact that he remained outside of the camp fighting for Zionism. The relationship between Abba and his father was ambivalent: significant reverence, but significant denigration that stemmed from the essence of the reverence, for one was dependent on the other. He regarded his father as sinning in defection, in escaping from the battle. He could not forgive him for standing afar when every Jewish person was obligated to enlist and come to the service of the army fighting for the redemption of their nation – for not passing by this historical opportunity. If not now, when?

Indeed, he denigrated the honor of his father in a coarse manner. However, was this not at a time of anger, when people do not control their speech? He judged himself favorably.

[Page 201]

Father had smacked his young son on the cheek, who did not bear the full responsibility for his actions and omissions due to his youth. He followed after his brothers who were years older than he was. Abba saw himself as dutybound to come to his aid, to help his weak brother. This has two meanings – both ideological and philosophically. His holy duty was to stand at his side during his time of difficulty, when he was attacked and punished for no transgression. The assistance and protection took on the form of exposing his cheek to the smacker and calling out: I am guilty. Smack me! I am responsible for him.

Is it possible to solve problems of convincing, of fundamental ideological difference, by smacking cheeks?! This was not a case of wantonness, of lack of restraint, breaking boundaries, or casting off the yoke. This was a clear case of an ideological dispute, a clash of outlooks, a clear desire to be consistent, to behave stringently as an enlightened person, as a Jew fighting for political and cultural liberation, of the new Jew who places his Judaism on pure nationalism as opposed to religiosity that had lost its luster -- i.e. behaving in accordance with specific principles without deviating right or left, principles of Hebrew historiography built on a mountain of arcane customs. Rather than bringing proofs to contradict their viewpoints, his father resorted to a slap on the cheek. Is this the path?! Had his father been a dark zealot, immersed in pious darkness, who does not know a thing about what was going on around him, about what was taking place in Jewish life, who does not know the essence of the streams and aspirations storming through the Jewish street, and not only of the Jews, Abba would not have been so angry. He would have been able to forgive him, claiming that he does not know in what era he is living. However, his father the rabbi had secular knowledge, was expert in philosophical problems, and was comfortable with Russian and German literature. How could he react in such a non-cultural way to the deeds of his sons, who had made it clear that they would not obey him, and would not accept the authority of old, Diaspora legalism, ways of life that were forged in the stifling atmosphere of the ghettos. "If you live in darkness and say dark things," they did dark deeds.

No, Abba could not forgive his enlightened father. However, he could not utter such denigrating statements, even though his father had not transgressed the current custom in the most severe fashion. However, Abba had crossed a threshold and transgressed all bounds of politeness. He regretted and felt pangs of conscience. But to go to his father and beg forgiveness – certainly not! His father had to beg forgiveness from him. They both sinned against each other. Since matters had reached this point, it was evident that they could not live under one roof. They must separate.

Abba would leave his father's house.

Abba and Zeev reached this decision during a long stroll and an exhaustive deliberation.

Zeev traveled to Warsaw. Abba prepared to travel to Dvinsk [Daugavpils].

Why did he choose Dvinsk, a city that he knew only by name and was hard to find on the map? This is the answer.

[Page 202]

The Rebbetzin felt guilty to some degree for the dispute taking place at home. She did not grasp at that time the depth and breadth of the chasm that opened between the two generations. She could not stand idly by this irreparable schism, for then she would silently accept the revelation she discovered regarding the *tallit katan*. She sought peace under all conditions and circumstances. Peace is greater than religious truth, and she pushed aside most of the practical commandments. Her sons had joined a bad crowd. This was a punishment from Heaven. The hand of the wanton times was involved in this. However, they are dear children, diligent, sitting and studying day and night. Secular studies are also not for naught. They are also involved in communal affairs, issues of the oppressed, downtrodden people, in accordance with their understanding. They are strange children, not concerned with their own good. They are complete wicked people, while simultaneously behaving like complete righteous people, exacting in their observance of "their commandments." "This is crooked as a spade" but their bent crookedness had a unique depth. They were prepared to give their lives for "their sins" without any benefit to themselves. They were sinners "for a righteous cause." They cast off the Yoke of Heaven to place a much more difficult yoke on their necks. Praying, putting on *tefillin*, reciting the Grace after Meals were considered as violations of negative commandments just as Orthodox people are diligent at keeping the laws of the Code of Jewish Law. They were curiosities, and their behavior was strange. All of their deeds were for the sake of heaven, but their heaven was different. They lived in accordance with the Code of Jewish Law[22], but their table was different. What is forbidden to us is permitted to them; and what is permitted to us they consider strictly forbidden.

Her heart, the heart of a mother, was agonized that they were forced to part. Her heart oozed blood. What could she do for her home? Could she try to find a compromise between the two sides? To mend the schisms? To promote peace amongst the disputants? How could she do this when the two sides were prepared to give up their lives[23] so as not to transgress? They would not give in. They were stubborn. She had great influence over her husband. He loved her. Through the force of love, she could lead him to compromise, but her sons would not listen to her. They were zealous for their beliefs more than their father. They would let themselves be killed over a shoe strap. They would not compromise on the jot of a '*yod*'[24] of their doctrine that was given by Herzl and Ben Yehuda[25].

She was tormented by the tortures of hell. Up until now, she was happy with motherhood. Her sons did not abandon her or leave. Other sons went out to places of Torah and traveled to study in Yeshivas. To her sons, the Yeshiva took place at home. They studied Torah from their father.

However, if it was decreed that they must part, and it cannot be retracted, let the parting be for a brief period. She recommended the city of Dvinsk to Abba since there are relatives there, who would receive him with open arms.

That is how it was. Abba left to Dvinsk. To the untrained eye, the parting was cold and tense. However, how painful and agonizing it was, it also tore at the strands of the heart!

Abba left home full of suitcases laden with a bounty of bedding, clothing, and shoes.

Yet, what was his spiritual luggage?

[Page 203]

He knew Hebrew well, and was expert in all areas of old and new literature. He knew Russian and German.

He would not lose his way. He would teach for pay, and busy himself with Hebrew and Zionist publicity, as well as volunteer work. I did not foresee that the effort would be in vain.

J. Leaving and Returning

He went to Dvinsk. He passed through Krâslava. He lived in Vilkomir, where he met elders who recalled Lilienblum, his "sin of his youth."

He took notice of the life of the Jews with which he came in contact in his role as a private Hebrew teacher.

The old way of life existed with the force of faith, despite the cracks in the walls. The new life had not yet begun to sprout. The young, new Jews who based the existence of the nation on three principles: the nation, the Hebrew language, and bustle, was not found even among faithful seekers.

However, he was certain that this "new Jew" would come. They would sprout from the ground. It was a necessity of the historical times. He, Abba, did not even take one rearward pace. He saw the assimilation taking effect on the youth both in the big cities and small towns. He now took on a new form –

a revolutionary. It was clear to him that it was bound to fail in Russia as it had failed in the Western countries. For is not assimilation a very ancient concept. "These are idol worshippers and those are idol worshipers." "That which comes to your spirit, that you say that we will be like the gentiles, will not be." The end course of assimilation is deportation from the country or annihilation by a nation in which it seems that the Jews are invading and setting up roots within their culture. Jews have tried this means of assimilation many times as a solution to the question of their oppression, and met with bitter disappointment. This time as well, bitter disappointment awaits.

The new life contains a form of grafting of the body and the soul of the nation of the People of Israel. This grafting that was effected by the Talmud and its commentaries, the various Codes of Jewish Law until the latter halachic decisors, was good for its time. It saved the nation from physical and cultural annihilation. However, the gain is outweighed by the loss, for it barely saved our nation from death. With a way of life that has no freedom of thought, no constant progress, but rather frozen tradition, is like the preservation of old wine that turns to vinegar over the years in worn out and broken vessels – there is no compromise no matter what. The "young Jew" – that is Abba as one of its representatives – will not compromise. The command of the historical times of the Nation of Israel is the creation of new forms, and the forging of new content into those forms. The Nation of Israel stands at the threshold of renaissance. It will renew its youth as an eagle. Out with all the rust, all the rot and mold that has collected during the long exile.

[Page 204]

He was imprisoned in Vilkomir. He participated in storming the jail and freed political prisoners.

He was freed before Passover, the Festival of Freedom. He returned home to Smorgon calmed, but not appeased and not tending toward compromise.

Passover passed quickly, as if one night chased the next, and one night the next.

Letters came to him from Vilkomir, asking him to return. They prepared for him lessons in the homes of the honorable people of the town. They even obtained for him living quarters in the bosom of a family. In short, they were waiting for him...impatiently.

Then the following took place:

His father called him to his room, and engaged him in a lengthy conversation. He detailed Abba's weak point. His father knew well that the strongest desire of his sons was to learn, and therefore, it would be good for he, Abba, to remain. Nobody would disturb him. He would be able to immerse himself in his studies. Why should he leave the home and suffer in a strange place, wasting his precious time giving classes to dull children? He should concern himself with wasting days. It is forbidden to do such a thing.

The mother knew of the letters that were received from Vilkomir, and she was concerned about two things a) that he might be caught by a girl who was not appropriate for him. b) that he might "intermix with strange things," be captured by the government, and deported to Siberia.

His father claimed, while they were all sitting at the table eating lunch, that Abba and Zeev could spend their entire time at study. That is how the sons of Rabbi Meisels of Łódź spend their time. With respect to Hebrew and Zionism, he apparently lowered the thermometer by a few degrees. If they dedicate all their time to acquire scientific knowledge, he would have no opinion about the painful issue of faithfulness to the Jewish religion. They could act in accordance with their best judgment with respect to Biblical and rabbinical laws. Even if it is said of them that they observe the commandments, how much time does such observance take? Ten minutes to put on *tefillin*. A few minutes to read the *Shema*. A few minutes to recite *Pesukei Dezimra* [the early part of the *Shacharit* service], and *Shmone Esrei* – and it is finished. Study is more important than prayer. He himself is not counted among the pilgrims, he does not abandon eternal life and occupy himself with temporal life.

Abba and Zeev remained.

Abba realized that he would waste time from learning in Vilkomir. This is a sin at any age, and at his age, this is a loss.

Abba and Zeev set times to study mathematics, geometry, and algebra. They also dealt with literary matters that soften the heart, and are the brokers of lust.

Abba was a fan of Spencer. He read his book "Education" over again in Russian translation. He judged: since he was an autodidact, having studied without a teacher or guide, he now can be a teacher and student in one person, and he must know how to teach himself, to invent pedagogy and become acquainted didactics if he wishes to succeed and see benefit from his studies.

[Page 205]

K. The *Rebbetzin* Prepares Provisions for Her Journey

It was 1907. The Rebbetzin was busy all the days of the weeks. She was occupied in charitable pursuits, especially in giving of charity in a discreet fashion. She did not collect for any philanthropic organization. Everything that she did was through her own initiative. She gave donations with an open hand, even beyond her financial ability. She had "materialistic" intentions and possibilities, so to speak.

She sat and thought about her situation: She had no merit of ancestors. However, the merit of her husband was greater than the world. But what could she derive, in actuality, from this merit? That is to say: to be his footstool in the Garden of Eden – that footstool would be below her honor and self-worth. She was proud to live in the World To Come on the "account of the wealthy person" her husband, and to merit crumbs from his table, to grab leftovers from the food served to him. She wanted her own account and her own merit. The merit of children? Behold, see what befell her fate. She knew their low level. They had turned away from the straight path, and apparently were not thinking of returning. She hoped that she would not bear their sins, "Fathers do not die for their sons,"[26] and that includes mothers. Was she guilty at all? Even though she was a woman and a Jewish *Rebbetzin*, the education of her children was fully in the hands of their father and under his supervision. How could she dare to mix in, even with a slight hint or a minor point, in a matter that is completely the monopoly of men? He taught them Torah. He tested them. They had been very diligent students and G-d fearing. All the people of the town were blessed by them when they were 13 years old. There were women in Ostrów who came to them and requested a blessing as if they were "child" Hassidim. The disaster came later. Their heart turned inside of them. It was as if a foolish spirit overtook them; Heaven save us.

And what type of a home does she have? From one side, her husband, the genius and *Tzadik*, a pillar of the world. From the other hand – there was a village full of gentiles. A short time ago, her mother came to visit her. Chiena Dreiza was astonished at the behavior in the home of her daughter and son-in-law. They get up in the morning, wash quickly, and immediately, without delay, sit down to eat breakfast: buns, milk, sour cream, butter, cocoa, eggs. Has such a thing been heard and seen? She was astonished. Is this how they conduct themselves in the home of the rabbi? Even an impure uncircumcised one crosses himself before sitting down to eat. She managed to reassure her mother with great difficulty. She pleaded with her to stop complaining, so that they will not enter again into a dispute. Her children were victims of the times that had gone off their path. She was concerned for their well-being, lest they become intermixed in affairs of the state, be arrested, and sentenced to harsh labor.

They saved the older one from army service. The solution cost 300 silver rubles. How did this happen? He was saved by an "angel" – that is, a person with a blemish sent in his stead. He received a white certificate. Everything was set in place by the "elder" from Sol, the sole official who remained in the entire Vilna district. He was a drunkard, but he appreciated rabbis. The matter of the angel was straightforward and practical. They exchange the pictures that come with a signature, tied in a crimson thread. They register in some remote corner where they do not recognize the candidate for draft. The angel comes and stands in his place and name. Since he is unfit, they reject him. The rest is done by the registrar. He exchanges the photograph, an everything falls into place. Of course, he received a fee for his extra efforts. The angel serves this role several times, year after year – however each time in a different place and under a different name. "Being an angel" is his trade, the source of his livelihood. He is not in danger. He is sure that he will be freed, for he is injured in all his limbs.

[Page 206]

This is the way they saved Jews from the hands of "Ivan." But one can fall into the hands of Esau in other ways. Several mothers were bereaved of their children who were sent to the gallows, and several wept for their sons and daughter who were locked in jail or deported to a far-off land.

She thanks G-d seven times a day for instilling a love of study into her children, so they do not have free time for any other matters.

However, how can she arrange her life in the World To Come and the Garden of Eden? Only one means remained to her, and that is charity, which saves from death, and leads to eternal life and a share in the World To Come. But how meager are her possibilities. Her heart was as open as the entrance to a hall to anyone oppressed and suffering, but her hand did not have the means. She was not a wealthy woman. She limited her food and clothing. She did not allow herself any external luxury. Everything that she saved from her stomach and wardrobe was distributed to poor men and women – such as fish for the Sabbath, to others, challas for the two Sabbath loaves. She knew the hidden needy people who were wasting away in their poverty and whose suffering was not public. They thought that their poverty was embarrassing. She gave the names and places of residence of the "recipients" to the fish seller and the butcher, and ordered them to keep it a guarded secret. They would send their portions to them every Sabbath eve, and not tell them who the donor and benefactor was.

However, all this was not enough. The small handful did not satisfy her appetite for giving. The Holy One Blessed Be He did not give her wealth, for had He done so, she would have provided sustenance for all the poor people of the area, all the orphans and widows. However G-d kept wealth and poverty from her. She stood in between those two economic extremes. Is there any wealthy rabbi with an abundance of property? Is the source of his livelihood not something that can be counted and measured, and there is no blessing on something that can be counted or measured? They live on a set salary.

Therefore, what could she do? She dedicated herself to charity. She donated with all her energy. She cared for the sick. There was no shortage of sick people during the winter season. Typhus and pneumonia epidemics spread during all the cold months, increasing the agony in the houses of the poor and on the narrow alleyways filled with trash.

She would leave her house early in the morning and return at dark. She did not concern herself with communicable diseases. She was an emissary for a good deed, and emissaries for good deeds are not injured. They are protected. If, Heaven forbid, sin takes its toll and she contracts a disease, she would accept her affliction with love. This is a part of the good deed, to sacrifice her single soul to save the souls of many – this was her duty.

[Page 207]

The *Rebbetzin's* mindset was not directed toward running and sustaining her household. In the city, there were so many houses of poverty and want, with forlorn families with nobody to concern themselves with them or to rectify their economic disgrace. Could she turn her eyes and thoughts from these many poor wretches and place her eyes on the small number of members of her household. The latter, thank G-d, were not short anything. Did they eat their bread in a meager fashion? Their table was full of all good. And the former were hungry for bread, Heaven save us, freezing from cold in the winter. They had no firewood. They slept on doleful beds, and they had nobody to change their bed during their illness. They had no money to pay for a doctor, and they had nothing with which to purchase medicine from the pharmacy. They came first. She preferred them to the members of her household. She did not have to worry after herself. The holy community concerned themselves with them.

L. The *Rebbetzin* Died

The Rebbetzin got sick. She lay on her bed for a few days. Her fever worsened. Two doctors tended to her – one Jewish and the other gentile. However, her situation worsened. Their diagnosis was incorrect. They thought it was pneumonia, but she was suffering from typhoid fever.

Her illness was serious. Her daughters and sons guarded her bed day and night. They divided up their days. Each of them stood guard at their designated turn.

Dr. Szabat from Vilna was summoned by telegram. He came. He gave the correct diagnosis, but he could not help. He was too late. He remained at the sickbed all night.

To our surprise, father noticed that her hair whitened overnight. That means that she used to die her hair. The doctor conducted himself strangely. He specifically spoke Russian. He did not even utter one Yiddish expression. Apparently, he was concerned lest his prestige as a doctor be lessened. He even attempted to speak Russian to the sick woman, even though he knew he was in the house of the rabbi, and was tending to the *Rebbetzin*. However, there was not much to talk about with her...

He returned early in the morning. He received 25 silver rubles for his visit.

Mother was dying. All the members of the household stood around her bed. These were her last moments on earth. It seemed as if she wished to part from her children and husband, and to deliver a testament to her household, but she could not express her will even with a small gesture or movement. This was the concluding moment of her life which was one large prayer, "A prayer of the afflicted when he grows weak"[27] Perhaps it was her will to give over to us the names of those who were in need... to concern ourselves with them and ask us to provide what is lacking on Sabbaths and festivals. However, she was prevented from doing this.

At the time of the departure of her soul Father gave a brief speech.

"She is dying because of you, for the sins of her sons and daughters. Now the time has come for you to return from your evil ways, to return to the G-d of Abraham, Isaac, and Jacob, to return to the *Beis Midrash*, to return to the *Gemara* and the observance of commandments. Promise that from this day onward, you will go in the way of G-d, and cleave to his commandments – perhaps He will have mercy. Even when a sword is resting on the neck, there is still hope. Repent, and save your mother.

[Page 208]

Abba was angry. He blamed his father for desecrating the holiness of the movement at which life and death meet and separate. On the other hand, he was astonished to see how great his father's dedication was to the sanctity of G-d and traditional faith, such that nothing can stand between it. Now he realized the greatness of the sacrifice that father dedicated on the altar of patience, as he saw their deeds and omissions of his sons, as he saw them trampling with their heels on his holy matters. And Abba held himself back, as if he was closing his eyes and being silent, controlling himself. He, his father, a servant of G-d, was falling to the depths of hell with his eyes on the one hand and ascending to the heights of heaven on the other. He surpassed all transient human bounds that have no actual existence, as he reached himself to the peak of godliness, to the definitive feeling of eternity, that he was above all physical, reality restricted by time and place. He, Abba, swore in his heart to follow his father in his traditions and ideals. No barricade could block the path as he forges his way. Such coarse, wild zealousness, and refined nobility – who merits such!

As they were about to be orphaned, they were full of sorrow, grief, and mourning, with the sense of impending disaster; they were feeling helpless, as they were standing face to face with the most terrible enigma, that breaks their body and souls with crisis – the death of a mother – at such a time he attacks them, that is he wishes to save them. He wants to exact from them a promise that they would return to their Father in Heaven, the Merciful Father, whose children they and their mother are, to whom the change and progress of generation is meaningless.

Mother died at the end of 1907. She was 48 years old when she breathed out her pure soul.

All the people of Smorgon accompanied her to her final rest. A crowd of widows and orphan followed her bier. They wailed and cried bitterly for their loss, the loss of their mother and patron.

Zeev, Abba and Moshe recited *Kaddish* next to the grave. Father restrained himself with all his strength from bursting out crying. No! He would not shed even one tear. He would not sob before the funeral crowd. His soul would weep and tremble secretly, but he would control his eyes. He stifled his tears.

The children sat *Shiva*. They read the book of Job. A prayer quorum gathered in the rabbi's home throughout the seven days. The three sons recited *Kaddish* three times a day.

"The time of human tribulation is a fitting time for one's G-d." Father now became a strongman. He wanted to utilize the confusion of his children, the sorrow of their souls. He went on the offensive against all their views. An opportunity came his way, and he would not waste it. If not now, when? His preaching increased. He demanded, he commanded, and he did not let up. They would sit *Shiva* in accordance with law and custom. They would rend their garments. Now they had to learn chapters of *Mishnah* for the elevation of the soul of their righteous mother who was taken prematurely. Their father grabbed a great deal. The recitation of *Kaddish*. Public prayer three times a day in the *Beis Midrash* was a small thing. This was the beginning, the first steps on the path to repentance. They must return to G-d and the Code of Jewish Law, to traditional Jewish life.

[Page 209]

Abba might have given in. His intention was to continue reciting *Kaddish,* and fulfil the other maximal demands of Father, and to turn a deaf ear. However, Zeev rebelled. He claimed, since their father is not satisfied with their concessions, he does not grasp the magnitude of their sacrifice, and how much spiritual health and life these concessions cost them. He demands more and more: give, give, and he is [still] not satisfied. They must retract from them, return to following their principles, and vow to refrain from Diaspora customs. Their father must not think that they are like clay in the hands of the potter, that their tragedy could softened them, and that he could knead and chew them to his will, as if their spine was broken by their grief and agony. The hammer of tribulation smashes class and forges iron.

Abba agreed that Zeev was correct.

The period of concessions ended.

When their mother died, the children lost their father as well – Abba said. At that moment, they decided to leave the home, but not the city of Smorgon.

Translator's Footnotes

1. A place for communal Jewish prayer
2. Pronouncing Hebrew in the Sephardic style was considered a divergence from eastern European Ashkenazic tradition and was considered a clear sign of Zionist affiliation.
3. A good wish for someone wearing new clothes or attaining new property.
4. See *Pirkei Avot* 3:2.
5. Proverbs 28:14
6. A reference to the rabbinical commentary that Jacob approached his meeting with Esau though gifts, prayer, and a preparation for war. See Rashi's comment on Genesis 33:9.
7. Deuteronomy 17:7
8. *Pirkei Avot* 1:6
9. See https://en.wikipedia.org/wiki/Mikhail_Bakunin

10. Yehuda Leib Gordon

11. "Of course" in Hebrew.

12. Likely due to Katriel's frequent travel, the wife and daughter groaned while he was away.

13. A fringed undergarment typically worn under the shirt, in keeping with the Biblical commandment.

14. Numbers 15:39.

15. Mizrachi is the Orthodox branch of Zionism, otherwise known as Religious Zionism.

16. Referring to the Hebrew slave whose ear is pierced if he does not want to leave his master after six years.

17. This sentence is a paraphrasing of the Ki Hinei Kachomer hymn of Yom Kippur eve. See https://www.chabad.org/multimedia/media_cdo/aid/140751/jewish/Ki-Hinei-Kachomer.htm

18. Psalms 42:9. Translation from Mechon Mamre: https://www.mechon-mamre.org/p/pt/pt2642.htm

19. Translation from Mechon Mamre (verse 8): https://www.mechon-mamre.org/p/pt/pt3101.htm

20. *Gematria* is an exegetical system of assigning numbers to each letter of the Hebrew alphabet, and deriving equivalencies. See https://en.wikipedia.org/wiki/Gematria

21. See https://en.wikipedia.org/wiki/Yitzchak_Yaacov_Reines

22. In Hebrew, the Code of Jewish Law is known as *Shulchan Aruch*, literally The Set Table.

23. So to speak.

24. The smallest part of the smallest letter.

25. Eliezer Ben-Yehuda, the force behind the revival of the Hebrew language. See https://en.wikipedia.org/wiki/Eliezer_Ben-Yehuda

26. Deuteronomy 24:6.

27. Psalms 102:1

Our works that were published in Smorgon

Translated by Jerrold Landau

A. A Reproduction [i.e., exact copy]

In 1908, we opened an independent school in Smorgon called Ivriya. A year later, we founded a book publishing house in Smorgon. The first fruits of our pens were published in 1909. The first booklet published in Smorgon was called "Theories of Material and Relative Naturalism." We published it in Russian. The primary idea of this relatively small composition, which was 20 pages in total, is brought down with great clarity, and served as the laying of the cornerstone of our pedagogic methodology, which is as follows:

> "In order to teach a child, one must first create an appropriate environment and to weave relationships into that environment. These relationships will awaken the recognition of the necessity of the studies to the student. It is not sufficient to teach in a psychological manner, a principle that Pestalozzi noted (1746-1827). It is necessary to teach in a sociological manner, that is, to consider the relationships between the student and the environment, as well as the relationships that are formed between the teacher and student and the students with each other. For example, when arithmetic is taught, one should set up, so to speak, a marketplace, open a store, and create an environment of commerce – a place in which it would be possible to utilize the knowledge gained in a practical manner, just as they developed in cultural history. The study of writing is the same. There must be some functional difference, for writing is used in the natural cultural environment as a means of interpersonal communication toward overcoming the physical distance in which the writers are located.

[Page 210]

> In this environment, the need for the study of writing stood out. In other words, one has to conduct the work in the environment quietly and silently, and use writing in place of speech in this environment as a means of communication between the teacher and students. One must maintain a postal system, so to speak. In short, one cannot teach in a vacuum. The necessity for studying the subject matter must come to

> fruition through a request felt by the student. The school must turn in to a miniature environment. *
>
> Foreign language must be taught by giving commands. The teacher commands, and the student obeys and fulfills the commands. In short, they suffice themselves with the understanding of the meaning of the illustrative words, and there is no demand for speaking in advance, forced by the teacher into the mouth of the student.
>
> The study of reading: One must not use the clever German method of dissecting the sounds and blending them into words. Rather, one should use an orderly foundation and a printing press. The children organize sentences, words, and pronunciation, and only after that, letters and punctuation. After some time – short or long depending on the shortness or length of time it takes for the individual student to comprehend – the student will grasp those sounds, that is the letters, as they repeat themselves over and over in various words. Thus, the students will develop their intellectual capabilities on the foundation of reading."

At the end of that year, 1909, our work on the teaching methodology of reading and writing was published in Russian, called "The Methodology of Imitation – Understanding."

B. Jewish Pedagogy

That same year, we published a booklet in Hebrew called "An Open Letter on Sources of Nationalistic Education." In that booklet, we developed the idea based on the foundation of "a theatrical kindergarten," with education based on commands rather than nouns, as is practiced in accordance with the "Hebrew in Hebrew"[1]. Therefore, we come to a performance of children and not a story, as is customary in schools. We must always be occupied with actions and activities.

We will bring a few sections from this booklet.

> "Until Pestalozzi came, the bent ear (mechanical method) prevailed. Pestalozzi came and promoted the idea of investigation (the observation theory). Fröbel came and put a brake on the absolutism of studying the

constitution of the limbs[2] (work and play). Now, republicanism of the limbs (work and play) came to the fore. The child is not full of eyes like the angel of death. The child has eyes that see, ears that hear, hands to work, feet to run, and a palate to taste, etc. Natural learning must be from the perspective of "all my limbs speak"[3]. The person benefits from the world with all his 248 limbs and 365 sinews[4]. The person does not look, but rather adapts. Humanity does not develop other than through the means of adaptation. Adaptation implies two things: to the physical surroundings as well as to the social surroundings. Therefore, we juxtapose: Just as humanity does not [advance] solely by observing but by adaptation – so too is education not solely by observing, but rather by adaptation. This is the pedagogy of its right hand limping on its thigh, with its father, Pestalozzi, the founder of observation, at a time when it needed to base itself on adaptation--adaptation to the physical surroundings. Pestalozzi based it on psychology at a time that it should have been based on sociology, on adaption to the social surroundings. Furthermore, adaptation to the physical surroundings is actualized by man in a social fashion. The pedagogy of its right hand looks upon man as upon a physical being. James (1842-1910)[5] advises the teacher to look upon education as "an associative mechanism" – woe to that pedagogy that forgets that man is also a social creature, and that education is in particular a social vision.

[Page 211]

Furthermore, as we researched the roots of Fröbel's kindergarten[6], we found one important principle missing. It has "work," it has games, but it does not have "life." It is lacking the drama of the children, the lens through which the children's lives peer upon all influences, in all their variety and colors, in all their light and shadows. We interpret that in a place where story is effective, drama should be effective, for drama is not like story. Drama is better than a story in content, feelings, movement, independent work, and educational-moral influence. Aside from this, drama should be nothing other than a game, and [why] should drama lose out because it is drama? Why is its place missing in the games of the kindergarten? Go and see how secondary this matter is! Among the games of the children, "art games" take a very important place. Art games are a ladder rooted in the ground, the head of which reaches heavenward[7]. Its bottom rung is playing with dolls; its top rung is Shakespearean drama. What is the game of kings, shopkeepers, teachers, childbearing women, the funeral, and more, if it is not drama on a hylic foundation? Are these games not the shadows of dawn of the human genius, when the sun at its height shines with its "material?" The place of stories should indeed be taken over by drama. The kindergarten will in the future become the theatrical kindergarten.

German pedagogy has eaten sour grapes, and the teeth of us Hebrew teachers are set on edge![8]. Has the time not come for the teacher to remove the German yoke from his neck? What do we have to do with German pedagogy that it shall rule over us?

But what? The Asian lion cub has become the European monkey!

Hebrew teachers! Remove the foreign idols from your midst! Abandon the imitation, the aping! Sanctify yourselves, purify yourselves – and create! The Hebrew genius will be your help."

C. Cosmism

That same year, in 1908, our Yiddish booklet titled "A Book to the Diaspora" was published.

The first chapter of the booklet deals with the despair that enveloped the Jewish street and which was expressed by the "Last Word" of Ch. N. Bialik.

> "From where did this black, dark despair sprout? From what foul wellspring does it draw is life? From the tribulations of the nation, from the flaming disasters? No, have we not made enough sacrifices, have we not built enough altars, have we not heard the word "deserving of death" until this day.

[Page 212]

> Do you know from where this despair grows? The oppression ekes at the faith in the heart. There is no faith in the spiritual powers of the nation. And there is no faith in the life of the world to come of the nation. All forms of thoughts in their hearts are that human progress is against us."

The second chapter expands on the statement of the urgent need for a raising of the soul on behalf of the Jewish nation from its perspective of an oppressed nation. The third chapter portrays the ideal from both a positive and negative perspective.

> "We must take the ideal from the life of the nation. The national ideal must grow its limbs from the life of the nation, the life of the festivals, holy Sabbath and weekdays, from the oppression and humor, from the tragedies and joyous occasions of the nation. The ideal must be saturated with the tears of two millennia. It must give an eternal response to the great question, 'why and for what reason, and to what purpose?' It is obligatory to give a logical reason and explanation for all the tribulations that we encountered in our Diaspora history, and reason and explanation for 'the days of blood and rivers of tears.' It must revive our martyrs, the rows of generations who put forth their necks for slaughter as doves. It must tie the long past, full of tribulations with the present filled with affliction and suffering, and must build upon them a new holy temple of restored humanity.
>
> Let us take it from the past to the present. We have a past of our prophets and their visions. We received that past as a legacy: The burning desire for truth, justice, and righteousness. This is the fire that constantly burns in our bones; impatience and pining for a raising of social consciousness of all of humanity, strong longing for the 'golden path' in which 'their swords shall be beaten into ploughshares, and their spears into pruning hooks[9]], to the time when the wolf shall dwell with the lamb – this is our pride, this is our crown, this is the breath of our nostrils. This prophetic ideal will be the soul of our national ideal, not a childish ideal, of a pottage of lentils or of a fleshpot, but rather the ideal that embraces the entire world and all that is in it, like the messianic ideal."

The fourth chapter is called "Cosmism".

> "No nation has the right to sustain the life and business of another nation. No language, no school can benefit from extra rights. Every national language has pathways among the members of the relevant nation and its national institutions. Human institutions, such as the post, the telegraph, and the like, use a general, international language. Every nation without exception is organized upon the communal principle.

In cosmism, the idea of the unity of the oppressed nations into one international group is presented. We regard the strife and disputes among them as a bitter, bloody error, national stifling, and especially as a blinding maneuver of the ruling nation, which takes into their hand the old principle: divide and conquer! However, sooner or later, the separatist egoism will fall away from the eyes of the oppressed nations, and the solidarity of interest of the oppressed will appear as bright as the light of day."

[Page 213]

D. The Creativity of Children

In 1912, we published a booklet called "Childhood Literature" anthology II of the students at the Ivriya School of the Gordin brothers in Smorgon. It was published by "The New Pedagogy."

I will include a section from the preface:

"**Literature to children or literature of children**. Earlier, literature was the acquisition of the upper classes, the monopoly of the ruling groups. High level people creations for high level people. Now, literature has descended to the masses, it dwells with the lowly and oppressed of spirit, it is with the poor people, and has even reached the depths of the tramps. The creative fathers of this literature are the faithful of the poor homes, people who dwell amongst their people, feel their pain, and shed their tears.

The child is like the nation. It is an actualization of the moment of the creation of the world[10] – the world of the child. Literature is created for the children. However, the purpose goes forward from there: not literature for children – but literature of children, literature of childhood itself; not the literature of 'childlike adults,' but rather of actual children, children for whom childhood life is their life, childhood thoughts are their thoughts, and childhood acts are their acts; children, with the sun of the joy of childhood over their children, godlike childlike naivete in their hearts, and the satanic blood of childhood in their veins. Bring to the child the freedom of creativity; bring to the child the freedom of the word!

Let us call the children and ask them – they will come and lift the edge of the kerchief covering the secrets of their souls that are covered by secrets. They will come and open for us the door like the hole of a needle to the unfathomable depths – the end and the beginning – which we call the soul of the child.

The methodology of creativity. The catechism that was conceived and born in the image of the Christianity of the middle ages, the catechism by which the principles of religion was taught in monasteries – this 'foreign branch,' the hidden treasure of Jesuit pedagogy, stood as our aid-detractor and was brought in to the *cheder.* To bring that clash with personal autonomy, that Jesuitism of which there is nothing more disgusting and filthy, that unseemly trait – to bring it in with its head, body, and entire being, with its outstretched boots and filthy dirt, into the soul of your friend and to make it as a person who does his own thing – this unseemly trait was tied with the knot of methodology; with its intellect not calmed until it overtook teaching the written language: questions and answers in writing, a hardening of the mouth and a hardening of the pen. Following this catechism comes the discourse. Not for naught, but rather that it is its child: from the hardening of words comes the hardening of the content, foreign words and foreign thoughts – parroting and aping!

The only result of this non-methodology is the sealing of the sources, the castrating of talent, the flattening of feelings, the clipping of the wings of creativity, the paralysis of thought, the drying of freshness, the dulling of the mind, the minimization of the heart, and the thinning of the soul.

[Page 214]

And the school was filled with this catechism, and there was no end to the astonishment. Europe has become filled with members of 'let us learn wisdom' and there is no end to the gleanings."

The date is listed at the end, 1 Nisan, 1847[11] years of our exile.

E. Education In Contrast with Enlightenment [*Haskalah*][12]

That year, a prospectus was published entitled "Our Composition."

I will bring sections:

> "We admit to the necessity of education. With this given, we point out the adaptation of the coming generation to its material and concrete surroundings, to its culture in the sense of practical, concrete civilization. We thus reject the rights of teaching in the understanding of giving over 'education'[13]. We reject the rights of the older generation to transmit the culture to the coming generation as a mountain over the head like a barrel [13], in the form of a collection of values, doctrines, theories, weltanschauungs, and life. We stand at the obvious point of an inter-generational battle, the battle of the culture of values between the elders and the youths that set the path for all of history -- between parents and children. This is the 'generational battle.'
>
> 'Educate a child in accordance with their way, and even when they age, they will not depart from it' (Proverbs 22, 6) – this is the principle upon which the *Haskalah* school is based, which the elders latched on to. Every founder of religious theory knows it and uses it to the detriment. They know that everything etched into the tablet of youth will not be erased throughout all the days of their lives. There are only a few special people who are able to uproot the plants that were planted in their hearts and minds at the age of childhood and youth, for this act of uprooting is accompanied by strong feelings of guilt. This guilt and pain were sufficient to frighten an average person to refrain from daring at all to think about or actualize such painful ideas. And fortunate is the person who is constantly afraid [14]. During childhood and youth, everything intellectual turns into an emotional matter, woven and swallowed by the feeling that he it is a matter of emotions. The person acquires a patchwork of youthful essence, which becomes soulful-internal-intimate, personal – and to free oneself from it implies cruelty to oneself, without knowing mercy, distancing a part of the heart, hurting the bird of the soul, erasing a complete section of poetry from the book of life. Doing something of this nature is only possible for those individuals for whom objective truth is more precious than their

essence, flesh, tendencies, and being. Therefore, the advocates state that forgetting what is learned is more difficult than learning.

During the days of youth, the intellect is as if it is soft and elastic, with no power of opposition. All theories of education[13] rely on this principle of acceptance of influence. The task of the school of education[13] seems to be the blending of old culture within the younger generation. Its goal is attained because the youth are easily influenced, because the young generation is immersed in an environment where opposition is seemingly removed. It is like iron placed before the heat of the smelter. Forge the upcoming generation while it is still soft and compliant. Bend the sapling while it is still pliable. In essence, the education[14] school is similar to a copier. It etches with the point of a diamond[15] of authority upon the wax parchments of the mind and the heart. Then it leaves them to cool, congeal, and harden. The etchings remain in their place in an indelible fashion. The 'educated' students are a wellspring of gramophones and copycats. What has been recorded in them is echoed from them. The old educational-scholastic hymn is spoken and sung from their throats.

[Page 215]

The educational-scholastic study is a form of 'flooding of the mind and the heart,' and is worse than regular propaganda. Propaganda, even with organized in a systematic fashion and presented under a government, ecclesiastical, or party rubric, nevertheless remains in essence a free expression. The propagandist and the propaganda target stand next to each other as two individuals with equal rights. However, the educational theory is completely based on spiritual, intellectual, and emotional subordination. It accepts from the outset that the intellect of the youth can be influenced and conquered with great ease. The 'educated' students will be won over for their entire lives. They will think, feel, and act as they were commanded in their youth. 'Educate a child... and even when he ages, he will not depart from it...'

The geriatrization. The educated population is the foundation upon which the older generation ages the younger generation. The elders who have successfully adapted to the life problems that have already existed for ages, are interested in perpetuating and guarding them so they will continue without end. The youth, on the other hand, are bothered by new problems that determine the more open line of opposition. This demands that they draw from energies that are relatively small. For that is the reason that they are created. They are invited to create new creations. They are fit to carry this out both psychologically and sociologically: from a psychological perspective due to their lack of t'he burdens of conservative apperceptions'; from the sociological perspective, because the old principles and ways of life are all captured by the elders. The youth carry on a harsh battle against conservatism, which they hate with all their souls. The elders, with their fear of the youths who come to push them away and remove them from the stage of ideas and the field of activity – in their fear, like Solness in Ibsen's play, in the face of the youths whose essence, arrival, and knocking on their doors – is the foundation of the school of education, which preserves the institution of authority and geriatrization (aging, and subordination to authority). This institution ensures and protects the rule of the older generation. It supports the 'geriatricization.' The school of education is the place in which the elders infect the virus of age upon the youths.

F. Aformism – Non-Structure

The meaning of aformism is the rejection of "education" – the recognition that education leads to damage, preventing the development of the human understanding. It endangers spiritual progress.

Aformism means an opposition to formism, to the forging of the soul of the young generation by a special institution existing to impart the form in the style of the older generation, according to its ideology and interests. To 'educate' means to impart the sum total of knowledge and doctrines that were formed and accumulated by the generation the older generation that is going and not returning – to the upcoming generation that is coming of age.

[Page 216]

Therefore it impedes its development, without allowing it to create the form of a new, fundamentally youthful world. It disturbs the youth from creating and accumulating its own perspective, from searching and finding its truths and lies, its pure path and its errors – in short, its direct path and empty non-paths.

The young generation has more talent and opportunities to find a new truth than those who are part of the older generation. However, the educational school sees its purpose solely as a means of imparting the old truths, science, arts and crafts to the young generation.

If it is our intention to raise a free young generation, a generation of free thinkers, who are free from previously accepted ideas, we must not burden their shoulders with the yoke of ecclesiastical faith or the yoke of university science, but rather give them the possibility to think their thoughts or to believe in their convictions in accordance with their soul and intellect, without anyone disturbing this. We must give the young generation the right of thoughts and feeling. The task and mission of the young generations is to forge new forms and to mint new coins. It is forbidden to impose on them the patterns of thought and usual paradigms of feeling, with an engraving that is completely lost on them.

The bearer of aformism is the younger generation, the youth. All who attempt to rectify the school complain unanimously against the lackadaisicalness and deliberation in effecting the changes. Procrastination is natural. The rectifiers approach the communal activists, the parents, and the teachers with their daring plans. They do not approach those whom they should be approaching, those who are interested with their full heart and soul in the improvements and rectifications – the young generation, to the youth studying in high schools and educational institutions.

Aformism directly approaches the young generation whose members are its bearers. Obviously, we do not denigrate the appreciation and assistance of all the preceding elements of humanity, of all those to whom cultural, moral, and social advancement was dear to them and close to their hearts. We especially value the collaboration of the four forlorn elements of society of our times: the worker, the woman, the oppressed nation, and the individual personality. These are the additional forces. However, the youth themselves, at the head like a pioneer, march under their banner, which is the banner of aformism, on the foundation of the international youth union. The youth guard strange vineyards, but do not guard their own vineyard. The are the tar-ointment on the wheel axles that pass over them and trample them. They give the lion's share with their sacrifice for every liberation movement. They fight for the liberation of the workers and nations, but not for their own freedom.

[Page 217]

It is impossible to explain cultural history and especially the migration of cultural centers unless one uses the law of conservation. Cultural material grows and progresses in cubes [i.e. powers of 3], and the propelling force is a square [i.e. powers of 2]. Therefore, as the large amount of cultural material gathers up, the propelling power dwindles relatively until it reaches a state of stagnation or freezing. The raw material grows at the expense of the processing. The example, formalism and arbitrariness enslave and chain the free, the drive for change and drive for duplication and tripling. The 'journeys of apperception,' the opinions

that we have adopted are not from the network of ideas that are spilling to enter, to burst inward. The inert principles decide the variable principles. The continuum of cultural development has moved from those 'barbaric' mechanisms, to nations lacking culture, and then to nations with a low cultural level, or, on the other hand, to the nation suffering from cultural hypertrophy, and tends to jump toward exaggerated conservatism – that is a crying contradiction with the environment that surrounds it, and that forces it to revolt – toward renewal. The idea that European culture has utilized will not disappear because the population is set in a moderate climate, not too cold or too hot. This theory, developed by H. Thomas Buckle (1921-1862)[16], is completely unfounded. The development of culture cannot be explained geographically or heteronomically[17]. The sprouting of culture as well as its wilting and withering are conditioned by its content, and the essence of the spirit and culture, by the psychology of the nations with a plethora of culture or a lack of culture. The blandness of the phenomena of culture must be exposed in all its essence, from its inner core.

The educational school serve as an intensely conservative institution, leading the younger generation on the path of preservation. Were it not for this education, the young generation, remaining free in spirit, uniting with its ideas, doubts, quests, and realities, would begin the culture of the spirit anew, from the beginning. They would pave a path toward the currently 'unrecognizable,' which has no border or end. Europe, according to our understanding, stands before a dilemma: either to accept the theory of aformism that will free the youth with a spiritual, intellectual, and emotional freedom, and remove the faith and science from the library; or it will be become irredeemably decadent after some time. It will become frozen like its sister Asia. Europe will be destroyed from a cultural perspective.

The new pedagogy is the pedagogy of the youth promising endless movement, 'a perpetuum mobile' [perpetual motion machine] of cultural advancement without reversals and congealing of the conservative ideals.

G. Historism

When we also use the principle of evolution in the realm of creations of the spirit, understanding that they develop, we are forced to accept the opinion, that they are also liable to breakdown and dwindling. With evolution comes dissolution. Science is the theory of explaining the world which stands to be dismantled, and anything standing to be dismantled is as if it is dismantled already. In the current historical era, it is accepted as a true principle, a true doctrine, since we do not yet have a better, more believable theory. However, we must recall at all times that it is sustained by the perspective of 'a working hypothesis' with a low efficacy, basing its correctness on practical, material results. For the true value of any opinion and idea is not from straightforward truth, but rather from the potential or actual ability to change the material in its environment.

[Page 218]

All the systemtology, all theories to explain and understand the world that are created by humanity are based on the search for the 'nonexistent' – on the desire to invent or create something that does not exist in reality. We can describe this activity in the following words: the anthropomorphism of the external world and the objectivity of the internal world at the time that it drifts as a burden.

All the following intellectual metaphors mislead the world: vitalism of the self with fetishism; psychism in accordance with animism, etc., politicism, monotheism in faith, pantheism, Paulism, Munism, or as it should more accurately be called, pannaturism, naturism, polynaturism and mononaturism in science – all these metaphors can be divided into two categories: teleological fiction and causal fiction. Fetishism stands at the sign of the teleological phantom. Each and everything seeks purposes and drives to achieve goals that are not presented before it, as if 'it wants.' That is, it is activated, if we use the scientific lingo, by outcomes, by hoped for results, expectations that he hopes to achieve.

According to science, each and every thing is causal; it is forced by urges and forces that act in its environment. Every event, every process is influenced by antecedents. Teleology is fictitious, it produces models of explanation that do not at all explain. For every purpose is based on a previous purpose, forever. The human intellect does not rest quiet until it brings the purpose to non-purpose, which is, to an independent purpose, and brings the teleology to an independent teleology, that is a world of purpose unto itself.

Casualism is seemingly a game of imagination. It is a deception of the imagination that is supported by intellectual tricks. That is to say, it stands on an extension of the chain of phenomena by the intermediate links of reason, so that it is difficult for the gaze of the intellect to gasp the two ends at the same moment of time. Every reason rests on the preceding reason, every cause rests on a precursor, such that every developed person is not satisfied until he arrives at the camouflaged cause, the sublime of the sublime, independent sublimity.

When we consider the systemology, we realize that all general theories that existed until this time were in in essence explicative, explanatory, interpretive, commentaries. From the outset they determine that they require explanation, that they have an essence that serves as a commentary, and that there are things that require explanation – at the behest of which the sought explanation is found. The supreme and most praiseworthy explicative is fetishism, which is the crown of objective rationalization. Everything, every phenomenon, every process is intelligent. Here, there is pure teleology, the path from fetishism to science seemingly lights up the degeneration of explicativity, of stumbling or the lack of the image of clarity. Animism is to a known extent a contraction of the reasoning of things: the behavior of a thing makes rationalizations through its living spirit and actions, which dwell within it and after some time are found outside of it. In polytheism, we already find agglomerates of things and processes that are united by essences, more accurately beings, reasons that are called gods. Therefore, the explicativities are separate from the essence of the things and dwell in creations that are specifically designated for such.

[Page 219]

As a result, the things themselves almost lose their entire intellect and reasoning. With monotheism, the world is completely denigrated as illogical and inexplicable. Intellect and explanations are centered around god.

Science makes an additional step, a large step, in the direction of inexplicativity. It takes from its interpretive charm, from the explanation of existence, the free well and understanding. Instead of god comes nature.

However, the action of explaining is completely a trick of the mind, an imagination of understanding. Every explanation demands a following explanation. Every interpretation is connected to postinterpretation, and there is no end. The derived conclusion is that the bounds of desire for explanation is the explanation itself. The explanation is explained from itself, which is a non-explanation. That is, the removal of the final chain from the model of reasoning from a fact that does not say 'interpret me,' or explain me. That is, we come to the idea that a fact as a fact does not require explanation. Every explanation of it is held within its essence as a fact.

The model of creation and essence. The two theories that are forced are those that pursue the intellect of man. In faith – creation; in science

– essence. The former is a technical concept. The second is a biological concept. Both of them desire to respond by subduing the fact, to bring something from nothing, and they fail. Faith is forced to come to independent creation of a creator, and science is forced to come to the independent essence of existence, to nature. Both create reality or something in order to explain things that cannot be explained and do not demand explanation."

("Our Composition" 1912, Smorgon)

H. The Arrangement of Children

In 1913, our composition "The Arrangement of Children" was published with five chapters: a. The value of the written language; b. the pleasantness of learning; c. the methodology of our reading; d. tools; e. curriculum.

We will bring a section from chapter 3, the methodology of our reading.

"Study and Reading

The methodology of the written language transgresses against the principles of pedagogy, against the natural principle. The written language is a language that stands on its own, and all teaching methods for a foreign language must apply to it. Written language is like a foreign language, and must be taught in a natural fashion, without the aid of the mother tongue, which is the spoken language. Since the foreign language is not taught through the means of translation to the mother tongue but rather through its own essence, it stands that the written language should also be learned via its own essence, without the intermediation of the spoken language, without translation to the spoken language – that is, without reading.

[Page 220]

For example '*shev*' used to be translated to the child. '*Shev*' means 'sit down.' Today, we are wiser, and we do not translate it to the student's language. We do not exchange a contract for a contract, a word for a word, but rather explain it within the context of the concept, that is, we tie the sum sounds of "*shev*" to the concept of sitting. The teacher says, '*Shev*,' and the child sits down (the theatrical kindergarten). It is thus even with the written language: the teacher shows the student the form of the word '*shev*' – and sits down; '*amod*' [stand] – and stands.

The sum of the letters of '*shev*' and '*amod*' are tied to the concept itself and not to a word that expresses '*shev*' or '*amod.*' Later, through the help and means of this vocalized word, one comes to the concept of sitting, standing, or the like. Why does the translation to the spoken language come, what does reading do? How superior is the power of vocal symbols than the visual symbol of letters? Why do we use the latter over the former?

You see – you remember – and you do. The eye sees, grasps the form of the word and sentence, the association arouses the related concept, and the strands are heard and filled in – not through lip reading, not by moving the lips, but by 'understanding' alone, the reading of the issues, seeing – and doing.

We have forged two ideals in linguistic techno-pedagogy.

The theater of the children – to the spoken languages

The school of the mute [the wordless school] – for the written language.

Reading is literally a translation, but whereas the translation from one spoke language to the next is an art known to expert translators – this translation from the written language to the spoken language is something equivalent for every person. It is done by set principles. The principles of reading are indeed the principles of translation.

The visual methodology is completely directed to the learning of the written language as an independent language. It is not involved with reading, with translating to the spoken language. The imitative method is a mixed methodology: it utilizes the written language, while not abandoning reading."

That year, and in that publication, our book "The Child" or "The Fivefold Covenant" was published in Yiddish. It is a dramatic poem with five scenes. This book presents the idea of the unity of the unity of the five forlorn individuals in our society: the worker, the woman, the oppressed nation, the youth, and the individual personality.

That year, our booklet "Our Cheder" was published in Yiddish.

* * *

In 1911, we edited the publication "Der Yunger Yid" (The Young Jew) in Smorgon.

Translator's Footnotes

1. A Hebrew educational methodology where the language is taught by using the language itself (a form of immersion).
2. I am unsure what '*Republikat -Haeivarim*' means.
3. A quote from the *Nishmat* prayer, recited on Sabbath and Festival morning services, as well as at the Passover Seder.
4. A traditional formulation of the human constitution, adding up to 613 – the number of commandments of the Torah.
5. See https://en.wikipedia.org/wiki/William_James
6. Fröbel coined the term "kindergarten".
7. Based on Genesis 28:12.
8. Based on Ezekiel 18:2.
9. Isaiah 2:4. The next phrase about the wolf dwelling with the lamb if from Isaiah 11:6.
10. The term used here for creation of the world is "*Harat Olam*" – known from the Rosh Hashanah *musaf* liturgy, following the three cycles of shofar blowing. This entire article is full of biblical and liturgical innuendoes – I am only pointing out some of the most prominent ones.
11. An unusual dating scheme. Since the destruction of the Second Temple was 70 CE, the secular year would be 70+1847 = 1917.
12. Often translated as "enlightenment" as the enlightenment movement, but here it likely means knowledge of a more or less secular nature. Perhaps "erudition."
13. A reference to the coercion at Mount Sinai (termed as the mountain being held over their heads like a barrel).
14. Proverbs 28:14.
15. Jeremiah 17:1.
16. See https://en.wikipedia.org/wiki/Henry_Thomas_Buckle
17. See https://en.wikipedia.org/wiki/Heteronomy

[Page 221]

"Ivria"

by Hanoch Levin

Translated by Sara Mages

Chapter in the history of Hebrew education in Smorgon

Smorgon served as a place for one of the pedagogical experiments in the field of Hebrew education on the threshold of the new century. Echoes of the educational movement, and the ideas laid at its foundation, traveled far from the town's narrow passages, crossed the borders of its district – between Vilna and Minsk, and spread to the wide domain of Russian Jewry until it knocked on the doors of H. N. Bialik and E. L. Lewinsky, who were not exempt from determining their opinion, and their position, on the voice that came from Smorgon, Lita [Lithuania]. This right was brought to our town by the sons of HaRav Gordin, Abba and Zev, who were later called the Gordin brothers. They were known in Russia as seekers of anarchism but remained in the spiritual life of our people to fertilize the generation's mind with original seeds of thought – from the school of Abba Gordin.

However, all that came later. Earlier, in 1905, the dynamic young men arrived at the home of HaRav, R' Yehudah Leib, author of "*Divrei Yehudah*" and "*Diglei Yehudah*," from the fanatical Hassidic Ostrow, to "free" Smorgon. They were deeply interested in knowledge and craved action. They were full of new thoughts and sought an outlet for their youthful vigor. They didn't come empty handed. The amazing autodidacts, "the Gordin brothers," already had the best minds of their generation. They were already familiar with the teachings of [Max] Striner, and knew whole chapters of his book, "The Individual and His Property," by heart.

Their rabbi and teacher was [Pierre–Joseph] Proudhon, and saw him as a strong spirit. Tolstoy captivated them with his educational–pedagogic teachings, and the new gospel from "Yasnaya Polyana" shook all the cords of their hearts. And above all – the deep-rooted knowledge of all the treasures of Jewish culture, the Talmud and its commentary, *Halacha, Midrash* and *Aggadah* – the legacy of HaRav, R' Yehudah Leib.

It wasn't long before the two began to implement their eclectic doctrine, in theory and in practice, in the field of education, and they started in Smorgon.

The advice was of Abba Gordin. At the beginning it didn't aspire to great things, all they wanted was to establish a new school, new in meaning, as an intermediate stage. "*Heder metukan*" [improved or reformed *heder*] served as the first layer of their educational structure, in the sense of a corridor to the parlor. They discussed and decided to set principles first:

[Page 222]

A. The teaching in "heder metukan" would be Hebrew in Hebrew.

B. The institution would be secular and free in its essence. It will not teach prayers and law, and will try to distance itself from everything that the religious spirit emanates from.

C. With that, its teachers will focus on the acquisition of original Jewish values, as expressed in the classical literature – the Bible, and at the same time teach the new Hebrew literature. They will try to also bring the generation's thinking, with its various streams, before the talented students.

D. "Yasnaya Polyana" will serve as an exemplary example.

Equipped with a fiery desire, clear principles and a well–tested plan, the two went out to conquer the uncultivated field, as they called it, of Jewish education in the town of Smorgon.

Although their father, the rabbi, stood aloof and his religious consciousness objected to the "youthful act" of his sons, he secretly blessed, from the depth of his heart, their exceptional daring out of hope that the work, and its framework, the concern for the matter and the difficulties of making a livelihood, will do their part and the "rebellious sons" will "grown up."

The rabbi placed the rear half of his spacious apartment at the disposal of the "brothers." Abba Gordin, and his brother Zev, went to work without delay. They collected furniture, everything they could lay their hands on – tables chairs and benches from the neighbors and even from Batei HaMidrash in town. With their own hands they distributed notices wherever they came: in the streets, in the shops, in the synagogue, in the *heders* and in the "small yeshiva," in these words:

Since the Gordin brothers, the rabbi's sons, are opening "*heder metukan*," our brothers, the Jewish people, are asked to come and register their children, in the place, on the day and the hour listed below...

And since the number of places is limited, we hereby notify everyone who is interested that, first come, first served.

The notices were written in three languages: Hebrew; Yiddish and Russian.

The results weren't long in coming. The day after the announcement was published many began to knock on the door of the town's rabbi.

Young mothers, daughters of homeowners, came to register their daughters. Also young fathers, "free," so to speak, who "walked with the time," were seen at the entrance to the rabbi's house. Some were anxious, some ashamed, with their little boys holding on the edge of their garment. And there was something to be anxious about: the Gordin brothers had a reputation of complete heretics. It was known that they dissociated themselves from the yoke of *mitzvot* and respect. Even on the Sabbath, and on holidays, they didn't come to the synagogue to pray and, there were those who said, that they would teach in "*heder metukan*" without a head cover...

Despite fears, 120 students enrolled in the first few days and it was necessary to stop the registration. The rabbi's rooms were too small to contain all this population and, in addition, the *melamdim* in town got up and "shouted": the oppressors of the Jews deprive us of our livelihood, they, Heaven forbid! convert this "holy flock," the Jewish children, who have not sinned, and, Woe for the calamity, at the rabbi's house, R' Yehudah Leib, author of "*Diglei Yehudah*." The *melamdim*, of the town of Smorgon, called for a meeting and threatened to delay the "reading" on the Shabbat.

[Page 223]

Under these conditions the Gordin brothers decided to move their school from the rabbi's house, so they wouldn't be an obstacle to their father – on one hand, and be free in their actions – on the other hand. They went and rented a suitable house, with a large courtyard, across the Minsk Street Bridge.

A few days later, on the house, on its facade, above the window cornice, a large sign, almost to the width of the house, was displayed with all its glory. Only one word was written, in a shade of gold, on its black background:

"Ivria"

On this day, the first Hebrew school was established in Smorgon (1908).

Loyal to their conviction and devoted to their opinions, the Gordin brothers set out to introduce to the new school, "Ivria," the new methods of the best thinkers of their generation who, in their opinion, ensured the natural development of the child and his progress in life, and sought new means and ways to ensure the success of their enterprise.

Needless to say, that the Jews of Smorgon were amazed at the sight of the "Torah" that was being taught within the walls of "Ivria." They wondered, and didn't understand... And how was it possible, sixty years ago, to explain these "strange" methods of education?

First of all, the children were free to do everything that was right in their eyes. They sang and danced at school, painted and sculpted, and engaged in all kinds of work and practical thinking. They didn't sit at all on their benches, they ran around all day long, and didn't read a book, even for a short while. Is this a new doctrine, and this is the reward? They also don't know how to hold a pen in their hand. The children of Smorgon will grow up, Heaven forbid! to be uneducated, and instead of becoming important people, they would fall into bad ways and become "actors." Yes, real actors. There was an urgent rumor that "plays" were being held at "Ivria," A "theatre," Heaven forbid! Such, and similar, was the picture that appeared before the Jews of Smorgon when they looked at the aspect of "Ivria" – and weren't in favor of it ...

The teachers, Abba and Zev Gordin, didn't notice what was happening around them. They were so engrossed in their new concept and were oblivious of the war that the religious circles, and the *melamdim*, were preparing against them. The two spent day and night at school. Here, they ate their meal... and here... they couldn't even fall asleep. "Ivria" was their only vision. They wrapped their souls in this educational enterprise. Even when students began to drop out, because of the hostile propaganda and whispers, they consoled themselves and said:

Leaves fall in the wind and the tree trunk stands firm.

The rate of leaving the school increased after a terrible incident took place within the walls of "Ivria."

A girl, the only daughter to her parents, was beaten by one of the students and the teacher stood by and didn't intervene – the girl has to fight back, she must capture her place in the children's group on her own. The girl run away from school – startled her mother, and she burst out with complaints: scandal, how could such a thing happen? Children are beaten and the teachers stand idly by. The rest of the children will see and learn from the teachers' behavior. And what do you think will happen in the end? They will grow up without manners, to be robbers and thieves.

[Page 224]

It must be published in the "*Gaztin.*" – – In the "*Gaztin*" – tells Abba Gordin in his book "Thirty years in Lita and Poland" – they didn't write but, they talked all over Smorgon about this "incident," and the conclusion, that the townspeople came to was – that the school, "Ivria," should be uprooted with everything in it.

And how do we do that? We will take the children out and the shepherds will only be left with their "flutes."

The incident was – stimulating, and it would have brought disaster to the educational enterprise, but, the Gordin brothers' "flute," with its clear beautiful sound, continued to play...

We must prevent disaster. The teachers of "Ivria" went out to the public in a publicity campaign. From house to house, in a face–to–face conversation, they tried to explain their way in education. The town's homeowners locked the doors in their faces. "We will not even allow them to stand on our threshold – these converts." But they didn't give up, they found a few sympathetic fans that understood their spirit and believed in them. Two of them stood to the Gordin brothers in their distress and they are: Rachel Lamdenski, daughter of the former community activist who enrolled her only son to "Ivria" out of recognition, and the second, Yosha Lvitan, that his son and daughter also studied at the school. They didn't spare any effort to explain to the public and spread the idea of the new Hebrew school.

Abba and Zev Gordin's new pedagogical doctrine ripened in those difficult days. It was modern in its foundation and preceded, in almost one generation, the patriarchs of the new Hebrew education in the Diaspora. The method was given a clear form, it was embedded in scientific patterns and was well explained – it is the method of instructional teaching (the imperative method) of the Gordin brothers.

From their little experience at "Ivria," they understood that the students do not grasp the method of wording. Not the verbal memorization and its numerous repetitions, but the liberating activation of the senses by direct contact – to do, perform and create.

In 1908, the year of the establishment of "Ivria" school, a textbook by S.L. Gordon was published by Tushia Publishing. With all its innovation it didn't answer all the pedagogical requirements of A. and Z. Gordin's school. Again, the boring statistics, and almost all of it words, words and names, and this is the innovation – pictures and drawings – but what will the children do with them?

The teachers of "Ivria" asked for a trigger which leads to movement. They wanted to start the child's mental mechanisms by means of short orders that give birth to actions and movements. From here came the name – the command system.

[Page 225]

In order to bring the children into free oral expression, sentences of command were thrown into the classroom, one by one – to do, to act, to play, to be in motion and create.

Sentences, of this kind, were easily absorbed by the students until, a short time later, they had a great treasure of sentences, not isolated words, orphan and abstract, unrelated to one another, and all the more so, do not bring the children into action, activity and practical work but, to miniature masks of human actions that are stored within the framework of logical connections that cause the child's activity. The young teachers, sons of Rabbi Gordin, preceded the members of their generation with new pedagogical thought of an active and working school, preceded – with complete faith.

Since the founders of "Ivria" continued to follow the path they had chosen, and constant movement, action and workmanship found a place at the school, there was no reason not to set up the theater in the institution. Its growth was organic. All that was left for the teachers to do was to arrange the sequence of actions that the commands provoked around one subject and before them was a dramatic novella, a miniature play.

But Smorgon, in the first decade of the twentieth century, what did it have to do with the new advanced method? For her, it was the "theater" that – "He that keeps his soul holds himself far from it" [Proverbs 23/7]. That – and no more?

So far oral expression, but, how to teach reading and writing? It turned out that these can also be acquired by a game. The teachers of "Ivria" ordered from a carpenter and a tinsmith, both parents of students, typesetting boxes of letters and vowels. Each student was given a typesetting box. The students created, without any difficulty, imperative sentences from their typesetting box, and as small printers they stood before the general typesetting box, which was located in their classroom, and pulled from it, wonder of all the wonders, letters and words which joined in their hands into sentences that all of them demanded: do, act and create. It was impossible to pull the little ones away from this "magic box." In turn, they composed written actions and built worlds.

At the same time, the teachers for beginners in Smorgon, Yankel Kazan, Baruch the *melamed*, and Itza Mechlis, stood before their flock and in a gesture ("*teitel*" in a foreign language) showed them the form of a holy letter in the "*Sidur*" and said: *Kamatz, Aleph*– A.

This is the way of A. and Z. Gordin, who couldn't settle for little in spiritual matters, and didn't rest until they published it in public. What did they do? They gathered strength, sat down and prepared a textbook for the children of "Ivria," and like them everywhere, by the name, "Theatrical Garden," which contained a series of gradual lessons for an entire school year, from beginning to end.

[Page 226]

When they finished their work they sent the manuscript to Moriah Publishing in Odessa. They didn't wait long for an answer, and the letter – the letter of H. N. Bialik himself and its exciting opening:

"Your work is useful and important" – and the first part and the last part is something like this:

Under the existing conditions (financial), the publishing house does not see the possibility of publishing your book (and again, the most useful and important), since, in the whole country, there is only a small number of institutions, "kindergarten" and "Ivria" such as yours, that can use your book. Therefore, you should send your manuscript to Eretz-Yisrael. Who knows, maybe your salvation will come from there.

Also, this time, the young educators didn't despair. Zev Gordin left for Warsaw, to Ben-Avigdor, with the recommendation letter from H. N. Bialik in his hand: helpful and important... Ben-Avigdor welcomed the teacher from Smorgon, praised their work, but he also rejected the publication of the book for the same reasons that H. N. Bialik rejected it – the generation is not ready for it...

And again, it was "Ivria" that saved its founders-teachers from loss of faith and despair. In their day-to-day work in the children's kingdom, although, a small kingdom (of the 120 students half remained) – they saw the whole vision. At last, they said, not the word written on paper is the essence of education, but the word engraved on the hearts of their students. Nothing else, only "Ivria" alone is the realm of desire, the promised land... "Theatrical Garden" wasn't published by Moriah, and not by Tushia, in 1909 it was published in Smorgon by the authors. After its publication booklets, on didactics and new methods of teaching, were added as loyal companions. This publishing house, which was born in Smorgon and called "The New Pedagogy," published an original book, the first of its kind – "From Children to Children." It was a collection of works by the students of "Ivria." The two, who stood out among the young participants of this literary collection, were: Pinchas Lamdanski in poetry, and Tzvi Hersh Kevito (the future famous announcer of Radio Moscow). In the story, Lamdanski's father, who traveled through Odessa for his business, visited H. N. Bialik and gave him the collection, "From children to children." The venerable national poet praised the book. When the story became known, the situation of the school improved and its virtues rose again. The teachers, Gordin, no longer had to fight for every child's soul. Many came to study with these "stubborn," "craftsmen of one craft." "Ivria" school in Smorgon developed a reputation throughout Russia and even overseas. An article written by A Litvin, who visited our town that year, was published in the American "*Forverts*." In amazement and enthusiasm he tells about the institution and adds: I examined its students and there was no end to my amazement at the sound of their fluent Hebrew speech, the extent of their knowledge and understanding. Also S. Ansky, the well-known writer of "The Dybbuk" who left to wander in the Jewish settlements to investigate the situation of the Jews and to collect folklore treasures, sent a positive opinion on “Ivria” to the company on whose behalf he was sent. Among the other visitors, who spent their days at the school to closely examine the methods used in it, were: the teacher and educator, Y. Y Glass, author the “*Heder*,” and Hochenberg the author of textbooks at the time. They published their impressions, both orally and in writing, in public.

[Page 227]

“Ivria” has long ceased to be just a school, a closed educational area in Smorgon. The institution began to serve as a source of inspiration and center for the new Hebrew education for the entire district of Vilna, and even beyond its borders. The extensive pedagogical work, which took place within its walls, found expression in many textbooks, the most famous of which was “*Alphon Mischak*” [Alphabet book with games]. On the occasion of the publication of the “*Alphon*,” Abba Gordin left for Warsaw. There, he made his first contacts with Hebrew teachers and educators, pioneers of Hebrew teaching in the Diaspora, Y. Alterman, P. Halperin and Pugachev who heard about “Ivria” and knew its process according to rumor. They were amazed by the young teacher, who stood before them and lectured confidently and enthusiastically about his pedagogical opinions. They didn't support everything, but the “innovation” – the new way – captivated them.

It was Fischel Lachower, the literary critic and historian of the new literature, who recognized the merits of the book “*Alphon Mischak*,” the fruit of six years of experimental work in “Ivria,” a theory, which can be carried into practice. It was he who blessed the completed work and published the book by “*Safrot*” Publishing.

Al off a sudden, the place became too narrow for the Gordin brothers in Smorgon, not they despised it, but because they knew a bigger world and new horizons were revealed to them.

The blessed acquaintance with the literary “lions,” I. L. Peretz, D. Frishman, young Sholem Asch and other “young priests,” who stood at that time in the eastern “wall” of Hebrew creation – all these, including their literary–pedagogical program, could no longer be stored within the walls of “Ivria” in Smorgon. The talent and dynamism, inherent in them from birth, now wanted a broader field of action. In their imagination, the teachers, from the home of HaRav Gordin, had already taken off beyond their town to evoke a general human–educational movement. For six whole years, from 1908 to

1914, the joy of small school children filled "Ivria" in Smorgon and, suddenly, its voice fell silent...

The school didn't open for the 1914 school year. The joy of the children of Smorgon ceased and the taste of childhood life was taken from them. They looked up with grief at the sign "Ivria," which hung orphaned on the school's façade, a painful reminder of what was, and passed.

The author, Elchanan Cajtlin, son of Hillel Cajtlin, immortalized "Ivria" in his book, "In the House of Literature," and so he wrote:

The Gordin brothers came to my father's house in Warsaw. Stood and preached before him about the new ways of education and unacceptable forms of teaching. In their hometown, Smorgon, they founded and managed a school that served as a laboratory for their daring ideas. They were the first among our people to lay the foundation for a school called, "Creative school." Thanks to them Smorgon was given the right to be the first Jewish town with new modern education.

[Page 228]

And as an end to the unfinished "pedagogic poem" of "Ivria" in Smorgon, and as an echo of orphan poetry, I bring one case that the hand of fate has made it a symbol:

After the First World War, in the early 1920s, the survivors, refugees of sword and famine, returned from Russia to the ruins of their hometown, Smorgon, the first thing they wanted to do was – to establish a Hebrew school for their children. In the "women's section" of the ruined Great Synagogue they installed a temporary house of prayer and housed the first classrooms there. They invited from Vilna the teachers, young Y. Tatarsky and the veteran teacher Beck.

Between classes, in one of the breaks, a group of children, whose members wandered every day among the mounds of their destroyed town, dragged kind of a strange beaten object – a tin sign whose shape had been lost and was covered with rust. They brought the sign to their teachers and together deciphered one word: – "Ivria."

The golden color didn't remain in its letters. On the ruins of the town of Smorgon the sign wallowed in ashes during the days of the war, as if it wanted to stay there and not be taken away. This is last remnant of a loyal testimony of interesting educational experience.

A. and Z. Gordin

[Page 229]

The Smorgon "Kibbutz"

by M. Ivenski

Translated by Yocheved Klausner

Smorgon was located between Vilna and Minsk. It was considered a small town in the district, but in truth it was livelier, if not even greater, than the district town Oshmien. It was easy to make a living in town – there were more than a few wealthy Jewish families. Although most of the residents were simple shopkeepers and workers, Smorgon was considered a rich town. There was enough "flour" and the Jewish residents sought to plant also "Torah" as much as possible.

The main source of livelihood in Smorgon was the leather manufacture. The owners as well as the workers were totally dedicated to their work; however, spiritual matters were not neglected and Torah study was always first. When the Volozhyn Yeshiva was closed in 1892, some of the *Balebatim* [well-to-do and respected leaders of the community, lit. "house owners"] brought a number of students and teachers to Smorgon, thereby establishing, amidst the "weekday" atmosphere of business, a *kibbutz* [group] of learners and worshippers, who were immersed in Torah study with body and soul.

Most of the members of this *kibbutz* (called "*kloizniks*"), were adult men ordained as rabbis. But the group included younger men as well, who had just left the yeshiva to begin their independent lives. There were no regular lessons at the *kibbutz,* but the *kloizniks* would study in pairs, learning from one another.

One of the *kloizniks* (1895) became later famous as the Yiddish writer A. Weiter. His real name was Aizik Meir Devenishki, and the *kloizniks* nicknamed him "the Bianiankener" after the name of his town of birth. Aizik Meir Devenishki was probably 15-16 years old at the time; he was one of the oldest of the younger group.

[Page 230]

Considering the standards of the times, the *kibbutz* was doing well financially. The *kloizniks* did not have to "eat days." They even received a weekly support that could amount to 2 Rubles and 50 Kopeks a week for those who had been ordained as rabbis. The others received 30 Kopeks a week, sometimes less. But nobody was hungry – the community would not let anyone fall. The money for the weekly payments was collected from various sources: at circumcision ceremonies, weddings, contract signing ceremonies, even at funerals. It was said that the community would collect money for that purpose "from the living and from the dead." The collector, who was also the supervisor in the yeshiva and the beadle of the synagogue, was a short Jew, with a face that looked like yellow parchment. His name was Feitel. This Feitel would fast for days, sleep on a bench in the synagogue and be content with very little, as long as his *kloizniks* were taken care of. He was for them a father, albeit sometimes a very angry father.

Life in Smorgon was peaceful and comfortable. Businesses flourished, as did Torah study. However, this serene situation did not last long. Something happened in the shtetl that caused an uproar. It was kept secret for a long time, but in the end the secret came out. "Horrible things" became known, and the entire town was distressed.

In the outskirts of Smorgon lived a former activist named Ivan Frantzovitch Sinitzki, who was considered trouble by most of the *balebatim* in town. Sinitzki was a true Russian (although Polish by origin), a fine, respected gentile, who helped Jews whenever he could. However, he was one of those who intended "to turn the world upside down" – change things that were there "since creation." He was part of the Russian intelligentsia and he devoted his life to "enlighten the masses." Among the Jews of Smorgon he found fertile ground for his ideas. Most of his students and followers were Jewish adolescents – boys and girls.

[Page 231]

Sinitzki's influence was definitely felt in Smorgon. The sons and daughters of the best Jewish families would go to Sinitzki's house to listen to his lessons. Among them were the rabbi's daughter Liebe Ginsburg (who later became Mrs. Lyessin) and her sister Beile. The *balebatim* in town were furious, but kept silent: their own children were involved in this.

Sinitzki's influence reached even the *Beit Midrash,* the study-house where the *kloizniks* studied under Feitel's supervision. Sinitzki had two representatives there: young Nuchimovski and Shimshelevitz; they preached socialism – the great and important meaning of Labor.

The idea of socialism we could understand and accept; but we could not consent to the activity of assimilators – assimilators were *treif*, "impure." We were nationalists.

Shimshelewitz, who was also a "Hebraist," recommended a Hebrew book, "The Enlightened Carpenter." This was a small book, part of a series of Hebrew books published by Ben Avigdor under the general name of "One-Groshen-Books." This book described a Torah student, a genius from Volozhyn, who left his studies and became a carpenter, an "enlightened carpenter," whose idea and goal was "to be useful to humanity." Shimshelewitz told me that this was a true story. He knew the young genius who became the hero of the book: his name was Avraham Walt. Shimshelewitz also revealed the secret: this Walt had been in Smorgon a while ago and had a long argument with Sinitzki. Walt was indeed a genius – he said – a socialist, a poet, but he had not yet left Judaism. He was a fiery nationalist... he was a genial person, a great personality...

"The Enlightened Carpenter" caused controversy and indignation, in particular among the *kloizniks*...

The book set forth among Jews the idea of "work" as a socialist concept. This idea was later adopted and promoted by A. D. Gordon, as the "Religion of Work" [*Dat Ha'avoda*].

[Page 232]

I was greatly impressed by Shimshelewitz's words...

Even before I met Walt personally, I felt the effect of his ideas. Shimshelewitz would bring us pages of poems written by that mysterious person, who had become the hero of a tale. The poems passed from hand to hand; they were full of Jewish suffering and pain, and willingness to sacrifice his life for Jews.

But Shimshelewitz brought to the *kloizniks* not only national poems by Walt; he brought also revolutionary poems.... this was actually his main goal. The poems had a significant effect; they greatly inspired some of the younger *kloizniks*.

The revolutionary poems were known not only among the *kloizniks*. Craftsmen and other workers were aware of them as well, and in 1896 circles of Jewish workers began to organize. Most organizers came from Vilna; among them was a friend of Walt (Lyessin), Shmuel Levine (Dr. Shmuel Levine, who died in New York about 30 years ago). Levine worked among the *kloizniks* as well and he talked with admiration about one of them, a genius, who became a great poet and socialist. He meant his friend Walt.

By that time, strikes began in town. This was already too much for the *Balebatim* – they were furious. At the same time, a preacher came then to our town, Simcha Cohen, who was a singer as well as a speaker. He would "sing" his sermons in a threatening voice that penetrated the souls of his listeners. In his sermons he asked the fathers not to spare their sons, but to do everything in their power to annihilate the "idol worship" [socialism] from their midst. The effect of the sermons was great: it caused trouble in many families, where sons and daughters of rich Jews helped enlighten poor laborers, show them how they have been exploited and organized strikes against their own fathers.

Even among the *kloizniks* in the Yeshiva incidents began to happen. Feitel the supervisor caught one of the students, Botwinik (from Rakov) reading from a book that he kept on top of his open *Gemara* [Talmud volume]. Actually the book was an entirely "innocent" book: it was a grammar book of the Russian language by Kirpitchnikov. But a rumor began, that the Rakover was one of Sinitzki's men. The result of Kirpitchnikov's grammar book incident was sad indeed. One of the Smorgon Jews, the rich man Baruch Nathan, slapped the Rakover and drove him out of the *Bet Midrash.*

[Page 233]

The fact that a *kloiznik* was beaten upset the entire *kibbutz* in the *Bet Midrash.* Older pious people were angry at Nathan, who dared to raise a hand on a teacher. The Rakover was a friend of mine, we lived in the same neighborhood; and although I did not always agree with him and we had many arguments about his friendship with the assimilates, I suffered the consequences of the well-known saying "woe to the wicked, woe to his neighbor".... Smorgon had become too crowded for me. Many of my acquaintances had moved to Minsk.

[Page 234]

Whenever I speak about her...

(A chapter of memories)

by Regina Helman

Translated by Sara Mages

Not without excitement and longing I bring up my memories today on the sheet of paper before me...As in a play, the images of my childhood pass before me through a bright transparent mirror, and I hold them one by one.

Smorgon my hometown – my cradle stood in you, I took my first steps in you, in your streets I learned my first lesson in human relations, and bought wisdom in your "*Heders*" and "schools".

My house in you was small, but the whole world resided in it. It was saturated with faith in God and love for the nation of Israel.

Untypical for girls, my father of blessed memory entered me to the "*Heder*" of Rabbi Gershon Yankel in Karka Street (Krever Gas). I was a small tender girl then. I was barely five years old.

Even now I can see in my dreams the long wooden benches adjacent to the tables. There were various strange engravings on them, birds and animals that the children's imagination carved, some with a small cheap knife, and some with a nail or a piece of glass. Next to this long table sat a congregation of babies, boys and girls, and learned prayers, the *Chumash* and the Bible. Next to the "class room" was a small room that served as the residence of the "Rabbi" and his "Polish woman", dark and narrow was this room and its entire space was filled with two wide beds. The naughty among us played "hide and seek" under the beds of this gloomy room.

Attached to the Rabbi's house grew a tree that its bough almost covered the roof and sloped towards the fence. I remember that the teacher's goat was tied to this tree. The goat, "the only daughter", was spoiled but kind hearted and overflowing with milk for the children of Rabbi Gershon Yankel. One day, the goat disappeared, and it was "*Tisha B'Av*" in the rabbi's house. The Rebbetzin clasped her hands, cried and shouted in a voice full of fear.

"The goat is lost and gone, Woe to me! our provider!" Needless to say, that we, the small children, participated in the great grief of the rabbi's wife.

My mother of blessed memory educated us in the spirit of tradition and religion. Every morning, when we got up, she placed us, the children, in a row and we repeated after her word by word: "*Modeh Ani Lefanecha*" ["I am grateful before You"], and at bedtime, when we climbed on our beds, she gave us a copper laver full of water and a bowl on its side to wash our hands and say: "*Hamapil hevlei sheina*" [the Bedtime *Shema*].

[Page 235]

Our mother insisted that also her daughters will pray "*Shacharit*", "*Mincha*" and "*Maariv*" every day.

And what is remarkable in this? After all, our mother was the daughter of a rabbi, the granddaughter of "R' Yosile der Villner", and also the uncles were teachers, judges and rabbis like R' Yodel der Zurferner, R' Zalman and others.

Every Friday, after "Kabalat Shabbat", my father used to bring a poor guest to the house, and mother brought a needy "Yeshiva Bocher" [an unmarried Yeshiva student] every Tuesday.

My father was a scholar, a "reader", a respectful man with a pleasant voice. His teaching was organized and in his spare time he taught us. How I loved to hear my father explaining the Bible. His explanations opened my eyes, and to this day I haven't forgotten the knowledge that I acquired from him in my childhood. On summer evenings and on the Sabbath he taught me "*Pirkei Avot*" and "*Barchi Nafshi*" in the winter.

The first planted words of wisdom and morals in my soul, and the second the love for poetry and the wonders of God. I grew up a little and started to study in the "*Reformed Heder*" ["*Heder Metukan*"] of the teacher Schinuk of blessed memory. He was an excellent teacher, a "grammarian", an enthusiastic lover of Zion, and an advocate of the Hebrew literature. Parallel to my studies in the "*Reformed Heder*" I also studied in the Russian Elementary School.

Nevertheless, I preferred my Hebrew studies over the Russian studies. When I started to read Hebrew books on my own – I didn't let them go. I was shaken when I read "*Ahavat Zion*" [Love of Zion] and "*Ashmat Shomron*" [The Guilt of Samaria] by Abraham Mapu. For many days I wandered dreamily and my eyes rose longingly to Zion.

Our teacher Schinuk had a large part in nurturing the Zionist dream among the children of Smorgon. He inspired us with his stories and lit a sacred fire in us for the love of our nation.

I remember a short essay that I wrote at that time under the influence and the teaching of our favorite teacher. The essay was about a way-of-a-dream, and this is its summery: One day the teacher Schinuk came and said to us:

children we are going on a trip. The teacher took us and transferred us on eagles' wings to Eretz Yisrael. And here, our feet are standing at the gates to Jerusalem. We climb the mountains around her and descend into the valleys. In a valley, between fields and vineyards, Jewish farmers are reaping with joy, and the sounds of happiness and joy are being heard from all sides. Blue sky stretches over our heads. Jewish shepherds are sitting on the hills playing their flutes and their sheep are dancing in front of them. We come to a vineyard and our teacher picks a cluster of grapes and tells us: let's carry it with a "pole for two"- we carry the cluster of grapes and bring it to our brothers in the Diaspora.

I woke up and it was a dream. The teacher Schinuk of blessed memory checked the essay and praised the writer (it's me) publicly. He asked me to give him my essay so he could read it before the members of the "Zionist Federation". I remember the phrase that the teacher wrote on the essay in addition to the grade:

[Page 236]

"Indeed, your feet will step on the land of Zion and your eyes will see the return of our people to their country."

Not before long, the "*Reformed Heder*" of Schinuk of blessed memory received a "burst of power." A young Jewish woman, a graduate of the Zionist School "Yehudia" in Vilna, who was qualified as a teacher, came to Smorgon, married our teacher Schinuk, and helped him with his revival work.

Maybe this teacher from "Yehudia" in Vilna was the cause of my deepen desire to be a teacher. That thought gave me no rest and I looked for ways to make it happen. My parents' financial status was strained, there were many children at home and my sisters came of age. O where will my help come from? My prayer and my secret tears were received in the heavens. Spirit and salvation came to me from a place that I've never expected.

In those days, Dr. Epstein of blessed memory lived in Smorgon. A precious Jew and an ardent Zionist. Though, he was a doctor for his people's illnesses, meaning, body illnesses, he didn't prevent himself from giving medicines for the illnesses of our people's spirit and soul. The city's Zionists gathered in his home for holiday parties or for reading parties from the nest Hebrew literature. And since I was gifted with a nice voice and read poems with the correct emotion, I was invited to one of these parties to read the poem "*Igeret Ketana*"[A brief letter] by Hayim Nahman Bialik. It seems that I succeeded in reading the poem, because soon after Dr. Epstein invited me and had a long conversation with me. He asked me about my aspirations, examined me carefully, and had made this decision.

The next day, Dr. Epstein came to my father, sat with him for a long time, and persuaded him to send me to a kindergarten teachers' school in Warsaw. My father didn't want to hear about Warsaw. Rumors spread: that "girls were abducted" in Warsaw in order to send them overseas... but my father accepted Dr. Epstein's offer to send me to "*Yehudia*" in Vilna. And thus I arrived to "Yerushalayim deLita". The gates to the Torah and knowledge opened before me in this Jewish metropolis, and I lived the life of national and cultural revival of that generation. On holidays I returned to Smorgon. In one of these days - we presented in this city "Chana and her Seven Sons" with Moyshe Kulbak, who later became famous. Smorgon, my Divine city, accompanied me in all the many stations of my life, in all my long wanderings around the world, in the steppes of Russia and Siberia, and in the European countries. And now, when I check my way of my life, I find that a lot of the grace and beauty of my hometown, from the good and noble, are embedded in...[the remainder is missing]

[Page 237]

The Worker's Movement
(According to Bayleh Ginzburg, Gershon (the Tanner) Feldman. Special research by A.Y. Goldshmidt, Vilna).
by A. Farsayt
Translated by Janie Respitz

We are providing here a few quotes from Goldshmidt:

> "In the titanic struggle of the working masses against Czarist Russia, in the struggle for a better and more just society, Smorgon played a very important role in the Jewish Worker's movement.

In contrast to the surrounding cities and towns in the Pale of Settlement where Jewish industry was based on small workshops, artisans who worked at home, Smorgon had its Jewish Bourgeois with a real Jewish worker's proletariat.

Workers who fought against their small artisan bosses crippled them. According to the expression coined by A. Liessen it was “the pauper striking against the beggar”. However, the struggle in Smorgon had the true character of class struggle.

It is no wonder that Smorgon was one of the fortresses of the Jewish Labour Movement.

All the new and up and coming political parties emerging on the Jewish streets tried to capture this fortress. Here in Smorgon, there was a dream of true Jewish socialism – broad Jewish working masses.

The Jewish worker element in Smorgon grew in numbers and strength together with the rise of the leather industry.”

Fifty–five to sixty years ago, Smorgon was still a small Shtetl.

By the outbreak of the First World War Smorgon was already a big city and one of the largest centres of the leather industry in Russia.

There were a lot of reasons that contributed to the fast tempo to which Smorgon grew and developed. We don't have dates to tell us exactly when. What we do know, is that even the old days Smorgon was the middle point between Vilna and Minsk and served as a centre for the surrounding towns and villages.

The wide road, lined with trees on both sides, which was a straight line between Vilna and Minsk, ran through the middle of the town. One side of the street was called Vilna Street; the other– Minsk Street. Leaving the town, the road continues between rows of trees.

If those trees could talk they would tell us about Napoleon's soldiers who came east against the hated Russian soldiers, and about the same soldiers who using the same road ran home, all stopping in Smorgon. Already then, 125 years earlier, Smorgon was a big village. It was here that Napoleon mad his escape leaving his exhausted army under the leadership of a general.

A memorial of Napoleon remained for us in Smorgon, the graves of his fallen soldiers in Litchnik Forest which we referred to as the "French Hills"

The trees would have also recounted how people came in an attempt to escape the suffering on the Polish manors in search of a bit of bread. They set up small industry to escape the primitive suffering of the surrounding area.

One of the industries to emerge was fur, especially sheep pelts for the winter. From this emerged a general pelt industry and then further developments: finishing, stitching and other branches of the leather industry.

The leather tanneries began to emerge around 60 years ago. The first to open a large tannery was Rotshteyn and Yisroel Shutkever (the new rich man).

In later developments, German masters would play a large role, introducing new methods. This is why the leather produced was called "Hamburg Leather".

The conditions in the tanneries were difficult – a 15-hour work day. Thursdays they worked until 12:00 and returned Saturday night.

The workers were divided in two categories: Masters – the aristocracy of the trade, and the rest who nobody cared about. In order to learn the trade you looked for talented masters. You would take them to the tavern and ply them with whisky and food. But for this you needed money. Since they did not have the money, they would steal

From this grew a worker's element. He was healthy and hearty, he could drink and fight. Spiritually, he was raw.

The first outbursts of revolutionary activity began as early as the end of the 1880s. They were initiated by two cultural leaders, Rubanov and Ivan Frantchevitch Sinitsky.

This is what we were told by Bayleh Ginzburg, Rabbi Menashe's daughter:

"Anna Mikhaelovna Rubanova was the most educated woman, stemming from nobility she followed the teachings of Tolstoy and chose a simple life as opposed to noble. When her husband Rubanov became the tax collector in Smorgon, they settled in a small village not far from town – in Ferevez. There, Anna Mikhaelovna worked in the fields with the peasants, dressed like them and tried to become one of them. However, she didn't find much interest in them. She began to look for friends among the youth of Smorgon. She had a large library and loved to read books. This is how she met a few Jewish girls; my sister Libe Ginzburg, Sarah Metlitzkaya, Olga Burshteyn and a few others. These same girls would later become pioneers in the workers' movement in Samrgon. Their fate would result in much suffering, at the hands of their parents, who were fanatics, the surrounding environment and the police

I would later become a student of Sinitsky.

Ivan Frantchevich Sinitsky was a petty bourgeois non-Jewish city dweller living in Smorgon. He spent his youth in large Russian cities where he studied. He was very well educated. When I met him, he was well into his thirties. He appeared young, strong and energetic. He was blond, with kind, smiling blue eyes. For a while he worked as a tax collector. People told a witticism about him. Every time he would have to go to the shops he would send a warning to be careful. He didn't hold this job for long and soon left to work the land.

Behind the town he had a large garden where he planted vegetables, fruit trees and beanstalks. Between the trees, vegetables and beanstalks there stood a small house built in the European style

When we began to go to Sinitsky's the house was not completely finished. His yard was filled with wood, brick and clay. I remember the first evening we went there. It was a Friday night late in the fall. It was dark and raining, but we, a group of five small girls wen tot Sinitsky's. Me, Doborah Shimshelevich, Sonia Shpalter, Revekah Donishevsky and Ida Heligman.

It was dark and scary. We couldn't see the road. We were frightened, but would not give up. We continued. Then we saw a small fire. That was Sinitsky's house.

We ran into the yard and OY VEY! We fell into a pile of clay and couldn't get up. We began to scream. Sinitsky came out with a lantern and with difficulty, helped us out. We were good and scared, but soon our fear turned into laughter. We laughed about everything – from our falling into the clay, washing our shoes and letting them dry beside the small oven. I think everything was laughing with us. Even the big table, the lamp and the book shelves on the wall. Our laughter rang out and filled the small room with joy. Sinitsky read something to us. I don't remember exactly what. I doubt if we even understood because we were still very weak in Russian. What I do remember, is that he served us homemade honey spread on bread and we enjoyed it very much. For a long time we went to Sinitsky's, at first once a week, and then twice. He would read to us and then give us books to take home. Then he would have discussions with us about the books. His goal was to help us develop and he gave us everything that according to him was useful and comprehensible for us

He also taught us to sing. He sang songs with us that bitterly cried over the fate of the Russian peasant. He taught us how to work in the garden, weeding and sowing. He tried to instill in us pride, self– worth, love of people, hard work and all that is beautiful and good

We felt very close to him and would tell him about all of our experiences. We had to fight our own parents who were afraid of a worldly education. As a Russian populist he stood to the side of the worker's movement. He was negative toward it. In order to weaken his influence among the intelligentsia, Shmuel Levin, one of the leaders of the movement in Smorgon, brought his good friend from Minsk, A. Walt, the now well– known A. Liessen, to Smorgon to debate Sinitsky. Walt was known for his sharp mind and strong debating skills. The debate took place in Sinitsky's house in the presence of 6–7 activists in the movement. Walt stressed his Marxist point of view and everyone stuck to his own.

We will continue to quote Goldshmidt:

"There was another source of spiritual suckling, Levin from Minsk. He earned his living as a teacher. He was among the Smorgon intelligentsia and an enthusiastic folkist who embraced Marxist theories. The group;

> Libe Ginnzburg, Sarah Metlitzkaya, Elke Burshteyn and others took on the issue of class struggle on and idealistic level. For them, going to the people meant gaining access to the working masses. The first step they needed to take was to awaken the working youth offering free courses in Russian and arithmetic."

Here is what one of the members of the first group, Gershon (the tanner) Feldman had to say:

> Our first teachers and instructors took us from darkness and brought us to the enlightened path toward a struggle for socialism. They organized a group and taught us to write and read Russian. When rumours about this began to spread through Smorgon, my mother called upon Libe, Rabbi Menashe's daughter, (Libe Ginzburg who later in America will be Libe Walt– Liessen):
>
> > Libe dear, they say you are teaching kids Russian. Is it true? Maybe you want to teach my son. He's constantly reading books.
>
> Libe looked at her father who was sitting quietly in the corner reading from his holy books. Her mother, the Rebbetzin stood by the oven her face reddening in anger and answered:
>
> > No. Who told you such things.
>
> My mother even wondered why Libe denied it. But, no is no. She left on her way
>
> She did not walk 15 feet when she heard steps behind her. Libe followed her. Libe poured out her heart and asked her to keep a secret. She told my mother she should go to Binke Shimshelevitch. This is where I found my circle. The members of this study group were: Yudl Kremer, Velfke Menkes,Binke Shimshelevitch and Bentshe Milikovsky.
>
> We all had a special feeling for our teacher. It was no small thing what they were doing for us!
>
> They put their heart and soul in teaching us how to serve the masses.
>
> Besides teaching they would also instruct. Our entire way of thinking had been changed

But now, the few professional Russian teachers in Smorgon began to shout:

–The Nihilists! The Nihilists are steering our youth off the path. They threatened to denounce them to the authorities.

The work was then taken over by Shmuel Levin. He ran it in a more clandestine manner and began to organize an aid fund. Our attitude was very negative. Why should we raise money? They don't have enough to get drunk on? Let them worry about it! No, we won't take it.

But when Tzivia's Leybke explained it to me and asked me to go with him to Levin, I went.

I shined my shoes, wore my cap to the side and without an invitation went the Leybke to Levin.

My appearance certainly did not invoke trust. Levin was in a dilemma. For a while the conversation did not connect. Levin was cautious. He was angry we came uninvited as he was busy with classes. But as he spoke to me, he calmed down and took me into the two groups; the first for knowledge of society, the second , nature. Each group had 20–30 people. It was 1895 and for the first time our group celebrated the 1st of May. We gathered deep in the Lichnik forest. Levin and a few others spoke. We ate and drank and in order to remember the day we carved the names of all present in a tree.

The work of our circle under the leadership of Levin, Libe Ginzburg and Sarah Metlitzky expanded. Our knowledge of society grew deeper. We began to comprehend the struggle that stood before us for better conditions and for fairer distribution of wealth that we could bring about with our calloused hands. Our aid fund acquired many new members

However, we could not conceptualize the real strength of our organization until the following event occurred. We brought in as a member our master – Mikhash Uknevitch. One Monday Mikhash came to work not yet sober from yesterday's drinking

Our boss got angry and sent him away. So four of us from the aid fund in our factory put down our work and left for the tavern.

We declared: A Strike! We will not go back to work until they allow our comrade Mikhash Uknevitch to return.

At first our bosses to not conceive what was happening. The word strike was very new in Smorgon. Neither the bosses nor the workers nor the police really understood what it meant

Moishe Zalman Shutkever was happy that his competitor was facing a strike. He sent his master, Hofman, to the tavern with a few coins .The master ordered whisky. The celebration increased. When people heard we were not returning to work and we were receiving whisky, more workers, sympathetic to our cause put down their work and joined us.

That's when our bosses understood that a strike is a terrible thing, and gave in.

But for us workers, this first success had great meaning. This was the first time we realized that if we unite, we have power and we will not be abandoned by the boss. Each of us felt more confident.

From that day on, spontaneous strikes would often break out, which would result in higher wages and other better conditions.

The movement strengthened and spread. Now the workers saw the truth in our slogan, that only through struggle will the worker obtain his rights. He received many new members, not all desirable. We didn't know then that within our ranks there were two moles. They were Gursky and Strashinsky.

Levin left Smorgon in 1896, but the seeds he and others from the first group of pioneers sowed spread quickly. The police were aware and were quite uneasy with our growth. They tried to capture the organizers. Most of all, they tried to get the book where all members were registered.

This was in 1896. There was a strike. Gursky who was on the executive and Eliyokum Malkes from the aid fund had to review the books and make a report. Gursky informed the police they could now have access to the book with all the names of the members.

When Yudke Kremer and Gusrky secluded themselves behind Batarayniya Street under a tree the Gendarme emerged and took them and the book.

A great fear overcame all the members of our group. For a short time, the movement was falling apart. We walked around with bowed heads, waiting and thinking that today or tomorrow, we too will be arrested. We were being watched. They arrested and exiled Yudl Kremer and Eliokum Malkes.

Yet, the idea of a workers' struggle did not die. Others came and began to organize the youth element of the finishers. Minke from Krakow, Nekhamkeh Ginzburg (wife of Yitzkok the tobacconist) and Aron Shimshelevitch led quiet, deep work. They tried to give the workers a better political consciousness. They provided a lot of literature in order to develop intellect.

There was no work for the tanners. The leaders claimed Binke Shimshelevitch and I were standing in their way. They suggested we leave Smorgon.

This really bothered us: What do you mean we are in the way? We want to help as much as we can. This is when we joined the organization.

The work of the organization began to grow. In 1897, 400 men came to the May Day demonstration and by 1898 we were already demonstrating in the streets.

The police, small in numbers, were unable to break up the demonstration and brought in a squadron of Cossacks.

The work of our organization spread to surrounding towns. Smorgon became the centre.

In 1901 the finishers called for a general strike to improve conditions. They had been working from 5:00 in the morning until 8:00 at night. The workers united, put down their work. The police could not stop them.

The last day of Sukkot, 1901, a squadron of Cossacks arrived in Smorgon. That night they carried out raids throughout Samrgon. They arrested 30–40 men and sent them to the Antokolsky jail in Vilna.

This did not scare the Smorgon workers. They took on the challenge of the police and called for a general strike. Now, it was not only the leather workers, but all workers.

Now the factory inspector came from Vilna. He called for a meeting of all workers in the provincial government building. It was on the largest gatherings. The room was packed.

The factory inspector said our demands for a 12-hour work day were correct.

But we workers, embittered by the recent police brutality were not prepared to stop there. We were upset and demanded: all those arrested must be freed, a 12-hour work day, freedom of the press and the establishment of a constituent assembly.

Hearing this kind of talk, the factory inspector refused to listen to us any further.

We threw our factory booklets in his face and left the meeting.

The strike lasted from the 12th to the 27th of October. They arrested all the organizers of the movement, around 120 people and finally broke the strike.

I was among the 120. I sat in jail for two years and then I was sent to Irkutsk province where I remained until 1903.

The only thing the workers achieved from that struggle was a 12-hour work day.

*

The revolutionary worker's movement was already so strong and deeply rooted in Smorgon, the mass arrests could not bring it down. Others came to replace those sent away. The struggle for a humane and just life against the greedy tyrants demanded sacrifices. Actually, all the early pioneers of the movement and the early activists suffered greatly. Almost all the pioneers of the first group left this world to soon

Libe Ginzburg (Rabbi Menashe's daughter), was an outstanding moral personality, with phenomenal talents, and always ready to devote herself to everything she believed in and held dear. Even as a child she was admired. It was said that her grandfather Reb Chaim Avrom would sit her on his lap when he had to deliver a ruling or solve a conflict, and he would ask her opinion. People were amazed by her clever answers.

She devoted herself to the movement with all the passion of her young soul. In the closed atmosphere of a small town her ideas came into conflict with the rabbinic ways of her parents. She suffered greatly from this. When she couldn't bear it any longer, she left for Warsaw. There she began studying dentistry. She did not like dentistry and she still had to hide from the police. In the end, she left for America. There she became a nurse following her likes and ideals. She married A. Liessin. This was the apogee of her joy.

The very difficult pioneering work in the worker's movement in Czarist Russia, the suffering of her Warsaw period (where she had one light filled moment; her friendship with the well– known revolutionary Fruma Frumkina) drained her of all her strength. On the 18th of August, 1912, she passed away.

Sarah Metlitzkaya, another from that small circle of pioneers also had a tragic end. We know a lot about her from the writings of Beyle Ginzburg who wrote:

> I was still a small girl, but as Libe's sister they trusted me and took me everywhere. They would send me on messages with illegal papers. Libe didn't like it and would get angry.
>
> Being very lively and unafraid I enjoyed my role. I was proud of it: This is where I am reminded of Sara Metlitzkaya. Fate was never good to her. Her parents died when she was very young. She was raised by an old fanatic grandfather. She suffered greatly and her proud firm nature hardened. She was a smart and good agitator, devoted to the movement with heart and soul. In her house, on a shelf, was the library. When the police discovered it and surrounded the house, the whole town was in turmoil. The street filled with people, young and old. No one had ever seen so many police in Samrgon. Everyone was afraid. People stood frightened and whispering. The entire marketplace where Sarah's house stood seemed like a fair. I looked up and saw Sarah standing at the window. She was looking out onto the street. Her face but pale, yet resolved. She was biting her nails. This is what she did when she was upset. I heard someone say:

Take a look at her nerve, how she stands so calmly by the window, as if nothing happened; like she is about to give a speech to the scoundrels. They should all be crossed out

This is all because she doesn't have parents, poor thing. Parents would not have permitted this to happen. A pity. A poor girl. Who will take care of her now?

"The Movement"! I felt like shouting out. And actually, that's what happened. Metlitzkaya was not arrested. The police took away all the books. They left Sarah alone. The same night, Sarah got dressed in men's clothing and with a wagon left for Minsk, and from there to London. She could not get organized in London. She felt pulled back to Russia. Then we learnt in Smorgon that Sarah Metlitzkaya was back in Minsk. Gershon Feldman and Binke Shimshelevitch went to Minsk to convince her to go to America. By now, she could not live without the movement. She arrived in America broken and exhausted. In the end, her nerves could no longer take it. She became very sick and would end her life in the hospital.

Another member of the small group of pioneers died young. Nechama Ginzburg (Yitzkhok the tobacconist's daughter).

Beyle, Rabbi Menashe's daughter wrote:

"I'm now remembering the evening before the general strike of the women tailors. Nechame's small room was packed with women tailors. A small lamp was burning on the table. Nechame stood on a box and made a speech. Her beautiful, smart face was shining. Her eyes were sparkling. Her voice rang out with great enthusiasm into all the hearts of those present. Everyone is swearing to be true to the strike. They sang the revolutionary song with heart, but quietly, not be heard outside.

The next morning the strike broke out. Parents were sending children to work, but nobody broke the strike. The strike lasted a few weeks and resulted in shorter hours and higher wages.

Nechame Ginzburg was also forced to leave for America, and she could not be calm. She too felt pulled back by the struggle. She returned and died suddenly in Kiev.

Shmuel Levin was truly a remarkable person. Great mathematician, well educated, devoted to the socialist ideal, he gave everything to the work of the pioneers. Among Levin's students in Smorgon were Meir Devenisky and A. Vayter who later play an important role in the 1905 revolution. He would become known with his works in Yiddish literature and would die a martyr's death at the hands of the Polish legion in 1919.

Also Levin was not fated to live to see better times. He came to America, became a doctor and 6 months later died of a stomach ailment

Those young pioneers and activists who died young did not die in vain. The ideals they fought for spread like fire among the youth and workers of Samrgon who continued in the struggle.

From the Smorgon Anthology
1934 America, New York.

[Page 250]

The Kibbutz and A. Veiter

by A.Y. Goldshmid

Translated by Janie Respitz

Isaac Meir Devenishsky
(1878–1919)

He came to Smorgon (which at the time was a centre of Torah study) in 1895 (17 years old) with a colossal amount of Talmudic and Haskala (enlightened) knowledge.

In those years in Smorgon they didn't follow the tradition of "eating days" for the talented youth that were preparing for ordination...they paid them 75–90 Kopeks per week.

Until 10:00 in the morning he studied with his teacher Levin (one of the pioneers of the worker's movement), after 10:00 he studied voice with great diligence, he had a very beautiful voice. He refused to accept the weekly wages. He received 10 Rubles a month from home. His mother would also send packages.

His best friend was the son of the Vendzigal Rabbi, Mordecai Rosenson (Raziel) (the father of David Raziel).

Another friend was Berl Bitchkovsky. They refused to support Rosenson because he wrote poetry.

Zalman Sutzkever took a risk for him and Bitchkovsky. Rosenson (Mordecai Raziel) was pardoned and his weekly wages were raised. (see in his interview)

In Smorgon there was a clandestine circle of self– education. They had a library. The “librarian” was “Sarah the Sour Kraut maker's daughter”, who was a midwife. She tried to acquire as many Yiddish, Hebrew, Russian and Polish books as possible.

Here you could find the works of Ahad Ha'am, the complete “Hashachar” by Peretz Smolenskin, Sholem Aleichem's “Jewish People's Library” , Spector's “House Friend”, Mendeles' “The Little Man”, “The Tax”, “Conscription” and “The Mare”. (In a few copies) “The Truth” by Aharon Lieberman, “Meeting of Scholars” by Radikson, from “The Voice” and “Voice of a Nation”, Y.L Peretz' “Jewish Library”, “Literature and Life”, and his “Pages”. Also Daniel Dirona amd and all the editions of Achyasaf

The library was illegal and secret, but had many readers from among the Yeshiva students and workers.

They began to organize small cells of workers in Smorgon led by intellectuals. The leader was the aforementioned Levin, who was Veiter's private teacher. Levin was friends with the half Russified Pole Sinitsky.

He had an estate in a beautiful garden near Smorgon. Sinitsky was a friend to the Jews. His job was a tax collector. Before he would go out collecting he would send notices that he was coming. He wanted everything to be in order

He was an admirer of Mikhalovsky, a populist. He knew Yiddish and devoted himself to propaganda among the Jewish youth.

Sinitsky had a rich library. Veiter spent a lot of time at his home and library. Here you could find the best works of European literature. Veiter divided his day. Until 10:00 he studied general studies and languages. From 10:00 until 4:00, Talmud and commentaries. After 4:00 he would read for a few hours. In the evening he would go to his new teacher, Sinitsky.

Saturday night he would go to the Lubavitch Hasidic shul. He would also go to Koydenov shul where they were more mystical. They would sing and dance with great passion.

A.Veiter wrote a lot. We have a poem that he wrote in Russian in Smorgon (see the poem below)

He began to publish a Hebrew and Yiddish journal "Organ of Smorgon Commentaries" in the spirit of Aharon Lieberman's "Truth" and Peretz' "Pages."

His parents new that Isaac Meir was involved in bad things. The play "The Travels of Benjamin the Third" was brought to Smorgon. Either Veiter or Mordecai Rosenson presented it on Purim. It made an impression. The very religious were shocked: they could not understand how the Yeshiva boys got involved with this.

Veiter considered this year in Smorgon to be the best period of his life. Smorgon was an enlightened city and he became familiar with all the new trends of the day. The Yeshiva boys in Smorgon were greatly influenced by Aharon Lieberman and Y.L. Peretz' "Pages."

During this time in Smorgon, new ideas were simmering among the Yeshiva students including Zionism, socialism, assimilation and political Zionism.

In 1905 A. Veiter was standing at the top of the Bund in Vilna, influential and powerful in the "Red City".

On April 19, 1919 (during the interim days of Pesach) the Polish army under Yosef Pilsutsky entered Vilna and celebrated their victory over the Red Army with bloody pogrom against the Jews. Seventy Jews were killed, among them the writer A. Veiter!

Go My Child

Go my child, over the field of death
Throw away the empty fear
The shadows will not emerge from under the graves.
The graves will be torn by the tempest
With wails and cries
Whistling they will awaken the dead –

They should not arise.
With what can they tempt the black night
In distress?
What did the world give them and death take away?
For what shall they emerge again from their graves.
There, where they wail sharply, tortured and burned.

This poem was undersigned "Smorgon" 1900. It was written in Russian and translated into Yiddish by Y. Goldshmid (A. Veiter, writings, p. 64 Kletzkin Publishing House with Goldshmid's introduction and biography, Vilna.)

[Page 253]

October 1905

(From the Smorgon book of collected works 1934)

by Nechama's Isaac

Translated by Janie Respitz

Business from years ago... Pushkin

In whose memory have those days not remained fresh until today? Who can forget the great hope, joy and enthusiasm of that holiday? Something impossible to describe filled the air. The defeat on the fields of Manchuria was such a slap in the face for the whole country. A quiet and deep unhappiness flooded all of Russia.

The youth and intelligentsia, the workers and peasants, the barracks and naval ships – all, all believed and felt that Czarist Russia was engulfed in anger and protest.

"Mayor Potemkin" lay deep in everyone's heart.

The intellectual and proletarian centres of Smorgon were brewing. At Peretz' the teacher in the shop was the correct "density", it was the centre of all the "Siberians", passionate protesters. They spoke very little and very quietly. But "they" knew..."they" knew..."they" were very, very serious. Peretz' place was open on Shabbes...there, they did not joke around...Note Miller's son became more pale, he was becoming more philosophical and his language smelled of “Capital”, dialectic and Plekhanov. The small, stiff youth, the hardened social – democrat looked very severe through his glasses.

Raphael the seltzer maker's house was also a “centre” – a gathering place. A short man who devoted all his time to study, with thick glasses would spend hours with his nose in the “Times” standing, while leaning his shoulder on the table. The black bearded mystic Rabinovitz was one of the central figures. Yosef Reznikovitz swallowed the newspapers and quietly mumbled to himself. Raphael himself would speak in allusions to my father...liberal politics... Potemkin...and would rock back and forth a bit. My father would respond with a glance and begin to rock...and both, Raphael and my father sweetly swayed. Another important “centre” was at the blond watch maker's shop. Here is where the true sect of clowns met. Straight from the train I would go there with a fresh pack of newspapers and I was truly made to feel welcome with a joke. The lead character was the blond watch maker himself. Beside him was the lame watch maker, the distinguished S. Savitz. The tall blond policeman would wait for me and want a newspaper for free; he knew I was not permitted to sell the papers ...so I had to give him and the other policemen “bribe” newspapers.

Besides Peretz the teacher's rascals and the blond watch maker's clowns there were many other centres of critics, philosophy and revolution. At Boyarsky's pharmancy, at Braverman's sausage factory, at Israel's Hirshke's used clothes shop they critiqued...even the Kalman the wagon driver on the new street offered opinions.

It is already a few days that the trains from Vilna and Minsk have not arrived. No newspapers. Slowly life town was expiring. The shops were closed. People were afraid to show themselves in the streets. It was cold. A bunch of policemen stood in the market and on Minsk and Vilna streets. Nighttime was dead silent; from time to time you can hear the hoofs of the Cossacks' horses. This is how the days passed. It's raining and it's wet and cold. But we wait to see what will happen. Why are the police so enraged? This is how almost eight days passed.

It was evening and I stood by the well with a bucket of water. I heard a whistle from the train station. The locomotive was approaching. The town awakens as if from sleep. It making livelier and livelier. A few hours later we heard a “Hooray” from Krever Street. There was a commotion. We heard a bang, shots. People were running in the darkness on to New Street, without hats, with one boot on, in the mud; they were coming over the fences and the gardens; it was dark, people were getting injured; people were running aimlessly. There was a demonstration on Krever Street. Cossacks attacked...it was, in short, revolution...we kids were in seventh heaven. But father was not happy with all the commotion and insisted that we stay home and not wander around. I didn't sleep all night.

I barely survived until morning. It was lively in the streets. Kalman's Alter with his big belly was on the street freeing the children . A functionary appeared. He was greeted with an “Hooray”. He took off his hat with a cockade...

A little later, around 2–3 in the afternoon, everyone was outside. The market and Vilna Street were packed...People were coming from all the side streets. It was a cold autumn day. A moment passed...people wereexcited. They were shaking hands, hugging, kissing, many were crying from joy...the Cossacks behind the church stood snuggled close together like lost sheep...there were no police around. A few workers were riding around on horses. People held hands and made a chain from Note Margolis' and further. Here they come...a large portrait of Karl Marx swayed in the air; on all sides red flags were waving in the sky. There was drumming. The Marseillaise resounded...people sang. A worker (Gershon the tanner) appeared on a horse with a bloodied shirt on a stick held high. This was the past work of the police...the crowd falls silent for a moment...many remove their hats...and they sang “You Fell As a Sacrifice”.

The cold, grey autumn day disappeared. There was joy in everyone's heart. It is the first omen of a new life. It was the first day of spring.

How can one forget such a day?

[Page 256]

The Last Days of Smorgon

(From the Smorgon book of Collected Works 1934, America)

by Nechama's Isaac

Translated by Janie Respitz

I'm turning the pages of a diary. The old yellowed pages in a torn notebook written with childlike naivety awaken in me past scenes

The old home of Smorgon swims before my eyes. I can see the panorama of winding streets unfold. Long narrow alleys, the marketplace courtyards and houses. The whole neighbourhood comes alive in my memory; Litchnik, Ashmen Way ,Pereves, the Vilija river, the Stop, and Sinitsky Way between two rows of trees. The pictures flash quickly. I see the old sharp life of the last days of Smorgon, the days when the town suffered in agony before its death that the war brought about

The summer of 1915 was catastrophic for the Russian army. Under the influence of a powerful German attack, the Russian army was about to lose.One town after the other fell to the enemy. The fortresses of Kovno and Brest –Litovsk fell. Grodno had already fallen and the Germans were standing at the gates of Vilna. Nothing could stop the march of the Germans.

Smorgon, from the beginning of the war was just a few miles from the front, suddenly became even closer. Fear of the coming events was strongly felt. There was a wince and the helpless just had to wait. The wealthier began to prepare to evacuate. The poor lived with blind hope.

There was not a large military presence in Smorgon. There were the bakeries and other divisions one would normally find.

The train connection to Vilna was paralyzed, but deep in Russia the trains were still running.

By the beginning of September newspapers ceased to arrive and we lived from rumours. Every day a new rumours that the Germans were very close to Samrgon. All of us in Smorgon did not believe these rumours.

On September 15th at 9:00 in the morning a rumour spread that the Germans were at the Vilija River. This appeared to be unbelievable. Everything was calm as usual. Smorgon had begun her regular day of activities. The shops opened. The factories were working and women went shopping in the market. Peasants came to sell their products.

Suddenly, from our side of the river, we heard the boom of artillery. The Germans were shooting at the train.

Panic broke out. Shopkeepers bolted their shops. The peasants harnessed their horses and in a wild gallop, whipping with all their might, left town.

The streets that had been full of life were now empty.

Soon shooting was heard nearby. The Russian soldiers tried to fight back. On Krever and Vilna Streets they began to shoot the attacking Germans. It did not last long. Within 2 hours the Germans managed to chase away the Russians. The shooting stopped and the people who hid in the cellars began to crawl out. They found the Germans breaking into the shops for groceries and other foods. Like hungry wolves, the German soldiers devoured everything. They did not treat the people badly. Some people opened their shops and sold things to the Germans.

By evening the streets were filled with people. The locals from Samrgon walked back and forth on Vilna and Minsk streets and could not believe their eyes. The city was unrecognizable. The shops had been broken into. The people, confused. People walked around stunned by the sudden changes. Only yesterday the city was happening. Only later did we learn that his was 100 miles from the war blaze and we were already in the middle of front fire.

We did not yet know, how this all transpired, thanks to the German breakthrough of the Russian front around Sventsian, they sent their best cavalry, infantry and bicycles and light artillery. They were behind the Russian army and cut off all communication.

From then on things happened quickly.

September 16th.

There were a lot of German soldiers in the city; artillery, cavalry and infantry. Something important was going to happen. As if poisoned, couriers were running back and forth. By evening, the Germans began to withdraw. We understood that no far away there was a favourable battle for the Russians. The night was unsettling. The sky was fire red. Nearby villages were burning.

September 17th.

The Germans are proceeding with their departure. Their mood is heavy. The battle is nearing Smorgon. The sounds of the canons are getting louder. Everyone gathered in the cellars and walled houses. The shul was filled with people. With pounding hearts, we are lying and listening to the sounds of the canons flying and breathe a little easier when we hear them land far away.

The battle, very close to Smorgon wages on. During the day a house on Slobodke Street caught fire from a burning coal. In no time, the wooden building was in flames. Me and my brother Mordecai were the first to arrive at the fire. The bombarding was strong and nobody dared to show themselves. Soon a second house began to burn. We realized if nothing resolute would happen soon, the whole town will catch fire. Meanwhile, more people began to appear. We all ran to the fire station and pulled out the buckets and pumps. Horses appeared from somewhere. As we carried the buckets through the horse market, a cannonball landed near us. We instinctively fell to the ground. We quickly got up and went on with our work. We put out the fire and left.

By evening the bombardment stopped. Just weak shooting continued. Small groups of Germans went around and robbed the abandoned houses. They took good clothing and preserves.

September 19th.

The attitude of the Germans toward the people worsened daily. They hung a fireman because they found a telephone. They also arrested a few Jews, among them Mendl Khosid whom they accused of espionage, in his attic they found pigeons. The Jews saved the entry of the Russians.

The battle raged on. The cannonballs are falling like hail, bringing destruction and death. No one dares to come out of the cellars. A cannonball landed on the corner near the shul with about two thousand people inside. A cannonball also fell on Bitshovsky's granary, but there was nobody there. By day the Russians attacked. They managed to chase away some Germans. We met the Russians with mixed emotions. On one hand we were happy that we once again belonged to Russia. On the other hand we were afraid because we heard that they did not stop provoking Jews. However, the soldiers did not treat the Jews badly.

From all these experiences we wanted on thing; to rest. We left the cellars and came out on the street. Smorgon suffered greatly. Many buildings were damaged by the bombardment. The feeling that the old way of life in Smorgon was shot which unwillingly seeped into our souls.

The robbed the remaining shops. The soldiers would take the expensive things and sell them cheap to the peasants. When the villagers learned of the banditry, they came to Smorgon. It took on the character of a pogrom, the only difference being, no one was hurt.

September 22nd.

The situation was the same. The banditry continued. When they were done robbing the stores they went to the houses. At night, groups of soldier – marauders went about. They were looking for Germans. But they looked for them in the dressers, men's pockets and lady's bosoms.

The bakeries worked all day baking bread for the soldiers.

There was a lot of military in Smorgon. People tried to go to Barun and Kreve. Many left town.

The moment we feared arrived. Cossack patrols came and told everyone to leave town. They told us in Russian they will shoot. It was not safe to remain. We packed a bag with underwear and a pillow. We packed a basket with food and went out to Minsk street. From all the streets and alleys people swarmed into Minsk street. We were running away from the sounds of the shots over our heads. Near Sinitsky's the Russian infantry dug small trenches in an attempt to stop the Germans. The faces of the soldiers were muddy and dark. Their eyes were sad and tired. They looked at us and said something. We only wanted one thing, to get as far away from this hell as possible. A few small scenes are sketched in my mind. Yude the carpenter, whose daughter suddenly fell ill, came running and took our 2 wheeled wagon. He tried to put the sick girl in the wagon, but she tore away and ran to the cemetery. Chana Aronovitch passed us with a sick child in her arms and a baby in her apron. I wanted to stop and help her, but bullets were flying over- head. We all fell to the ground and lay for a while. When I stood up, I could not find her. We believed then, we were leaving Smorgon for a short time. We would hide in the forest for a while and then return home. No one could conceive that we would be leaving forever, our childhoods and youth, our joys and our sorrows our beloved home.

[Page 261]

A testimony

by Pesach Taburiski

Translated by Sara Mages

I was born in Smorgon in 1903.

I studied at the Russian Elementary School which was located in Minsk Street. There were five classes in the school. The school's principal was Skott, and the teachers were Horowitz the author of the grammar book, Dubkis, and Filler. Mrs. Scott was the principal of an elementary school for girls.

In 1911, at the age of eight, I entered the Elementary School's preparatory class. The school had about 250 students. Each student, who was accepted, had to be able to read and write Russian, be versed in the multiplication table and the four rules of mathematics.

Skott taught the Bible which was translated into Russian. We also prayed in Russian. We started the morning with a prayer for the king.

I studied four years in the school. The studies continued without interruption even during the war which broke out in 1914.

The big recruitment day came. The recruits, meaning, the reserves up to age 45, were transported to Oshmene [Ashmyany]. Their number reached tens of thousands.

During the first year of the First World War, convoys of Jewish refugees from Kovno, Jonava, Kurlandia [Courland] and also from cities in Poland arrived to Smorgon's station.

Immediately, our city organized a “War refugee aid committee.”

We welcomed the refugees in the train station. We brought them food. Smorgon's notable women worked in an improvised kitchen. Samovars were brought and tea was boiled. We watered and fed the poor people who fled from the German's sword, or deported from their place of residency according to the decree of the commander-in-chief of the Russian Army, Nikolay Nikolayevich, the Jews' enemy. We received the refugees who wanted to remain in our city with open arms. Some of them stayed with us for a whole year.

The Germans entered the city and captured it on the eve of Rosh Hashanah. They robbed the grocery stores and the wine stores. They handed out chocolate to the city's children to earn their trust.

The Jews treated them with open sympathy. Not out of love for Wilhelm [Kaiser Wilhelm II], but out of hatred for Czar Nikolay II, the Czar who was hostile towards the Jews. Under his orders, his wicked people, who pretended to be nationalists, carried out pogroms against the Jews in the cities of the Pale Settlement.

The conquerors didn't harm the civilians.

One fine day we heard shots from the Firibeiz? side, meaning, across the Viliya River.

[Page 262]

The Russians built a new bridge over the river, because the Germans demolished the old bridge and also blew up the railway line. The battle was fought almost within the city limits, buildings were ignited and fires broke out.

The Russian infantry seized the city and took it from the Germans. Cossacks' troops arrived after the infantry.

After a few days, an order arrived from Nikolay Nikolayevich to burn the whole city and expel all of its Jewish residents.

Those who refused to obey, about forty people, gathered in the Koidenav Shtiebel. The Cossacks burnt the house on them.

The Cossacks stormed the few dozens men and women who hid in Kovrsky's liquor workshop. They tortured the women and set the distillery on fire.

All of us, who were expelled from the city, walked towards Minsk. We arrived, some in a cart and some by foot, to Maladzyechna. From there we traveled by train to Minsk. In Minsk they put us in the synagogue. We were welcomed by the workers of the Red Cross and the members of the "Refugee Aid Committee." Only a few refugees from Smorgon remained in Mink. The majority of the refugees traveled to various cities: Bogorodsk, Krakow and Poltova. Some traveled farther and reached Siberia. Some immigrated to the United States through Harbin [China] and Japan.

When we were expelled we didn't have the time to take food, clothing or underwear with us, we left with nothing. A few refugees bundled a little food in a tablecloth and the women took Sabbath candles.

We had a big oven in our house and the neighbors used to keep their Sabbath meals in it. Our uncle lived in the Bears Street. He was a busy factory owner and didn't know what was happening in the city. As usual he came to our house on Saturday to attend the Shabbat meal with the family. He entered, and to his astonishment he saw the Cossacks sitting around the table eating Jewish food, fish, meat and cholent, that they took out of the oven. They showered him with blows and he fled for his life

After the feast, they took kerosene from our storeroom, poured it on the Jews' houses and set them on fire. - - -

In 1920, some began to return to Smorgon. These were the forerunners... meaning, the families who lived in Minsk and their return journey wasn't long. Most of Smorgon's residents returned in 1921-1922. Some of those who returned stopped on the way and lived temporarily in Vilna, and some came straight to Smorgon. They settled in the cellars of the surviving buildings. A few busied themselves in building new houses to replace those that were burnt. For building material they used the wooden beams that they removed from the trenches which remained intact. They were built two, three, or even four stories below ground.

[Page 263]

Memoirs

by Harry L. Hofman

Translated by Janie Respitz

The experiences and recollections that occurred more than 1/3 of a century ago have become more and more pale. Many have already disappeared from my memory. But now when I dig deep into my memory – remarkably the events of my last six months in my hometown Smorgon, come alive

These last months were the last of Smorgons existence as a "City of the People of Israel". An industrial town, with a Jewish traditional and cultural life

When these scenes and recollections appear in my memory, they are tied to the pain and the cries that have been ringing in my ears for the past 37 years:

Smorgon Jews, You too?! You, who were all such kind people!

The truth is, the people of Smorgon were really nice and good – hearted.

The month of May 1915.The Czar Nikholai Nilholevitch, may his name be blotted out, the head of the Russian army, issued a command that the entire Jewish population of the area living within 50 miles from the active battle theatre must immediately leave their homes. This very decree, I believe was known as "the expulsion from Kovno".

Hundreds of thousands of Jews, men and women, young and old, weak and sick were forcefully packed into freight trains with their belongings, the bare essentials, and sent deep into Russia and even further to Siberia.

I believe this horrible edict fell upon Smorgon's Jews in the first days of May on a Thursday evening. A small group of comrades and friends improvised a meeting on the sidewalk of Vilna Street. It was decided there to try to do something to ease the suffering of those being sent away. We set up small stoves on the sidewalk and prepared food for old and young. We even warmed milk for the children. We took our prepared foods, challah, bread, cigarettes and other articles and went to the train station

A few freight cars, packed with those being sent away, were on the side tracks not far from the station.

There on the spot we decided to do more than just distribute food. We decided to take as many as possible off the trains, bring them back to the city and temporarily organize things.

Even the station guards in Russia were corrupt. The bible says that bribes blind the seeing. Those guarding the wagons were blinded during the short time it took us to complete our action.

We carried children and adults out of the train cars on our shoulders. The Jewish wagon drivers were ready to do their part. Wagon after wagon came to town packed with passengers

The next morning was Friday, Erev Shavuot. Tens of Jews went around town with wagons collecting food, clothing and pieces of furniture for the homeless.

In the following days, we met at the station by day and by night. We waited for the trains filled with refugees and distributed food clothing and other essential items. We also removed tens of wanderers and brought them to town.

We found them lodgings. We found place for almost 500 people.

Around the middle of May, our group of active workers had a meeting with the secretary of Baron Ginsburg who was helping every city and town care for war victims.

At this meeting it was decided to set up a food centre, or a city kitchen and dining room where refugees could receive cheap meals.

For this purpose, we rented Dina Grinhoyz' dance hall on Vilna Street. Three meals a day were prepared and served to the needy for a nominal fee: 3 kopeks for breakfast and 6 kopeks for lunch or supper. We charged this small amount so people would not feel like it is a donation or handout.

Tens of workers helped in this sacred work, which was not easy. Foods such as butter, cheese, milk, potatoes and other vegetables were collected from stores and the market where the merchants donated them. We also received cash donations.

All the meal preparation was done for free by women and young girls, who worked many hours, day and night.

I can't give you all the names of those who helped, but I must mention two. They worked 10–12 hours a day in the hot summer months. They cooked in the kitchen and never refused to do the most difficult tasks. This was Mrs. Lieberman, Pesach's Rivka's daughter in law and Mrs. Markovsky.

The kitchen soon became popular among the military in town. High ranking officers would come in Friday night and see a few hundred people being served tasty meals, served by young ladies from the finest families in the community. Some of the military personnel would sit down at a table to eat, and would leave a nice tip. This is how we made some money.

The work of the kitchen had a great reputation that spread widely. When the government had to evacuate an institution, 800 people had to pass through Smorgon. The writer of these lines had to get up in the middle of the night and help provide good meals to those passing through.

Once, I was called upon to bring food from Moladechne. By instructions from the above-mentioned Baron Ginsburg, the warehouses of the commissary were opened for us. We loaded eight wagons with flour, rice, sugar, tea and other products. They also provided us with all the necessary documents so that no soldiers guarding the road could stop us from arriving in Smorgon as quickly as possible, and wouldn't confiscate our products.

Besides providing food, as I already mentioned, we provided refugees with housing and furniture. We also helped with medical and legal services and provided teachers for the children. We opened special schools and courses.

In the days when Smorgon was occupied by the Germans, and also in the days when battles were taking place in and around Samrgon, with shrapnel and bullets flying through the sky, we the aid workers went around the city in danger, looked for cellars and warehouses where locals and recently arrived refugees could hide. We distributed among them sugar, cookies and other products we carried with us in order to maintain and delight them.

Catastrophe was nearing. Destruction has arrived.

Smorgon was burnt. Smorgon was emptied.

Those of us who escaped Smorgon came to Minsk. Together with others from our aid committee, we created a committee which became part of the "Minsk Society to Help Jewish War Victims".

We were given the assignment to provide help and support to those living in a part of Minsk called Kamarovke.

In this neighbourhood there were many refugees from surrounding cities and towns. We housed them in the study houses, schools and also government buildings. We hammered together wooden planks and built beds for sleeping, sitting and eating. The over crowdedness in town was unbearable. There were by now 300,000 refugees in Minsk. Under my supervision and responsibility in Kamarovke there were many refugees from Smorgon, and many refugees who came to Samrgon, we helped to get settled and then had to run for their lives with us.

My work was extremely difficult. Daily I had to witness the suffering of acquaintances and friends. Some of the wealthiest were now receiving aid. They were not only broken economically, but physically and spiritually as well. Every time I visited the other side of the river. They would look at me, and without saying anything tears would begin to flow without stopping. The visits with the Jews from Kovno, Svalk, Shavl were painful and heart wrenching. We once were responsible to ease their suffering, and now we found ourselves in the same desperate situation.

Thirty – seven years have passed, but they could not erase the memories of those terrible years of destruction.

Rochester, New York
The United States of North America

[Pages 268-270]

Smorgon Exploding

by A. Raple's

Translated by Janie Respitz

From the collection "Smorgon", 1937 (America)

The wave of people who left Smorgon under the hail of bullets, went to Zaliese. There they spread out on a large meadow on the riverbank, lit fires and tried to supress their hunger with the bit of food they brought with.

Night fell. After all they experienced that day, they just wanted to rest and forget. Everyone found a spot and tried to sleep.

No one could fall asleep. Everyone thought to themselves – what do we do next?

Many believed that the Germans, in their quick attack, would soon capture Zaliese and we would return to Smorgon. Those that believed this, remained in Zaliese a few more days under the free skies. The majority forged their escape deep into Russia.

We passed through Zaskevich, Lebedova. These towns were completely empty. We ate vegetables that were still remaining in the gardens. We would find a few potatoes and a Jewish soldier gave us some bread. This was a real meal.

In Lebedve, soldiers surrounded the house where we stopped to sleep and demanded that they *play* around with the young women. We barely managed to escape them.

We finally arrive in Molodechna. From there, trains were running to Minsk. The freight cars were filled with refugees.

Luckily, the days were sunny and warm, lessening the suffering of the refugees.

Minsk was over packed with refugees from the entire front. They all arrived at once. In vain, we tried to offer comfort and solace to the first escapees from Kovno province. Minsk was exhausted from the refugees.

Every school, government building, every corner that was still free – was used to house refugees.

The over crowdedness and filth brought epidemics. There was no reason to remain in Minsk. They were just waiting for a repetition of events that took place in Smorgon. At the first opportunity we decided to move on.

Where to?

It did not matter where, as long as moved further away from the front. They began to hand out train tickets for free, the Pale of Settlement was now abolished. The war brought about such a large stream of refugees, that there was no other choice than to allow them to travel deep into Russia.

We took the first military train and travelled at God's mercy.

This is how Smorgon, a city of more than 30,000 people, was dispersed throughout big, wide Russia.

There was not a large city where you could not find anyone from Smorgon. Kharkov, Yelizivatgrad, Yekaterinaslav, Simferopol, Mariupol, Rastov on the Don, Tsaritzin, Samara, Kazan. Some even made it to Kharbin and from there made their way to America.

But then something remarkable happened. The economic situation of Smorgon's Jews was closely related to the leather industry. This led to the creation of leather centres where Smorgon Jews fled.

From the beginning a few Smorgon factory owners discovered “Sela Bogorodskoye” in the Nizhnenavagorod province. Leather tanneries already existed making it easier to settle in. They brought tanners, finishers, and leather cutters from Smorgon and set up a mini Smorgon.

More leather factories emerged. The village quickly came alive, like a city.

A second centre was founded in Kharkov, the largest commercial city in Ukraine. The city was always a large importer of goods from Smorgon. In those days there was a lack of leather goods. The motivated Jews from Smorgon quickly built a leather industry. Here too they brought leather workers: tanners, finishers, and cutters who were dispersed in various towns and cities. The second largest leather centre, after Smorgon, was created in Kharkov and still exists today.

The third centre was in Rostov on the Don. The same thing happened there.

The Smorgon Jews who settled in these places exhibited extraordinary friendliness to everyone from Smorgon looking for help. We could fill many pages with moving stories how in this critical times one helped another.

So let us all, Smorgon Jews living in a free America, remember this good trait of Smorgon Jews in the past. We must and we will continue the old tradition of Smorgon:

Anyone who stretches out a hand to us will not leave empty handed.

[Page 271]

The Kibbutz and Mordecai Raziel

by Esther's Meir

Translated by Janie Respitz

The witness (testimony) of Rabbi Reb Yehuda Leyb Gordin, the grandfather of David Raziel.

(From an interview)

I studied in "Kibbutz B'nei Torah" in Smorgon, in the years 1895 – 1897.

The spiritual leader and examiner was Reb Yakov Shmuel Katz, an ordained Rabbi, the son in law of Avraham Heilikman, whom we called "Black Avreml."

Every young man in the religious study group received a stipend of 1 Ruble and 50 Kopeks.

They called me, within the group and in town Motl the Venzigal's Rabbi's son. In the days when I was part of this study group it included: A. Veiter, Chaim Shloyme Varshavsky (he was the son in law of Forseyt from Smorgon and later a Rabbi in Brooklyn). Mendl Danishevsky (Mendl Poltaver) and Moshe Uzder, (the brother in law of the great scholar Reb Chaim Heller, may he rest in peace).

I dramatized and staged Mendele Mokher Sforim's The Travels of Benjamin the Third, and as an introduction I wrote a poem.

I still remember one of the verses: They know about Pushkin, Bern and Heine, they do not know about Moses.

The performance took place on Purim in the home of Magid's Frade. The actors were boys from our study group.

Because of my sin of writing poetry, they didn't give me my financial aid, the 75 Kopeks a week that the younger boys in our group receive.d

Interceding for me for this injustice were Zalman Sutzkever, Berl Bitzkovksy, Skapinker and Yosef Zalman Reznikovitch. And so, they resumed my subsidy with an additional 75 Kopeks. Now I got payed like the older boys, 1 Ruble and 50 Kopeks a week.

The enlightened Jews in town said: “We didn't know that we have a Pushkin in the religious study group. Should we let him be mistreated?!”

[Page 275]

The Town and Its Residents

B. Between the Wars

My Town

by Baruch Sutskover

Translated by Ehud Sutzkever and Jerrold Landau

In memory of my brother Shlomo Neta and his family
who were killed in the Nazi Holocaust

The gate I build for you my town Smorgon
Is not a gate of victory.
It has no laurel wreath on top
but rather interwoven memories
of Bereavement and Doom.

You were full with versatile activity, work and creativity,
Bourgeois, merchants and farmers.

Small with widely open landscape
Surrounded by forests,
crossed by rivers on which banks your children
grew roots as deep as your ancient trees[1]
During those times, to you
People would come
To work in you, to conduct business
– Also to acquire Torah and light.
You received everybody
And you always sheltered then,
Until the time came
And destruction overtook you.

[Page 276]

This was during the time of the
First World War
Battles which took place within you
And you remained destroyed.
Your population was deported
From the destroyed city.
No residents remained within you,
They wandered afar
And became refugees.

You remained desolate for years
Until the end of the war.
Then your children returned
To rehabilitate you from your ruins.
And again –
The echoes of hammers–
New houses were built
The howling of the wolves was exchanged.[2]

Your form as a city was renovated.
With buildings, factories, and fields.
Institutions were also set up within you
To help the needy and impoverished.
Thus, slowly and quietly
Your life began
Anew.
You arose and became a community
As before
Splendorous and praiseworthy.
Your youth – alert and vibrant,
Set up its organizations in an exemplary fashion
For culture, to mold the pioneers
They got accustomed to work in *hachsharah*
To actualize their aims
To aliya to the Land of Israel.

[Page 277]

You, the city, also had,
Those who did not want to mention the name of Zion.
And as opposed to those who made aliya to Israel
They remained to await
The arrival of the redeemer.

But the Messiah did not come
New tribulations began.
And this time –
The city was not just destroyed
But rather the community was wiped out completely.

I cannot write on paper
That which the Nazi enemy perpetrated upon you
How you, my dear ones, your hair stood on end
When they took you to be killed and annihilated
In Ponar.
How the children were torn to pieces
Before the eyes of their parents.
How you were hauled like sheep
To the gas chambers.
How you fertilized fields that were not yours
With your body and blood.
It is impossible to mention everything.
Thus was your fate set, oh city.

You, oh beautiful one, will not be rebuilt
The dead will not re–establish a community.
We from here, from Zion,
Will perpetuate you, Smorgon
On a tablet in the Chamber of the Holocaust

Hadera, Nisan 5623 (1963)

Translator's Footnotes

1. This marks the end of Ehud Sutzkever's translation (end of line 17 in the original). Jerrold Landau continued translating from this point.

2. Exchanged evidently for sounds of construction.

[Page 278]

My hometown Smorgon

by Rafael Weinstein

Translated by Sara Mages

A

My hometown Smorgon, what was this community before the First World War and after, in other words, what was its contribution to the Lithuanian Jewry and to the country of Israel?

When I was a boy I loved you, my hometown, I loved your streets and everything that was around you, the forests and the rivers. I clung to you, because from you I nursed my devotion to return to Zion and the holy city of Jerusalem, because you inspired me with your spirit, the spirit of religious nationalism. I was born at the beginning of the new world. The days were quiet and peaceful and everything was quiet around us. Peace and tranquility prevailed in the big world, and in our city people respected each other. There were distinguished men among us, whose concern for the community and their fellowman was greater than the concern for themselves.

It is possible to say that I was born on the knees of Zionism. In those days, a star shone from the darkness and lit up the dark roads on which our nation walked. A large movement rose, a great awakening to return to Zion, to redeem and build our country from its wilderness.

We lived in Avraham Zuckerman's house in the courtyard of Beit HaMidrash. All the houses of worship, the "*Kloyzn*", the "*Shtiebelekh*", and even the hospitality house were concentrated there. I was a curious boy by nature and I loved to hear the Hasidim sing when they danced. Their songs captured my heart and charmed my soul with the grief and joy that merged in them. Many times I forced my way, without being asked, into the circle of excited dancers, who danced and sang to the depths of their souls for the sanctity of the Sabbath or a festival. I felt that the whole world "Was good!" and there was nothing more superior and improved. At home, I received a national-religious education. My father was middle-aged then. He devoted all of his will and strength to public work, and engaged in the distribution of the Zionist idea with great enthusiasm. Our house was spacious with eight rooms. One of them was dedicated to the office of "*Gemilut Hasadim*". On Saturdays and holidays it was used as "*Mikdash Me'at*" [minor sanctuary] where Jews from all the social classes prayed. It was called the "The Zionists Minyan" by the residents of our city. Every day there were many visitors to our house, and words of Torah, wisdom and piety were heard in it at all times. I absorbed the words of the visitors and debaters, who didn't intend to teach me, it was educational.

[Page 279]

I remember the Fridays, around the time of lighting the Shabbat candles. Hirsh Yehudah Rodenski walked from street to street and loudly announced that it was time to welcome the Sabbath. When he approached the side of the shops it was like terror fell on the merchants: Hirsh Yehudah is getting closer, meaning, that we need to close the shops. In an instant the bargaining ceased and all the work stopped in the city. A dense Sabbath atmosphere hovered over Smorgon's alleys and yards. There was no need for policemen and threats of fines. Hirsh Yehudah's voice was enough to stop all the secular wheels of commerce. The sanctity of the Sabbath took over on its own. Jews flocked to the houses of worship dressed in their Sabbath clothes, hurried to welcome the Sabbath Queen. Great voices, full of poetic effusion and holy longing, were heard in the courtyard of Beit HaMidrash and echoed in the distance.

My birthplace, Smorgon, was a Jewish metropolis in Lita. Great Torah sages lived there and the generation's geniuses studied there. The genius rabbi, Rabbi Avraham Yitzchak Kook, May the memory of the righteous be of a blessing, studied in a Yeshiva in Smorgon. A number of Smorgon's rabbis were famous in Russia for their knowledge, wisdom, and piety. I will only mention two of them. HaRav Yehudah Leib Gordin, and Rabbi Menashe Gintzburg. There were many "*Hadarim*" [Jewish religious schools for young children] in our city, most of them taught from the old system and a few from the new. There were reformed "*Hadarim*" where the teaching language was Hebrew. It is worth mentioning the names of the outstanding teachers: Yakov Shenzon, Leib Gilinski, Avraham Buck, Shmuel Milikovski and others whose names escaped me. All were certified teachers who finished their studies in education. Dr. Epstein of blessed memory served as a doctor in our city and supported the founders of "*Tikvah*" School. Among the founders and educators were the activists: Mr. Gershon Weinstein, Mr. Liberman and Mr. Mendel Yanovsky. The pride of our city was the writer and poet Moyshe Kulbak, who earned himself a respectable place in Yiddish literature. And we can't ignore the artist and sculptor, Mr. Etking who was born and lived in Smorgon and earned a world reputation. The great author, Abraham Aharon Kabak, also wrote his memories about the community of Smorgon. And it is impossible to ignore the family of Avigdor Koussevitzky, who were distinguished cantors with a fine singing voice.

A winter view

[Page 280]

B

The economic and public life

Before the First World War there were nearly thirty thousand people in our city Smorgon. It was known as an industrial city and its residents engaged primarily in curing hides. The products were of the best quality and found buyers in many markets across Europe. There were also a lot of tradesmen in the city like tailors, seamstress, shoemakers, carpenters, sheet-metal workers, fitters, plasterers, oven-builders and more. There were also banks in the city. The owner of one of the banks, Meir Bronda of blessed memory, was considered to be the most respected proprietor. He was a biblical scholar, a philanthropist and a diligent activist. The city paid tax to fashion: there were two cinemas, "Gignet" and "Eden". I went to see a movie by the name The Western Wall." The excitement in the audience peaked when they showed the mountains around Jerusalem.

During those days the following political parties were active among the Russian Jewry: the "Zionist", the "*Bund*", and "*Agudat Yisrael*". They took up their stand in the social life of our city. My father's house, as I said above, was a communal house because my father was a diligent activist in the Zionist movement and in the community. My father's coworkers, Shmuel Fein, Yosef Reznikovich, Ajzik Bronda, Ben Meir Bronda, Chaim Alperowitch, Mendel Yenovsky, Gershon Broide, Zev Melkis, Rapoport, Ripkin and others, came to our home. They negotiated matters of Zionism, argued about the modes of propaganda and the methods of work. I was a boy, and of course, I didn't understand their discussions and debates. But I knew that they were talking about Eretz Yisrael. I saw young men and women going down to our cellar where they packed the "*Keren Hakayemet*" boxes. They wrapped them in white cloth and sent them to the nearby towns. This work was done in secret, underground, because it was forbidden. Every Saturday evening my father's acquaintances gathered for a national Zionist "*Se'udat Melaveh Malkah*" [Escorting the Sabbath Queen meal]. They sang songs of Zion and also Hassidic songs. Once I asked my father: who is Herzl? and what is "*Keren Hakayemet*"? My father answered me, when you grow up you will know and understand, but added and said: my son, Herzl is the man who wants to bring the whole Jewish nation to his homeland and "*Keren Hakayemet*" collects money to redeem the land from the Arabs. I was filled with astonishment and asked him again: what do we lack here in our homeland that we should look for in another country? We live in peace and quite, each in his own home, we keep the Sabbath, celebrate our holidays, and no one bothers us. His answer was: we aren't in our own country. We need to redeem our Holy Land and settle there.

During the elections to the *Duma*, the Russian parliament, a strong war flared up between the Zionists and the "*Bund*" movement in the city. The Zionists had the upper hand. My father and his helpers engaged in propaganda in favor of Zionism, and fought the city's "*Bund*" members, because our city was an industrial city with a lot of factory workers.

[Page 281]

The Russian revolution appealed to the "*Bundists*" [members of the "*Bund*" movement], who waited for it to erupt and change their lifestyle. The "*Bundists*" mocked us, the Zionists, and claimed that we should build our future here, in the Diaspora, and abolish the Zionist aspiration. Great Zionist speakers visited our city and gave their speeches. I will mention the most distinguished among them: Dr. Shmaryahu Levin, Dr. Mosenzon, Ze'ev Jabotinsky and others. No wonder, that many young people emigrated from our city to Israel, settled there and engaged in agriculture. Many of Smorgon's people live on their land in Hadera and established a generation of farmers in Israel. On this occasion I'll comment, that Smorgon had a suburb by the name of "Krake". Jews, who worked the land and lived on their crops, lived there. We called them the "Krake's Jews". They had sort of communal autonomy: their own rabbi and slaughterer.

Wilenska Street in Smorgon

When the First World War broke out we were expelled from our homeland. The city was set on fire. We fled for our lives to the vastness of Russia and Ukraine. In our places of exile we formed a Smorgon's group, the Zionist movement continued to operate, we cared for each other and offered a helping hand. When we arrived to Minsk, my father and Mr. Yakov Perewoski, the veteran activist of our community, provided the inhabitants of our city with identity cards that were stamped with the seal of our community that they hadn't forgotten to take with them when they were expelled from the city. This identity card served as an official passport for everything. Many refugees from our city settled in Kharkov, the capital of Ukraine. They immediately organized and concentrated around the Zionists' synagogue, which was located at the home of the well known philanthropist Abraham Yehudah Zuckerman of blessed memory. I remember the time of the Balfour Declaration. How great was the happiness of the refugees from Smorgon.

[Page 282]

A great assembly gathered in Zuckerman's home, and my father preached about “the beginning of the desired redemption”.

Our community's activists remained faithful to their public work until they return to Smorgon at the end of the war, and helped to rebuild it and restore it.

In 1921, when the civil war was at its peak, different squadrons consolidated, fought against the Bolshevik regime, and carried out pogroms against the Jews. The Bolshevik authorities allowed the war refugees to return to their homeland, and many refugees returned to Smorgon.

And when the first refugees returned, what did they find? destruction and desolation. It was hard to find the road to the city because it was completely covered with grass and shrubs. Foxes and wolves walked in it. They started to clear it off. They cut down the trees, uprooted the shrubs and exterminated the weeds. The returnees flowed day after day, and family came after family. When we returned we found one house standing alone in Wilenska Street. The family of Moshe Kagan lived in that house. My father left to wander around the city. He searched and after a lot of efforts he found the veteran activist Mr. Yakov Perewoski, Moshe Sherira, and a number of families residents of “Krake”. The three activists came to a decision that there was a need to establish a temporary immigrants' committee which will design a program to rebuild the ruined city, speed up the return of Surgeon's scattered residents, gather the deposed, and offer assistance to all the needy. These are the members of the committee: Gershon Weinstein, Yakov Perewoski, Moshe Kagan, Yakov Boaz Horowitz, Shmuel Greis and Moshe Sherira. Gershon Weinstein was elected as secretary. The first action was to rent an apartment from a Gentile. The house had two small rooms and its roof was made of straw. The committee took up residence here. The diligent secretary started to send letters to our townspeople "Relief" (Aid) committee, which was established in the United States. In his letters he described the destruction of the city, the shortages, the poverty among the returnees, and stirred the hearts of our merciful brothers. The response came immediately and crates full of food and clothing arrived. A short time later, delegations of behalf of "Relief" arrived, and donations started to flow. There was also a Jewish relief committee for war victims in Vilna called "*YEKOPO*" [acronym of Yevreyskiy komitet pomoschi zhertvam voyny] which gave construction loans to the needy. A short time later, houses for the returning refugees were built with the help of the two committees, "Relief" and "*YEKOPO*". The first building was built in the courtyard of Beit Hamidrash. The returnees lived there until they received loans to build their own homes.

A large sum of money was received from the aid committee in the United States, about twenty thousand dollars. With this money they fixed the Great Beit Hamidrash and the fence around the cemetery which lay open. They filled the trenches that were left from the days of the war, established a bank for the residents, opened a library and also built a number of public buildings. Those who came from afar lived there temporarily.

The secretary and treasurer of the bank was Gershon Weinstein. Chaim Tarachan was the primary bookkeeper. And these are the members of the bank: Shlomo Katz, Mordechai Mirski, Yeshaya Kovarsky, A. Schulman, Chaim Alperowitch, Reuven Rodenski, Meir Goldberg, and Padulsky.

[Page 283]

Gradually, the social life started to flow in a normal rate and it was time to organize a community where all the representatives of the Jewish population will be found. The leaders of the community were: Yakov Perewoski, Moshe Kreinis, Natan Kovarsky and Shlomo Katz,Gershon Weinstein was elected as the community's secretary.

Dov Bindman and G. Weinstein established a school by the name of "*Tarbut*" [culture]. Most of the city's children studied there. It was located in a two storey building. The orphanage boarding school was also located in this building. The studies of all the subjects were conducted in Hebrew. A "*Talmud Torah*" school was founded, and Rabbi Menashe Ginzburg cared for its existence. There was a "Small Yeshiva" and young men from the city and the region studied there. At the head of this religious institute stood: HaRav Yakov Boaz Horowitz, Moshe Sherira, Dov Bindman and Avraham Eliezer Gurevich, of blessed memory.

C

In 1923, the first pioneers left Smorgon and immigrated illegally to Israel: Yona Megidai, Zampkin, Shmuel Weinstein and Galinsky. They belonged to the end of the "*Third Aliya*" [immigration].

After that, a chapter of "*HeHalutz*" [the pioneer] federation was established in our city. The member Rasish came to our city to organize the "*Halutz*" activities. At the head of the local "*Halutz*" organization stood the members: Mordechai Cohen, Shmuel Rodenski, Eliakum Lamdansky, Eliezer Schlemowitz, Zalman Katzkowitch, and more. A few years later, all of them were able to immigrate to Israel. When they arrived to Israel they joined the "*Haganah*" ["The Defense"] and participated in the building and the defense of the homeland.

And here, the pioneering training period started in Poland, and a group of young people from Smorgon left for a "*Hachsharah*" [pioneering training] Kibbutz in Klosow [Poland]: Binyamin Marshak, Zalman Alperowitch of blessed memory, Pergament and others. After their training they immigrated to Israel, settled in Hadera where most of the immigrants from our city concentrated.

"*HeHalutz*" wasn't the only active organization in our city Smorgon. There were a number of other organizations like the "*General Zionists*" federation, the "*Hitachdut Zionist Labor party*", "*Poalei Zion Right*" and "*Hashomer Hatzair*". All of them strove for one purpose, the redemption and the building of the land of Israel, and the revival of the Jewish culture in the Diaspora and in Israel. All the organizations offices were concentrated in the most magnificent building in our city. The name of the building, which previously served as a school for Smorgon's orphans, was "*Internat*". This building was the cultural center of our city, and in it, as it is mentioned above, was also "*Tarbut*" School. Quiet a few students of this school serve as teachers and counselors in elementary schools in Israel. Among the teachers of "*Tarbut*" School were: Yosef Bernstein, Moshe Fisher, Shmuel Katz, may their memory be blessed. Yosef Bernstein and Moshe Fisher preached the Zionist idea from the synagogue's *Bimah*. They aroused the congregation to act for the benefit of our people and their settlement in their own country, and they repeatedly emphasized that our nation is facing annihilation in the Diaspora.

[Page 284]

The members who were active in the "*Hitachdut* Zionist Labor party" were: Eliezer Schulman, Raphael Weinstein, Reuven Greenberg, Zalman Pergament and Yisrael Gass, but the driving force of the party was Yosef Bernstein. The members who excelled in the management of "*Hashomer Hatzair*" and "*HeHalutz*" were: Avigdor Jacobson, David Perewoski, Ahuva Bronda, Bracha Jacobson and Etka Meltzer. Most of the best young students in our city were concentrated in "*Hashomer Hatzair*" movement. Most of them spoke Hebrew and were imbued with a national pioneering spirit. To our joy, many of them are now in Israel. They were able to immigrate to Israel before the Holocaust.

A branch of "*Tarbut*" acted vigorously in our city. Its duty was to ensure the existence of a school bearing the name "*Tarbut*", spread the knowledge of the Hebrew language, bring the Hebrew book into the Jewish homes, and educate to youth in the spirit of Zionism. The branch also provided the tuition for children of families who were unable to pay because the community couldn't allocate sums of money for this purpose. Six members represented the Jewish community in the municipality. They lobbied before this institution to support the school with a set amount of tax money that was collected from Smorgon's Jewish residents. Their efforts were unsuccessful. They encountered the anti-Semitism that existed between the members of the municipality, and we alone carried this financial burden. The writer of these modest columns spent quite a lot of efforts and energy to collect the necessary funds needed for the needy students. Occasionally, the active members of the drama club and lovers of the stage staged plays for this purpose. We plotted to invent all kind of tricks in order to collect contributions from various parties.

There were also other difficulties that we had to overcome and remove from the path of Hebrew education. The Polish government schools in the city tried to absorb the Jewish children, and plotted for the souls of the children of the poor. They offered them varied inducements in order to capture them into their network like: studies on Sunday instead of Saturday, and various discounts. During enrollment days we recruited our friends and placed two of them in each region to speak to the parents' hearts, and explain to them the national sin of giving their children to a foreign culture and to assimilation. We worked in secret to avoid capture by the hostile Polish police. The members who excelled in these actions were: Reuven Greenberg, Zalman Pergament and the writer of these lines.

It is impossible to ignore our community's library and the great reading room. There were Yiddish and Hebrew books in the library. Most of them were reading books and a few were textbooks and encyclopedias. The library was given to the Zionist administration by the members who were active in the community's culture department. We the youth, developed, nourished and expanded the library. All the activists worked voluntarily. There were seven members in the administration which was elected for a period of one year. The library's revenues were meager and we filled in the deficit by charging admission to lectures, literary debates, films, and also plays. In this manner we were able to purchase new books every year. In the reading room it was possible to find newspapers from all over the world.

[Page 285]

The writer of this article served as the chairman of the board, the secretary was Reuven Greenberg and the board members were: Natan Lepkin of blessed memory, and may they live - Chana Aleprowitch and Alte Denishevsky (today Shoshanna Plowsky).

A drama club existed in our city. The first and foremost amateur actor was Shmuel Rodenski. We predicted a bright future for him on the stage and our prediction was fulfilled. He became famous in Israel as one of the great stage artists. The following members participated in the performances: Feigale Leggat, Zipora Rubin, Gitila Bronda, Malka Bronda, Liba the seamstress, Hinda Lipkir, Etka Meltzer, Aharon Rubin, Pesach Taborsky, Zila Schar, Mordechai Cohen, of blessed memory.

We will finish our review with a society named "*Linat Tzedek*". This charitable organization played an important role in our city. Most of its activists were women: Rachel Rabinowitch, Sara Denishevsky, Chana Bernstein, Alta Denishevsky (Shoshanna Plowsky), Bertha Horowitz, Margalit, Bracha Bronda, Ema Rudnick. Tzedek Rudnick was the head of the organization.

"Hashomer Hatzair"

Right to left. Standing in the first row: Chaim Bronda, Avigdor Jacobson, Z. Cohen, H. Schulman, B. Berlin, R. Greenberg, Skelit, L. Pruss.

Second row: P. Denishevsky, M. Katz, H. Koplovich, A. Bronda, A. Meltzer, H. Kirzner, K. Lagget, H. Greenberg, L. Pergament.

Third row: A. Badnes, A. Koplovich, L. Schulman, K. Kagan, R. Weinstein,Viz. Pergament, S. Denishevsky.

Fourth row: S. Rodenski, Y. Gass, M. Denishevsky, G. Denishevsky.

Fifth row: H. Vitkin, B. Taborsky, S. Chadash, Y. Friedman.

[Page 286]

My Home in Smorgon

By Golda Shalem

Translated by Sara Mages

It seems to me, that it is difficult and almost impossible to come up with any kind of memories about the image of the city and its character that don't carry a strong personal character. These memories should be part of their writer's autobiography, because fate wanted that we - the natives of Smorgon, a generation who was born at the beginning of the 20th century and reached the days of the Holocaust - will also know two world wars. All the hardships of this period left their mark and molded the character of the child and the youth, who were born in Smorgon, from the beginning of their lives. Each one of us who wants to write what he can still remember from his childhood in his birthplace - will find out that at the dawn of his life he only had a few years of peaceful life at his parents' home, with his family, relatives and friends, in a typical Jewish town. But this life, idyllic life in a quite densely populated town, which was adorned with a beautiful rural landscape of fields, forests, farms, and Belarusian farmers with their rural way of life - disappeared in 1914, the first year of World War I. In 1915, the Russian army ordered all the city residents to leave their city, because the Russians had to retreat and the army headquarters had chosen the tactic of "scorched earth". In no time the city turned into mounds of ash and burning embers. I still remember the shocking image of the burning city - which started to burn before we left. Each child only took a small bundle in his hand, and we also took our cow (because we lived out of town). On the road, the cow was the source of life for the nine small children. And so, in an instant, we and the other residents of the city, turned into a great huge camp of refugees who trudged their way south on the road leading to Maladzyechna, and from there to Minsk which at that time was still far from the front. And so it happened, that the peaceful quiet life of the children and youth in the background of a town, its environment and its rural landscape, stopped overnight and was replaced with other living arrangements and other ways of life in the large expanses of Great Russia. So, naturally, if we just want to reminisce back to that period of our lives in our birthplace in the Diaspora - these childhood memories should contain all the secrecy and romance that were reflected in the mind of a Jewish child in his early childhood. And here comes the main obstacle, and it is the poor eloquence of an ordinary person, a worker, who never wrote his memories, despite this he tries his best, because he has a strong desire to rescue from obscurity all that he can still save: and I'll start with this.

[Page 287]

I'm from a family of a laborer who worked in the tannery industry, a family with many children who tasted the life of a hired worker of those days. My father worked a long and arduous day, and received a very small salary which was barely enough to support his large family and pay all types of expenses. It is very possible, that the difficult economic situation of the Jewish worker in the towns of those times - determined my future as a member of a collective farm in Israel.

[Page 288]

My earliest memories relate to the period of my life when I was 4-5 years old. I remember that we lived in a rented apartment, one in a row of apartments that shared one yard. The buildings stood in a long line on the right side of the yard, on the other side, across from the buildings, was a wooden fence. It was a totally sealed fence without a single crack and it separated our yard from the slaughterhouse yard.

The smells and the sounds that came over this fence didn't add pleasure or peace to the residents of our yard. I remember that my parents had a very strong desire to move from this place, even to a place farther from the city center where the shops and the market were. And indeed, my parents found a way to fulfill their wish.

During that period, the head of the Russian Orthodox Church in Smorgon decided to lease plots of land by the size of 1-2 Dunam to Jews who wanted to build a house outside the densely populated area. Previously, these plots of land were part of a public garden that also belonged to the church. It was leased to the city for all kinds of social events, like masquerade parties and summer concerts by the firefighters and the police orchestras. The plots, which were leased to the Jews, lay in a semicircle around the garden, and therefore, each plot owner had a common border with the public garden and was able to watch all the events in the garden. Of course, it wasn't easy for a hired worker with a large family to save money to build a house, even the simplest one. Nevertheless, the idea became a reality, and the houses were built, for some earlier and for some later, in the form of a new street with its new houses. Each house had a beautiful well-maintained flower garden and a narrow wooden walkway for pedestrians according to the needs of that time. Our new street was given the name - the Gardens Street. In a short period of time it turned into a "nature" road, a place for a summer stroll for the residents of the crowded areazv who once a week, on a Sabbath afternoon, enjoyed the sight of green fields and fresh air because our Gardens Street was only built on its right side, and fields of grain, barley, oats and abundance of wild flowers lay on its left side. Shortly after we settled in our new home a new Catholic Church was built in town (until then the Catholics didn't have a proper church). The church was built at the continuation of Minsk Street on the left side of Sinkzki's gardens, and Gardens Street ran in a semicircle on the right side.

And we, the Jewish children, from the street near the church, were uninvited guests to almost all the weddings that took place there and also to the funerals. It opened a new religious world for us, the religious ceremonies of the nation in which we lived. We also became proficient in the Gentile's language, something that helped us to befriend the neighborhood's no-Jewish children (because there were also non-Jewish families in the new neighborhood).

[Page 289]

Here, in the new place, an ample space opened for us, the children, for activities and games. During the winter, when the snow piled up and covered everything in the yard, we had to sweep it sideways to open a path to the primitive cowshed which was built from wooden beams, and a path to the well which was located in the street and served several neighbors. We, the children, threw snowballs at each other while we were clearing the snow, and we also built snowmen. Not once the game was at the expense of helping our mother (we only helped our mother because our father left early in the morning while we were still asleep - and came home from work in the evening, not before the hour of seven, and sometimes later. I remember that only the older children were still awake at this hour). But, we saw the real "life" during the summer. Then - "who will resemble us and who will compare to us". Who needs a more ideal place for a game of hide and seek than a high flour field, almost as tall as an adult? (they were fields of rye). As time went by, we weren't allowed to play hide and seek in the fields before harvest for obvious reasons. And if not the fields, we found other hiding places. The passion for the game was very strong, and I remember my brother Zalman, who was forced to retire from the game for a few moments in order to pray the Mincha prayers as he always did at twilight. But it was almost impossible for him to be totally disconnected from the game, could it be? If so, he found a way. He stood near the corner of the house, muttered the prayer verses quickly, and his eyes followed the course of the game (of course, all of that not in the presence of our father). In brief, the new house opened a whole world for us. A pine forest stretched behind the fields and a train paved its rhythmic course thought it. We always heard its whistles and we could see the thick smoke that rose from the locomotive's chimney. But as the saying goes: "There's a fly in the ointment". It was heaven on earth for the children and additional difficulties for our parents. Mother was forced to carry the family's food baskets and the concentrated food for the cow over a great distance. To this day I can't imagine how my mother could do it all, the specious new home added more work and also the garden next to it. Every year, in the spring, we took the manure out of the cowshed, spread it over the designated area, and a gentile, the owner of a horse and a plough, came in one of the spring days, ploughed the plot for us and mixed the manure with the earth. We planted potatoes at the farthest plot from the house, and vegetables closer to the house. Of course, we really worked hard at that. We spread all over the garden, 3-4 children together with our mother, and the work was done for the best because we ate from the fruit of our garden all summer, each vegetable in its season. There was a payment for the work in the garden, and the family's food budget balanced more easily. Mother saved money from her food budget and spent it in other areas, like clothing and footwear. In those days every Jewish child was guaranteed a new outfit and new shoes for the holiday of Rosh Hashanah, and it wasn't a trivial matter for our family.

[Page 290]

There were also two purple palm bushes in our plot of land, and at the back of the plot stood a bent multi branches old apple tree. Every year it bloomed in early spring and was covered with flowers. Almost every year the flowers turned into "Antonov" apples, which ripped late, almost in the fall. But the most important thing, that delighted the children's heart, was an ancient elm tree with a stork's nest at the treetop. At the beginning of the spring, we, the children, watched the treetop to see if the storks returned from the warm countries. And when the pair of storks finally returned, they began to repair and pad the nest, and get ready for hatching. But we were not rewarded to see a lot of generations of storks, and were not rewarded to see our only apple tree blooming in the spring, because the war broke out and uprooted us from our new home, and from a beautiful corner of an outstanding rural landscape with all the nice things in it. We were uprooted from our home shortly after we won it and after so many yearnings - and we never returned to it.

Unconsciously, I divided the stories of my memories into two conflicting authorities. Like series. One is the home - that is to say, mother and children, and the other authority - the father, who was barely noticeable in the life of the family and in his children's education. After all, he had no choice but to accept this unwanted partition that is solely the result of the reality of life. The only day of the week, in which the whole family sat together around the table according to the traditional ceremony, was Friday eve. Father blessed the wine and sliced a slice of white challah for each child. All the Sabbath dishes were good and plentiful as in a home of a wealthy family. After eating, all the participants recited the blessing on the food, and almost all of us knew the blessing by heart. At the end came the Sabbath songs that I remember to this day. After the Sabbath came six more days of hard work that we can't ignore. Maybe I'll write about it in more details.

The tannery work, in which my father worked as a laborer most of his life, was the primary industry in Smorgon and a source of livelihood for many. It was the processing of crude skins, mainly for the upper parts of shoes and boots. Those were small factories which employed a small number of workers. Next to them were bigger factories that the number workers in each one reached to a few dozens. The tanner's wage was higher than the wage of a worker in a workshop. The tannery industry, which started in a small scale, spread and grew. Of course, something from this profitability was also felt in the wages of all the workers. I remember that my father's salary in those days reached to twenty-five rubles a week, which was considered to be an acceptable salary. It was already during the time when my father was promoted to foreman (a master in his field).

[Page 291]

Every Jewish teenager preferred to work as an apprentice in a tannery than working as an apprentice in the tailoring or the shoemaking industry. The dignity of the tannery industry was in its organization. Every Jewish young man, who began his professional career in a tannery, advanced over the years and also received a higher salary, something that helped him so save for his future.

These factories spread mostly south of the city and concentrated on a side street. The street, or rather - the alley - was built diagonally on a slope. The Jews called this alley the Bathhouse Alley, but much later it received the official Russian name - the crooked street or the winding road. I especially remember this winding road because it led to the factory where my father of blessed memory worked, and because in one of the houses, on this street, I learnt the Hebrew alphabet from Jewish teacher with a curly yellow beard.

It was a year before the outbreak of the war. I turned six and was given to this Jew so he could teach me the beginning of the art of reading and writing. Every morning I ran from our house in Gardens Street, passed a section of Minsk street, the square with its many shops, and went down to this alley where the honorable "*Heder*", that I liked very much despite all of its deficiencies, stood. And the deficiencies were mostly - the place itself, because in that street there wasn't even a single courtyard which wasn't used for tanning hides. The courtyards were filled with large tubs and giant boilers in which skins were soaked in a chemical solution that produced unpleasant odors, and there wasn't a shortage of flies in the summer. We, the group of children, in this narrow crowded corner, didn't have a suitable place to play games during the break between classes. Yet, I was proud of the place where I bought my first knowledge and where learned to read. And I was very proud when I visited my father's place of work with my mother. There, in the factory, was a world in itself. Jews with beards and sidelocks worked alongside Jewish and non-Jewish teenagers.

It was late fall 1915, when the war took us far from our birthplace and from our home. For a short time we lived as refugees in the big Jewish city of Minsk that received us with a lot of love and kindness. We were housed in its many synagogues. From there we left for the interior of Great Russia, and arrived to the northern expenses of the Volga near the city of Stalingrad, (then

Tsaritsyn). Father got a job with the same factory owner from Smorgon who moved his factory there. Relatively to others, he was a large factory owner and his name was Hut (Gut in Russian). A whole new world full of experiences opened for us, the children, another environment and another human landscape, a lot different from what we were used to. The Russian language began to replace the Yiddish, but only in the street, at home we continued with our usual traditional life of a simple Jewish family.

[Page 292]

When I was accepted to the Russian Elementary school of that time - I was the only Jewish girl in a class of 60 children (at that time there were very few Jews in the Russian cities because of Pale Settlement that existed during the days of the Czar). During the Russian Orthodox religion class, when the priest explained the stories of the Bible according to the New Testament and showed pictures of characters from the Bible, I could also raise my hand because these stories were not strange to me, I still remembered them from home. But when I entered High School these memories started to fade. I no longer saw a printed Hebrew word. Eventually, we became like the children of the country except for the Yiddish language that we kept at home and within the family circle. The environment, the street and the school, impacted me, and when the 1917 revolution broke out I was drawn to the revolutionary ideas which flowed like a tidal wave that flooded everything and everyone. I started to love the vast country and its people who held such lofty ideas. When the new regime established the "*Komosol*", the national organization of Russian youth, we, the High School student of the seventh class, were ready to join. The grand state ceremony was going to take place in the large city square and in the presence of a rabbi.

But meanwhile something happened - the authorities announced that each citizen, who wasn't born in Great Russia and wanted to go back to his native city, may do so. My father of blessed memory held on to this one and only opportunity. We packed our belongings and left for the road - to Smorgon, which was already in independent Poland. My father had two reasons: the religious and national assimilation of the Jewish youth, and the severe economic crisis that struck Russia at the same period (it was right after the Russian civil war when famine and epidemics ravaged the population).

And here came the fateful turning point for us and for everyone who returned from Russia. After a lot of wanderings, that lasted about six weeks, we arrived to Smorgon. New houses started to emerge from the scorched earth, public buildings were built, the synagogue was restored, and the city came back to life. But for me it was as if I fell from heaven to earth. I stood on the verge of despair. Suddenly I found myself detached from my studies and from my friends, and I didn't see any possibility to renew my studies.

[Page 293]

In great desperation I started to look for a reason to continue my life and found it when I started to give myself a report of what was there - it wasn't mine - not the earth, not the people and not their ambitions. Very slowly I started to get closer to myself, to my origin, to the young Jewish generation and its aspirations. And here again, a new world opened before me, but its source was ancient. First of all I remembered the Hebrew alphabet that I once learned from the yellow-bearded rabbi. I started to search for a Hebrew written word. At first I read books in Yiddish and became familiar with its great extensive literature. This reading brought us to the source of our origin and the recognition of our strength. I read Fiarberg's fascinating short story "*Le'an*" [where to] and "The way of our world" by Shalom Asch. But in order to peek into the modern Hebrew literature of the time, like "Masada" by David Shimoni, "Days and Nights" and "A beautiful heart" by Natan Bistritzky [Agmon], sing patriotic songs and more and more..it was necessary to know the language in which they were written, the language of our forefathers and our country that came back to life after centuries of stagnation. So, we started to study Hebrew from the "*Tarbut*" schoolteacher Yosef Bernstein of blessed memory.

He was a veteran Zionist, dedicated with his heart and soul to the Zionist idea. He maintained close ties with the pioneer youth movements, which conquered almost all the Jewish streets, mostly the Jewish youth who returned not long ago from the cities of Russia after the establishment of independent Poland. At that time, the youth federations "*Gordonia*" and "*HeHalutz Hatzair*" and the political parties "*Hitachdut*" and "*Social Zionists*" were established in Smorgon. In the meetings of the youth organizations we heard for the first time the echoes from Israel, about the organization of the Jewish worker in the country, about the "*Histadrut*" [General Federation of Laborers in the land of Israel], but the emphasis was placed on the way of life of the Israeli laborer - and it is the kibbutz idea. A labor battalion was established in the name of Yosef Trumpeldor, the "large group" and the "small group" of those days. And all the settlement movements, who at that time marched their first steps in Israel. There were close to one hundred members in "*HeHalutz Hatzair*" chapter in Smorgon. The "*Halutz*" chapter was one of the largest and strongest in the area. Members started to leave for *Hakhshara* [pioneer training] kibbutzim to get ready for their immigration. But the immigration policy of the Mandate government of that period appeared, and many members were left in the *Hakhshara* kibbutzim until their immigration to Israel. In each quota of certificates [visas] that were received at the Zionist office, there were also certificates for us, the youth of Smorgon. The yearning and the joy to immigrate were felt in the whole city and in each Jewish home. Parents accompanied their children with joy and hope that one day they will join them and immigrate to Israel. After all, all of them gathered and came to the ruined city from all corners of Great Russia to fulfill their Zionist historical designation. Indeed, many of the members' parents, who immigrated to Israel after their children, live to this day with us in the country.

[Page 294]

My home in "Kreke"

By Leah Rotbart

Translated by Sara Mages

About seventy Jewish families lived in "Kreke". I'm the third generation of the first settlers. My father's name is Chaim Malkes. Kreke's Jews were framers and engaged in agriculture: they planted wheat, barley, oats and potatoes. They also had vegetable gardens and orchards. There were cows, sheep and horses in the farms.

1914. The First World War broke out.

Shots were heard from the direction of the village of Firibuz? which was located on the banks of the Viliya River. We saw plumes of smoke rising to the heavens. The battle between the Russians and the Germans attackers intensified and got closer to "Kreke". Great fear grasped the tranquil residents.

Our family consisted of seven persons: father, mother, two sons - Avraham age fifteen and Mordechai age thirteen, and three daughters - Rachel age nine, Chava age seven and me Leah age four and a half.

The seven of us left our home, our farm and all of our belongings, and fled to Smorgon.

We were housed as war refugees in the synagogue's courtyard.

1915. The Cossacks entered. They expelled the entire population of Smorgon. We walked and came to Minsk where we only stayed for a few months.

Idelson had a tannery in Smorgon. He moved to Elisavetgrad [Ukraine] with all of his workers. One of his workers was my uncle Shlomo Levin. He came especially to Minsk to transfer his parents. We traveled with him to Elisavetgrad and stayed there for five years.

My father and my brother worked in Idelson's factory. Father as a carpenter, he repaired and prepared work equipment for them, and my brother - as a tanner's apprentice.

1918-1919. A civil war raged. There was an exchange of regimes in the Ukraine, Skoropadsky, Denikin, Petliura. A regime left and a regime entered.

Riots broke out. On one Saturday they carried out a terrible massacre on the Jewish residents of Elisavetgrad. It was on the eve of the Bolsheviks' entrance to the city and its conquest.

We hid with a Staroöbriadtsy family (a Greek Catholic sect of religious conservatives). The fear was awful. We were not sure of our lives. That night the city was occupied by the "Red Army" soldiers.

The economic conditions were favorable, but we were afraid to stay in a city where our lives were in danger. But my brothers stayed and continued to work at the factory. We left at the end of 1919 and came to Smorgon. We traveled in the coach of the "Red Soldiers" who retreated from the Polish Army attack after Poland gained its independence.

[Page 295]

A house in the "Kreke"

1920. Our father returned several weeks ahead of us. The mother and the three daughters returned. Our family was one of the first families to return to their homeland. When we arrived we found a number of people in "Kreke". They made up their minds to leave the place and escape the wrath of the Polish legionnaires who captured the village from the Bolsheviks in 1920.

When we returned to our native village we didn't find a trace of our house and our farm. We sat outside on the packages that we brought with us and burst into tears. The mother hurried to go and search for the father. She found him a after a careful examination. He worked as a carpenter for the farmers in Firibuz? There weren't any houses in the whole neighborhood because all of them went up in flames during the battles that took place in the area. We moved to one of the trenches that were left from the war between the Russians and the German invaders. Also now it was not quite in the country because of the war between the Russian's "Red Army" and the Polish legionnaires. The Russian's camp was on one side of the Viliya River and the Polish - on the other side. They exchanged artillery fire regularly.

We moved to live in the village of Klapi, which was at the rear and a little farther from the battlefield. We lived in this village for half a year. Our father built us a timber house, meaning that he only erected the skeleton, walls without a floor and without a ceiling. Later, we moved the skeleton of this house to Smorgon when we returned in the summer. Meanwhile, other families returned from the Diaspora. "*YEKOPO*" (a Jewish aid society) sent a certain amount of money. An apartment building, which was divided into small cubicles, was built with this money. It was possible to place two beds in each small cubicle.

[Page 296]

1921. Gradually more families returned. The city of Smorgon recovered a little, but it didn't return to its first economic strength.

Four families lived in the apartment building. At that time there wasn't a bakery in Smorgon and my sisters, together with children from other families, walked to Lebiedzieva (a small town whose Jewish residents weren't deported during the war), and bought flour in the shops. They brought a sack of flour weighing half a pound, and we baked a rye bread from it. There wasn't a single doctor in the whole area. All of us got sick and suffered from severe abdominal pain. There wasn't anyone to turn to for advice or medicines. Yankel Febuzki's firstborn son served as a sanitary nurse in the army and tried to be our doctor. He advised us to pick wormwood leaves, boil them and drink the water. We followed his advice and recovered.

The cemetery was completely destroyed. The children went to the cemetery and collected the scattered bones. The adults dug a grave and brought them back to a Jewish grave.

The cellar of Kovarsky the medic served as a place of worship. There, they gathered and prayed on weekdays, on the Sabbath and even during the holidays.

Every Wednesday was market day. The farmers came and brought the products of their farms, meaning, eggs, butter, cheese and even linen. We bought our food from the farmers, delivered it to Vilna, sold it for a profit - and made our living.

We drew water from the stream which flowed near Strashinsky's mansion.

Thorns and weeds grew in Smorgon's streets during the years of our absent.

The men went to the surrounding villages or towns to search for work, and the women and children stayed at home. At night we heard the mewing of cats, the howling of various small animals, the creaking of the ruined synagogue's tin roof which was swinging and banging in the wind. These strange noises, which joined other loud noises, terrorized us until the blood froze in our veins.

At the end of 1921 we moved to "Kreke". We engaged in farming again. We plowed, seeded and also harvested.

A special messenger came from the United States and brought each and every family a gift of help and relief from their relatives in America.

At that time Smorgon was under Polish rule, and its ruler was Pił?sudski.

The stream of the returning families increased. All the places of worship and Beit HaMidrash were restored. A school, with eighteen boys and girls, was established. Our teacher was Tetraski who knew Hebrew. He was the brother of the Rebbetzin from "Kreke". A university student, who was left without means, and couldn't continue with his studies. He came to Smorgon and engaged in teaching. After him came a second teacher by the name of Beck.

[Page 297]

The school grew and there were a number of classes. The school with all of his classes resided in women's gallery of the ruined synagogue.

The teacher Gilinski, a native of Smorgon, returned and taught us the Bible. Another teacher appeared, his name was Katz, he taught us general studies and his wife taught us crafts, meaning, sewing.

There was a "*Hekdesh*", a hostel for poor travelers, in Smorgon. The "*Hekdesh*", which remained intact, was located next to the cemetery. The Hebrew School, with its five classes, was housed in this "*Hekdesh*". In it we studied both religious and secular subjects. The teachers were Katz, Bernstein and Shoshanna Denishevski. Among the students was also Hanoch Levin who now lives in Israel. He is the principal of "Ilanot" school in Ramat Aviv.

Later on, the school was transferred to the big building that the Jewish community of Smorgon built with the aid that it received from the United States and from "*YEKOPO*".

This building served as a cultural center: the library, the theater, the youth clubs, and other institutions were located there. The building was called "Internat".

[Page 298]

The Rebirth of Smorgon

Perl Ginsburg-Teisner

(Daughter of the Rav Menashe)

Translated by Yocheved Klausner

Our Smorgon has suffered very much during the First World War. The town was entirely destroyed, the population was evacuated and the Jews were dispersed and scattered over the seven seas. When the war ended, the population began to return and started to rebuild the ruins, and some time later I came back as well.'

I entered town through Krever Street. It was impossible to recognize anything. Here and there some houses or parts of them have been rebuilt, standing between heaps of barbed wire, half-burned walls and ditches. Wide-open cellars could be seen, and lone chimneys rose to the sky. I intended to tell my coach driver where to stop, but it didn't take long and we found ourselves out of town. I had hoped to recognize our own new house, but the streets were overgrown with wild, tall grass and the remnants of the houses were barely seen.

Most of the townspeople who had returned were still living in the cellars. They slept on wooden boards that they had found scattered around, and the place was full of various merchandise that helped them make a living, more or less. Geese, chickens and goats were trampling around, feeling at home. A cat was impossible to be found; we had to "import" cats from Vilna. However, the people who had returned did not feel lost; on the contrary, they were hopeful and full of courage. A few were disappointed and regretted their return from Russia, but when they remembered that this place had been their only hope while in exile they did not give up: smiles were seen on faces and even jokes were told...

Everyone was hospitable to the extreme. Every returnee was received with open arms and was immediately given an honored place. In our house I found Meir Feivel, very sick, and my father z"l was taking care of him.

[Page 299]

The most important wish, for everybody, was to be able to leave the cellars. The motivation and drive to rebuild was enormous. The sound of hammers was heard everywhere. Logs and other building materials were found among the rubble. But we did not have enough workers, because we had no money to pay them. We were happy to be able to erect four walls and a ceiling and the floor was tolerable, but we didn't even begin to think about dividing the area into rooms. We thanked God for the roof over our heads. In the middle of the house we had a stove and it kept us warm.

A group of returning emigrants cooking a meal for themselves – 1922

The economic support of the town was the weekly market, on Wednesdays. If it rained on that day, the market was postponed to the next Wednesday.

There were very few shops, and most of the trading was done on little tables, set on the street. We would buy from the peasants dairy products, eggs and chickens and we would take the merchandise to Vilna and sell it there. When the market closed on market day, men and women and even young children could be seen on their way to the train station, carrying heavy baskets.

[Page 300]

Traveling to Vilna was a problem: the train authorities did not allow merchandise on the train, so it had to be hidden. But the chickens were naturally noisy, and not once did the owner jump off the train at some station, out of fear of being discovered. Many times I would take with me, arriving in Vilna, baskets full of merchandise that didn't belong to me and wait at the station, sometimes for hours, until the owner arrived on the next train.

The most important cultural center was, at first, the women's synagogue. Men and women would assemble there. Right after prayer, the place turned into a *Talmud Torah.* The community meetings were held there and important matters were discussed. For the refugees who returned from Russia it was the first place where they could rest, temporarily. One could see there, at the same time, one person sleeping, another eating and still another putting on his prayer-shawl for the morning prayer; sometimes children were seen, waiting for their teacher.

The town was in the process of rebuilding. The relief organization YEKOPO helped a great deal. Some people were supported by their relatives in America, until they could stand on their own two feet.

America was perceived as a country that can make one happy. Shortly before I arrived in Smorgon, an emissary from America had visited the town, and he was talked about for a long time after he had left. At the farewell party the community arranged for him, everybody wished to be "next year in...." – and no more was said.

A very important step was the grounding of a Children's Home. Orphans and children of poor families were taken out of the moist, cold cellars and given a warm home, as well as food and drink. What was still missing was a bit of *Yiddishkeit* (Jewish religious atmosphere). The children themselves, most of them from traditional Jewish homes, complained that they were not given *arba kanfot* [a traditional small fringed prayer shawl] to wear. Still, it would have been a great tragedy for the children and their families if the home was closed. Poverty was terrible, all around. The sources of aid and support were gradually drained out and YEKOPO was forced to retract the loans. And yet another misfortune befell the population: the rate of the Polish Zloty kept falling and it became impossible to return the loans with the same value, which brought chaos to the commerce and money change. Even the American relatives became tired of helping and the need increased. However, in spite of all these difficulties, the townspeople tried to help each other as much as they could. There we found the really good-hearted people, who were ready to help discreetly and modestly: they would bring bread to the hungry, help the sick, and bake *matza* for the poor on the eve of Passover.

[Page 301]

In time, these good people formed a committee, which grew to include 22 persons and I was among them as well. The committee was very active, and it became an important and useful institution, for the good of the town.

Not far from Smorgon was a Jewish Colony called *The Land*. Before the war, the inhabitants of the colony would hire workers to till their land and they would look for work in town – they found this to be more practical. This arrangement brought them no great luck, however, and they were, in general, poorer than the townspeople. After the war they were in a much better situation than their friends in town: they had their own potatoes, beets and other vegetables – what can be better than that?

I spent in Smorgon about three years. During that time, the town has made progress. The wild grass in the streets was gone, the streets were cleaned and leveled out and wooden boards were fastened to the openings of the cellars, so that, in the darkness of the night, people would not stumble and fall in. The half burned houses, which upset and scared the passers-by, were demolished and life became more normal. The community members began to restore the buildings of the Jewish institutions, the Talmud Torah began to function in its own building and the men were able to pray in their own *shul* [synagogue].

The Talmud Torah was in a good situation. The teachers Katz and Bernstein were devoted to the children heart and soul and the children were happy there. They received a full Jewish and general education. In addition, the children from the poorest families received a good meal. The fine and charitable woman, Alte Danishewski, helped by several other women, took care of these meals.

[Page 302]

The house that had once been the bank became the center of all cultural and social activities. The meetings of various institutions were held there. The house contained also a large library, managed very skillfully by the adolescent members of the community.

In general, very few young people returned to Smorgon after the war. Those who did return left after a short while, because there was nothing to do for them there. However, their place was soon taken by the children who began to grow up and became the youth of the town.

When Usischkin, the well-known Zionist leader, visited Vilna, his visit made a very strong impression on the Smorgon Jews.

I remember as if it was today, when my father z"l came home from shul on holiday, his face shone and he announced with joy: "Usischkin is in Vilna and he is collecting money to redeem Eretz Israel." The brothers Akon were visiting with at the time. They were fanatic members of the *Agudat Israel* religious party, although they wore their beards short. My father's joyfulness upset them a great deal and they asked: "Did you know, Rabbi, what the Zionists are doing in Eretz Israel? They eat *Chametz* on Passover, in public, so everyone would see." "I know, I know everything," my father interrupted, "I also know that they travel on the Sabbath. But, as R'Tevele has said: before the *Huppa* [wedding ceremony] the servants clean the place and make it ready." It was a beautiful sight to look at my father, his face like that of a saint, declare: "Eretz Israel, the Holy Land, a home for the Jews." The brothers Akon were silenced.

The emigration from Smorgon to Eretz Israel increased, but mostly because there was no other country we could go to. Those who managed to receive a "certificate" [a British official permit to immigrate to Eretz Israel] were happy. With every group that left, Smorgon became smaller. No Jew came to take the place of those who had left. The news from Smorgon did not encourage people to come.

The picture of my saying farewell to Smorgon and leave for America is alive in my memory to this day. With tears in the eyes, my friends and family shook my hands and wished me a "safe and healthy journey." Nobody doubted my joy and happiness for being able to take that step and going to America.

[Page 303]

The Tarbut School, From its Beginning to its End

by Henoch Levin

Translated by Deborah Horowitz Nothman

1921. "On the ruins of Smorgon from World War I, the Hebrew School was founded on the Great Synagogue."

After the Great Revolution and World War I, all of Russia was seeped in "mourning". Roads were soaked with the blood of Israel's Jewish (the Jewish people), and our "nations' dwellings" were lit by fire (burned to the ground). There were miles of stretched out lines—masses of refugees returning westward to rebuild their ruined lives. Amongst these masses of refugees were the Smorgoners, a "unique tribe". They were recognizable and distinguished by one noticeable feature, "Brotherhood". These Echalons (Russian word) (likely echelons in English) of long trains transported human beings, as if they were cattle, and who lumbered along, weeks and months in caravans, on the winding and destroyed roads of Russia–were the families of Smargon (note: common variation of Smorgon spelling). Indeed, they were a rare breed! They sat bent over and huddled in one car. Men and women, old and young, sitting on their bundles, the only remainder of their worldly possessions, trying to figure out what their future holds for them. In these freight cars, the seed of the first and renewed community of Smorgon was born, and from which sprouted a new social order (activism). The main concern, however, concentrated on the livelihood and education of the children.

In one of these cars sat the teacher Katz, the first postwar educator to the children of Smorgon. At the end of 1921, there were about 51 remaining families in Smorgon. Perhaps, some returned earlier, but no one remained in this destroyed city. At the end of the year, the first assembled class of the Hebrew School met in a temporary abode.

Tarbut School
H. Sarachan, Margosia, M.Fisher, B.Weinstein, Katz, Z.Perga'ment, Bernstein, Scultz, R.Weinstein, A.Brudno, Y.Grinberg

[Page 304]

The teacher Yosef Bernstein

This temporary abode was housed in the "woman's section" of the ruins of the Great Synagogue. No longer for women only, the section became the "House" for all of Smorgon. So, the house of learning was now called the "women's section". The long narrow building that once stood in all its glory with prominent pillars was the complete opposite–this "House of G–d" that was once so magnificent but now ruins of its former glory. The synagogue was now the home to the school. All activity occurred on the second floor.

Immediately, after the adults attended morning prayers, the children would take over the space for Torah and higher education. Wooden benches, built by the carpenters of Smorgon were installed in the "women's section" as our first Holy contribution. The window panes were yet to be installed, and the window openings were stuffed with anything that was found suitable. The wind howled in the chimney, and the two groups of children, who sat huddled together, made the best of this saddening situation. The class was divided into two sections to indicate the difference in age and knowledge. There was no wall between them during the lessons, just empty space.

In one section, Mr. Katz taught, and in the other section, Mr. Beck, and alternately, a Mr. Masersky taught. Mr. Masersky was a young student who was from Vilna who happened to be passing by. On his head he wore a cap which was white with a red stripe all around (the colors of the Polish flag)– which created much amazement to the young children. The curriculum was agreed upon and compulsory–a first in the country. Learning was through improvisation, without textbooks. Instruction was taught orally; the Siddur was learned through prayer.

[Page 305]

An ordinary day for our students consisted of recitations from the "Chumash". Slate boards were used to write and erase. A notebook was provided for all, and publications from the Widow and Brothers Romm from Vilna (they were in the publishing business) were provided (donated) to further instruct and teach. When the Hebrew textbooks arrived, it was like "Mana from heaven"! Greetings from another World! And what books!!–one had never seen such books: a book with pictures? And no more Chumash. With an annotated Bible and a history book by Trivitzh, Nudel and Kutik—–a whole new world enfolded! The pupils started to read and understand Hebrew, pronouncing it in the Ashkenazi pronunciation. They tried to impress their younger brothers and sisters by speaking in this "Holy" tongue and it was a great miracle: they would also sing the songs in Hebrew and read simple stories with great satisfaction.

The language of the state, Polish, was not yet instituted in Smorgon by 1922. As the government was not yet a functioning entity, it was still a time of political chaos; the education system was in a Russian/Lithuanian limbo.

Even so, the teacher's wife, Julia Katz, who herself was educated in Lisbegrad, decided to continue with Russian education in the "women's section" of the Hebrew school. She asked permission from the parents first, "Who knows, perhaps (they would mind)... in any case, knowledge never hurts!"

Although the school was small and poorly equipped in its first year and only with the very basics—the building radiated warmth and laughter from the over the 150 children. Already, in the first days of its existence, the teachers of the Hebrew school of Smorgon laid the foundations of educational instruction. The education materials, although sparse, and funds were also not readily available, these teachers did everything to enlighten and brighten the lives of these children. Through songs, poetry, games and crafts, they ensured that this knowledge was readily and enthusiastically absorbed.

The First Class of the Tarbut (Culture) School

[Page 306]

Every Friday, the end of the week, an hour before the last lesson, Mr. Katz would assemble the students (there were three classes already) and teach them a Sabbath song and tell them a story for the Sabbath. The first song he sang was:

Tomorrow is Sabbath, tomorrow is Sabbath
To school we will not go
Only rest
Only take a walk
And play all...day.

And since this song had no rhyme at the end, a group of jokers from among the pupils rewrote the final clause in Yiddish as: "az gehn zal a reich" (to go for a smoke). The reference is probably because teacher Katz always had a cigarette in his mouth!

The financial support of the school was made possible, right from the start, by contributions from "YEKAPO" (JEWISH COMMUNITY RELIEF WAR VICTIMS). Tuition and distribution of "chits" by the school board to the teachers (used like cash for merchandise, meats, vegetables and other produce) was donated though Yekapo. This first phase in the development of the Hebrew school in Smorgon soon came to an end. The people remember it as the era of the "women's section", appropriately named from the place where the school was housed.

Smorgon continued to grow, and eventually the upstairs place of the Old Synagogue was too small to house its students. The leaders of the community, namely Rabbi Yacov Pererofski, Rabbi Gershon Weinstein and others, decided to transfer the school to another location! Do you know where? To that hostel (poor house) that stood at the outskirts of the city. A place that was locked up so it could be available should your distant relative, a second or third cousin, even a first cousin, should wander back from exile and need a place to stay. People were still hopeful that some may still return. No way! The hostel stood empty, looking out at the cemetery.

In that case–we will put the school there! First of all, we will get rid of the noisy children (after all, it was also a synagogue) by sending them far away! And secondly, the cemetery might instill a sense of respect and obedience—

meaning it would produce a more moral youth (even in those days). So, instead, a closeness to the cemetery could be a blessing!

[Page 307]

Even today, it is not known if this was exactly the reason the community leaders made the decision to move the school to the hostel, but the reason is attributed to the jokers who used to meet at the barber shop of Berl Levin (father of Henoch), may he rest in peace. While they waited for a haircut or a good shave every Thursday evening and Friday, they would discuss local matters and news of the world–of course, with the usual clowning and joking! And thus, the school was relocated! After Succoth in 1923, the school moved and now the second phase of the school began——known as the "hostel" era.

What was the uniqueness of this place? For two years, the Hebrew School of Smorgon was in the hostel that belonged to the community. The cemetery did not frighten its small occupants. On the contrary, "the Children of Israel" learned the truth of the passage "the dead will not praise G–d, nor any worldly beings". In addition, they learned the lessons of life and death, owning possessions versus not having anything: a lesson found in Tikkun Olam. The school had four classes, with a total of seventy pupils. All was orderly and the teachers were well excelling. Report cards were distributed at the end of the year to indicate the child's progress. New subjects of study were introduced; this was a period of enlightenment. The old subjects of Torah and Hebrew were still taught, but the focus was on broader subjects of knowledge. Mr. Katz taught botany and mathematics. The Russian mathematic books were well known, especially one by Varshchgin, and were made available to these students who understood their importance in the larger world. (So close and yet still far from their little shtetls where they would go into the Litchnik forest on Lag B'Omer, with bow and arrow). The material was understood by the fourth-grade students. A new teacher has arrived!

One day, a young Jew is seen in the town, reportedly from the town of Krasna, wearing a Polish military uniform. The coat suits him well, offsetting his virility and youthful expression.

[Page 308]

On his head is the Polish, four cornered army hat (called "rogatywka" in Polish), adding a sense of mischief to his demeanour. He is lodging with his relative, Damta, the butcher, and Rabbi Cohen. After several days, there was a rumour in town that he was the new teacher of Hebrew subjects. Shortly after, he changed out of his uniform, and appeared at the school. He brought with him a new vitality to the school. His name was Joseph Bernstein. It was quite apparent that he was the exact opposite of the teacher Katz.

There were of two different temperaments: Katz, the peaceful and calming individual, and Joseph Bernstein, the tempestuous and effervescent one. Katz was completely calm, walking and smiling with his understanding eyes, immersed in his own world, and deep in thought. And Bernstein, one does not exactly know [what he was thinking?]. He was excitable and full of laughter and energy. This is what the students needed!

The teacher Bernstein, was the leading force behind all the Zionist activity in Smorgon. All cultural activities in the school were met with great enthusiasm by the students. His appearance in the school led to new cultural activities and a renewal began for all.

One day, in the year 5684, a functionary from the Tarbut School of Vilna came to Smorgon, by the name H. Tzemel, may he rest in peace. He resembled the writer Y. L. Peretz: same build and mustache. He walked proudly, laughing and full of energy. Once, Tzemel assembled the parents of the pupils and praised the study of the Hebrew language, the teachers, and the existence of the school. He then said "Here, Yosef, (I) come to bring you enlightenment"– and all eyes turn to Yosef Bernstein, who smiles, as if to say, "I deserve that!"

And Katz, like a true Cohen (the name consists of two letter" kaph and tsadi, short for Tsadik–a righteous one) sits in his corner, a true gentleman. He sits stooped, his head bowed, rolling a "papyros" (cigarette) and sticks it in his mouth. He is impervious to what's going around him.

After this general meeting with the parents, the meeting continues with the school committee to discuss finances. From this aspect, the school has not been as successful. The amount of tuition collected was low, and some parents could not afford to pay at all. The teacher's salaries were not paid.

"Aha!" said Reb Sutzkever when he was asked to pay his son's tuition.

[Page 309]

"Outside the frost will eat
The north wind blows free!
And tuition we must pay!...

But never mind! Merriment reigned in the schoolhouse. During the breaks, the children hurried to the schoolyard–which was the cemetery–to collect snails (berelach), along the ditches that still remained from the wartime days and to play hide and seek amongst the tombstones rooted in the ground.

It must be mentioned to greatly praise the older pupils who helped their fathers immensely in those first few days when they returned to Smorgon.

These older pupils helped with the task of bringing the bones of the deceased Jews “from the valley of bones”—to a Jewish burial site.

From this “hostel” school, the Hebrew language emerged in this town. It was quite an achievement, to speak it with the Sephardic accent that was taught by Mr. Bernstein, and all teachers followed the same course. The schoolchildren had a great sense of achievement: they wanted desperately to please and also to prove their abilities. Not to speak in the Holy Tongue would mean punishment. Trouble however started brewing: grandmothers and grandfathers of those pupils attending the Tarbut school started grumbling amongst themselves that a common language was needed between them and their grandchildren. “See how these outsiders (teachers) insisted on speaking only in their Holy mumble jumble? They decreed a silence on us and there is no one to prevent this disaster...”

Kindergarten class under the direction of Shoshanna (Alte) Danishevsky and Rachel Gass

[Page 310]

In this period of the Tarbut School—social activities sprung up from which many youth movements originated. The first Hebrew play that was performed by the pupils under the direction of the teachers–who were very generous with their time and effort–was "Two Melodies" or otherwise titled, "The Kidnapped". From Succoth until Passover (the first term) the rehearsals took place. During all those days, especially during the winter, the children were enthusiastically engrossed in the play. Not only the actors who participated, but also all the children in the school. Sorrow and mourning descended on all, as they were engrossed in the fate of Dudel Bendes (who played the part of the kidnapped child). They prayed for his safety; they pleaded for mercy! It was a great day for Hebrew in Smorgon–the day when "Two Melodies" was performed and for the many days following when the song "This is a Great Day" from the first act–was echoed in the houses of Smorgon on Sabbath nights. This degree of devotion and love of Hebrew plays and everything literary and cultural attributed to the Hebrew language, was an indication of the social activities that these pupils engaged in after school hours. Many of the readers amongst us till today, can still remember our childish attempts to re–enact plays on Friday nights and holidays in our own homes: giving out parts, rehearsing, and culminating in using one room for a stage and the other for the audience, with a curtain in between.

How much apprehension was generated from the point of view expressed in "Rejoice with Trembling" (Psalms ll, 11)? How much joy of creation?! There were such joyful times in the house of Rivka Danishevsky, a young girl in the first graduating class of the Tarbut School, and also in that gloomy house of Gudel, one of the owners of the lumber yard (on the way to the train station). (Remembering or reflecting on the days of his youth)

The pupils of the Tarbut school, in the time of the "hostel" era, were also partners in an archaic quasi–framework of a children's movement before the pioneering youth movements that sprung up in the Vilna district. The "Agudah", the first such organized group which originated in the "slaughterhouse" was the precursor to the other social movements. Cold and dark, the building was unsurprisingly available, and the club began to meet there.

This four-room building served as storage for all kinds of produce. In one of the rooms, we held meetings for the boys and girls. From this place, the ideals of Zionism started to enfold: a new club was formed, with Hebrew as its language, to consider and discuss new and idealistic ideas. From the original "Aguda" (a religious group), the new movements of Hashomer Hatza"ir, Gordonia, and Hechalutz Hatza"ir began to take shape. (Note: ir as in the first era—which ir refers to the "women's section")

[Page 311]

So, the "second era", was a continuation of the "woman's era", and ended in 1925. The foundation was set: standards of higher learning and the planted roots for the Hebrew language to be spoken in Smorgon. Culture and education was now in the forefront. A new building, which we shall now call the "third era", was now transferred to the new building called the "Internat".

This building was erected after World War I by Jewish Welfare Agencies from the U.S. in order to service the poor and needy that returned to Smorgon. It housed the poor and the displaced war orphans and provided assistance and food so these people could renew their physical and spiritual strength to ensure an easier transition into moving forward with their lives and education.

Of course, there were always, different opinions expressed by the people of Smorgon: who should have access to these welfare facilities? Only the needy, or, was it available to all? Remember the commandment, "Love thy neighbour as thyself"? It is a "Mitzvah" to provide welfare assistance and encouragement to one's brothers! But, they must also think of their needs. As a result of a committee meeting, the Tarbut School was transferred to this new "Internat" building. Large crates started to arrive, a gift from "Yekapo" (the Jewish agency at that time) and books from the Smorgon library to the classrooms, then the school equipment, desks, chairs, blackboards, benches, and closets that filled the large classrooms.

The Library Board of the World Jewish Aid Agency, 10–11–1938

[Page 312]

Management: 1. Rafael Weinstein, 2. Anzelevitz, 3. Grinberg, 4. Mira Danishevsky, 5. Hannah Alperowitz, 6. R. Cohen, 7. Katz

Rafael Weinstein officiated as Chief Librarian of Smorgon. He founded the library with boundless dedication and as a result of the effort through his work over twenty years, created a cultural institution concerned with the social activities of the youth of Smorgon. The library became a cultural meeting place, a stage for free discussion and debate. And for many years, the library served as a reading room which provided daily newspapers and periodicals in both Yiddish and Hebrew. "Writers and fighters" (the Children of Israel) descended upon Smorgon. Books were becoming the new order of the educational forefront.

The large, two story "Internat" building also housed a large auditorium on the first floor, with an imposing stage and beautiful wall hangings. The school, with the classrooms and books (some rooms on the first floor) also had room for an auditorium. The auditorium became a cultural center of Smorgon; it had great lighting, a curtain on the stage, and hosted many Yiddish and Hebrew plays as well as literary events, concerts, and dances. It attracted large crowds. Smorgon was finally enjoying a cultural revival and the town became known in the area. Visiting troupes came to perform, some of a very high caliber. Appreciation for literature, education, and a better quality of life began once again in Smorgon.

The Tarbut School, took up seven rooms on the second floor (it shows you how large the building was). They had definitely outgrown the "hostel" school. There was more room to breathe—more pupils were added, new teachers arrived, a new administration was elected!

The principal was Mr. Fisher, may he rest in peace. He was a veteran teacher and a graduate of the first class of "Tzerna" in Vilna, a native of Glubokie. He was very friendly and created a warm atmosphere amongst the community.

[Page 313]

He was active in all cultural events and voiced his opinions, introduced new pedagogical learning methods in the school, and established a healthy and growing framework for the school. He was considered "a worthy proprietor" who was constantly looking to improve the quality of "his baby"– the School. He was very involved with the drama group where he performed with his pupils. In the play, "The Sale of Joseph", he played the role of Joseph, the Patriarch, alongside his students. On the initiative of Fisher, the teacher, the first choir was formed under the leadership of the teacher Yitzhak Zuckerman (Y. Ben Abraham, may he live a long life). The young teacher knew, being a graduate of the Vilna Tarbut Seminary, how to introduce to the children, as well as the adults of Smorgon, praises (likely liturgical songs) to "the Holy One", Blessed Be He. He introduced all types of songs: folk, songs of Zion, songs of the labour movement. The choir "Zamir" that was founded by Yitzhak Zuckerman was one of the best in the area. Its success was no doubt to Zuckerman's professional knowledge and good taste. The "Nightengale", and its accompanist, the string orchestra "the Organ", under the leadership of S. Magid, the violinist of Smorgon, (a native and a graduate of the Vilna Conservatory), contributed a large impact to the cultural heritage of Smorgon.

The Tarbut school was merely a part of the foundation that became rooted in the city of Smorgon. From that foundation sprang many ideas and areas of growth. "What will the fields create" (what lies ahead, what can these students create, where can they go, what contributions to society can they develop? Thus the reference to the garden of fields).

And what light will history shine on them? As in the play, "The Land of Israel", the much anticipated homeland of the Jews, where brothers and sisters had already immigrated to and toiled the fields and forests of Hadera (Israel) [see David Shimonowitch, The Jubilee of the Carriage Drivers] as well as in the Valley of Jezreel.

In 1936, the school had 7 classes as well as a full–fledged elementary school, which was recognized by the government of Poland. This was quite an achievement for us, a school of 390 pupils. The school was considered a second home for the children of Smorgon, second to their parents' homes: their lives had new meaning, full of contentment, spiritual and educational, with high hopes to bring them to a higher level in society.

These 300 plus schoolchildren, our"nightengales", became the renaissance of our city, and were armed with wings to fly. Who knew what lied ahead? Neither the children, nor their parents, that this illustrious, enlightened and progressive Tarbut School would have to shut down. A new world order was to begin, the arrival of the Nazi "killing machine" would soon be upon us.

[Pages 314-315]

Lag Ba'Omer in Tarbut school

by Mariashe Yentes

Translated by Anita Frishman Gabbay and Frieda Levin Dym

The holiday was a time of much anticipation and enjoyment. We went to school—not as a day of learning, but to assemble there with our teachers and to begin our hike to the forest (which the Smorgon Jews) named "Litchnik". With much joy, we prepared everything the evening before, the food and the eggs--those colored eggs! The eggs were hard boiled with the shell together with an onion so they would turn yellow. If we wanted blue eggs, we would put a blue dye, "shinka", in the water. We used that for our wash. If we wanted another color, we used paper of different colors and made such beautiful designs!

And, in addition, we needed to have a "kasinke" (headscarf). This was absolutely necessary for our outing. The kasinka had to be white, with 3 points, starched and stiff.

We came to school to prepare for such a festive and joyous holiday and we assembled in rows. We marched on “Chasercher Gas” (Pig street) and through the cemetery, passing the “matzevas” (tombstones), which made us feel sad and uneasy. Then over the railroad tracks. After a half an hour, we arrived in the thick of the forest.

If on the way we passed a peasant with his horse and wagon, we greeted him loudly and mocked him by shouting “Pritzel” (which means landowner). We started singing and pranking him to look under the wheels. If the peasant bent down and looked under his wagon, we started laughing and continued to sing. But when one of our teachers heard what was happening, we knew what to expect: he would reprimand us with harsh words.

The nightingale chorus with A. Toker

In the forest. Each teacher assembled their class and addressed the holiday, the uprising of the Bar Kochba and about Rabbi Akivah and his followers. The words were free, but the talmudists were divided.

Then we would gather around, and start singing song about Eretz Israel and we ended with dancing.

From a distance, we could see the peasants and the shiksas working in their fields, and we were envious of them: they were working their own fields and their own land, and we yearned to come to our own Eretz Israel, to work in our own fields and if need be—to camp bravely like the Bar Kochba military amongst our own people.

[Page 316]

The Pioneering Movement in Smorgon

by Beni Marshak

Translated by Sara Mages

In the winter of 1923 the first branch of "*HeHalutz Hatzair*" [Young Pioneer] was established in my hometown Smorgon. Its founders were the members: Pinchas Rashish (the mayor of Petah Tikva) and Aharon Berdyczewski a member of Kibbutz Yagur. Both arrived to the border district of Eastern Poland from faraway Warsaw to organize the Jewish youth for the doctrine and the "theory" of Zionism, and to prepare it for the **revolutionary mission** of the generation.

It's no coincidence that the first branch of the pioneering movement was founded in Smorgon. Masses of discouraged youth, who sought a new path in life, wandered in the city in the first years after the First World War. They clung to the Zionist-pioneering message that came to them from Israel. This fermentation of youth had deep roots in the history of the city of workers. The "*Bund*" movement was established in Smorgon, the "Leather Workers Organization" was founded and cells of workers gathered in the bakeries (the famous bagels). Also the proximity of Vilna, the "Jerusalem of Lita, " helped to bring the theory of the revolutionary activity. Moreover, the regime of the notorious Władysław Dominik Grabski in Poland, the corruption that has spread throughout the society, the suppression of the workers in general and the Jews in particular, the dispossession of the minorities from the economic positions - all of these served as the cause for the establishment of the revolutionary pioneering youth movements "*HeHalutz Hatzair*" and as a result of a transition of ages - "*HeHalutz.*"

[Page 317]

1929, the "*Halutz*" federation in Smorgon

The first organizers of "*HeHalutz Hatzair*" in the city, who expanded and deepened its ideological ideas, were the members: Zalman Alprovitz, Gita Brodny, Mordechai Cohen, the writer of these lines and others. The founding meeting was held in the "*Hekdesh*" which was in the ground of the Jewish cemetery on the outskirts of the city.

From the first days there was a feverish activity in the young branch. Every evening the house was crowded with groups of boys and girls, "night owls, " who talked about the events in Israel and in the movement. They clarified current issues, learned about the Jewish labor movement, studied the Hebrew language and waited impatiently to do the real work. In 1924, when the slogan of the pioneering movement in Poland: "Pioneers for training and physical work" was thrown in the Jewish street - it was like a "note from the heavens" for us in Smorgon. One feeling filled the hearts of the members - the desired moment, the time for expansion and fulfillment - has arrived. In the coming days more than thirty *Halutzim* [pioneers] left Smorgon for the first *Hakhshara* [pioneer training] points in the district - to the Maladečina Forests. Boys and girls, who have never held a tool in their hands - not a saw, not an axe and not a hatchet - are now clutching them in their hand and see them not as tools for physical labor but as spiritual-ideological conduits. Although the work was grueling, the trees of Maladečina Forests succumbed to the young Jewish men. The trees were cut down, sawn, sorted, and tied in bundles. On Saturdays, when one of the members visited the "local" chapter of "*HeHalutz,*" he inserted a new spirit, a spirit of joy and creativity, a sense of freedom and release from the anxiety which accumulated during the week. The visits of these tourists from the *Hakhshara* points in the forests created a tension in the hearts of the members. This stream of activities stretched and passed until it evoked every house in the city, "startled" it from its tranquility and incited its young sons.

Smorgon was fortunate that most of the members of the "*HeHalutz*" in the city immigrated to Israel during the limited immigration of 1924. Almost all of them joined the "Work Battalion" named after Joseph Trumpeldor. The letters, which came to the branches of "*HeHalutz*" and "*HeHalutz Hatzair,*" testified that the "Smorgon group" didn't embarrass their place of origin.

In those days, a joke circulated among the *Hakhshara* kibbutzim about the young men from Smorgon.

[Page 318]

The "Litvaks" claimed that the young men from Smorgon weren't able to distinguish between right Shin[1] and left Shin[1], and that they pronounced the name of their city "**Sh**morgon" not Smorgon.

This is the place to mention that our town was one of the few places in Poland that its young men and women, who joined "*HeHalutz*" and "*HeHalutz Hatzair*", left for pioneering training and immigrate to Israel - didn't anger their parents. On the contrary, the parents showed sympathy to their children's actions and supported them as much as they could.

Not once the reading was delayed in the synagogue when the public found out that a pioneer from a needy family didn't have the financial means for his immigration to Israel. Needless to say that solution was found on the spot for that *Halutz.*

The pioneering movement in Smorgon also radiated its light on the city's Hebrew School "*Tarbut.*" This school was one of the most organized schools in the district and contained hundreds of students. The cooperation between the teachers and the pioneering movements was a blessing for both. This interaction existed for many years, and deepened the common values of the "*Tarbut*" movement and the pioneering movement.

All these years the city was poised towards the pioneering activity and lived in the movement's atmosphere. The glorious revolutionary tradition of Smorgon was renewed, and was transferred from the adults to the youth.

We can't forget that our city was destroyed for the first time during the First World War. Although it was almost rehabilitated at the beginning of the liberation of Poland, every Jew knew and felt that it was only a temporary fix, and that the Satan of extinction lay at the entrance to their home in the Diaspora. This premonition brought the positive attitude of the residents of Smorgon towards the pioneering movement.

In 1925, two members from Smorgon, Zalman Alprovitz z"l and Beni Marshak, were drafted by central headquarters of the "*Halutz*" movement in Warsaw for the first national seminar. The first delegation from the "*Halutz*" federation in Israel participated in it, and its members were: Y. Trenkin, Tarshis and Zisling. When Zalman and I left for the seminar we continued our ties with the chapter in Smorgon. Two matters encouraged us: A) The affiliation of our members in the "Work Battalion" in Israel. B) The expansion of the branch in our hometown. At the end of the seminar we were sent to the *Hakhshara*'s central points in Poland - Zalman to "Shaharia" and I to "Klosowo. "

During the three and a half years that I've stayed in Klosowo, I had the opportunity to meet *Halutzim* from my town who came to the *Hakhshara*.

[Page 319]

I always wondered about the pioneering spirit that pulsed in them, their willingness to participate in missions and their strong will to overcome obstacles. Many of the *Halutzim* from Smorgon, who received their training in Klosowo, live to this day in kibbutzim in Israel.

The transformation of Kibbutz Klosowo into a permanent training point in the life of the movement in Poland caused my separation from the chapter in

Smorgon but, I always knew what was happening in the chapter and followed its activities from afar.

From the right: Y. Magdy, Herzl Antzlevitz, Eliezer Zipkin, Binyamin Gilinski, L. Danishevsky.
Sitting: S. Rodansky, M. Danishevsky, G. Weinstein, M. Weinstein.

My last visit to Smorgon was on 2 October, 1929, the day before I immigrated to Israel. I only had a few hours to say goodbye to the family that I haven't seen during my stay in Klosowo. I arrived secretly to my hometown to receive its blessing for the road - and said goodbye to my loved ones and to my friends clandestinely because the Polish authorities were looking for me. If they managed to find where I was, they would have delayed my immigration. On the next day I left Smorgon and crossed the border near Kopyczyńce in Poland. I left behind me a Jewish city and its inhabitants, a city of vision and action that was completely destroyed by the Nazi criminals. Among city's martyrs - the elderly, women and children - was my mother of blessed memory. My sister and her daughter, who managed to visit me in Israel in 1939, returned to liquidate their interests in order to return immediately to their son and their brother in Kibbutz Givat HaShlosha. They returned in August, and the war broke out in September 1939.

[Page 320]

You can find the Smorgonim everywhere in the country: there are those who realize their aspiration in a kibbutz, and there are those who work in a city or in a village. Today, as in the past, they are spiritually united to the same "original" cause, to the same guideline in the history of Smorgon, and its unique sociological development within the Polish Jewry. The *Halutzim* of Smorgon wrote a special chapter in the Israeli wars. I will be content with one of many. The most noticeable is Mordechai Cohen z"l, the son of the city's slaughterer. In 1923 he was one of the founders of "*HeHalutz*" movement in Smorgon. He was educated in a Zionist family, and was among the first who immigrate to Israel and joined the work battalion of Yosef Trumpeldor. Since his arrival to Israel he was an active member of the *Haganah* ["The Defense"] and a revered instructor and commander. In 1941, when the best young men in the country were called by Yitzhak Sadeh z"l for operation "*Kaf Gimel Yordei Ha'Sira*"[2], it was clear that Motke will be one them. Their mission was to sabotage oil refineries in Syria. May his memory be blessed together with the memory of his friends who fell in the battles to liberate the State of Israel. May the right of Smorgon, whose streets were filled with the cheers of young fighting pioneers, will stand for us. We, the few survivors in Israel, will not shame the spirit of our ancestors and our daring friends - for the bright future of our position in our independent state.

Translator's footnotes:

1. The Hebrew letter Shin represents two different phonemes. The two are distinguished by a dot - a dot above the left-hand side of the letter for **S**, and dot above the right-hand side of the letter for **Sh**.
2. "*Kaf Gimel Yordei Ha'Sira*" - "The 23 Who Went Down at Sea" - http://en.wikipedia.org/wiki/Operation_Boatswain

[Page 321]

The Beginning of the "Halutz" Movement in Smorgon

by Tzvi Horovitz

Translated by Sara Mages

Dedicated to the memory of my brother Nehemiah, his wife and their son Reuven who perished in the Kovno Ghetto, May the Lord avenge their blood.

In the midst of the First World War (1915) all the Jews were expelled from the city. All of a sudden, by order of the military authorities, all of them became refugees. They left in a hurry and scattered across the cities of Russia and the Ukraine. Most of them remained in their new place of residence also after the war and at the beginning of the revolution. Terrible pogroms were carried out against the Jews during the exchange of regimes in the Ukraine. The war refugees, including the Jews of Smorgon, started to return to their homeland after the Bolshevik regime was established and reached a relative stability. They returned with their elderly, children and young men. When the youth, who grew up during the war and revolution and during the bloody pogroms against the Jews, returned to Smorgon they found it burned and desolated. They began to calculate their life and the question that pecked in their mind was: Is it possible to build a future here? Is it possible to plant a safe life here? Until when are we going to be sacrificed on the altar of regime changes!?

The youth began to organize itself for immigration to Israel. Of course, there were many obstacles in their new way. Their parents objected. They couldn't accept the idea that their sons and daughter will leave them, and more, that they will go to the desert and to an unpopulated country. They claimed: we wouldn't object if you wanted to go out into the big free world, immigrate to the United States or to Argentina, but it's a total madness to wander to the wasteland.

However, the young people's desire to build a homeland and the realization that the Jews had no future in Russia, were so strong that they didn't pay attention to their parents and nothing could have delayed or stopped them. Emissaries came to Smorgon from the central headquarters of the "*Halutz*" movement. They established branches, sent the members to *Hakhshara* [pioneer training], and after they completed their training season - they arranged their immigration to Israel.

Some of our members have completed all the stages of preparation, immigration certificates were obtained for them, and they, the lucky ones, immigrated to Israel. I remember the first letters that came from our members in Israel. We used to get together specially for the reading the letters. We read them seriously and swallowed every word like hot cakes. The desire to do the same throbbed in every heart, and each one of us wondered and asked himself - when will I be able to reach the land of our longings?

[Page 322]

Slowly slowly the pioneering movement, which was a movement of a few brave and bold individuals, has become a national movement which encompassed almost all the Jewish youth. At that time, "*Hehalutz Hazair*" movement was established to fill the vacant places of those who left for pioneer training and immigrated to Israel.

The question of educating the children in the Zionist spirit arose, and as a practical answer it was decided to establish a Hebrew school which was called "*Tarbut* School. " Classes in Hebrew for adults were also opened. Here, I need to mention the dedicated diligent teacher, Gilinski z"l, who devoted all of his energy to teaching the language in evening classes. Every Sabbath, after the reading of the Torah, he climbed on the synagogue's stage and asked the congregation not to interfere with their children's decision to immigrate to Israel.

Our activities also included the founding of the library. Over time, thanks to the devoted work of the librarian Rafael Weinstein, the library became known as the best and the largest in the Smorgon region. Sometime later, Zionist political parties were established among the youth like: "*Zeirei Zion*," "*Hitachdut*," "*Hashomer Hatzair*" and others. At times, the arguments between the members of the various political parties and their fans lasted till midnight. The youth found a purpose in life and an interesting content. Our influence started to show its signs in the Jewish street. Also the sedated elements within the community considered us, against their will, as a rising active force which took up a position in the public life.

I will mention two valuable activities that were executed by "*Zeirei Zion*" I was among their initiators.

A. In the municipal elections we wanted to enter one of our members to the city council. The delay was caused by the age requirement law. We faced a serious problem since we were younger than the required age, so, we turned to Mr. Potashnik who was a fan of our party. Since he was entitled to be elected under the regulations, we asked him if he would agree to be our candidate. He gave us his permission. We entered his name to our list, and thanks to the hard work of our members he was elected to the city council. It was a significant accomplishment for the pioneering movement in Smorgon. We can't forget that Smorgon was an industrial city, and the "*Bund*" movement was very strong even after the First World War. We had a hard and bitter struggle in the council with the members of the "*Bund*" who opposed to any Zionist activity.

B. The second activity was also important. With great effort we were able to penetrate the administration committee of "*Tarbut* School. " The committee was represented by conservative community dignitaries, and we weren't willing to accept the fact that the school wasn't managed according to the Zionist spirit.

[Page 323]

Our decision was determined: we will spare no time and effort in order to enter into the committee that set the school's rules. What have we done? We consulted.

Since there were orphans in our city that their mothers couldn't pay their tuition at "*Tarbut* School, " which was relatively high, (at that time the Polish government didn't support the minorities' independent schools. "*Tarbut*" existed from the support of the community and from tuition fees), we committed ourselves to pay the tuition of these students. To obtain the necessary funds we got a job, a hard unskilled job - to clear the rubbish from the ruins which was plentiful in those days. We also recruited our friends for this purpose. After a hard struggle we received representation in the school administration, but in the eyes of the city's officials it was a bad thing. The old activists, who were rich in experience, didn't agree with the intervention and the penetration of the young people to their area of activities. We didn't give up and with the help of the teachers, who quarreled for us and fought our war, we entered our representative.

Gradually, step by step, we penetrated into the daily life of the community. Bit by bit we expanded our operations and entered the various areas that were in the hands of the "community elders. " Many of our rivals, the young members of the "*Bund*" or the P.P.S. - who objected the Zionist idea - joined our ranks. I will mention only one of them, and he is the member Yisrael Rappaport z"l. He was an educated man who fought against the idea of the rebirth of the nation Israel in its ancient-new homeland. Eventually, he was convinced that we were right. He became active in our movement and helped us a lot.

We set up *Hakhshara* points, which were managed by volunteers, near Smorgon. Our member Beni Marshak (today a member of Kibbutz Givat HaShlosha), was sent by "*HeHalutz*" to a seminar in Warsaw, and was absent from his home for a long time. One day he came home to visit his family. I, as a member of "*HeHalutz*" committee, came to his home in the morning to clarify a number of issues, but, I didn't find him. The young man was gone. I asked his mother Where is Beni? She told me that he went to bed with the rest of the family, and when they woke up in the morning they didn't find him in his bed and the bedroom window was wide open. Apparently he left the house through the window because he didn't want to wake us by closing the door behind him.

There was a *Hakhshara* kibbutz in Soly. I traveled to Soly and found him there. He walked the whole way and came to visit the kibbutz.

When our movement grew and became stronger, the question of funding stood before us in all of its severity. Among the members of the *Hakhshara* were young men who didn't have the necessary funds to immigrate to Israel. There were also those who came from affluent families but their parents, who objected to their children's immigration, clenched their fists and refused to give them the expenses for the long journey. In those days, the "Jewish Agency for Israel" didn't cover the expenses of those who immigrated to Israel. This was the common practice: if, for example, the branch received twenty five immigration certificates and the numbers of candidates, who were ready for immigration, was larger, then, those who had the financial means were favored over the poor. We opposed this unjust arrangement. We said that the members should immigrate according to their place in line, if they had the financial means or not. Therefore, we started to look for ways to obtain the financial means, and here, an idea flashed in our mind - to establish an amateur drama group: we will present plays, sell tickets, and with the money we'll finance the immigration. We cooperated with all the Zionist parties. We invited an actor from Vilna to instruct the amateur actors. At first we presented light skits, and then we proceeded to serious plays. Of course, apart from the instructor, all the work was done voluntarily. Even the hall was given to us free of charge by a school called "Internat."

[Page 324]

I consider it my duty to mention our member, Mordechai Cohen z"l, who was the son of Smorgon's slaughterer. He successfully played the main role in Victor Hugo's drama before his immigration to Israel. At the end of the play, the Polish police officer, who was present at the show, shook his hand and thanked him profusely for his wonderful acting.

He immigrated to Israel in 1926, and was one of the excellent commanders of the "*Haganah*" ["The Defense"]. During the Second World War he was one of the 23 members of the "*Haganah*" [*Kaf Gimel Yordei Ha'Sira*[1]] who left for a military mission on behalf of the country and didn't return. May his memory be blessed.

We presented a play each time we needed money to finance the immigration of our members. We informed the public in advance that we'll use the proceeds to finance the immigration of our members, and the hall was always full. There was always someone in the city council that was willing to help us to obtain a license for the shows.

Finally, I would like to dedicate a few lines of thanks and recognition to the memory of Rabbi Plutkin zt"l, who served as the town's rabbi in the period before the outbreak of the Second World War. He helped us a lot with our pioneering work, and despite his poor health he always came to the train station to bless the *Halutzim* who immigrated to Israel with "*Tefilat HaDerech*" [traveler's prayer]. Even the "*Halutz*" meetings were held in his home. He was admired by all the residents of Smorgon, and was always ready to help them before the local authorities who valued him. May his memory be blessed.

The full name of the teacher is Yehudah Leib Gilinski. He was born in 1873 and came to Smorgon in 1893. He immigrated to Israel in 1925. In 1927 he traveled to the United States to visit his father but he didn't live to return to Israel. In 1936 he died of a brain hemorrhage that caused to him by a Jew who claimed that the Israelis dispossessing the Arabs of their lands. He got angry when he heard these words of slander - and died.

Translator's footnotes:

1. "*Kaf Gimel Yordei Ha'Sira*" - "The 23 Who Went Down at Sea" - http://en.wikipedia.org/wiki/Operation_Boatswain

[Page 325]

Zalman Alperowicz – a Monument to the Soul of a Pioneer

by Y. Bankover

Translated by Jerrold Landau

I went through those days under unique circumstances and unusual conditions. There were the conditions of a new place, and questions of acclimatization in all areas. My time and my head were not free. Nevertheless, throughout the entire time – from the time of Zalman's death – I do not forget his image even for a moment.

Zalman passes before my eyes from the first day that I knew him. This was in Smorgon, when I came for my first visit after I arrived in the Vilna District. I found an active chapter there with vibrant youth full of enthusiasm – Zalman among them. He stood out already at that time, serving as an example to many who moved on to a life of actualization. The news that I received at all times from Smorgon validated my opinion: Zalman was among the active ones who urged others to action. I met him in the seminary in Warsaw after some time: he had grown up, he was exuding pleasantness and a thirst for knowledge. I did not have a chance to know him from up close. I took leave of him on my journey to the Land with only this first impression.

In the Land, news reached us about the permanent *Hachsharah* movement, about Klosowa and Shacharia, as a symbol and a path. Zalman was among the activists and the living spirit of Shacharia. He and his friends inaugurated the Fifth Aliya[1] for which we had awaited so greatly and prayed for its advent. The meeting point between the previous *aliya* and the new *aliya* was not simple, and went through constant struggle over mutual influence and acclimatization. Not only did the newcomers face the task of getting used to the conditions of reality in the Land, but first, and foremost – the penetration of the new spirit of maximal actualization that they, the newcomers, brought with them. The question that concerned and worried all of us was: how will the *aliyot*[2] meet[3]: from mutual understanding, or from a deepening chasm? Therefore, our meeting with the Fifth Aliya was accompanied by a blend of joy and trepidation: joy for the newcomers, for those who were continuing the path in faithfulness – and trepidation for the means of acclimatization. For us, the people of Hakovesh, the meeting with Shacharia and its founding kernel headed by Zalman – was a meeting of encouragement, mutual learning, and movement-based understanding. We knew days of mutual struggle as well as the joy of mutual life and creativity.

Years, many years passed. The path was long: from the young group during the days of the Fourth Aliya in Kfar Saba to the period of settlement in Ramat Hakovesh – a very long, difficult path of becoming independent, achievements, overcoming, and growing up – as well as days of obstacles. We knew our stance on Hebrew labor in the *moshava*, and our group suffered in this battle. We tasted the taste of abandonment, with all the depression that comes with such. Those were years of great efforts, debates on the time of our transfer to Ramah (i.e. Ramat Hakovesh), on transferring the children, and on leaving the *moshava*.

[Page 326]

The dispute was stormy at times, fraught with serious differences of opinion. Zalman participated in all these deliberations, not only with advice and recommendations, but also with personal dedication and boundless readiness for actualization. From the first bunk in Ramah that served as both the dining hall and dormitory, to the well that we dug (we dug but did not reach water), to the fortified, firmly-based point as Ramat Hakovesh was in those days – it was one long chain of communal efforts. He, Zalman, was among the activists and responsible ones in all of these. He was always prepared to participate in bearing the yoke. He did not evade the work and impose it on others – he always served as a personal example of readiness. During the years of the disturbances, when everyone and everything was involved in the bloody battle that Ramah was tried with, Zalman was given the concern for day-to-day communal life of the group. In that too, as always, he excelled as a member who bore the burden under all conditions, prepared to carry out the most difficult and responsible tasks. Thus did he go among us throughout all the year, until the illness afflicted him.

He already felt the illness before he went out on a mission to Poland – but he was not subdued, for in his life he never knew what sickness was. He regarded all sickness and ill people as if a spoiled, delicate individual. Before leaving for the Diaspora, during the times that we guarded the orchard together, we discussed meeting at the upcoming congress. I would come from the Land, and he from Poland. We wove joint plans of visits and meetings in the countries of the Diaspora. I arrived at the congress, but did not find Zalman there. The illness had begun to overcome him, and he remained in a convalescent home in Poland after a difficult operation. I received a greeting from him, worrisome about his state of health, but joyous regarding his work in Łódź – he was an exemplary comrade responsible, dedicated and beloved by the entire group. I decided to visit him in Poland on my way back to the Land. However, the war broke out, and my plan was canceled.

About a month later, Zalman arrived in the Land, as the first of the emissaries [to return]. He was broken in body, with worrisome signs of illness on his face. He battled his illness for more than a year, and never made peace with the fact that he, Zalman, could be ill. He laughed at illness all the years, and did not understand what illness is, for he was very, very strong in body throughout all the years. He suffered unusual suffering throughout that year. He moved from the hospital to a convalescent home, and then to his home, as his illness progressed. He was powerless to stop it – as it ate away his body. With our eyes, we saw death on his face. Great was the sorrow of the group, who did not want to come to terms with the fact that he would leave us and not return.

In the latter period, it was difficult to visit him both at the hospital or at home. I refrained from doing so, for I did not want to arouse words or thoughts with him about his illness or his situation. I went to bid farewell to him before I left for afar. By chance, I found him in good spirits, as the pain had abated. He asked about my work and my plans. He took great interest in all questions of the movement. When I parted from him, he extended his hand to me with difficulty, for it was all bones. He said to me, “I have heard that you will return here in about three months. During this time,

[Page 327]

I will certainly get better, for the great pain that I have and the frequent attacks are a sign of impending recovery. And then...” I grasped his weak hand and agreed with his recommendation, even though I had only a faint hope in my heart that we would merit to such a meeting.

I received the news of his passing about six days into my journey. I do not know about his final moments of life. I was far, far from home, but very close. Close and participating in the grief of the group over the great tragedy that overtook us. Our cemetery, which had taken in so many good and dear male and female members over the last few years – took in one more of the best and most dedicated among us. There is no comfort for the group, only grief and great feelings of loneliness afflicting me, for I am together with the entire group in mourning the death of our Zalman.

I write these lines here in haste, and under conditions not conducive to writing – almost lying down, and with very weak light. I hope that these lines will reach you at the *Shloshim*[4] of the death of Zalman, and will join with the words of appreciation that will be delivered by the members who lived and worked together with our faithful and dedicated Zalman.

Translator's footnotes:

1. See https://en.wikipedia.org/wiki/Fifth_Aliyah
2. I.e. the arrivals from the different waves of *aliya.*
3. i.e. meet [ideologically].
4. The observance of the thirty-day mourning period – and also the ceremony that marks the end of that period.

[Page 328]

Political Parties and Youth Movements in the City

by Mordechai Taburiski

Translated by Sara Mages

Vibrant Zionist life pulsed in Smorgon even though it wasn't a big city. There were many political parties and youth movement in the city, and most of the youth and adults were members of these movements.

The branch of "*HeHalutz*" ["The Pioneer"] in our city was organized immediately after the First World War when the first refugees returned to the ruined city from the vastness of Russia and began to rebuild it. At the beginning of the 1920s members of "*HeHalutz*" were sent to *Hakhshara* [training camps] in Poland, and participated in regional and national conferences. From 1924, and until the outbreak of the Second World War in 1939, many of them reached Israel. In those years dozens of *Halutzim*, who received training in kibbutzim in Poland, immigrated to Israel and today they're scattered all over the country. "*HeHalutz*" opened a broad organizational operation and all the proceeds of the drama club were dedicated to the immigration of members to Israel. In addition, Zionist and cultural activity was conducted among the youth.

[Page 329]

The chapter of "*Hitachdut*" gathered around it the activists of "*Tarbut*" school and its teachers. Hebrew was the dominated language in the chapter, and blessed cultural and social activities were also held there. Some members managed to immigrate to Israel until the Holocaust, but the vast majority was destroyed in the terrible period which passed over the city in the years 1941–1944.

The youth movements, "*Hashomer Hatzair,*" "*Gordonia,*" and "*Freiheit,*" which concentrated hundreds of youth, conducted an extensive educational and Zionist work together with "*HeHalutz.*" They made "pottery" for the Zionist parties and conducted seminars, summer camps and conferences. They educated the youth to life of work, scouting and love of Israel.

The chapter of "*Hitachdut*"

"*Tarbut*" school served as an important repository for the youth movements, and the children were taught the value of Zionism and love of Israel. The teachers invested a lot of efforts in this direction despite the financial difficulties of the school which only existed from tuition. It taught the Hebrew language to the youth who studied within its walls. Some of the students continued their education in Hebrew high–schools and seminars. Over time, they continued the tradition of teaching the Hebrew language to the next generation.

The youth movements conducted their activities within the walls of the school. I still remember the chapter of "*Hashomer Hatzair*" on the ground floor, "*Gordonia,*" "*Hitachdut,*" a library for adults and youth, and a hall for performances on the second floor. The building was full, during all the hours of the day and evening, with adults and youth who came to find the content of their life in Zionist and communal activity. Impressive parades, sports activities and scouting games were held in the schoolyard.

[Page 330]

On the other hand, the problem of employment and the continuation of higher education were difficult for the Jewish youth in the Polish towns. A small part of the youth continued their education. Most of them were forced to help their family because of its difficult economic situation.

"*Vitkinya*" federation in Smorgon – the Scouts level

Top first row: **Magidey Chava, Zigel Dov, Magides Tova, Schwartz Nacha, Kreines Baba, Sutzkever Pola, Rivka, Galperin Chaya, Podolsky Sara, Alprovitz Avraham, Koversky Leah**

Second row: **Karpel Avraham, Karpel Dvora, Libman Guta, Grinberg Reuven. Jacobson Nechama, Weinstein Rafael, Goldberg Belah, Levin Batya**

Third row: **Koversky Lusia, Chadash Manya, Kraines Zipora, Pomoznik Leah, Yablonovitz Meir, Danishevsky**

"*Hapoel*" group in Smorgon

[Page 331]

A Polish high school for commerce was established at the end of the 1920s, and some of the Jewish youth studied there. However, after they completed their studies at this school it wasn't easy to integrate in the life of commerce and services because of the discrimination against the Jews. They couldn't get a government job, even the lowest, and were forced to work as junior accountants in Jewish stores.

The Polish students, who came from out of town and other remote locations, brought the poison of anti–Semitism to our city. I remember the guards that stood next to the Jewish shops and the wild incitement of the farmers who, more than once, planned to carry out a pogrom on market day. Thanks to the relations with some of the non–Jewish residents and the connections with the local authorities, who have taken preventive measures, these plots have been foiled.

The local Jewish youth stood honorably in the battle, and from time to time skirmishes broke out with the anti-Semites. It should be noted that we always had the upper hand.

The chapter of "*Hashomer Hatzair*" in Smorgon

This situation continued until the outbreak of the war between Poland and Germany – on 1 September 1941. The Red Army entered the western part of Ukraine and White Russia after two weeks of battles and the German–Russian agreement. The Jews were relieved. Despite the economic difficulties and adaptation to the new regime they didn't have to fear physical extinction. Most of the Jewish youth received government jobs and the children continued their studies.

Most of the youth accepted the reality and aspired to settle down and move forward in life. At that time the Soviet regime was quite liberal towards the Jews, all the roads were opened before them and they didn't feel racial discrimination. Those who came from affluent families found it difficult to get a job, but most of them overcame that too. The relations between Jews and

Christians have improved. Proper working relations prevailed between them and they spent their free time together.

[Page 332]

A group of gymnasts coached by Gadosowicz

This situation continued for a short period, until June 1941. Everything collapsed with the outbreak of the German–Russian war which brought the terrible Holocaust of the Jewish nation. Only a few remained from Jewish Smorgon, survivors of death camps, partisans and those who returned from across Russia. Most of them came to Smorgon and left it immediately because it was completely destroyed and they didn't find a relative and a savior. Most of them moved to Vilna where all the survivors of the nearby towns and the survivors of the Lithuanian Jewry were concentrated. At the first opportunity, after the signing of the Russian–Polish agreement, almost all of them left Vilna for Poland, and from there in various ways Israel.

[Page 333]

Our Fields and Forests

A. Ish–Ahuvi

Translated by Jerrold Landau

Ish–Ahuva

Of Hechalutz in Smorgon

Our people had forests
We – only young trees
Every forest protected soldiers
Ours protected the guard.

Every forest has old,
Wide crowns of branches.
Under the thick branches
There were wild beasts.

[Page 334]

It is possible that the sun does not cast
Its rays, a prankster.
And thicker become the shadows
In the forest deeper.

Our sun is flowing
Thirstily swallowing rays.
In the earth, the young roots
Seeking sources of water.

And we rejoice like children
When a branch grows bigger,
When the young, green fruit
Is first cut by the knife.

The other forest covers miles
Our – only spans.
However, hope in the heart
Is available therein.

The Market in Smorgon

They come in from the entire region
Gentile men and women in sleds,
And flax, pig hair and hens
They hold inside.

They are traveling to the market,
Which takes place very Wednesday in Smorgon.
And then they all arrive
With the first crow of the hen.

They began to carry around the market:
Cloth, soap, matches, bread,
Waiting a long time for the purchaser,
In the meantime, becoming red from cold.

[Page 335]

The businessmen run to the sleds
"*Shto maesh, kury, swiny, wolosy, len?*"[1]
They feel it and they haggle,
Until the gentile shouts, "*Pashow von!*"[2]

But the businessmen do not yield,
Until they purchase it

They drive the farmer crazy
And pay him the price.

Everyone drags back a customer
And it is jolly in the shops.
The gentile who has purchased something from another
It is obligatory to accompany him with mocking.

A young gentile sits on a wagon
Having a snack and a drink,
And to the gentile woman opposite him
Casts a wink.

The market

[Page 336]

The butchers hire an animal
And make an agreement.
But then the people from Vilna come
And pay more, as if to incite.

Lads come around
Through the streets,
Seeking to earn something
Where to eat.

It was also jolly at the horse dealers
Who replace a bad one with a good one.
They bang with the whips and smile
To demonstrate their might.

The gentile sells his bit of merchandise
Then he goes to the tavern for some liquor
He finishes the last cup
And staggers out to the street.

They hug and kiss
The wife in the middle of the street,
Until they fall off their feet
And they set out on the sled.

Evening, after the market day
The wholesaler demands his many loans,
He closes the window with the shutters,
And counts the money in the silence.

Smorgon has now been sleeping for a long time
The snow continues to fall in pieces,
Only from Banczer's tavern
Does Malinowski the drunk drag himself.

Somewhere from afar, are barking
Dogs tied to chains
Trudging in the snow and glaring
A silhouette, then it disappears.

With his long, thick cane
In his wide, torn coat
Lopej the guard creeps around the market
And watches over the stores at night.

Translator's Footnotes

1. This is a mix of Polish / Ukrainian / Russian: "What do you have: hens, pigs, bristles, flax?" Thanks to Lukasz Biedka, project coordinator of the Przemysl Yizkor Book, for his help on this phrase and the following phrase.

2. This means "Go away" in Russian, but has more of the implication of "bugger off."

[Page 337]

On my "Stage" Smorgon

(A chapter of the history of drama activities in Smorgon)

by Chanoch Levin

Translated by Jerrold Landau

The beginning of the drama activities / Heshel Wynzinger from Brody / Illusion comes to Smorgon / The window / Shmuel Rodansky – doing wonders / Sofia Juliwana "Mirele Efrat" / The son of the King and the Pauper / Feigele / "The Dybbuk" comes to the city / Roza Szar / Three Gifts / The Light of the Crowns

The drama club before the First World War

From left: **Avraham Danishevsky, Freda Ajzenstat, Ida Aharonowa, Zlata Ceitlin, Elisheva Jebzorow, the son of Sheina-Saraka, Linka Chazonow, Sara Dniszbesk, Eliezer Meirowicz**
Bottom: **Natan Rozowski, Yehuda Nianka – Polkes**

[Page 338]

1.

The times of the theatrical activity in our city were like the times of independent consciousness of the youth there. That is to say: on the day that the youth of Smorgon stood on their own, uncovered their world, and began to seek their own paths and to involve themselves in the new life that arose in the wake of the various ideological streams at the end of the 19th century – that was the same time at which the drama activities in our city began. The essence of this activity was the desire for fine artistic expression for those spirits who broke through the doors of the new life. In any case, the first initiators found [the theatrical] stage to express themselves with voice or image, dialogue or plot, whether their heart's longing tended to Chibbat Zion or their source of pride was the Bund, or even faith and devotion to the Rock of Israel[1].

The theatrical activities in all forms lasted for nearly a half century, encompassing all strata of the youth in all the ideological streams in Smorgon. The enchanting theatrical tree in the city was not planted with ease. It was a thin sapling whose beginnings and sprouting was clouded in the clouds of legend.

In those days, I was a student who moved to Vilna, the locale of Torah. As a student, I had to write a composition on the topic, "The first buds of Hebrew theater for children in the Haskalah literature." In addition to the sources in the Strashun Library[2], my mother of blessed memory told me the following instructive story. Not her own story, my mother received it from her father of blessed memory, Reb Shmuel Shimshon Danishevsky, who owned a tanning factory on Vilna Street, where the road split, with one direction leading to the railway tracks, and the other toward Soly, and from there to Oshmyana.

Grandfather, my mother's father of blessed memory, did not produce large hides. He produced a special type of hide from which to make thick soles for shoes, called "*filshefner.*"

My grandfather was a young man at the time, and was helping his father in the tanning business: whether through the work of his own hands, or through supervising the group of Jewish workers from the town.

One day, a non-local Jewish young man came to the tannery, and requested work. He explained that he had worked in the manufacturing of *filshefner* from somewhere else. From where? --- Brody. Why did he come from Brody to Smorgon? Something happened, causing the communal administrators [*parnassim*] to throw him out for mocking them.

How did he mock them? He belonged to that "group of scoffers" known as "Brod Singers." He would gather together a chorus of lads in the city market to sing verses and to disgrace the communal administrators as "strongmen." Seeking to root this [mocking] out, the parnassim threatened to damage the livelihood of his father, who was a solitary tanner and earned a meager livelihood. The young man fled for his life. He had heard that far from Brody, approaching the land of Rus, there was a city called Smorgon, the majority of whose inhabitants worked in tanning, earning their livelihoods in an ample rather than a meager fashion. Therefore, he placed his knapsack on his back, took his walking stick into his hand, and now he stood here full height, with his *peyos* and beard that had not yet sprouted.

[Page 339]

His name was Heshel, and his surname was Wynzinger. It is easy for a wise person to understand that deeds of levity, jokes, and games capture the hearts of the workers even more than practical work. The soul of Heshel of Brody especially attracted the soul of grandfather of blessed memory, that is my mother's father, who was a young man at the time. A year after he arrived in Brody, our Heshel demonstrated his capabilities, and the entire "glory of his kingdom"[3] as he played the role of Achashverosh in the Purim play which was performed in my grandfather's tannery, to the enjoyment of the large crowd that filled the factory, which was grey and gloomy all year, but that day was full of joy and light.

At the wedding of my grandfather Reb Shmuel Shimshon Danishevsky to my grandmother Henia, Heshel of Brody served as the jester along with a group of young tanners. They entertained the invitees with a skit called "Beautiful and Gracious Bride," composed by Heshel in honor of the young couple. Composed from his heart, Heshel wrote melodies to the songs and taught them to the musicians. The house was filled with applause.

The Hebrew theater in Smorgon before the First World War participates in the performance of "Chana and her Seven Children."

Top from left: **Shmuel Fine, Ida Shulman the sister-in-law of Kalman, Nachum Szapir, Basil Wincz, Aharonow the Russian teacher, Mrs. Szimszelewicz, Kalman, Nachum Szapir, Lyula Chazonow, Kribicki, Nathan Rozowski**
Top: **Esther Shulman, Genia Abramowicz Helman**

This "first performance" of Heshel of Brody was a topic of conversation of people for many days. Furthermore, after the wedding of my grandfather, the rest of the honorable householders asked Heshel to return and perform at the weddings of their sons and daughters, and even offered to pay him generously. Before additional facts are revealed (and who knows if [later research] will reveal), we can see in this story the beginning of Jewish theater in Smorgon. The founding father of this [art in Smorgon] was Heshel Wynzinger of Brody – he and none other. Who knows the path of the spirit? Apparently, the merit of Heshel went around, and two of the daughters of Reb Shmuel Danishevsky found their place in the theater – Fania on the national stage in Rostov, and the younger one, Rachel (Rachil) for a short time in Kharkov.

[Page 340]

2.

Before the end of the 19th century, proclamations were issued publicly in Smorgon:

"To all Jewish men, who are like minded,
There is news in the country, wonderful in our eyes,
For the first time in the community of Smorgon
Illusion has arrived.
In pictures of light, you will see – it is not for naught,
The Western Wall, the remnant of our ancient sanctuary
And the grave of Rachel our Mother on the way to Ephrata
And a redeemer shall come to Zion in our day, now."

These verses [above] – language of exaggeration; however proclamations in this literal form, written in the vernacular, as well as Hebrew and Yiddish, were affixed:

To the walls the anteroom of the *Beis Midrashes* of the city.
And on the gates of all the tanneries.
And on Kowarski's liquor distillery.
And on the awning of Barberman's confectionary.

As well as on the hut, which is the government's "Budka." Budka is a platform in the flower market opposite the Pravoslavic Church, where the collector who collected the market-day tax from the farmers of the area and the Jews who came from the near and far towns sat. The name of the collector was Fuma, and it was said that he was an apostate. The Jews called him, in a mocking manner, Fuma Fumszcyk (landowner).

The people of Smorgon, men, women, elderly, and youth gathered on the date set in the announcements. Even children were not missing from the crowd. Everyone came and gathered in the large hall of Grynhaus-Szimszelewicz, which later became the performance hall of Smorgon prior to the First World War.

3.

With the luck of this "illusion" the first movie theater in the town was born, called Gignet. When Jewish Smorgon was "crazy with illusions" and saw in its eyes, and more so in the eyes of its spirit, the Western Wall, Rachel's Tomb, and, to differentiate, acts of juggling in "pleasant pictures on the cloth" -- the wide-branched theatrical activity in all public areas of Jewish life began[4]. The first to begin was the Beit HaUlpana in the garden and school of Ivriya. Its entire educational scope was based on theatrics. The grammar book of this institution was called nothing other than "The Garden Theater" of the Gordon brothers, that appeared in Smorgon in the year 5689 / 1929, that is 55 years ago.

[Page 341]

There were performances of stories of the Bible, as well as "Living pictures" such as "About the Bird" by Ch. N. Bialik, and "My Soul's Longing" by M. Tz. Maneh, in the Hatikva modern Zionist cheder of the Chovevei Zion committee. The crowning achievement of their performances was a full play in Hebrew called "Hannah and her Seven Children" immediately followed by Goldfaden's "Bar Kochba." The Hebrew teacher Mordechai Lus, Szinon, Kalman Nachum Szefer, Shmuel Fine, and others were the doers behind this – as well as the actors, who were the students of the modern cheder and older people from the Young Zion circles in our city.

Not long passed before the poor "maidservant," that is the Yiddish language, was envious of the "mistress" (Hebrew), and gathered all "workers for the Russians," workers in the factory, apprentices in the workshops, toilers and supervisors in the official offices, some of them Poalei Zion members and others from Bund – and they founded the Drama Club. About 20 male and female youths began to involve themselves in the theatrical works. They read and worked on "Koldonia, "The Witch" of Goldfaden, and prepared it for the stage. For some reason, those people found in that theatrical creation, a complaint against the ignorance of "those who sit in darkness and the shadow of death," and against the oppression perpetrated by various types of wealthy "fine Jews" against their impoverished Jewish brethren.

The group was involved in learning the roles by heart and rehearsing the scenes until the stage performance.

What are the scenes?

Two members appear in a workshop, and discuss:

“Tell me, my friend, what are you busy with now?”<> “I am busy with a scene [*atiod*]”

“What does that mean, idiot?”

“Not “idiot” but “*atiod*”[5].

“Oh, at.. yod, that is how it is said” – the last one finished off and got back to his work, as he continued to discuss with himself the meaning of the word that had not been explained to him. It seems that the pair, Aharonow and the girl Tania Szapira, found themselves, explained it for themselves, translated it to the actual language, and brought it to the club as a foundation, as the first attempt at theatrical work.

[In the play] there is a point that the two lads are supposed to attack the policeman (on stage, of course) on the market day and take revenge upon him for disrupting the poor peddlers. How was this scene carried out in actual fashion?

One moonless night, the two attacked the “Gordoboy” (local policeman) of the city, placed a sack on his head, tied the opening of the sack on the bottom to his belly, dragged him below the bridge, and left him there “groaning.” The next day, they found the “Gordoboy”, released his [tied] bonds, and he could not speak.

[Page 342]

It is superfluous to state that our two “actors” carried out their role in the finest possible manner. Why not? Did they not begin from the “scene”?

4.

This “consuming fire” of “the players' theaters” did not go without notice by the “kibbutz” of Smorgon, that is the religious scholars, remnants of the Yeshiva of Volozhin, who came to the city. The players joined the studiers to become one group called the “kibbutz.” (See the article elsewhere in the book[6]). At first secretly and later openly, the Yeshiva lads began to involve themselves in the preparations for the play – which one you might ask? They desired no more or no less than “The Travels of Benjamin III” of Mendele Mocher Seforim.

One day already, the hands of the beadles [*shamashim*] of the city were full of work. The three *shamashim* were Reb Itzik, the chief *shamash* of the Great Synagogue; Reb Velvel, the *shamash* of the *Beis Midrash*; and his brother Reb Yuda, the *shamash* of the Kloiz. All of them toiled to take down the posters in the holy courtyards and areas, the print of which was as follows:

"With the help of G-d
Let it be known that on day ... of the week of the Torah portion of ...
Year ... from the creation of the world, we stand
To tell all who come to the hall...
About
The great story of
"The Travels of Benjamin III"
By Rabbi Mendele Mocher Seforim
He is the sword, and he is the scribe, the rabbi of Israel
He is
Sh. Y. Abramovich from Kapyl, currently Odessa
The story will be performed through conversation and gesticulation
And for anyone who does not understand, Tishbi will explain the questions and problems.[7]"

If you think that they just spoke these thoughts, you are mistaken; they spoke and carried them out. They performed "The Travels of Benjamin II" in the home of Rish'a in Korska.

5.

[Page 343]

During the brief period between the end of the First World War and the tragic closing of the final destruction, from 1922 until 1939, [the] new Smorgon that arose from its ruins, bustled with great activity. The majority of the youth joined the pioneering vision. The soul of the city residents went out to "the place where cedars are planted." Within the ranks of Working Land of Israel, the progression of the nation actualized before their eyes – it was a blow on the head like the blow that an angel delivers atop a young tree, saying to it: grow.

In the gloomy huts that were built provisionally immediately after the war, in the cellars of the multi-story Russian houses that were renovated, and in the first houses that were built, the first cells of social and Zionist activity in the city were born.

One group gathered in a certain place and decided on the "program" – and behold, there was Poalei Zion before you. The second group gathered in the Hebrew school in the poorhouse, and behold, the Young Zion party arose, which later became Hitachdut.

Lads and girls would gather together in the evenings, light sooty candles, and break out in song and dance. During the break between the song and dance, they would discuss the "world and what is in it," as they looked for ways to rectify society in a kingdom of righteousness and peace. At times, when the young Dr. Namiot of Vilna came to visit (Y. Ohel, currently a teacher in Israel) or Tzvi Rozensztajn from far-off Warsaw, the editor of the Hechalutz publication "Heatid", the youth of Smorgon would gather together, whether from Hechalutz, Young Hechalutz, Gordonia, or Hashomer Hatzair. All the local meeting places were full. Several of them already went to prepare themselves with hard work in anticipation of future *aliya*. Then, the pioneers would return to Smorgon, with the certificates for *aliya* arranged and in their pockets.

But where would they find money [for *aliya*]?

Aside from travel expenses, it was necessary to dress the son or daughter and to prepare a wardrobe. Mother would knit a coat of many colors out of farmer's white linen. Grandmother would put her hands to the muskrat[8], and the older sister would sew undergarments. And Father? He was busy and occupied with issues of livelihood. He would spare his bread to give cash to his pioneering son. However, the handful does not satiate the lion. After all the "bundles" were searched, it was found that they were still missing a great deal.

What did they do? They made a theater.

The youth consulted together and decided to arrange a play in honor of their friend who was making *aliya*. The income would be dedicated to the travel expenses and other needs.

The drama club that was set up was an umbrella institution for all the organizations of the city. It was the "demilitarized zone" where ideological debates were forgotten, and everyone devoted themselves to the theatrical act, to the poetic word, and to the practical work toward the artistic tapestry that is called a play.

The first meeting place was in the home of the brothers Shmerl and Yisrael (call Izrail) Rappaport.

I was a child and I stood behind the window of the brothers on winter nights. I would stretch my neck and my entire body to peer through the windowpane at what was taking place inside the house.

[Page 344]

Shmerl Rappport walked with confidence, slightly bent. His arms were extended, knocking together, with his low voice. At times his voice thundered, and at times it whispered. His younger brother, Yisrael, who was not blessed with the dramatic voice of his brother, watched him and corrected him here and there. Yisrael Rappaport was an autodidact in the best and complete sense of the term. He was familiar with all streams of Jewish and secular literature. He would frequent people of wisdom, and had progressive ideas. He was the living spirit in all cultural activities of Smorgon.

The child behind the window of the Rappaport brothers stood in wonder and astonishment, and prayed in his heart that he would obtain an "entrance ticket" to the world of "dreams."

Mula Rodansky – that is Shmuel Rodansky, the actor in Habima[9] – also belonged to the first group of the Drama Club. He made his debut on the stage in Smorgon, and was the producer of "The Lunatic in the Hospital." He took the city with a storm, but he made *aliya* to the Land of Israel immediately after the performance, along with his entire cast. The first pioneers and "actors of Smorgon" were Mordechai Cohen of blessed memory (who forged the image of the eternal matchmaker), Lamdansky, the Weinstein sisters, Rodomin, and others.

They left and others joined the club. Some of them had expert talents who learned the art of the stage. Had the destruction [of Smorgon] not overtaken them, they would certainly have graced the stages of Israel, like their older brother and friend Sh. Rodansky. However, they did not merit.

The drama section of Hechalutz in Smorgon

Woe to that splendor![10]

Later, theatrical Smorgon exposed the Jewish actor Yaakov Gordin, only in the middle of the 1930s. However, we have to consider that the city was in ruins those years, and was empty of Jewish settlement, and "when the cannons thunder, the muses are silent."

[Page 345]

However, when they found out about Yaakov Gordin, he [i.e. his plays] never left the stage, and they did not pass over even one of his plays.

Gordin's theatrical compositions were not all of a high artistic caliber, and most were composed of motifs foreign to the Jews. Nevertheless, the plays were able to capture the soul of the youths and to quench their thirst for dramatic exposition of the struggles of man and society, with their stormy drama, pathos, and practical lessons.

6.

It seems that with Sofia Juliwana (Dniszowska), the city dentist, the esthetic expression of the stage arts blended together with the ideological and educational values of the vision of the artistic creator.

Sofia Juliwana watered the open field in the soul of the youth following the First World War. With her first performance on the stage of Smorgon in the role of Mirele Efrat, in the play of the same name by Yaakov Gordin, she metaphorically brought down nobility from the works of adornment. Before the audience that filled the Intarnat Hall, the Jewish mother stood with her full essence of splendor and pain, with the glory of her life wisdom, with her great love and mercy. The writer of these lines recalls that on that evening when the Song of Songs to immortalize the Jewish mother was sung by Sofia Juliwana, her older sister Sima approached the family matriarch and kissed her on her cheeks...

What does this mean?

It is unclear whether the youth understood the depth of the meaning of the words that her sister said:

"Every mother is Mirele Efrat..."

Thus, Sofia Juliwana Dniszowska ignited in the hearts of both her audience and those who studied her role, the love for the nation, for humanity, and for everything created in the [Divine] image and through the many characters she portrayed on stage.

With her natural refinement, the understanding of her cultural mission in the city, her connection to beauty and goodness, and the grace of her values and influence, she knew how to turn the drama club of Smorgon into a united troupe of actors. Equally important, she wanted to expose to this "small group" of the best of the youth of the city to new horizons, and to teach them, some for the first time, the essence of good prose, of fine poetry, of artistic truth, and proper appearance. She was the one who found and tutored one of the promising young talents: Feigele Leget from the Karke, a settlement of Jewish farmers on the other side of Smorgon. She was an up-and-coming dramatic talent who was forever lost to the Jewish stage due to the tragic events of the Holocaust. The memory of all the female characters whom she played with enthusiasm, energy, and true characterization – characters from Gordin, Sholem Asch, Peretz Hirshbein, and the pinnacle, Leah from Sh. Ansky's Dybbuk, is guarded in the hearts of all who knew her as an anguished monument of artistic glory that has set forever...

[Page 346]

7.

With similar luck, a charmer of short stature [height] was born to the Jewish stage: Asher Galperin (Asherke), with his brief, stormy life. (He and Yisrael Rappaport were tortured to death in one of the cellars of the market warehouses by the Nazi wild beasts.) His essence actualized the legend of the "King and the Pauper" for he was both in his life's situation.

He was the son of a poor family. He started out by delivering newspapers. He went from door to door with a bundle of periodicals and proclaimed their names out loud: Heint and Moment from Jewish Warsaw; Zeit, Der Tag, Vilna Kurier, and Rodio from Vilna, and the only Hebrew weekly, Baderech.

The Drama Club before the First World War

On the way, as the newspapers were being distributed to the houses, the short, ebullient, alert lad stood, and a group of curious people, youth and adults, gathered around him to find out what news was brought by the newspapers under his arms. Then Asherke began to "perform" the news on the "Daftak" – which was the walking path of the Smorgon promenade on Vilna Street, whose name later changed to 3rd of May.

Next to the city announcement pillar, opposite the clock fragment and Yisrael Itzi's coffeehouse, was the "bourse" of young Smorgon, where all the world's problems were dissected for the rod or for grace.

Asherke Galperin performed his first roles in the cast through the newspaper and the monthly: libel of the day, and a curse upon me if the "Comedy of Art" was not performed on the streets of our city with the improvisation of the newspaper deliverer, a poor lad who turned into a "son of a king" at that time.

[Page 347]

At the time, he was not aware of the meaning of this vernacular [or worldly] concept, just as he was missing many fundamental concepts. Asher Galperin did not acquire organized education. Everything he knew later, and he knew no small amount, was acquired through his own power. With time, this "newspaper deliverer" became an agent for newspapers and books in the city. There was a veritable library in his house. He was engrossed with his library during any free hour. He had a large collection of plays in their original [language] and in translation, organized by topic.

His first performance on stage was in the play "The Man from Vilna." His acting was a topic of conversation among the youth of the city for many days after the performance. They prophesied greatness for him, and several fans even wanted to send him to the Young Theater of Warsaw, which was famous in the Jewish world at that time. However, words had limited help, and the prophecies of greatness were fulfilled only within the bounds of the town.

This platform is too small to detail the names of all the lead roles in tens of plays that were forged with unusual ability by the amateurs in a remote town that lived its life in the wake of the events and currents of the Jewish world in the third and fourth decades of the 20th century. Nevertheless, we cannot pass over some of them: the roles of Chanan and the Rabbi from Miropol in the play, The Dybbuk by Sh. Ansky[11].

8.

This is the story of the Dybbuk that entered the town:

During the 1930s, a young man named David Kac came to live in town. He was a native of Smorgon, but he spent the war years with his family in Vilna. He received his knowledge and education from the Real Gymnasja in the Yiddish language. He spent time with the Yiddish "sages" of Vilna.

He gained education and knowledge of the stage after spending several years in the studio of the Vilner Troupe, as one of the up-and-coming participants in the artistic Jewish theater. His arrival in Smorgon was a juncture in the drama activities of the city. This juncture was expressed by the raising of the artistic level of the Drama Club, and the search for new manners of theatrical expression.

He brought with him two plays, The Dybbuk and The Book of Stage, from his membership in the Vilna Troupe. Performing this great, classic play in a provincial city was a very daring act. Dovidl Kac struggled with this material and mastered it. Were it not for the powers of the Drama Club, and their enthusiasm and desire to measure up to the new [ideas], who knows if the theatrical talents of the youth would have been sufficient. In any case, he spent days and nights in rehearsals of this play. David Kac played the leading roles of Chanan and the Rabbi of Miropol.

Leah[11] – Feigele Leget, shall be remembered positively.

[Page 348]

Sender Brinitzer[11] – Shmerl Rappaport and others.

The actor Y. Wislic from the Vilna Troupe was present at the opening performance, and issued full praise for the performance.

David Kac saw that he had someone upon who he could depend. He transferred his roles to Asher Galperin. The latter raised the two roles to a such a level that the producer of the play was astonished at the abilities he displayed – until he concluded:

"I do not have anything to do on the stage when Asherke is standing on it...". The "hammer" found its faithful "anvil."

At the end of the 1930s, David Kac left the city and crossed the border to Russia. He worked in the Jewish theater in Kharkov during the few "good years" for Jewish culture in the Soviet Union. When this culture was destroyed, he was also lost in the depths of oblivion. His tracks [of his life] were lost.

9.

For a long time thereafter, "theatrical" Smorgon drew its substance from the remnants of the stage "feast" of the young "rabbi" – that is David Kac. The sparks of his art showered down with the light of teaching in the artistic endeavors of the city.

After him, it was impossible to return to Y. Gordin as before, even though the light stage[12] in Smorgon received an infusion of energy during those years in the personality of the actress Roza Sar-Pocznik, who originated from Smorgon and returned there from the Folks Theater of Vilna. She knew the "Smorgon of on High"[13], for the artistic reality and the characteristic value of the theater was not in the light operettas such as Yankele or Blumen-Kenigen [Flower Kings] that were performed, not without talent, to the enjoyment and appreciation of the audience – hidden in the best of popular song and story that was dressed up in festive garments of beauty and truth in the creations of Y. L. Peretz and Shalom Aleichem.

After the Drama Club stood for this opinion, it attempted to impart its path and knowledge to the young guard of the stage of Smorgon.

As a final, orphaned echo of the drama activities in the city, there was the performance of the stories of Y. L. Peretz: "From the Head of the Dying Man" and "Three Gifts." The writer of these lines adapted the literary material and give it a theatrical form, and A. Galperin paroduced the "Young Guardian" of the Drama Club.

It seems that Y. L. Peretz never spoke to the hearts of the youth as he spoke at that time on the stage in the Intarnat Hall of Smorgon. The displaced Jewish soul searched for the "gifts" to bring them to the Throne of Glory: a bag of soil from the Land of Israel, the modest covering of a Jewish girl saturated with her blood, and the thread from the yarmulke of a Jew who had become a martyr [Sanctified the Divine Name], the actualization of the love of G-d, the modesty of the daughters of Israel, and the love of the Land of Israel.

Then, on the day of the physical destruction, sparks flew, of course, as in the eyes of the audience of "The Additional Soul" of the Jewish people that is never destroyed; on the day of the physical destruction, sparks escaped from this soul to become the lights in the crown of the Holy One Blessed be He, and in the crown of creation.

Translator's Footnotes

1. This last sentence states, in very flowery language, that those interested in artistic expression may have come from Zionist backgrounds, non-Zionist Bund backgrounds, or even religious backgrounds.
2. See https://en.wikipedia.org/wiki/Mattityahu_Strashun
3. Paraphrased from Esther 1:4.
4. This early move theatre screen was probably made of cloth.
5. A play on words.
6. See page 95.
7. A rabbinical reference to the belief that all unanswered questions from the Talmud will be answered by Elijah the Prophet (the Tishbi) upon his return.
8. i.e. she would prepare furs.
9. Mula is a nickname for Schmuel; Habima is the national theater of Israel.
10. i.e. to that splendor that was lost.
11. A role in The Dybbuk. See https://en.wikipedia.org/wiki/The_Dybbuk
12. Light state here probably references lighter entertainment or lighter productions.
13. i.e. The sublime Smorgon: a takeoff of the Jerusalem of Above or the Heavenly Jerusalem, in contrast with the earthly Jerusalem.

[Page 351]

Few out of Many

Images from the town

Dov Bindman

by Benjamin Bindman

Translated by Sara Mages

HaRav Bindman

My father adhered to the Torah since the dawn of his childhood. Of his four brothers he was the only one who has devoted his life to this noble cause and saw it as his main vocation in life. He was able to fulfill his ambition in life despite the many obstacles that stood in his way.

He headed for the famous Yeshiva in Slabodka, Lita. At that time this Yeshiva was at the height of its splendor and glory. Talented young men, who were superlative in the Torah, were accepted as students to this Yeshiva and distinguished personalities headed it.

Since its establishment this Yeshiva accepted the teaching method of R' Yisrael of Salant zt"l, and became famous as the center of the "*Musar* Movement[1]."

My father always mentioned, with love and admiration, the names of his distinguished teachers like: R' Nota Finkel - the "grandfather" who founded the Yeshiva, R' Yitzchak Yakov Rabinowitch - R' "Itzale of Panevezys, R' Yitzchak Elchanan Spektor - the Rabbi of Kovno, and R' Moshe Mordechai Epstein *Rosh Metivta* [head of the Yeshiva].

[Page 352]

He always remembered their sayings: "In all situations, troubles and torments, in all conditions of a human being, a person shouldn't lose his balance, the image of God which lies within him." "The main ambition is to always point out the superiority of man. It trains him to rise until he's worthy of the crown of God's creation." The greatest obligation in life is the burden of the Kingdom of Heaven."

He absorbed the principles of the Torah and they left their mark on him and guided him throughout his life.

However, the spirit of the "*Haskalah*"[2], which blew at that time, didn't skip him. He read, like many other Yeshiva students, the literature of the "*Haskalah*," and studied night the works of Judah Leib Gordon, Avraham Mapu, and "A wanderer on the path of life" by Peretz Smolenskin. Although he delved into these books they didn't led him astray. He continued to study, with great diligence and zeal, the six orders of the *Mishna* and ***Poskim***, and found in them healing, balm and consolation to the pain and indecisions of the human soul.

He lived in poverty during his stay at the Yeshiva and ate every day at a different home. Over time he received, as an outstanding student, private *Gemara* lessons at the homes of wealthy people. In one of these homes he met Rubinstein, a young Yeshiva student who came to study secular studies (later, he was the Chief Rabbi of the city of Vilna and a member of the Polish Senate).

In this new environment he learned to appreciate the value of secular studies, and realized that it's possible to be educated and along with it to remain a God-fearing Jew.

He spent most of his childhood and adolescence at the Yeshiva in Slabodka. He stayed there until his marriage to my mother Rivka, the daughter of Meir Leib from the city of Smorgon. I, his only son, was born in this city.

Although my father was ordained as a rabbi he didn't use the Torah as a source of income. He began to engage in trade and dedicated his free time to the Torah.

At the outbreak of the First World War my parents wandered far and wide until they reached the city of Romny, Ukraine.

During the First World War, and also a short time after it, we lived in poverty in Russia but we didn't suffer from the shame of hunger. We suffered a lot during the period of the Russian Civil War, and more than once we were saved by a miracle from the pogroms of Petliura's people and others like them.

Even in these chaotic days my father z"l continued to study the Torah and prayed every day in public. He devoted a lot of attention to my education. He entered me to "*Cheder Metukan*" in which sacred and secular studies were taught in "Hebrew in Hebrew."

I studied in this *Cheder* for a short time. The Bolsheviks rose to power and my father realized that they wouldn't allow him to engage in trade to support his family and pursue his traditional lifestyle.

[Page 353]

He was especially troubled by the thought that he wouldn't be able to educate his son on the lap of Torah and Judaism. Therefore, he decided to leave Russia and return to Smorgon.

My parents returned to Smorgon in 1922. The city was destroyed to its foundations and only a few of its previous residents returned to live in it.

The main activity of my father z"l concentrated in the field of education. Without noise and without advertising he planned to establish a primary school. He turned to "*Tarbut*" institutions in Vilna and discussed the matter with Mr. Zemel. The latter sent the teacher Katz, an educated man with a noble spirit, to Smorgon.

In this manner the primary school "*Tarbut*" was established in Smorgon. He also cared for the study of the Bible and *Gemara* and established "Talmud Torah." To do this he brought two talented teachers: "Chaskil the white" who excelled in his special teaching method and his interpretation of the Bible, and "Chaskil the black" who was an expert in the teaching of the *Gemara*.

But it wasn't enough. He quickly realized that a primary education wasn't enough and took care of the continuation of the studies.

In this manner he found the appropriate way to merge sacred and secular studies.

At that time a high school didn't exist in Smorgon. Therefore, he brought a teacher, a young energetic man named Zuferner who was a graduate of "*Tarbut* Gymnasium" in Vilna (later he became famous as a distinguished resistance fighter in the French Maquis and was known by the name Leonard. Not long ago he died in France in middle age). This teacher lived in our house and my father z"l gathered groups of students who have received additional lessons so they could be accepted to "*Tarbut* Gymnasium" in Vilna. These lessons took place in our home.

All the efforts and the hard work that my father z"l invested were not wasted. Over time, his blessed activities yielded results: the Zionist movements found a wide-open field and mature youth who were able to understand their doctrine.

My father devoted his free time to the Torah. Every day he gave a Talmud lesson in the *kloyze*, not for a personal gain but to make the Torah great and mighty. He was careful to leave his business and financial worries at the fixed time in order to give the daily lesson.

At night, he took out the "*Masechet*" from the packed bookcase and trilled the Gemara's pleasant melody in a silent tone. He was hunched over it until late at night and no one dared to bother him at these moments.

During the lesson at the *kloyze* he knew how to examine and distinguish between the real diligent learners and the superficial learners. In his teaching he visited the common sense instead of using the method of dry and sterile debate. He also put an emphasis on logic.

[Page 354]

He was very sad when he saw that I, his only son, was moving away from the *Gemara*. Therefore, he asked me to also add my good friend and taught us a page in the *Gemara*.

My father z"l was an avid lover of Zion and told me about Theodor Herzl and his achievements. He especially appreciated Sokolov and enjoyed his witty newspaper articles. He also instilled in me a deep affection for Zion and taught me from the songs of Zion like "*Sham Bimkom Arazim,*" "*HaShushana*" and others.

He always contributed generously to charitable organizations, religious organizations and also to the Zionist funds.

The townspeople treated him with respect and affection because he was a humble man by nature. He loved people and pursued peace.

I remember that a quarrel broke out in the city during the elections for the city's rabbi and the holy Jewish community split into two rival camps. He was troubled by the controversy that broke out and worked very hard to make peace between the opposing sides. For that reason he was accepted by both parties.

A poetic spirit also nested in him. He especially liked the poetry of Bialik, and from time to time he recited sections from "*HaMatmid*" ["The Talmud student"] which expressed his way of life at the Yeshiva in Slabodka.

He gave *Gemara* lessons at the Hassidim "*Stiebel.*" He got closer to the Hassidut even though he was educated on the knees of the sworn "opponents" of the Hassidut in Lita. Most of his students were Hassidim and he got closer to the way of life of these simple and innocent people - craftsmen and small merchants, people with a special soul that their heart was full of joy even in times when the livelihood wasn't plentiful.

I remember "*Simchat Torah*" and how he danced between them during the "*Hakafot.*" His eyes sparkled with joy when he sang Hassidic songs with them with great devotion and enthusiasm.

However, sometimes I think that his heart felt that something bad was about to happen to him, that he foresaw his bitter end. During the "Days of Awe" he wrapped himself in his prayer shawl and extended the prayer "*Shemoneh Esrei.*" He continued to pray even after the congregation and the rabbi completed the prayer, and said the "*Viduy*" [confession] in silence out of heartbreak and restrained tears.

He poured his heart weeping and said the prayers "*Unethanneh Toqef*" and "*Aseret Harugei Malchut*" [The Ten Martyrs] in a trembling voice. Apparently, he felt that fate would be cruel to him, that he will not die of natural causes but in the hands of inhumane executioners, in one of the cruel deaths of the Ten Martyrs.

[Page 355]

In the 1930s my father realized that many of the best youth were swept by the stream of Communism. He clearly understood that only the Zionist movement can save the youth from the clutches of Communism. Therefore, he agreed, without a choice, to part from me and to accept my immigration to Israel.

In his twilight days he also planned to immigrate to Israel. Despite the many difficulties, which involved in adjusting to a new life, he decided to rebuild everything in his old age. But Hitler's soldiers came and preceded him.

My beloved parents gave their pure souls into the hands of mass-murderers, and died for the sanctification of God's name with all martyrs.

May their memory be blessed and peace to their ashes. May God avenge their blood.

Translator's footnotes

1. The *Musar* Movement: Eeducational movement and ethical program designed to promote and develop the teachings and practices introduced by Yisra'el Lipkin (Salanter; 1810–1883).

2. The Jewish Enlightenment, or *Haskalah*, was an ideological and social movement that developed in Eastern Europe in the early nineteenth century and was active until the rise of the Jewish national movement in the early 1880s.

[Page 356]

Betzalel Magidey – lines in his memory

by Refael Weinstein

Translated by Sara Mages

We're obliged to mention in our book the name of our friend Betzalel Magidey, who was the living spirit and the driving force in all areas of public and cultural life of the community of Smorgon. He was one of the active leaders of the Zionist movement in our city.

He has done a lot for the benefit of "*Tarbut*" school. Day and night he made sure that poor children, who didn't have the means to pay tuition, will remain without a Hebrew national education. He, together with other members, the writer of these lines was also among them, has done a lot for the benefit of Hebrew education. He struggled diligently and persistently with the "parents committee" who objected to the right that was given to the poor to study at half the regular tuition at the aforementioned school. To cover the budget deficit he organized all sorts of activities - dramatic plays, special funds, dances and movies. He carried out his plans with devotion and stubbornness and devoted all of his energy to this noble cause.

It wasn't easy to recruit actors for these plays. Sometimes, it was necessary to persuade the parents, talk to the mothers' heart and ensure them that their daughters will return within an hour. Typically, the plays lasted for two hours or more.

He organized the society of "stage enthusiasts." The revenue from the performances was divided between the educational organizations, "*HeHalutz*" and the library.

Betzalel Magidey stood, like a sentry at his post, in a constant effort for the benefit of the Zionist and cultural-national activity.

The wick of his life was cut short prematurely. He passed away at the age of 29. He was not able to fulfill his personal dream of settlement in Zion, and he always made sure that others would be the first to immigrate.

Few were like him among us in those days. He was a great friend who accomplished a lot. We will remember his deeds, his name and his memory are etched deep in our hearts.

May his soul be bound in the bond of the eternal life of our nation.

Jerusalem, 4 August 1962

[Pages 357-358]

Shloymale (Shalom) Magid - a Pleasant Musician

by Beile Magid-Bear

Translated by Anita Frishman Gabbay and Frieda Levin Dym

A.

Shloymale Magid was born in Smorgon in the “Karke” to poor parents. He was a kind soul, a sweet and respectful individual. From the time of his early childhood years, he showed musical talent. His studies did not come easily to him. He came from very meager means, but this upbringing did not deter him from studying. He saved penny after penny, by giving private lessons to Jewish children from Smorgon. Acting in plays, he would provide the melodies for the silent films until he was able to accumulate enough money to attend the Conservatory in Vilna. Here he excelled as a student, director and virtuoso.

In later years, when he finished at the Conservatory, he started to compose plays, which were performed in front of audiences in Vilna concert halls. It was the “horrible and unthinkable events” that cut short the beautiful life of the young Shlomale Magid. Deep in my heart, those beautiful melodies still resonate in me, his sweet smile is etched in my memory forever/

By Beila Bear, formerly Magid, Montreal, Canada

B.

Who in Smorgon didn't know Shlomale the Fiddler? Everyone knew him and loved him. He and his fiddle were one. His whole life was filled with melodies and beauty. His musical talents started while he was still in the Tarbut School where he taught the children to play the fiddle. Later he started an orchestra in which his students were participants. After the First World War, when I was still a young girl, I remember the background music he provided to the silent movies by Smolenski at the Theatre on Garbersha (Garber) Street.

He accomplished a lot in his short life. His renown did not come to him easily. Shlomale, a child of not so young parents who fled Russia, started to show his artistic talents at age 7. When the family returned after the war to the destroyed city of Smorgon, Shlomale had to both work and study extremely hard. He had to go to Vilna several times a week to study in the Conservatory. In order to earn tuition money and meet his daily needs, he would take with him small packages to sell in the Jewish homes.

In 1937, he married my aunt, Beila Katz. At the outbreak of the war in 1941, he was mobilized into the Russian Army and was killed on the Smolensk front. Shlomale Magid died and what became of his fiddle?!

Beila, his wife, like an "eye belongs to one's head", she wanted to make sure that the "prized possession" and last memento of his life, the fiddle, would be guarded with her life. From one camp to another, she hid this fiddle and it never left her company. As long as the fiddle was whole and by her side, she believed that her Shlomale will return to her. After 3 years, day by day, until March 27, 1944, in the Kushadar Ghetto, she clung to the last memories of Shlomale. On that dark and gloomy day, the Hitlerite murderers robbed her of the fiddle and took away their 6-year-old daughter, beautiful and talented, from their mother (and Shlomale). This was a day of great pain and suffering.

The night before, the beautiful Hindele (as she was called) was sitting on the step of the Ghetto Barrack and singing to herself because it was her birthday. With her sweet and melodious voice, she was singing a children's song from the Ghetto:

"The commandant (woman) in her green coat
Stands at the entrance
I sing myself a little song, and in my heart there plays a fiddle.
Full of tears and heartbreak".

[Page 359]

The Fiddle Song

by Hirshele-Zvi Levin[1][a]

Translated by Frieda Levin Dym

After a Concert evening produced by virtuoso Shlomayle Magid from Smorgon.

Quiet
A Song

A Klezmer
Is playing on his fiddle.

He plays in a trance
He plays, lost in his thoughts
Like he is frozen
He lost his senses
He plays on his fiddle
His very old song.

And the Strings---

They are crying,
They are screaming
And complaining bitterly,
Like nasty weather.
Such a beautiful fiddle
Letting out so much pain!
They fly above
Feeling the winds and torment.

From a place of "KOVOD"

From Generation to Generation
Our enemies
Bring us new disasters:
Holy of Holies...
From the alter of jealousy
Into the flames of "Nations" hatred.

[Page 360]

Burnt and chased away, in his
loving name
Tortured and beaten
Seas of blood are pouring!
Hearts are pierced
My blood is boiling over,
More and more than ever
He screams in a piercing voice----
"REVENGE"

The Klezmer ends his song
On that twisted and broken fiddle.

Footnote

1. This poem was sent by Zvi-Hersh Levin, son of Berl and Minetze Levin of Smorgon, to his brother who was a teacher in Pinsk in 1937. It was published in the same year. He was not yet 13 years old, still (the boy) captured the emotion of the coming days of bloodshed. The young heart knew what lay ahead; he was killed on the way to Ponar.

Translator's footnote

a. Cousin of Frieda Levin Dym

[Page 361]

R' Ze'ev Wolf the *Shamash*

by Shoshana Pelavski

Translated by Sara Mages

R' Ze'ev Wolf the *Shamash*

The world of my father z"l was in Beit Hamidrash. Not because he served the Torah all his life, also not because he was in the company of wise scholars and learned from them – but because of his **love** to the building itself. He devoted his life and narrowed his being within its four walls.

We, the children, saw very little of him at home, among his family. And not only us, all the townspeople knew that R' Ze'ev Wolf the *Shamash* [beadle] is always in Beit Hamidrash, most hours of the day and until the still of the night,

Our mother, Pasha, sent us, the little ones, to see what father was doing in Beit Hamidrash because he was late to return home, forgot to fulfill the needs of a person and walked for days without a light meal.

When we were ordered, as mentioned, by our mother to visit our father, we found him in the big Beit Hamidrash, walking quietly in the darkness of the building in order not to disturb its silence. He walked around the inner walls, sliding his hand on every object, running his fingers over the copper sink and the big hand–washing cup, cleaning the reader's desk with a rag in his hand and polishing the "*Shiviti*" before him. Then, he passed between the rows of benches and peeked into the worshipers' cubicles, which were attached in an incline along the benches, to see if they were also clean and tidy. In this manner he walked and checked the "house of his life" every day.

[Page 362]

Father, we turned to him in a low voice, father – mother sent us to ask when you come home, the meal is getting cold.

If, at that time, R' Ze'ev Wolf was in a different world, or didn't feel that we arrived, he didn't say anything. He only looked at us with affection and a good smile spread on his bearded face. He put his finger on his lips, waved it and whispered: indeed, indeed... to himself, and we didn't know then if it was an expression of agreement or an expression of embarrassment.

In any case, father always agreed to our request and left with us. Our walk was a happy walk. Not that we, God forbid, acted recklessly, even though my brother, Pesach'ke, wouldn't oppose to it – happy was our walk because **all of us** walked together, with our father, walking from a place of *mitzvah* and we might go back there tomorrow.

On the way home we passed by the store of our uncle, R' Yudah. Our uncle, R' Yudah, was also a *Shamash* in a "*Kloiz*" but, unlike my father, he didn't dissociate himself from the matters of the world and his livelihood was a leather shop in the street leading to the market. Our uncle knew the timing of his eldest brother and waited every day for the time of his arrival to greet him as he passed by the threshold of his brother's leather shop. It seemed to us, his escorts, his children, that this shop, which always smelled of tanning, is now slightly, slightly perfumed with the scent of the Torah.

And R' Yudah used to say:

– You know, Velvel, my brother, only when the **two** of us are together in the leather shop, a large portion of the smell of tar and grease is taken from it and all this thanks to synagogues in which we are *Shamashim* ..."

Our mother, Pasha, had a small bedchamber in our big house. There, she engaged in the task of baking. After all, our livelihood wasn't provided by our father z"l because, as our uncle R' Yudah used to say – "the cheeks shrink from the dew of heaven." Therefore, our mother was a "woman of valor" and from her came "the fatness of the land." When mother saw father coming, she quickly wiped her hands at the edge of her apron, rushed to greet him and prepared the meal.

After "*Birkat HaMazon*" [grace after meals] father left for the "big room." So was called in our house the room in which stood the big bookcase. R' Ze'ev Wolf the *Shamash* stood before the bookcase and checked whether, God forbid, the sacred mixed with the secular. There were **his** books and **our** books.

[Page 363]

Only in the book room father enjoyed "two tables": sometimes he took the "secular" from the bookcase – studied from "Ahad Ha'am," read a chapter in " *Ha–To'eh Be–Darke Ha–Ayyim*" by Peretz Smolenskin, and quenched his thirst from an article in "*Mei HaShilo'ach*" [living waters]. Later, as if he wanted to purify himself from excessive immersing in a secular book – he took out the Gemara, sat at the table and started to study it. Father's practice was: he washed his hands between a secular book and a sacred book...

My father was silent. We never heard him raise his voice on us or on any other person. He barely spoke to us and yet, we had a feeling that nothing escaped from him. If there was a sick child at home, he spent a long hour by his bed. He shook his head and said nothing and as he left the house, he put a "Golden" (gold coin), his pay for a month, for the doctor and for other things needed for the body. During this act he used to say to mother: – "Pasha, invite the **best** doctor." In this statement he meant the young doctor, Dr. Epstein (who would be the founder and director of the first "Hebrew Gymnasium" in Vilna that was named after him after his death).

Doctor Epstein was noble, affable and respected the scholars. He was known for his great affection for children. It's told about him, that whenever he heard the cry of a child from a house on his way to visit his patients, he immediately entered that house, checked the child and endeared himself on him with words of praises and sweets that he kept in his "doctor's case."

Doctor Epstein wrote one "prescription" in Latin, as is the custom of all doctors, and one in the Holy Language, and asked that the Hebrew version of the drug will be written in the long "card" that, in those days, was attached to the medicine bottle. Father z"l was among those who honored the doctor and when he preached a sermon on the Sabbath about "the long road of our people" in the present of a "Minyan of Zionists," my father left his synagogue, gave orders to his helper, and went with joy to savor the words of doctor Epstein the Zionist.

In 1914, when the first war broke out, our family left the city and arrived to Poltava. Father remained in Smorgon to guard his synagogue. All pleadings, even the intervention of the city's rabbi, R' Menashe Ginzburg, didn't help. He insisted – I'm not leaving, God will have mercy.

[Page 364]

Only after learning that the front was getting closer to Smorgon, we urgently summoned father to join us until the rage passed. From the great fire that burnt the city, from the ruins of a holy community, R' Ze'ev Wolf the *Shamash* rescued two Torah scrolls. One he gave to a Jew who traveled with his family in a cart to Molodechno and from there to Minsk. He took the second book with him to Charkow [Kharkiv], where we moved from the city of Poltava. We lived in the big yard of our townsman, "master" Zukerman, the chief agent for the trade in leather in Smorgon, all of Greater Russia including the districts in the north and in the south. Many refugees of sword and fire, members of our city, gathered in this yard. In order not to cease prayer and Torah from the remnants of the community in exile, master Zukerman stood and built Beit–Midrash in his yard, in terms of a "sanctuary." Obviously, father returned to be its *Shamash*.

R' Ze'ev Wolf placed the "book" in the Holy Ark and asked to only read it in order to draw the radiance of the destroyed city on the members of his community and on himself. In Zukerman's "*Kloiz*," in Charkow, they used to pray in a "First *Minyan*," mostly on the Sabbath. Once, my father didn't return from Beit–Hamidrash after prayer. A long hour has passed and R' Ze'ev Wolf the *Shamash* was gone. At noon, they searched for the *Shamash*, maybe he went to a "*Mitzvah* of joy" – but they didn't find him. The day darkened, three stars have already risen in the sky of Zukerman's yard – and he hasn't returned. Concern entered our hearts and we left to search for our father throughout the city. He returned at a late hour.

Where was he?

It was a calm Sabbath. He left to visit all the synagogues, the "*kloizin*" and the "*shtiebelekh*" in the city of Charkow and walked from one house of God to the other. Looked and saw that indeed God is found in this place. Counted all the synagogues in the city and found out that there were 18 of them...

The war ended and we returned to Smorgon. The family dwindled. Mother passed away in Russia. Father returned to the ruins of his city. His synagogue was destroyed and until the ruins were rebuilt his world was also destroyed. At an old age he became be the chief *Shamash* in Smorgon.

When the "beating" intensified in Poland and the hatred of the Jews increased in all areas of life, father wanted to immigrate to Eretz-Yisrael.

R' Ze'ev Wolf the *Shamash* turned to Rabbi Kook zt"l. He knew him when he was a student in Smorgon Yeshiva. In his letter, the rabbi promised to make all the efforts to advance his immigration.

My father didn't live to do that. In 5694 he passed away in purity. On the "*Shiv'ah*" to his death his family found the exchange of letters between him and Rabbi Kook zt"l. Many residents of the city came to comfort the bereaved and share their grief with the family. From them, some came repay debts...

How? – It turned out that R' Ze'ev Wolf the *Shamash* was engaged in "giving charity in secret" all his life.

[Pages 365-366]

The Tehilim Jews of Smorgon

by Yakov Danishevsky

Translated by Anita Frishman Gabbay and Frieda Levin Dym

In 1915, we were expelled from Smorgon. In 1922 we returned. We came back to a destroyed city. I was sick for 3 years, with a heart condition. Doctors advised that I should be fed pig meat and fat. They assured me that this diet is how I could be cured of my heart condition.

My father was a religious Jew. How can he allow his son to become "treif" (unclean)? So he went to the synagogue to daven (pray) tehilim and to ask advice from the rabbis so that his son might be healed by eating a lot of butter instead of pork fat.

So they gave me large quantities of butter to swallow instead of pork. I started feeling better and eventually I became healthy again. My father told everyone that he believed that the Almighty, as a thank you for saying Tehilim, saved his son.

My father fervently believed in the mitzvah of helping the poor. Often, after praying in the synagogue, and especially on Friday nights, he lingered, looked around, and saw who was left behind or uninvited, and brought them back to our house.

On one particular time, he invited back six people. When my mother saw such "piggish eaters", she started to scream, "Baruch, what did you do? Are you crazy? Six beggars!" She almost cried from disbelief. He replied, "Gitel Tzertze, do not consume yourself and eat your heart out! From a mitzvah, one does not become poor. Helping the poor is a great deed, and the Almighty will pay us back with many blessings and make us rich in this way and not poor."

On Erev Pesach, he would distribute smurah matzah and our own charoset to all the Jews on our street. When he was done sharing with our neighbours, he would carefully put on his kitel and start preparing for the seder with great "zeal" and with a choir-like a capella. All the sons and daughters (in our family) had good voices, so in our house, the seder would go well into the night. The neighbours, who already finished theirs, would stand under the windows at our house to listen and admire the beautiful melodies.

Before dawn, our father would get up and go pray with the first minyan. He would take with him a large loaf of black bread and share it with the poor people who had slept in the synagogue overnight next to the warm ovens. The "yatka" (butchershop) that belonged to us was next to the shulhof. Because of my Dad's praying and saying tehilim, and afterwards taking his time, the yatka was crowded with goyim waiting to buy the treif meat from a cow that became treif (or the other half of the behind of the cow or ox).

If one of the Baruch's children came to open the yatka with the key, the customers would come around and ask, "Baruski? Baruch? Little Baruchlings, where is Baruch?"

The answer was usually just one word: "praying". Happy are those whose way is perfect. Psalm 119.

Every Shabbos from Mincha until Maariv, Baruch would pray. He had a very sweet and likeable voice.

[Page 369]

Chatzkel, the Blacksmith

Translated by Anita Frishman Gabbay and Frieda Levin Dym

Yamim Noraim or "Days of Awe" in Smorgon: it is a holiday observed in a solemn style. In the evening, every Jewish window with its bright, shining candles looked just like the stars in the sky. Everyone, both old and young, was happy with scarves on their heads, eying each other, not to be late for "Kol Nidre".

In the small synagogue on "Krever Gas", the (cantor) Bal Tefilah" Katzkel (Chatzkel) the blacksmith is praying. Everyone is rushing to listen to him. Folks say that when he prays, you are holding back the tears of joy listening to such a beautiful and melodious voice. Also, the main thing about Katzkel, you know where you stand with him.

Katzkel the blacksmith was not only a great “Bal Tefilah”, but also a very honest man, a loyal worker, and a Jew held in high esteem in the city. He was always on the side of honesty and righteousness. Therefore he made himself available to the town's folk and workers, as they looked up to him for advice. He was a community leader and an active committee member of “Gemilat Hesed” (loan society) and the “Tarbut” School board.

He was also involved with “Linat Hatzikah”, a group composed of mainly women who looked after the sick and needy, providing help or food. Some members were Minzcha Levin (Frieda Levin's aunt), a midwife (kushninetze) Fisher, and others.

One time, Katzkel was going home from a meeting of “Linat Hatzikah” and was attacked by some Polish drunkards. He was badly injured and had to be bedridden for a long time.

But this did not scare him when he went back to work because the residents needed him and his assistance to help the poor. He was full of energy and blessed with a good heart to help others. Helping others is what he lived for! His fame was renowned, even among the Christians, from near and far. People sought out his advice and help, and he never turned anyone away.

But it was by the Nazi's murderous hands that ended his life so tragically at age 49.

May his memory live on!

[Page 370]

R' Meir *Sofer Setam*

by Moshe Mekler

Translated by Sara Mages

R' Meir *Sofer Setam*

R' Meir *Sofer Setam* [the scribe] from Smorgon. R' Meir the scribe, or, as he was called by people, R' Meir the Hasid, was a well-known figure in Smorgon. He was born in Vilna, a descendant of a family of learners and authors. His father - the preacher, was a diligent Torah scholar and the author of religious books. His brother, Peretz Wiernik, an author and journalist, was for many years the editor of "*Der Morgen Zshurnal*" [*The Jewish Morning Journal*] in New York. R' Meir was a wonderful figure, multicolored and rich in content. He was studious and knowledgeable in Hassidic literature. There wasn't a Hasidic book, from the days of Baal Shem Tov to authors of his time that he didn't purchase or obtain, read it and almost knew it by heart. After he unintentionally "turned" a Hasid (his family strongly opposed the Hassidut), he became one of the central pillars of Koidanov's Hassidim. After he settled in

Smorgon he realized that his main mission was to bring communities together and spread the idea of the Hassidut to the public. He was gifted in all the talents required for this task: tremendous knowledge of the subject, was articulate and had a polished style. When he opened his mouth with words of Torah or Hassidut, and stories of Hasidim, he charmed his audience and kept his listeners in suspense. I remember that there were those who spent the whole night, until dawn, in his presence.

What he preached to his followers was mainly the value of joy and damage from sadness, because sadness is the mother of all sins. R' Meir saw in sadness the lack of vitality, submission and acceptance of fate. According to him, melancholy is the reason for apostasy.

[Page 371]

And from here he came to the main objective of playing music and singing. He saw in music the revelation of God's will. He heard in it the music of creation, and believed that it has the power to release small matters and inferior issues from daily life. For that reason he held many parties at his home which excelled in singing and dancing to the depths of the soul. He prayed fervently and purposely because he considered it the main foundation of his being. This story, which I've heard from him, testifies to his devotion, faith and confidence. "Once I was in agony and all kinds of sufferings - the pains of parenthood, etc. and wanted to pour my heart before the rabbi. I came to Koidanov on Friday, the eve of the Holly Sabbath, at 11 before noon, and before I finished my prayer I've been told that our holy and glorious rabbi, the *Admor*, may he live a good and long life, was sitting at his table. I entered to receive his greeting and he ordered me to wash my hands for the meal. As I sat at the table I arranged in my mind all the things that I was going to tell him. At that time our rabbi, the *Admor*, started to tell a story:

When the brothers, the holy R' Peretz author of *Hapeliah,* and his brother the *Mohorosh* [our teacher the rabbi Eliezer Shlomo] from Nikolsburg came for the first time to the Holy *Maggid* [preacher] from Mezhirichi and entered to receive his greeting, they asked him to tell them the meaning of the Gemara - "Each person is bound to bless for the bad in the same way as for the good?. " Is it possible? After all, from the good you feel good and from the bad you feel bad.

And the Holy *Maggid* said to them: "I don't know how to reply you. Go to my Beit Midrash. There sits a man named Zusia and ask him." The respected holly Zusia was known to the entire world as a poor and needy man, oppressed with many difficult and bitter sufferings that were not like them around the world. The holy brothers entered Beit Hamidrash and said to him: "our rabbi sent us to you, to rationalize and explain the meaning of the above mentioned Gemara. R' Zusia answered them and said: what the rabbi wants from me, how can I answer you? Such a question should be asked from a man that his situation is sometimes good and sometimes bad, but I, from the day of my birth to this day, feel very good and never had a bad moment, so I cannot know answer you on matters that don't concern me.

And the holly brothers understood that their holly rabbi sent them to R' Zusia because this holy man would give them the proper solution to their question.

I immediately realized that the honorable rabbi, the *Admor*, may he live a good and long life, felt my thoughts and this story served as a answer for everything that was in me. In this manner he infused his faith in his followers and taught them to overcome the ravages of life and their sufferings. R' Meir was immersed in religious ecstasy and thirst for God all his life, and hence his compassion for people .He lived up to his principles. His heart was full of sadness for people who had to take care of wives and sons and had no sources of income to support them and fulfill the practice of moral order: "Share your bread with the hungry, because you saw the naked and covered him."

[Page 372]

Every month he received sensible amounts from his brother in America. When he received them, he set aside for charity, gave presents to the needy and benevolence to the poor, and on the next day he had nothing left. He never slept more than five hours a day, went to sleep at midnight and got up a three in the morning to study and read books.

He did his work, the scriber's work, with holiness and purity, owe and reverence, without uttering a word during his work, his writing.

I only a told very little about his activities and actions, I'm not the man who can describe the outstanding great man who spoke with fine words. It's a shame that his writings, which contained a treasure of thoughts and contemplation, were lost together with him and his family in Vilna in the great Holocaust of the Polish Jewry.

[Page 373]

Berta Shein *z"l*

by Baruch Sutzkover

Translated by Sara Mages

Was born in Smorgon in 23.12.1900 to her parents, Ester Riva and R' Avraham Eliezer HaLevi Horvitz, who is known by the name Avraham Leizer the Hasid. At the age of 16 she, her parents and family, lived as refugees in Russia like all the people of Smorgon.

In Russia she married Aharon Shein from Smorgon, and in 1924 she returned to Smorgon as Berta Shein. They opened a shoe store until their immigration to Israel in 1935.

In Israel they settled in Hedera and as new immigrants started to get used to the new country. Berta, who had a lot of energy and wasn't able to manage in trading as she has done in Smorgon, worked for the first time in constriction and painting. In 1937, Berta returned to work in trade and opened a grocery store together with Reuven Rodensky. After her partner left the country and returned to Smorgon, Berta and her family remained in Israel and adapted to the conditions of the country.

In 1945, when the former residents of Smorgon in Israel came to the help of their brothers, the Holocaust survivors, it was natural that Berta was among the first. She was elected as a member of the Association of Former Residents of Smorgon and since then, and until her last days, was its living spirit, the activist who activated others. Berta, who had a good memory, common sense and quick and right judgment, dedicated herself to the work of the association. She divided her time between the care of the family and the Association of Former Residents of Smorgon.

[Page 374]

In 1949, the Shein family started to build their home. However, in 1950, her husband, Aharon Shein, passed away. Berta, the widow, that all the burden and worry of the home fell on her, also found the time needed for the association's work. Berta's difficult financial situation didn't prevent her from coming to the aid of the people of Smorgon, the Holocaust survivors, who arrived to Israel. Her house was open to all and those who needed help and advice, the depressed and the bitter, came to Berta and she helped everyone. Berta housed people in her home until they were able get an apartment. At her home they received shelter, food and clothes. Berta also organized weddings at her home for the survivors who came to Israel and had no one to help them. She was satisfied with little but helped others with generosity and kindness.

The burden that she had taken on herself impacted her health and in 1956 she became partially paralyzed in half of her body. Also, in this condition, when she wasn't in full health, she continued to devote herself to the help of others and saw it as a sacred work. At the end of her life, when she was no longer able to move, was confined to her house and later to bed, she showed interest and concern to the work of the association. Our heart ached when we saw her in her last days. Is this Berta, the energetic and full of life? Also, when it was already difficult for her to talk, she inquired about the work of the association.

All those who knew her and worked with her, and all those who have been helped by her, will remember her for the best.

She died in Hedera on 13 Tamuz, 5722, after a long and serious illness.

[Page 377]

The Holocaust and the Destruction

Chapters of Testimony

"The City of Slaughter"

H.N. Bialik

Translated by Israel Efros

Edited by Jerrold Landau

...ARISE and go now to the city of slaughter;
Into its courtyard wind thy way;
There with thine own hand touch, and with the eyes of thine head,
Behold on tree, on stone, on fence, on mural clay,
The spattered blood and dried brains of the dead.
Proceed thence to the ruins, the split walls reach,
Where wider grows the hollow, and greater grows the breach;
Pass over the shattered hearth, attain the broken wall
Whose burnt and barren brick, whose charred stones reveal
The open mouths of such wounds, that no mending
Shall ever mend, nor healing ever heal.
There will thy feet in feathers sink, and stumble
On wreckage doubly wrecked, scroll heaped on manuscript,
Fragments again fragmented–

*

Pause not upon this havoc; go thy way.
The perfumes will be wafted from the acacia bud
And half its blossoms will be feathers,
Whose smell is the smell of blood!
And, spiting thee, strange incense they will bring–
Banish thy loathing–all the beauty of the spring...

Editor's (Jerrold Landau) Notes: This English version of the poem, presented above, is sourced from the *Complete Poetic Works of Hayyim Nahman Bialik*, Israel Efros, ed. (New York, 1948): 129–43 (Vol. I). It was translated with literary license, and does not exactly match the Hebrew text in the Yizkor book. The asterisk denotes the beginning of a significant diversion from original Hebrew.

Two Songs (Poems)

by Liba Elgin

Translated by Anita Frishman Gabbay and Frieda Levin Dym

My Devorala's Portrait

On the wall, to the left of my bed
Hangs my Devorala's portrait
Once...in the middle of the night-
When I am longing for her and I think
I see: She is looking at me...
I hear: She is talking to me...
Mother, I know, you are lonely,
The war will be over soon.
For three years you gave me your bread
While you endured the hunger and pain.
Mother, I remember, during your night sift
You saved a potato for me

And in the end, you remained alone
In front of a closed door...

Kaiser Wald

I remember you well,
Your yellow sands
Bathed in our blood..

Kaiser Wald,
Murders of humanity
You devoured our people
Without reason, my blood is also here,
In your woods.

[Pages 379-399]

The Destruction of Smorgon

by Mariasha Yentes

Translated by Janie Respitz

In memory of all my friends, together with me in the summer 1942, left the Smorgon ghetto for the camps. We had no idea where we were being taken, and it did not dawn on any one of us that this [departure] was the end. We would never see Smorgon again.

* * *

From the first transport, only twenty, perhaps less, survived.

Let us all, the survivors, not forget the innocent who believed that justice would rule the world, and they would see the Land of Israel – but were killed. Let's tell them: You, dear friends, will always be remembered.

When I pass railroads (we all worked near a stretch by the mountain Shzvir) and see people working with pickaxes and spades, or whenever I walk along railway tracks, I see all of you. I see Esther, Fanke, Roske, Basia, Isaac,

Yoshke, Avreymke and others. They are standing and working there. I just have to approach, look and call out, and they will respond and complain to me:

Why do you always leave for the village? We always had trouble with you. Yoshke always had to sing, and Avreymke had to distract the supervisor so they did not notice someone was missing.

I want to respond and show them that I brought a piece of bread and a piece of torn newspaper with "news" that was two months old.

I go to them. Other people are working. Where are the [Jewish] patches? Where is the fear in their eyes? Where are they? Where? Where?

Then I remember this [conversation] was twenty years ago, and I say to myself, "You are the one that survived. You have the duty to tell what happened. No one will believe that the weak Mariasha survived it all and endured. And you, [the] heroes of Smorgon youth, are gone. Woe is me."

* * *

In the summer of 1942, the majority of Smorgon youth were sent to the camps. In the first transport there were about 100 young people. Only a small amount survived.

They take us from the ghetto to the train station. Everyone needs to bring a knapsack with a few things to wear [along] with a wooden box or a small suitcase for small products. Parents give their children the best and nicest things they possessed. They (the parents) remain at home, in Smorgon, among their own. We are travelling to a far away foreign place, and no one knew where or even thought this would be our end, that they were leading us to our death. Even if this thought crept into someone's mind, he would not talk about it for fear that others would laugh at him. We are sure they were taking us away to work, because what value was it to them to kill us? They [already] destroyed entire towns. They forced all the Jews into a barn and lit the barn on fire. Anyone who ran out of the barn was shot.

The Germans had time to fuss with us, and besides, who sends people to death in passenger trains?! And for what reason would they kill us? We are healthy and able to work. The Germans needed workers; therefore, the truth is, they are sending us to work.

With us on the train are some refugees from Vilna. They say that perhaps they were taking us to Ponar. But we had to be patient and wait until we got closer to Vilna [to be certain].

Meanwhile, we pull ourselves together and find places on the train. We take out food from our wooden boxes. We did not think about what lay ahead or about those who remained at home and if we would ever see them again.

Tears run down from our eyes. It is dark in the train, and we are still in the Smorgon station. The cars bump into each other as they are being connected to the locomotive. Yoshke Katz shouted, "Kids, no tears! Especially you girls! Whoever cries will be thrown out!"

We hear a song, "I'm going away, who knows where." Yoshke Katz sings and Manke Khadash sings along.

We begin traveling. Yoshke and Manke are singing "Sing Your Troubles". We want to forget the circumstances of our travels. Where [are we going] to?

Yokhel's Rozke is sitting beside me, "Mariasha, lets' close our eyes and pretend we are going on a field trip to Vilna. I'll tell you where we will go, what we will see." (Yokhel had lived with her parents for years in Vilna). She begins to name places and remember names of friends.

Yoshke and Manke continue to sing. Everyone joins in. Monke Khadash starts a new song. "Who Sings on the Other Shore".

Suddenly we stop; the iron door creaks. I open my eyes. There is pushing, jostling, noise, and shouting.

The people for [the town of] Sal are coming. They will ride with us. They took all the youth from Sal.

Where are we going? What will happen to us?

Don't worry. All will be good. Hearts are throbbing. What's this about Ponar? We were afraid to ask one another. We travel on and try to sleep.

At dawn, we arrived in Vilna. From far away on the tracks we saw Jews. We recognize them by their badges. Up close, we see pale faces and fear in their eyes.

Where are they taking us? Where are we? We look at one another. Perhaps we will see a relative? Maybe an acquaintance?

We pull further [along the tracks]. The train is swinging; we're going. The two refugees from Vilna are standing by the windows and looking out, their faces white as chalk. We are almost at Ponar. They are biting their tongues so they do not speak. We tell Yokhele's Rozke to go to the window and take a look and see if we are at Ponar. They [the two refugees] do not let her approach. It does not look good as they are whispering. Suddenly both shout out!

We pass it. We are going to live.

Folks began to joke around. Moshe Danishevsky (son of Boruch Velvel) began to sing: "Miracles", a Chanukah song—the most appropriate song under the circumstances.

Now we were sure they are taking us to work.

We pass [the town of] Lanerverave, and the train seems to be going faster.

The train stops. Through a small window we saw "Radzhisky" written [on a sign]. We never heard of such a city or town. The door opens, and the Germans take a few men off. They force the people from Sal and a few from Smorgon to climb down.

Finally we arrived in Oran. Here, they forced everyone down. We were about 60-70 people.

Dusk falls; it is raining. We are in a small town and on the road. From a distance we see Germans. They surround and line us up with our knapsacks on our backs and our boxes in hand. How difficult! You have to go but to what and where? We understood [that we will be put to] work. Will we have the strength to carry on? A question, a thought: What happened with the others? A qualm [comes across us], and we pulled ourselves to continue. "Oy! I can't walk any further! I am sure I'll soon fall over. "

We are walking through a forest, and I remain standing. Fanke Kreyn is beside me. We have no energy to continue, especially carrying our packs. Isaac Gas comes to us and takes our packs and carries them for us. Yoshke Katz tells a joke, but he is not singing. Here one does not sing. No singing. We enter a fenced-in yard with barracks. We put down our packs and march—for inspection and enumeration. They line us up and told us to remain standing;

the camp commander will soon talk to us. We were trembling, hungry and wet from the rain. We stand in the yard and wait. Our hearts pound, "What will he say to us?"

Then the commander arrives wearing a green uniform. He has a sadistic expression on his face. He begins his speech. We obviously did not understand everything (although what Jew does not understand [some] German!). The main points we caught. We were nothing. We had to work hard; if not, they would do to us what they did to the Jews from Oran. He tells us all to look to the right. "You see that hill? That's where they are, and that's where you will be." He calls Yoshke Katz out of line. He was the tallest of all the boys.

"You will be in charge. Remember! Work! Work! And now return to the barracks!"

They separated the men and the women.

A great fear takes over. Who knows what they will do with us.

We become familiar in the darkness with our four cornered room. In the middle are three levels of wooden plank beds. They are strewn with straw. From all four sides there is a narrow passage. On one side there were two benches and a red plank on a scaffold which is apparently our table.

In the darkness we climb into the bunks. Me, Manke Khadash, Kreyne's Fanke, Yokhele's Rozke, Merke Kapalovitch, Esther Kapalovitch, and Baske Levin took the top bunk. We assume there would be more air [up top].

We lay down but we cannot fall asleep. One thought worried us: what will happen tomorrow?

* * *

All of us, boys and girls, are on the railway tracks. The older women work in the kitchen. The Germans do not treat us too badly but the food is inedible. Most of us are able to trade things for food. From work, we sneak into the village and barter a dress or a blouse for butter, eggs and cheese.

We receive mail from home. Bad news: it is bad in the ghetto. Most of the youth are sent to Shezhmir. What kind of place is that? We did not know. At work we meet people from Smorgon and a few women from Alkeniky and from

Radzhisky. We work long hours, from darkness to darkness. We have a half hour break for lunch.

During the short break, Yoshke Katz sings. Even the Germans enjoy his singing and as a result are kinder and in better moods. We use that opportunity to sneak away to the village and pay a peasant woman to bake us bread.

Now the question [to ask]. How do we bring hot bread back to the camp? Luckily the bread is ready after work. Everyone returns to the camp. Avrymke Danishevsky remains with us. We can trust him; he is brave.

It is my job, together with Avreymke, Rozke and Isaac Gas to deliver the bread. How we manage, with luck, to bring it to the camp, I have no idea. A few friends wait for us impatiently at the gates of the camp and when they see us coming, one of them strikes up a conversation with the guard. We then quickly toss the two bags of bread over the fence. The bread, thank God, is now in the camp. But how can we now enter the camp unnoticed? We have an idea: Avreymke Danishevsky would be the fall guy and run toward the gate holding a package. The guard catches him, hits him and takes away a half loaf of bread. When the guard is preoccupied with him, we sneak back in.

Once again we are all together. We are working hard but not starving. We help one another, and we all go to work. Only the older women stay in the camp during the day.

Suddenly, girls from Vilna arrive. Among the girls are [soon to be] wonderful friends and a few profiteers. One that we called "Rozke Cossack" is the so-called camp leader. She wants to profit at our expense. She begins to bully everyone in the kitchen, taking the substance from the soup and leaving us only the liquid. We then learn from the Vilna girls about the cruelties of the Vilna ghetto. They shared with us the songs from the Vilna ghetto.

Yoshke Katz quickly learned the melodies, and sang "I Want to See My Home Once More". He also sang Dr. L Buznansky's song "Bombs". We sang along.

Bombs, bombs, my dears,
We are waiting, any minute now you will come and throw fire,
And if on us – that's also good.
A beautiful life led by haste

Now you have become a slave.
Children, women and the aged
They continually slaughtered us.
Bombs, bombs, my dears,
It haunts my thoughts, my soul.
Will we people still remain
The heart yearns for revenge
For our troubles and pain.
Bombs, bombs, my dears.

When we would sing "Bombs, Bombs", it would make us feel a little better. God!, let us live to see the bombs fall and put an end to all of this [suffering]. Who has the strength to endure?

In the camp, we are able to approximately calculate when Rosh Hashana would begin. Ten days later was Yom Kippur. While working, Moshe Danishevsky and Yoshke Katz would sing like cantors, and they sang Kol Nidre. Among us still are some very young children like Hirshke Levin (the son of Berl, the barber) and Yankele Khadash. God neither hears our cries and nor sees how our tears pour over the ground we worked. We fast all day. At night we lie on our cold bunks and think about home, the holidays, Rosh Hashana and Yom Kippur in Smorgon. We cry and cry.

Later, our group is divided. Some, including me, are sent to Ignolina, and the rest are dispersed to other camps.

When I arrive at Ignolina (near Svintzian) there is already snow and frost. We gather in the women's shul. There are 30-40 of us from Smorgon: 8 girls, 2 couples, 2 families, and the rest are young men.

It is cold outside and hard to dig into the frozen ground. The guards are evil. We are no longer singing. When we "return home", everyone tries to warm up a bit by bringing a few small pieces of wood to heat. Then we would tell anecdotes as it is impossible to fall asleep in such cold. When we finally fall asleep late at night from exhaustion, it is soon time to wake up.

When I open my eyes, I would see Leybl Akerman, a sixteen-year-old boy, standing and praying. He did this ritual every morning.

This is how the days and months drag on, without any major changes in our miserable lives.

We learn the horrible news about the Smorgon ghetto from Isaac Gas. He went with a German to Smorgon to bring us warm clothing. He did not find one Jew in Smorgon. A few are in Ashmene, many are in the camps near Ashmene and a few are in Zelyonki.

They take us to Svintzyonke. A typhus epidemic breaks out. Some of the sick are taken to hospital in the Vilna ghetto. Avreymke Danishevsky devotes himself to the sick. Such a strong man will not get sick, but he did, and died in Svitzyonke.

The majority of our sick are in the Vilna ghetto hospital. With great self-sacrifice and fatherly concern, we are cared for by Dr. Shumelisky. In the hospital there are patients from Smorgon and also from Zhezhmir. The plague is rampant there as well.

How good it was to lie in the hospital, on white sheets on a soft bed with a pillow under my head. On one side of me lies Manke Khadash, on the other side Basia Levin and across from her, Ete Podberesky. We are running high fevers and hallucinating, but we still recognize each other. Our heads are shaved, but who cares. We are lying in kingly beds. We have splitting headaches, and we can barely speak. If we are to die, better here and not like Avreymke who never even warmed up before he died. Basia Levin jokes as usual and Manke Khadash takes charge. We are slowly recuperating. Manke is already singing. We began to realize we are in the Vilna ghetto hospital. We knew we have to get out of there as soon as possible in order to escape danger.

Our feet were shaking, our heads spinning, everything is topsy – turvy. But we have to leave. Where do we go? To whom do we belong?

I go to the barber from Minsk Street who is now in Vilna ghetto. I go with my last bit of energy. I look around. What's going on? People are dressed as people. There is a theatre and a Jewish police force.

The Smorgon Jews from the first transport live in the Vilna ghetto at 8 Ashmene Street and work on the railroad. Among them there are friends who are well settled; for example, one is an assistant to the head chimney sweep. This is the best profession in the ghetto. Who can compare to a chimney sweeper! Who will be like him, who will be equivalent to him! He struts around like a peacock. He distributes products through the chimneys. He's a Jew, a notable man. He acquired his affluence thanks to the luck that goes with him as he climbs over the roofs and goes through the streets and barriers undisturbed.

Friends from Smorgon come to me and help me to return to the Ashmene ghetto to my mother and sister. The story goes like this: the Ashmene ghetto needed someone who can work in an isolation room. I go to the Vilna Jewish Council. I have pain in my feet and can barely take a step. People help me by holding me up from under my arms. We meet a girl from Vilna who was previously in Aratz. She was walking with her boyfriend, a policeman. They invited us to come for cholent (a Sabbath stew) on Saturday.

I remembered my head was shaven. Everyone can see that I had Typhus. Woe is me! People have pity on me. Jews are merciful people.

We go and eat cholent: real Kishke (entrails) and potatoes. The potatoes get stuck in my throat. If only the tears from my heart could soften them.

Some of the people of Smorgon in Vilna talk of escaping to the forest, but for this we would need weapons. The partisans would not let us join without weapons and we have no money to purchase weapons. Besides this obstacle, I am still sick. Perhaps it would be easier to go to the forest from the Ashmene ghetto.

We talk about our sad situation. The girls from Smorgon have tears in their eyes. Yoshke Katz notice the sadness and says a song is better than tears. Better to tell jokes and laugh than to pity yourself. We remember the cholent and the girl with her policeman.

Yoshke Katz sings the song "The Policeman" written by L. Rosenthal.

Who says that falling in love can only happen in palaces and I in the ghetto it is a disgrace?

I was smitten over my head, actually, with a simple policeman. This was Avreyml. I loved every bone in his body. He was a guard at the gate.

He took all the girl's packages. From me, he took nothing.

He calls me "beautiful" (in Russian), "my love", - I will guard you with my life. With me you will lack nothing, if you agree to be mine.

He comes to my room every evening. All weak he is faint. I serve him buckwheat cookies that I made myself.

We go walking from Rudnitzker to Kamnitzker and back.

My friends point at us: “Oy, Basia has found such happiness”.

If God wills it, there will be a wedding.

The neighbours of my room will burst with jealousy.

* * *

I must go to Ashmene ghetto. I begin to work in the hospital. It's hard to be confined in the ghetto. If only I could work in the “space”, to get out of the enclosure once a day. Such “luxury” is not for me. The Judenrat (Jewish Council) brought me here and I must work for them.

In Ashmene ghetto, there is a pharmacy and a pharmacist. He is not ashamed to ask us to wash the floors in his house .This task is one of the worst insults for a young girl, especially because he has a daughter my age at home. How many tears did I shed! More than in the camp. Who can handle this humiliation!

We work in the hospital with great devotion. There are many from the camps brought here from Baranovitch with horrible abscesses on their skin and various diseases caused by hunger, cold and uncleanliness. For them, the hospital is home. They feel so lonely and lost. Later I work in the isolation room with Typhus patients.

A part of our first transport arrives in the Ashmene ghetto including Baske Levin and her brother Yoshke. Fanke Kraines and Issac Gas also arrive in the last days before the liquidation of Ashmene ghetto. We know we will have to leave Ashmene. Those who have relatives in the camps can go to them. Some will go to Vilna ghetto. Some are talking about going into the forest.

What do we do with our parents? How can we leave them? If we save ourselves, what will happen to them? If we have to die, we all die together.

It is 1943 and the Ashmene ghetto is liquidated. We are given the opportunity to go to Zhezhmir. I go with my mother and sister on a wagon to [the town of] Sal. In the Sal ghetto, we find people from Smorgon, among them, the teacher Katz. They come to the station to meet us. Katz is aged! He's very happy to see us. He asks us what has happened to us and where we suffered.

I look at him. Something is missing, but what? Oh, yes! His pipe. In school it was always in his hand. If only we could help him find a bit of tobacco.

We sleep at our friends in Sal. Who can sleep? Our hearts pound and say that we will not see them again. In the morning, my school friends Baske Grays and Merke Engar come to say goodbye to me. We go to our teacher Katz. He's not working today and accompanies us to the train station. We say goodbye to him. It's so hard to separate from our teacher; he showed us our first numbers, taught us math and history. How did he sin, how did we sin, so we should suffer like this!

We travel in a freight car and do not stop until Vilna. We remain in Vilna for a few hours. Some people from Smorgon snuck in but the Germans did not see them. We continue en route to Kovno. Once there, we all get off with our packs at the Kashudar station and are loaded onto trucks and taken to the Zhezhmir camp. I'm with Eta Fadberezky, Lybe Berkman, the one that prays, Merke and Khaimke Mirsky, and Yoshke Katz. These are [my] friends from the first transport and we stay together.

We are already in Zhezhmir. It is a small town on the Vilna – Kovno highway. The local Jews were killed by the Germans and Lithuanians, and buried half alive. Now they bring Jews from Smorgon, Olshan, Kreve, Svir and Mikhalishko. The women are in the Shul – the men in the women's section. Wooden planks used as bunks were brought into the Shul. We are put in a room with 10 other families. We take up two planks. With us are Alte Yablanovich with her sister and little brother, the Karpels, and many others. People are pushing, it's crowded. With difficulty we climb onto our bunk.

I'm already used to these troubles but always among familiar people I know from home. Here, there are a thousand people, many unfamiliar.

I meet a childhood friend Khaike Sadavitch. I am happy to see her as it has been a long time. She informs me on how to get settled in this place. Seeing Khaike me gives me hope, and she tells me that "Georg" will come in the morning and take me to work. He is a mean German and looks only for full grown and healthy girls.

Until [the following] morning I have a whole day and a whole night [to acclimate]. Khaike takes me to their building and shows me her bunk. The camp commander is in the second building and is a Jew from Fadbrozh but now a refugee in the Smorgon ghetto. A little further on is the infirmary which has two doctors and a nurse who were sent here from Vilna. There is a big bakery where they bake bread for the entire camp. There is also a kitchen. Almost all the inmates eat from the kettles although the soup is made from horse meat. There is a bath and our boys from Smorgon heat it every week. We can get some hot water from them. There is business in the camp as things are traded, bought and sold. There is Tzipe – Bayle – Reyze[1]. You hand overt things and she brings you goods. She earns from this [business]. Most of the business is in the hands of people from Alshan. It is said they bring in meat and other good things. But you need to have money; whatever they had was stolen from them.

A few girls work in the German's barracks. They steal medication and bring it into the camp. A few girls also work in the office. We get some news from them about what the Germans are planning next. In the German's barracks there is a carpentry shop, and the weaker older women work there. Golde Tabarisky is among them. I try to get my mother work there as the carpentry work is not too difficult. It is warm in the workshop; you can even cook something there. My mother and Golde would cook a yellow bean stew. It was delicious. I did not know there was such an amazing dish in the world of gastronomy. I was that hungry.

Whatever we anticipated and predicted, happened. “Georg” took me to work on the tracks. Railroad work was not new to me. I would sometimes run to the village and trade something with the farmers. My sister is still a child and she too is working on the railroad, but her work is easier. There are a lot of small children in the camp.

Every morning there is roll call. A few Jews from the Judenrat are guarding us; one is better, one is worse. One holds a stick in his hand (to hit us) but rarely uses it. The other one does not even have a stick. The German camp commander likes to receive bribes. With someone like him, a taker, we can get by. We call him “the guy with the hoarse voice”. He knows there are typhus patients in the camp. However, when a German commission come to investigate, he hides the sick. He does this [subterfuge] for his own benefit. He understands very well, if he is not commanding a [productive] Jewish camp he would be marching on the front!

We meet Jews from the other camp. We share news: sad news from Vilna and greetings from the Kovno ghetto. About 20 men from Zhezhmir work for a German company in Kovno. The news from Vilna is that when they liquidated the Smorgon ghetto, some Jews asked to be sent to Kovno. Together with the Jews from Sal, they went through Vilna. The kids working on the railroad jumped into the train cars their parents were in. Instead of going to Kovno on April 26, 1943, they were all taken to Ponar. From the group from Smorgon, one man from the outskirts was saved. I do not know his name. Issar Mirsky from Krever Street jumped out of his [certain] grave and escaped. Yabitch and his daughter were shot when they tried to run away.

In Zhezhmir there are many children without parents. Their parents are in Sal and Svir. A sadness hangs over the camp: who knows what will happen to us tomorrow.

There are rumours spreading that we will be sent to Estonia and Latvia. Some of our inmates leave from the Vilna ghetto to join the partisans in the forest. Some fell on the way. We are also talking about escaping to the forest. But how could I leave my mother and little sister?

The mood in the camp is uneasy. Everyone is apathetic and indifferent to everything. Every time a vein pulses, we want to live and escape from this place.

The Kovno police arrive with trucks and want to take us to Kovno. We have no choice as the work in Zhezhmir is ending. If we must leave, it may as well be to Kovno. My mother and sister are with me. We enter the ghetto. They call us Polish or Russian Jews.

In Kovno, there are Jews who had been rounded up in Czechoslovakia, Austria, and France but they were held in the 9th or 7th fort.

The Jews in Kovno ghetto accept us warmly. They find us places to live in the church and movie theatre. They set up 20 bunks, distribute products, and ask us about friends. With luck, they bring some packages of food for the children. They invite us over. Their small rooms are poor but warm. Families live together.

A few days pass and we observe everything. We understand that if something were to happen, us "Polish and Russians" will be the first scape goats.

People are needed in Kushedar. Kushedar is three kilometres from Zhezhmir. We are familiar with the area, and we think, maybe, we will succeed in an escape. The majority of our youth sign up for the transport to Kushedar. I remain because my sister is sick; she is in the Kovno ghetto hospital. The rest are ordered to work. Khaya Melnik and I are ordered to work in the trench near the railroad. We sort military items brought from the front. At work we could "profit" by putting on a few sweaters, a pair of boots and yet careful not to be caught. We are surprised: German military coats, with bullet holes, soiled from battle.

We did not know how to begin. Our hands were trembling, but we had to work. We are very excited each time we find a piece of newspaper in a pocket. Even though the story was a few weeks old, it was still news for us. From work we are able to sneak into the village. I thought perhaps I can send some help to my mother and sister from here.

They transported me to Kushedar with some friends. It was a small camp, almost exclusively composed of the young. We work in peat. The guards are White Russians and Ukrainians. The master is Dutch and the camp commander is a German. We are permitted to go to Zhezhmir on Sunday afternoons with a guard. We do not work on rainy days, and we sneak out of the camp and go to the village. We trade things and we send food to friends and family in Kovno ghetto. The Jewish camp overseer is a Czech Jew. The doctor and nurse are from the Zhezhmir camp. The food from the kitchen is not bad. The barracks are small, but not over packed. There is a girl from Svintzin , Leyke Svirsky. She writes poems describing our life in the camp.

We whisper about joining the partisans.

One dark night they kill the Dutch master and the German camp commander. The Russian guards tell us to run away. We are afraid to obey them; perhaps this order is a provocation. None of the Jews leave the camp. All night we heard horrible shooting. We are struggling with the idea: on one hand, run away and be free; on the other hand, we are afraid the murderers, the Germans, would take out their anger on our parents who are in the ghetto.

A week later I take my mother from the camp. She wants us to remain together no matter what happens.

With a heavy heart I say goodbye to my childhood friends. Who knows if we will ever see each other again.

I return to the Kovno ghetto. I work in fields of potatoes, cabbage and beets. It is a good place as I do not need to steal; for good work, they give us enough food. The problem is we have to carry aheavy bag two kilometres back to the ghetto. We want to fill the bag as much as possible.

We live in the cinema. We are more comfortable than in Zhezhmir. My mother is working in a brush factory. I receive letters from my friend in Kushedar.

They do not let us stay. They sent us to a camp in Paliman, and we are the only ones from Smorgon there. Everyone in the cinema helped us pack. We say our goodbyes and cry. Golde Tabarisky and Sananike ran to the Judenrat asking they not separate us. It did not help. Our hearts told us we were seeing each other for the last time.

A short time later, they send everyone from Smorgon in Kovno to Latvia as part of Action 3,000.

In Paliman, they refer to us as the people from Zhezhmir. They order my mother to the kitchen so we would all have something to eat. We are the poorest in the camp. The other inmates help us in a very delicate manner so we would not feel insulted. We are extremely sensitive.

I work in a brickyard. It was difficult work. Others work on the train tracks. A year passes. I know that the boys from Kushedar went to the forest. We also speak about leaving. After the liquidation of the Smorgon ghetto, Kayle and Simke Shwartz, Leybl Kapelovitch, his wife Chana and their children arrive in Paliman.

My mother has a heart attack. The people from Kovno now in Paliman look after her. They even bring the best doctor from the Kovno ghetto. They do so much for her, and she actually gets better.

I am at work. The Gestapo surround the land, and they take all the children and adults who appear sick or weak. My mother hides in the kitchen; however, they find her. My little sister sees them take away our mother and cries and begs them to take her too. Nothing helps. She was not a small child anymore. The German respond to her, “Next week they will also take you from here”.

Our mother left for the train station holding the hands of two unknown children.

My sister does not move, as if frozen.

They bring us back from work after the kids and sick adults were moved. The tears and cries of parents who returned from work to learn their children had been taken away is too difficult to describe.

In this operation, Actions Against Children, the following adults and children from Smorgon are killed: my mother Khaya Sore Entes, maiden name Axelrod, Leybl and Khane Kapelovitch's son a little girl, Tzipe, her sister and two children.

The very same day, Actions Against Children took place in Kovno, Kushedar and Zhezhmir.

We are still hopeful they take them all to a work camp, or perhaps to Germany because the front is nearing.

We work on the railroad that went from Minsk, Vilna, and Kovno through East Prussia deep into Germany, and we observe how the White Russians run away with their families by train to Germany. Minsk is already in the hands of the Soviets; Smorgon as well too. Oh, if we could for a moment, look into the faces of our enemies! They celebrate our tragedy. Our evil neighbours are joyous when they see how the Germans torture us! But the Russians are returning!

We did not have the privilege to see Smorgon freed from the Germans! They send us further. The entire camp is being sent back to Kovno and we go by foot. We are indifferent. We think: should we escape? They will capture us, and we have no strength to run and hide. Early in the morning we arrive in the Kovno ghetto. I find my friend from Kushedar. They brought her here as well. A few [friends] ran away. I go look for them. I come with my sister and they do not ask about my mother. They understand what happened to her.

They keep us in Kovno for two days. We hear shooting. Are they bombing? No, it is heavy artillery. Maybe a miracle will happen and they will not take us from here to Germany. We have no luck, and they take us by train to

Germany. Some jump from the train when it slows. They do not feed us or give us any water. We arrive at the determined place and we all disembark, numbering one thousand. They separate the men and the women. The women are put in wagons and drive around German towns and villages. We arrive at the second place. The gates open and S.S let us in. We enter a yard and we look around to see plants, flowers, and beautiful buildings. What kind of place is this? From a distance we see tall chimneys. It is a metal casting factory. Is this where we will work?! They take us a little further, and we see barracks surrounded by electrical wires. They lead us into a yard and order us to give up our money and precious items. I did not possess anything; I already sold my mother's rings in the Kovno ghetto to buy her medication when she was sick. I remember how my hands trembled when conducting the sale. The Jew who bought the jewelry from me also sighed: woe to the daughter who has to sell her mother's wedding ring in order to save her life. So, I did not have any precious items left, except for photographs of my parents, uncles, aunts and their children. I now also had to part with the pictures. How difficult it is to part with the images of their lives, from their dear, loving faces. Everything is thrown into a big pile. They will certainly burn everything. Nearby there is a pile of shoes, tall as a wall. Shoes, dresses and coats are thrown separately. Everything is done with the famous German accuracy. Naked, we undergo a gynecologic exam. It is the first time in our lives we saw such a chair. We are trembling. Who knows what they will do to us? We then go through a bath. We wash ourselves, and they give us striped shirts and pants to wear. Whoever is short gets long pants, and those who are tall get short pants. They make us look like freaks. We can hardly recognize one another. Hungry and cold, they lead us into the barracks. Only now we learn we are in Katzet Shtuthof near Gdansk. Hundreds of women are in one room, with five levels of bunks. From dawn until 8:00[AM] we stand on our feet for roll call and drills. For breakfast, we receive a cup of coffee, a piece of bread with margarine from the tip of a knife—an added blow (insult). For lunch – soup made from nettle and other grasses. The female guards are White Russian and Ukrainian murderers. The head guard is a Pole named Max, an evil man. One morning he enters our room when we are still asleep, and a woman in her sleep shouts: “Fire!” Hundreds of women wake up from her screaming; everyone is confused and frightened. We all begin to shout, “It's burning!” Panic breaks out. Max is outraged. He begins beating and flogging left and right. Many women die.

An operation takes place. They gather the children and the elderly and burned them in the local crematorium.

Four weeks pass. They give us (but not all of us) wooden shoes, a wooden spoon, a bowl or a cup and send us to work digging trenches. There are 1200 women in the transport. They house us in tents. We march to work in rows of five, each with a shovel on her shoulder, accompanied by the S.S.

In this camp there were a few people from Smorgon: me and my sister Rokhele Leah – Mera, the sisters Khieni, Esther and Sore, Male Gurland, Tzirl with Bayle Katz, Toybe Magids, Feygele Alperovitch, Fruml and Khane Alperovitch, Khaye Melnik, Frume Khadash, Rokhele and Ete Fadberezky, Kaze Legat, Frume Golde and Imke Lasikov, Elke Pamatchnik, Rokhele and Dobe, the tailor's daughters, Sheynke and Yehudis Danishevsky, and a few girls from the outskirts. We are 10 in a tent. We stay together at work. Esther Luria was with us in the camp. In her book “Jewish Women Enslaved”, published in Rome, she describes our pain and our appearance in the rags that we wear.

Among the women from Smorgon, only a few receive shoes. My sister and I walk to work barefoot, trudging through the snow. A Christian takes pity on us and tosses us an old pair of slippers. I cannot express the joy this gift brought to us. Later – what luck! – we receive wooden “clogs”. But the snow would stick to the wooden “soles” and before we could pull them out of the snow, we receive blows from the guard.

* * *

We are free. The Russian soldiers tell us to go on the road that leads to Chekhochinek. We fill ourselves with potatoes and we also raid a warehouse of food. We attack the food like ants, taking bread, canned meat, cheese, and we go on our way. We arrive at Alexandrova station. The Christians do not let us in as we are neglected, dirty Jewish women. We wait at the station. I go into town and beg for warm water and some rags to “clean up” and get dressed.

We continue to make progress, and we arrive in Chekhochinek. The Russians tell us to go to a pension. I walk in and look into the mirror on the wall. I am frightened by my own appearance. It was more than a year since I combed my hair. I feel like my whole body is stinging.

I think: how can such a creature become human again?!

God, how can we live to rid ourselves from the neglect and lay down to sleep in a warm bed? We go to the baths every day. I can sit there for hours. As much as I wash, it is not enough. We receive cloth and sew dresses and blouses. They give us military coats.

I want to go home. I want to go to Smorgon to see who has survived.

We arrive in Grodno. We undergo an inspection and interrogation by the NKVD[2]. They keep us locked up for a week. After that hell, they give us tickets to Vilna. From Vilna, I will go to Smorgon. My heart wants to see my birthplace, and the next morning I leave. I arrive at the train station in September 1945. It is the same station [I remember]. The same peasants surround the station. Where are the Jewish wagon drivers? It is dead silent. I walk down the tracks. This is where Axelrod's house was. No! This is not Smorgon! Everything is burnt. Burnt houses, burnt Jews. Where are you? Here I become stubborn. I cannot make peace with the reality of the destruction. I want to see the dormitory. What I see is the cemetery. All of Smorgon is one big cemetery, from Sinitsky until the church.

I was told in Vilna that there were a few Jews in Smorgon who are staying at the Kapel's or with Rivka Glezer. I arrive at Rivka's in the evening. Yes, I find a few Smorgon Jews. They told me Motke Tabarisky recently returned from Russia. I go to Kapel's. There too I found a few who returned from camps in Russia.

Remaining in Smorgon is impossible. The Christians in town look upon us with open hatred. We are too big in their eyes. They look at us with hatred as if they were asking: You survived? Too many of you have survived!

I return to Vilna. Yitzkhak Dnishevsly tells me about the Kibbutzim in Poland and the Zionist Movement. From Poland, they go to Israel, and Sore Alperovitch is in Israel and lives in Hadera.

In December 1946, I travel to Lodz. I choose a Kibbutz. It is a training place where they prepare you to go to Israel. [Finally] going home. I am with my sister in the Kibbutz until 1948. The same year, we arrive in Israel.

Translator's Footnotes

1. The three names likely represent three different women who conducted trade/business. The "she" in the next sentence likely refers to one or any of them.

2. NKVD is the People's Commissariat for Internal Affairs, https://en.wikipedia.org/wiki/NKVD

[Pages 400-418]

In the Ghetto and in the Camps

by Rivka Markus (Yamnik)

Translated by Janie Respitz

I was born in Smorgon. My father's name was Yakov Markus. My mother's maiden name was Tsilia Danishevsky.

We were three children: me, Taybele and Notele.

We had an iron business in the market. Our father was a community activist and a general Zionist.

It is 1941; the war breaks out. There is a panic in the city. We don't know what we should do. Everyone is running away. My father said we will do what the others do. We packed, taking as much as we could, and left Smorgon.

We left by foot, burdened with packs and bags. We left our house in a mess, we didn't even lock the door.

We walked all night without stopping. In the morning, when it was light, there was a squadron of German airplanes bombing. We laid down on the ground. The bombing lasted a few hours. When it ended, we continued on our way. The peasants spread rumours the Germans were throwing gas-bombs.

Hungry, exhausted and petrified, we entered a peasant's house and asked for food and a place to rest. The peasant and his wife took pity on us. They gave us fresh bread and milk and allowed us to spend the night. We stayed with them for a few days. However, their neighbours arrived and told them if they don't send us away immediately, they will massacre us and murder them.

We had to continue our journey. My mother's aunt lived in Lebedove. We decided to go to her. We stayed with her one week. The town was relatively quiet. It was bombed by the Germans and the local non-Jews did not persecute us. The problem was with food. It was hard to get produce. The peasants were afraid to come to town on market days. Mother and father decided we should return to Smorgon because there was no place to escape the Germans. A truly safe place was impossible to find.

Mother was afraid to have father travel with us. The Germans would capture him and take him to work. So, our father and the youngest Notele, remained in Lebedove. My mother, my sister and I headed back to Smorgon. If we find it quiet in Smorgon and the road is not dangerous, we will return to get them. We were sure our separation would be for a short time, so we barely said goodbye to our father.

We arrived in Smorgon. We were happy to find our house not burned. We found our grandfather, Berl Danishevsky, our mother's father, in our home. His house was burned so he came to ours.

Mother returned to Lebedove to get our father and brother. My sister and I remained with our grandfather. When she arrived in Lebedove, she could not find our father. The S.S came and took him away with all the other men. They took them all to Molodechne on foot. She actually found him in a camp but was unable to free him from the Nazi claws. With a broken heart, she returned to Smorgon to look after her small children.

When we saw our mother return with Notele and without our father and how sad she was, we broke down with bitter tears, as our hearts told us we will never see our father again and we were now orphans.

Rumours reached us that they sent them from Molodechne to Sal or to Lide. Mother wanted to go look for our father, but our grandfather did not permit her. An old man, he was afraid to be left alone with the children during such terrible times. We never heard from our father again. None of those captured in Lebedove and other places and sent to Molodechne survived. The Nazis shot them.

Every day brought new troubles. Within a short time they created two Ghettos, one on the outskirts and one in Smorgon in the Shul court. We took a few things and went to the ghetto. We joined a family by the name of

Sarakhan. Living with us in the same house were my uncle Meyer Golberg and his family. This means his wife Mania, their daughter Bayla – Estherke, and my father's sister, Sorele; The Pamachnik family (father, mother and four children); The Mirsky family (mother, father and two children); my grandfather Danishevsky; The Perl family. Also, Sarakhan's sister. One can imagine how crowded it was. So many people living in one house. We did not complain. At least we were among friendly Jews.

We had some ideas how to obtain food. My mother would sneak out of the ghetto and trade possessions for food with familiar peasants. We even had a young refugee eat with us one day a week, just like the Yeshiva students used to do.

Every morning we gathered for roll call. Then the overseers would send us to work where we tore up grass or cleaned the pavement. Our overseer was a Polack named Kashekovsky. He was a young gentile who had gone with us to the same high school. He would beat us brutally, insult us, order us to sing and demand how to carry our brooms.

There was a Judenrat (Jewish Council) in the ghetto. It was comprised of Rabbi Markus and Rabbi Slodzinsi, Yavitz, Noyekh Goldberg, Mirsky, Perl, Abrasha Tsirulnik, Sarakhan and a few others.

Every day there were new edicts. Now the commissar demanded gold, then, Persian lamb coats, leather coats, ordinary clothes and boots. Because we lived with people from the Judenrat, we were informed. Every demand from the Nazis was accompanied by a threat: if it will not be obeyed by the determined time, we will all be shot. We spent many sleepless nights.

My mother packed the clothes that had to be delivered.

As there were a few wealthy Jews, the Judenrat was able to fulfill the demands of the commissar.

Every day we would receive terrifying news: in Lebedove they burned the Jews alive and at Ponar, they shot hundreds of Jews. The same things were happening in other cities and towns.

We lived in great fear. Who knew what tomorrow would bring?

Fortuitously I was sent to work with my mother. We had to keep the school clean and run it as a soldier's residence. The soldiers would come to sleep and then leave for the front. We would also clean the field kitchens. For this work, we received provisions. As long as we had our own food, like bread and potatoes, we were able to avoid non-Kosher food. We distributed our provisions among the needy, hungry families in the ghetto. Our work had another advantage: we received from the Germans news about what was happening at the front and throughout Germany.

Besides cleaning we had to heat the ovens, do laundry and mend [clothes]. I was only 14 years old. Working with me were ten girls around my age. I remember a few of the names: Bayle Goldberg (killed in Estonia), Esther Pamatchnik, Musia Melnik, Berta Perl (killed near Danzig) and Fania Rubinchik.

Our fate was in the hands of the commandant. When he was less of a wild animal than your average Nazi, our lives were a drop easier. We were permitted to go the village and trade goods with the peasants. In exchange for food we would give clothes, jewelry or money. But when the commandant behaved like a mean dog, things became terrible. We could not bring any food into the ghetto, and we suffered grave hunger.

Early one dark morning they ordered everyone, small and big, old and young, to line up in the yard. There was a great panic and we all thought our last hour was approaching. They counted us to be sure no one was missing. The Judenrat prepared a list for the commander of all the young people, one from each family, to send to a work camp.

I was on that list. Because I was working for the local command, the administration held me back and sent my younger sister Taybele. It broke my heart to say goodbye to her. My mother and I were very frightened. She should not, God forbid, perish as my father did.

I continued to work for the local commander. Our troubled life went on as before. They began to talk about the liquidation of the Smorgon ghetto happening soon. We had a good idea how this would transpire. We knew a large number of ghetto-occupied Jews will be killed. [Yet] We were desperate and helpless. What could we do except live in fear of death. I could not rid myself of the thought of them taking me, and without any reason, kill me. Under the ash of dark despair, there was a spark of hope and a will to live. Under these circumstances, the will to remain alive was strong.

One day they informed us of the need for more people in the work camps. Anyone who had a relative in a work camp can choose to be transferred to that camp. I chose to go to the work camp in Zhezhmir because my sister was there.

2

They took us to the station and packed us into freight cars. We took some clothes to wear and something to eat. Before I left, my mother had the shoemaker make me a pair of boots. They were red. Mother was afraid they would pull the boots off my feet. They were too nice for a "Jewess" so my mother smeared them black.

We spent three days on the train. The cars were very cold, and they did not give us any food--not even a drink of water. They kept us confined and would not even let us out to go to the bathroom. When we arrived, the Germans opened the doors, saw what was going on inside the train car, and shouted that we were filthy pigs.

When we arrived in Zhezhmir they took us to a closed gate. When we entered we saw a synagogue and another building that was a hospice.

They counted us to make sure no one escaped on the way.

They housed us: 300 women in the synagogue which had three rows of bunks. Everyone was at work so the building was empty. I impatiently waited for them to return from work so I could see my sister. Late that evening, my sister arrived. I was thrilled to find her alive and healthy, although hard-worked.

We received our first lunch in the work camp. It consisted of potatoes in a lot of water with bits of garbage and leftovers from the Germans' meals added to it. What the Nazis left on their plates, the cooks would add to our "soup". Along with this dish, we would receive a small piece of bread, the same size for everyone, and margarine. When the supervisor saw my boots, he immediately wanted to remove them from my feet.

I found a bunk on the third level near my sister. I accepted the hardships of camp life. There was very little water. We had no water to drink or wash with. I decided to cut off my braids as I couldn't [would not need to] wash my hair. Water was such a rare commodity in the camp that looking for water meant risking your life. Near the synagogue there was a Mikve (ritual bath) and bathhouse, but they were so neglected you became even dirtier if you washed there.

There was no lighting. We would light small pieces of wood we brought from work. Every woman would light a piece which smoked and emitted carbon. In the morning the women's faces would be black from the soot. The air was smoky and stifling.

Early every morning, bells rang to wake us. They gave us black coffee and we tried to wash our faces and hands.

We worked at paving the road. We worked very hard, digging earth and carrying large stones. Twelve o'clock brought us lunch: water with potato and a bit of flour mixed in. If they slaughtered a pig, the cooks took the water from washing the pig and poured it in.

A few women would risk their lives and sneak out of the camp to try and trade clothing for food. Those who did not have extra clothing would take from those who were better off. In gratitude for their efforts of trading clothes for food, they would receive an (another) equal share of the food.

From time to time, a truck transporting the supervisor of the work camp would arrive. The supervisor loved to take bribes. He would bring provisions that parents in the Ashmiene ghetto would [package and] send to their children in this (Zhezhmir) work camp. He would also bring letters and other items.

My mother, her father and my little brother Nosn were in Ashmiene ghetto. Smorgon ghetto had already been liquidated.

The sanitary conditions in the Zhezhmir camp were so terrible, a large percentage of women and men contracted typhus including myself. There was a Jewish nurse in the camp who looked after the sick. As I was recovering, I had a dream I was at home in my bed with white sheets. When I awoke I took that dream as a sign that I would recover quickly. The nurse told me that in my feverish state, I shouted and asked to be taken away from the window because the Nazis would shoot me. She took care of me and gave me coffee, kasha with water without a drop of milk. When I recovered, I was so weak, I could not take a step. I leaned against the wall. It took a while until I could stand on my feet again. It was dangerous to let anyone know you were sick as they would take the sick out of the camp and shoot them. The Jewish camp supervisor would isolate the patients, and would make excuses why they did not show up for work. There was no medication and people were afraid to ask for some. The German administration should not learn about the sick.

I was lucky to have extra clothes. I gave them to my friend. She snuck out of the camp, and traded them for bread, a piece of butter, and pork fat. Thanks to the extra food, I regained my strength and returned to work.

One evening we returned form work exhausted, only to learn that the Jews in the Ashmiene ghetto, where our families were, had been shot. Of course there was nothing we could do. We cried and wailed for our loved ones all night. In the morning, having calmed down, we hoped that the news was just a made up rumour, and we did not have to accept it as truth. Instead, we hoped they liquidated the ghetto and sent the Jews to other camps. As my heart told me a few weeks later, the parents from Ashmiene ghetto arrived at our camp. Among them, my mother, grandfather, and my little brother Nosn. The families united and everyone was very happy. Such joy! Suffering, but together. They enlarged the camp and we were able to live together. Work continued as usual without interruption or calamities.

3

Suddenly, tens of trucks appeared. We were very worried. We thought they came to take us away. When we inquired, they told us we were being transported to Kovno ghetto.

They [ended up] liquidating half of the Zhezhmir camp. Only 150 persons remained. Among those who remained was my grandfather. After arriving at the Kovno ghetto, the Jews there received us warmly and put us up in the synagogue. I was together with my mother, sister and brother. My uncles' family, the Goldberg's, were also with us.

One late evening, we heard a knock. Who could be knocking? The Jewish police of the ghetto. Terrified, we opened the door. We asked, what do you want? Who are you looking for? The police replied, "We are looking for someone named Rivka Markus." That's me! I got ready to go with them. My mother began to cry, and asked where they were taking me. They replied I was on a list of people who were being sent to another camp. It was difficult to separate. We were afraid we would never see each other again. The crying of my mother, sister and brother did not help. They walked me for a while through the dark streets and brought me to a jail. There were other women there who were also on the list. We all cried through the night and did not sleep a wink.

Early the next morning, the Germans arrived to take us from the jail and put us on the trucks. I succeeded in hiding in a corner and was the last one remaining in the jail. On her way to work that morning, my sister Taybele spoke to the head supervisor of the factory and told him I was being transferred to another camp. He interceded on my behalf and I returned to the place I had been working [at the Kovno ghetto].

One day, many Germans entered the camp. They went from house to house removing the people. We did not know what was happening. However our neighbour, when she saw the Germans approaching, took me and a few other girls, mainly children, and threw us into the cellar, locking the door[1]. We remained there for 24 hours, dazed and afraid to breathe, fearful the Germans may find us. We heard their steps on the floor--their boots over our heads. We heard shooting but did not know what was going on outside on our small street. When all was quiet, a few crawled out of the cellar. They returned to tell us that thousands were sent to Estonia. Among those sent were my uncle Goldberg and his entire family. We never saw them again. They were all killed.

For a short while, life in the ghetto was jeopardized. They sent us all to another part of the ghetto. My sister and I continued working in the same factory. Our mother also continued to work at the same place.

One day as we were sitting and working in the rubber factory, people began to discuss terrible news. Hundreds of trucks with S.S entered the ghetto, and they were removing all the children from the ghetto. Many workers had left children at home when they left early that day for work. We could barely wait for the hour when we could return home. We were still hopeful we would find the children at home.

As we approached our house, our brother Nosn did not come out to greet us as he did every day. We have not yet lost hope because our mother left for work, she told Nosn, if anything should happen, he should hide. He [assumed] he was hiding somewhere. We searched for him in the cellar, in the attic, in the yard – Nosn was nowhere to be found. We now fully realized our tragedy.

We sat in our winter coats and cried all night from despair, and did not go to work in the morning.

We assumed the Germans, the evil animals, were satisfied with the [number of] victims, but we were fooled. The next day, more S.S. arrived with dogs and searched for more hidden children. When they found children hiding, they threw them from top story windows, or tore them to pieces, or dragged them by their hair through the streets beating them to death. This [savagery] is how the wild Germans romped through Kovno ghetto for the entire day.

In desperation, we wanted to accompany the children, but they chased us away. Rivers of children's blood [ran] and seas of mother's tears poured for many days. In cases where the mothers were able to stay with their children, they notified us that all the children taken were brought forth and shot.

We spoke to the supervisor of the factory and asked if our mother could work with us. This way we could be together even at work. He agreed.

There were rumours that the Nazis were going to liquidate the Kovno ghetto. Some Jews began to build "Raspberries" (hiding places) under or inside the houses. Some people achieved [created] outstanding "architectural" accomplishments. We had nowhere to hide and we were resigned to our fate: what will be, will be.

4

One Sunday we were ordered to gather. They lined us up and led us through the streets of Kovno. Where to? Is this the end? After a few hours of walking we stopped by the riverbank. We saw a barge. They put all of us on the barge and began to think: what kind of death awaits us? Shooting or drowning?

It was spring, 1943.We are sailing on the boat (barge). They gave us bread and sausage to eat. We travelled like this, in fear, for a week. We saw a big city and they tell us it is Kenigsburg. We remain in Kenigsburg for half a day. [At least] a quarter [if not] half of the Jews from town brought us bread. We sail on and arrive at shore. We deboard, and they lead us on foot. We see a sign, "Shtuthof"[2]. We knew there were crematoriums there and a great panic ensued. There were more than one thousand people arriving and knew no one left alive. Those who had money, gold or jewelry, threw it into the toilets, just to be sure the Germans did not get their hands on it. Parents kissed and said goodbye to their children. Everyone was crying. We chewed on our dry bread and thought this food was to be our last feast. This is how we spent the night--in a barrack waiting for our verdict.

In the morning, the Germans, together with the camp Kapos, came and took us to the baths, made us undress, took our clothes and anything we had with us. We remained silent. One thought consumed us: these were our last hours, if not, minutes.

After washing, we were taken from the bath and made to wear the things the Kapos gave us. We dressed and did not recognize one another in the comical clothes we were wearing.

I actually chose a pair of slippers with high heels. They came in handy. Next they lined us up and sorted us. My sister and I were together, but we pretended to be strangers, since these evil people tried to separate relatives and tear apart families. We stood four in a row: my mother, my sister, Basia Glezer and me.

They directed us to the barrack, gave us bread and margarine, and distributed mats to spread on the floor. We were trying to figure out [their plan]: we were ready to die and now they are letting us live. It was unbelievable.

We slept the night, rested from our journey and our moods improved. We are hopeful that the Germans apparently needed us to work for them.

Early the next morning there was roll call. A Russian woman was the supervisor of our block. We were standing and waiting to be counted for over an hour. Then they told us to return to the barrack. A few people stepped out to see where we were. In front of our eyes was a huge area filled with barracks. On one side there were barracks for men, on the other side for women. Down the middle, there was an electric fence so we could not approach.

We were very happy when we saw our grandfather on the other side of the fence. We exchanged a few words.

A week later we were commanded to exit the barrack and line up in [groups of] fours. When we saw the Germans, we understood something tragic was about to happen. They began to sort us, some to the left and some to the right.

My high heels made me appear taller and in good shape. We also tried to make my younger sister look older. We placed sand under her feet so she would appear taller and pinched her cheeks so she would look healthier. Our efforts did not work. They took my younger sister out of our line and sent her to the left. My mother immediately realized what was happening and when the German looked away, she grabbed my sister and brought her back to the right side.

5

They took us out of Shtuthoff and made us walk for a few days. We arrived at an empty place, without any barracks or shelter. The Germans told us they would hold us here to work. They immediately began to pitch tents. We were 10 to a tent and laid on the bare ground, not even having straw to lie on. It was already the fall [season], and we slept on the frozen ground. They sent us to work digging trenches. We worked from dark to dark, from early in the morning until late in the evening. Returning to our tent after work, we received watery soup. This was our lunch and supper. There was no water for washing or drinking.

It was the beginning of 1944, and it was getting colder. We did not have anything warm to wear. The supervisors were S.S., mean murderers. They beat the women at work for no reason, just for the pleasure of beating and scaring us. We lived under these conditions for four months.

Once again they divided us. The weak and sick were being sent to their death.

The rest of us, the strong and healthy and able to work, were taken to a train station, and placed on passenger trains. We understood that something was not right in Germany. We had no idea what. We were so downtrodden, we had no strength even to hope or await something better.

We arrived in Debek. From there we walked an entire day and arrived at a place filled with barracks. Again we were divided and were placed 30 women in one barrack. In the morning they woke us, gave us coffee and bread, and took us to dig trenches. Here [in this barrack], there was straw on the floor and mats. The head of the camp was an S.S evil man. Before they took us to work, they counted us and the commander said we should work hard until blood pours out from under our nails.

We had nothing to eat, and it was cold. The ground became harder from the frost making digging even more difficult. Later, they gave us coats. We tried to figure out how to stay warm. We took straw from the mats and stuffed our coats. We looked like monsters. Many among us died from various diseases. Water was a rare commodity, and if they caught a woman stealing water, they beat her to death.

A thick snow fell. I was without shoes. How does one go to work barefoot in the snow? Luckily, they brought us wooden shoes. I was happy to have something to put my feet into so I could go to work and not catch a cold. A few more months passed.

6

Suddenly chaos [erupted]. They dragged us out of the barracks, lined us up, and ordered us to walk. Under strict supervision of the S.S., we walked all day without stopping until late at night. We were hungry and frozen, and it was snowing. Where were they taking us? Finally they took us to a stable and informed us we would spend the night here. They gave each of us 3 overcooked potatoes. We slept in horse dung and without any straw. Early the next morning they took us out of the stable, lined us up, counted us and ordered us to march again. We hoped we were going to a specific place, and we would arrive there quickly. We continued walking for days without any food. We slept in stables. Some of the women had frozen hands and feet. Those who lagged behind were shot. Our rows were diminishing; we were becoming less and less. When we saw a woman die and left on the road we thought: this will be our fate.

After weeks of walking, we arrived at an estate. They led us into a barn with cows that were well maintained and clean. We were happy. There was electricity and water for the cows. We washed and warmed ourselves near the animals. We also stole potatoes and potato peels from the cows. My mother, finding a small box which she used as a pail, milked a cow and gave each of us some milk to drink. We were jealous of the cows. They were clean and calm and were sure of their lives. They were not anticipating death any minute.

The following morning, after sleeping in the barn, we received three potatoes and set out again on the snowy roads. It was hard to leave the cows and the clean, tidy barn.

By chance, we learned that many women were hiding in this village where the estate was situated. But we did not know which of the farmers would take pity on us and take us into hiding. So we continued to walk where we were being led.

We walked and walked. We were exhausted and searched for our last bit of strength. Starving and faint, if we found a bone of a dog or a cat on the road, we shared it: for example, everyone would have a lick, then hide it for later.

The road was sown with the women our escorts shot. We were in such a state of despair we did not even notice the area we were walking through.

I was so distraught. I was thinking of committing suicide and putting an end to this painful march. I decided not to budge, thinking they will just shoot me. I tell my mother and sister my suicide plan and say my goodbyes. They both began to cry and begged me not to do it. I tore myself from their arms and remained the last one in the line of marchers. I stood beside a tree and waited for an S.S to approach. My mother and sister cried and called out to me, but I remained standing as if nailed down. When the S.S. approached, I said to him, “I'm not walking anymore! I can't go on with this march any longer.” The S.S. looked at me with amazement and said, “Go on, you young goat!” I did not understand what was with him [his response] and why he did not shoot me. He shot so many other women. Perhaps he enjoyed spite. He would not shoot me because that's what I wanted. He was punishing me by not fulfilling my wish and making me suffer longer and continuing on the march.

It was New Year's night. The S.S took out a cookie from his pocket, gave it to me and told me to join the others in line.

My mother and sister were overjoyed. They wondered however, about the strange behaviour of the S.S guard. I shared my cookie and left with them. This miracle gave us strength. We regarded it as a sign that we will be saved from the Nazis and will live to see better times.

7

During our march we came across a German military division running haphazardly as well as a number of German citizens running away with their belongings. We understood they were running from the Russian military which was approaching and marching victoriously.

We worked up a bit of courage, but fearfully thought: before we live to see revenge, and wait for consolation, we could lose our souls as we were so exhausted.

We continued to walk in this manner for 10 days. We arrived at a place that looked like a camp. A gate opened wide, they counted us, and we were led in.

We were handed over to others and brought into a large barrack without electricity. The barrack was packed with women, and we all laid on the ground. Those who had frozen noses, hands or feet screamed from the pain. No one could help. Dying on the floor with us were women including Alta Yablanovitch and Berta Erl.

The filth in the barrack was beyond description. The air was infected from the gangrenous feet and hands. We sat awake all night, and in the morning we tried to figure out where we were. We were surrounded by a high fence. The women who had already been there a while told us there was an airfield and our location not from Danzig. On our own initiative we looked for a barrack with running water and faucets. The [new] barrack was cold and damp, but cleaner and without the horrific scene we experienced the previous night. On our own, we moved there. They gave us bread and soup with potato peels.

A few days passed. They did not send us to work, and on the third day, they told us to prepare to leave. Coincidently, our friend Basia Glezer met a woman she knew that worked in the kitchen. The woman told her to return to the barrack and remain there. She should not leave because they will make us walk until we die. We decided to stay. What will be, will be. Another reason we stayed is that my mother had frozen feet and could not walk any more. Together with my mother, sister and Basia Glezer, we went to the other woman's barrack. It was clean and the bunks were covered with straw. There were electric lights and a wood burning oven. There was warm water for washing, a luxury we could not even dream about. I found a bunk with a straw bag, and my mother and sister found another. We were actually very happy. The women in this barrack were healthy and brave, and they influenced us with their faith and confidence.

There was a men's section in the same camp. Among the men we found a friend from Smorgon, [his name was] Kraynes.

8

We remained, and the other women from our group continued walking. At night, many trucks came into the camp, and we thought our hours were numbered. In the morning we learned they took all the sick women away. Life in the camp was risky. Some people were sent to work in the camp, some outside. I worked 10 metres outside the camp. When I arrived at work I saw a large grave filled to the top with hundreds of female corpses, piled one on top of the other.

The same week, they sent us to work in the middle of the city, digging trenches. We found the streets, houses and free people very interesting. It had been a long time since we had seen such remarkable things: people dressed like people, not like wild wrecks.

That is how the days passed. We dug trenches regularly. Suddenly we heard a siren, and the guards shouted to us to fall to the ground. We knew these were Russian planes and bombers. We got pleasure seeing our guards prostrate and afraid. Their pride and arrogance disappeared completely. We understood the Russians were approaching quickly. Our camp was situated on an airfield that was vulnerable. We knew that at any minute it would be destroyed and we would be buried in the ruins.

At this time a few women in our barrack contracted typhus. My sister Taybele was among them. She had a high fever and lost consciousness. My mother and I left for work and the sick remained in the barrack. My mother snuck away from work, took off her yellow patch and went to the hospital to ask for medicine. I had no idea where my mother disappeared during work, and I was very worried. During the day, sirens continued to go off numerous times. Again, Russian planes. I finished work, and had to return to the barrack. My mother was still not around. Basia Glezer calms me down and convinces me that my mother is waiting for the other women to return from work so she can return with them. I calm down because I knew I could trust my mother. But I am remained distressed. Later, my mother arrived, medication for my sister as well as bread and a chicken. We all delighted to have a bit of chicken broth.

The following day they did not send us to work. The German supervisor came in and told us that in a few minutes, the entire airfield will be destroyed. Whoever has any strength should run away as far as possible.

We took the nurse and brought her to where the supervisor showed us to go. There was a deafening bang from the explosion. We fell to the ground. Suddenly, the middle of the day was dark from smoke and ash. We lied down like shadows, and when all was extinguished and quiet, the same German came back to us and told us to return to our barrack. Yet, we returned to find everything destroyed. The barracks were down, and those who did not escape in time, died in the barracks. We found a barrack not totally ruined and moved in. Night fell and [the skies] darkened. We realized we were on the front. We thought: who knows if the Germans will let us live to see our liberation which seemed to be very near. In the middle of the night, we heard the guards call the girl who worked there, to leave the camp with them. Basia Glezer looked outside to see what was happening. The Germans took the girl and sent her away. Their intention was to show an example of a camp woman, healthy and good looking.

The Germans gave up. Before leaving they threw hand grenades in the bunkers. We still did not believe the Germans were running away, and we remained without guards. We thought we would wait a few days to figure out what to do.

March 29th, 1945. We see two Russian cavalries approaching. Three weeks later, my sister recovered from delirium and regained consciousness to learn she is free.

Translator's Footnotes

1. As the author states later, some houses created 'outstanding' hiding places.
2. Stutthof Concentration Camp: https://en.wikipedia.org/wiki/Stutthof_concentration_camp

[Page 419]

In Hospital in Smorgon

by Mariasha Yentes

Translated by Janie Respitz

Who from Smorgon was not in the "Tarbut" dormitory and does not remember the neighbours?

When playing hide and seek, we would hide in the vestibule of a neighbour, or when a naughty boy chased us we would also hide in the vestibule of a neighbour. One of the closest neighbours was Leah, the bathhouse attendant. Who in Smorgon did not know Leah the bathhouse attendant?

When at school, if someone hurt his hand, foot or nose, the best place to go was to Leah. She would give us a cold compress. Leah's vestibule was dark and black. A white goat stood there. To hide there was a real pleasure. When the boys, may they rest in peace, wanted to harm us, Leah would save us. She would take us from our hiding place under her large shawl and take us away. The boys had no idea where we disappeared to.

Leah's married daughter lived in the same house. She also knew us very well. On many occasions our running and yelling woke her babies.

Years passed. In 1937 we graduated from the "Tarbut" school, and practically forgot about Leah and her daughter and grandchildren.

However, I met her in the ghetto. As soon as I saw her, I remembered her, never to forget.

It was 1943. I had already been in a few camps. I was recovering from typhus. I arrived in the Ashmen ghetto. There were no longer any Jews in Smorgon. The remaining Jews from Smorgon were in the Ashmen ghetto.

They opened a hospital. There were a few doctors and nurses working in the hospital. There were many sick people. All the beds were full. There was no medication. I was sent to work in the hospital. I was to pay attention and learn practically how to care for typhus patients because having had typhus, I was immune. They created an isolation room because the typhus epidemic was spreading through the ghetto and camps.

The hospital was full. The patients were mainly from the Baronovitch camp and other places.

On Saturday they brought a patient on a stretcher, barely alive, emaciated. She was burning up.

I approached the patient trying to help the nurse. The patient whispered:

> "Mariashinka, you don't recognize me? It's me Sheyne Eshke—Leah the bathhouse attendant's daughter: Save me. Run, get the doctor. I have four babies at home. They killed my husband."

I ran to the doctors, woke them up and asked them to come quickly. They knew about her condition and told me openly: the woman is dying. If we had medication we would try to do something. With bare hands, there is nothing we can do.

I cried, begged and argued.

> "Save her. She has small children. What will happen to them? Who will care for them?"

I remember the extinguished look in Dr. Seliver's eyes that were filled with tears, and the blueness of his lips.

Dr. Dalinsky said: She will today and tomorrow; it is better not to think about it.

I sat by her bed all day. In my mind I saw her children. That night she died in my arms.

It took me a few days to get over it. It was the first death I witnessed from hunger and cold.

I kept thinking of the fate of her children. I did not yet know what the German murderers could do to innocent babies. Later I saw what they did to Jewish children and I curse the German people. All the mothers from other nations, that saw our tragedy, could have helped save us, but did not want to save any Jews, any Jewish children.

[Page 422]

Ponar

by Sherke Kaczerginski

Translated and Edited by Jerrold Landau

Quiet, quiet, my child, let us be silent
Graves are growing here,
They were planted by the haters,
As they passed through here.
All the roads lead to Ponar now,
Father went, not to return,
And with him our light.
Still, my child, don't cry my jewel.
Do not cry in pain!
Our pain, in any case, the enemy
Will never understand.
Seas and oceans have their border,
Prison also has its end,
But to our plight
There is no border,
There is no border.

[Pages 423-432]

What I Survived

by Elka Baranovsky

Translated by Janie Respitz

My maiden name is Krochmalnik. We lived at 10 Gzhive Street. My mother's name was Etl. Her maiden name was Laskov. My father, Avrom Krochmalnik, was a tailor and according to the townspeople, he was an honest and clever Jew. As I remember, my father was active in municipal committees and societies.

It was 1922. Many people who had previously left Smorgon began to return. Our family returned to our hometown as well and we started our lives all over again. It was not easy to get organized. We did not complain. We were used to these problems of poverty and suffering.

My father had a brother, Itche Blum, in America. He came back to Smorgon and helped us out. He was very generous. After a few years in Smorgon, Itche got married and returned to America with his wife. He left us his house. We moved into his house and rented ours.

At this time, my brother Chaim went to Zionist training camp in Grachov, and my sister Rivka went to Tel Chai near Lublin. In 1929 after 2 difficult years of preparation, Chaim and Rivka left for Eretz Yisrael. In 1933 my sister Chana left for Eretz Yisrael as well. I graduated from the Polish school "Pavshechnia" and went to work as an assistant bookkeeper for Mr. Rosenblum, the owner of a store.

It was the 1930s. In town there was an old Rabbi named Plotkin. He had two daughters, Bella and Hadassah, and a son. The Rabbi died, and one side brought another Rabbi named Sladzinsky. Bella married a Rabbi called Marcus. As he was the son-in-law of Rabbi Plotkin, he inherited the Rabbinate in Smorgon. A huge fight broke out between the two sides. They held elections to determine who will be the next Rabbi. They fought bitterly. People were buying votes at high prices. My father stood firm for Sladzinsky. Rabbi Marcus ultimately was chosen. This story is the occasional example of the religious communal life, that we, the youth, did not get involved with.

The youth had more important matters than fighting over a town Rabbi. We founded an organization called "Vitkin". We had a few members. The majority of the youth in Smorgon belonged to "Hashomer Hatzair", Freyheyt", "Poalei Zion", and "HeChalutz".

Our leader was Ruven Grinberg, who now lives in America. A few years later we became "Gordonists", and at the same time we accepted "Unity", led by the teacher Bernstein, may he rest in peace. We also joined "HeChalutz". Chaya Brudne, Nechama Yakobson, and I were chosen for the committee. We organized the youth from the "Tarbut" school. Each one of us led a group where we had to do actual work. We organized a few parties and undertook "flower –days". We collected money for The Jewish National Fund and the Jewish Agency. The most difficult task was collecting money. Collecting 10 or 20 groshen a month was like the parting of the Red Sea. However, difficulties did not stop us. The work we did for Eretz Yisrael was not only a holy obligation, but also an honor.

I definitely remembered the conferences. One was a get together with "Gordonists" from Vilna and our branch. We rented a barn and a peasant's hut in the village Shvitlan. We held our meetings in the barn. Arye Tishler from Lodz was the leader. After interesting deliberations and resolutions were passed, we formed a choir. We sang and danced and felt like one family. We all ate from one pot in which we cooked and brought to the table. Romances also sprung up. People corresponded. Personal letters went from Vilna to Smorgon and from Smorgon to Vilna.

Then there was the conference for Smorgon "Unity" together with "Unity" from Old – Vilayke. We rented wagons and set out on our journey. Except for the pouring rain, the event was very sweet. The anticipation of meeting new devoted friends warmed us up and fostered a sunny atmosphere. Among the male leaders were our teacher Bernstein, Grinberg, and friends from the older group. The female leaders included myself, Batia Kaplevitz, and Baila Megida. They received us very warmly in Vilayke. Dubin, who was from Vilayke, led the conference. We made a lot of new friends from the Vilayke members of "Unity".

We also actively participated in the organization bazars. We spent entire evenings knitting and embroidering items to raffle at the bazar. Our friend Riva Grinberg, may she rest in peace, was very active. So was our teacher Fisher, may he rest in peace, and others. I do not remember all the names.

Until 1939 I worked as a bookkeeper for Rosenblum as I mentioned earlier.

The end of that year I got married. My husband's name was Zelig Levinson. In 1940 I gave birth to a son. In 1941, the Russians entered Smorgon. They sent Rosenblum to Siberia. He was a rich man and they considered him a class enemy, a bourgeois. Now he lives in Holon, Israel.

I begin to work at "Utilny Artel", sorting rags. Jews from Smorgon went through the villages collecting rags and brought them to the warehouse. We sorted them and shipped the rags on to packed trains heading to Russia. My husband worked in the regional distribution centre. They would bring the farmers flax, mushrooms, chickens, eggs and other produce. My husband, Zelig, was the buyer of the produce and the manager. He supervised the distribution to various places.

The Second World War broke out on June 22, 1941. My husband was mobilized into the Red Army. The city of Smorgon went into a state of panic. People were trying to leave. My brother-in-law Levinson harnessed his horse and wagon and packed all he could. The whole family was ready to depart. I ran into my parents and asked them to leave with us. My father refused to leave the city. My begging did not help. He explained. "If we are fated to die, that's how it is inscribed. I want to die at home, not wandering somewhere strange."

I said goodbye to my father, took my child and joined my father-in-law and mother-in-law. On the road we caught up to my husband. He escaped from his mobilization point. He hoped that with all the mess they will not find him. We traveled together to Horodok and planned to go further. However, they told us the Russian border at Minsk was blocked. They were only allowing party members with special papers through. We had relatives in Horodok and decided to stay with them for a few weeks until it became clear to us where we could hide. Until the fear passes and the war ends. After a few weeks we left for Zaskevitch, my husband's hometown. There we stayed with his aunt.

On July 22, 1941 a Lithuanian porter came to town with Rebak Brosh, a gentile from Smorgon. They entered our house, found my husband's cousin Hirsh – Dovid Levinson, and took him away. Rebak was angry. At that moment my husband and I were not in the house. We came home to the tragedy. When the porter and gentile saw my husband, they told him to go with his cousin. The next morning, the murderers took them to Zalesie and shot them. I thought then that my father was right. There is no escape. It's better to remain at home.

I picked up my child in my arms and began to walk home, to return to Smorgon. It is about 17 kilometres. I don't know where I found the strength. After arriving back home I faced another tragedy. When I asked where my younger sister Feygele was, they told me a non-Jewish neighbour on our street shot her. My husband Zelig, Zelig's cousin Hirsch, and my sister Feygele were the first victims taken from our family.

In October 1941 they set up a ghetto. They sent us to “Karke”, the outskirts. They put one, two, or sometimes three families in one small room. They sent us to work. We worked on building the Zaliyes train tracks. We worked hard from very early until very late. Day in, day out, we toiled in hard labor, tormented and fearful. The winter changes to spring.

In the summer of 1942 they transport us back to Smorgon, specifically to the Smorgon ghetto in the Shul courtyard, enclosed with barbed wire. We find a small room at the Kube's. Life is terrible and frightening. My father is working a bit as a tailor. They sent me to different difficult jobs. I feel “happy” when they send me to work in the baths, as I can wash myself. I will always remember the screams of the tortured Jews. In the middle of the marketplace, next to the fire department, stood the Sadeviche wall. Underneath in a dark cellar some Jews were imprisoned. Among them were: Yisrael Rapaport, Avrom Katz, the bookkeeper Chaim Yavitch and many others whose names I do not recall. There they tortured and beaten. We heard their screams throughout the marketplace.

They lined up the girls and women with brooms in our hands. They made us sing songs and run through the marketplace. The screams from the men in the cellar were deafening and tore at our hearts. But what could we do except pray for the salvation of those tortured.

In 1942 my sister Leah with other young people were sent to work in Zhezhmir. Later, the Smorgon ghetto was liquidated and we were transported to the Ashmen ghetto. There also were a few families living in one room. My father worked as a tailor at a workbench. I worked as well. Before work we would receive a piece of bread and a few other products which barely kept us alive and the strength to work.

After a few months in the Ashmen ghetto, there was military action. Early in the morning we were forced to leave our homes and line up in rows of five. We are told to march, and we head to the Shul. On both sides there were German police and Lithuanians. There are also Jewish police who say they are also mean murderers. We are told that the Jewish police participate in beating and murdering Jews, and if they find out a Jew is hiding, they turn him in.

We are standing and wavering between life and death. Whoever gets a wave of a finger must immediately leave the line and go off to the side. That means you lose. At the last moment, my father took my child in his hands and begins marching. Then me, my uncle Itche Blum and his wife go as well. We marched not dead, not alive. Then they took my uncle from the line as we continued to march. I turned my head to see what happened. Firstly, I see my uncle pitifully standing with his head bent down, forlorn. He was always so proud and self-assured. He looks with extinguished eyes at his wife for the last time, at me and at his brother, (my father).

They led us into the Shul. I cannot even describe what took place. One person tore out his hair, the other banged his head on the wall. One was missing a mother; another was missing a father, or a husband, or a wife.

The weeping and wailing was strong, as if it were a new found voice, capable of taking down the walls of the shul. The sound could move the heart of an animal, yet not the hearts of the Nazis, Lithuanians or Jewish Kapos. They kept us in the Shul until late in the evening. Those singled out were taken to Zeliyanke and shot. When the murderers returned from their murderous work, they let us out and told us to return to our homes. The Asmen ghetto was to be liquidated. Some will be sent to Zhezhmir labour camp, some will go to Panievezh. They were sent in closed train cars. Many Jews from Smorgon were shot in Panievezh.

When I arrived in Zhezhmir I found my sister Leah. We were happy our parents are with us in the camp. My father is taken to work in the tailor shop. My sister and I are sent to work on the railroad. My mother takes care of my little son. We eat from a communal pot. They keep us half hungry.

In 1943, the Zhezhmir labour camp was liquidated. Some of the labourers are sent to Pleskov; others are transported to the Kovno ghetto located in Slabodke. After arriving in Slabodke, we live up in the Shul. Our beds were made of planks of wood. There was no shortage of bedbugs.

In the Slabodke camp, my father worked as a tailor again, and my sister Leah had a job at the laundry. I worked in the clothing department. It was on the outskirts of Kovno in a place called “Shans”. We came to work, scared to death, but we did it. The will was strong. Especially when there are children involved. I still had my little Dovidl.

What would a mother not do for her child? We will do whatever possible. We went to work without shoes, wearing a small dress. At the department, we get dressed. The shoes were military. We made clothes from pieces of fabric.

We received shoes and clothing and our job was to sort it out. The German guarding us was an invalid. We paid him off and he pretended not to see. We took as much as we can and put it on. The most dangerous part was to smuggle it into the ghetto when we returned from work. The items we smuggled in, we sold in the ghetto. We then took the money and bought food from the farmers. We then fed ourselves and our children. As I said, mothers risked their lives to ensure their children would not starve to death.

Suddenly there was a command to bring forth 5,000 workers. The Germans provided trains and told us to take all our possessions and put them on the trains. We believe the Germans when they tell us they are taking us to another labour camp. We packed our things and got on the trains. First they took us to the workshops in the ghetto. There we saw trucks. They told us to get into the trucks. Our belongings were on the train. We are scared to death: we have no idea where they are taking us, maybe to our death.

We continued traveling. We were stopped by Ukrainian bandits. They made us give them what we had on: gold, jewelry, watches. My father took out his pocket watch and gave it to them. I had a wedding gift from my mother-in-law--a gold watch that I hid in my child's bag. I took it out and gave it to them.

We traveled on further. We arrived at the ninth fort. I looked out. Lithuanians and Germans were standing. They stopped the trucks. They made the passengers climb out and they were sorted. I shouted: “We are lost!” I asked my mother to watch my child. Our truck stopped and we heard the command: “Climb out!”

My sister Leah went out first. I handed her my child. They grabbed him from her arms and flung him to the side. They pushed me and my sister to the other side. They pushed my mother and our youngest sister Kaylinke to the same side as my son. My father was sent separately. Within five minutes our family was torn apart to pieces. One cannot see the other. I began to shout and cry: “My child! My child!” I got hit in the head with a rubber stick. I could not see anything. They told us to march. They shove us into freight cars, boarded up and locked. I did not know what was happening to me. I lay on the floor. The train did not start to move until evening. The crowdedness was indescribable, like herring in a barrel. We traveled in this packed environment for a few days and nights. The older people and children were in the front train cars. (We later learned they were transported to Auschwitz). My mother was killed in Auschwitz. Together with her, my sister Kayla and my child Dovidl, born in 1940 – killed in 1943.

At a certain station, they stopped the train and told everyone to get off. At that time, I got a glimpse of my father. They began to sort us deciding who will go to which camp. After being sorted, they told us to get back on the train. They were taking us further. We arrived in Estonia. We stopped at Ereda station. And were told to climb out. We were supervised by the head of the camp, Shneider. He lined us up and told us to march. We walked for four kilometres and arrived at the camp. At the camp there were only men. Jews from Vilna. Among them were two women dressed like men.

We are sent to barracks with rows of wooden planks. In the morning they sent us off to work. I told them I was a tailor. They sent me to the workshop at the train station. I was happy not to be working outdoors but under a roof, in a building with walls. However walking back and forth from the stationwas quite a distance and tired me out. I was using my last bit of strength. This waswhere I stayed for almost a year. One of the worst people was Meir Chayt, a Jew from Vilna. He bullied the female inmates and would beat and kill the men.

It was 1944. The Ereda camp was liquidated. A group of men escaped to the forest and joined the partisans. The camp commander, Shnabel, tried hard but did not capture them. They packed us into freight cars and took us to a place called Lagediye. We remained in Lagedive for three weeks, living in tents. From there they transported us in freight cars to Danzig. Here, we found Jews from all the Estonian camps and I meet up with my dear father.

In Danzig they put us on a ship. When we came closer to shore they put us on smaller boats and brought us to shore. From there we walked to Shtuthof.

In Shtuthof camp, I was sent to Block 19. The Kapo of our Block was called Shurka, a Ukrainian woman. No pen can write about the suffering and pain we experienced. The camp was surrounded by electric wires. On the other side of the wire was the district where they kept the sick. We saw how they threw people from the trains and sent them to the gas-ovens, day in and day out. They were sent to burn and suffocate. Then I saw a group of women marching in rows of four. They went through the gate. Among them I recognized women from Smorgon. There was the Rabbi's wife from the Karke, Zukerman, Leah Mishkin and others from Smorgon.

I spent three weeks slaving in Shtuthof. During this time I was selected twice to be burned. Each time I managed to escape to my sister Leah in Block 19. This was the workers' Block.

They took us to the bathhouse. After washing they give us prisoners' clothes. They sent us to work at a place not far from Bramburg. My father remained in Shtuthof. We became separated. This time permanently. He died in Shtuthof.

They later put us in barracks with wooden bunks. They fed us a bit of soup once a day. We were building a railroad.

On January 24, 1945, they took all the women and sent us toward Berlin. The frost burned us in pain. We were lightly dressed in rags. Walking in wooden shoes that stuck to the snow, we continually fell. This trudge continues all day and night. In the morning we realized we are now alone; the S.S and our commanders ran away. We saw a group of Russian prisoners marching. They told us to be strong and persevere because the Russian army will soon come to free us. Their words comforted us. Some women were brave and entered a farmers' house and asked for food. The lady farmer gave us bread and hot water. She then prepared straw on the floor as beds. We fell asleep instantly. While sleeping, we heard knocking. It was 1:00 in the morning, and we were afraid. We began to hear shouting in Russian. Opening the door and to our great surprise, we saw Russian political instructors enter the house. They told us, "We came to free you. We are also Jews." It all seemed like a dream.

After liberation on January 26, 1945, we traveled to Lublin, then from Lublin to Lodz. I got re-married in Lodz and went to Germany. We spent two years in a Kibbutz. In 1947, we left for Israel. It is five years now that we are living on a Moshav. We are happy. Most important, our children are happy.

In closing, I would like to remember my husband Zelig Levinson who was shot in Zalesie, as I recalled earlier. Zelig's entire family was killed—they were confined in a barn and burned alive.

Our best neighbours were killed: Velvl Shvartz and his family, and Elye Shvartz and his family. I would like their names to be inscribed in our memory.

May God avenge their blood.

[Page 433]

In the War

by Shalom Sneidman

Translated by Eilat Levitan and Ona Kondrotas

Summer of 1941

When the war started I was serving in the Soviet army. Together with the rest of the soldiers in my brigade, I fell as a POW near the town of Orsha (Mogilev, Belarus). All the POWs were taken by the Germans to the camp. I was able to change my uniform to plainclothes and escape imprisonment, intending to somehow get to Smorgon, even if I would have to walk the entire way. In the first village I entered, I encountered a German solider.

"Are you a Jew?" he asked.
"No."
"Are you a soldier?"
"No."
"So who are you?"
"I am a prisoner."

Upon hearing this, the German intended to stop and return me to the camp I came from. All of a sudden, from afar, he saw another POW escapee, and so he started walking toward him to arrest him, too. I used this moment while he was busy with the other to escape. The first thing I did was to exchange my soldier boots for wooden clogs so that I might be mistaken for a villager. Thus I arrived in Minsk.

When I arrived, I saw a POW camp surrounded by barbed wire. When I looked at the inmates, I recognized some of them as people who had served in the same division as I. I went all around the camp to avoid it and reached Minsk. This occurred on the same days that all the Minsk Jews were put in a ghetto. I knew that I could not rely on my costume and wooden clogs to disguise me and so, quickly I left the town. On the road between Minsk and Smorgon, I met a farmer returning from Smorgon. I asked him if the situation was still calm in Smorgon and its neighborhood. He answered me in a very angry voice, saying, "Smorgon is burned to the ground. All of this happened to you because you Jews breached your union with God. This is the punishment from the Heavens."

I used only isolated trails and out-of-the-way roads in my travels, avoiding any main roads so that I would not encounter Germans. I entered the town of Horodok (near Volozhin), where I met other people from Smorgon. A Jew by the name Berl Greiss, from Smorgon, confirmed the reports of the farmer, saying the town had been burned to the ground. He, together with other locals, had found a temporary haven here. In Horodok, I also found my brother and sister. There, I worked as a carpenter for some farmers until May 1942. That month, we were caught by the Germans and sent to work in Krasne, where the Nazis ran a concentration camp. All the Jewish residents were locked in the ghetto, and the strong among them worked in the labor camp.

In 1942, some brave Jews started escaping from the camp and joining the partisans. Good contacts between the ghetto, the war camp prisoners, and the resistance were established. A resistance movement now started within the camp. Propaganda calling people to escape from the ghettos and go to the forest circulated. The main issue was obtaining weapons, because only with weapons could one survive outside of the ghetto. Anyone who had any money bought weapons from the farmers or from Germans who were not of Nazi beliefs but had come here to profit. They would sell to the Jews for a large amount of money the personal weapons that they had received as soldiers, or other weapons that they stole from the barracks, but some Jews among us did not have any money, and had to steal weapons instead of buying them.

My workplace, a warehouse, often housed weapons brought there for repair. One time, I broke in between midnight to 1AM, broke through the door, and was thus able to obtain guns for my sister and I, as well as some grenades and other ammunition. Since we also worked in the forest, cutting wood, we hid the weapons in a manger. The original Jews who had escaped prepared an escape for the rest of us. We learned that anyone who had a gun or grenade, or, better yet, a rifle, would be happily received by the partisans. When I escaped to the partisans in the forest, my sister stayed in the ghetto.

Before I left, I said to her, "I'll go to the partisans and see if its an appropriate place for you, and if so, I'll come back secretly to the ghetto and take you out."

Pesach Binder, from Smorgon, escaped and joined the partisans before me, leaving his wife in the ghetto. When we decided that the partisan camp was sufficiently safe and women could be incorporated into our life there, we decided to return to the ghetto and bring the women. Just before we were ready to do so, Binder became sick. In the partisan camp, a Russian doctor diagnosed him with typhus. As no typhus medicine was available, the partisans decided to execute the sick so that an epidemic would not take root. There was another man from Volozhin who was also sick with typhus, and both were executed by the partisans.

There was a group of eleven Jews in the camp who came shortly before us. They were now isolated in a separate location, for the partisans feared they would get typhus. I was put with them, and although we lived separately, we received food from the brigade. The Jewish members of the brigade were fearful that all of us would be executed and were very downcast, fearing that they could not save us. We were very lucky, for a Jewish doctor who came to the camp and checked us found that we did not have typhus. We returned to the brigade and arranged a new unit made up of all the people who had recently arrived from the separate group.

Shortly after, we learned that the Russian doctor who checked us was really a spy serving the Germans and planned to kill us. The head of the brigade was a Soviet man by the name of Ivanov. In this brigade there were hundreds of Jews, but in spite of it, or perhaps because of it, the brigade was riddled with Anti-Semitism.

Two weeks later, before the Jewish holiday Purim, we sent a carriage to bring my sister from the ghetto, but were too late. Jewish Krasne had been annihilated, and all its residents had been killed the previous day. Everyone had been killed except for the wife and child of Binder, who were miraculously saved from the execution and arrived at the camp. [editor's note: contrary to this account, others who came from Horodok and Krasne hid and later escaped to the forest. There were close to a dozen, amongst them were members of the Gringaus family.

In May of 1943, Germans narrowed in on our camp, and many of our comrades were killed in the ensuing scuffle. During that year, the Red Army parachuted some forces near our camp, and among them were Jews who had been in my paratrooper unit. The Red Army met and liberated us in the early summer months of 1944. On October second of 1944 I returned to Smorgon. The entire town had been burned to the ground by bombs and shelling. From Smorgon, I traveled to Lodz in Poland, and then to Italy. From there, I finally immigrated to the land of Israel.

[Page 436]

A Page from the Holocaust...

by Ida Levin (Canada)

Translated by Yocheved Klausner

The year was 1942, in the autumn; I and my family were in the labor camp in Zsezsmir. We arrived at the camp six weeks earlier, from the Smorgon ghetto. My daughter, a 13-year-old girl, was already there, and with the liquidation of the Smorgon ghetto we obtained permission to choose a camp where we had family relatives.

The Nazis demanded from the Judenrat to supply 300 Jews. Since we were the last to arrive to the camp, we were counted among the three hundred. We were 180 women and 120 men, frightened to death, because we were certain that this was to be our "last road." We were packed into box cars; the doors were shut and bolted. Late at night the train began to move. We traveled a certain time, which to us seemed an eternity; however, some of the travelers, who knew the way, informed us that the train was going in the direction of Vilna. Suddenly the train began to slow down – we were approaching Ponar. Jews from Vilna and the neighborhood towns knew very well what Ponar meant: it meant certain death. Thousands of Jews from the Vilna ghetto perished there. The nearer we came to Ponar, the slower the train moved. As it stopped finally, we all froze in our places. In the deadly silence we heard how the car doors opened, and then the well-known shout of the SS: Raus! [out!]

We went out of the wagons, more dead than alive of fear. Apart from our guards, many SS men were around us. They ordered us to form lines outside the wagons, counted us again and again and left us standing there a long time. All that time they discussed our fate, trying to decide what to do with us. We had no doubt that this was to be our end. We were finished. What we have experienced during those hours, waiting for certain death, was more frightening than death itself.

[Page 437]

After a long discussion the SS ordered us to climb again into the cars. Again the doors were shut and bolted, and the train began maneuvering back and forth and finally began to move slowly forward. Where are they taking us? Our terror rose from minute to minute. Finally we felt that the train began to accelerate, and Ponar was behind us. A spark of hope rose in our hearts, and we slowly regained some measure of calm.

We were kept in the bolted, moving train for eight days. We didn't know where we were taken, or to what purpose. Finally we arrived to a total wasteland, a place called Makritza, near Paskow.

On the way we experienced another deadly fright. The partisans have planted mines on the railroad and one of the cars was destroyed entirely. Luckily it was the car occupied by the guards; all were killed.

Makritza was a primeval forest where no human being had ever set foot. Through this impassable forest we were given the task to build a railroad line. Seven months a year the forest swarmed with wild flies and gnats that bit us until blood ran from our hands and feet. Our guards had special covers that protected their faces; we had no protection against the blood-sucking insects and the blood-sucking Nazis.

Yet, despite the difficult circumstances, we did build the line, stretched over a great number of kilometers.

As the battlefront became nearer, we were again transported, to another working place.

[Page 438]

The Experiences of a Partisan

by Eliezer Karpel

Translated by Yocheved Klausner

We possessed some 29 hectares of land, and we were farmers, working our land.

I lived until 1925 in Rodno, a village, where five Jewish families lived, all of them connected through close family relationship.

From 1925 I lived in Smorgon, on Skapinka Street.

After Smorgon was destroyed the first time and we were driven out, we came back and settled there again. This time only a few thousand Jews lived in Smorgon.

1941: Heavy fighting between the Russian army and the Germans. The houses around the town square were all burned down.

On 23 May 1941, I joined the Red Army. The chief commander was Voroshilov. I was sent to the front in Viazme, where I remained four months. In October I was taken prisoner of war by the Germans.

The Germans drove us, a group of prisoners, to Smolensk. I managed to hide in the villages – every day and every night in a different place – and worked with the peasants, as one of them. In November, I was again captured by the Germans, who were looking for young men, and was sent again to a camp of war-prisoners. We worked in the forest cutting trees, we chopped wood, built side roads connecting to the main highways, cleaned the snowed-in roads.

Almost two years we endured the hardships of the prisoners-camp, until 20 September 1940.

Since we were young men without papers, the Germans treated us as war-prisoners. I called myself Alexander Karpov, and pretended I was a Christian, a "white Russian" [from Belarus]. The camp was located near Smolensk.

August 1943. The Red Army approached Smolensk, and the camp was transferred to another location, near Orsa.

[Page 439]

We received information that there were partisans in the nearby villages. In the camp near Orsa we worked in the cavalry unit: we cleaned and brushed the horses, we fed them and gave them to drink and we cleaned the stables. This way we were a little less restricted in our movements and the guards were not too alert and strict. So we decided – two prisoners and I – to escape. It was on the 20th of September 1943. Two days and two nights we hid in the forest. We had nothing to eat during those two days, because we were afraid that we would be discovered and shot.

Finally we met a group of partisans and we joined them. The group was part of the 16th Smolensk Brigade. It numbered 1,500 White Russians and Russians, among them just one Jewish young woman from Minsk. Among the partisans, I became a Jew again and readopted my true name. The unit included men with high military education and fighting experience. Many of them had escaped from German prisoner camps. I became a lookout and a commander of a small military unit.

On 3 July 1944 we joined the Red Army, a unit located between the towns Swir and Michaelishek. After a short time the Red Army began to move, proceeding in the direction of Germany. Our partisan brigade remained, with the task of cleaning up the forests from hiding Germans and units of Polish partisans, who have fought against us. When we completed this task in the forest, we united again with the Red Army and were sent to the front near Riga. Later we fought at Memel, Koenigsberg and Danzig.

I was wounded twice, first in Memel on 20 September 1944 and the second time in Koenigsberg on 10 February 1945. However, the Germans payed for my wounds with tens and hundreds of lives. Our unit blew up bridges, railroad lines; four train cars were blown off the destroyed rails – two loaded with tanks and two with German soldiers. We captured a military base from which soldiers were sent to the front. We participated in battle until the 12th May 1945. Then I was sent to Lignitz near Breslau to supervise the military economics, until 1947.

For bravery in the battle I received five medals of "The Order of the Red War-Flag."

[Page 440]

Smorgon was Destroyed Twice

by Margola Hurwitch

Translated by Yocheved Klausner

In 1915 the Cossacks stormed into the town. Immediately they drove out all the Jews.

We started to walk through the Zaljes forest in the direction of Maladetchne. We left the town on Friday, taking with us only candles and Challah: candles to light on Friday before the beginning of Sabbath and say the blessing, and Challah for the blessing over bread at the Sabbath meal. We spent the Sabbath in the woods. We stuck the candles in the sand – candlesticks were too heavy to carry.

As Sabbath ended, we set out through the Zaskiewitz forest to Lebedove. We didn't find anybody in Lebedove – all have run away. We spent the night in the synagogue, crowded like herring in a barrel. In the morning, after we had rested a little, we started to walk on the way to Maladetchne. From there we took the train to Minsk.

There was not enough food in Minsk for all the refugees who had arrived there. A cholera epidemic broke out among the refugees, and following this a rumor spread that the doctors were poisoning the sick. The people were afraid to consult with a doctor and when somebody contracted the disease it was kept a secret. Those who did call the doctor and took the medicine he prescribed died, and those who were not cured remained alive – thus the rumor went on among the refugees.

We spent only one week in Minsk. Since the Red Cross committee gave us free train tickets to go wherever we chose, we reached the Rami Poltovne Gubernia [province] and stayed there until 1922. The most difficult times were under the rule of general Deniken and the White Guards, who adopted only one solution: "Kill Jews and save Russia!" They robbed all we had.

[Page 441]

On *Rosh Hodesh Elul* [the first day of the month Elul] 1922 we came back to Smorgon. We found it in ruins. The leather factories were not reopened. The factory owners could be found in various Russian cities: Kharkov, Rostov on the Don, Nizhny-Novgorod, Samar; some even went as far as Siberia.

In Smorgon, the rebuilding began – small houses, seldom a two-story house. People returned to the leather trade, in Smorgon itself and at the various fairs. We also received aid from America. Finally Smorgon was rebuilt, but it never recovered entirely – not as it was before the destruction. Now Smorgon was under the power of the Polacks.

In 1939, Soviet soldiers entered Smorgon, and the Soviet regime was instituted. In 1941, they left and Nazi soldiers came in.

I left Smorgon on foot, walking in the direction of Zaljesie, and I managed to reach Orsa. On the way, German airplanes bombarded constantly. I was evacuated to Pozno, from there I was transferred to Samar, which was named at that time Kubishow. From there I was transferred again, this time I was sent to a Kolkhoz. I worked in the Kolkhoz for six months.

My daughter became a nurse and went to the Ural region. She worked there from 1943 to 1948, when she returned to Vilna. I came to Vilna as well, and since we were considered Polish citizens, the Soviets allowed us to leave. In 1947 we left Vilna and went to Warsaw, then we managed to go to Israel, by plane.

At that time, my sister Hene was looking for a husband. She met a Yeshiva student, but as soon as they began to talk she realized that he was not religious enough. She asked him – is there in your Yeshiva a young man who is more observant than you?

Yes, he said, there is, and his name is R'Zelig, from Grodno.

So my sister married R'Zelig Shapira, who was famous in *Musar* [study of morals] circles of the Yeshivas. He is mentioned with great respect in the book "Higher than the Sun" by David Zaretzki, dedicated to the students of the Chafetz Chaim Yeshiva who perished in the Holocaust. Stories were told about miracles that he performed. He studied Chumash [The Five Books of Moses] and Talmud with the children in the Oshman ghetto, where he lived with his wife.

In 1938, my sister became very ill.

[Page 442]

R'Zelig Shapira gave her a gift – five years of his own life. Together with five *dayanim* [rabbinical judges] he went to the grave of the great scholar to pray for her recovery. After that, she lived another five years.

When my sister and her husband were taken from Oshman to Ponar, they jumped off the train. The Germans shot them on the spot. This happened in 1943, exactly five years after her recovery. Jews recognized their bodies and gave them a Jewish burial.

[Pages 443-448]

Emotional Experiences of Survival during World War II

By Leah Bubis

Translated by Janie Respitz

It is the month of June in 1941. War broke out. I was an employee in a Soviet store. Sonia Alkin and I were standing by the store, with the keys in our hands. We were ready to open when we noticed the Soviet leader and supervisor are confused and are running from place to place (along the street). There was a lot of noise and confusion. We were in a dilemma and did not know what to do. Should we close or not. We approached one of the directors and asked him. He told us nothing happened and we should open as usual. Then he disappeared. We were still uneasy. We begin to ask other Jews in Smorgon what was going on. That was when we learned the war had begun.

Where do we run to? Many Jews from Smorgon left on foot toward Minsk. My mother, Sheyne Yente Budgar and I did not have the strength to walk. My brother Boruch was with us, but my brother Yakov went to a village near Svir. We decided to wait for him to return with a horse and wagon. He returned that night and we took as much as we could pack in the wagon and left to a village to farmer acquaintances.

On our way, we soon encountered German soldiers. I was frightened but I managed to smile at them so they would not think we were running away from them. We arrived in Khatchelyevitch. Yakov took us to his farmer friend. We were hoping to find temporary shelter. The farmer took us to his barn, and we went to sleep.

In the morning a peasant entered the barn with an ax and shouted, "Jews, I'll kill all of you!" When he saw my brother Yakov he became gentler and said, "If not for Yankl, my friend, I'd chop all of your heads off!" We sat and cried in the barn for a few days in total fear. It was particularly difficult on Friday night when we remembered how our mother would light candles and we all felt so safe at home.

Every day, the farmer whose barn we were hiding in, came in and asked us to leave because he feared the Germans would learn he was hiding Jews. I said to my mother, "Mother, let's go to the Svir ghetto. Whatever will happen to all the Jews, will happen to us." Mother agreed to go to Svir ghetto. We took some of our belongings; the rest we left with the farmer in Khatchelyevitch.

There were only Jews from Smorgon in the Svir ghetto: Nechama Yakobson and her mother and her brother Moishe and also Esther and Hinde Katz with their mother and father Yisroel Katz were a few I remember. I would meet all of them at work. We had to work every day.

I lived with my family in the Shul court with relatives. The situation was intolerable: we worked hard and as payment, we saw death every day of the week. There was never a minute we were sure of our fate as we endured troubled, hard earned lives.

One day I went with my brother Yakov to the farmer in the village to get some of our belongings we had left behind. On our way, near the town of Lishnitze, two peasants spotted us as they were coming from Svir. It was late at night. They wanted to shoot us. With a bitter cry I asked them to let us return to the Svir ghetto and to our mother who was waiting for us. They let me go but not my brother. They pointed their pistols toward him and took him in their wagon to head into the forest. I kept my composure and grabbed the reins of the horse and did not allow them to go to the forest. I begged for pity: I lamented and wailed: what is my life worth without my beloved brother! Their murderous hearts softened and they let us both return to the ghetto. We were in the Svir ghetto until the end of 1941. At that time, they only allowed artisans, useful in their professions, to remain. They sent me and my mother to the Mikhalishko ghetto; my two brothers, Boruch and Yakov were sent to a labour camp near Vilna.

When we arrived at the Mikhalishko ghetto, they assigned us to a house with 30 other people. The sanitary conditions were horrific. One who has not experienced it, could not possibly imagine the dirt, hunger and cold. I often pushed through the barbed wire surrounding the ghetto to exchange clothing for a bit of food from the farmers. At night, I snuck back in. It was very dangerous but hunger drove me to risk my life. I observed that the same families from Smorgon in the Mikhalishko ghetto were also with me in the Svir ghetto.

At the end of 1942, an order came to leave the ghetto. If you had family in a labour camp, you can request to be transferred there. We were also given another privilege. Those who had left belongings with the peasants could return and take their things on the long journey ahead. The trip took seven days.

We were being sent to the Vilna ghetto. The enclosure there was very high and the guard, who was very strict, told us that we could not leave to trade our belongings for food. Instead, we would have to trade only from within the ghetto. If not, we would die of hunger. My mother walked to Batchilevitch, took some things and began her return. A peasant killed her on the road and took everything she had. I was left totally alone and helpless. I could not stop crying. I cried so much I nearly went blind.

Everyone in the ghetto was packing. I did not know what to do. I was completely lost. One day my brother Boruch came and took me to a labour camp near Vilna. The others from Smorgon unfortunately went to Kovno. They were all killed.

I lived in the Vilna ghetto with my two brothers, Boruch and Yakov.

It was 1943. They sent us to hard labour without food or drink. We suffered greatly and with constant fear. Every day, the guards grew stricter. The hangman Weis and Murer, the Gestapo man, arrived. A few times, while we were working, the officers surrounded us with a chain of Gestapo men. I looked around; perhaps there was an opening for escape to save my life.

My two brothers and I were sent to work in a vegetable garden in Kupernishek near Vilna. Rumours were spreading that the Germans were planning to liquidate the Vilna ghetto. We began planning to take refuge in the forest to join the partisans. We knew the partisans took in refugees who came with weapons. We sold some of our clothing and bought revolvers. We joined a group of 18 men who shared the same goal. We threw away our yellow badges and left. We passed a row of villages. We walked at night. By day we hid in the bushes. We had nothing to eat and finally decided to take the risk and enter a peasant's home and ask for a piece of bread. But the dogs attacked us, almost to the point of biting. We returned to the forest and continued walking every night until we arrived in Naratch forest.

The peasants in Naratch told us there were partisans in the forest. We were very happy to hear that news since reaching our goal now seemed closer. As we were deciding where to go, a group of partisans approached. They took our weapons and told us to go deeper into the forest. We listened and eventually came to the commander of the partisan division. He asked us, not sure whether seriously or jokingly, "Where are your guns and grenades?" We replied that we only have revolvers but the partisans took them from us. He asked, "How did you get the revolvers?" When we told them they were purchased in the Vilna ghetto, he laughed and said, "What kind of partisans are you. You should have killed a few Germans and taken their weapons. That would make you true partisans!" He then refused to allow us into his division. He suggested there was a group of Jewish partisans in the forest and we should join them.

So that is what we did. Thankfully, the Jewish partisans were pleased to have us. The commander of the partisans, Yosef Glazman, came from the Vilna ghetto. The Jewish group fell apart toward the end of 1944. Individual partisans joined the general partisan division. They assigned me into a workers division, with a group of tailors. Soon after, the forests where the partisans held their positions were attacked by the Germans. There were approximately one to three thousand German soldiers. They began an offensive against the partisans. I was assigned to help the Russian doctor and had to watch over the wounded partisans. They took me and the sick to the Neva swamps. I told the doctor that if the Germans ever come real close to us,

I will run away and leave the wounded. He did not answer and walked away, leaving me alone. The shots were so deafening, I became confused. I believed by waving my arms I could keep the bullets away from me and the patients. I soon ran away. About 100 metres from the sick camp, I hid in the bushes. After a few minutes I heard the German soldiers trek through the mud in their rubber boots. I lay there motionless, holding my breath. The Germans left quickly and I managed to stay alive. It was nighttime and pitch black. I head back to the sick and wounded but not sure of the exact way. Luckily, I saw my kerchief on the ground which I lost while running. I returned to the patients to witness a horrible scene. One of the patients committed suicide by shooting himself in fear that the Germans would leave him half dead. I spent a few days with the sick men in the swamps. It was extremely cold, and we did not have any warm clothing. When things quietened down, they took the patients back to the forest. They promised to find me a new place to go. During the German attack, my brother Boruch and18 other men, were killed. Among them was Glazman, the commander. The Germans surrounded them. In order not to fall into Nazi hands, they exploded grenades.

I remained with my older brother Yakov. We heard, not far away in Neva Oyzle, that Jews were hiding in mud huts. We traveled to them. We received a bit of food from the peasants, who changed their attitude toward the Jews realizing that the Germans lost the war and will be chased away.

A few months later the war ended with the defeat of the Nazis.

I was free. But where should I go? home?

When I returned to Smorgon I found our house burned down. Only the Gentile's homes on Krev Street remained standing. All the Jewish homes were destroyed.

It was 1945. There was no future for me in our devastated city. I went to Lodz, and from Lodz to Germany. I spent one year in Germany, then left for Italy in 1946. I married in Italy in 1947 and in 1948 came to Israel.

[Page 449]

Words of Testament

By Tova Donski

Translated by Eilat Levitan and Ona Kondrotas

I was born in Smorgon in 1923. In June 1941, the town of Smorgon was heavily bombarded by the Germans. I, together with many other Jews, escaped from the town and hid in the villages of the surrounding area. We soon realized that we were not safe from the bombardment here, and so returned to town. The Germans took over the town and established two ghettos: one in the yard of the synagogue and a few neighboring streets and the other in an area known as Karka. Our entire family lived in one room, since there were very few valuable spaces and it is was very crowded in the ghetto.

Daily, the Germans would come with some Belarussian collaborators who were residents of Smorgon. They would arrive at the ghetto and take people to work. Both men and women were forced to work. We worked from an early morning hour until the evening. In the Karka area, there were a few Jews that were millers. Having flour, they divided it among all the needy people. Some people had money and they were able to buy food from the villagers. People who by this point had lost all their money gave their clothes and other valuables to the villagers in exchange for bread, potatoes, and other food supplies.

In August 1942, during the third transport, I was taken together with many other young men and women. They told us we would be taken to work on a job that would last six weeks. They transferred us in trains normally used for livestock on a journey that lasted four days. On the road we were given only stale bread to eat. The train cars were locked and the windows were clouded so that we would not be able to see where we were and where we were being taken. It was very crowded. All of us were young men and women able to do any physical labor.

They brought us to Zasmir, a small town near Kovno. We were put in a labor camp: the women lived in the synagogue, and the men lived in the synagogue yard. The manager of this camp was a Jew from Podbrodze by the name of Ring. Every morning he woke us to drink breakfast coffee. The coffee was prepared by the residents of the camp. We worked from early morning until dusk fell, building a new road.

One time, when we were taken to roll call, the head of the work camp, whom we nicknamed the Hoarse One due to his raspy voice, asked us, "if there is any man or woman that does not like this work, or cannot perform, you should come out and tell me, and you will be returned to the place you were taken from." Twenty-six people came forth, and said the work was too difficult for them. Immediately, they were put on a truck and a few more people were added to their count as helpers. They were taken outside of the camp where they were all shot and then the helpers buried them, at the order of the Nazis. When the helpers returned to the camp, they told us of what had occurred. It was a miracle I survived, because I had intended to inform the Nazi officers that this work was too hard for me, as well.

At our camp there were around a thousand workers. At one point, typhus spread in the camp. We had a doctor by the name of Anulik with his wife Miriam, who was a nurse. They were brought to the camp from Vilna. The doctor and the nurse did not let the Germans know that a typhus epidemic was spreading through the camp, because they I knew that most likely everyone would be killed if the Nazis found out. When people were too sick to work, they would say that the harsh weather prevented them from arriving to work. In reality, twelve people died of typhus. When people became delirious from the high fever, they often began to curse at Germans and Hitler. We were very fearful that the Germans would be notified of this by the guards of the camp and find the true nature of the disease.

Eventually, I received the information that my entire family was taken to Ponar and killed. Ponar was a suburb of Vilna. I spent eleven months in the work camp. When the camp closed, we were transferred to the Kovno ghetto. We stayed there for a month and were then taken to Koshadar, and here we worked digging peat bogs for fuel. Most workers became sick with rheumatism in this damp and dark environment. We also worked in the forest, cutting trees and making boards of wood from them. Men and women worked together. With us worked also gentiles, amongst them twenty-four Ukranians and Uzbeks, and six Communist Germans. They started a rebellion, killing the two Ukrainian policemen guarding them, as well as the Dutch engineer leading them. The German sergeant who was guarding them they hit on his head and his brains spilled out onto the barbed wire. They collected the weapons of the guards and escaped to join the resistance in the forest.

The next day, German soldiers surrounded the camp. They did a headcount and found that none of the Jews had escaped, and ordered us to return to our barracks. In Koshadar, there were Jewish families who were brought from the Kovno ghetto. With them they had about twenty-four children. One time, the Germans collected all the Jewish children and put them on a train, taking them all to be murdered.

This was the last straw. Finally, the Jews realized that their end would soon come, and forty-eight of them now escaped and were able to reach the resistance. This showed the Germans that there was not sufficient guarding in this camp, and they transferred us to Alikshut. In Alikshut, we worked at filling train tracks with sand, and whoever was not fast enough was beaten mercilessly. The people responsible for our job here were the SS. We worked at this camp for a month, and from there we were transferred to the war camp by the name of Kozlovaroda, where we once again worked in a peat bog for three months. From here, we returned to the Kovno ghetto.

When the ghetto was annihilated, we were put in a locked livestock train car and we traveled between five and six days. The Nazis brought us to Stutthof near Danzig. This took place in the spring of 1944. Our camp was located in the forest, and we had to walk by foot from the train tracks all the way to the forest. When we reached the camp, we saw that in the yard lay a pile of shoes. We now saw that this was a death camp and was surrounded by electric barbed wire.

We were made to walk to the barracks for showering. The Nazis ordered us to undress and leave all our belongings and any jewelry we might have in a pile outside, and divided us into groups of twenty. The groups were taken away from each other. The Nazis checked us, and the weak among us were sent to be killed, either by shooting or burning. The ones who were still able to work were sent to live and work for the time being. When my turn arrived, they checked me and sentenced me to work and physical labor. Thus, I was to survive. They shaved my head and gave me a uniform - a prisoner's dress. Three hundred women were taken to the barracks and were all to sleep in one room. It was horribly crowded. You couldn't even find a place to stand and there was no air to breathe. Every day, the Nazis organized a headcount and would check us, and occasionally they would organize selections of those who would remain alive and those who would be killed. We were divided into two rows: one on the right and one on the left. The people who were given a 'life sentences' were sent back to the barracks. The women who were fast and entered the barracks first did not receive beatings, but the slower ones were hit mercilessly.

The commander of that camp was a Polish man by the name of Max. The women in charge of the barracks were Ukrainian. Once a day we received cabbage soup. Some would try to cheat and stand in line twice. If caught, they would be beaten for their greed. I was in Stutthof for six weeks, and was then transferred with about a hundred other people to a war camp in Germany.

During the winter of 1944-45, we lived in very low tents where one had to crawl on one's knees to enter. It seems like the forced hard labor we did was busy work that did not really serve anyone. We shoveled snow from one place to the next, for instance. This was a very cold winter and we were all in summer clothes. This camp contained 800 women. The Jews in this camp were from Lithuania and Belarus. We slept on hay; there were no mattresses. We didn't receive any blankets; they let us cover ourselves with tablecloths. We wore clogs for shoes. When women got sick, they did not let anyone know they were sick, for they were fearful of being executed.

In this place there was one doctor - she was really only a medic. We found out that in the camp that was located next to us, they killed all the prisoners and we were very fearful that this would be our fate as well, soon. At one point, the Nazis transferred us to Lubic in Galizia, in the environ of Tran. Shortly after, they changed their minds, wanting to return us to Germany, but had no time.

For a week, we hid, together with our enemies, in the forest while planes would shell the area. Little children who lived in a nearby village came to us one day and announced that the Russians were nearing. Soon we found that they told the truth. The Russians came, but we could not believe our eyes. We were so fearful, depressed, and disillusioned that we thought they were only Germans who wore Russian uniforms as a disguise. It was impossible for us to accept the fact that liberation had come.

Finally, a Jewish soviet soldier arrived and began speaking to us in Yiddish. Only then did we comprehend that we had made it, we had survived!

We had come from slavery to salvation, from death to a freedom and a future. The Soviets collected us and brought us to a camp that was free of Germans. There, we found a cauldron filled with cooked food. Some people jumped on this food and filled their stomachs with it. Since they were starved for months or even years, many died of the sudden shock of plentiful food in their bodies.

The Soviet soldiers took us to a market and told us to take what we wished. All of us chose bread. In our eyes, this was the most delicious delicacy possible.

[Page 453]

Testimony

by Sh. Greis

Translated by Jerrold Landau

Our family, the Greis family, who lived in Karke, was a wide-branched family of hundreds of people. It was a family of tillers of the soil who sustained themselves through the work of their hands.

In 1941, during the Second World War, with the advance of the Germans in the direction of our city, men were drafted to the Red Army, including my older brother who fell within three days. We left Smorgon in the direction of Russia. Some people, including my parents, abandoned the journey and returned to Smorgon.

At the beginning of the occupation, there were two ghettos in Smorgon, in the city and in the Karke. Within a few months, only one ghetto remained in the city. As a young child, I wandered around the Judenrat offices and saw the decrees that the Germans issued. At times, they demanded 100 furriers, etc., and at times, they demanded laborers. When there were not enough to meet the demand, I volunteered to be one of the workers. I worked in a woodcutting factory.

After a short time, they began to liquidate the ghetto. Only protected people remained, my family and I among them. The people were sent to Kovno, Zazmir [Žiežmariai], and Vilna. My oldest sister, her husband Shimshon

Asinowsky, and their children were among them. They perished on the way to Ponar along with the rest of the people. We traveled in the direction of Zazmir, where there was a very harsh labor camp. People, including my sister, became ill with typhus. After a few months, they selected people for work from there, and sent us to Plashkov. We worked on the railway tracks that led a distance of six kilometers to the front. We worked under very difficult conditions. We chose Mottel Mirsky as the leader, who concerned himself with the wellbeing of everybody. After some time, that group was transferred to Mokrava in Estonia. From there, we were transferred to the Kaizerwald camp in Riga. The most difficult period began in Riga. We were greeted with murderous blows when we arrived in the concentration camp. They took our clothing from us, and we received camp uniforms. Groups of men were sent to the old cemetery of Riga to remove the dead and burn them. After the work, the Germans would burn that group.

After some time, a large group was sent to Dundaga, which was called a death camp. The S.S. chief was Zorki. He was known as "Iron Gustav" [Eizner Gustav] by the camp inmates. He had two Jewish deputies, one named Werner, a well-known metrograph[1] from Berlin; and the other Hubert. Both were murderers in the fashion of the Germans.

We, my father, my mother, my brother, my sister, and I, also ended up in that camp, along with many other people of Smorgon. This was a camp of death and torture. They would beat people until death. Many people from our group perished there.

[Page 454]

With the advance of the Russians, we were transferred by foot on a long, difficult journey. We crossed rivers and forests. Several of our people attempted to escape to the partisans in the forest, but they did not reach their desired destination. The small portion of us who remained alive arrived on foot to Stutthof. There, the Germans conducted an action [action]. The people were divided into a work group, and a group destined for death. My brother Shalom and I were in the ranks of death. I succeeded in jumping to the work group through my father, and thereby survived. My mother and brother Shalom met their deaths in Stutthof. From there, we were sent by train to Buchenwald. Only approximately 60 men were left of our group of 450 people. From there, we were transferred to the Rimsdorf camp, where there was a factory of coal fuel. They worked us very hard, and people fell like flies – my father of blessed memory among them. There were approximately 12,000 people in the camp in February 1945, including a few who remained from our death march. We walked for days and nights without food or drink, and people fell like flies. Only Zalman Pragmant and I remained from our group among those who arrived in Theresienstadt. The Red Army liberated our camp from the accursed Germans on May 9, 1945. I became ill with abdominal typhus after the liberation. After I recovered in a Russian military camp, I remained alone, the sole survivor of the entire family. I was a youth of about 16, and I looked like a child of no more than 12. I was sent to the direction of Smorgon. Along the way, I found out that there were many Jewish survivors in Łódź, and I arrived there with difficulty. As I rode the train, I had to hide from members of the AKA who wanted to kill Jews[2]. I arrived in Łódź by miracle. We were first housed on a Jewish floor. The next days, the Krochmelnik sisters visited me and informed me that the center of Smorgon natives was at their home[3]. There, I met Moshe Bernsztajn, my school friend.

We moved to Częstochowa with the group of 105 children from age 13 to 17. From there, they transferred us to Prague and Germany as Greek Jews. They caught us along the way and sent us back several times, until we finally succeeded in arriving in Munich as German Jews. From Munich, they transferred us to Feldenhing, where they prepared us for *aliya* in the Hebrew language. I made *aliya* in 1946 on a ship of Maapilim from Marseilles. We arrived at the shores of the Land after 14 days, but we were stopped by two British boats. After a battle[4] lasting an entire day, they transferred us to Haifa, and from there to Cyprus.

I remained in Cyprus for eight months with a group of youth *aliya*. I arrived in the Land and enlisted in the Israel Defense Forces. My school friend Moshe Bernsztajn of blessed memory fell during that period in the first days of the War of Independence.

Translator's Footnotes

1. Metrograph, as the word implies, is likely a reference to a person who recorded train speed and number of stops and durations.
2. AKA was likely a Polish organization unfriendly/hateful to the Jews.
3. Smorgon jews from a gathering place in Lodz were in their home.

4. Lacking additional information, the "battle" may be referring a heated argument between authorities or a situation where shots were either threatened or fired. The immigration process was historically heatedly contested.

[Page 457]

A Yizkor Prayer

Translated by Jerrold Landau

May the nation of Israel remember its precious children, pure ones the children of pure ones, who were stolen from the bosom of their parents at the hands of the human beasts and brought like sheep to slaughter; whose backs were broken, and who were murdered in strange deaths, and piled up in piles outside. Infants and nursing children who were smashed against stone walls, tossed off walls and cast live in sacks into the depths of rivers. Their lives were cut off in their youth by cruel hands – in sanctification of the Divine Name.

May Israel remember and preserve in your bundle.

[Page 458]

First to be Annihilated by Yitzchak Katzenelson

(A dirge for the murdered Jewish children]

Translated by Jerrold Landau

The first for annihilation – the babies were, orphaned children, wanton on earth
Indeed, they were the best of the world, the finest of charm in a world of darkness!
Hah, many orphans! Among them, the forlorn of the world in orphanages.
Shine comfort on us,
From the gloomy faces, mute and darkened. We have said, the light of the day will yet
Break forth upon us!

Behold it was, at the end of the winter of forty-two, in the orphanage, there was such an indigent.
I saw children, who had just now been taken in from the street. And I brought in to me a corner
From the corners,
And I see at the bosom of the teacher, a baby, less than two years old
Thin, very thin, pale – death is in her face, and she has eyes, serious they are, serious.

And I consider her, I consider this elderly two-year-old girl, like a grandmother – a hundred years old
And she is a Jewish daughter, like a hundred years old. The seriousness and torment
That her grandmother never saw in a dream she saw while awake,
The afflicted baby girl.
And I weep, and this I say to my soul: Do not weep, the agony will end, but will remain
The seriousness!

The seriousness will remain. It will be poured out to the bosom of the world, to the bosom of life
To deepen them.
This is the Jewish seriousness. It will sober up, light up, open up the blind eyes, establish itself;
It is like Torah to the world, like prophecy, like a holy letter with a seal.
Do not weep, do not weep. Eighty million murderers will be the atonement
For a child of heavy contemplation in Israel.

Don't weep. At this "station" I saw another girl, about five years old.
She was feeding her younger brother. He was crying. The brother was ill.
She dipped crumbs of toasted bread into thin jam,
And with great wisdom, snuck it into his mouth. My eyes merited to see this!

[Page 459]

To see the mother, the five-year-old mother, feeding him, listening to the conversation
As she spoke to him. My mother, one on the face of the earth, was not as wise as that in reality.
She wiped his tears with laughter, feeding his heart with joy,
A girl of Israel! Shalom Aleichem did not make them better than her.

I saw this! I saw the orphan in the home, the older one;
I entered a different hall. There was a fierce chill – here as well as there.
Far off there was a coal oven – its glow fell upon a group of children
The naked babies – almost stood around the flame of the coal.

To the hot flame, one stuck his foot. This one, a small hand, almost frozen.
And another one his naked shoulder. One pale, with dark eyes, a very tender child,
Told her story. No, this was not a story! It was stormy, it was enthusiastic.
Oh, the son of Amotz! [1] You were not as zealous, and in the Israelite language,
You had no such thing.

The Jewish girl spoke, intermixed with the holy tongue. No, the holy tongue is in everything!
Hear, hear, see his eyes, the Jewish ones, and his forehead, how he cast
His head up... Isaiah! You were not small like him, and you were not so large,
And as good as him you were not. There was no truth such as this in your mouth, and you did not believe this!

Indeed, more than this is the child in the orphanage, the child who spoke so movingly
Great was the appearance of his brothers and sisters. Every one of them with a small mouth opened
Listened to him, hear.

Hah, all the lands, large cities in Europe, old and new,
You will no longer see such a form on the earth, and there has never been such on the face of the earth.

I looked and I saw: they lowered a sack onto the thin back of a Jew
And the sack wept. It was a child of Israel! The wrath of the officer burnt with rage:
Where is the father! And to the child with a warning: Recognize him!
The child understood,
With glazed eyes as someone paralyzed,
The father looks and does not cry. He looked into the eyes of his father and no longer recognized him!
This little child! And the German comes out, then another Jew from the row, a man
"Innocent" – you are!

And he joins the two of them with the thousands sentenced to death – such scorn he desired.
And I further saw – but go from me and do not ask, when? Where? What more did my eyes see?
I adjure you: do not ask about anything, and in the depths, and the rumors of the street, let it be forever.

[Page 460]

They, the children of Israel [i.e., of the Jews], were the first to be sentenced to tragedy.
Most of them without a father or mother. The ice, hunger, and lice consumed them.
Holy anointed ones, sanctified through torment. Say please, about these, in what did the sheep sin?
Why in the times of destruction were they the first to be set forth to the evil ones, they were the first?

The first to be taken to death, the first on the wagons,
Thus were they tossed on the wagons, the large ones, like sacks of garbage, like dung on the earth.
They transported them; they killed them; they murdered them, without remnant or memory.

The best of my sons! Perished! Hah, woe unto me, and alas! A travesty and a ruin!

Translator's Footnote

1. The Biblical Isaiah, the son of Amotz.

[Page 461]

One Childhood

by Chanoch Al-Domi

Translated by Jerrold Landau

In memory of the martyred, pure children of Smorgon – with a mournful heart.

—The author

a. Ask your father, and he will tell you[1]

My children, more than once you asked, as I was sitting reclining on my back, about this book, saying:

"Father, what do others say about this book, for anytime it is before you and you read it, a wave of nervousness covers your face; and you do not put it down until you sit me down next to you and ask to read to me one of its chapters. And I dear father, whenever this happens, I conclude by telling you:"

"It is too heavy for me, it is like a sealed book to me. Its black cover and the agony coursing through its pages, and to me – books are abundant when they are happy and enjoyable."

"My son, if it is truly difficult for you to read it, and the things written on the hundreds of pages of the book are far off from you [and] from a different world, then at least listen to the words of my mouth and hear the story of the small town, the birthplace of your parents and grandparents over many generations. You will learn to know about the entire mass of people, their joy and grief. You will unite with a chapter of life that was cut off by the enemy.

And who knows if you will not find, after all this, that your pleasant tree is planted on those springs of life, and its roots suckle from the sources of life of your ancestors."

b. A Place Under the Sun

In the geographical maps and textbooks of the Land that you have, the name of the small town is missing.

However, in order to describe its place under the sun, let us go together to search for a small place in the wide world, and we will find it:

It is between Minsk, the capital of White Russia, and Vilna, which is the "Jerusalem of Lithuania," the city of the Gr'a (the Gaon Rabbi Eliahu), a major Jewish city of Torah and doctrine.

The place is a large strip of land. Vast forests grow in it from the six days of creation. Rivers, streams and ponds spring forth from clefts within its expanse. Bears walk among its forests. This is the brown bear whose fame spread through the land: a glutton and drunkard who loves to lick things up. As time went on the fathers of the city strengthened the bear and made it into a sign on the city emblem.

[Page 462]

Your ancestors knew how to tell many legends about the meaning of the name of the city of Smorgon, about its bear school, about its bakery dough – the famous cakes of Smorgon, about the legends of its two rivers Groyat and Okna, tributaries of the large Viliya River.

If you enjoy legends, read at the beginning of the book about the legends "A Conversation from Ancient Times"[2]. If you like to delve into questions, then read the chapter on the history of the city from its beginning to its destruction.

c. The World of One Child

All the rest is a story of childhood, experiences, impressions, joy, pain, and dreams. As you look through the lens of one child to the background of life in the small city, you will find that the following chapters are only one of many in the story of the life of a person.

* * *

1. The Home of the Hat Maker

The Home of Reb Shlomo the hatmaker stood on Kirovai Street next to the well from which all the residents of the street drew water for their needs.

Reb Shlomo's house was one story with an attic, called *szlaka* in the vernacular.

The house was a house of boards. It was said about the hatmaker: when he was about to build the house for himself, he went out and declared before the gentile residents of the village, that anyone who would bring him a choice board from a mighty, strong tree with lots of foliage, would receive a gift over and above his salary: a winter hat made of fur, with ears sticking upward, called *naoshnik*. The farmers brought wood for the building, two or three boards in one sleigh. They unloaded them before the yard and traveled on. The Czeslars came out – they are the builders who built the house. As they were covering the roof, Reb Shlomo the hatmaker came out and told them.

"As you put up the "hat" that is the roof of the house, make it two stories, that are connected toward the top. The structure of the roof will hover over them – *naoshnik* – that is the winter hat with ears.

The house left the hands of the builders rounded and smooth. Not more and not less, and exact in all details.

You will ask, why did the hatmaker need his house built with two stories? Would one not have been sufficient for him? He needed it. The first story would serve as the workshop. There sat Reb Shlomo's two daughters, Tzirel and Feigel (the other girls [of Shlomo], pure doves, flew from their nest overseas, to America). They sewed hats for the Jewish population and the masses of villagers. Some of the hatmaker's sons were on their own, and others were apprentices with the tradesmen of the city: tanners and barbers. And what about the second attic? It was empty all year. Only on the eve of Passover did they bring down the holiday dishes which were guarded there all year, through a hole in the first attic.

[Page 463]

However, I want to tell you about another hole in the ceiling... The one found in the ceiling of the hat shop, opening into the room of Tzirel and Feigel.

You would enter the hatmaker's shop. The bell would ring immediately, and through the resonance of the bell at the entrance, and through that hole from above extending downward, the form of a women – either of Tzirel of Feigel the daughters of Reb Shlomo, appeared through the hole. The image through the hole, with a face round as the moon in the middle of the month, would call out loudly with either a chirp or a whistle, apparently coming through the tube leading to the hole in the ceiling, toward the customer in the space of the store below:

"Father, it seems that a customer entered the store."

The hatmaker came out from the den, that was a sort of room – a small room at the side of the store – and he saw the customer, a certain gentile, one of the children of the land. He stood, looked upward, and smiled between his mustache and his full beard together, and said:

"See how far these people have come with their inventions?"

Do you want to know whose invention was this hole in the ceiling? I swear you do not know. Only one child knew. In short, this was the child or the little one of the story, the son of Berl, Reb Shlomo the hatmaker's oldest son. He knew and was a witness that this was the invention of his father.

This is the story: The father of the child had a bright face, and was not a master of any pranks. One winter day, when nobody was walking in the market, and when there was no money in the pocket, father came. He was already self–sufficient and a householder in his own right, with all his pride directed to this child who had grown up in the interim and now tells stories [of his own]. To whom is he coming? To Grandfather Reb Shlomo the hatmaker, and he said the following:

"Father, you should listen to me, and we will make a hole in the ceiling of the store, connecting it to the attic of Tzirel and Feigel"

Grandfather looked at his son, a type of gaze the meaning of which was more or less the following:

"Go somewhere else with your ideas." He added more or less the following:

"I see, my son, that you have no other worries. If you want a hole in the ceiling, fine, do what you say – only do not make a hole in the head. Perhaps I am allowed to ask my son, the fruit of my body, why all this?"

"The sign will be tomorrow," the father answered in brief, mysterious words. He smiled a smile that had an inkling of mischief and jest. He said goodbye to his father and left.

[Page 464]

2. The Hole that Father Made in the Ceiling, What is its Use?

The next day, Father went to the attic of his sisters Tzirel and Feigel, and called through the floor of the attic, which was the ceiling of the store. He made a round hole about the size of a human head, to the surprise of all the members of the household. Father sawed and opened the hole. The bystanders turned away and pushed against each other with their elbows, back to shoulder, and said in laughter:

"What will be the end of this matter?"

The end of the matter was that immediately after the conclusion of this work, Father ran to his house that stood in the flour market (he earned his livelihood from a fur store and from cutting hair). He took in his hands the boy, who was small and could not yet keep up with the quick pace of his father – and brought him to Grandfather's hat house. They came, and father immediately placed the small child under that hole in the ceiling, which was now covered by a wooden cover as large as the opening, and said, "

"My son, close your eyes, and do not look up."

Father said this, and went up to the attic of Tzirel and Feigel. He lifted the cover and moved something over to the circle in the ceiling – do you know what? – a new hat, tied on a string woven with gold and silver, aimed directly at the young child's head.

The young child stood below, and the hat, a gift from above, was on his head. He squinted his eyes and laughed with joy, as he saw the bright face of his father through the hole in the ceiling – as the shining sun.

What can I tell and add – there were no days for Reb Shlomo the hatmaker as good as those days from when the hole in the ceiling of his shop was made. The issue of the hat that rolled down and descended from above in the store of Reb Shlomo the hatmaker became known to the children of the city of Smorgon – these brazen children – who then urged their fathers to come to see the "magic" and to merit this great thing of a hat sent from above.

The children of that city were opinionated and stood their own [ground]. The fathers did not object. Probably, in the hands of the children who were so impressed by the house of the hatmaker, it is written in the book about business that for a long time, Grandfather Reb Shlomo's shop was never empty, and he was never lacking a coin in his pocket.

Eventually, the father of the child, Reb Dov–Ber Levin, was requested to provide help in the matter of hats. What did he do? He tied together hats hanging from above, with a bag for every hat, and with all types of sweet and treats in the bags. On Tu B'Shvat there was something extra – a small dry carob (*bokser*) for the enjoyment of the children.

Lest you think that with all this, comes the end of the story that began with the hole in the ceiling, and ended with hats hanging from it? – no, no:

The final result of this was revealed once and not again, in the childhood experiences of that child, as is told in our next chapter.

[Page 465]

3. How the Nickname "Plomp" Came About for the Wells Dug in our Area[3]

The wells of our city were dug by Jews.

In the merit of Mendel "Plomp" and Getzel Gliniarnik, the Jews of Kirovai Street drank their good water. How?

Kirovai Street was a long street. Its head was opposite the fish market, and its end reached the railway tracks. Before the wells were dug, the residents of the street would drink their water in measure from the turbulent river, a distance from *Hodu* (to G–d for he is good), until *Aleinu*[4], as our brethren in this city used to say when describing a long distance.

The Jewish women, the housewives of Smorgon, would groan and moan with their young daughters, the "water drawers" next to them, with bent heads from the pails around their necks. It was not enough that they went down every Monday, in rain and frost, on hot summer days and during the cold of winter, to wash the clothes in the river. Then they had the additional burden of hauling water from afar. This was until the merit of Getzel Gliniarnik and Mendel "Plomp" stood for them, and put an end to the suffering of the women of Kirovai Street and their daughters.

Reb Mendel the flax merchant dug the first well. He was wealthy householder with five sons who divided up the "entire land" amongst themselves, with the "kingdom" of each one not encroaching on his brother. Each would go out to the nearby towns twice a week to make purchases, that is to purchase flax from the farmers. They were strong, stubborn men who crowded out other Jews. They would follow close after the heels of the gentiles to purchase their merchandise, with the curses of the pushed–aside Jews following after them. Reb Mendel was a widower, and all the housework was done by his only daughter Mirele. He saw that she was becoming more and more stooped over each day, groaning and moaning. Reb Mendel said to himself, "This is only because it is hard for her to bring water from the rivers." He spoke, and he carried out his promise. He dug the first well with his own hands. The Jews of Kirovai Street stood in astonishment about that man, and stared at him with awe and respect. After Mendel finished his work and water bubbled up from the bottom of the well, he got up and brought benches and tables from his large house, placed them around the well, and made a large celebration for his brethren of the city. First, Mendel cast a large rope with a pail at the end down to the bottom of the well and drew "the first waters." The sons, who had all gathered and came together that day, distributed the water in earthenware cups to each of the Kirovaites, and drank *Lechaim*! Then Mirele and her friends left the house with large platters of honey cakes. The mouths will be fed! A honey cake for everyone. The Jews rejoiced and celebrated the joy of the well.

And when Mendel's heart was glad with water, he asked that they lower him to the bottom of the well, so he could see with his own eyes how the water bubbles up from the ground. His sons tied him with a rope and lowered him to fulfil the commandment of honoring one's father. Apparently the "dunking" was too strong, and the water in the well was very deep. Mendel shouted and called out: "Plomp... plomp.." His sons quickly grabbed the rope and raised their father from the well while he still had his breath within him. They lay Reb Mendel down and took turns sitting beside him. His sons slapped his cheeks from each side to remove the water and restore the breath of his nostrils. Reb Mendel made sounds of bubbles of water: "Plomp". "Plomp".

[Page 466]

The next Sabbath, Reb Mendel stood up and recited the *Hagomel* blessing in the synagogue on Kirovai Street.

From that day onward, the nickname Plomp stuck with him. He was Mendel Plomp, and every well in the city, old and new, was called by that name.

4. Getzel Gliniarnik, the Man of The Land

The well of Grandfather Reb Shlomo the Hatmaker was dug by Getzel Gliniarnik in the *Karka.* What is the meaning of this? As it sounds: land of tilled soil and field. How did the Jews of Smorgon reach this "status" of "all the gentiles"? This is the story that took place.

A new king, that is Czar Alexander II, rose up. He ruled all the land of greater Russia, and proclaimed a decree for all the Jews in all the lands of his kingdom, living legally or illegally: whomever wishes to gain real estate should come and register in the royal registry. He will then receive land from the government in his place of residence – the best type of land upon which to live – for him to till and guard. He would be able to live there in his city until the advent of the redeemer, our righteous Messiah.

From all the Jewish settlements between the cities of Minsk and Vilna, only the Jews of Smorgon responded to this "worker of good," that is the Czar of all Russia, Poland, Lithuania, etc. Alexander II.

From the documents and writings of those days, we learn that 78 heads of families, tradesmen and day laborers whose livelihood was difficult and who did not even have a rubbed–out coin in their pocket, registered and determined to leave the "city of hides" on account of the oppressors – i.e. the owners of the tanning enterprises – who "elongated" the days of the workers service and oppressed their lives down to the smallest coin... The main thing was that these people escaped the prickliness that came from the tanning centers that the city was full of.

Where would they find the money? For they do not distribute land for free, even the land of the Czar. They went and sent a letter to Baron Hirsch, the doer of good and benefactor of his nation. They explained to him their request and placed their petition before him, asking him to stand with them at their time of their difficulty.

[Page 467]

If we say that the aforementioned Baron was moved and answered them, we would not have said everything. A hasty messenger was sent by him to purchase gentile lands near Smorgon. They settled the requesters on the land and left them with *karbons* (currency of the country) to build houses and plant vineyards: for each person to sit under his vineyard and fig tree. And how will they settle!?! The Jews were tied to the Karka land with their navels and ate the bread of the land through the sweat of their brow.

Getzel Gliniarnik was among the first to settle on the Karka. However G–d prevented him from reciting *hamotzie* on his morsel of bread. His fate was that his field was allocated where the large river, the Viliya, was located, winding its route in a tortuous fashion and sending streams of water without any order, in branches and sub–branches near the river and the passageway to the lands of the north.

The Jew Getzel was tied to the flow of the Viliya. Every few years, it would overflow its banks, at the beginning of the spring when the snow and ice melted. It would flood Getzel's fields and soak the full toil of his hands with its strong stream. The field of this person was flooded over, but the stubborn person was Reb Getzel. He did not sell his land due to the treacherous Viliya, and did not even abandon it. He continued to work it faithfully, whatever may be. You will ask, how did he feed himself and his family? From plastering. From here, Gliniarnik, who plastered the houses of the Jews with cement during wintertime, set up and fixed the large ovens that wore out over years and from the rain. He plastered the floors of their house of the residents of Karka, and did other such jobs that were needed at the time, or were desired by his fellow brethren. As has been noted, he, Getzel Gliniarnik, dug the well at Grandfather's house.

5. What Happens to the Child who Wants to be a Drawer of Water?

That child had an additional level of love for that well at the home of his grandfather Reb Shlomo. Every time that he went to visit the "house of the hatmaker" with his father, he would urge his father to take him on his shoulders and show him the opening of the well, to see its depth and darkness, and look at his shadow in it.

In particular, the heart of the child fluttered from joy when Reb Shaulke Pozarnik the firefighter, a redheaded, stubborn Jew, famous throughout the city for his haste and bravery in putting out fires, approached the well. Shaulke the firefighter earned his livelihood from the bucket of water that was resting on his cart, that he himself hauled to provide the weak housewives with sufficient water for their needs on weekdays and Sabbath eves.

When a fire broke out in the city, Shaulke Pozarnik would harness the horse of Itza the "postmaster and owner of horses" to his cart, take the shofar of the *shamash* [beadle] of the damaged synagogue in his hands, gallop through Kirovai Street and shout with all his might "Fire!"

[Page 468]

Thus was the custom of that Reb Shaulke next to the well of Shlomo the hatmaker:

At first, he would tuck the edges of his *kapote* into the area between his belt and his loins.

He washed his hands and immediately leaned against the well and recited a silent prayer to chase away the demons and evil spirits that live in the depths of the well. He did all this, then he lowered the pail that was tied to a rope, wound around wheels that were anchored into two hooks attached to the opening of the well.

He would roll the wheels and lower the pail, as he hummed to himself. The pail filled up. He raised it, and poured the water into the barrel on his cart.

Since Reb Shaulke was careful that the water in the pail would always be close to full, that is full to its rim, it was natural that gushes of water spilled out of the bucket, and there were veritable puddles on the ground outside the well.

The young child enjoyed standing in this puddle, dancing with his small shoes in the cool water, splashing jets of water about for his pleasure.

You probably understand that his father, Reb Berl, when he saw the disgrace of his son, immediately took him, brought him into Grandfather's home, and always placed him on the warm attic of Tzirel and Feigel to dry his wet feet and socks. The child of course shouted...

Once the aunts Tzirel and Feigel distracted the young child, who took a flask of water that was used to spray the hats during ironing. Somehow, he tied together a chain of hats that were scattered on the floor, went to the hole in the ceiling, and removed the cover.

He then did the same thing that Reb Shaulke Pozarnik did next to the well. He began to lower the flask – which was the pail of the well – the well being the hole in the ceiling.

However, this child did not tuck the edges of his *kapote* into his belt. He did not roll up his sleeves. He did not whisper a prayer.

He only stood at the mouth of this "well" in the ceiling and called out as loud as he could: "Water! Water! Water!"

Water sprinkled and poured out from the hole in the attic onto the heads of the customers in the hat store of Grandfather Reb Shlomo, wetting the hair of the village gentiles.

They moved to the sides, crossed themselves, and called out.

"*A Atu Cztu Wom*?" (These, why so much?) The elderly hatmaker appears the gentiles with smooth, logical words, and concluded:

"Do you not see, this is a prank of a young child"

[Page 469]

After this last act, the aunts moved out of the attic in the roof and descended to their home below for some unknown reason

Or maybe it was because the war broke out in the interim, and a shell damaged and sealed the well. The hole in the home of Grandfather Reb Shlomo the hatmaker never again bothered the gentiles and the young child.

6. An Incident with a Magnifying Glass

It Is said, to whom are you beholden for good all the days, and their mercy is bound up with you, if not to he who first taught you how to literally walk on your small feet?

If not to this – then to he who brought joy to your hearts and lit up your faces with a gift and a game.

If not to this – then to he who participated with you in all your childhood creations.

If you have no such person, by your life, you lose out in the long run.

To that child whose entire world is confined to the area between his parental home, which stood on the Flour Market, and the home of Reb Shlomo the hatmaker on Kirovai Street – it was like this:

There was someone who broadened his world.

This was another elderly person, a pleasant man, the second grandfather, the father of the child's mother Reb Shmuel Shimon.

All that the child remembers from the appearance of that grandfather was that he was a head taller than anything around him, even taller than the high gate of his yard, for he had to bend his head every time he went through it.

Even taller than the tall trees in the plain behind the spacious house.

Taller, even, than the...clouds. How? He said to his grandson:

“If you want, I will take you for a ride on one of them. Perhaps you think that the child was not tied to tops of these â€˜heights of the world'?”

The child squirmed and trembled with his entire body when his grandfather Reb Shmuel Shimon tossed him up, and then caught him with his two arms. After this manly game, his grandfather kissed his grandson to calm is fear, pushed his thumb into the cheek of the child and rubbed it around in order to arouse his laughter. He would them immediately toss him up again to the "Heavenly court". If as time went on, the child, who had by now grown up, walked about with his "head in the clouds", the role of Grandfather Reb Shmuel Shimon was more significant than the role of the rest of the people and things that led him to this path in the world.

To the extent that this grandfather's stature grew in the eyes of the child to that of a giant, one of the Nephilim, to that extent he became [myopically] nearsighted.

The child was always concerned that the giant may not pay attention to his short stature, at home or in the yard, and hurt or trample him, Heaven forbid, with his large feet. For that reason, the little one lowered his stature further, and pushed himself into every corner and wall in the home of his grandfather, cried silently, and tried to avoid being seen.

[Page 470]

Reb Shmuel Shimon wanted to provide glasses for his eyes, but he could not find glasses appropriate for his nearsightedness anywhere, neither in his city or in other places from Minsk to Vilna. Having no choice, he fashioned for himself a magnifying glass on a rod.

That rod was a work of an artisan, prepared by Pesach Elkes the craftsman. He was the man who built the large synagogue and the holy ark after the large fire. He built them in a splendid fashion with lots of moldings and carvings. He etched the image of the tabernacle and its vessels in them, as well as the image of Aaron and his sons and the forms of the ophanim and holy seraphim. The eye could not have enough of seeing it, especially the eyes of the children of Talmud Torah, who would enter the anteroom of the synagogue with their teacher to learn the stories of the Torah from the images.

Everything that went out from the hands of Pesach Elkes was in a fine state. Even this rod of grandfather's was certainly not like those of the rest of the world. First, there was a handle made of bone. If it was not ivory, it was probably a bone of the wild ox[5]. Etched on one side of this handle was the blind Lemech holding an arrow, killing his grandson Tubal–Cain, as stated in the *Midrash.* Etched on the other side was the Binding of Isaac, with the angels fluttering on high, shedding tears onto the eyes of the lad Isaac – from which his sight was later affected. Above the handle, on the rod itself, Pesach

Elkes etched the image of a bearded, barefoot gentile – with the sun shining and light blinding around him. This gentile held a lantern in his hand to provide illumination.

The child knew how to pronounce the name of Isaac our Forefather, but he could not contemplate the name of Diogenes – a philosopher according to Grandfather – or to pronounce his name. Eventually, he learned that he was a Greek, who went to search for man with the flashlight in his hand.

Finally, what is your opinion of the rod of Grandfather's magnifying glass? You also think that it is one of the "wonders of the world." In truth, there was no other object in the large home of Reb Shmuel Shimshon that it could be compared to and could serve such a purpose.

Go and see, at times, the giant, the child's grandfather, would place the little one on his lap, bring the magnifying glass close to the child's eyes, and search in them.

You might ask, why was Grandfather interested in the eyes of his grandson? The little one himself asked such a question. The giant with the magnifying glass on a road answered as follows:

"I wonder, what will your eyes be involved with in future times, when you grow up?" The child did not understand anything of these words.

Just as he did not understand the knowledge of his grandfather, who made a "search" in his eyes, in all his views, his own and not those of others, so did he not understand the interest he had in his ears, the canals of which were inspected by that rod along with his eyes.

[Page 471]

Grandfather Reb Shmuel Shimon said, "It seems that through the ears, one can see what is laying in the container of the head of man".

For a long time, the child felt his ears and squinted with his eyes – until he was redeemed [i.e., figured it out].

7. Grandfather Reb Shmuel Shimon and his Family

Reb Shmuel Shimon's house stood "outside the boundaries" of the Jewish settlement in the city of Smorgon, on the gentile street.

This main street, Vilna Street, ended at this place and split into two branches. The one on the left led to the railway station, and the one on the right led toward the "Dark Forest," from which the road to Vilna, the Jerusalem of Lithuania, continued.

Reb Shmuel Shimon did not build his house among the gentiles because they scorned his brethren of his nation.

It seems that he did this specifically out of his love for his fellow Jew. How, you might ask? Tuesday night would foreshadow the great market day of the city. At the light of the morning star and the crow of the rooster to wake up the slumberers, Grandfather would go and stand in the path outside his house to return the gentile Kirila and the rest of his friends who were tipsy, and who had disrupted the market day of the previous week. How did he bring them back? He would grab one of them with the flap of his fur coat, and grab the second one similarly. He would bring them together, and bring them into a great "conflict," to "wrestle" with each other.

Kirila and his friends would return to their village, beaten and subdued, and would not enter the crowd of their brethren at the entrance to the market. The land, that is Smorgon, would be quiet for thirty days, with no outburst or outcry.

You could not enter the house of Reb Shmuel Shimon until you went through that tall gate, made of boards, clumsy and high. Above the gate fluttered some sort of "heroes sign," unique of its kind and unique in the city. The round sign was carved and engraved. Upon it was a rubbed–out image of the banner of the Tribe of Simeon.

Apparently, this grandfather had decided that he, his father, and all his ancestors, all previous generations, were members of the Tribe of Simeon. He opened up the *Chumash* and found the flag of the tribe. He looked into the *Midrash* and found the coin of that tribe. Since he found what he wanted, he immediately affixed this image of heraldry atop his gate.

I will not describe all the details of the rubbed–out image. I will only say this, that under the image, to the right and the left, engraved and etched deep into the copper, were two letters *Shin*, one on each side – the initials of his name: Shmuel Shimon.

[Page 472]

Until the man calmed down from this act, all the idlers and unemployed of the city of Smorgon entered, stood in front of his gate, straightened their stature, lifted their heads up to see what was written on this *rav* (sign in the vernacular). Their eyes rolled from one side to the other, as they read Sh. Sh.

After they pronounced the initials out loud, they put their fingers to their mouth, and repeated over and over: Sh. Sh.

From then, the nickname Rash'ash stuck with Reb Shmuel Shimon.

The empty, good–for–nothings of Smorgon saw the elderly man as he walked about for his business. They immediately hid behind every abandoned fence, and secret corner, mocking him out loud to disturb him, calling out through the street:

"Rash'ash is walking, clear the way for our rabbi Sha'sh!"

If you think that Shmuel Shimon cared, you do not know anything about the first nickname that he had, and that actually always bothered him.

On the contrary, he was happy with his second nickname, that made people forget the first.

What was the first nickname? Reb Shmuel Shimon the "Kalte Loksh" – that is the cold noodle.

How did this bespectacled man get such a strange nickname? This is what happened. And it did not happen to him, but rather to his grandfather, Reb Michael of Daniszew, who was a merchant and a scholar, modest, and a great giver of charity. In his day, he saw that nobody was concerned about the poor people of Smorgon, whose administrators were immersed in controversy, and had no time to help those were in distress. He went and set up a sort of private kitchen.

He called together his entire family, his wife, sons, and daughters, and taught them to occupy themselves with the commandment "disperse your bread to the poor"[6].

The daughters would make the dough, roll it thin, and cut it into thin slices. These are the noodles.

His wife would cook soup.

His sons would bring the food every Friday in two large vats to the houses of the poor, and pour out soup for the Sabbath into their vessels.

Since this food reached the houses of the poor of Smorgon for the most part when it was cold, they called Reb Michael of Daniszew "Kalte Loksh" (cold noodle).

This was the story, and this was its reward.

This nickname passed down as an inheritance from Reb Michael to his sons, and from them to Grandfather. Certainly, this nickname was honorable and merciful. It continued on to all the descendants of the family until the final generation. However, two great wars came, wiping the people out of the book of life – them, their names, and their nicknames.

[Page 473]

However, until the drafting of the gentiles to beat each other began[7], and the world got confused, the city of Smorgon was quiet and successful. Its Jews were written in the names of their fathers, and were called by their nicknames. For example, that little one who, about whom we are more or less interested, was called the following on Kirovai Street.

"Henech Berl's Shlomo's the hatmaker's

That is:

Henech (that is the child), the son of Berl (that is his father), the son of Shlomo (the grandfather), the hatmaker.

That same area of the city, spreading from the flour market where his father's home stood, until the home of his grandfather Reb Shmuel Shimon, for the entire length of Vilna Street until the crossroads leading to the railway station, and the Black Forest, was called by the child as follows:

Henech Mintza's Shmuel Shimon's the Kalte Loksh.

That is:

Henech (the child), the son of Mintza (his mother), the daughter of Shmuel Shimon (the grandfather) the cold noodle (the nickname).

8. How Did the Child Stop Being Afraid of Mitran's Dog, [named] "Paskody"

How does one go down to the cellar of the giant? You could go down from inside, or you go down from the outside. There was a hole in the floor in the middle of the large kitchen of Shmuel Shimon's house. The opening had a cover as large as itself, and the cover had a hook at the edge. If you wanted to go down to the cellar, you would just have to remove the rope tied to a peg on the nearby wall, tie it to the hook, and pull.

The cover would then rise, and you would be standing "at the threshold of the lower abyss" – that is, next to the opening leading to the cellar. A ladder was resting on the floor, with its top reaching the edge of the opening. You could go up and down to your heart's content. That was in the house.

From the outside – you would go down the steps under the porch (*genikl* in Yiddish) of the back door of this large house. By your life, if you did not know from hearing, or through this story, you would not find the entrance to that cellar in the house. Why is this so? Because in the kitchen, from where one goes down to the cellar, there is a sheet of hides made up of interwoven pieces that were brought from Grandfather's factory. You would also not find the outside entrance to the cellar, for it was hidden beneath the porch.

Why did Grandfather do this? Perhaps he looked up at the stars and realized that disaster was about to afflict the world, so he prepared the cellar as a hiding place.

Whenever the child was at his grandfather's house, he wanted to go down to the cellar to see what was hidden there.

[Page 474]

Once the child begged him and said:

"Grandfather, I want to go [in] there" and he hinted with a nod of his head and a wink to a place over there.

"Where do you want to go, my child?" asked Grandfather.

"To the cellar."

"And what will you do in the cellar, my little one?" Asked grandfather.

"I will search for treasures."

"What treasures will you search for there?

"The treasurers that you told me about, Grandfather."

"And what will you do if you do not find treasurers there, my son?"

"Grandfather will look for them and find."

"Okay" was the answer.

The child did not know the meaning of this cut–off word.

"And when, Grandfather, will we go there?" The child did not let up.

"When you get bigger," answered Reb Shmuel Shimon in brief.

"And when will I be big?"

"When you will be as strong as you need to be!"

"And how will I be as strong as I need to be?"

"When you are not afraid of Mitran's dog," answered Grandfather.

"I am already no longer afraid of Mitran's dog."

"If that is so, then let us see if you are truly strong. We will go to Mitran's dog," concluded the giant man, the grandfather of the child. They both left the house.

Mitran was Reb Shmuel Shimon's neighbor. He was an adult gentile who hobbled on one leg. It was said that he lost his leg due to the evil eye[8]. Once when he was properly drunk, literally drunk as Lot, he told his gentile friends who joined him in the "bitter drop" that he has no fear of that "slithering beast" on the tracks – the train. They stood up with him, wagered with him, and promised him such and such gallons of liquor if he displays his bravery...

He spoke, and he did: Mitran went to the railway tracks, rested his large body on the gravel area next to the tracks, putting only one foot on the track. The train passed by and severed his foot. Mitran was in pain and afflicted with terrible afflictions for many months. His wound opened and closed, opened and closed. When his pain strengthened, he washed it away with the liquor that he received from his friends. He finally went and prepared himself an artificial limb (Kula in the vernacular). One day he brought in the despicable dog, called Paskody by the gentiles, to frighten people.

This dog was a despised creature. It would always stand up and scratch itself in front of its excreta with the pole that was tied to its leash. All the passers–by on the street were afraid to walk by due to its bark.

When this child would reach Grandfather's street when walking with his mother Mintza, his entire body would begin to tremble. They would even avoid Mitran's house by crossing to the other side of the street.

[Page 475]

In truth, the gentile Mitran and his dog Paskody did not threaten Grandfather. They liked the Jew.

The handicapped man's livelihood was found through Reb Shmuel Shimon. From the day that gentile went on "amnesty" because of his injury and abandoned his work in the fields – he was dependent on the kindness of his Jewish neighbor. Grandfather would purchase oak bark from him for his tannery. This was mixed with a type of liquid called export, and used to soak the hides. Grandfather would purchase it and pay generously.

The two of them, the grandfather and the grandson, went to visit Paskody, Mitran's dog.

The beast leaped out of the pole quickly. The leash to which he was tied stretched and recoiled backward. Paskody stood up on his hind paws and showed his teeth.

The dog did not bark.

And it did not move.

It calmed itself.

And it folded is legs underneath and laid down.

It only gazed at the grandfather and his grandson with good eyes, and calmly murmured, “hum... brr... humm... brrr”. The child was not afraid of Paskody at that moment, and the next day, they went down to the cellar.

9. What Did the Child Do with the Barrel of Cabbage Stocks?

The entire city gathered in Reb Shmuel Shimon's cellar.

Were all those terrible tribulations not to have come, the ones that wiped out the city and all therein, and froze our world until all joy was removed from the hearts and laughter from the lips–Grandfather's cellar would still exist to this day. We would not read about it in a story, but rather go and see what was in it.

Language is insufficient to describe what that child found in this underground place of his grandfather. Before his eyes got accustomed to the darkness of the cellar, and opened a bit, the aromas of cooked dishes and the spices of the city wafted to his nostrils.

The cellar was made up of compartments. Some were for food and drink, and others were for all sorts of belongings that were lovely in their time, and were still nice now, but it was best to hide them away because of the evil eye, so that wrath not break out against us.

All the food and drink were arranged in barrels, containers, trunks and chests, or were hanging from hooks and beams.

[Page 476]

There was one pantry for potatoes for the winter. They were buried in thin sand, with their “eyes” sticking out. They were not rotting. One large pantry was for pickled food, where there were barrels of purple cabbage (sauerkraut), and pickled cucumbers.

The daughters of Reb Shmuel Shimon, the older ones and the younger ones, worked especially in preparing that pickled cabbage.

In the evening, when the light of an autumn day was fading, a red splendor covered the roofs of the houses and the foliage of the maple trees that grew next to the kitchen window. Then *di muter*, that is the wife of Grandfather Reb Shmuel Shimon, who was called that by the household out of respect, to differentiate her from his first wife who died young – placed a long wooden shelf on top of the tables (*kozals* in the vernacular), and summoned all the daughters of the household to the kitchen with a loving voice.

Mintza the eldest, who was summoned to come while it was still day, brought her son. The mother would cut cabbage and the child would entertain the hearts of those who came to the kitchen.

There was Sarah, who was small and refined, and married to Shmuel Fajn, an enthusiastic Chovev Zion (lover of Zion), and the first of all the youths in the city who worked at the holy task of reviving the nation.

There was Fania. No place in the house was free from her pranks. She was an actor from her early childhood, and was the first participant in the amateurs' circle on the stage of Smorgon. Later, she was an actor in the government theater of far–off Rostov in Russia.

There was Rechil, that is the dark, pleasant Rachel, proud of her beauty, young, and already a teacher in the Russian girls' school. She corresponded to that Tolstoyist (a student of the well–known Russian writer Tolstoy) named Gabriusha. She was as tall as one of the Nephilim, and as innocent as a child.

They were all daughter of Reb Shmuel Shimon who were born to him from his first wife Henya (and the child was called after her name). They stood on one side of the cabbage shelf.

And the other side of the shelf – who stood there?

All the young ones, including the lads. These were Chayale, the daughter of Reb Shmuel Shimon's old age who was born to him by *di muter.*

And the sons: Alterke and Shayke, the first quiet and bashful by nature, and the second "mercurial" who never rested for a moment. He was called Sambatyon, but this one did not quiet down even on the Sabbath.

And finally – the child. Jumping around the legs, falling and getting up, and chewing lightly on the cabbage that was called *kacan* (in the vernacular).

"Where is our child?" asked Reb Shmuel Shimon, who entered the kitchen to see all of his children reclining around the cabbage shelf, cutting the leaves finely.

"Certainly under the table," responded Mintza, the mother of the child. Grandfather immediately put the magnifying glass to his eyes, bent down a bit, searched, but the child was nowhere.

[Page 477]

"You are rebelling against me, my children," said the old man. "You have hidden the child from me."

"Father, behold he is in the barrel!" Uncle Shayka burst out in laughter. All the members of the household looked toward the large barrel and saw the child riding on the cabbage heads: It was to the good fortune of that child that there was not much water in that barrel.

"Catch it, Grandfather!" the child called out, and tossed a head of cabbage, as large as the hand of the grandchild, to the grandfather. Grandfather caught the cabbage with one hand, lifted the child from the barrel with the second hand, and said:

"Now let us go down to the cellar! The child thought that Grandfather might punish him, and now he was going to take him down to the dark place – but it was not so!

"Let us trash the cellar, and see if the rest of the miracles and wonders are better than those of the barrel." Reb Shmuel Shimon concluded the words of the child.

10. In the Cellar

You certainly want to know what are the rest of the wonders that the child saw that evening in the thick darkness of the cellar of the house? Go out and descend in the footsteps of time down the stairs under that porch that was called *genikl*, located behind the house.

I have already described to you the cells, the chambers, and small pantries for all types of pickled foods. However, you have not yet figured out how to tell the difference between bitter and sweet in the vats of drinks and receptacles for food – starting with the carboys of mead and raisin wine, and ending with the cherry and apple juice of various sorts – all of these in the chamber of wonderful stuff in the cellar. On the shelves, in an important manner, were plates and jars, each different from the other, containing various concoctions of the house of Reb Shmuel Shimon: the sweet cherry and its brother, the sour cherry (called *czerszany* in the vernacular). Some of them spiced up the winter nights as the warm drinks were served, and treated the "sons–in–law" who came to see the "brides," the daughters of Reb Shmuel Shimon, who were invited with a gesture and the words:

"So, let's put our *kirshlech* on the table, that is from the famous cherries."

Other concoctions were close to them in place and taste: fox grapes[9] (called *agrast* in the vernacular), with their eyes like glazed blue, hard and whole, without any blemish.

Various berries, from black to red, which were a medication for colds and beneficial to make sick people sweat to relieve the dampness of the illness.

The preserves to garnish the bread were in a unique compartment. These were the black plum jam, and currant (called *brusznicze*s) jam.

[Page 478]

The first was a desirable food for children, and the second, very sour, to serve as an appetizer before a full meal, and as a condiment for all types of meat. The types of meat in the cellar cannot all be counted, but it would be inappropriate to not mention that which was present at all times in that large house: salted brisket in round barrels, preserved tongues, livers and kidneys in *barban* – that is a type of drum that was taken after use from Grandfather's tanning factory. There were jars of duck fat and hard fats designated for frying the Chanukah latkes and potato kugels.

All of these were things that the stomachs of grandfather's house required. However, the fineries in the cellar were delicacies that the hearts of a person desired due to their fine nature, and the soul always wanted.

In one of the resonating corners, next to the wonderful boxes of childhood, "So much stuff in the boxes, Grandfather!" the child called out with a glow in his spirit and a sparkle in his eyes.

“You want to know how many there are, count them my child!” said the giant in the cellar. The child began to count them one by one, and did not reach the end of the count, whether because of lack of ability, or because Grandfather opened one of them and took out copper or perhaps gold coins.

“For whom is all this treasure, Grandfather? Is it true that the coins are dwarfs? Uncle Shayke said that they were dug from a tunnel to the cellar, did Shayke tell the truth?” the child asked and asked without letting up.

“Go ask your uncle Shmuel Fajn,” said Grandfather.

11. The Land of Israel Rings

Eventually, the child asked this uncle, who told him that these boxes were – the wonder of the redemption of the Land of Israel. It was forbidden to keep them in the open and use them in public for fear of the government. Therefore, he took them down to Grandfather's cellar, where they are waiting for better days. Until those better days come, the good eyes of Uncle Shmuel watched over them to protect and save them.

The child received from his Uncle Shmuel one box whose lock was broken. His eyes feasted on it for many days until its image became etched in his heart until this very day. It looked like the blue glassy appearance of the large flower vase that stood on a narrow, tall stand at the corner of the guestroom of his parents' house facing the flour market. The child placed it, standing on a chair, next to that vase. The shape of a Magen David shone on one side of the cover of the box. A star reflecting light was etched into each of the corners, the inside of which had the image of a man following his plow, with the rising sun opposite him.

[Page 479]

Two lions were crouching on the other side of the box, facing each other, holding the blue and white flag with their bodies.

The child did not know if this box was more wonderful than the other boxes in the cellar, but he felt that the secrets of great ones are etched within it. He would feel it in the day, and see it in his bright dreams at night. All the coins that the child received were placed into that box. How? He would remove this precious treasure from the stand, place it on the fur carpet on the floor, take the coin and toss it inside. He would continue until he reached the last of his coins. When all were in the box, he would immediately lift it up, walk around the room, shaking the box strongly. The coins would jingle inside like a bell. It would seem like many bells joined together, resonating throughout the house and its inhabitants.

"Berl, what is this that is 'shaking up the worlds' with you?" all those who passed through Father's door would ask.

"Do you want to see the tricks of my little one? Come and see!" Father would say not without a trace of pride.

Dov–Ber would bring them to the door of his room. They would stand and see the child making his circuits with the box. The little one would notice the crowds of people watching him with their eyes. He stood bashfully before them.

"What is it that is ringing with you?" Father asked his bright–faced child, as he tossed a handful of coins to the feet of the child, to appease him and assuage his confusion.

"The Land of Israel is ringing" said the child.

The adults heard the answer of the child, peered at him and were astonished. They moved their lips, but their voice was not heard. They raised their heads to Father and looked at the bandage[10] that circled his head, wondering in their hearts: This bandage comes from another flag, and how do we settle it?" It is a question.

12. The End of the Pristov [Police Chief] Who Injured Father

The other flag stood in the cellar of the giant, that is Grandfather Reb Shmuel Shimon. It was fastened to the sandbox with all the accessories and wonders, various articles of clothing and colored liens that served as props for the actors of the city and the daughter of the owner of the house, Aunt Fania, who was responsible for this burden. The flag was red – and the child imagined in his heart that he was dripping with its colors – drop by drop, into the sand in the box, apparently as if it was wounded.

If – an actual injury was not seen on the flag – its canvas was torn and ripped: All its threads, woven together, the work of the child's mother Mintza – were frayed, with the strands hanging down from the textile.

[Page 480]

It once happened that all the workers of the city, tanners and tradesmen, craftsmen and day workers, apprentices and students, went out to demonstrate the brotherhood of workers on the first of the month of spring, that is what they call May in their language. All together, they went out to protest against the government oppression, and the disgrace and pressure on their lives. Mother went out as well, holding the flag that she embroidered during the nights, marching upright at the front of the camp.

The Pristov, that is the police chief of the city, saw this act of rebellion of the *zhyds* – as the gentiles called the Jews. He immediately commanded the Cossack brigade that was camped opposite the city to hitch up their horses, take their whips, and scatter these rebels with shouts of Hurrah!

The Cossacks stormed out to the streets of the city. They broke through the rows of marchers, beat them the butt of their rifles and whipped them right and left with their whips.

The father of the child was also there. He did not mix in with the throng of demonstrators, but only watched the parade. He saw that evil was about to take place, and his wife, who did not pay attention due to her great enthusiasm, was marching toward the danger. He broke through the crowd, reached his wife, removed the flag from her hands, and dropped it behind him to protect her. A Cossack noticed him, and made his horse gallop straight toward him.

Were it not for the agility of Berl the son of Shlomo the hatmaker, he would certainly have been trampled, and she would have caused the child to be orphaned from his father.

However, it was impossible to free oneself from this danger unharmed. That Cossack made him taste the taste of the whip, which had a lead tip.

Because of that flag, Father remained at home for a month with a bandage on his head.

Those days of Father's pain and affliction, when he had nothing to do – were happy days for the child. It was not that his heart was hardened, and he did not feel the gloominess of Father and Mother. On the contrary, the little one used all the meager energy of his soul and his feeble imagination to figure out how to comfort and encourage his father. He was certainly happy that Father was fully connected to the home and to him during that period. Furthermore, the child sought, so to speak, to prove the depth of his love for his Father, for he too was saddened by all the suffering and pained by all the agony. The child stood up and became ill.

This was not a fake illness. It was actual. Father had one bandage on his head, and the child – two. One was bound on his little head to reduce his fever, and the second was tied as a yoke on his neck to ease his warm, heavy breathing. The sick child accepted his suffering with love because his Father, who was sitting with him, would caress him, comfort him, and kiss him. He would hold the burning hand of the child in his large, merciful hand, and even tell his son stories that were desirous to the small heart of the child.

[Page 481]

Once as evening was falling, the room of the sick child moved, and his bed flew about. Father was sitting at the head of his son and telling the end of the story, about this anti–Semitic Pristov, the evildoer may his name be blotted out, who wanted to destroy us and would have killed mother with the lead tipped whip. After several days, this Pristov was found with his arms and legs tied in a sack, the opening of which was also tied. The sack was under the bridge over the river, passing by Minsker Street, where it divides into two.

The police found their leader, that is the Pristov, in the sack under the bridge. They released him, and placed him on the pavement next to the bridge. They wanted to stand him up, but a hook[11] fell on that wicked man. They tried to talk to him, but he did not answer – he lost his power of speech. They gave him liquor, and he began to cry. They returned and asked him how he got there, and he began to laugh. He alternated crying and laughing. They found out from the relatives of that wicked man that it was not only the power of speech that he lost, but his mind became deranged. They sent him somewhere, and that was the end of the sentence.

"Father, what is the end of the sentence," asked the sick child in a weak voice, as he struggled with his sore throat."

"The end of the sentence, my son, is the end of the story."

"It is not good, Father, for the story must have an end" said the child.

"And so – what do you want the end of the story to be?" asked the father.

"Let it lead to another story."

"How?" asked the father in astonishment.

"That there should not be another Pristov. There should also be no more Cossacks, the whips in their hands should be broken, and the wooden marbles should only be used by the children to play, and that we may all go in the way of the rising sun."

"What sun?" asked Father, not delving into the depth of the thoughts of his son.

"Like those that are drawn on the blue box of Uncle Shmuel."

The child rested his head on the pillar that stood in the corner of the room where that box was located. Father also turned his head to that side, and it seemed to both of them that the sun was indeed shining from there.

13. The Singing Box and the Death of the Giant

During those days that the child was sick and Father was resting in his bed, Mother was not at home. Where was the mother of the child? In the house of her father Reb Shmuel Shimon. Mother would leave the house in the morning and return at night. Before she left, she would open her son's room slowly, approach his toes on his bed, stand for a bit silent and sad, look at the face of her son, lit up with the light of a final dream, and kiss him. Her lips would move as she touched the hot forehead of her sick child. She would mutter something in her heart and leave slowly, so as not to wake him. Once the child was semi–awake and felt the tears of his mother on his cheek. He opened his sleepy eyes, and saw that she was mournful, depressed, and wearing black. He wanted to ask why she was so sad. He could not, as she disappeared quickly and left the door open. Father came, sat beside his son, and said.

[Page 482]

"Did you see a good dream, my son?"

"I forgot my dream, but I only remember Mother's sad face."

Father was silent and perplexed. The child saw that his father was also joyless, which was unusual. His heart soured, and he burst out crying.

"Why are you crying, my son?" asked Father.

"I want Mother" sobbed the little one.

"Mother will return in the evening."

"Take me now, Father, to Mother."

"I cannot do so, my son."

"Why not, Father."

"You are sick, and Grandfather is no more!"

"How is it that Grandfather is no more?"

"He passed away, and is no longer with us."

"Where did he go, my grandfather?"

"To a far–off place."

And when will he return."

"Grandfather will not return, for the place is far off – very far."

"I want to go to Grandfather. Let us go to Grandfather. Even if it is far – far, let us go to him."

The father could not end the talking of his son. He saw that his tears were flowing, his eyes were blinking, and his mouth was talking, and he tried to calm him in a different manner.

"You are no longer a little child, my son. You are older, and you have understanding. It is not fitting for you to cry. Come and listen, and I will tell you what happened to Grandfather?"

"When the child got sick, Grandfather Reb Shmuel Shimon wanted to visit his grandson. He had left the house, and was prepared to go through the tall gate of his yard to go out on to the long Vilna Street. He realized that he was going to the child emptyhanded. He stood and said to himself."

"It is impossible for you, Shmuel Shimon of Daniszew, that the matron whose name you forgot is ruling over you, for you are a very old man; Is it not that a great treasure is hidden in that cellar for that child to whom you are going. How could you forget, an old man such as you?" Everything that he was saying to himself – Grandfather was thinking of nothing other than the musical box that he brought as a gift for the child from his last trip to the city of Minsk.

Reb Shmuel Shimon went to Minsk three times a year to bring his tanned hides there – the hides that were called *pilszpaner* in the vernacular, to sell to a certain German who came from his far–off estate on the great Volga River.

[Page 483]

This is what happened: after the two reached an agreement regarding everything related to the business transaction, they concluded the deal with a drink and a snack, and exchanged gifts. One to the "*shkotzim*" of this German, who sail on the great waters of the Volga. The other to the grandson of that "*Staro–Zakonik*", that is the Jew of the old faith from Smorgon.

The gentile received a chest of cakes, small and large, soft and hard, from "Samuel Semion Levovich Daniszewski." These were the cakes that his city was famous for. He gave the Jew a musical box, the workmanship of the German craftsmen.

He remembered what he forgot. Grandfather returned to his house to fetch the box that was placed in a hiding place in the cellar with everything else hidden there.

Then Reb Shmuel Shimon took his kerosene lamp that was called *kerosinke* in the vernacular, which was hanging from a hook in the anteroom of the house. Grandfather lit it with a match, and turned toward the back entrance to the cellar under that porch that was called *genikl*. The old man went down the stairs calmly, with his heart happy that he was going to be doing a good deed for the sick child. He found the music box, that beloved treasure, by feeling and groping his way. He wrapped it in a velvet cover that he found among the stage props of his daughter, Fania the actor.

Grandfather now wanted to return through the way he came, but at that time, the Satan lured him, and he smelled the aroma that he loved – that is the hot lentil soup called *lindzn*. That soup has the consistency of dough or potato dumplings, pleasant to the palate. Reb Shmuel Shimon could not withstand his appetite, and tried to shorten the path by going up the ladder leading to the kitchen. He went up with the wick in his lantern, as he ascended the rungs and knocked his head on the cover of the cellar. The cover lifted. It did not stay up, but rather fell back down, injuring Grandfather's head. He rolled off the ladder from the knock, and fell heavily down to the cellar, banging his head on a heavy keg. The members of the household realized that he fell, and found Grandfather lying there, with his breathing fluttering. They brought him up, laid him on a bed, and hastened to summon the good physician, Dr. Epstein. He was the one who founded the large Hebrew school in the city of Vilna, where our young child would eventually study. The physician examined him, made a sign of despair, as if to say, "May G–d have mercy." He commanded the Orthodox members of the household to refrain from moving Grandfather from his place. The look on the face of that giant changed, as contortions of pain overtook his body.

Reb Shmuel Shimon suffered for three days and nights with terrible afflictions, until he returned his soul to his G–d.

A heavy mourning descended upon the house. The sons and daughters of the deceased sat Shiva as their souls wept silently. The daughter Mintza, that is the mother of the young child, left her sick son every day and returned at dusk, forlorn and mourning.

[Page 484]

And that music box, that hidden treasure, a gift from Grandfather of blessed memory, what became of it? The box shattered into smithereens when it slipped from the hands of that giant as he was falling off the ladder. It broke apart, and its shards rolled to a dark corner of the cellar.

Woe to the loss. The child did not merit to make music with the enchanting box of Grandfather of blessed memory. Its chords disappeared forever. At that moment, the internal reality of the child stood at the threshold of the locked gate of the great secret, dark and forlorn, about the loss with no solution.

The giant crouched and fell down, and a world of grace and light disappeared with his fall.

14. The Night Travels of the Child

The shloshim [30–day mourning period] for the child's grandfather, Reb Shmuel Shimon of Daniszew, had not yet passed.

He, who was a giant in the eyes of his grandson, like the Nephilim in the land.

He, the owner of the magnifying glass on a rod that enlarged the world and its contents.

He, Rasha'sh, who was called such by all the local jokers because of the *harb* – that is the sign that fluttered above the high gate of his yard.

Not long thereafter, there was great preparation in the house of the little one. Doors were opened gently, and all sorts of people entered both houses, one on Kirovai Street, and the other on Vilna Street, on the route that leads to the Dark Forest.

Those entering waited a bit in the anteroom. They removed their hats and placed them on the long peg in which animal horns were fastened, with the colors of the wild ox or perhaps, as is written in the books, from the deer to the buffalo. Out of doubt, the child called those pegs – just horns. However one thing he knew beyond the shadow of a doubt that it was his father, and none other, who one day brought this fine object from a large chest in the city of Vilna with all the merchandise that he got there.

And what did Father get from the city of Vilna? He would get all sorts of furs, which were originally the garb of various foxes.

This is the common fox whose body is grey with a thin tail. This is the noble fox, for it had a streak of silver in its fur, and sparks of light in its ample tail – this is what was frequently found in the yards of the noblemen, the princes of the land, who sewed their fur coats – the inside as the outside –

from this type of fox. Immediately after removing them, father took out all the other types of furs from the chest: large, medium, and small.

[Page 485]

Some were from martens and others from white rabbits and its mate, the grey rabbit. Some were from moles, and other from the black, wild cat called *kotik*. Finally, there was the precious fur of the Karakol goat, black and grey. In truth it can be said that our little one, unlike other children his age, was not afraid of the wild forest animals that entered his house. It seemed that he pulled out their glassy eyes from their heads and played with them quietly, or would pull the hair from their tails to hide between his bedding.

When nobody was looking, he would spread the furs on the floor of the room, and would set sail with all the animals to their forests.

"What are you doing, my son?" His mother would ask as she caught him in this game.

"I am riding on this young fox, who is taking me to his hole."

"And what will you do, my son, in the den of your friend the fox?" asked Mother in complete seriousness, as if the words her son were completely true.

"I am invited to the feast hosted by the old fox for all the residents of the forest and the fields."

"And through whose hand did the old fox send the invitation to my son?" added Mother, to verify the truth of the imagination.

"The old fox always sends all the invitations via the white rabbit who jumps from tree to tree in the forest."

In his night dream, the child went out on his travels with his friends the animals, and returned in peace in the morning, with his eyes lit up with visions. His mouth did not stop telling about the miracles and wonders.

15. A Sister is Born to the Child

You probably recall that we were standing for a short while in the hallway of the house, where we tarried a bit at the horned hanger affixed to the wall. The entire story that we told above, from beginning to end, was on its account.

If so, let us urge, therefore, all those entering to move from the anteroom to the parlor.

Our little one sees masses of people standing at the door, and calls out in his heart to each one to find out for himself if this call might catch their attention.

Here is his grandfather, Reb Shlomo the hatmaker from Kirovai Street and his wife Grandmother Hinda. Immediately after them are their sons, dragging their sisters Liba, Tzirel, and Feigel, behind. That is all one group. They all entered and made room for others. Uncle and aunts from here and there, descendants of Reb Shmuel Shimon, who came to rejoice with the head of the house. They all surrounded the large table, took a cup of wine or liquor in their hands, raised the cups, knocked them together, and wished Lechayim and Mazel Tov to the father of the little one, Berl. Father responded to them with joy and a lit–up face, "To you too!" The child heard the blessings and knew that they were directed to none other than that small being, red and white, lying in the cradle, who shrieks loudly when she is not asleep. In those days of agony and grief, the sister of the little one entered the world. The house had not recovered from the death of the Grandfather when they stood up, entered the house, and called her name Shima, to continue on the life and the name of the deceased Reb Shmuel Shimon of blessed memory.

[Page 486]

There is nothing that brings comfort to people more than a baby who proclaims with motions and shouts to them and to the life ahead, with bright smiles and joy. That baby was lying in the cradle made of reeds, rocking on its round legs attached to its walls.

At that time, the little one stood next to the cradle, stood up on his tiptoes to the extent possible, but could not reach. He stretched his head between the reeds and saw that his sister was sleeping, with her splotched face trembling. Her wrinkled face seemingly announced her gloomy existence, and within a moment she has a bright smile on her face, as if she already saw the 310 worlds of contentment and happiness in her dream[12]

"Why is it that you are standing and laughing?" said the father of the child. "You will wake up your sister."

"See, she grimaces like Aunt Fania." The child broke out in loud laughter.

"Stop it, my son, leave the cradle and go to the adults."

The adults do not pay attention to the child. They are only interested in eating and drinking, chit–chat, and stories of times gone by.

The child was astonished from the masses of people and afraid of the tumult. He certainly escaped from the noise to the silence of the second room where the mother was resting. He snuggled between his mother's arms to seek a hiding place. However his young uncle called Shayke saw the perplexed, abandoned child, and quickly rushed to him to calm his fear and return calmness to his soul. Shayke saw the child slunk in a corner. He approached him and said:

"Come with me, little one, we will leave the house, wander around the marketplace, skip over the yards, and go to the shops." The child was happy knowing that Shayka was not a joker. He would not take him around for naught, and he would fulfil all that he promised.

[Page 487]

16. In Front of the Firehall

This was how their walk through the streets of Smorgon at the end of the summer went, one year after the end of the war, the thunder of which echoed from afar and the smoke of which rose up from fires that were approaching.

At first, they opened the door, and heard the ring of masses of small bells tied together – to accompany them with the blessing of the ringing. The went down the steps of the house and stood on the sidewalk next to the street. The eyes of the child immediately saw the firehall, *pożarna* in the vernacular. Opposite his house, to the left was the *Carkawna*, that is the church of the gentiles with a tin roof, sparkling in the light of the son, with three onion domes growing from the roof, round and potbellied, similar to the toy doll with a lead ball in its belly – called *wanka wastanka* because every time you put it down, it would jump and stand up by itself. The onions of the roof were swallowed up by the blue of the sky.

There were red barrels resting atop red wagons in front of the iron gate of the fire station. Since the horses were not hitched to them, they were certainly roaming about the meadow behind the bathhouse across the bridge. The only pump, called *di pumpe*, the pride of the firefighters, stood in a gated area with a long pipe, twisted as a snake, attached to its side. Small ladders were resting on the walls of the station. Among them was a large ladder with a mechanism to lengthen and raise it. The scoffers of the city called it *yaale veyavo*[13].

Melech Klopot sat dozing next to the gate, on a rock to which the horses were tied when needed. He was the emissary of the firefighters. He had a brass helmet on his head and an alarm bell in his hand.

This Klopot was an apprentice. Why was he called by that name?

Every time a fire broke out in the city, or as people say, "the red chicken" was sent to the gardens – he immediately rang the bell, summoned the firefighters, and called out loud:

"Here are new *klopot*!"[14] That is to say, perplexity, confusion, and troubles – a disaster and tribulations are fluttering over this city.

The young uncle, called Shayke, approached Melech Klopot, shook him gently, and asked him:

"Reb Melech, sir, do you think that a terrible *klopot* is approaching?"

The good firefighter smiled into his beard and responded:

"What do you think my son. If there is *klopot*, I am here." However, the heart of the child did not agree with the words of his uncle and Reb Melech at that moment. His soul trembled and turned toward to the shiny brass helmet that was polished and glimmering in the sunlight – one cannot remove one's eye from it.

[Page 488]

"That, my uncle" gestured the child with his thumb, blinking his eyes and pointing his head toward Klopot's helmet.

It seems that the uncle understood the concern of the child. He removed the helmet from Melech's head and placed it on the head of his young nephew. The helmet was larger than the child's head, which was hidden inside it. This too was a problem, that the heavy helmet descended and obscured the light of the day, leaving our child in darkness. Indeed, the little one did not forgo all the pleasures of childhood that he had at that moment of happiness, brought to him by the helmet of the fireman. Shayke gave Reb Melech Klopot as payment for wearing this brass helmet one *fajm*, that is a coin and a half that is the price of a glass of liquor in Yunta's tavern – he is Reb Yom–Tov – for it is as if everyone who enters his tavern comes to a great festival[15]. The child walked by the side of his uncle, and his small heart rejoiced inside him, for G–d had prepared such a nice day for him.

He still felt the heavy, shiny brass firefighters' helmet on his head. It was as if he was wearing a royal crown.

17. On the Streets of the City

How does one go on the streets of the city? One walks upright on the wooden sidewalk, and steps over the cracks that come from slats that are missing or that have rotted because of the rain and snow.

Then, one passes by the narrow doors and looks to see what is inside. One goes to the main road, and walks on a wide path, with one's feet pounding against the sharp, unhewn rocks that stick out, leaving a mark on the shoes. One finds puddles after the rain, jumping in, and crossing them.

If the puddles are too big for a person to jump over, one takes a stick or a pole from a nearby fence, spreads them across the puddle, and crosses in peace.

The two of them, our uncle Shayke, and the little one, stand near a puddle on the route. The uncle wants to take the little one in his arms, but the child protests, saying:

"I am big already. Let the uncle make a bridge."

The child requested, and the uncle acceded. A slat or a pole was immediately spread over the puddle in the road, a bridge by all standards. As this was happening, the uncle did not forget to roll up the legs of the little one's long pants, for had he not done so, he would eventually have to answer to the mother of the child – his oldest sister Mintza.

Thus did they walk, while the heart of the child continued to rejoice.

[Page 489]

Suddenly, there is the sound of wheels, the whoosh of horses, and pillars of dust: From the curve of Vilna Street, from the direction of the railway station, a large carriage with two wagons speeds by. Pinia the Red is sitting in the cabin of the carriage. He is the lead wagon driver of all the "holders of reins" in the city. His sons Hershel and Shepsl drive behind him, sitting on a seat, stretching and pulling with their hands, and whistling to the horses: "Whoa!" They crack the whip.

Their father, Pinia the Red, saw that his children are erring, and acting improperly with the horses. He calls out loudly:

"Hey, you rebellious ones, put the reins down, drop the whips from your hands!"

Pinia's sons Hershel and Shepsl are chastised, and lower their heads. Their whole bodies are trembling from the verdict of their father. The horses, however, raise their heads with pride. The merit of their ancestors, the swift horses, certainly stood for them this time. They shake their manes, neighed joyously, as if to say in horse language.

"It is clear—you rebellious sons will get your punishment."[16]

18. Everything for Free!

More than the child coveted in his heart those sitting on the platform, and was jealous that they are leading fine animals like these horses – he placed his attention toward the strange people sitting in freedom and luxury in the carriage and wagons of Pinia the Red. Those people had colored kerchiefs on their heads, and wore multicolored cloaks. The had some sort of candle-like shaft in their mouths. It looked like a snake. Whenever they chirp at them, they make noise and roll up to their original state. They had scepters in their hands. They were apparently kings or noblemen. Two were sitting in a wagon, displaying a long banner with large letter, with the statement in Polish, Hebrew, and Yiddish:

It is *darmo*![17]

It is free!

It is free!

The net day, Wednesday, was the market day in the city. These strange people stood in the open area in front of the firehall, and unfurled these enchanting banners that were resting in this wagon, now traveling behind them.

The people took out all the wonders of the world from the carriage, spread them on the stalls to the light of the day. They set up a splendid platform, and ascended the steps, clothed in their splendid cloaks, and wearing jagged hats on their heads. Two of them made their proclamations, with trumpets and pipes – declaring all types of bargains that they had, showing them to the people:

[Page 490]

There was a small round mirror, a small, colored comb, bows and ribbons for girls, bobby pins and safety pins, a flowered and polka-dotted kerchief, full of colors, fluttering in their hands above the heads of the onlookers, everything almost free, for a small coin – that is *darmo*!

One of the group rolled a carpet in front of the central stall and acted like a clown: he put a red bulb on his nose, painted his face and whistled, put a linen wig on his head, rolled his eyes, and jumped and danced until he looked like a triangle in the air, doubled over – like a somersault, which is called *koziołki* in the vernacular.

He eventually stood on his feet to the applause of the audience, and coins began to fall into his overturned hat resting in the middle of the carpet.

As he did all this act, his other friend stood nearby, walking around with a music box, below which was a wooden pole. The box played a sad song in the language of the country, with a hoarse, shrieky sound. A lattice cage with a secret case below rested on the carpeted top of the box. A green parrot swayed on a platform of branches at the opening of the cage. Its mouth was not closed, and its tiny tongue fluttered inside without stop. As the motto goes, not to swallow and not to vomit.

"Gather around me, and come, beautiful girls"

Thus did the owner of the music box shout loudly.

"Come all and gather, come and listen to my words:

Who of you does not want to know what will take place in the future? The future is shrouded in darkness, but fate is etched on a hidden note in this case." (He spoke, and showed the crowd the hidden box).

"For a coin, my learned friend, the praiseworthy Geronimus, the master of all birds, shabby and hot tempered, babbling and overflowing like a well, conducting himself in anger, will take out the note.

> Wise and learned, expert and smart
> His tongue is sharp and unstable like water
> An emissary sent to the city of Smorgon
> With praise, welcome him with applause!"

And to the parrot:

> "Did I speak the truth, wise Geronimus
> And did I not contradict you in front of the crowd and the people?"

The parrot, Geronimus the apprentice, opened its mouth in the language of people, to surprise of all those who came to the market, the purchasers of wheat and merchants of flax and other merchandise.

"It is true, my *gospidin* [boss],

[Page 491]

Bring a coin, and you will hear that which is hidden!"

And this *gospidin*, his master, the owner of the music box, pointed his thumb toward the parrot, who jumped down and flew up from the platform of the cage, and covered his master's finger with his wings.

A young farmer girl, named Stastinka, took down the coin that was tied to the edge of her kerchief and gave it to the owner of the music box. The *zadarmnik*, the group from the carriage and as members of this religion are called, brought Geronimus the parrot close to the hidden box, and opened it before him. With its twisted beak, the parrot pulled out one ballot of all those arranged in the box.

The villager daughter moved to the side. From her face, it could be seen that her heart was palpitating inside. Certainly, before the end of that suspenseful day, she would take that ballot to the village head who would understand and read everything that was in store for her.

It seems that the farmer girl would return to her home happy and glad. She would run the entire way, jumping and dancing. When she would return to her parents' hut, she would sing. The members of the household would be surprised, and say:

"What has happened to our Stastinka?"

Our Stastinka, as all the members of the household, did not know that all the fortunes in the secret box of the owner of the music box were all good ones.

19. A Cake called "Kushit"[18] and an Emblem called "*Kokorda*"

This, and similar things to this, passed before the imagination of the child on account of that walk with his uncle called Shayke. The little one stood in his thoughts, with a yearning glance to the carriage and the wagons of Pinia the wagon driver.

The uncle noticed the thoughts in the heart of his little nephew, guessed what he wanted, and said:

"Prepare, my child, for tomorrow. We will go to the market tomorrow, and I will buy you a snake whistle."

"Will we also go to the parrot Geronimus?" asked the child.

"We will go to him as well."

"And now where are we going, my uncle?

"Now we are going to a place that is all sweets, to the *Proznia*, that is the confectionary of the Berberman sisters."

The child knew that shortly he would have a moment of literal enjoyment – while awake and not in the dream that he had seen previously. His eyes would see. His hands would take, and his mouth would taste.

From all the types of sweets offered to him by the red–cheeked Bererman sisters: sugar coated cakes and fruit, twisted dough dotted with nuts and almonds, colored candies in the shape of beasts and animals placed on sticks – from all these the child did not choose even one. His heart, desire, and palate were on something called "Kushit", cakes on a tall stand, black and lovely, sweeter than wine, and topped by a ring of chocolate.

[Page 492]

"My uncle, will you buy me the Kushit?" asked the child of his uncle, hurrying his steps.

"Of course I will by you the Kushit."

Do you know how to make a shortcut? – that is to jump over the path in front of you, and to go around and around until you arrive at the place without an obstacle.

The uncle wanted to cross through a straight yard and go out on the second road, from where he would head to the confectionary. However, he met the ire of the students of the Ivriya School. What does the uncle of the little one, who is no longer a child, have to do with these school children? This is the story.

There was a school in the city of Smorgon, unique of its kind, of which there is none like it in the entire country. It was founded by Rabbi Gordon's two sons, Abba and Zeev. Eventually, they became well known amongst the Jews and the gentiles in the country. They were great in thought, different in their ways, and strange in their vision to rectify humanity under the rule of freedom and justice. When they were still young, they founded the Ivriya School, in which everything was taught in Hebrew, with an accent that we do not speak, and in a manner that had never been taught in any other place: with work and play. This was a great innovation in our times, which became known in the city of Smorgon, for better or for worse.

Uncle Shayke knew how to play music. He had several musical instruments in his house. Some of them were dual harmonicas. If you wanted, you could play them with your mouth, and if you wanted, you could play them with your hand. That harmonica was prepared to entertain the children of Ivriya. On every festival and holiday, to those that adhered to the tradition of the ancestors, and those that guarded the school according to their hearts – Uncle Shayke would come and accompany the students in song, as he would play for their many performances. That day, the well-known teacher Abba

Gordin sent two of his students, one of them still studying in the *Beis Midrash* and the other who was older and served as an assistant to his teacher, to look for the young musician, the son of Reb Shmuel–Shimon.

The students found him while he was walking on the city streets with the little one, talking to him.

“We were looking for you for some time. You are summoned to our teacher, Abba.”

“Are you not jesting with me?” answered my uncle.

“If you want, we will swear by taking hold of an object,” interjected the oldest of the group.

“For example?” asked my uncle.

“On that emblem of honor that our teacher is placed on our hats today, called *Kokarda* in the vernacular.”

He said this, took off his hat, and showed him the emblem. A sheet of copper with the letter *ayin* engraved upon it.

[Page 493]

Buds flowered at its edges, as if to say that Israel will sprout from the Ivriya School.

The child heard that they call that emblem *Kokorda*. He laughed out loud, as he pronounced each syllable Ko–kor–da forward and backward.

“My Uncle, when will I get a *Kokorda*?” asked the child. The uncle did not have a chance to give an answer that would satisfy the questioner, when the oldest of the group said:

“If you want, child, you can have mine.”

He opened the pin that held the [metal] sheet inside the hat, removed the engraved copper emblem, and gave it as a present to the child. The child was happy with this object that came to him unintentionally. Since he did not know how to thank him, he uttered a nonsense phrase:

"May it be that your voice be heard from one end of the world to the other!" He said this thinking that perhaps there is nothing greater for a person than for his voice to be heard.

He did not know that he had uttered a prophecy with his mouth that would be fulfilled by that same lad from whom he had received the gift. Eventually, he became well known as a major radio announcer on Radio Moscow. The student's name was Leviatan, and he composed nice poems in Hebrew during his youth, published on the pages of "Hagan Hateatroni" whose editor was his teacher, Abba Gordin.

20. At the Synagogue of the City

Before those two, the child and his uncle, arrived at the Ivriya School, they passed the Great Synagogue of the city.

The entrance way, formed of a rectangle of hewn stones lead from Vilna Street opposite the Flour Market, directly to the lane of the synagogue. At that time, Michaelka Slop, a tall, hunchbacked, Jew, thin as a tree twig, was standing there. He was nicknamed Slop, which means pillar, because of all those traits that I have just described.

The communal administrators deliberated and agreed to make him the guardian and the lighter of the lanterns on the Jewish streets, including the large lantern at the entrance to the lane of the Great Synagogue. The child saw that Reb Michaelka was standing before the pillar, and circling the pulley at its side. He lowered the lantern, slid it down on a metal wire, until it reached his height.

He opened the lantern, cleared the wick, and poured kerosene into the receptacle. He checked it from all sides, and then raised it to the top of the pillar.

The little one stretched his head upward and stared at the bird standing on the lantern and shaking it in the wind. The lights of sunset reflected off the lantern, blinding the eyes of the child. He wanted to lower his sight, but he could not take his mind off the bird. He clapped his hands, and the feathered being flew off the top of the pillar, and stood on the bright, round molding on the eastern wall of the Great Synagogue This joyful bird joined a good group that attracted the heart of the child. Two doves from the cote [shed] of Bentza the carpenter, whose house was opposite the synagogue were fluttering back and forth and in a circle, with a sense of importance, skipping and perching on the molding. The feathers of the doves were colored as if they dipped themselves in eyeshadow.

[Page 494]

"As long as you stand looking at the bird and the doves, the sun had already set, and we will not get to the place where we said we would go," said the young uncle to the little boy, as he moved him from the place. The little one was dragged against his will as his head was still pointed toward the molding of the synagogue, which looked like a rainbow with its colors, and which was the sitting place of lovely winged creatures.

The synagogue of the city was built half of bricks and half of stones. It was tall and stately, and fitting in every way to be a house of G–d and of His people Israel.

Stairs led up from the women's gallery on the second floor to the flat roof of the synagogue. A wooden fence rose up around the length of the edges of the roof. That fence had round windows as well as holes made by people. There were cannonballs and balls of cast iron, pipes and metal bars, basins made of pitch and utensils to light a bonfire – all of these were arranged at the side of the fence. The shaft of an old cannon stuck out from one of the holes.

The city elders were able to tell about the brave deeds of their ancestors from previous generations. Were it not for the power and bravery of the early fathers, who knows if this community would have survived in peace through the times of war and tribulations, the armies of wild disturbers, who pillaged and murdered, and stood ready to kill, wipe out, and destroy all the Jews, from youth to elderly, from child to woman. From the roof of the synagogue, the men would conduct war against the gentile riffraff below, to protect the unfortunate souls who were locked in the synagogue. They would throw cannonballs and fiery torches on the heads of the gentiles, and pour boiling water from boilers and basins. Supports of bricks and stones fortified the walls of the building from the outside. Since they were constructed on a slope, they served as a kind of sled rink for the Jewish children studying in the Talmud Torah, which was located on the ground floor in the anteroom of the synagogue.

Our little one is now standing in front of the holy building, listening to the voices bursting forth from it:

Rabbi Yaakov–Boaz was teaching his chapter of *Mishna* and *Ein Yaakov* to his audience, the simple folk: tradesmen, tanners, storeowners who were able to leave their shops in the hands of their wives and children, guests passing through, and those who attended the *Beis Midrash* as they had nothing else to do. The *Beis Midrash* of Rabbi Yaakov–Boaz took up the entire right wing of the ground floor, and was too small to accommodate all those who knocked on its gates. To the left of that wing, the quiet sound of the melody of the group of Hassidim sitting in the *kloiz* of the Kojdanow and Lubavitch Hassidim rose up.

Even though they did not all form one tight group, for this one cleaved to his Rebbe and this one to his Rebbe, to whom he traveled – they formed one group for the purpose of prayer.

[Page 495]

The voices were not the main thing for the child at this time.

What was the main thing for him? The lads exiting the Talmud Torah, placing their lanterns next to the wall of the synagogue, and climbing up those supports. They went up, and slid down with resounding shouts of joy.

"Uncle, I too want..." said the child, without explaining what he wanted at the end. A hint was sufficient for Uncle Shayke, and he responded.

"And how can you stand up to them, for you are small and they are big?"

The child recalled his grandfather Reb Shmuel–Shimon, and the story with the gentile Mitran's dog Paskody, before whom he stood bravely without flinching. The child responded to his uncle:

"Do you not know, my uncle, that I am no longer afraid of Mitran's dog."

"Okay," said the uncle, "If you are as brave as you say, let's go."

They approached the place and asked to join in.

21. The Trip to Oblivion

The Cossacks!!!

The sound of the shouting of disaster rose up from the lane leading from Vilna Street to the Great Synagogue.

"The Cossacks are coming!" The call was heard from others who were going from the house to the yard, and from one road to the next.

A great pall fell upon the lane, and confused the mind of the child. Mothers burst forth from their house in weeping and shouts to look for their children and take them home. The bells of the tanneries rang and alarmed, summoning the workers. Shopkeepers closed their stores and hastened to their wives and children. The shutters were lowered. Doors were closed and locked. The streets emptied of people.

Uncle Shayke quickly grabbed the young child. He covered him with the edge of his coat under his arms. He left the slide at the Great Synagogue and ran with all his might toward the Flour Market – to the home of the parents of the little one. When they approached the house, they heard the agonized cry:

"Where is the child? Who has seen the child?"

The uncle burst inside and placed the child before his father and mother, as he said:

"Here he is!"

Tears of joy following fear welled up in their eyes.

* * *

[Page 496]

The Cossacks flooded through the streets of the city like a stream of mighty water. They were fleeing from the German brigades who were pursuing them. They arrived and camped in the city. Then they went out to mark the Jewish houses with signs, some for pillage, and some for burning.

That day, the child, his father, mother, and baby sister who was named Sima descended to the cellar of Grandfather Reb Shmuel–Shimon of blessed memory.

When they got there, they found sitting crowded there all the sons and daughters of this tall grandfather who had built the house and the cellar to serve as a safe refuge.

We sat in the darkness of that cellar for three days and nights. During those days, our child wandered the entire length and breadth of this subterranean place, as someone searching for his lost object. He looked behind every barrel and under every bench. He peeked into the storehouses and felt all the shelves.

"What are you looking for, my son?" asked Mother.

"I am looking for Grandfather."

The mother kissed her son as her tears flowed down her cheeks.

During the nights, the smell of fire and smoke reached the nostrils of those sitting in the cellar. Everyone understood that the Cossacks were burning their city.

After three days, Father exited and went to the neighbor, the gentile Mitran, asking him to hire horses and wagons.

The gentile did what Father asked. He got wagons and hitched them to horses. We sat in them and set out on our journey.

Father drove one of the wagons, with its passengers. Uncle Shayke stood strong and firm in another one, driving the horses with a steady hand.

Mitran sat on the platform of the third wagon. His dog Paskody followed along at the side of the wagon, walking leisurely and humbly.

The escapees were now some distance away. Minsk Street was already behind them. They went along the route leading to Karka, that is the village of the Jewish farmers. They stopped their horses at the orchard of Sinicki, which extended over the length of both sides of the main street. The owner of the orchard came out. He had returned not long ago from the plains of Siberia, where he had been exiled by the evil regime. He said:

"They won't be in power forever. The evil regime will disappear completely from the land. A new world will arise. I say to you in truth, you will yet return, dear brothers, to your home in peace." Sinicki's daughters approached the wagons, and gave the passengers fruits from the garden. They repeated what their father had said:

"May it be that you will return soon."

The child saw that they were covered with white clothes, with sheets over their shoulders, apparently like wings. He looked at their pale faces, that did not appear like gentile girls, and saw that they were very sad. Tears began to choke his throat. He could not control himself, and burst out crying. One of them said:

"You are already big, my child, and it is not appropriate for you to cry. Take these as well for the journey."

[Page 497]

She gave the child a linen sack with fruit that he had always liked: fox berries – called *agrast* in the vernacular, glassy and transparent. The child took out one berry, looked at it, and saw that it resembled the tear that fell from the eye of the good maiden whose appearance was similar to an angel. He could not restrain himself, and cried more.

While this caravan was standing near Sinicki's orchard, two additional wagons approached and arrived.

In one of them sat the rabbi of the city, Rabbi Menashe Ginzburg and his daughter Perel. The rabbi of the city, a righteous, upright man, sat and whispered a prayer. A Torah scroll rested in his bosom, and his *tallis* covered the holy object. Meir "Kanbal," brave, and corpulent, who instilled his fear upon the gentiles of the city and the villagers sat in the final carriage, with his small wife, Breina, beside him.

"Rabbi," said Kanbal to the rabbi of the city, "You travel in front of me. I vow that not one hair of your head will fall to the ground."

If Meir Kanbal promises such – one depends on him, for his nickname came from the gentiles of the city, who compared his might and power to a praised army commander from history, and imagined in their hearts a trait of cruelty which he did not have.

"Rabbi," Kanbal again turned to the rabbi of the city, Rabbi Menashe, "It seems to us that you did not pay attention to us, to what we said. Please your request first to G–d, and then to us. And you, the community of Israel," as Meir turned to those sitting in the wagons, "take what is in your hands, and go forth and camp." He only uttered such words of urging to bring the travelers out of the black melancholy that had overtaken their spirits.

The caravan had not yet moved from its place when the sounds of the shouting of Hurrah came from afar. The travelers turned their heads in fear in the direction from where they had come, to the Minsk Street and saw that the skies were red from the flames of the fire.

The city behind them was burning.

The mothers sobbed discretely so as not to cause their children to be afraid. The fathers urged on the horses to drive the wagons.

A stray bullet, a harbinger of bad things, passed over the wagon in which the child was sitting.

“Woe to me, the girl was hit!” She dropped her head and fainted. The members of the household stood over her and restored her with cold water and drops of valerian. The mother opened her eyes and saw Father and her son hugging her.

“It is well with our infant, praise to G–d that He saved her,” said Father. He could not restrain himself and began to cry.

“You Berl, are crying!” smiled Mother, and wiped Father's tears.

They looked at each other, clasped their hands, and were silent.

[Page 498]

And the child, as this was happening, moved from his parents, approached Uncle Shayke who was driving the horses, raised himself to him, and said:

“And when, my Uncle, we will return to visit those placed that we did not get to?”

“Don't worry, little one, about those places. We are going to new places, large and wonderful.” The child cast his eyes afar, wanting to know about what plots were awaiting him.

“There – there, at the edge of the horizon, the Zelsia Forest, were two of the faithful companions ready to greet the child: the impetuous rabbit, with upright ears, will bring the little one into the secret language of the trees. The squirrel that leaps from branch to branch for its thick nut, will make nuts fall to eat and to play with.

Across the forest, further along the road leading to the city of Minsk – stands a train. The locomotive moved quickly, spewing forth its smoke. The chains connecting the wagons grated.

A shriek of the whistle and a wail of the siren. The world shook, and moved with the child

Translator's Footnotes

1. Deuteronomy 32:7
2. See page 31.
3. *Plomp* means pump in Yiddish.
4. Two obscure phrases. *Hodu* means India. The phrase *Hodu Lashem Ki Tov* means "Praised is G–d for He is good". *Aleinu* means to us, or upon us. *Aleinu Leshabeach* is a reference to a thrice daily prayer. From *Hodui ad Aleynu* is a play on words that would mean from India to us – or something that comes to us from afar.
5. *Shor Habar* – a mystical wild ox from the Messianic era.
6. Isaiah 58:7.
7. A reference to war—likely World War I
8. See https://www.myjewishlearning.com/article/evil–eye–in–judaism/
9. See https://en.wikipedia.org/wiki/Vitis_labrusca (Could also be gooseberries).
10. The reason for the bandage is told later in this chapter.
11. Perhaps a curse.
12. See https://www.mishnahyomit.com/articles/Uktzin/310 Worlds
13. *Yaale Veyavo* (may it rise and ascend) forms part of the prayer service of festivals and Rosh Chodesh.
14. *Klopot* is troubles in Polish.
15. A play on the words *yomtov*, meaning a festival, but also a first name.
16. This sentence is repeated in Aramaic and Hebrew, with the sentence "and in the Jewish language rather than Aramaic:"
17. Free in Polish.
18. Kushi is a term for a black person.

[Pages 499-541]

Memorial Pages (Necrology) Smarhon, Belarus

Transliterated by Shalom Bronstein

יזכר
זכרם הקדוש
של אבותינו
אחינו אחיותינו
וילדינו שנרצחו
בשואה.
תהיינה דמויותיהם
חקוקות בלבותינו
ויזהירו שמותיהם
עד בוא הגאלה
השלמה

יזכר
געהיילקט דעם אנדענק פון
אונזערע טייערע און אומ-
פארגעסלעכע וואס זענען
אומגעקומען אויף קדוש השם
אין די געטאס און לאגערן
איכה יועם זהב
ישנא הכתם הטוב
תשתפכנה אבני קדש
בראש כל חוצות.
(איכה ד׳)
(ווי אזוי איז פארטונקלט דאס
גאלד פארביטן דאס טייערע
פיינגאלד די הייליקע שטיינער
צעשאטן אין אלע עק-גאסן)
די פארבליבענע משפחות
אין אמעריקע

These page numbers refer to the original Yizkor book and not this translation.

Family name(s)	First name(s)	Maiden name	Gender	Father's name	Mother's name	Name of spouse	Remarks	Page
א Alef								
AZRACHIN	Elyusha		M					503
AZRACHIN	Esther	MAGIDS	F					503
EPSTEIN	Michael		M	Zev	Sarah			503
EPSTEIN	Bella	POTASHNIK	F	Zalman	Esther			503
AROTZKER	Meir		M	Shabtai	Chaya Sarah			503
AROTZKER	Bushka	MAGIDEY	F	Michael	Chana			503
AROTZKER	Nachum		M	Meir	Bushka		On the list his mother's name is recorded as Biksha, apparently in error	503
AROTZKER	Gershon		M	Meir	Bushka		On the list his mother's name is recorded as Biksha, apparently in error	503
AROTZKER	Michael		M	Meir	Bushka		On the list his mother's name is recorded as	503

							Biksha, apparently in error	
AROTZKER	Sarah Mara		F					503
AROTZKER	Wolf		M	Shalom Yona	Tzvia			503
AROTZKER	Liebka		M	Shalom Yona	Tzvia			503
AROTZKER	Berel		M					503
AROTZKER	Moshe		M					503
ANTZLEVITZ	Baruch		M	Azriel	Feiga			503
ANTZLEVITZ	Sheina	DANISHEVSKY	F	Shimon	Marisha			503
ANTZLEVITZ	Feiva		M	Baruch	Sarah			503
ALPROVITZ	Binyamin		M	Chaim	Fruma		On the list it states that he fell in battle on the German front	503
ALGIN	Chana	JAVITZ	F	Chaim	Rivkah			503
ALGIN	Sarah		F	Shmuel	Chana			503
ALGIN	Etka		F	Shmuel	Chana			503
ALGIN	Chaim		M	Shmuel	Chana			503
ILSHANSKY	Kasal	BABRATZ	F	Yoel Baines	Esther			503
ILSHANSKY	Batya		F	Moshe	Rasel			503

ILSHANSKY	Micha		M	Moshe	Rasel			503
ILSHANSKY	Chaim		M	Moshe	Rasel			503
ALPROVITZ	Mulia							503
ALPROVITZ	Lama	DANISHEVSKY	F					503
ALPER	Sonia		F					503
ALPER	Buma		M	Yochanan	Sonia			503
ALPER			M	Yochanan	Sonia			503
ALPROVITZ	Ya'akov		M	Shalom	Chaya			503
ITKIND	Moshe		M					503
ITKIND	Reiche		F	Berel				504
ITKIND	Hirshel		M	Moshe	Reicha			504
ITKIND	Sonia		F					504
ITKIND	Chana		F	Hirshel	Sonia			504
ITKIND	Ya'akov		M	Hirshel	Sonia			504
ITKIND	Yoel		M	Hirshel	Sonia			504
ITKIND	Leibel		M	Moshe	Reicha			504
ITKIND	Zenia		F					504
ITKIND	Esther		F	Leibel	Zashenia			504
ITKIND	Shmuel		M	Moshe	Reicha			504
ITKIND	Rachel		F					504
ITKIND	Azriel		M	Shmuel	Rachel			504

AROTZKER	Leizer Wolf		M					504
AROTZKER	Mariasha		F					504
AROTZKER	Chaya		F	Leizer Wolf	Mariashe			504
ALPROVITZ	Abba		M					504
ALPROVITZ	Golda		F					504
ALPROVITZ	Sarah		F	Abba	Golda			504
ALPROVITZ	Koppel		M	Abba	Golda			504
ALISHKAVITZ	Eliyahu		M					504
ALISHKAVITZ	Shosha	RABINOWITZ	F	Yitzhak	Liba			504
ALISHKAVITZ	Zalman		M	Eliyahu	Shosha			504
ALISHKAVITZ	Hadassah		F	Eliyahu	Shosha			504
OBSOIVITZ	Minna	YORESHNER	F	Leib	Batya			504
OBSOIVITZ	Eliezer		M	Ya'akov Shalom	Sheina Rachel			504
OBSOIVITZ	Asher		M	Eliezer	Minna			504
OBSOIVITZ	Rachel		F	Eliezer	Minna			504
OBSOIVITZ	Ya'akov		M	Eliezer	Minna			504
ANGOR	Shalom Yona		M					504
ANGOR	Tzvia		F	Leibel	Chasia			504
ANGOR	Miriam		F	Shalom Yona	Tzvia			504
ALPROVITZ	Velvel		M					504

ALPROVITZ	Menucha		F					504
ALPROVITZ	Zalman		M	Velvel	Menucha			504
ALPROVITZ			F	Velvel	Menucha			504
ASINOVSKY	Yerachmiel		M				On the list the family name appears as ASINOVSK, apparently in error	504
ASINOVSKY	Chana		F					504
ASINOVSKY	Gottlieb		M	Yerachmiel	Chana		On the list it states 'in the [Concentration] Camp' as place of death	505
ASINOVSKY	Chaya		F	Yerachmiel	Chana		On the list it states 'in the [Concentration] Camp' as place of death	505
ASINOVSKY	Meir		M	Yerachmiel	Chana			505
ASINOVSKY	Chana		F					505
ASINOVSKY	Lipa		M	Shmuel Moshe	Chana			505
ASINOVSKY	Peiva		M	Shmuel Moshe	Chana			505
ASINOVSKY	Shimshon		M	Shmuel	Chana			505

				Moshe				
AROTZKER	Leibel		M	Yitzhak				505
AROTZKER			M					505
AROTZKER		SHER	F					505
ALPROVITZ			M				On the list it states that 'he is the brother-in-law of SHER'	505
ALPROVITZ	Sonia	SHER	F					505
ALPROVITZ	Bila		F					505
ABRAMOWITZ	Ya'akov Leib		M					505
ABRAMOWITZ	Rachel		F	Ya'akov Leib				505
ABRAMOWITZ	Frimel		F	Ya'akov Leib				505
ASINOVSKY	Sarah Feiga		F					505
ASINOVSKY	Liba	GREIS	F	Chaim Baines	Devorah Maral			505
ASINOVSKY	David		M		Sarah Feiga			505
ASINOVSKY	Ya'akov		M		Sarah Feiga			505
AROTZKER	Chatzkel		M					505
AROTZKER	Sarah Feiga		F					505

ב **Bet**

BRODNA	Yehoshua Leib		M	Shalom	Devorah			505
BRODNA	Fraydel	BRODNER	F	Shlomo	Ada			505
BRODNA	Devorah		F	Yehoshua Leib	Fraydel			505
BRODNA	Dasha		F	Yehoshua Leib	Fraydel			505
BLUM	Yitzhak		M	Leizer	Keila			505
BLUM	Rachel	RABINOWITZ	F					505
BODGOR	Yeshayahu		M	Zalman	Leah			505
BODGOR	Sheina	LEVIN	F	Leib	Donia		On the list it states the place of death was Mikhalishok	505
BODGOR	Nachum		M	Yishayahu	Sheina			505
BODGOR	Zalman		M	Yishayahu	Sheina			505
BODGOR	Baruch		M	Yishayahu	Sheina			505
BERNSTEIN	Yosef		M					506
BERNSTEIN	Chana		F					506
BERNSTEIN	Shmuel		M	Yosef	Chana			506
BRODNY	Eliyahu		M					506
BRODNY	Batya		F					506
BRODNY	Cheina Esther		F	Eliyahu	Batya			506

BRODNY	Mariasha		F	Eliyahu	Batya			506
BRODNY	Shama Leib		M	Eliyahu	Batya			506
BRODNY	Moshe		M					506
BRODNY	Chana		F					506
BADNAS	Ya'akov Nute		M					506
BADNAS	Gittel		F					506
BADNAS	Yudel		M					506
BADNAS	Yehoshua		M					506
BADNAS	Chana		F					506
BADNAS	Itka		F					506
BRODNY	Batya	DANISHEVSKY	F					506
BRODNY	Menasha		M					506
BRODNY	David		M					506
BRODNY	Chava		F					506
BRODNY	Riva		F					506
BRODNY	Chaya		F					506
BRODNY			M		Chaya			506
BOROVSKY	Yisrael		M					506
BOROVSKY			F			Yisrael		506
BOROVSKY	Baruch		M	Yisrael				506
BOROVSKY	Hinda	TOLTZ	F					506

BOROVSKY	Rosa		F					506
BOROVSKY	Hirsh		M				The list states the place of death was Sol	506
BOSHKNITZ	Meir		M	Shmuel	Riva			506
BOSHKNITZ	Gershon		M	Shmuel	Riva			506
BERNSTEIN	Velvel		M					506
BERNSTEIN	Sarah Feiga		F					506
BERNSTEIN	Yosef		M	Velvel	Sarah Feiga		A prisoner of war; the list states that he died in captivity	506
BERNSTEIN	Moshe		M	Velvel	Sarah Feiga			506
BERNSTEIN	Reiche		F	Velvel	Sarah Feiga			506
BERNSTEIN	Gittel		F	Velvel	Sarah Feiga			506
BERNSTEIN	Bracha		F	Velvel	Sarah Feiga			506
BONIMOVITZ	Baruch		M					507
BONIMOVITZ	Moshe		M					507
BONIMOVITZ			M	Baruch	Masha			507
BOSAL	Aharon		M					507
BOSAL	Hinda		F					507
BOSAL	Mordecai		M	Aharon	Hinda			507

BOSAL	Leizer		M	Aharon	Hinda			507
BOSAL	Shalom		M	Aharon	Hinda			507
BOSAL	Leah		F	Aharon	Hinda			507
BADNAS	Batya	SHINYOK	F	Aharon	Devorah			507
BADNAS	Devorah		F	Yosef	Batya			507
BADNAS	Rachel		F	Yosef	Batya			507
BADNAS			M	Yosef	Batya			507
BOROCHOVITZ	Matla	BORON	F	Shepsel	Chaya			507
BOGLAR		LEVKOV	F	Yoel	Leah			507
BERKMAN	Shalom		M					507
BERKMAN	Feiga		F					507
BERKMAN	David Leib		M	Shalom	Feiga		The list states that he was a Partisan	507
BERKMAN	Esther		F					507
BERKMAN	Sima		F	Shalom	Feiga			507
BERKMAN	Rachel		F	Shalom	Feiga			507
BERKMAN	Ida		F	Shalom	Feiga			507
BERLIN	Devorah Batya	RUDOMIN	F	Avraham	Masha			507
BROIDA	Chaya		F					507
BROIDA	Wolf		M				His personal name on the	507

							list is Wolf	
BROIDA		SHAPIRA	F			Wolf	On the list the name of her husband is recorded as Wolf	507
BERNSTEIN	Avraham		M					507
BERNSTEIN	Risha		F					507
BRODNER	Pesia		F					507
BRODNER	Koppel		M	Zisel	Pesia			507
BRODNER	Motel		M	Zisel	Pesia			507
BRODNER	Yeshayahu		M	Zisel	Pesia			507
BRODNER	Yitzhak		M	Zisel	Pesia			507
BRODNY	Moshe		M	Avraham	Minna			507
BRODNY	Minna		F	Moshe	Mira			508
BRODNY	Reuven		M					508
BRODNY	Chana		F	Avraham	Minna			508
BRODNY	Leah		F	Avraham	Minna			508
BINDMAN	Ber		M					508
BINDMAN	Rivkah		F					508
BRODNY	Ber		M					508
BRODNY	Reizel		F					508
BERGER	Velvel		M					508

BERGER	Sarah	SHAMASH	F	Avraham Chaim	Rivkah			508
BRANDWEIN	Mira	SHERTOK	F					508
BRANDWEIN			M			Mira		508
BRODNY	David		M					508
BRODNY			F				The first sister of David BRODNY	508
BRODNY			F				The second sister of David BRODNY	508
BRONZNIK								508
BRODNY	David		M	Bar				508
BRODNY			F			David		508
ג **Gimmel**								
GOFSOYVITZ	Leah	MOSTBLISHAKER	F	Elazar	Esther			508
GOFSOYVITZ	Shmuel		M	Zalman Leib	Ahuva			508
GOLOB	Miriam		F	Avraham	Rachel			508
GOLOB	Alter		M	Noach	Miriam			508
GOLOB	Chana		F					508
GOLOB	Chaya		F	Alter	Chana			508

GOLOB	Aharon		M					508
GOLOB		MILIKOVSKY	F			Aharon		508
GILMAN	Rosa		F					508
GALPRIN	Yisrael		M	Mordecai	Chaya			508
GALPRIN	Feigel	KIDDUSHIN	F	Bunia				508
GALPRIN	Sonia		F	Yisrael	Feigel			508
GREIS	Aharon Shlomo		M	Shimon				508
GREIS	Matla		F	Menachem				508
GURVITZ	Guta		F					508
GURVITZ	Nechama		F	Kopel	Gita		The list states the place of death was Kovno	508
GURVITZ	Rachel Leah	DANISHEVSKY	F				The list states the place of death was Kovno	508
GURVITZ	Reuven		M	Nehemia	Rachel Leah		The list states the place of death was Kovno	508
GALPRIN	Avraham Mordecai		M					509
GALPRIN	Zelda	BOTWINIK	F					509

GALPRIN	Asher		M			Esther		509
GALPRIN	Esther	GALPROVITZ	F			Asher		509
GALPRIN			M	Asher	Esther			509
GALPRIN	Sender		M					509
GASS	Yechiel		M	Shimshon	Sheina			509
GASS	Sarah		F					509
GALPRIN	Eliyahu		M					509
GALPRIN			F			Eliyahu		509
GITLITZ		MAGIDEY	F					509
GREIS	Meir		M					509
GREIS			F			Meir		509
GREIS	Avraham		M					509
GREIS			F			Avraham		509
GRINGAOZ			M					509
GRINGAOZ			F					509
GREENBERG	Chaim Yitzhak		M	Binyamin	Temma			509
GREENBERG			F				On the list it states that she died as a partisan	509
GALGOR	Chanoch		M					509
GALGOR			F			Chanoch		509

GALGOR	David Yitzhak		M					509
GALGOR			F			David Yitzhak		509
GALGOR	Sheina		F				It is probable that the family name was different	509
GALGOR	Hinda		F					509
GREENBERG	Heshya		F					509
GASS	Shimshon		M					509
GASS	Sheina		F					509
GASS	Tzipa		F	Shimshon	Sheina			509
GASS	Ayzik		M	Shimshon	Sheina			509
GASS	Saral		M					509
GASS	Zalman		M	Sherel				509
GASS	Yisrael		M	Sherel				509
GASS	Rachel		F	Sherel				509
GASS	Yitzhak		M					509
GASS	Batya		F					509
GLAZAR	Feiga	KATZ	F	Yosef	Yacha			509
GLAZAR	Tzipa		F	Avraham	Feiga		On the list the date of her death is recorded as 1952 in	509

							Zhezmor	
GLAZAR	Yechiel		M	Avraham	Feiga		The list states the place of death was Kovno	509
GLAZAR	Nachman		M	Ya'akov	Tzipora			509
GLAZAR	Moshe		M	Ya'akov	Tzipora			509
GLAZAR	Nechama		F	Ya'akov	Tzipora			510
GLAZAR	Perl		F	Ya'akov	Tzipora			510
GURVITZ	Ama	TABORISKY	F	Avraham	Devorah			510
GARLIK			M				Profession listed as scribe; the list states the place of death was Lebedevo	510
GARLIK			F				Wife of the scribe; the list states the place of death was Lebedevo	510
GARLIK	Pachma		F				The list states the place of death was Lebedevo	510
GARLICH	Tuvia		M				The list states the place of	510

							death was Lebedevo	
GARLICH	Leib		M				The list states the place of death was Lebedevo	510
GARLIK	Hinda		F				The list states the place of death was Lebedevo	510
GANZBURG	Alter		M					510
GANZBURG	Rachel		F					510
GORLAND	Gutel		F				A prisoner of war; the list states that she died in captivity	510
GURVITZ	Sarah		F					510
GALPROVITZ	Nechama	SCHWARTZ	F	Eliyahu	Liba			510
GALPROVITZ	Zelig		M	Yosef				510
GALPROVITZ	Moshe		M	Zelig	Nechama			510
GREIS	Leah	DANISHEVSKY	F	Shimon	Masha		The list states the place of death was Sol	510
GREIS	Bryna		F	Shmuel	Leah			510

GREIS	Batya		F	Shmuel	Leah			510
GREIS	Leib		M	Shmuel	Leah			510
GREIS	Efraim		M	Zvi	Rachel			510
GREIS	Chana		F	Shlomo	Aliza			510
GREIS	Zvi		M	Efraim	Chana			510
GREIS	Aliza		F	Efraim	Chana			510
GREIS	Shalom		M	Efraim	Chana			510
GREIS	Reuven		M	Shlomo	Aliza			510
GREIS	Devorah		F					510
GREIS	Alter		M	Avraham Reuven	Devorah			510
GREIS	Shlomo		M					510
GREIS	Sarah		F					510
GREIS	Leah		F					510
GLAZAR	Reuven		M					510
GREIS	Sarah		F					510
GLAZAR	Matla		F					510
GLAZAR	Chaim Yisrael		M	Reuven	Matla			510
GLAZAR	Shmuel		M	Reuven	Matla			510
GLAZAR	Chana		F					511
GLAZAR	Miriam		F	Chaim Yisrael	Chana			511

GALPROVITZ	Gutel		M					511
GALPROVITZ	Rachel	LIPKER	F					511
GALPROVITZ	Rodel		F		Gutel Rachel			511
GALPROVITZ	Keila		F	Gutal	Rachel			511
GALPROVITZ	Yosef		M					511
GALPROVITZ	Reizel	DAUL	F	Yitzhak	Feiga			511
GREIS	Shalom		M					511
GREIS	Berta		F					511
GREIS	Leib		M	Shalom	Berta			511
GREIS			F	Shalom	Berta			511
GURVITZ	Sarah		F					511
GURVITZ	David		M	Elyakim	Sarah			511
GREENBERG	Chana Rachel		F					511
GREENBERG	Riva		F	Chaim Avraham	Chana Rachel			511
GREENBERG	Elyusha		M	Chaim Avraham	Chana Rachel			511
GREENBERG	Temma	KATZ	F					511
GLAZAR	Rivkah	BERLIN	F	Shlomo	Devorah Batya			511
GLAZAR	Yitzhak		M					511
GLAZAR	Tzipora		F	Yitzhak	Rivkah			511

GLAZAR	Shulamit		F					511
GURVITZ	Ya'akov Boaz		M					511
GURVITZ	Etel		F					511
GREIS	Berel		M					511
GREIS	Ama		F					511
GREIS	Chana		F	Berel	Ama			511
GREIS	Hirsh		M					511
GREIS	Mara		F					511
GURVITZ	Abrasha		M	Shlomo				511
GURVITZ	Rosa		F	Shlomo				511
GOLDBERG	Meir		M					511
GOLDBERG	Minna		F					511
GOLDBERG	Bila		F	Meir	Manya			511
GOLDBERG	Esther		F	Meir	Manya			512
GERSHNOVITZ	Avraham		M			Mara		512
GERSHNOVITZ	Mara		F			Avraham		512
GLOV	Raphael		M			Sarah Feiga		512
GLOV	Sarah Feiga	MIADLER	F			Raphael		512
GLOV	Shaul		M	Rafael	Sarah Feiga			512
GLOV	Yona		M	Rafael	Sarah Feiga			512
GREIS	Shimon		M			Mara		512

						Devorah		
GREIS	Mara Devorah		F			Shimon		512
GREIS	Chaim		M	Shimon	Mara Devorah	Sarah		512
GREIS	Sarah		F			Chaim		512
GREIS	Meir		M	Shimon	Mara Devorah			512
GREIS	Chaim Beinas		M			Devorah Merl		512
GREIS	Devorah Merl		F			Chaim Baines		512
GREIS	Leibel		M	Chaim Baines	Devorah Maral			512
GREIS	Pesach Hirsh		M	Chaim Baines	Devorah Maral			512
GREIS	Baruch		M	Chaim Baines	Devorah Maral			512
ד **Dalet**								
DWORKIN			M					512
DWORKIN			F				On the list his profession is listed as 'the baker from Lebedevo'	512
DANISHEVSKY	Avraham		M	Shmuel	Esther			512

DANISHEVSKY	Doba		F						512
DANISHEVSKY	Shimon		M	Shmuel	Esther				512
DRYN	Chaim		M						512
DRYN	Pesia		F						512
DRYN	Leibel		M	Chaim	Pesia				512
DRYN	Sachne		M	Chaim	Pesia				512
DRYN	Yosef		M						512
DRYN	Bila		F						512
DRYN	Chaim David		M	Yosef	Baila				512
DRYN	Meir		M	Yosef	Baila				512
	Batya		F						512
	Eliyahu		M						512
	Ita		F	Eliyahu	Batya				512
	Yosef		M	Eliyahu	Batya				512
	Rachel Leah		F	Eliyahu	Batya				512
	Fruma		F	Eliyahu	Batya				512
	Liza		F	Eliyahu	Batya				513
DRYN	Batya		F						513
DRYN	Leizer		M						513
DRYN	Sarah		F						513
DANISHEVSKY	Saral	ANTZLEVITZ	F	Moshe				On the list it states that the place of	513

							death was Vilna - Ponar	
DANISHEVSKY	Leizer		M					513
DANISHEVSKY	Gittel		F					513
DANISHEVSKY	Lealke		F	Leizer	Gittel			513
DANISHEVSKY	Yache		F					513
DANISHEVSKY	Dalia		F	Lialkel	Yacha			513
DANISHEVSKY	Shmuel		M					513
DANISHEVSKY	Leib		M	Shmuel	Bryna		The list states the place of death was Kovno	513
DANISHEVSKY	Feiga		F	Leib	Doba		The list states that the place of death was Kaisiadorys	513
DANISHEVSKY	Bruker		M	Leib	Doba		The list states that the place of death was Kaisiadorys	513
DANISHEVSKY	Yerachmiel		M					513
DANISHEVSKY	Hertzka		M	Yerachmiel	Rivkah			513
DANISHEVSKY	Shimon		M	Yerachmiel	Rivkah		On the list it states that the place of death was	513

							Alt-Vileike	
DANISHEVSKY	Baruch		M	Yerachmiel	Rivkah		On the list it states that the place of death was Alt-Vileike	513
DANISHEVSKY	Sarah		F	Yerachmiel	Rivkah			513
DANISHEVSKY	Gusia		F					513
DANISHEVSKY	Meir		M					513
DANISHEVSKY	Henya	GREIS	F					513
DANISHEVSKY	Reuven		M					513
DANISHEVSKY	Nechama		F					513
DANISHEVSKY	Michael		M		Nechama			513
DANISHEVSKY	Sheina		F		Nechama			513
DANISHEVSKY	Luba		F					513
DANISHEVSKY	Avraham		M	Baruch	Gittel			513
DANISHEVSKY	Yeshayahu		M	Shimon	Miriam			513
DANISHEVSKY	Baruch		M					513
DANISHEVSKY	Velvel		M	Baruch	Gittel		On the list it states that 'he was a prisoner of war'	513
DANISHEVSKY	Moshe		M	Baruch	Gittel			513
DANISHEVSKY	Ayzik		M	Reuven				513

DANISHEVSKY	Eshke		F					513
DANISHEVSKY	Chana		F	Ayzik	Eshka			513
DANISHEVSKY			M	Ayzik	Eshka			513
DANISHEVSKY	Shimon		M					513
DANISHEVSKY	Shmuel David		M					514
DANISHEVSKY	Gittel		F					514
DANISHEVSKY	Rachla		F	Shmuel David	Gittel			514
DANISHEVSKY	Baruch		M	Velvel	Gittel			514
DANISHEVSKY	Rachel	BOROCHOVITZ	F	Dov	Matla			514
DANISHEVSKY	Shmuel Ber		M	Shalom	Rachel			514
DANISHEVSKY	Chaya		F	Shalom	Rachel			514
DANISHEVSKY	Shalom		M	Shmuel	Esther			514
DANISHEVSKY	Sarah		F	Dov	Matla			514
DANISHEVSKY			F	Leib	Sarah			514
DANISHEVSKY	Nachman		M	Leib	Sarah			514
DANISHEVSKY	Leib		M	Yosef	Tzipora		The list states the place of death was Lebedevo	514
DANISHEVSKY	Chaim Leizer		M					514
DANISHEVSKY	Reizel		F		Hoda			514

DANISHEVSKY	Sarah		F	Chaim Leizer	Reizel			514
DANISHEVSKY	Hoda		F	Chaim Leizer	Reizel			514
DANISHEVSKY	Yisrael Yitzhak		M	Shalom	Chasia			514
DANISHEVSKY	Raphael		M	Yisrael Yitzhak	Chaya Sarah Rivkah			514
DANISHEVSKY	Gronya		F	Yisrael Yitzhak	Chaya Sarah Rivkah			514
DANISHEVSKY	Batya		F	Yisrael Yitzhak	Chaya Sarah Rivkah			514
DANISHEVSKY	Pesia		F	Yisrael Yitzhak	Chaya Sarah Rivkah			514
DANISHEVSKY	Shmuel		M					514
DANISHEVSKY	Chana		F					514
DYOL	Leib		M					514
DYOL	Alta		F					514
DYOL	Yitzhak		M	Leib	Alta			514
DRYN	Ya'akov		M	Eliyahu				514
DRYN	Mordecai		M	Ya'akov	Malka			514
DRYN	Sonia		F					514
DRYN	Yosef		M	Ya'akov	Malka			514

DRYN	Rivkah		F	Ya'akov	Malka			514
DRYN	Bunya		F	Ya'akov	Malka			514
DANISHEVSKY	Batya		F					514
DANISHEVSKY	Berel		M	Reuven				514
DANISHEVSKY	Rachel Itka		F	Aharon	Nechama			514
DANISHEVSKY	Baruch		M	Yisrael				514
DANISHEVSKY	Yenta	DANISHEVSKY	F					515
DANISHEVSKY			M			Yenta		515
DANISHEVSKY	Yosef		M					515
DANISHEVSKY	Tzipa		F					515
DANISHEVSKY	Yisrael		M	Yosef	Tzipa			515
DANISHEVSKY	Batla		F					515
DANISHEVSKY	Feiga Bella	DANISHEVSKY	F	Noach Eideh	Matla			515
DANISHEVSKY			M			Feiga Bella		515
ה **Hey**								
HALPRIN	Avigdor Moshe		M	Ya'akov	Feiga			515
HALPRIN	Bella	RUBIN	F					515
HALPRIN	Yosef		M	Avigdor Moshe	Bila			515
HALPRIN			F	Avigdor Moshe	Bila			515

HORWITZ	Esther Rivkah	PARVOSKY	F	Shimon Yosef	Sarah Bila			515
HORWITZ	Sheindel		F	Avraham Eliezer	Esther Rivkah			515
HORWITZ	Shimon Yosef		M	Ya'akov Boaz	Etel			515
HORWITZ	Alla		F	Shimon Yosef	Sheindel			515
HORWITZ	Chana		F	Shimon Yosef	Sheindel			515
HORWITZ	Avraham Eliezer		M	Shimon Yosef	Sheindel			515
HORWITZ	Yisrael		M					515
HORWITZ	Leah	YANOVSKY	F	Sinai	Chaya			515
ו **Vav**								
WINHAUS	Eliyahu		M	Zalman	Tzirl		The list states that the place of death was Kaisiadorys, Lithuania	515
WINHAUS	Zalman		M				The list states the place of death was Lebedevo	515
VITKIN	Reizel		F					515
VILNER	Eliezer		M				The list states the	515

							place of death was Lebedevo	
VILNER	Kreina		F				The list states the place of death was Lebedevo	515
VALINSKY	Genya		F				On the list the family name recorded is VALINSKY	515
VALINSKY	Chaya		F	Shlomo	Genia			515
VALINSKY	Yisrael		M	Shlomo	Genia			515
VALPOV	Yoel		M					515
VALPOV	Dora	GILMAN	F	Shabtai	Rosa			515
VALPOV	Shmuel		M	Yoel	Dora		The place of death is listed as Shinberg	515
WEINER	Chasia	ALONSKY	F	Moshe	Rosa			515
WEINER	Moshe		M	Aharon	Chasia			515
VEITZ	Eliyahu		M				On the list it states that he was the father of Malgosia the teacher	515
VIDSKY	Alter		M					516

VIDSKY	Frimel	MIADLER	F					516
VIDSKY	Sarah		F	Alter	Frumel			516
VIDSKY	Hirsh Yehuda		M	Alter	Frumel			516
VIDSKY	Tzila		F	Alter	Frumel			516
VILENCHIK	Leib		M					516

ז **Zayin**

ZAVODNIK	Shmuel		M					516
ZISKOVITZ	Ozer		M					516
ZISKOVITZ	Eliyahu		M	Ozer	Sarah			516
ZISKOVITZ			M	Ozer	Sarah		On the list it states 'the son of Etel'	516
ZARTZER	Reuven		M					516
ZARTZER	Rachel		F					516
ZARTZER	Koppel		M	Reuven	Rachel			516
ZARTZER			F			Kopel		516
ZAMIEVSKY								516
ZOVISKY			F					516
SILVERMAN	Elka	SHNITT	F	Nachum Reuven	Shprintza			516
SILVERMAN	Shmarya		M	Leib	Elka			516

ח **Chet**

CHADASH	Chava	MALKAS	F	Chaim	Batya			516
CHADASH	Moshe		M					516
CHADASH	Shlomo		M	Moshe	Chava			516
CHADASH	David		M	Moshe	Chava			516
CHADASH	Lipa		M					516
CHADASH	Chaya		F					516
CHADASH	David Yitzhak		M	Lippa	Chaya			516
CHADASH	Sima		F	Lippa	Chaya			516
CHADASH	Tzvia		F	Lippa	Chaya			516
CHADASH	Chaim Meir		M	Lippa	Chaya			516
CHADASH	Slava		F	Lippa	Chaya			516
CHADASH	Yudel		M					516
CHADASH	Pinchas		M	Yudel			On the list it states 'he fell on the front during the war'	516
CHADASH	Ben-Zion		M					516
CHADASH	Riva		F					516
CHADASH	Ayzik		M	Ben-Zion	Riva			516
CHADASH	Sonia		F	Ben-Zion	Riva		On the list it states - Partisans	516
CHADASH	Fruma	SITZKEVER	F					516

CHADASH	Yeshayahu		M					517
CHADASH	Chaya		F	Yishayahu	Fruma			517
CHADASH	Avraham		M	Yishayahu	Fruma		On the list the year of birth appears as 1829 apparently in error	517
CHADASH	Golda		F	Yishayahu	Fruma			517
CHADASH	Ya'akov		M					517
CHADASH	Reuven		M	Ya'akov	Hinda			517
CHADASH			F			Reuven		517
CHADASH	Simcha		M	Ya'akov	Hinda			517
CHADASH			F					517
CHADASH	Bumka		M					517
CHADASH	Idel		F					517
CHADASH	Yosele		M					517
CHADASH	Chaim Reuven		M					517
CHAYAT			M				On the list it states 'the father,' probaby of Freyda, Bilah & Ya'akov	517
CHAYAT	Frayda		F					517

CHAYAT	Bila		F					517
CHAYAT	Ya'akov		M					517
CHOREG	Dr.		M					517
CHOREG			F				The wife of the physician	517
CHOREG			M				The son of the physician	517
CHEN	Leib		M					517
CHEN			F			Leib		517
CHEN	Mordecai		M					517
CHADASH	Yoshe Pinya		M					517
CHADASH			F			Yosha Pinya		517
CHADASH	Cheina		F	Yehoshua Pinya	Leah			517
CHAZAN	Gutman		M					517
CHAZAN	Hinda		F					517
CHAMARKSY	Hirshel		M					517
CHAMARKSY	Bila		F					517
CHADASH	Chaim Leib		M			Henya	The family status and relationship is conjectured	517

CHADASH	Henya		F			Chaim Leib	The family status and relationship is conjectured	517
CHAZAN	Reuven		M					517
CHAZAN	Sheina		F					517
CHAZAN	Baruch		M					517
CHAZAN	Avraham		M					517
CHADASH	Moshe		M					517
CHADASH	Avraham		M					517
CHADASH	Moshe		M					517
CHADASH	Levi		M					517
ט **Tet**								
TABORISKY	Golda	AXELROD	F	Yisrael				517
TABORISKY	Sarah Sonia		F	Natan	Golda			518
TABORISKY	Sheina Riva	MISKIN	F				The list states the place of death was Sol	518
TABORISKY	Yosef		M	Baruch Natan	Bryna			518
TABORISKY	Devorah	GONZBERG	F	Yehuda				518
TABORISKY	Yona		M	Baruch Natan	Bryna			518

TABORISKY	Feiva		M	Feiva			It is not clear whether Feiva is his personal name or that of his father	518
TABORISKY	Chana	KOVERSKY	F	Avraham				518
TABORISKY	Ida	HALPRIN	F	Ya'akov	Feiga			518
TOLTZ	Henya		F					518
TARKINSKY	Moshe		M					518
TARKINSKY	Esther		F		Chaya			518
י **Yod**								
YABLONOVITZ	Isser		M	Meir	Chaya			518
YABLONOVITZ	Aidel	GERSHOWITZ	F	Leib	Feiga			518
YABLONOVITZ	Alta		F	Isser	Aidel			518
YABLONOVITZ	Moshele		M	Isser	Aidel			518
YABLONOVITZ	Azriel		M	Meir				518
YABLONOVITZ	Miriam		F					518
YABLONOVITZ	Yosef		M	Azriel	Miriam			518
YABLONOVITZ	Tzvia		F	Azriel	Miriam			518
YUDELVITZ	Chana		F					518
YUDELVITZ	Yitzhak		M					518
YUDELVITZ	David		M					518

YORESHNER	Batya		F					518
YORESHNER	Feivel		M	Leib	Batya			518
YORESHNER	Berel		M	Feivel				518
YORESHNER	Chaim		M	Leib	Batya			518
YORESHNER	Sarah		F					518
JAVITZ BERMAN	Nachman		M	Chaim	Rivkah		On the list it states 'Nachman JAVITZ from the BERMAN family'	518
JAVITZ	Golda	BRODNA	F	Avraham	Minna			518
JAVITZ	Gita	KARPEL	F	Nachman	Golda			518
JAVITZ	Chaim		M	Nachman	Golda			518
JOACHIM	Yitzhak		M	Mendel				518
JOACHIM	Bila		F	Ya'akov	Chasia			519
JOACHIM	Sioma		F					519
JOACHIM	Nachum		M					519
JOACHIM			F					519
JOACHIM	Yenta		F					519
JOACHIM	Chaya		F					519
JOACHIM	Yechiel		M	Chaim	Bryna			519
JOACHIM	Dalia	KATZ	F	Yitzhak	Chana Riva		It is probable that her personal	519

							name was Tzila	
JOACHIM	Chaim		M	Yechiel	Tzila		It is probable that the personal name of his mother was Dalia	519
JOACHIM	Sonia		F	Yechiel	Tzila		It is probable that the personal name of her mother was Dalia	519
YINES	Sarah		F	Avraham	Rivkah			519
YOKOB	Avigdor		M					519
YOKOB	Sheina		F					519
JACOBSON	Mordecai Leib		M	Avigdor				519
JACOBSON	Tzvia	MILIKOVSKY	F					519
JACOBSON	Moshe		M	Mordecai Leib	Tzvia			519
JACOBSON	Noach		M	Mordecai Leib	Tzvia		On the list it states 'he was a prisoner of war'	519
JACOBSON	Shlomo		M	Mordecai Leib	Tzvia		On the list it states 'he was a prisoner of war in	519

							Germany'	
JACOBSON	Yerachmiel		M	Mordecai Leib	Tzvia		On the list it states 'he was a soldier who fell on the front in the army'	519
YOKOB	Bella		F	Mordecai Leib	Sheina			519
YOKOB	Moshe		M					519
YOKOB	Leib		M					519
YOKOB	Yekutiel		M					519
YOKOB	Yisrael		M					519
JAVITZ	Elka		F					519
JAVITZ	Sonia		F	Melech	Elka			519
JAVITZ	Moshe		M					519
JAVITZ	Bila		F	Zalman	Masha			519
YOCHLIS			M				On the list it states 'the baker from Vilna'	519
YOCHLIS			M				On the list it states 'the baker from Sol'	519
YAZGUR	Fraydel		F					519
YAZGUR	Luba		F					519

כ **Kaf**

KATZ	Tzila	BELIN	F	Shlomo	Devorah Batya			519
KATZ	Ya'akov Yashka		M	Gedalyahu	Tzila		On the list it states that he fell as a partisan in battle with the Germans near Svir	519
KATZ	Asher		M	Shmaryahu	Chasina			520
KATZ	Sarah		F					520
KATZ	Leah		F	Asher	Sarah			520
KATZ	Yochanan		M	Asher	Sarah			520
KATZ	Yisrael		M	Chaim	Hinda			520
KATZ	Esther	TOLTZ	F					520
KATZ			M	Yisrael	Esther			520
KATZ	Moshe		M	Chaim	Hinda			520
KATZ	Chaim		M					521
KATZ	Hinda		F					522
KATZ			M	Chaim	Hinda			520
KATZ	Avraham		M					520
KATZ			F			Avraham		520
KATZ	Ida		F	Avraham				520

KATZ	Yosef		M					520
KATZ	Avraham		M	Yosef	Yocha		On the list it states the place of death as 'in the Concentration Camp'	520
KATZ	Gita	SHINYOK	M	Aharon	Devorah			520
KATZ	Ya'akov		M	Yosef	Yocha			520
KATZ	Gensia	GARLINSKY	F		Sarah Gita			520
KATZ	Shaul		M	Ya'akov	Genesia			520
KATZ	Chana Riva		F	Zvi	Sarah	Yitzhak		520
KATZ	Hirshel		M	Yitzhak	Chana Riva			520
KATZ	Yitzhak		M	Hirshel	Etel			520
KATZ	Itche Meir		M				On the list the personal name recorded is Atza Meir	520
KATZ	Gensel		M					520
KATZ	Sarah		F	Eida Meir	Gensel		On the list it states the place of death was 'in the Concentration Camp'	520
KATZ	Leibel		M	Eida Meir	Gensel		On the list it states the	520

							place of death was 'in the Concentration Camp'	
KATZ	Zelda		F	Eida Meir	Gensel		On the list it states the place of death was 'in the Concentration Camp'	520
KATZ	Shmuel		M					520
KATZ	Chanya		F					520
KATZ	Lonia		F					520
KAGNOVITZ	Shaul		M	Yoel			On the list it states 'a soldier he fell in battle in the army'	520
KAGNOVITZ	Ita		F	Yoel			On the list it states the place of death was 'in the [Concentration] Camps'	520
KAGAN			M				On the list it states 'the father,' he was probably the father of Yitzhak and the husband	520

							of Esther	
KAGAN	Esther		F					520
KAGAN	Yitzhak		M		Esther			520
KAGAN	Tanya		F		Esther			521
COHEN	Etel	PERGAMENT	F	Yisrael	Fruma			521
COHEN	Chaim Yitzhak		M					521
COHEN	Nechama	PERGAMENT	F	Chaim Yitzhak	Etel			521
KAGAN	Nisan		M					521
KAGAN			F			Nisan		521
KAGAN	Pesia		F	Nisan				521
KAGAN	Naftali		M	Nisan				521
KATZ	Leizer		M	Chaim Zelig				521
KATZ	Zelig		M	Leizer	Esther			521
KATZ	Avraham		M	Leizer	Esther			521
KATZ	Yeshaya Shiya		M	Leizer	Esther			521
KATZ	Stasia	MAGIDS	F					521
ל **Lamed**								
LEVINSON	Avraham Yitzhak		M	Berel				521

LEVINSON	Rosa	DIMENSTEIN	F	Yehuda				521
LEVINSON	Gutel		F	Avraham Yitzhak	Rosa			521
LEVINSON	Yehuda		M	Avraham Yitzhak	Rosa			521
LEVINSON	Bracha		F	Avraham Yitzhak	Rosa			521
LEVINSON	Frieda		F		Gutel Genia			521
LIEBERMAN	David		M	Gedalyahu	Ita			521
LIEBERMAN	Genya		F	Gedalyahu	Ita			521
LEVINSON	Zelig		M	Moshe	Rachel			521
LEVINSON	David		M	Zelig	Elka			521
LIPKER	Yisrael		M	Leizer			He was a prisoner of war; the list states that he died in captivity	521
LIPKER	Chava	KATZOVITZ	F		Sima			521
LIPKER	Chaya		F	Yisrael	Chava			521
LIPKER	Yeshayahu		M	Yisrael	Chava			521
LIPKER	Rivkah		F	Yisrael	Chava			521
LAZBANIK	Ya'akov		M					521
LAZBANIK	Kisha		F					521
LAZBANIK	Tzira		F					521

LAZBANIK			F		Tzira			521
LIZEROVITZ	Yerachmiel		M					521
LIZEROVITZ	Fruma Mina		F					521
LIZEROVITZ	Efraim		M	Yerachmiel	Fruma Minna			521
LEVINSON	Feigel	GREENBERG	F	Moshe Leib	Chaya Sarah			522
LEVINSON	Meir Shepsel		M					522
LEVINSON	Eli		M	Meir Shepsel	Feigel			522
LEVINSON	Isser		M					522
LEVINSON			F			Isser		522
LIEBMAN			M				On the list it states 'the old man'	522
LIEBMAN			F				On the list it states next to her husband's entry 'the old man'	522
LIEBMAN			F				It is likely that her family name is different; on the list it states 'the daughter' and she was probably the daughter of	522

							LIEBMAN 'the old man'	
LIEBMAN	Yisrael Yitzhak		M					522
LIEBMAN	Sonia		F					522
LIEBMAN	Sioma		F	Yisrael Yitzhak	Sonia			522
LEVIN	Rivkah	YUDELVITZ	F	Moshe	Chana	Yishayahu		522
LEVIN	Yitzhak		M	Yerachmiel	Sarah			522
LIMON	Azriel		M	Yishayahu	Rivkah			522
LIMON	Sheige	GREIS	F	Shlomo	Leah		On the list it states the place of death was 'in the [Concentrati on] Camps'	522
LIPKER	Mordecai		M	Eliezer			On the list it states the place of death was 'in the [Concentrati on] Camps'	522
LIPKER	Chana	KARPEL	F	Leib			On the list it states the place of death was 'in the [Concentrati on] Camps'	522

LIPKER	Gershon		M	Mordecai	Chana		On the list it states the place of death was 'in the [Concentration] Camps'	522
LIPKER	Chaim		M	Mordecai	Chana		On the list it states the place of death was 'in the [Concentration] Camps'	522
LEVIN	Reuven		M					522
LEVIN	Rachel	SARCHAN	F					522
LIPKER	Avraham		M	Chaim				522
LIPKER	Devorah		F					522
LIPKER	Hinda		F					522
LIFSHITZ	Alexander		M					522
LIFSHITZ			F			Alexander		522
LEVKOV	Shimon		M	Yisrael	Zinia			522
LAPKIN	Natan		M					522
LAPKIN			F			Natan		522
LAPKIN			F	Natan				522
LEVINSON	Moshe		M					522
LEVINSON	Rachel		F					522

LEVINSON	Chasia		F					522
LEVINSON	Sima		F					522
LIPKER	Leizer		M					522
LAPIDUS	Itka	YORESHNER	F					522
LAPIDUS	Yitzhak		M	Leib	Batya			522
LAPIDUS	Gitla		F	Yitzhak	Itka			522
LEVIN	David		M					523
LEVIN	Fruma		F					523
LEVIN	Yisrael		M					523
LEVIN	Frimel		F					523
LASKOV	Mendel		M	Chaim Matityahu	Leah			523
LASKOV	Sima	GIRZON	F	Yechiel				523
LEVKOV	Yoel		M	Reuven	Sheina Sarah			523
LEVKOV	Leah	GURSTEIN	F	Moshe Mordecai	Nechama			523
LEVKOV	Moshe		M	Yoel	Leah			523
LEVKOV	Berel		M	Yoel	Leah			523
LAGET	Rachel	SHKOLNIK	F	Mordecai	Chana			523
LAGET	Avraham Yasia		M	Pesach	Pesia			523
LAGET	Miriam		F	Avraham	Rachel			523

LEVIN	Chaya	MAGIDEY	F	Michal	Chana			523
LEVIN	Yosef		M	Shlomo	Chaya			523
LEVIN	Chanan		M	Shlomo	Chaya			523
LEVIN	Yisrael		M	Shlomo	Chaya			523
LEVIN	Hirshel		M	Shlomo	Chaya			523
LASKOV	Ya'akov		M				On the list it states the place of death was 'in the [Concentration] Camp'	523
LASKOV	Rachel		F					523
LEVIN	Zvi		M	Arieh	Matla			523
LEVIN	Rachel	ZOFRENER	F	Zev	Bluma			523
LASKOV	Yeshayahu		M	Chaim	Leah		The list states the place of death was Kovno	523
LASKOV	Esther		F	Yishayahu	Rosa		The list states the place of death was Kovno	523
LASKOV	Chana		F	Yishayahu	Rosa		The list states the place of death was Kovno	523

LASKOV	Chaim		M	Yishayahu	Rosa		The list states the place of death was Kovno	523
LAPIDUS	Chaya	KATZKOVITZ	F	Yitzhak	Sarah			523
LAPIDUS	Yitzhak		M	Avraham	Chaya			523
LAPIDUS	Aidel		F					523
LAPIDUS	Gittel		F	Yitzhak	Aidel			523
LEVIN	Chaim		M	Shlomo	Hinda			523
LEVIN	Shlomo		M	Chaim				523
LEVIN	Liba		F					523
LEVIN	Lazer		M				On the list it states the place of death was 'in the [Concentration] Camp'	523
LEVIN	Rivkah		F	Lazer	Fania		On the list it states the place of death was 'in the [Concentration] Camp'	524
LEVIN	Chaim		M					524
LEVIN		PARVOZKY	F	Ya'akov		Chaim		524
LEVIN	Chava Liba	VILENCHIK	F					524

LEVIN	Perl		F						524
LEVIN	Yeshayahu		M						524
LEVIN	Moshe		M	Yishayahu	Perl				524
LEVIN	Sheindel		F						524
LEVIN	Eliyahu		M	Yishayahu	Chava Liba				524
LEVIN	Mila		F						524
LEVIN	Sheindel		F	Eliyahu	Mila				524
LEVIN	Moshe		M	Yishayahu	Chava Liba				524
LAGET	Henya		F						524
LAGET	Gronya	LAGET	F						524
LAGET			M				Gronia		524
LERNER	Dora	BARACCINI	F	Dov				On the list the family name is recorded as LERNA, apparently in error	524
LERNER	Mula			Shmuel	Dora				524
LEVIN	Dov Ber		M	Shlomo	Hinda				524
LEVIN	Mintza	DANISHEVSKY	F	Shmuel Shimon	Henya				524
LEVIN	Sima		F	Dov Ber	Mintza			On the list it states 'in the [Concentrati on] Camp' was place of	524

							death	
LEVIN	Batya		F	Dov Ber	Mintza		On the list it states 'in the [Concentration] Camp' was place of death	524
LEVIN	Zvi Hershel		M	Dov Ber	Mintza		On the list it states that the place of death was on the way to Ponar	524
מ **Mem**								
MALKAS	Chaim		M	David Leib			On the list it states the place of death was Zilonka Forest	524
MALKAS	Batya	LEVIN	F	Leibe Yishayahu			On the list it states the place of death was Zilonka Forest	524
MELTZER	Polie		M					524
MELTZER	Leah		F					524
MELTZER	Mordecai		M	Polie	Leah			524
MELTZER	Rivkah		F	Polie	Leah			524
MIADLER	Chana Reiza		F					524

MIADLER	Ayzik		M		Chana Reiza			524
MIADLER	Chaya Gittel	DANISHEVSKY	F					524
MIADLER	David		M	Ayzik	Chaya Gittel			524
MIADLER	Shaul		M	Ayzik	Chaya Gittel			524
MIADLER	Ya'akov		M					524
MIADLER	Sonia	LIPKER	F	Chaim	Fraydel			524
MIADLER	Hinda		F					524
MEMPEL	Yona		M					524
MEMPEL			F			Yona		524
MILIKOVSKY	Michael		M					524
MILIKOVSKY	Rachel		F					525
MELNIK	Yocheved	ZUSMANOVITZ	F	Matityahu	Musia			525
MELNIK	Aharon		M	Shlomo	Tamar			525
MALKAS	Alter		M					525
MALKAS	Bella		F					525
MALKAS	Etel		F					525
MALKAS	Hirsh		M					525
MALKAS	Shmuel		M					525
MALKAS	Aharon		M					525
MALKAS	Miriam		F					525

MALKAS	Sonia	ASONOVSKY	F	Yerachmiel	Etel			525
MIRSKY	Gutel		F					525
MILIKOVSKY	Hirshel		M					525
MILIKOVSKY	Etel		F					525
MILIKOVSKY			M	Hirshel	Etel			525
MILIKOVSKY	Zalman		M					525
MILIKOVSKY	Batya		F					525
MILIKOVSKY	Ben-Zion		M					525
MILIKOVSKY	Chana		F					525
MILIKOVSKY	Pesia		F					525
MIRSKY	Aharon		M				The list states the place of death was Lebedevo	525
MIRSKY	Risha		F					525
MIRSKY	Nachum		M					525
MAYEROVITZ	Hillel		M	Shlomo				525
MAYEROVITZ	Hinda		F	Leib			On the list it states that the place of death was Ziezmariai	525
MAGIDEY	Asher		M	Michael	Chana			525
MAGIDEY	Sarah Minna		F	Avraham Chaim	Sima			525

MAGIDEY	Shima Ata		F	Asher	Sarah Minna			525
MISKIN	Chana	STEINMAN	F	Zundel	Feiga			525
MISKIN	Lipa		M	Shimon	Chana			525
MILCHMAN	Chaya Riva		F				On the list it states the place of death was Fastov	525
MOSTBILISHKER	Leah		F	Leizer	Esther			525
MAGIDEY	Peiva Leib		M					525
MAGIDEY	Lazer		M				The list states the place of death was Lebedevo	525
MAGIDEY	Riva		F				The list states the place of death was Lebedevo	525
MAGIDEY	Chava		F	Lazer	Riva			525
MAGIDEY	Sonia		F	Lazer	Riva			526
MAGIDS	Baruch		M					526
MAGIDS	Fania	SARCHAN	F					526
MARGOLIN	Ben-Zion		M					526
MARGOLIN	Moshe		M					526

MAGIDEY	Aharon		M					526
MAGIDEY	Sheina		F				The list states the place of death was Sol	526
MAGIDEY	Alta		F	Aharon	Sheina		On the list the personal name of her father is recorded as Aharon, apparently in error	526
MAGIDEY	Leah		F	Aharon	Sheina			526
MAGIDEY	Yitzhak		M	Aharon	Sheina			526
MISKIN			M				On the list it states 'the father of Shimon & Yehudit MISKIN'	526
MAGIDS	Shlomo		M	Eliyahu	Elka Liba			526
MAGIDS	Hinda		F	Shlomo	Bila		The list states that the place of death was Kaisiadorys	526
MAGIDS	Fruma	NORMAN	F	Zvi	Tova			526
MAGIDS	Avraham		M	Yitzhak	Miriam			526
MAGIDS	Rachel		F	Avraham	Fruma			526

MANDEL	Yona	KAVRATZ	M	Alter	Rachel Leah			526
MANDEL	Malka		F					526
MADOLKSY	Lipa		M	Avraham	Sarah Chana			526
MADOLKSY	Leah		F					526
MALKAS	Mordecai		M	Chaim	Basha			526
MALKAS	Nechama		F	Mordecai	Chaya Sarah			526
MACHNITZKY	Genya	TABORISKY	F	Feiva	Esther Rachel			526
MIADLER	Yekutiel		M	Yisrael	Devorah			526
MIADLER	Devorah		F	Yekutiel	Liba			526
MAYEROVITZ	Michael		M					526
MAYEROVITZ			F			Michael		526
MATLOVKSY	Nechama	MAYEROVITZ	F					526
MATLOVKSY			M			Nechama		526
MAGIDEY	Ya'akov		M					526
MAGIDEY	Michla							526
MAGIDEY	Baila		F					526
MAYEROVITZ	Malka		F					526
MAYEROVITZ	Chanan		M					526
MAYEROVITZ	Sheina		F				It is probable that the family name	526

							was different	
MARNITZKA	Chana	TABORISKY	F					526
MAYEROVITZ	Pinya		M	Hillel	Hinda			527
MAYEROVITZ	Sheina Rachel		F	Hillel	Hinda			527
MANS	Moshe		M			Masha	The pronunciatio n of the names, gender and family relationship is according to the Pages of Testimony	527
MANS	Masha		F			Moshe	The pronunciatio n of the names, gender and family relationship is according to the Pages of Testimony	527
MANS	Ya'akov		M	Moshe	Masha		The pronunciatio n of the names is according to the Page of Testimony	527
MANS	Devorah		F	Moshe	Masha		The pronunciatio	527

							n of the names is according to the Page of Testimony	
MANS	Bila		F	Moshe	Masha		The pronunciatio n of the names is according to the Page of Testimony	527
MANS	Eliezer		M	Moshe	Masha		The pronunciatio n of the names is according to the Page of Testimony	527
MAYEROVITZ	Leib		M					527
MAYEROVITZ	Chasia		F					527
MAYEROVITZ	Asher		M	Leib	Chasia			527
MAYEROVITZ	Avraham		M	Leib	Chasia			527
MAYEROVITZ	David		M					527
MAYEROVITZ			F	David				527
MARCUS	Ya'akov		M					527
MARCUS	Rabbi		M			Bella		527
MARCUS	Bella		F				The rabbi's wife	527

MAGIDEY	Michael		M	Nachum	Bishka			527
MAGIDEY	Nechama	PLOTKIN	F					527
MAGIDEY	Sarah Itka		F	Michael	Nechama			527
MAGIDEY	Feivel Hirsh		M	Michael	Nechama			527
MAGIDEY	Rachel Masha		F	Chaim	Batya			527
MAGIDEY	Fruma		F	Feivel	Rachel			527
MAGIDEY	Leib		M	Feivel	Rachel			527
MAGIDEY	Sarah		F	Feivel	Rachel			527
MAGIDEY	Asher		M	Michael	Chana			527
MAGIDEY	Minna		F					527
MIRSKY	Motel		M	Eli Meir	Mana			527
MIRSKY	Nechamia		M	Motel	Leah			527
MIRSKY	Chano		M	Motel	Leah			527
MIRSKY	Eli Meirim		M					527
MIRSKY	Chana		F					527
MIRSKY	Gutel	TZAPLOVITZ	F	Yitzhak Leib	Feiga			527
MIRSKY	Yerucham		M	Eli Meir	Chana			527
MIRSKY	Feiga		F					527
MIRSKY	Feigel		F	Gutal	Hoda Batya			527
MIRSKY	Yisrael		M	Gutal	Hoda Batya			527

MIRSKY	Liba	BADNAS	F	Avraham Meir				528
MIRSKY	Ya'akov Hirsh		M	Yisrael	Liba			528
MIRSKY	Shalom		M	Yisrael	Liba			528
MARKMAN	Zelig		M					528
MARKMAN	Pesia Leah	GURVITZ	F	Ya'akov Boaz	Etel			528
MELTZER	Zisel		M	Zelig	Dosia		The gender is according to the Page of Testimony	528
MELTZER	Gita Mara		F	Yitzhak Ya'akov	Etel			528
MELTZER	Etel		F	Zisel	Gittel Mara			528
MILLER	David Dondzik		M					528
MILLER	Liza		F					528
MILLER	Ida		F	David	Liza			528
MILLER	Yitzhak		M	David	Liza			528
MAGID	Shalom		M					528
MAGID	Liba		F					528
MALKAS	Leah		F					528
MALKAS	Moshe		M		Leah			528
MALKAS	Malka		F					528

MALKAS	Nachum		M		Leah			528
MALKAS			F			Nachum	The wife of Nachum MALKAS	528
MALKAS	Chana		F		Leah			528
MALKAS	Malka		F		Leah			528
MAGIDS	Elka Liba		F					528
MAGIDEY	Chana	EKES	F	Leibik	Chaya Rachel			528
MAGIDEY	Leizer		M	Yitzhak	Minna			528
MAGIDEY	Eli		M	Eli	Chana		It is probable that his family name was different	528
MAGIDEY	Yitzhak Itzia		M					528
MAGIDEY	Minna		F					528
MAGIDEY	Shalom		M	Yitzhak	Minna			528
MAGIDEY	Liba		F					528
MAGIDEY	Chanaleh		F	Shalom	Liba			528
MAGIDS	Minna		F					528
MAGIDS	Moshe		M					528
MAGIDS	Eliyahu		M					528
נ **Nun**								
NAROTZKER	Elka		F					528

NORMAN	Dina		F					529
NORMAN	Buma		M					529
NEWMAN	Bryna	RODANSKY	F	Berel Ayzik		Reuven	The family status and relationship is conjectured	529
NEWMAN	Reuven		M			Bryna	The family status and relationship is conjectured	529
NORMAN	Bella		F					529
NIBOSHTZIK	Esther		F					529
NEFACH	Mafanizia							529
NEIFACH	Reuven		M				According to the Page of Testimony It is probable that his family name was NIFACH	529
NOFECH	Bryna	RODANSKY	F	Berel Ayzik			It is probable that her family name was NIFACH according to the Page of Testimony	529
NOFECH	Yehudit		F	Reuven	Bryna		It is probable that her family name was NIFACH	529

							according to the Page of Testimony	
NOFECH	Leib		M				According to the Page of Testimony It is probable that his family name was NIFACH	529
NORMAN	Moshele		M	David	Gita		The list states the place of death was Kovno	529
NORMAN	Avremeleh		M	David	Gita		The list states the place of death was Kovno	529
NORMAN	Minhala		F	David	Gita		The list states the place of death was Kovno	529
ס **Samech**								
SUTZKEVER	Itka	SHAMASH	F					529
SUTZKEVER	Nachum		M	Moshe	Etka			529
SUTZKEVER	Misha		M	Nachum	Malka		On the list it states that he was a prisoner of war of the	529

							Germans	
SUTZKEVER	Avraham		M	Nachum	Malka			529
SUTZKEVER	Gary		M				On the list it states that they lived across from the Tarbut School	529
SLODZINSKY	Rabbi		M					529
SLODZINSKY	Rabbanit		F					529
SWIRSKY	Zalman		M					529
SWIRSKY			F			Zalman		529
SUTZKEVER	Chaim		M					529
SWIRNOVSKY	Zina	LEVIN	F				On the list it states the place of death was Turetz	529
SWIRNOVSKY	Chaya		F		Zina		On the list it states the place of death was Turetz	529
SWIRNOVSKY	Raya		F		Zina		On the list it states the place of death was Turetz	529
SWIRSKY	Yehoshua		M					529

SWIRSKY	Batya		F					529
SWIRSKY	Sioma		F	Yehoshua	Batya			529
SOLOVY	Grisha		M					529
SOLOVY	Rivkah		F					529
SOLOVY	Sarah		F	Grisha	Rivkah			529
SUTZKEVER	Shlomo Nute		M	Yitzhak Mordecai	Batya			529
SUTZKEVER	Chasia	BIROVSKY	F					529
SUKOVINSON	Sarah		F	Moshe	Malka			530
SUKOVINSON	Tzvia		F					530
SUKOVINSON	Rachel		F	Ya'akov	Tzvia			530
SUKOVINSON	Chaim Eli		M	Simcha	Chana		On the list it states he fell on the front	530
STROCHINSKY	Yona		M	Avraham	Devorah			530
STROCHINSKY	Feivel		M	Yona	Rivel			530
SARCHAN	Chaim		M		Bella Chaya			530
SARCHAN	Gita	ALPROVITZ	F	Binyamin	Tova			530
SARCHAN	Zalman		M	Chaim	Gita			530
SARCHAN	Batya		F	Chaim	Gita			530
SARCHAN	Meir		M	Chaim	Gita			530
SARCHAN	Moshe		M					530
SARCHAN			F			Moshe		530

SACK			M					530
SACK			F					530
SARGOVITZ	Liba	GREENBERG	F					530
SKLOT	Mira	KATZ	F	Shmuel	Henya			530
SWIRSKY	Nechama		F					530
ROTZKEVER	Sheina		F					530
SUTZKEVER	Yosef		M					530
SUTZKEVER	Bila		F					530

ע **Ayin**

ETINGER	Avraham		M				On the list it states that the place of death was Vilna - Ponar	530
ETINGER	Sarah Yudis	GURVITZ	F	Ya'akov Boaz	Etel		On the list it states that the place of death was Vilna - Ponar	530
ENTAS	Chaya Sarah	AXELROD	F	Ya'akov	Slava		The list states the place of death as Kovno	530
EKES	Leibik		M					530
EKES	Simcha		M	Leibik	Chaya Rachel			530

EKES	Sarah		F			Shmuel	On the list it states it states that she was a seamstress	530
EKES	Shmuel		M			Sarah		530
פ **Peh**								
PODOLSKY	Max		M	Shmuel	Miriam			530
PODOLSKY	Dora	WAKS	F	Mordecai	Rachel Leah			530
PODOLSKY	Sonia		F	Max	Dora			530
PODOLSKY	Fania		F	Max	Dora			530
FENSTER	Michael		M	Shmuel	Batya		On the list the personal name recorded is Machal, apparently in error	530
FENSTER	Sima Eta		F	Michael	Miriam		On the list it states the place of death was 'in the [Concentrati on] Camp'	530
FENSTER	Shmuel Chaim		M	Michael	Miriam		On the list it states the place of death was 'in the [Concentrati on] Camp'	530

FENSTER	Yitzhak		M	Michael	Miriam		On the list it states the place of death was 'in the [Concentrati on] Camp'	530
FRIEDMAN	Mendel		M					531
FRIEDMAN	Raiza		F					531
FRIEDMAN	Yosef		M	Mendel	Reiza			531
FRIEDMAN	Sonia	RAPPAPORT	F					531
FEIBUSHVITZ	Liba		F	Leizer	Esther		On the list the family name is incorrectly recorded as FEIBOSHVIT S	531
FEIBUSHVITZ	Peiva		M	Avraham				531
FEIBUSHVITZ	Doba		F	Feiva	Liba			531
FEIBUSHVITZ	Avraham		M	Feiva	Liba			531
FEIBUSHVITZ	Esther		F	Feiva	Liba			531
FEIGENBAUM			M				On the list it states 'the father,' and that he died in the [Concentrati on] Camp, probably in 1944	531

FEIGENBAUM			F				On the list it states "Mother;" and that she died in the [Concentration] Camp	531
FEIGENBAUM	Moshe		M				On the list it states "Daughter;" and that she died in the [Concentration] Camp	531
FEIGENBAUM	Peivke		M				On the list it states "Son;" and that he died in the [Concentration] Camp	531
FEIGENBAUM			M				On the list it states "Son;" and that he died in the [Concentration] Camp	531
FISHER	Moshe		M					531
FISHER	Esther	BAUDEN	F					531
FEIGLIN	Feiga		F					531
FEIGLIN	Moshe		M					531
POPISKY	Alter		M					531
POPISKY	Shoshana	KARPEL	F	Leib				531

POPISKY	Bella		F	Alter	Shoshana			531
POPISKY	Berel		M	Alter	Shoshana			531
POTASHNIK	Pinya		M					531
POTASHNIK	Yosef		M					531
POTASHNIK	Rosa	SHER	F					531
POTASHNIK	Ya'akov		M	Pinya	Rosa			531
POTASHNIK	Tzila		F	Pinya	Rosa			531
POTASHNIK	Sonia		F					531
PERGAMENT	Feya	RAPPAPORT	F					531
PERGAMENT	Yisrael		M	Zalman	Peia			531
PERGAMENT	Henya		F	Zalman	Peia			531
PUPKO	Yitzhak		M					531
PUPKO	Eli		M					531
PUPKO	Sima	LIFKOVITZ	F	Yitzhak Ya'akov	Etel			531
PUPKO	Etel		F	Motel	Sima			531
PUPKO	Yosef		M	Motel	Sima			531
PARVOZKY	Idla	GORDON	F		Bracha			531
PARVOZKY	Eliyahu		M	Moshe	Idela			532
PARVOZKY	Esther	GITLITZ	F		Shifra			532
PARVOZKY	Moshe		M	Eliyahu	Esther			532
PARVOZKY	Shifra		F	Eliyahu	Esther			532

PARVOZKY	Chaim		M	Moshe	Idela		On the list it states he was a soldier who fell in battle	532
PARVOZKY	Altzka		F					532
PARVOZKY	Mira		F	Chaim	Alta			532
PODBERZKY	Ayzik		M	David Leib	Esther			532
PODBERZKY	Chaya Liba		F	Ayzik	Rivkah Leah		On the list it states the family name is recorded as PODBERZKIT, apparently in error	532
PODBERZKY	Moshe		M	Ayzik	Rivkah Leah		On the list it states the family name is recorded as PODBERZKIT, apparently in error	532
POMOTZNIK	Milach		M	Yosef	Klara			532
POMOTZNIK	Avraham		M	Milach	Bella			532
POMOTZNIK	Yosef		M	Milach	Bella			532
PERGAMENT	Fruma	KOZLOVSKY	F	Gamliel	Feiga			532
PODOLSKY	Mara		F					532
PODOLSKY	Michael		M					532

PODOLSKY	Rosa		F					532
PODOLSKY	Chana		F	Michael	Rosa			532
PODOLSKY	Mulka		F	Michael	Rosa			532
PRESS	Ya'akov		M					532
PRESS			F			Ya'akov		532
צ **Tzadik**								
ZIMMERMAN	Shmuel		M	Ya'akov	Hinda		On the list it states that the place of death was Vilna - Ponar	532
ZIMMERMAN	Rashel Atla	KAGAN	F	Reuven	Chaya		On the list it states that the place of death was Vilna - Ponar	532
ZIMMERMAN	Chanan		M	Shmuel	Rashel		On the list it states that the place of death was Vilna - Ponar	532
ZUCKERMAN	Elka Pesia	KRINIS	F	Yitzhak	Rivkah		On the list it states that the place of death was Vilna - Ponar	532
ZUCKERMAN	Natan		M				On the list it states that the place of death was Vilna - Ponar	532

ZUCKERMAN	Rabbi Chanan		M	Yosef	Zelda		On the list it states it states that the place of death as 'in the [Concentration] Camp'	532
ZUCKERMAN	Hodel	TATRASKY	F	Moshe	Liba		On the list it states the place of death was 'in the [Concentration] Camp'	532
ZUCKERMAN	Ya'akov		M	Chanan	Handel			532
ZUCKERMAN	Leib		M	Chanan	Handel		On the list it states the place of death was 'in the [Concentration] Camp'	532

ק **Kof**

CHERTOK	Lipa		M					532
CHERTOK	Manya	RAPPAPORT	F					532
CHERTOK	Avraham Yitzhak		M					532
CHERTOK	Malka	WEITZ	F					532
CHERTOK	Levi		M	Avraham Yitzhak	Malka			533

CHERTOK	Eliyahu		M					533
CHARLNOSKY	Shmuel		M					533
CHARLNOSKY	Esther		F					533
TZIPIN	Reuven		M	Efraim	Reizel			533
TZIPIN	Devorah	ALPROVITZ	F	Ya'akov				533
TZIRULNIK	Chanoch		M			Ama	The family relationship is according to Pages of Testimony	533
TZIRULNIK	Ama		F			Chanoch	The family relationship is according to Pages of Testimony	533
TZIRULNIK	Sonia		F	Chanoch	Ama			533
TZIRULNIK	Avraham		M	Chanoch	Ama			533
ZIMMERMAN	Shmuel		M					533
ZIMMERMAN	Tzila	YAMBROW	F					533
ZUCKERMAN	Mordecai		M					533
ZUCKERMAN	Hinda	SCHWARTZ	F	Yitzhak	Peia			533
ZUCKERMAN	Leib		M	Mordecai	Hinda			533
ZUCKERMAN	Ya'akov		M	Mordecai	Hinda			533
ZUCKERMAN	Rachel		F	Mordecai	Hinda			533
ZUCKERMAN	Yitzhak		M	Mordecai	Hinda			533

TZIMBLER			M				Profession listed as pharmacist	533
TZIMBLER			F				The pharmacist's wife	533
TZIMBLER	Yitzhak		M					533
TZIMBLER	Chana		F					533
TZIMBLER	Luba		F					533
KALMANOVITZ			M				On the list it states 'the father'	533
KALMANOVITZ			F				On the list it states 'the mother'	533
KALMANOVITZ	Reizel		F					533
KALMANOVITZ	Ya'akov		M					533
KABAK	Leah	LEVIN	F	Yishayahu	Chava Liba		On the list it states the place of death was Turetz	533
KABAK	Feivel		M				On the list it states the place of death was Turetz	533
KABAK	Sheindel		F	Feivel	Leah		On the list it states the place of death was	533

							Turetz	
KONONVAL	Bryna		F					533
KARP	Leibel		M					533
KARP	Sarah	DRYN	F					533
KARP	Ben-Zion		M	Leibel	Sarah			534
KARP	Batya		F	Leibel	Sarah			534
KARP	Yerachmiel		M	Leibel	Sarah			534
KAGANOVITZ	Zavel		M					534
KAGANOVITZ	Yocha		F					534
KAGANOVITZ	Yisrael		M					534
KAGANOVITZ	Alta	GREIS	F	Zavel	Yocha			534
KAGANOVITZ	Piva		M					534
KAGANOVITZ	Zlata	GREIS	F	Zavel	Yocha			534
KATZOVITZ	Sima	LEVIN	F					534
KAVRATZ	Yehezkel		M	Yoel Baines	Esther			534
KAVRATZ	Etel	MATZOLSKY	F	Avraham	Sarah Cheina			534
KAVRATZ	Avraham		M	Yehezkel	Etel			534
KAVRATZ	Fruma		F	Yehezkel	Etel			534
KAVRATZ	Menasha		M	Yehezkel	Etel			534
KATZELNIK	Ben-Zion		M					534

KATZELNIK	Fraydel		F					534
KATZELNIK	Feivel		M	Ben-Zion	Fraydel			534
KATZELNIK	Avraham		M	Ben-Zion	Fraydel			534
KATZELNIK	Nechama		F	Ben-Zion	Fraydel			534
KARPEL	Avigdor		M					534
KARPEL	Feigel		F					534
KARPEL	Ya'akov		M	Avigdor	Feigel			534
KOZLOVSKY	Batya		F					534
KRAVITZ	Moshe		M					534
KRAVITZ			F			Moshe		534
KIRZNER	Moshe		M					534
KIRZNER	Leah		F					534
KIRZNER	Chava		F	Moshe	Leah			534
KIRZNER	Hasel			Moshe	Leah			534
KIRZNER	Shlomo		M	Moshe	Leah			534
KIRZNER	Sarah		F	Moshe	Leah			534
KIRZNER	Rivkah		F	Chaim	Rodl			534
KIRZNER	Chaim		M	Aharon	Rivkah			534
KATZOVITZ			M				On the list it states 'the tailor from Damsk'	534
KOPLOVITZ	Aharon		M					534

KOPLOVITZ	Etel	KAVRATZ	F	Yoel	Esther			535
KOPLOVITZ	Mirala		F	Aharon				535
KATZOVITZ	Shlomo		M					535
KOPTZOVSKY			M				Profession listed as dentist	535
KOPTZOVSKY	Eliyahu		M					535
KOVERSKY	Tzipa		F					535
KOVERSKY	Grisha		M					535
KOVERSKY	Liosia		F	Grisha	Anya			535
KOVERSKY	Sima		F	Grisha	Anya			535
KOVERSKY	Chaim		M	Grisha	Anya			535
KOVERSKY	Ovsey		M					535
KOVERSKY	Sonia	GREENBERG	F					535
KOVERSKY	Bryna		F	Ovsey	Sonia			535
KOVERSKY	Feigel		F	Ovsey	Sonia			535
KRAINES	Tziril		F					535
KRAINES	Rachel		F	Moshe Yehuda	Tzirl			535
KOSTIN	Poleh		M					535
KOSTIN		KOPLOVITZ	F			Pola		535
KRAINES	Itza Ayzik		M					535
	Lena	KRAINES	F	Itza Ayzik				535

			M				Lana	Wife's maiden name was KRAINES	535
KRAINES	Manya		F	David Moshe	Rosa				535
KICHELMACHER			M					The brother of Regina the teacher	535
KOPLOVITZ	Leib		M	Chanan	Feiga				535
KOPLOVITZ	Sarah	SHNEIDMAN	F						535
KOPLOVITZ	Shoshana		F	Leib	Sarah				535
KOPLOVITZ	Chanan		M	Leib	Sarah				535
KOPLOVITZ	Shmuel		M	Chanan	Feiga				535
KOPLOVITZ	Liza		F						535
KOPLOVITZ	Sarah		F	Shmuel	Liza				535
KOPLOVITZ	Chanan		M	Shmuel	Liza				535
KOMINER	Chaim Leib		M						535
KOMINER	Sarah	EPSTEIN	F	Michael	Baila				535
KOPLOVITZ	Berel Motel		M	Abba	Mera				535
KOPLOVITZ	Rhoda	POTASHNIK	F	Zalman	Esther				535
KOPLOVITZ	Chaim Abba		M	Berel Motel	Rhoda				535
KOPLOVITZ	Chana Gittel		F	Berel Motel	Rhoda				536
KOPLOVITZ	Chana	BADNAS	F					On the list it states that	

							the two children of Leib and Chana KOPLOVITZ perished in Kovno in 1943	
KOPLOVITZ			M				On the list it states that he lived in the lane next to the Great Synagogue	536
KOPLOVITZ			F				On the list under her husband's details it says that they lived in the lane next to the Great Synagogue	536
KOPLOVITZ	Batya		F					536
KOPLOVITZ	Dina		F					536
KOPLOVITZ	Esther		F					536
COOPER	Avigdor		M					536
COOPER			F			Avigdor		536
COOPER			M	Avigdor				536
KAGAN	Shimon		M					536
KAGAN	Rachel		F					536

KAGAN	Yisrael		M	Shimon	Rachel			536
KARPEL	Ya'akov		M					536
KARPEL	Yitzhak		M				On the list it states 'A soldier who fell in battle with the Red Army in Berlin'	536
KARPEL	Liba		F				On the list the year of birth appears incorrectly as 1982; the place of death is listed as Kaisiadorys	536
KATZOVITZ	Meir		M					536
KATZOVITZ	Shalom		M					536
KATZOVITZ	Chaim		M					536
KRAINES	Sheina	ALPROVITZ	F	Yitzhak			On the list it states that the place of death was Ziezmariai	536
KRAINES	Miriam		F	David Moshe	Rosa		On the list it states that the place of death was Ziezmariai	536

KRAINES	Shlomo		M	Arieh	Rivkah			536
KRAINES	Rachel		F					536
KRAINES	Bryna		F					536
KRAINES	Feigel		F					536
KRAINES	Golda		F					536
KAGANOVITZ	Shmuel		M	Noach	Golda		On the list it states that the place of death was Vilna - Ponar	536
KAGANOVITZ	Golda	RAPPAPORT	F	Avraham Zalman	Yenta		On the list it states that the place of death was Vilna - Ponar	536
KAGANOVITZ	Zecharia		M	Noach	Golda		On the list it states that the place of death was Vilna - Ponar	536
KAGANOVITZ	Chaim		M	Noach	Golda		On the list it states that the place of death was Vilna - Ponar	536
KAGANOVITZ	Noach		M	Chaim			On the list it states that the place of death was Vilna - Ponar	536
KAGAN	Eli		M	Reuven	Chava			536

KAGAN	Berta	KOPLOVITZ	F				On the list it states that the place of death was Vilna - Ponar	536
KAGAN	Eliezer		M	Eli	Berta		On the list it states that the place of death was Vilna - Ponar	536
KAGAN	Chaim		M	Eli	Berta		On the list it states that the place of death was Vilna - Ponar	536
KROCHMALNIK	Avraham		M	Eliezer				537
KROCHMALNIK	Doba		F					537
KROCHMALNIK	Feiga		F	Avraham	Doba			537
KROCHMALNIK	Keila		F	Avraham	Doba			537
KREITZIK	Elchanan Nuta		M	Eliezer Zev	Masha			537
KREITZIK	Sarah Zlata	LAPKIN	F	Yosef Eliyahu	Rivkah			537
KREITZIK	Eliezer		M	Elchanan Nuta	Sarah Zlata			537
KREITZIK	Fruma		F	Elchanan Nuta	Sarah Zlata			537
KREITZIK	Moshe		M	Elchanan Nuta	Sarah Zlata			537

ר **Resh**

RAPPAPORT	Yenta		F	Zecharia			On the list it states that the place of death was Vilna - Ponar	537
RAPPAPORT	Menucha	SWIRSKY	F	Yisrael	Rivkah		On the list it states that the place of death was Vilna - Ponar	537
RAPPAPORT	Bryna		F	Mendel	Pola		On the list it states that the place of death was Vilna - Ponar	537
RAPPAPORT	Moshe		M	Mendel	Menucha		On the list it states that the place of death was Vilna - Ponar	537
RAPPAPORT	Mendel		M	Avraham Zalman	Yenta			537
RABINOWITZ	Rivkah		F	Noach	Miriam			537
RABINOWITZ	Ya'akov		M					537
RABINOWITZ	Rachel		F	Ya'akov	Rivkah			537
RABINOWITZ	Avraham		M	Ya'akov	Rivkah			537
RABINOWITZ	Shoshana		F	Ya'akov	Rivkah			537
RABINOWITZ	Rachel	NIBOSHTZIK	F	Yitzhak	Esther			537

RABINOWITZ	Avraham		M	Yitzhak	Frieda			537
RABINOWITZ	Miriam		F	Avraham	Rachel			537
RABINOWITZ	Yitzhak		M	Zalman	Rikla			537
RABINOWITZ	Liba	SCHWARTZ	F	Ya'akov				537
RABINOWITZ	Peiva		M	Yitzhak	Liba		On the list it states he fell in battle in the army	537
RODNER	Chaya Batya		F					537
RODNER			M				On the list it states 'the father,' probably of Chana & Yosef	537
RODNER	Chana		F		Chaya Batya			537
RODNER	Yosef		M		Chaya Batya			537
RODNER		DANISHEVSKY	F			Yosef		537
RODANSKY	Pesach		M				Profession listed as watchmaker	537
RODANSKY			F			Pesach		537
RINDZONSKY	Uri		M					537
RINDZONSKY			F			Uri		537
RINDZONSKY			F	Uri				537

RINDZONSKY			F				On the list it states 'the mother of David RINDZONSKY	537
RAPPAPORT	Shmerel		M	Mordecai				537
RAPPAPORT	Sonia		F					538
RAPPAPORT	Moshele		M	Shmerel	Sonia			538
RAPPAPORT			M	Shmerel	Sonia			538
RAPPAPORT	Yisrael		M	Mordecai				538
RAPPAPORT	Hadassah	PLOTKIN	F					538
RAPPAPORT	Luzer		M					538
RAPPAPORT			F			Luzer		538
ROTZINSKY	Rachel		F					538
ROTZINSKY	Avraham		M	Yitzhak	Rachel		On the list it states - Partisans	538
ROTZINSKY	Shimon		M	Yitzhak	Rachel			538
RAPPAPORT	Kalman		M					538
RAPPAPORT	Chaya Rachel	AROTZKER	F		Sarah Mara			538
RODANSKY	Reuven		M				On the list it states the place of death was 'Ghetto'	538
RODANSKY	Ita		F				On the list it	538

							states the place of death was 'Ghetto'	
RODANSKY	Berel Ayzik		M					538
ROSENBLUT	Rivkah	MAHARSHAK	F	Shmuel	Esther		On the list it states the place of death was Lemberg	538
ROSENBLUT	Fruma		F	Mordecai	Rivkah		On the list it states the place of death was Lemberg	538
RUDNIK	Moshe		M	Meir	Chaya Golda			538
RUDNIK	Regina	KICHELMACH ER	F					538
ROGOVIN	Bluma	MAGIDEY	F					538
ROGOVIN			M			Bluma		538
ROSENBLUM	Shimon		M					538
ROSENBLUM	Sheina	MAYEROVITZ	F					538
ROSENBLUM	Ya'akov		M					538
ROSENBLUM	Pesia		F					538
ROSENBLUM			F		Pesia		The first daughter of Pesia ROSENBLU	538

							M	
ROSENBLUM			F		Pesia		The second daughter of Pesia ROSENBLUM	538
ROSENBLUM			F		Pesia		The third daughter of Pesia ROSENBLUM	538
RODANSKY	Hinda		F					538
REINES	Velvel		M					538
REINES	Sarah		F					538
RAZNITZKY	Sachne		F					538
RAZNITZKY	Risha		F					538
ש **Shin**								
SHAMASH	Avraham Chaim		M					538
SHAMASH	Rivkah		F					538
SHAMASH	Pesia		F	Avraham Chaim	Rivkah			538
SHAMASH	Moshe		M	Avraham Chaim	Rivkah			538
SHIVITZ	Sima	MATZAR	F					538
SHAMASH	Shmarya		M	Eliezer	Yenta			539

SHAMASH	Sheina	LEVIN	F	Otniel	Mapia			539
SHAMASH	Otniel		M	Shmaryahu	Sheina		On the list it states the place of death was Shamburg, Germany	539
SHULKIN	Idel		F					539
SHULKIN	Manya		F					539
SHNEIDMAN	Reuven		M	Baruch Zevulun	Susia			539
SHNEIDMAN	Ya'akov		M	Baruch Zevulun	Susia			539
SHOCHMAN	Rivkah		F	Isser	Raya			539
SHMUKLER	David		M					539
SHMUKLER	Nachum		M	David				539
SHMUKLER	Feigel		F	David				539
SHMUKLER	Henya		F	David				539
SHMUKLER	Shlomo		M	David				539
SCHWARTZ	Godel		M				The list states the place of death was Lebedevo	539
SCHWARTZ	Tzvia		F					539
SCHWARTZ	Nacha		F					539
SCHWARTZ	Hirsh		M				The list	539

							states the place of death was Lebedevo	
SHULOMOVITZ	Itza Moteh		M					539
SHULOMOVITZ	Manya		F					539
SHULOMOVITZ	Shalom		M	Kalman	Bluma			539
SHULOMOVITZ	Batya		F					539
SHULOMOVITZ	Nachum		M					539
SHULOMOVITZ	Ovsey		M					539
SHULOMOVITZ			F			Ovsey		539
SHULOMOVITZ	Mones		M					539
SHULOMOVITZ	Shprintza		F					539
SHULOMOVITZ	Moshe		M					539
SHULOMOVITZ	Rosa		F					539
SHULOMOVITZ	Margalit		F					539
SHAMASH	Leibel		M					539
SHAMASH	Leah	ALPROVITZ	F	Binyamin	Teiba			539
SHAMASH	Bryna		F	Leib	Leah			539
SHAMASH	Batya		F	Leib	Leah			539
SHAMASH	Chana		F	Leib	Leah			539
SHULOMOVITZ	Yehoshua		M	Shalom	Margalit			539
SHULOMOVITZ	Leah	SWIRSKY	F					539

SHNEIDMAN	Arieh Leib		M					540
SHNEIDMAN	Stisha	KAGAN	F	Avraham Yitzhak	Bracha			540
SHNEIDMAN	Yitzhak		M	Shlomo Chaim				540
SHNEIDMAN	Sonia	TZIGEL	F	Velvel	Rachel			540
SHNEIDMAN	Shlomo Chaim		M	Yitzhak	Sonia			540
SHNEIDMAN	Rachel		F	Yitzhak	Sonia			540
SHAFSNAVAL	Malka	JAVITZ	F	Chaim	Rivkah			540
SHAFSNAVAL	Bila		F	Avraham	Malka		On the list the family name appears incorretly as SHPANSNAV L	540
SHAFSNAVAL	Chaim		M	Avraham	Malka			540
SHAPIRA	Rachel Leah	KAVRATZ	F	Yoel Baines	Esther			540
SHAPIRA	Alter		M					540
SHAPIRA	Yehuda		M	Alter	Rachel Leah			540
SHAPIRA	Asher		M	Alter	Rachel Leah			540
SHAPIRA	Tzila		F	Alter	Rachel Leah			540
SCHWARTZ	Eliyahu		M	Yitzhak	Peia			540
SCHWARTZ	Liba		F					540

SCHWARTZ	Moshe		M	Eliyahu Leiba				540
SCHWARTZ	Velvel		M	Yitzhak	Peia			540
SCHWARTZ	Chana		F					540
SCHWARTZ	Fruma		F	Velvel	Chana			540
SCHWARTZ	Feiga		F	Velvel	Chana			540
SHNEIDMAN	Chaya Golda		F					540
STEINMAN	Zonvil		M	Dov			The list states the place of death was Kovno	540
STEINMAN	Feiga		F	Alter	Yehudit		The list states the place of death was Kovno	540
SHAPIRA	Zelig		M				On the list it states that the place of death was Vilna - Ponar	540
SHAPIRA	Henya	HORWITZ	F	Avraham Eliezer	Esther		On the list it states that the place of death was Vilna - Ponar	540
SHULMAN	Liebka		M	Avraham	Frieda Rivkah		On the list the year of birth appears incorrectly	540

							as 1973	
SHAPIRA	Shlomo		M					540
SHAPIRA	Raya		F					540
SHAPIRA	Yosef		M	Shlomo	Raya			540
SHAPIRA	Feya		F					540
	Shlomo		M				Profession listed as sexton of synagogue	540
SHULMAN	Ya'akov		M					540
SHULMAN			F			Ya'akov		540
SHULMAN	Pesia		F	Ya'akov				541
SHULMAN	Yitzhak		M	Ya'akov				541
SHULMAN	Liebka		M	Ya'akov				541
SHULMAN	Sonia	ZARTZER	F	Reuven	Rachel			541
SCHWARTZ	Yitzhak		M					541
SCHWARTZ	Nusia	KABATCHNIK	F					541
SHULMAN	Eliezer		M					541
SHULMAN	Feigel		F					541
SHULMAN	Avraham		M					541
SHAMASH	Yisrael		M					541
SCHWARTZ	Leib		M					541
SCHWARTZ	Moshe		M					541

SHINYOK	Aharon		M					541
SHOCHMAN	Raya	RABINOWITZ	F	Yitzhak	Liba			541
SHOCHMAN	Mordecai		M	Isser	Raya			541
SHOCHMAN	Ya'akov		M	Isser	Raya			541

[Page 542]

Translations by Jerrold Landau

בקשת סליחה ומחילה

מנשמות הקדושים האלמונים

בני עירנו סמורגון

ששמותיהם לא נזכרו ברשימות

דפי־יזכר

אם בשל חולשת הדעת והשכחה ואם בשל חוסר עדות

יאצר יגון־חדלונם, בלבנו עד עת

„ונקיתי דמם — לא נקיתי"

ועד ארגון יוצאי
סמורגון בישראל.

Memorial tablet in the Chamber of the Holocaust on Mount Zion in Jerusalem

A request for pardon
From the souls of the anonymous martyrs
Of our city Smorgon
Whose names are not mentioned in the lists
On the memorial pages
Where because of lack of knowledge and forgetting, or because of lack of testimony
The pain of their destruction will remain in our hearts until the time of

"And I will hold as innocent their blood that I have not held as innocent"[1]

The organization of Smorgon natives in Israel

Photo from Martef Hashoah – Holocaust Chamber in Jerusalem. It includes the tablets of Smorgon, Vilna, Olknik, and part of Brisk – likely to show the placement of the Smorgon memorial tablet. The Smorgon tablet is as follows:

In memory of the martyrs
Of the Community of Smorgon, may G-d avenge their blood
Who perished during the time of the Nazi Holocaust
Memorial day is 27 Cheshvan

May their souls be bound in the bonds of eternal life

Perpetuated by Smorgon natives
In Israel and the Diaspora.

Translator's Footnote

1. Joel 4:21, also included in the Av Harachamim prayer of Sabbath mornings and Yizkor. I have taken the translation from Mechon Mamre: https://www.mechon-mamre.org/p/pt/pt1404.htm

[Page 543]

The Activities of the Committee of the Organization of Smorgon Natives

by Rafael Weinstein

Translated by Jerrold Landau

Committee of the Organization of Smorgon Natives, Hadera, Israel

What were the activities of the natives of our city in the Land for the survivors of our city of Smorgon?

[Page 544]

Through the efforts of the veteran activist G. Weinstein, the following members gathered together: Baruch Sutzkever, Pesach Twborski, Zalman Kackowicz, Tzadok Rudnik, Batya Shein, Alta Dniszewski, and others, and founded "The Provisional Committee of the Organization of Smorgon Natives." A large meeting was convened from amongst all the settlements in the Land in 1945. Everybody donated to the extent that they were able, giving their donations to the charitable fund that extended assistance to those in need through interest free loans. The members of the committee who worked tirelessly were not content only with the help that our fellow townsfolk extended to the survivors. The budget was insufficient. The secretary of the board, B. Sutzkever and the chairman Weinstein approached our townsfolk in the United States with a call to come quickly to the aid of their fellow townsfolk who miraculously survived the Holocaust by the skin of their teeth, and were now in serious material trouble and distress. At that time, Mr. Avraham Furseit of blessed memory stood at the help of the "Assistance Committee of Smorgonites in the United States." He immediately answered their request, and dedicated all himself to this assistance work with all his energy. He conducted a campaign for the charitable fund. A. Furseit did not suffice himself with this. In addition, he organized the sending of packages of food and clothing to the survivors in the Land, as well as those who remained alive in the city of Smorgon. He worked incessantly and tirelessly for years. He fulfilled the commandments of "And your brother shall live with you"[1], and "You shall love your neighbor as yourself"[2]. He lived up to the adage "All the people of Israel are connected to another" in the clearest practical terms. He connected the survivors with their relatives in the United States. He toiled, found them, and roused them to open their hands to their kinsfolk and fellow townsfolk.

"The Committee of Smorgon Natives" stood on its guard throughout the entire period of the Holocaust. Every survivor from Smorgon who made *aliya* was greeted with open arms. Everyone was given initial aid in the form of 25 liras. The committee members concerned themselves with finding lodgings, and, to the extent possible, with arranging work and livelihood. Not only this, but the committee also organized the sending of food packages to those who remained alive and returned to live in our city [of Smorgon]. May it be [the Divine] will that we will know no more war, tribulations, and grief. May we merit to see all the natives of our town Smorgon gathered and absorbed in our flourishing, growing country.

Jerusalem April 8, 1962

Translator's Footnotes

1. Leviticus 25:36.
2. Leviticus 19:18.

[Page 545]

The Smorgon Help Committee

by A. Tchipkin (New York)

Translated by Anita Frishman Gabbay and Frieda Levin Dym

The Smorgoners in America wholeheartedly looked after the needs of their dear brothers and sisters. From time to time, other organizations would send help to Smorgon. This assistance was initiated when the need arose. Occasionally, one organization got help from several different places at one time, and others did not get any help. So this made it difficult for others to operate.

We hoped that eventually, with our help, that their situation would improve and they would no longer need our aid. We now see that they were forced to flee their land. The situation for all our people and our Smorgoners became even more sad. It became clear to us that our help, up to this time, was not sufficient and would likely become permanent. Because of the need and the poverty over there, additional help and support was of the utmost importance. It also became clear to that that more planning and organization was needed when conducting relief work.

With this knowledge, all the Smorgoners in New York, reorganized themselves. We all embarked on this Holy task: to help our unlucky brothers who were unfortunate and in such crisis. But the Relief Committee did even more, and especially, for us Smorgoners, here in America. We were definitely the "bride" amongst the Jewish American life (perhaps, treated, better)—[than] our fragmented...[1]

[Page 546]

For the first time, we Smorgoners, from all different backgrounds, came together to unite to perform this "Holy" duty. In no time, the immediate need to sustain our dear brothers on the other side of the ocean, to help them sustain their daily existence, became a priority to everyone of us. Every minute weighed heavily on our hearts and minds. It was of the utmost importance to organize ourselves and the general public to consolidate into one central committee to deliver help as soon as possible.

In order to succeed, we must forget our personal politics and work together. The Smorgon Relief Society exists, and must continue to exist.

SMORGONER! A Holy task stands in front of us--a sacrifice that stems from humanity and brotherhood!

[It is] a sacrifice. We cannot rest until our work is done!

Our brothers, our neighbours and all our friends in Smorgon, are fighting with their last breath to stay alive.

SMORGONER! You must not remain silent! You must help them. Get involved with the Smorgon Relief Committee.

Translator's Footnote

1. A likely reference to the Smorgoner's who immigrated to America had a better life and received more help (and felt like a newly wedded "bride") in comparison to other Jewish Americans and their torn and fragmented community back home.

[Pages 547-548]

The Society of Smorgon Natives in America

by Y. Miller

Translated by Anita Frishman Gabbay and Frieda Levin Dym

Friends of Anshei Smorgon B'nei Chaim Avraham

In a united voice from our immigrant society, who left Czarist Russia to escape from the programs and other hardships, and who had to leave their homeland and start new lives in new places, we were once Smorgoners!

Coming to America, in a strange land, they were helpless and lost! The contrast between a little shtetl in Lita [Lithuania] and the bustle of New York was colossal. Slowly, but surely, we settled in. Now, that we have a "small piece of bread" (started earning a living), we were missing our neighbours (a friend), someone from our own (town).

On May 8, 1887, a group of Smorgoners assembled on a top floor on Hester Street and pledged to start a Smorgon Relief Committee. The first founders were: Gerhon Blum, Yehuda Anshelevitz, Zundel Rabinovitch, Rafael

Schwartz, Max Elentuch, Sam Yafitz, Barnet Lapkin, Barnet Ash, Sam Alpert, Lipa Goldstein, Berl-Moishe Ashinofsky, Maurice Horowitz, Shlomo Hurwitz, Barnet Krivisky, and [?] Dlot. This handful of old immigrants, remembering their old homestead of Smorgon, with respect for their former friends and relatives in and around Smorgon, and with great respect for their learned and devoted Rabbi Chaim Avraham, used his name to found: Friends of Anshei Smorgon B'nei Chaim Avraham.

With the help of the initial group of Smorgoners, newly arrived immigrants to America had the opportunity to receive financial assistance for their daily needs. The Friends of Anshei Smorgon B'nei Chaim Avraham started to grow in size to over 200 strong. A brotherly and friendly atmosphere was created between everyone. We looked to help each other in difficult situations as well as share in each other's pride and sorrow.

After the war (World War 2), our relief committee played a very important part. It seemed that Smorgon suffered more, and since it is our town, we tried as much as possible to heal the wounds that our brothers were still haunted by. From that time forward, the Friends of Anshei B'nei Chaim Abraham undertook to involve itself in all matters concerning the town's wellbeing and livelihood and its relief societies.

With warmth, friendship and brotherhood, we, our Friends, pledged, whether in America or in our homeland, to help you in need. [The pledge was as follows:]

Our Friends, the “Mother” of all Relief Committees, welcomes you all [and] the well renowned relief committees to the Committee of the Smorgon Relief Society. We pledge to help in relief and to work hand in hand in order to improve our efforts by working together. Our common goal is to improve the lives of our brothers and sisters across the ocean.

[Page 549]

Stories through Photos

Translations by Jerrold Landau

Pictures obtained by Larry Gaum

[Page 551]

Minsk Street before the War

[Page 552]

Rabbis of Smorgon,

see the chapter Rabbis of the Community of Smorgon

Rabbi Rafael Shapira

Rabbi Moishe Danishevski

Rabbi Slodinsky, 1930-1931

Greeting Rabbi Slodinsky in Smorgon on his appointment as rabbi of the city, 1930-1931

[Page 553]

Stories through Photos (cont.)

Institutions of Smorgon

[Page 555]

Committee for Feeding Children
Board of the Soup Kitchen for Refugees of the First World War

From left: **Yosef Rusnikovitch, Sutzkever, Rivkah Alodoch, Hary Hofman, Mrs. Markovski, Mrs.**[1] **Liberman, Lyulka Chazanov, Lyuba Greis, Yosef Sholomovitch, Natan Ruzufski, Perla Ginsberg-Toizner, daughter of Rabbi Menashe, three of Markovsky's daughters**

Women's Committee for the Providing of Clothing for Poor Children

From right: **Shprinze Sholomovitch, Brochel Brudne, Surel Danishevska(i), Sonia Danishevska(i) (dentist), Bassil Gas, Alte Danishevska(i),(Danishevsky)**

[Page 556]

Gemillut Chassidim Committee

Standing from right: **V. Berger, Israel Rappaport, M. Broide, Tzadok Rudnik, Kraines**
Sitting from right: **Hisherver Broidna, Faiva Taboriski, Moishe Antzelevitch, Moishe Brudne, Badanes**

Va'ad Ba'alaey Melacha of Smorgon[2], March 9, 1935

Sitting from right: **M. Tzkerman, A. Shein, Z. Pergament, I. Rapaport, Krochmalnik**
Standing from right: **A. Galperin, A. Shulman**

[Page 557]

Va'ad Linat Hazadek

Translator's Footnotes

1. gv' is short for Mrs. Not for Gabi
2. Committee of Tradesmen of Smorgon

[Page 559]

Stories through Photos (cont.)

The Zionist Movement in Smorgon

[Page 601]

The Hebrew speaking club in Smorgon before the First World War

In the center: **The teacher Pesach Sheinuk**
From his right: **Leah Shenzon, Alte Dnishevsky, Alta Shtulper**
From his left: **Leah Greis, Rochel Balzam, Stasia Magids**

Gathering of the Committee of the League for Labouring in Israel
March 16, 1932

Standing from right to left: **Etke Meltzer, Chana Kruchmalnik**
Sitting from right to left: **I. Shiner, Menashe Brudne, Meir Bushkanetz, Mendel Alperovitz, Clara Lickt (or likely Leget)**

[Page 602]

Po'aley Zion meeting before World War 1

Standing from right to left: Eliahu Itzhak Alperovitch, Leah Ushevitz, Rafael the son of Zindel the Melamed - teacher, Arieh the son of Shmuel the butcher
Sitting from right to left: **Natan Rusuvski, Rashel Berberman, Chaim Alperovitz, Nachum the son of Meir the watchmaker, Shmuel Madvinsk[1] , Abraham Danishevsky**

A meeting of Hechalutz from Smorgon with the "Arzia" Hachsharah group in Ashmiene

[Page 603]

A group of activists of the Zionist movement of Smorgon before the First World War, with Dr. Muzinson

Natan Ruzufski, Warszawski, Shmuel Fine, Itzik Brudni (Bar-Eli), Dr. Muzinson, Yosef Ragovitch (or Ranikovitch), Faivel Rapaport, Avraham Biderman, Gershon Broide, Chaim Alperovitz

Keren Kayemet gathering in Smorgon

Standing from right: **Z. Alperovitz, B. Maharshak, M. Gilman, S. Rapaport, S. Shein, Z. Pergament**
Sitting from right: **A. Abramavitch, Berenstein, G. Veinstin, A. Lemodinski, A. Ish-Ahuvi**

[Page 604]

Stories through Photos (cont.)

First group of Chalutzim to make Aliyah to Eretz Israel after WW1 (Zionists Movement of Smorgon)

Standing from right: **Z. Tzarbin, A. Shmuelson, Z. Rudumin, S. Rudinski, A. Tzipkin, C. Alperovitz, M. Cohen,**
2-Standing from right: **S. Berlin, I. Helperin, (Vilna), C. Alperovitz, S. Shein, A. Lamodinski, A. Sholomovitch, D. Grinberg,**
3- from left: **A. Danishevsky, M. Brudna, Penina Shapira(Lefer)(Vilna), Margalit Krinski (Vilna), Rochel Berlin (Vilna), Ida Lifshitz (Vilna),**
4-from left: **S. Vinstein, A. Kisin (from Vishneva)**

A group of Lithuanians take the first row of tents

Twenty tents in number, and thus are they divided by town:
Nine tents for Vilna, five for Kovno, and two
Each from the outlying cities of Smorgon, Koshdor (Kaišiadorys), and Jastolin (Azdelin??).
Most are learned in Torah
And have dreamt of Zion from their early youth
They work in the field in training and in "Tarbut" and are setting up the camp.

From "the Jubilee of the Wagon Drivers" by D. Shimon

[Page 605]

Ha'chalutz Organization in Smorgon 1924

Standing from right: **A. Danishevsky, M. Katz, Israel Rabinovitch**
Second row: **K. Tablovitch, S. Rudnitski, Z. Alperovitz, Z. Rudamin, B. Grinberg**
Sitting in third row: A. Grinberg, A. Abramovitch, M. Katz, A. Ish-Ahuvi, Z. Pergament, Z. Katzkavitch, Z. Rudamin
Seated below: **D. Grinberg, A. Lemodinski, A. Sholomovitch**

Translator's Footnote

1. Another interpretation is that Madvinsk is "from Dvinsk" – i.e. Shmuel from Dvinsk

[Page 606]

Stories through Photos (cont.)

In Martef Hashoah
on Mount Zion, Jerusalem[1]

Jerusalem: Baruch Sutzkever, opening the memorial gathering

The Vow: "Through the insight of my eyes, which saw the destruction / Laden with screams, to my bowed heart / With the insight of my mercy that guided me to forgive / Until came the days that threatened to never forgive! I have vowed the vow: to remember everything / to remember – and speak, to not forget.

Avraham Shlonsk

Chanoch Levin delivers the eulogy
Let us remember

"... In all your questions I hear voices
-- My brethren, gathered in flocks to the slaughter –
From transit points from isles of destructions
From cities and towns – altars for sacrifices
Moaning over their loss frightens my nights."

Sh. Shalom

[Page 607]

Survivors from the community of Smorgon at Martef Hashoah

"... My brother, my brother Refael – in your extinguished eyes flames from all the ovens still flicker, and in your stormy heart is preserved the screams of the victims, from man to woman, from elderly to child."

(from the book)

The crowd recited chapters of Mishnah for the elevation of the souls of the victims of the Holocaust

"... Our rabbis taught: our brothers do not cause [i.e., require] sackcloth or fasting, but rather repentance and good deeds."

[Page 608]

Baruch Sutzkever unveils the plaque for the martyrs of Smorgon in Martef Hashoah

"The strands of my heart are in tatters at the sound of the bitter screams: is this not an echo from the vale of weeping, of the son and the daughter who saw their honored mother be martyred, when the throat of the father was slit – children bleat out to G-d – and the spirit of their outcry will be torn?!"

Reuven Avinoam

Eliezer Sholomovitz lighting candles at the dedication of the memorial tablet

"How will we live with this sadness, with this pain in our consciousness
We cry out by day, and from night to day,
If the bearer of good news does not come to our street suddenly
And gives us the news: There will be a day of peace from the heavens.

A. Tz. Greenberg

[Page 609]

Chanoch Levin, Margalit Bilevski, and Bracha Brodno

"And as our children march to the gallows,
Jewish children, wise children,
They know that their blood is not considered as blood.
They only cry out to their mother: Do not look!"

A. Elterman

Memorial candles...

The children of Maharsha'k light candles in the candelabrum of six (million)

"The crematoria were not yet locked
From every furnace
The smoke still winds upward
The world is still given over to the hand of Cain"

[Page 610]

With the survivors...

The children of Maharsha'k light candles in the candelabrum of six (million)

"The crematoria were not yet locked
From every furnace
The smoke still winds upward
The world is still given over to the hand of Cain"

(The sections of poetry and eulogy were cited in the eulogy of Chanoch Levin.)

Translator's Footnote

1. Holocaust Chamber:
   https://en.wikipedia.org/wiki/Chamber_of_the_Holocaust

[Page 611]

The Activities of the Board

by Baruch Sutzkower

Translated by Jerrold Landau

When we, the Smorgon natives in Israel, learned of the bitter situation of our townsfolk at the outbreak of the Second World War; and we, who felt with our bodies and flesh all the tribulations and oppression that we endured as refugees in Russia during the First World War, as well as the terror of the pogroms and disturbances in Ukraine, and we returned to destroyed and ruined Smorgon – we knew and felt the situation, and girded ourselves to help our brethren.

With trepidation, we gathered many of the natives of our city. During the normal times prior to the Second World War, we would offer help and support for the new immigrants who arrived from Smorgon, until they acclimatized to the Land – and we did all this without a special organization for this. Everyone did what they could, and offered the needed help in accordance with their means.

However, this time, we knew that additional large–scale help would be needed, in proportion to the needs, on account of the terrible Holocaust that afflicted our townsfolk. This would be in greater magnitude and form than the previous efforts.

The Organization of Smorgon Natives in Israel was founded for this purpose. It was headquartered in Hadera. It began to prepare for the first urgent aid activities for the Holocaust survivors, whose arrival we awaited. We had no possibility of physically arranging aid in the Diaspora. This was done by various bodies and institutions, in which several of our people participated in the aid activities. However, as an organization, the only thing we could do was to prepare to greet our surviving brethren and help them acclimatize and set themselves up here in the Land.

At the first meeting, which took place in Hadera, the first committee was elected. It was composed of Gershon Weinstein, chairman, Baruch Sutzkower, secretary; Eliezer Sholomowitz, treasurer; Berta Shein; Pesach Taboriski; and Zalman Katzkowitz.

In 1942, we held the first memorial gathering in Hadera in memory of our community of Smorgon, which was annihilated during the Nazi Holocaust, and no longer exists. From that time, we arranged a memorial gathering on an annual basis.

We began by collecting money. We opened an account in the Loan and Credit Bank. We created a benevolent charitable fund to help the members. Our chairman Mr. Gershon Weinstein directed it, concerned himself with its development, and dedicated a great deal of activity to it, to the best of his ability. With his great experience already from Smorgon during the period of assistance after the First World War, through his efforts the work for the charitable fund developed, and many members in need were helped. In time, we distributed about 300 loans totaling close to 40,000 liras. We attempted to offer help to the best of our ability, given that the help that we hoped to receive from our fellow natives in America was very meager, almost zero.

[Page 612]

The Organization of Smorgon Natives in Israel

In the photo from right to left: first row: **Eliezer Sholomowitz (treasurer), Baruch Sutzkower (secretary), Pesach Taboriski**
In the second row: **Shoshana Danishewski (Polawski), Gershon Weinstein (chairman), Berta Shein of blessed memory**
In the third row: **Avigdor Jakobson, Zalman Katzkowitz, Mordechai Taboriski**

[Page 613]

The aid was not only offered in the form of monetary loans. There were also cases where we had to offer physical assistance to those liberated from the camps and ghettos. We made efforts and worked in this direction as well.

From among our committee, Mrs. Berta Shein had an open house to everyone. Anyone in need found assistance there. During the time after their first arrival, we housed them in the homes of members until they found permanent dwellings.

When we found out about the realities of our fellows who returned to Smorgon, we sent them care packages of food and clothing.

In 1953, after our brethren the Holocaust survivors stopped arriving, we decided at our memorial gathering to publish the Book of Smorgon, to perpetuate our city and community for the coming generations.

We made efforts and searched for an appropriate person for this task. We found our member A. Ish Ahuvi (Isser Liberman) of blessed memory to be an appropriate person for this activity. He indeed accepted this work upon himself, and began to carry it out with full seriousness and willingness.

During the course of the several times I met him regarding the book, I realized that our choice was correct. He was a man capable of drawing out anything connected to "Smorgon" from the books into which he delved. He knew how to extract that which was effective and useful for us. However, to our sorrow, he did not finish his work. His sick heart could not hold out. The life of this man, all his activities, including our activity regarding the publishing of the book, all ceased.

At the following gathering in 1954, we already memorialized our member Ish Ahuvi of blessed memory along with the rest of those who had passed on.

Let these lines in our book be dedicated to the memory of our member I. Ish Ahuvi, thanks to whose commencement of the work on the book, we were able to continue and bring it to conclusion.

We broadened the number of memories and included the members: Avigdor Jacobson, Shmuel Weinstein, and Shoshana Danishewski (Polawski).

In 1960, we contacted the writer Abba Gordin of blessed memory to edit the book. A book committee of eleven members was chosen, including the following:

Chanoch Lewin, Baruch Sutzkower, Avigdor Jacobson, Leah Bodger (Bubis), Shoshana Danishewski (Polawski), Mordechai Taboriski, Leah Lewinson, and Yisrael Lewinson. The editorial board of the book was chosen from among them, and we began to gather material and continue with the editing.

However, luck did not favor us this time as well. The editor of the book, Abba Gordin, who was also considered to be a man of Smorgon, and who approached the task of editing not only as an editor but also as someone from our community, did not complete the work of editing. On one occasion during a discussion with me, he said, "Be diligent with preparing and collecting the material, for I am an old, sick man. Who knows what will be." His heart prophesied to him that he would be unable to complete the work. Indeed, that is what happened. He did not know that his heart would cease to function a short time after this.

When he was in the hospital, and we visited him several hours before his passing, he still thought that he would leave the hospital the next day and continue the editing. He did not know that his prophesy was to come true. He was not able to complete his work, and he did not merit to see the completion the book that he had worked so hard on, and wanted to see published with all his heart.

[Page 614]

The photograph of our editor Abba Gordin of blessed memory appears at the beginning of our book with two dates (1887–1964)[1].

May his memory be guarded with us forever.

This time, we approached the task of finishing the book through our own powers. Thanks to our member, Chanoch Lewin, who already played an active role in the editing as well already (during the life of the editor Abba Gordin), and who took upon himself the task of finishing the editing, dedicating a great deal of his time to it – the book of "Smorgon" was concluded and published.

Our gratitude is hereby expressed to all the members who helped us in publishing the book, and finding the material , to our members who prepared the list of those who have passed away, and to the member Leah Bodger (Bubis) who dedicated a great deal of time to the book.

The city of Smorgon no longer exists as a Jewish community.

We have perpetuated it with a memorial plaque in Martef Hashoah [Chamber of the Holocaust] on Mount Zion in Jerusalem, along with all the holy communities the names of which we unite with memory. The Book of Smorgon will be an eternal memory for future generations.

Let this be a testimony that despite the great, terrible Holocaust that was perpetrated upon our community, as in previous generations where they arose against us to annihilate us[2], our response to those who rise up against us is:

We exist and will continue to exist. We live and will continue to live. We will live, and we will outlive them.

[Page 615]

A meeting of a group of women from Smorgon in Israel 20 years after the liberation from the camps

First row, seated, right to left: **1. Marisha Entes (Pialko), 2. Sima Laskow (Ratzin), 3. Hiene Liborski (Fejer) from Swir**
Second row seated from right to left: **1. Fania Rubinshtok from Wilejka, 2. Keize Legat (Tal–Shor), 3. Mira Ogolnik (Straz) Vilna, 4. Rubinshtik from Wilejka, 5. Fruma Golda Laskow, 6. Chana Alperowitz, 7. Frumel Alperowitz, 8. Nechama Stranocki (Bar–On) from Swir.**
Third row standing from right to left: **1. Fania the nurse from Kovno, 2. Onia Rubinshtok (Ogwir) from Wilejka, Dora Kweskis from Kovno, 4. Tova Magdis (Donski), 5. Eta Pedevzki (Orlich), 6. Masha Cukerman (Poznik), 7. Chaya Sadowicz (Ziskind), 8. Sara Alperowicz (Epstein), 9. Ella Pomochnik (Shapira), 10. Rachela Entes (Gershon), 11. Rachel Podbarski (Miller), 12. Leah Swirski (Holcman) from Sventzian**[3]

{Following this page there are 5 unnumbered pages. They are blank memorial pages for the owner's own recording. Heading is:

In Memory of our dear ones
Father, mother, brother, sister, son, daughter, relative, friend, and acquaintance}

[First unnumbered page following the memorial pages]

On Your Heights You have Fallen...[4]
by Baruch Sutzkower

In Memory of Those Who Fell in the Liberation of the Homeland

"Blessed is their sacrifice in the death–mystery"

[Second unnumbered page]

On Your Heights You have Fallen
Baruch Sutzkower

In Memory of Those Who Fell in the Liberation of the Homeland

"Blessed in their sacrifice in the death–mystery"[5]

Mordechai (Motka) Cohen

He was born in Krasna in the district of Vilna in Tevet 5666 (December 1905) to his parents Matilda and Tzvi. He received a religious education in his parents' home. He studied in the Yeshiva of Vilna at the age of six.

He was already imbued with a military spirit in 1918. He joined Komsomol, which at that time fought street battles during the times of regime change in Russia.

They returned to Smorgon in 1922, and his father Reb Tzvi served as the cantor and shochet [ritual slaughterer] in the city. He was a graduate of the Tarbut School, and educated in the Hebrew Gymnasja of Vilna. He was a member of the Hechalutz movement from his youth. He was active in the drama club. After *Hachsharah*, he made *aliya* in 1925 and settled in Hadera. He worked in agriculture in the citrus orchards. When I made *aliya* in 1929 I found him as the work director in the Meirson orchard, where I also worked. We were the only Jews among many Arab workers. Once during the rest break, one of the Arabi workers expressed during a conversation that the Jews were "*wlad al mavet*" (sons of death). Motka immediately got up, and, despite the fact that we were few among the many, gave the Arab a ringing smack and said, "I will show you who is '*wlad al mavet.*'" The Arabs were never again so brazen as to mock the Jews.

This is the way Motka was. He was daring, with both a fighting and mischievous spirit. He was a member of Hapoel, where he served as the head of the steward division. He was a dedicated member of Haganah from the day he made *aliya*. He was a counselor, commander, and a good friend. He was active during the disturbances of 5696–5698 (1936–1939). He participated in the bringing in of the illegal immigrants on the Samaria beach. He was a commander of the guard brigade in Hadera, and a commander of several new points in the country during the time of their establishment during the "Tower and Stockade" period[6]. He was among the first to participate in a course for seamanship and sabotage operations. He was beloved and admired by everyone with whom he came in contact.

In 1941, the Jewish Agency was requested by the high British command of the Middle East to enlist a number of volunteers to a daring military operation aimed at thwarting the efforts of the enemy in Syria before its conquest by the allies. Since daring, brave men were requested for this task, it was natural that Motka was among the 23 choicest members of the Haganah who went to the boat, and took upon themselves the commando tasks. The lads set out on the journey at 8:00 a.m. on May 18, 1941. They set out but did not return.

Just as their departure was secret, aside from the few who knew of the activity; their end is enveloped in the mystery of death. Who knows if we will ever find out for sure how they died. At the time I am writing this memorial to Motka, 24 years have passed. The image of Motka with his serious facial expression, or his mischievous character, is etched in my imagination.

He left behind a wife, two children, friends, and acquaintances throughout the country.

As we memorialize him, we are proud of him.

[Third unnumbered page]

Moshe (Moshele) Bernstein

The child Moshele, the son of Chana and Yosef Bernstein (my teacher), is etched in my memory. Whenever I visited the home of my teacher, I would see the child [Moshele] with the round face and dark eyes that expressed tenderness, simplicity, and good–heartedness.

He was born in Smorgon in the year 5684 (1925). He was 13 when the Germans attacked Poland. He was in the Buchenwald Camp. He endured all the terrible tribulations in Europe along with his mother and younger brother. He was the sole survivor in his family. He was liberated from the camps, and was among the first to be deported to Cyprus. When he returned to the Land, he settled in Hadera. He was among the first to enlist at the outbreak of the War of Independence. He successfully concluded the training in Camp Dora near Netanya. To the request of his acquaintances that he take care and be careful with himself since he was the sole survivor of the entire family, he responded: "If I have succeeded in enduring all the terrible tribulations of the Nazi Holocaust, I am certain that I will overcome here too as well." However, fate had it otherwise.

He was sent to the front in Ramat Hakovesh–Qalqilia, and fell on 11 Nisan 5708 (April 20, 1948) as he was guarding the workers in the fields of Ramat Hakovesh. He was brought to burial there.

May his memory be guarded with us forever.

Mordechai Glazer

He was born in Smorgon on 14 Adar 5689 (March 26, 1929) to his parents Tzipora and Avraham. He graduated the Tarbut School with excellence. He was an alert youth, diligent at his studies, and talented. He was beloved by his teachers and friends. He was thin in body and strong in spirit. He endured all the tribulations of ghetto life in various places. He was cut off from his family at the age of 12, and sent to forced labor. He escaped from the camp and [then] smuggled out friends who were sentenced to death. He lived in the forest. He was captured and sent to Dachau. He succeeded once again in smuggling Jews. He endangered himself by bringing food for his friends who could not maintain themselves. He was captured a third time and beaten cruelly. When he was liberated, he had no energy. He quickly recovered and immediately prepared for *aliya*. He found his mother in a dramatic fashion on a train traveling to Germany, after five years of separation. He organized his friends to sneak through the border by foot via tortuous mountain routes. He encouraged those who were falling behind. His friends would say, "If Motel is going, we will all go." He made illegal *aliya* to the Land, and was imprisoned in Cyprus. There, he disguised himself as a sick person, and succeeded in making *aliya* to the Land and joining a youth group in Masada.

With the Syrian invasion, he participated in the defense of the Jordan Valley, and fought in Tzemach and Deganya. He fell on 9 Iyar 5709 (May 18, 1948) with a Molotov cocktail in his hand during an anti–tank storm operation by the enemy in Chatzar Deganya. He was the sixth, after his five brothers who were murdered in Europe. His parents settled in Hadera. We did not merit to see him again.

[Fourth unnumbered page]

Ninth Memorial Gathering in Hadera
August 1954
With the participation of Cantor M. Koussevitzky of blessed memory

Cantor Koussevitzky

[Fifth unnumbered page]

Moshe Koussevitzky of blessed memory

by Baruch Sutzkower

The child Moshe was born to his parents Alte and Avigdor Koussevitzky on 22 Elul 5657 (1897). He was destined in his life to conquer the world as a world-famous cantor.

He was educated in his family, who were prayer leaders, and received a traditional education. He studied with his grandfather Reb Shalom Szulman, and later in the progymnaszja of Smorgon. At a young age, he enthralled his audience with his sweet voice and pleasant singing. At that time, young Moshe Koussevitzky also dedicated himself to sculpting and drawing. He began to sing in the Smorgon synagogue choir.

When Smorgon was burnt down and completely destroyed at the outbreak of the first World War, Moshe Koussevitzky and his family left along with all the people of Smorgon as refugees, and reached Russia. They settled in the city of Rostov. Despite the fact that the economic situation of the family was good in Russia, they returned to destroyed Smorgon, and Moshe Koussevitzky was among those who rebuilt the city anew. Later, he moved to Vilna where he completed his studies in music. He sang in the opera, and made his first steps in the Choral Synagogue of Vilna. There, he started to gain fame as a cantor with a pleasant voice. After a period of serving as a cantor in Vilna, he was invited and accepted a position at the Tlumacza Synagogue in Warsaw until the outbreak of the war in 5699 (1939).

He miraculously succeeded in saving himself from the Nazi Holocaust. He left Warsaw and arrived in Russia. At the end of the war, he traveled to America and was accepted as the cantor at the Beth El Synagogue in New York, a position which he held until his death.

During that period, Cantor Moshe Koussevitzky became famous throughout the world. He appeared throughout the world, and earned bountiful praise and great esteem.

The voice of the world-renowned Cantor Moshe Koussevitzky was silenced on 7 Elul 5626 (August 23, 1966). He was appreciated and accepted by his audience of listeners and many fans throughout the world. News of his death after a malignant illness, which overtook him and silenced the voice that many people listened to in every place, was received with great agony.

He was buried in Israel, where he visited often and performed throughout his life. He was buried on Har Menuchot in Jerusalem on Thursday, 9 Elul, 5626.

[Sixth unnumbered page]

The ninth memorial gathering in Hadera, August 1954, with the participation of Cantor M. Koussevitzky of blessed memory. Opening of the gathering.
From the right: **Mayor of Hadera Y. Viderker, P. Taboriski, B. Sutzkower, G. Weinstein, M. Koussevitzky of blessed memory, E. Ish Ahuvi of blessed memory**

M. Koussevitzky of blessed memory greets the gathering
From right: **E. Ish Ahuvi of blessed memory, Y. Viderker, A. Sholomowitz, Sh. Meirson (seated) of blessed memory, M. Koussevitzky of blessed memory, B. Sutzkower, G. Weinstein, P. Krinis, B. Shein of blessed memory**

[Seventh unnumbered page]

M. Koussevitzky of blessed memory singing

Smorgon natives at the gathering

[Eighth unnumbered page]

Mrs. B. Brodna presenting flowers to Cantor M. Koussevitzky of blessed memory

Cantor M. Koussevitzky of blessed memory exiting the hall of the gathering, bidding goodbye to his fellow townsfolk. Standing next to him are P. Zuckerman, and Reb Yitzchak Mordechai Sutzkower of blessed memory

[Ninth unnumbered page]

The three young Karpel brothers, who were in the camps, and later met in the forests. They were the first Jews who arrived in destroyed, pillaged Smorgon.

In Israel. The Karpel brothers as soldiers in the Israel Defense Forces

From the right: **Yosef, Yerucham, Yisrael**

[Tenth unnumbered page]

The Jewish faction in the Smorgon city council before Mr. G. Wajnsztajn (Weinstein) made *aliya*
Standing from right: **Nathan Taboriski, Chaim Lewin**
Seated from the right: **Yeshayahu Kowarski, Libman, G. Wajnsztajn, Meir Goldberg**

[Eleventh unnumbered page]

The 90th birthday celebration of Mr. G. Weinstein, chairman of the Smorgon Organization of Israel

Mr. G. Weinstein seated at the head of the table
From the left: **Mordechai Taboriski, Pesach Taboriski, Baruch Sutzkower, Tova Sutzkower, Leah Bubis (Bodger), Refael Weinstein, Eliezer Sholomowitz, Dov Morochowski**
Opposite: **Zalman Kackowicz, Shoshana Plawski**

Standing from the right: **Rachel Kackowicz, Yafa Lubelinski (Sholomowitz), Leah Sholomowitz, Binyamin Sholomowitz, Yisrael Levinson, Mordechai Taboriski, Eliezer Sholomowitz, Dvora Sholomowitz, Batya Weinstein, Baruch Sutzkower, Tova Sutzkower, Leah Bubis (Bodger), Shoshana Plawski, Zalman Kackowitz, Z. Taboriski**
Seated from the right: **Rudnik, Tz. Rudnik, Shmuel Weinstein, G. Weinstein, Refael Weinstein, Leah Levinson, Pesach Taboriski**

[Errata page]

Errata

Page 268 line 2: *tzeshpreitung* rather than *tzeshpreinug* [hail – of bullets].

Translator's Footnotes

1. See https://en.wikipedia.org/wiki/Abba_Gordin
2. A direct reference to the *Vehi Sheamda* song of the Passover Seder, "Indeed, in every generation, they rise up against us to annihilate us."
3. Although unclear, the parentheses likely contains the married Hebrew name. Any reference to a "from *town name*" also likely indicates that the woman was born in the mentioned town and not in Smorgon.
4. This part of the verse is from II Samuel 1:19. Note, the TOC translator did not translate it literally, but rather took a different part of the same verse: "How the Mighty Have Fallen."
5. The title page of this section is repeated verbatim at the top of the first text page.
6. See https://en.wikipedia.org/wiki/Wall_and_tower

Addendum

The story of the tombstone

This part was dictated in 1996 by Motke Taburiski and Lisa Levinson now living in Hadera , Israel. In 1942, when the Ghettoes in Smorgon where liquidated, the Jews of Smorgon were sent to Oshmiane. The youngsters were sent to work in Germany and Littuenia. In Oct 21, 1942 - 750 people were killed. among them were the Jews of Oshmiane, Smorgon, Krevo, Olshan.The killing took place in Zelonka (between Smorgon and Oshmiane)After the war, in 1952, the Jews from Vilna made the first tombstone. They collected the human bones under the tall grass. A kerchief that was found in the grass was recognized by relatives. The tombstone deteriorated in 1967. The government in Belarus created a new one, but Wrote on it "in memory of the victims of WW II. They never mentioned that they were Jews. In 1995 we contacted the director of the museum of Smorgon. Mrs. Maria Leonidovna Moiseyev. She was very cooperative and efficient. Some money and a script in memory of the Jews of Smorgon were transferred. She created a board with the script. This board was fixed on the wall of what used to be the great synagogue and is now a bank.

On one a regular day, that was formally made a complete day of rest in Smorgon, together with the mayor - the pupils of the local high school gave a performance, and a new tombstone was erected in Zelonka.

Tombstone in Zelonka

Memory board in Smorgon

1- Museum director, 2- Mayor of Smorgon, 3- Mrs. Lisa Levinson, 4- Mr. Motke Taburiski

The Nazis Next Door[1]

....How America Became a Safe Haven for Hitler's Men

By Eric Lichtblau

The Road to Ponary [Ponar]

The bastard [Lilekis] must have signed his name somewhere. A scrap of paper, a death warrant, an order rounding up the Jews—there must have been something with that name scrawled at the bottom. *Alexandras Lileikis.* But if it was there MacQueen wasn't finding it. MacQueen, a race car driver turned historian for the Justice Department's Nazi team, had spent days rummaging through the dog-eared war files at the archives in Lithuania, but he was coming up empty.

This was the fourth trip to Lithuania in the last few years for MacQueen, who had taught himself Lithuanian for the job. The secrets held in the Lithuanian archives, opened up to American researchers after the fall of the Soviet Union two years earlier, had turned up plenty of grim, eye popping details about the Nazi massacres in the Baltics, but nothing on the man MacQueen most wanted to nail: Lileikis, the onetime chief of Lithuania's security police and a proud Massachusetts resident for the last thirty-five years.

The old man practically dared the Justice Department's Nazi hunters to find something on him when Eli Rosenbaum had first come knocking on his door in Boston years earlier Sure, his men in Vilnius might have rounded up Jews, Lileikis had scoffed, but that didn't mean he had ordered it. He knew nothing about any executions, he told Rosenbaum. “Show me something that I signed,” he said in a cool, defiant manner of his. He was taunting them. He knew if the prosecutors couldn't find evidence that he played an active role in the massacres in Lithuania all those years ago, they had no case. MacQueen figured that unless he could find something on him, Lileikis would live out his days in America.

As he scoured the records, MacQueen was growing frustrated. In Vilnius, the Nazis had wiped out one of the great meccas of Jewish civilization in all of Europe, machine-gunning to death nearly all the city's sixty thousand Jewish men, women, and children at a notorious pit outside town. It was inconceivable to him that the chief of the special security police-the dreaded Saugumas force-wasn't involved. Could there be nothing with his John Hancock on it? Impossible, MacQueen thought. The Nazis wrote down everything, a macabre testament to their own brutality. He knew the Germans had burned many of their records as they fled Vilnius but still, there must be something that survived with Lileikis's stamp of approval on it.

That's when MacQueen realized that he had been going at his search backwards. Instead of looking for the files on the murderers, he began looking for the files on their victims. He searched the record for a prison in Vilnius where he knew many Jews were jailed before they were killed. In the prison records, he discovered a canvas-bound book with the names of nearly twenty-nine hundred wartime prisoners typed in Russian. He pulled the files on the ones with Jewish-sounding names. There were hundreds. Some of the documents were lightly signed; it looked like the Nazis had started burning the records on their way out of town, but ran out of time.

In the batch, after some digging, he found a red file with the record for a young Jewish man named Rachmiel Alperovicius who was arrested by the Lithuanian security police on September 4, 1941, and executed two weeks later. Like farmers advertising their livestock, the security police described the young Jew's physical attributes: big, flattened ears; strong body; broad shoulders; small teeth. And there at the bottom of the page, in thick, black ink, was the signature MacQueen had been struggling to find for more than three years now.: Alexsandras Lileikis, chief of the security police in Vilnius.

Soon MacQueen found the records for another Jewish prisoner with Lileikis's signature at the bottom, then another, then another. Suddenly, Lileikis long-elusive name was everywhere. MacQueen worked through lunch, taking photos of the documents and typing notes on his laptop as he dug deeper into the file. He had been at the Justice Department for five years since he first answered an ad for a war historian on the Nazi team Nothing topped this moment......

A handwriting expert compared the signatures to another one on file for Lileikis in Germany. It was a match. To MacQueen, the signatures were a smoking gun-evidence that Lileikis had ordered Jews in town to be rounded up and turned over to the Gestapo for certain death. Lileikis, he was convinced, was a Schreibtischtater-a desk murderer. He gave the orders....

He had directed the carnage in concert with the Gestapo. The distinguished looking gentleman from Boston, he believed, had been the Nazi's henchman in Vilnius, the man with the blood of many thousands on his hands.

MacQueen studied the names of the victims, reading the stories of their unmourned murders in the long-buried files: Beila Levinson, Danielius-Antanas Konas, Chaja Lapyda[2].......

1. Here is an excerpt from the book The Nazis Next Door: I chose to include this in the Smorgon Addendum as it should be a constant reminder to future generations, that the Holocaust was real! Never forget!
   Anita Frishman Gabbay [grand-niece of Yehuda-Leib Gilinski, husband of Elka ?, teacher in the Smorgon Tarbut school-father of Benjamin Gilinski (Hadera), Michal (Brooklyn), Miriam(Mexico ?)] return
2. Chaja Lapyda (Lapida/Lapidus) was the grandmother of Frieda Levin Dym, mother of Ida Levin of Smorgon. Chaja Lapidus [nee Katzkovitch] was murdered together with other members of her family in Ponar. return

Mollie Feldman's Family

Smorgon, Belarus

Submitted by Marjorie Greenspan Kaufman

My maternal grandmother Mollie Feldman lived in Smorgon before emigrating to the United States. Born in 1911, Mollie (Margalit) Feldman was one of 11 children. Her family worked in the leather tanning business, fashioning gloves. At the time, Smorgon belonged to the Russian Pale of Settlement. Following WW1, Smorgon became part of Poland. My grandmother told us when she was young girl, she and her friends would walk up to the top of a nearby hill to watch the soldiers fighting. She didn't convey much more about her family and life in Smorgon as her parents and most of her siblings were murdered by local pogroms, antisemitic riots and eventually the Holocaust, and the subject was simply too painful. Mollie was sent to the U.S. as a teenager in the early 1920's. In New York, she reunited with a cousin from Smorgon, Abe Gordon, and they married and settled in White Plains, NY. Abe had been conscripted by the Russian army but managed to escape and make his way to New York after an unexpected two-year hiatus in Havana. Years after my grandparents passed away, I found a box of postcards and letters sent to Mollie from her family in Smorgon in the mid 1920's. The collection included beautiful Rosh Hashana greeting cards, studio pictures of her sisters and their families and souvenir postcards from nearby towns, with Yiddish or Ukrainian writing on the back. Thanks to the wonderful people at Jewish Gen, particularly Anita Gabbay, I was able to obtain translations of the inscriptions. The postcards and letters form a rich, warm and fleeting snapshot of Jewish life in Smorgon in the 1920's, of Jewish holidays and family gatherings, of tales from a best friend who stayed in Smorgon and was finding her way through life with her new husband and baby, of a sister and a male cousin who were among the early Zionists who emigrated to Israel. When I look at them now, I feel a strong connection with my ancestors from Smorgon and I thank God that my great grandparents had the means and foresight to send my grandmother to America. I can only imagine how difficult and painful it was for her to leave her entire family behind, to receive an initial smattering of postcards and letters, and then, silence.

Dedicated with love to my grandparents, Mollie and Abe Gordon, z"l, may their memory be a blessing.

Figure 1. Mollie Feldman age 14 (middle) and sisters 1925 Smorgon

Figure 2. Feldman sisters 1926 Smorgon

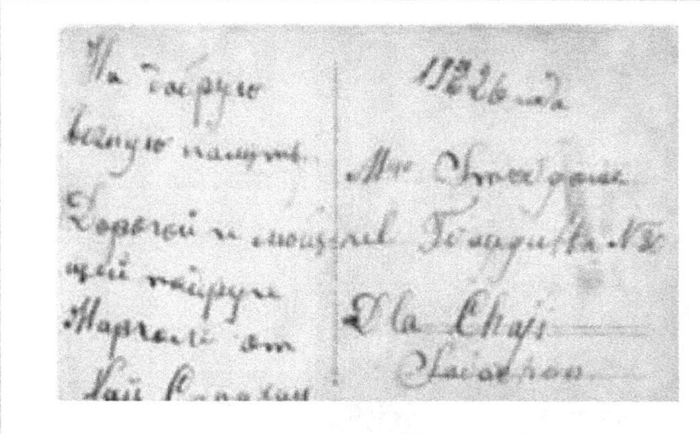

Figure 3.

Figure 4. Older Feldman sister with husband and two sons, date unknown

Figure 5. Sister, 1927

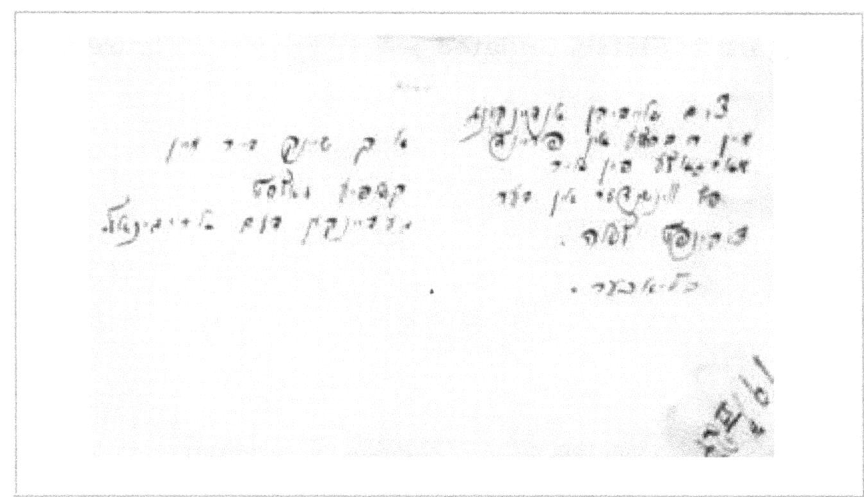

Figure 6. Reverse of Image 5. Yiddish

Figure 7. Sister. Undated

Figure 8. Sister? Smorgon 1928

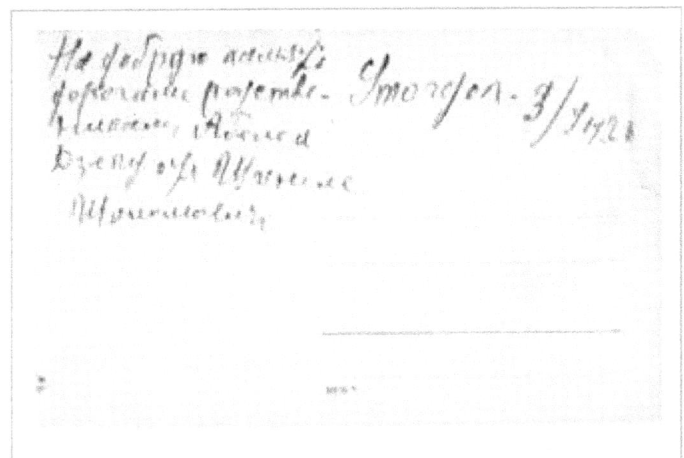

Figure 9. Reverse of Image 7

Figure 10. Sister?

Figure 11.
Brother? Smorgon
1927

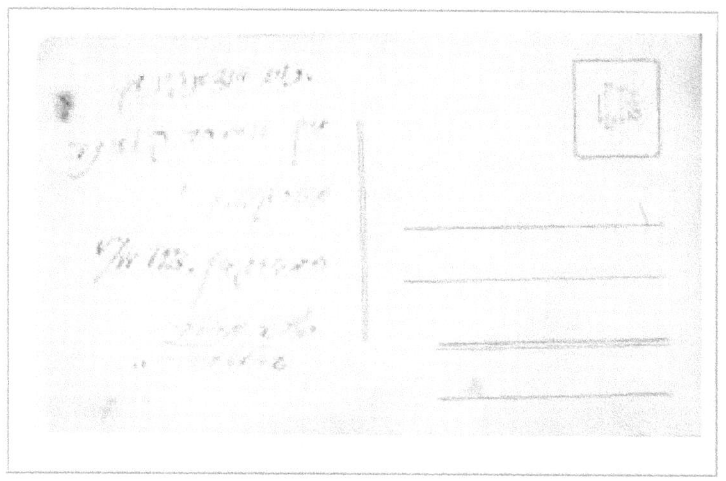

Figure 12. Reverse of Image 9. Yiddish.
"Dear ......Margalit (Mollie) Smorgon 1927.
Shana m'touka (Sweet New Year)"

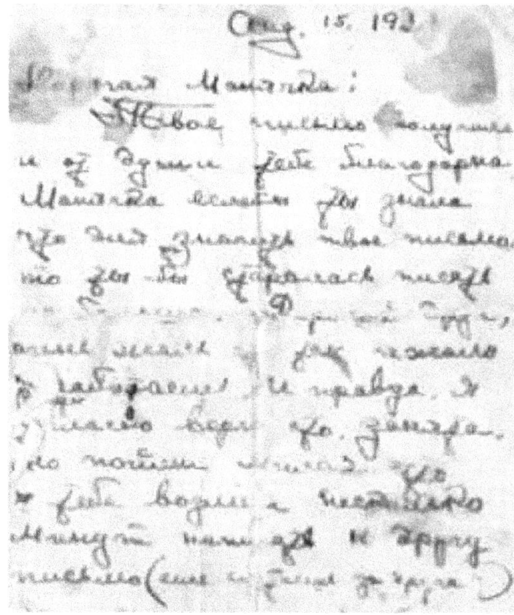

Figure 13. Letter to Mollie from her best friend, 1928

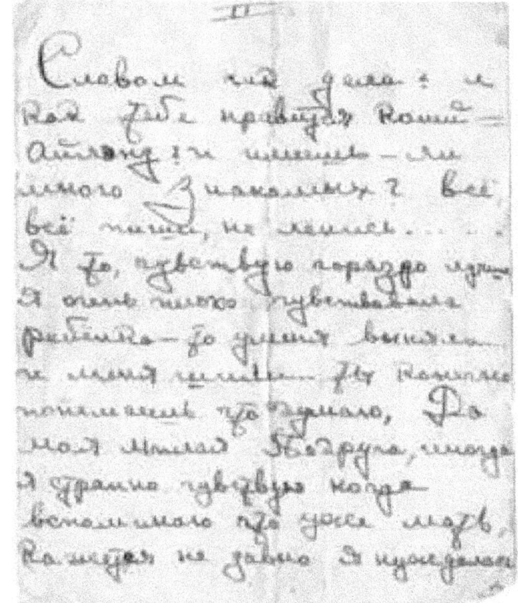

Figure 14. Letter to Mollie from her best friend, 1928

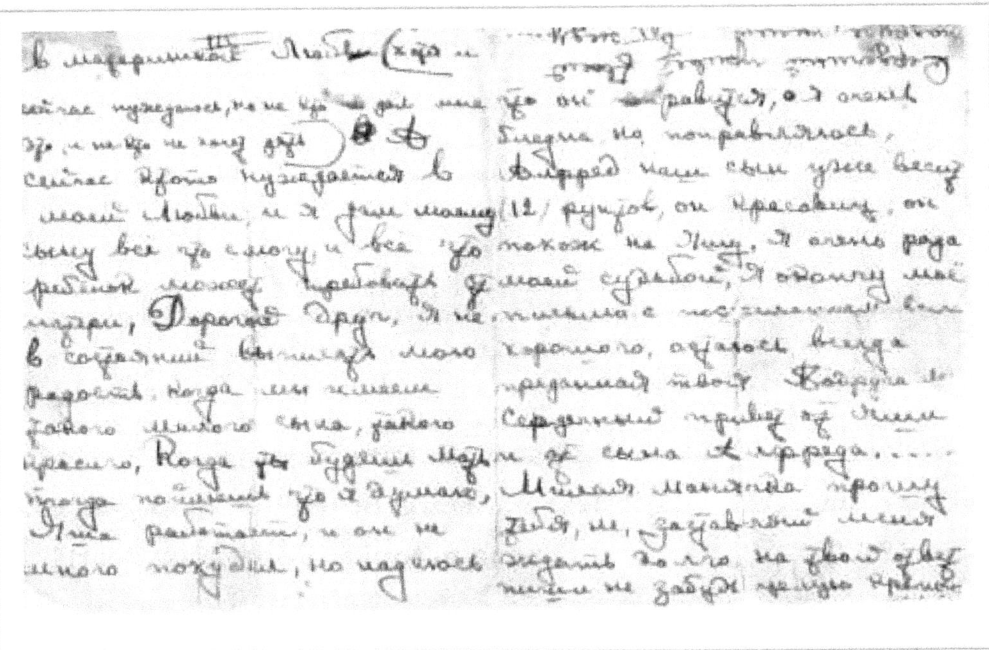

Figure 15. Letter to Mollie from her best friend, 1928

Jewish Life in Smorgon 1920s

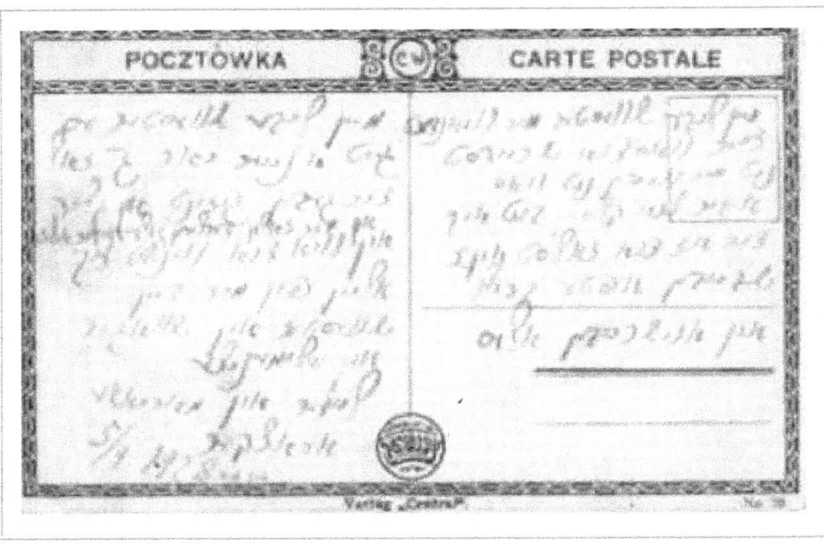
POCZTÓWKA
CARTE POSTALE

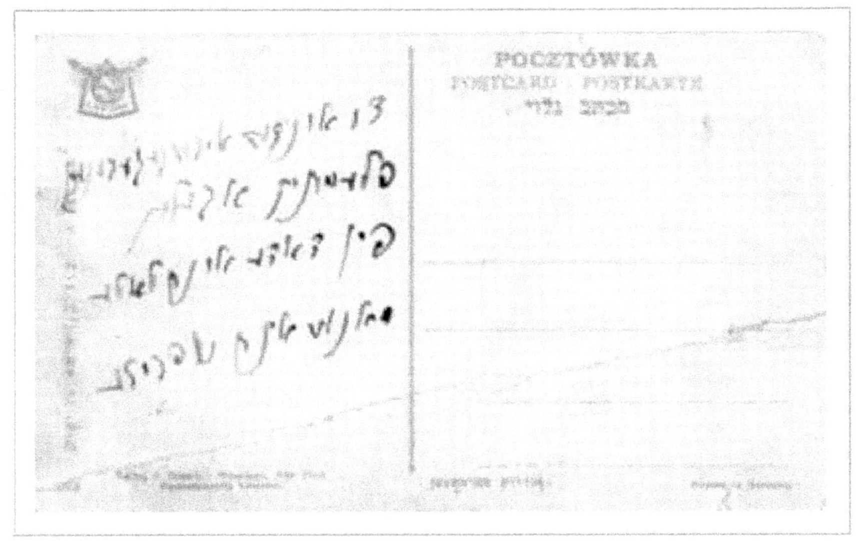
POCZTÓWKA
POSTCARD · POSTKARTE
מכתב גלוי

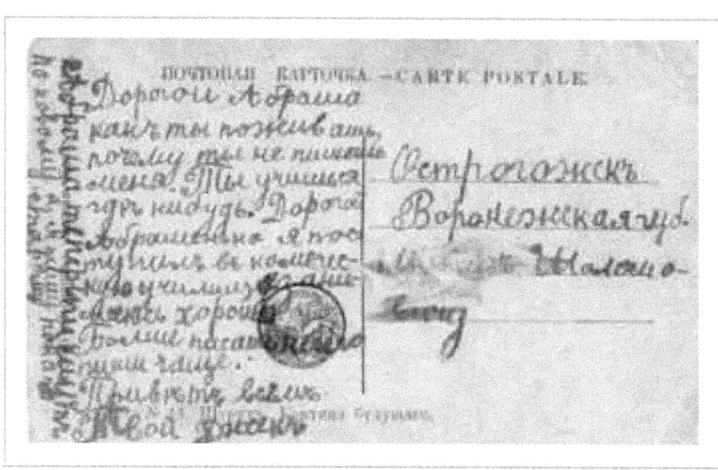

ПОЧТОВАЯ КАРТОЧКА — CARTE POSTALE

Дорогой Абраша
какъ ты поживаешь,
почему ты не пишешь
меня. Ты учишься
где нибудь. Дорогой
Абрашенька я пос
тупилъ въ коммерче-
ское училище. Зани-
маюсь хорошо.
Больше писать нечего
пиши чаще.
Привѣтъ всѣмъ.
Твой [illegible]

Острогожскъ
Воронежская губ.
[illegible] Шалмо-
[illegible]

[illegible]

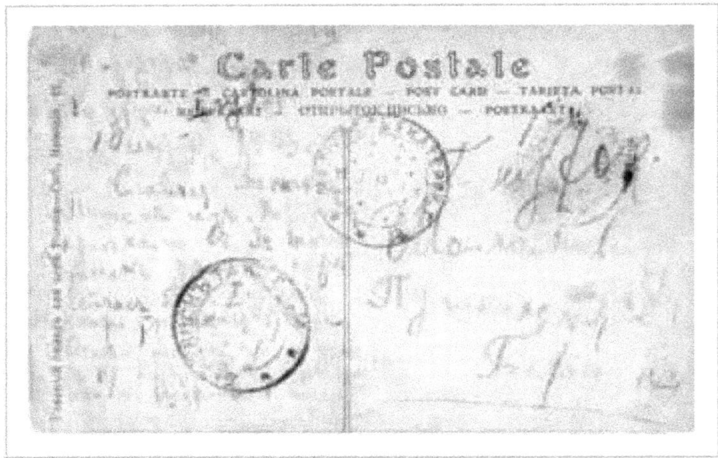
Carte Postale

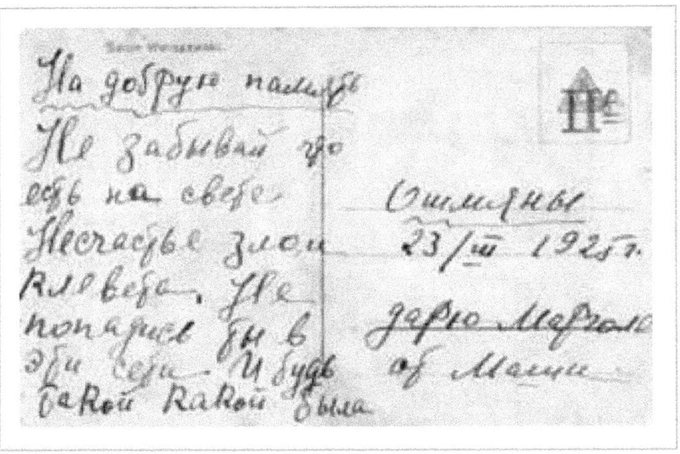

На добрую память

Не забывай что
есть на свете
Несчастье злой
человек. Не
попались бы в
эти сети. И будь
такой какой была

Ошмяны
23/III 1925 г.
дарю Марьяше
от Маши

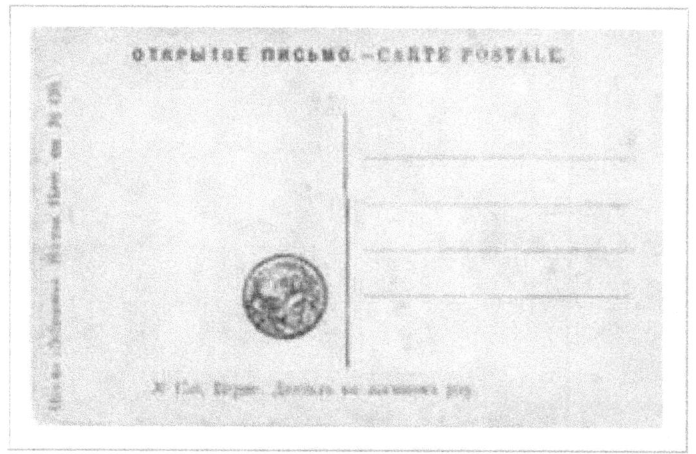
ОТКРЫТОЕ ПИСЬМО.—CARTE POSTALE.

Feldman Relatives in Israel 1920's

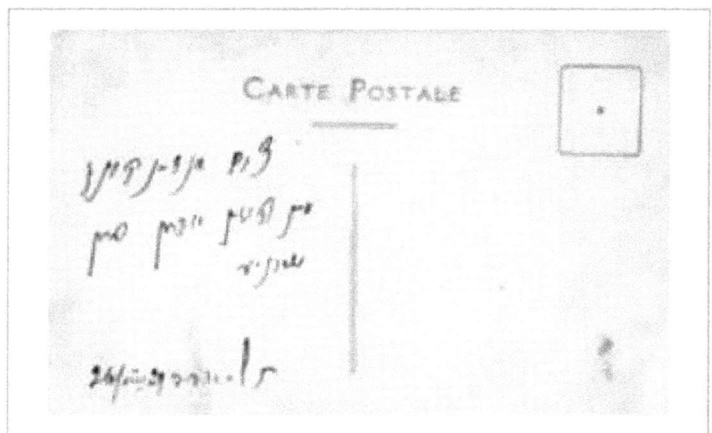
CARTE POSTALE

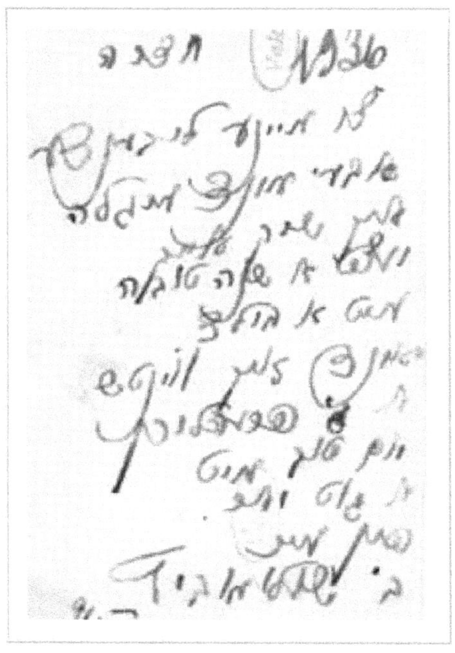

Tel Aviv, 1929

לשנה טובה
שער ציון

שנת פריחה וברכה
חדרה
תרצ"ז

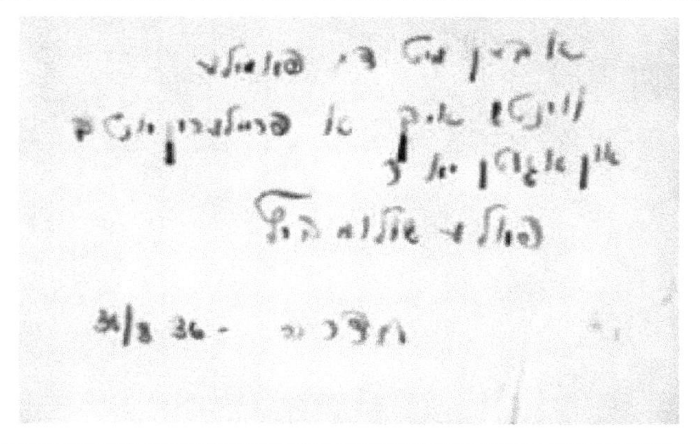

לשנה טובה ומבורכת
92
COPYRIGHT BY „PALPHOT" – MADE IN PALESTINE

INDEX

A

B

C

D

E

F

G

H

I

J

K

L

M

N

O

P

R

S

Z

www.ingramcontent.com/pod-product-compliance
Lightning Source LLC
Chambersburg PA
CBHW062021090426
42811CB00005B/914

* 9 7 8 1 9 3 9 5 6 1 8 5 5 *